The Early Diary of Anaïs Nin

Volume Two

1920 – 1923

WORKS BY ANAÏS NIN

*With a Preface
by Joaquin Nin-Culmell*

———

Harcourt Brace Jovanovich, Publishers
New York · London

Anaïs Nin, 1903-1977.

THE EARLY DIARY

OF ANAÏS NIN

VOLUME TWO 1920-1923

Library of Congress Cataloging in Publication Data
Nin, Anaïs, 1903–1977.
Linotte, the early diary of Anaïs Nin.
Vol. 2– pub. with title: The early diary of Anaïs Nin.
Vol. 1 translated from the French by Jean L. Sherman.
Includes index.
Contents: [1] 1914–1920 — v. 2. 1920–1923.
1. Nin, Anaïs, 1903–1977 — Diaries.   2. Authors,
American — 20th century — Biography.   I. Title.
II. Title: Early diary of Anaïs Nin.
PS3527.I865Z522   1978   818'.5203 [B]   77–20314
ISBN 0–15–152488–2 (v. 1)   AACR2
ISBN 0–15–127183–6 (v. 2)

Printed in the United States of America
First edition
B C D E

HBJ

𝔎 *Editor's Note* 𝔎

It is now well known that Anaïs Nin kept a diary from 1914 to 1977. The original journals comprise more than 35,000 hand-written pages with no erasures and almost no corrections. Until 1947 Anaïs wrote in bound volumes that she called "diary books." (After 1947 important correspondence had grown too large to be recorded in the pages of diary books, and, with a few exceptions, Anaïs wrote her diary on loose sheets of paper.) When she began to edit the diaries for publication, she numbered these books from one to sixty-nine.

This second published volume of Anaïs Nin's Early Diary is drawn from books nine to nineteen, covering the years 1920 to 1923. These diary books were usually inexpensive "date books" with allowance for a page a day. Anaïs ignored this arrangement and wrote as much or as little as she pleased for each entry, which she usually dated accurately but sometimes identified only as "Monday" or "Evening." Books fifteen and seventeen are larger and more luxurious than the others and are bound in leather. These were given to Anaïs by her cousin Eduardo Sánchez and are inscribed respectively: "To my lost princess . . . Time can never crumble a true devotion!! E.S." and "To Anaïs from one who is economical in diaries—Eduardo, *The Mysterious!* I am presenting this diary to you, but I fervently hope that it will, when stored with your secrets, run away and come back to its original owner. So, I pray you, cuisine, not to clasp it in chains—it may come back! ¿Quien sabe?"

The opening page of volume eighteen contains Anaïs's first title for a diary book: "Journal d'une Fiancée." Almost all of the later diary books had titles (see Volume VI of *The Diary*, pages 55–56); the titles were written when Anaïs first opened a new diary book and were usually prophetic.

The present volume was prepared from a typescript made by Anaïs in the late 1920s. As she typed, she left out passages she considered schoolgirlish or those in which she went on a little too long about nature. Most of these deletions have been respected, but in some instances significant material has been restored. The editorial approach is the same as for *Linotte*. Cuts have been made in repetitious passages, extended quotations and routine entries of little interest to the reader. Also, Anaïs's arbitrary and frequent use of capitals and exclamation points has been kept to a minimum. Occasionally a cloudy passage has been edited for clarity.

As with *Linotte*, the material is presented as it was written, chronologically, and in Anaïs's astonishingly sound but distinctive English, which was subject, as she herself realized, to the influence of whatever author she happened to be reading. At times, the chronology is confusing. Anaïs, never able to resist the lure of a new diary book, sometimes wrote in it before she had finished the old one. Then, fearing that the feelings of the old diary might be hurt, she would go back and fill in its blank pages at the end.

Anaïs wrote that Spanish was the language of her ancestors, French the language of her heart, and English the language of her intellect. Occasionally in this diary, the first that she wrote in English, Anaïs unconsciously lapses into the language of her heart. Because her father did not read English, she continued to write to him in French and copied most of these letters in her diary. Faced with her father's constant corrections, she once playfully included in one of her letters an entire page of accents, punctuations and other torments of the French language, writing "you may put them wherever you wish!" She resorts to French also, for reasons of discretion. The frank sensuality of Marie Bashkirtsev's journal so shocked her that she confided to her diary, "I can only write about this book in French." Her comments and other long passages in French have been translated by Jean L. Sherman. Short passages in French or Spanish have been left as they occur in the text and appear in footnotes translated by Anaïs's brother Joaquin Nin-Culmell.

Joaquin was also most helpful in resolving questions concerning people and events of the period. We are grateful to him and to others, especially Ian Hugo (Hugh Guiler), who assisted in the preparation of this volume. But the real guidance came from Anaïs herself, particularly during the last years of her life.

Rupert Pole
Executor, The Anaïs Nin Trust

Los Angeles, California
October 1981

LIST OF ILLUSTRATIONS

[Between pages 176 and 177]

Anaïs Nin, c. 1922

The Nin house in Richmond Hill

A. N.'s brother Joaquin

Rosa Culmell Nin

A. N.'s brother Thorvald

Joaquin Nin-Culmell

Miguel Jorrín

Enric Madriguera

Eduardo Sánchez

Hugo Guiler

A. N. as a model, 1922

A. N. as a cover girl

A. N. as Cleopatra, 1922

[Between pages 368 and 369]

Hugo Guiler

A. N. with Juan Manén

Rosa Culmell Nin with Manén

Finca La Generala, Havana

A. N. in Havana

A. N. in Havana

A. N. in a Cuban newspaper

A. N. as a Gibson girl

A. N. in Havana

A. N. in Havana

A. N. and Hugo Guiler in Havana, 1923

Anaïs and Hugo Guiler

❧ *Preface* ❧

This volume of Anaïs Nin's Diary and two yet to come bridge the important gap between *Linotte* (volume I of The Early Diary, 1914–1920) and the diary volumes already published (volumes I to VII, 1931–1974). They are significant for many reasons but primarily because they introduce and describe for the first time the man Anaïs referred to as "my husband, my lover, my collaborator. The axis of my life. He who made my own work possible with much harder work than my own, whose faith breathed life into me." Better known to Anaïs's readers as Ian Hugo, the gifted illustrator of many of her novels and an artist in his own right, Hugh (Hugo) P. Guiler carefully nurtured Anaïs's growing mastery of English and offered her that rare combination of courageous literary criticism with glowing support for her talent. His devotion to her was complete, and her love for him would, as she put it, "outlast time." The birth and growth of this relationship in Richmond Hill (Long Island, New York), which culminated in marriage, is the main subject of this second volume of The Early Diary.

As in all of Anaïs's diary volumes, the events jump rather than walk, explode rather than flower, reach out impetuously rather than cautiously. Anaïs always lived primarily for the future, sometimes in the past, only impatiently in the present. This did not prevent her from living the reality of the present to the fullest.

Cocteau once wrote that he was the lie that always told the truth, an idea somewhat akin to Bergson's *mensonge vital*, a term that Anaïs loved to quote. It is difficult, almost impossible, to know with Anaïs where the fiction that always tells the truth begins and the Diary whose truth changes from day to day ends. The more her diaries are published, edited or not, the deeper the mystery. The more telling the clues, the more difficult to trace the motives. The more doors are opened, the more doors are closed. The more light, the darker the shadows. Anaïs was a human bathysphere who could endure and describe pressures beyond the depth of most people. Out of this endurance and because of her observations, she came to believe in the poetic truth of myth. She would have been much surprised and even perhaps a little disappointed had she discovered that Aristotle's definition of myth approached her own intuitive perception of truth as a prismatic illusion.

In this volume, the Diary itself is still the central core of Anaïs's inward life and so it was to remain to the end. It is not "a mere book," alive, comforting, faithful, an understanding yet mute witness to her hopes and illusions; the Diary is, rather, a confessional, an ever changing blueprint of her extraordinary and eruptive development, an objective record of her contradictions and doubts. Nevertheless, she knew that the Diary was but a shadow of herself, a pale reflection of her own strong perceptions, a mirror of her own troubled images, an inner garden safe from the intrusions of the outer world. Safe but not isolated, for Anaïs's imperious need to communicate was the real reason for her writing at all, and certainly the reason for her change from French to English. Perhaps her Diary began as an imaginary letter to her absent father, but it rapidly became a real letter to the world, to *her* world, which at that time included her cousin Eduardo Sánchez.

Eduardo's French was somewhat sketchy. He easily confused *cousine* (cousin) with *cuisine* (kitchen), and the mix-up soon became a family joke. More important, the two cousins confided in each other and English became their common bond. French, like the "one, great longing" of Anaïs's life, the great emptiness of her father's absence, was not forgotten but merely stored away.

Boys became more important in Anaïs's Diary. At Columbia University in New York, where she spent a brief time, at home, in Richmond Hill, or at work, she was surrounded by friends, artists, family and admirers. Anaïs, who never really considered herself beautiful at that time but whose photographs belie her every statement, must have dazzled her *chevaliers servants* of those years. In addition to Eduardo Sánchez, who remained her steadfast friend for many years, there were her cousin Charles (Carlos de Cárdenas); Miguel Jorrín, younger brother to Tío Enrique's wife, Julia; Enric Madriguera, the violinist and, later, conductor; and a score of others. Concerts were organized at home, books were read and discussed, diaries compared, lofty themes introduced and tossed about as if they were being discovered for the first time, and flirtatious dances attended. Anaïs was the catalyst in all of these activities, and yet she was happiest—as she wrote to her father—when she could "write, read, study, meditate, dream."

It is interesting to note that her "passionate desire to write" always came first. It was already thus in *Linotte*. Even before she met Hugo, Anaïs was determined to share with the world all that lies within, "whispering in a language I understand but cannot yet translate." She was determined, as only Anaïs could express determination, to learn to write of those things she heard but that "others have not heard." She was no less determined "to tell all that is vague and nameless, give visions to those who cannot visualize, share fancies, dreams, make the world listen to unseen and delicate music and to the stories of worlds they have no time to discover and explore." What a goal for a maturing Linotte! What a secure sense of direction, what an unbending vocation, what an anticipation of her own adventures in seas yet to be discovered!

Even then, Anaïs read voraciously, and her appetite developed a logic of its own, quite apart from any structured plan. She oscillated wildly between Bossuet and Emerson, Lamartine and Poe, Descartes and Darwin, Rostand and Tennyson, Henri Murger and Sinclair Lewis. In reality, however, she was more especially drawn to diarists like Maurice and Eugénie de Guérin, Marie Bashkirtsev and even Amiel. Books didn't influence her as much as they fed her own ideas, vague as they were, unstated and untried perhaps, yet always recognizable as indisputably Anaïs's in spite of their germinal state. For Anaïs, books were like people—something to be enthusiastic about, quickly assimilated and retained for what they could offer to her own immediate development as a person or as a writer. In Anaïs it is dangerous to differentiate between the two. She once wrote that she would have liked to have been a book and, indeed, for her, people were like books.

But books were not enough. Anaïs had yet to find the human companion she so ardently hoped for in her dreams. "Now and then I plunge into the depths, am balloted and storm-tossed and wind-lashed, or gently carried away on the crest of the waves and blessed by a vision of shores and harbors. My hands are tightly gripped around Experience's very hair; I go wherever it leads me until I tire of her strenuous company and swim back to my Ship." Hugo became her ship, the captain of her turmoils. Her happiness, her cure, her refuge, her talisman, he was all of these things for her, and yet she found him "utterly bewildering." She wanted to understand his point of view without necessarily sharing it. She wondered if her imagination, her dreams, had not made her quite unfit for reality; if her talent for *describing* life had not progressively weakened her ability to *live* life. And yet, a great force unerringly drew them together in spite of Anaïs's bewilderment, in spite of her own doubts, in spite of her propensity to criticize in depth not only herself but those closest to her.

Hugo was torn between his growing love for the girl with the French accent who wrote incessantly in her diary and the loyalty he felt for his concerned family. He went to Europe to resolve the painful conflict and to weigh the heavy consequences of an early marriage. Among the questions he asked himself were the following: Could he support Anaïs and could he support Anaïs's commitments to her own family? Meanwhile, spirited Tia Antolina invited Anaïs to visit her in Havana, where she would be sure to be caught up in a whirl of social activities and become, as usual, the center of attention. The possibility of losing Anaïs was not lost on Hugo, and in the midst of his travels he proposed by cable. Anaïs accepted also by cable and they finally met in Havana, where the marriage took place in March of 1923, a few weeks after Anaïs's twentieth birthday.

Joaquin Nin-Culmell

Berkeley, California
September 1981

The Early Diary of Anaïs Nin

Volume Two

1920 – 1923

❧ 1 9 2 0 ❧

Summer. Richmond Hill. From afar our house looks like those they paint on Christmas cards. From near you can see it needs paint, that the porch is not very steady, that the railing which comes up to the entrance is rotted, and that the squirrels who run up and down the roof have found plenty of holes in it in which to make comfortable nests.

At night it is at its best. You see only the lights shining through the windows, shining the better because there are no shades, and you see the outline of its sharp slanting roof against the sky.

We moved in last night. Only part of the furniture had come. We ate by candlelight, and all slept in the same room, because it was stormy outside and we felt strange and lost in the big house. The candles threw fearful shadows on the walls, and many doors we were not used to opened unexpectedly into dark rooms. Our voices sounded hollow and dismal. We asked, however, with impatience: "Mother, whose room will this be?"

"We'll see tomorrow, in the daylight."

Tomorrow was long in coming. We were awake all night, with the sound of the rain and wind, with the shaking of windows and, worst of all, with strange footsteps on the roof.

Once, I walked to the window, and when the lightning flashed I saw that Joaquin's[1] eyes were wide open and that he was frightened too.

---

[1] *A.N.'s younger brother.*

"What is that noise on the roof?" he whispered.

"That is what I'm trying to see."

"What are you doing by the window?" asked Mother.

"There's a noise on the roof."

"That's nothing," said Mother, and went to sleep.

Meanwhile Joaquin's head and mine were imagining stories. A man was surely looking down on us through the holes in the roof, to see what the people were like who had bought the old house. What did he think of us? Why was he running back and forth on the roof? Would the morning ever come and frighten him away? No. He was taking advantage of an endless night, of the rain, of the lonely hill.

When Mother slept I went to the window again. Joaquin watched me with enormous eyes. All night the man ran up and down the roof, very fast, very nervously. All night it rained. Joaquin and I waited for the morning, and as soon as it came we dressed, and slipped out of the room, and went slowly downstairs and out of the house. We began to examine the roof anxiously. Immediately we saw the squirrels hurrying back and forth, in great excitement, up and down the slanting roof, in and out of mysterious holes, and along the very edge of it—the squirrels, disturbed by our arrival, restless and unable to sleep too, angry perhaps, and fearful of being chased out of their home. They had nothing to worry about. We fed them, and they came down from the roof to look into the house, at the new furniture, old to us, but new to them, I mean.

The rooms were distributed. The corner one is mine, because everybody can see I need the sunshine the most. It has a fireplace and four windows, two looking toward the woods, and two toward the village, of which I can only see a few housetops.

Joaquin has a smaller one next to mine, with one window toward the woods and the other toward the station. Opposite these, and giving onto the garden, Mother and Thorvald[1] have their rooms.

We spent the morning opening trunks, hanging pictures and curtains, pushing furniture around. My books are on the mantelpiece, with my journals, so I consider myself settled down.

July 9. There is a little volume I often turn to at night after my daily tasks are all accomplished, for sweet, mute sympathy. I call

---

[1] *A.N.'s older brother.*

it my Diary, and have grown to love it very dearly, adding always so much of myself and my life that it has all grown into many many little books, in which I am never tired of writing. You are today made one of them, and perhaps the only distinction I make in my treatment of you is the use of the English language in place of the French. It makes little difference, after all, what language the tongue employs if it speaks from the heart, does it not? Habitually I find myself quite alone in carrying out this little daily-life chronicle, but now Eduardo,[1] my cousin, admits he has begun his in school, and so many things, a myriad of them, bring us together, whether it be our inclination to regard life as poetically as possible, or our love of books, our ambitions, our ideals. Somehow we are led to believe that our lives will not be uninteresting . . . to ourselves . . . and to each other. Eduardo does not read French as freely as I read English, and we wish to show each other parts of our diaries.

I begin today then to confide in you, little Diary of mine. These are now the best years of my life, for I have hope. I have heaps of friendly thoughts in my head, and an immense quantity of hope, of illusions. When these things leave me, I prefer to die, and until then I will live with all my heart this glorious life, which is a strange mixture of monotonous tasks and delicious emotions, sprinkled now and then with little incidents out of the ordinary, and the realization of some sweet, tender daydream.

I had dreamed of someone whose intellectual life would be, somehow, in harmony with mine, that I might realize all is not madness, that others, too, experience the emotions and thoughts I guiltily wrote in the pure white pages of my life record. And my dream came true, for Eduardo accidentally came to my house, and as we spoke he responded in every way to the flights of my imagination.

I may write more later. I have to tell you how I suffered a great disillusionment, the fall of one of my idols, and yet it has passed like a nightmare; it is only a memory of a bad night after the sunshine penetrates my room and my heart again.

July 10. There is something now that makes the days seem like a drop of water in an ocean; the hours flit by, uncounted, the days are never too long. I cannot understand this wonderful contentment. I am supremely satisfied with the sunshine, with those

[1] *Eduardo Sánchez.*

around me, with everything, and yet there is a great deal to do in the house, and Thorvald and Joaquin still at times tease me mercilessly, but those little things which at other times are the superficial causes of my unreasonable sadness pass now almost unnoticed.

Charles[1] has come to see us. His mother[2] and Antolinita[3] are at the hotel and will come tomorrow. Charles has not changed very much. He is quite his old self, now, as he sits quietly reading downstairs, with no need of what we call company (for true companionship is not often found in people but in books and dreams).

Eduardo and I went to the theatre last night. You know that usually I speak to you of theatre, dances and things of that kind very superficially and without interest, still less with comments. I think it is because I find myself such a poor judge in matters of amusements, lacking as I do the quality of being sociable. Yet last night you would have loved to be near me, as we spoke between the acts of the things you and I love, of the things I thought I would only speak of to you, secret. And the play itself was well acted, although neither Eduardo nor I could find it in our hearts to admire the characters. It was the *Famous Mrs. Fair*, with Blanche Bates, and all those who supported her role seemed so very sincere in their parts that at times one's emotions were truly roused and we sympathized deeply.

How strange it is! Just now Eduardo allowed me to read his diary. I write "strange" because I feel so blind, so blind at times, wondering how other people see life, how other people think and what they wonder about. Eduardo tries to fathom the deep, strong, passionate emotions music arouses, beautiful music particularly and perhaps only; and the meaning of it all. I can see that Eduardo understands people better than I do and it makes me thoughtful. I wish I knew his secret and then I would not suffer so. There is one thing now of which I am certain. All the confidences I place in my cousin, on account of mutual likes and dislikes, are not ridiculed . . . too much. The proof is that while he is here I somehow do not fear to show him what I write, and yet I would rather burn every page of my Diary than allow Thorvald to see it, and for that matter, Charles also, he is so sarcastic.

We spoke of our neighbors at lunchtime. People say I am distant, cold perhaps. It is strange, is it not? I am thinking of this

[1] *Carlos de Cárdenas, a cousin.*
[2] *A.N.'s Aunt Antolina.*
[3] *Antolina de Cárdenas, a cousin, nicknamed "Baby."*

now because I am alone, and wondering . . . When all around me is still, I can hear my thoughts whisper to one another, laughing very sweetly, very softly at me. Soon the house will be gay again and perhaps I will laugh often or oftener than the others. Cold and distant indeed . . . But through all the days, until I grow old and wise and weary, I will be kept wondering by many things.

July 13. I am disconsolately writing in bed, being ill, both Joaquin and I, since yesterday. At times I would not care so much; in fact, usually I enjoy this confinement, which harmonizes with my indifference toward certain things, but just now Mother has a great deal to do, and I can't help her, and every hour I waste away weighs heavily upon my conscience. The trouble is that my head aches so that I cannot walk. Poor little Joaquin is lying very still and angelically in the tiny room next to mine. I cannot even take care of him. Yesterday when I tried to lie still, I began to think and think until my eyes were full of tears. Then I fell asleep and dreamed that I was dying and that nobody missed me or cared. I thought of this so much that when Mother came at midnight to see if I wanted anything, I asked her if she loved me. I am sure Mother does love me, and Joaquin also, but Thorvald? Oh, Thorvald grows more like a rock every day. When I told him *perhaps* Joaquin and I were going to have the measles, he answered: "I hope so," which, even being said for fun, sounds . . . like Thorvald!

I am afraid Eduardo finds it very dull here. It seems like a hospital, and the house is lonesome and still. The leaves rustle all day long. As I noticed today the soft, rich, warm color of the branches, I compared them with their winter disguise, the cold brilliant, icicle-laden branches. It makes me think that what I like in trees I like in people too, because I prefer by far the warmth and softness to mere brilliancy and coldness. Some people remind me of sharp dazzling diamonds. Valuable but lifeless and loveless. Others, of the simplest field flowers, with hearts full of dew and with all the tints of celestial beauty reflected in their modest petals.

July 14. What strange and complete loneliness! I do believe that it was not my real self who took the days so lightly, but now it is, because I am lonely again and undescribably sad. I went to the theatre with Antolinita and saw *Honey Girl*. I could not appreciate its versatile charm and could never smile at the correct moment. It was very hot, oh, so hot, and people seemed tired, and though Antolinita was in a wonderful humor, I continually followed two trends of thought—one in harmony with her own, the other fearfully contemplative and vague.

Two things are apparently the cause of my crisis. A storm, a beautiful, terrifying storm, is about to break; there are lightning and thunder and strange, heavy gray clouds, but the rain remains up there; the thirsty grass seems to long for it—just as I long for the second cause of my reflective mood: I think it is Eduardo's companionship I miss. The week we spent together was perfect, because our correspondence in some magic way opened the golden door to the world we each created alone, but allowed us to go in together. Our conversations were like spells, which were broken always regretfully. Eduardo never ridiculed anything and understood everything. The sketch I would like to make of him for you I am powerless to draw, not for lack of mere words, but because I cannot materialize or explain or understand him. I just *feel* his sensitiveness, his love of beauty. I know what he dislikes and what appeals to him, and of all things, when I watched him listening to music I was thrilled by the realization that melody arouses his emotions to the edge of the infinite. One night we visited Tia Coco[1] at the inn, and before leaving we slipped into the dance hall for a few minutes: It was like flying through the clouds. He is generous too; he brought me flowers to adorn the house, and a pink Kewpie doll while I was ill. Being with Eduardo I realized Thorvald's indifference, Joaquin's baby age, Mother's absorbed life, and every night this week I remembered to pray to the blue heavens for having given me a cousin like Eduardo and the vision of what perfect companionship truly is—even for only a week's lifetime!

The rain is pattering, soft and soothing. I had to leave the porch and come to my room. A great many thoughts are crowding into my foolish head, and I must write until bedtime. In the beginning of this book I told you I wanted to confide to you my disenchantment, and then the days seemed so full of sunshine that I forgot Marcus[2] absolutely. But now, if I am to write of the people who come into my life, and go away, and if I am to describe life as I see it, I have to write everything. This was a lesson, a

[1] *A.N.'s Aunt Edelmira.*
[2] *Marcus Anderson, a young admirer of A.N.'s.*

severe and cruel lesson. I must not, I must not idealize people. It is unjust to them, and unjust to me also, but until what age am I going to be totally blind?

One afternoon, the day Eduardo came, Marcus also came to see me. We spoke of books, of artists, of a great many things, with long, awkward silences now and then. It was torture for me because all my ancient instinctive yearning to fly possessed me, and I noticed how Eduardo watched Marcus with twinkling eyes, and realized vaguely that I was strongly, oh, so strongly, tempted to laugh with him. After a few hours Marcus went home, and I, thinking how far he had come just to see me, was still blind, but I was glad it was not Eduardo who was going—which proves? Nothing at all!

That evening we all walked for the mere pleasure of walking and I was teased and teased about the unfortunate Marcus. When the jests ended and Eduardo and I found ourselves walking a little apart, I asked him earnestly to give me his opinion of Marcus. He spoke seriously and truthfully. I was very thoughtful afterward.

The next day I met Marcus to visit the Museum of Art. He called me twenty times, very gravely, "my dear child." It was our last day together because he was going somewhere to study, and as he spoke I felt a great wave of pity, and wondered whether I liked the unhappy boy just because no one else could endure him, and the boys thought him contemptible, effeminate . . . and then my castle was shattered.

The boy I once idealized enough through his letters, his poetry, to call a Prince, the boy I thought no one liked because he was simply "different," the boy I once admired and respected asked me to kiss him goodbye! I believe he saw the surprise, the *pain*, the anger, in my eyes. I could not speak. Marcus knew I did not and would never love him, but he thought so lightly of what I hold most sacred and precious that he dared to ask for it. "Will you?" he asked again, "Will you?" I said no very quietly, and feeling sorry, I added softly, "Don't be angry, please." But since then I cannot control my sentiments and deep in my heart I feel I cannot even like my poor shattered idol. Now it is all written. It seems as if I am always climbing the dangerous ladder to reach romance and always slipping down again. But wait—I am going to leave romance for other things now and climb the ladder of knowledge. Perhaps the most perfect friendship in the world is the one that does not ask for anything. And perhaps there is nothing lovelier reserved for me than this week of delicious harmony with my cousin, because we gave each other the best we had, and asked for nothing but sincerity and sympathy. Perhaps I have gray hairs today. Who knows? It is not easy to learn, and to learn by experience.

July 15. To write a poem is not painful, and yet after hours are spent on it, polishing and retouching, there is a certain touch of despair mingled with our other feelings that indicates the lack of perfect, undoubted satisfaction, a certain self-reproach because the lines do not carry the entire beauty of the sentiment. I wrote something which, as I read it, and each time I read it, thrills me profoundly. This morning, while I worked with Mother, visions of waves, of foam, seaweeds, sand and moonlight danced before my eyes, and my fingers laboriously completed the calculations while my head wandered.

This afternoon I played a game of wild tennis with intense dislike, played atrociously, and then I sat in my room to ponder over Frances's[1] letter; it is very much unlike her, and I do fear this last friend is "going away" from me too. There is perhaps something wrong with me, although I always seem to give so much when I love and like, and do not ask for the moon.

People say I look like a ghost. To look like a ghost is a very new and fresh sensation. At first, as you watch the effect of your countenance upon those on whom it is inflicted you feel heartily sorry for yourself. And then you grow slightly bored by the remarks, particularly if one is told that one is lovesick, at a time when I have made all the imaginable resolutions to banish all thought of love (having so far succeeded that the only place in which I find love now is in the dictionary). The third stage is a sudden rush for my room, a pause before the mirror, and the detested rouge is employed for lack of the real thing. Oh, vanity, vanity!

Today I find I miss Eduardo, and that I am looking forward to his letter. I am wondering too (oh, futile thought) whether he misses me as much. He is traveling now, night and day, and will arrive in Cuba Saturday.

July 16. I appeared today in the presence of my family with a tan shoe on my left foot and a black shoe on my right foot. Much

---

[1] *Frances Schiff, a former classmate.*

derision followed and I proceeded in my taciturn way to fill the day with similar impossibilities. Some days of the year are useful, but today I can say that I am ashamed of myself. Yet I have written another poem.

July 18. The day before yesterday Antolinita appeared on the scene to remain with us until Saturday night because her mother had gone to Lake Placid in her auto, and my little cousin was following her by train. She left us last night, and I saw the beloved name on the train schedule, Lake Placid. What hosts of dreaming hours the name brings forth! Golden hours of unbroken magic, which I shall never forget, for every nook and cloud, each scented forest path, the moonlight on the lake, are engraved on my memory for always. Perhaps when I was there I did not feel its beauty so, but now I see the wonders of Lake Placid in my dreams, and I yearn to touch the waters, and yearn for the smell of the pines.

Sunday now to me has its enchantments too. I have grown to like that universal peace, and as the organ's melody floated softly above our heads I prayed a little, and wondered what prevents me from being good. Why can't I endure Thorvald's teasing? Why does Joaquin's selfishness seem so unbearable and cruel? Suppose I were sweet and light-hearted, and suppose I were good; it would be different, would it not? Nothing could ever make me angry or unhappy. It would be wonderful! I soliloquize a great deal during the day, but I am not eloquent. It's useless.

I dreamed last night of Eduardo. He was telling me that Rita Allie[1] was an angel, and she appeared with jewels in her lovely hair and blue wings, and with a soft, clinging dress. "You will be very famous someday but you must follow me," she said. Her voice was like music, and I watched Eduardo go away with her. In my dream I felt an impending danger and called Eduardo back, but he did not listen, so I followed them. A great mirrorlike lake stretched before us. Rita Allie floated above it with her blue wings, but Eduardo was drowned. Then she laughed and I awoke.

July 19. Thorvald has gone to camp. He is never very kind and yet I miss him, although I would not tell him so for all the world. I wrote him a letter with a borrowed sense of humor.

Marcus wrote me a short, childish letter. But all the little

---

[1] *Rita Allie Betancourt, a family friend noted for her beauty.*

things that took place today seem very very little. On my tiny stage where the day's things are acted stand many strange and interesting characters, because I have been reading the History of English Literature. The three famous monks of the Northumbrian School, Bede, Caedmon, and Cynewulf, were strangers to me, but I recognized Chaucer and Spenser. I can hardly write because I am so anxious to return to my book. There are so many things I have to tell Eduardo. I could write a letter 16 pages long but he has not written yet. I am almost sure he has already forgotten. Speaking of Eduardo makes me forget my book. Of all our interminable conversations I have written nothing. It was, as a whole, a thing which cannot be pinned down on paper, made of ourselves, our ideals, our reflections, and varying with our moods, but so sincere and loyal and unaffected. I never thought conversation could be a pleasure, nay a necessity, yet now it is one of the things I miss profoundly.

Once, Eduardo turned to me suddenly and asked me if I were going to be a suffragette.

"Heaven preserve me!" I exclaimed, "I despise the mere idea." He breathed a sigh of relief, as I added, "I have the old-fashioned idea that a woman's place is in the home."

"Oh, I am so glad," said Eduardo. "I have almost fallen in love sometimes and then the girl told me she believed in woman's suffrage. No sooner was it said than my ideal was destroyed."

We laughed. Sometimes I said very foolish things and laughed a great deal because I was quite contented. There is one serious thing, however, to which Eduardo would not listen: that I should become a business woman. When we spoke of this he was so terribly grave that I had to confide to him the vague doubts that linger in my own mind as to the exactness of this fact. Perhaps if during my course at Columbia I find that I have no talent I may undertake what I call the "selfish career" without talent. Who knows?

I am making a character study of Lucy.[1] I have taken three long walks with her, and I have been tempted a myriad of times to shake her violently because her language is a perpetual shock, a painful experience for me. But I want to know how girls, common girls, talk, and what they think about, and whether they have hearts, also if it is true for them that: "my mind to me a kingdom

[1] *Lucy Kruse, a neighbor.*

is." I cannot place the sketch in my Diary. I do not believe I would like to read it very often.

July 20. This morning I awoke smiling to myself and I got out of bed on my right foot, which according to superstitious beliefs is a sign of good humor. Good humor in me is a rare mood, and the more I thought of it, the happier I felt to be able to experience the novel sensation. I dressed in bright colors and accompanied Mother to New York, and we separated at [Pennsylvania] Station. She was to shop and I to present myself at Columbia University.

I was intimidated by the impressive buildings, but when I saw the statue with its inscription "Alma Mater," I smiled at it. I had to inquire for Philosophy Hall, and then to wait for Professor Gerig, to whom I had written a month or so ago after deciding with Mother that I wished to take a course. I believed he was going to be old and rickety and so when he appeared, a comparatively young teacher, I almost lost my mental equilibrium. All the speeches I had prepared in the train made their exit and I spoke most foolishly, I believe. But he understood and took me to Prof. Chinard. Here I was told that the Winter courses were not even planned yet, and that in my anxiety not to lose my opportunity for enrolling I had really overdone the thing, and that it was not necessary for me to appear there until Sept. The Professor told me I could indeed take as many courses as I pleased, and on the whole I left the University just as light-heartedly as I had come.

I had occasion to notice how hot and crowded the city was, and how blessed the pure, refreshing air of the fields, bringing waves of the scent of flowers to me as I stepped from the train. And then the dreamy stillness . . . A little boy and girl, in bathing suits, played around a garden hose and shared the cooling sprays with the plants and the grass. I almost laughed.

At home I found a letter from Emilia[1] and, it being nearly a mile in length, the enjoyment lasted long. Then I wrote a wild letter to Thorvald, and stood dreaming near my window, overwhelmed with a new wave of sensuous joy for the mere right of living. Yes, how new that I should feel life throbbing and tingling in my veins, I, who am so much given to contemplation, and lack-

[1] *Emilia Quintero, a family friend and a pianist who served as accompanist to Metropolitan Opera singers.*

ing every form of animation except the eternal intellectual enthusiasms burning like a thousand flames and finding expression in my dreams and thoughts. How new, and how wonderful.

I am wondering at what I have done today. I was nearing the station when a sign caught my attention at Macy's: Books $.39. Very few times can I buy a book without remorse; it seems a luxury and only for myself; other things I can share, but I am the only bibliomaniac in the family. So today I decided I would buy just one book—only one. I was dazzled by the collection of shelf-worn books. Irving, Thackeray, Hawthorne, Dickens, Shakespeare's plays; treatises on spiritism, which are the fad today, and volumes of poetry tempted me beyond description. I almost bought one of Merimée's works, out of pure curiosity, then forgot it in the contemplation of [Bulwer] Lytton. Then Emerson caught my fancy; I smiled at a voluminous dictionary, as this was beyond my means, and hesitated among Scott, Eliot, Ruskin, Addison and Austen, not wasting one moment on the unloved modern novels, and jingling my pennies with the exultant spirit of future possession. Finally I caught sight of a cookbook! It is useful, I thought to myself, but?! The choice was a test of my will power, and a good, well-needed lesson on *usefulness*, which is undeniably one of the qualities I lack and grieve for. The saleswoman approached me. "Let me have the cookbook," I said, not too loudly, and wondering if she would give me Dickens's tantalizing little volume instead. But she had heard, and I dropped the money in her hand and proceeded to leave the shop. She had to run after me: "Here's your book, miss," she said, and I stared and took possession of my valuable property. I soliloquized until I convinced myself that I was satisfied with myself. A test of my will power it had been, and I was victorious. One of the strongest arguments in favor of the book of recipes is that someday I will have all the books I had seen, in my library, which is to reach the ceiling and completely surround me. Beloved prison. I will give the recipe book to my daughter.

I fell asleep last night reading one of my 1917 Diaries again, not because I was bored, exactly, but because I lost count of:

All the stories I began to write
All the good resolutions I made
All the foolish things I did
All the grammatical horrors I piled in one word.

The writing was abominable, the phraseology unthinkable, and most of all, it now appears to me a painful fact that I exaggerated and dramatized things beyond reason's bounds. I wonder if I do now? And yet I cannot say I am ever sorry I began and continued this Diary, even if I am to laugh at my foolish self, each year making me abler to criticize and condemn. One consolation remains, however: I am sure that while I am abusing or praising myself, I leave those around me unabused and unpraised, therefore doing what is considered, in pure American slang: Minding my own business. And another consolation exists in the fact that although I find much to ridicule in the chronicle of my life in 1917, I read with true enjoyment, living again the lovable hours in life's mauvais quart d'heure.[1] Oh, no, I do not regret the hours I spend transporting my eloquent ink to these white pages.

July 21. I write a voluminous letter to Emilia, with illustrations to accompany my epistle: photo of Thorvald, hay cart, and me.

This is a memorable day in my life. Listen to my story: A letter was waiting for me on the breakfast table. Probably a rejected poem, I thought, as I recognized my own handwriting. And I opened it. After reading a few words I jumped from my chair with joy. It was a kindly, encouraging letter from the Verse Editor of the Delineator,[2] accepting my Elegy and promising to send me a dollar soon. I laughed and danced and could hardly swallow my breakfast. I flew to my typewriter and proceeded to send away several of my manuscripts. Oh, what strange results are brought about by encouragement. I have dreamed dreams today like those I created as a child, dreams of literary fame. A wonderful pageant unfolded before my eyes of those whose pens had achieved so much, and had finally written their names on the tablets of posterity. This ease in relighting fires that I believed to be only smoke shows what a silly, unreformed child I am still. Not a thought in my head is really settled. I seem to be full of contradictions and doubts. I wonder how people acquire that precious serenity and firmness of decision which I have noticed in them with unbounded admiration. To be as calm as a rock— Fancy me today, tossed and balloted by my joy just because a little poem of mine was accepted, heavens knows why, and heaven only

[1] *Bad moments.*
[2] *A monthly magazine.*

knows also if it was not for lack of something better. This last thought is a great consolation, is it not? But I do deserve a bit of ice to cool me down, and if no one else manufactures it, then I must. So I am going to bed thinking that my poem was taken faute de mieux.[1] This will cure my conceit, but nevertheless, I am terribly happy!

Oh, if Eduardo would only write. My imaginary letters to him are assuming ponderous proportions. Perhaps he has nothing to say. But if my cousin disenchants me, then I will never like a boy again in my whole wise life. (Which is a very foolish thing to say, but what can you expect from Mademoiselle Linotte?)[2] There is already one thing which is painful to me—that is writing to Marcus. I wish he would vanish from my life as he came. It hurts me continually to think how blind, how utterly blind and imaginative I can be. A friendship I once compared to a star—it is more now like a tinsel star—and yet I must keep the sad secret, in my Diary. Please note I did not say in my heart. I doubt its existence. I doubt other things also, not many, although when Charles, Eduardo and I discussed religion I found myself calmly expressing my disbelief in Heaven after death. I am certain of the causes of my disbelief, and certain of their accuracy, and yet I cannot yet pin them down on paper. Someday I will express my thoughts more clearly and convince you.

July 22.

Petit Papa Chéri:[3]

You should learn English, that's all there is to it. You see, even this minute I would like to tell you how much pleasure your letter gave me and my French stumbles, whereas in English (also in Spanish) I can find hundreds of words. Luckily, I am sure you understand. Imagine, when we receive Madame Quintero's letters (veritable epistles, I assure you) I am able to answer her with 12 pages in Spanish, with a microscopic number of mistakes compared with those I make in French. However, cheer up. In September, si Dios quiere[4] (I love that fashion of passing off a responsibility), in September, little Papa, I am going to begin very seriously a course at Columbia University: languages, literature and philos-

---

[1] *For lack of something better.*
[2] *A.N.'s nickname for herself.*
[3] *Letter translated from the French.*
[4] *God willing.*

ophy. I am very much afraid of remaining an ignoramus and have decided not to be one. Then later on I will be able to write letters like yours, like music.

What do you think of Mademoiselle Linotte? I sent a poem in English to a journal and they accepted it and sent me five francs. That was so encouraging that I have begun to dream again as in the old days. No doubt at the University I shall find out whether I have a talent to cultivate. Don't make fun of me!

In rereading your letter, I stop just as I did the first time at certain lines that sadden me. You shouldn't think about death, Papa, at your age. You are younger than Mother, and she seems so young, so full of energy, tireless, smiling and as beautiful as she is courageous. You should think that you preferred to give your whole life completely to art instead of to your children, and now you understand that art asks everything and gives nothing in return, isn't that so? The greatest sacrifice is to do what one doesn't want to do. I understand so well, so well, how much you would like to see us again, and when that day comes it will be every bit as happy for us, you know that. And that day will surely come, first because none of us wants to spend his life in the United States, and also because I have wanted it my whole life long. Try to believe that, Papa, I beg you.

It's to give you pleasure that I go on taking snapshots. Enclosed are some new ones. Sometimes I think I send you the same ones more than once because I forget which ones I selected for you. You will soon have an albumful. I am glad to know that my picture pleased you. People who know me say that it makes me look older. No doubt the picture makes me look very intelligent, but really I am still a featherhead.[1] Sometimes I go on preparing for a conversation with a certain person. I soliloquize, I make speeches to my mirror, to the living-room chairs, the trees and the walls. Then when the moment comes—Good Evening—I find I am guilty of banalities and other horrors.

Joaquin has been studying Gounod's *Ave Maria* just because it interests him. He plays it very well and with a touch that astonishes his listeners. Near our house we heard a pianist playing and took Joaquin to play for her. The lady listened to him and said, "I don't know if I have anything to teach this boy." Nonetheless, Joaquin goes to see her often, until such time as Mother finds him another teacher. He is on vacation now and plays all day

[1] Tête de linotte.

long. Thorvald is at Boy Scout camp for two weeks. Outdoor life is what he likes best and of course the result is splendid.

I don't know how it happens, but the days slip by in such a delightfully quiet way that we forget to count them. Every Sunday I write in my Diary: Oh, Sundays. Everyone looks so angelic and peaceful . . . Warm weather, a pale sky, quiet trees, quiet people. The little church is half an hour's walk from here. Mother is going to sing there next Sunday. Instead of reforming me, all this makes me dreamier and more philosophical than ever. A tennis game doesn't excite me, the theatre doesn't interest me much, I have only one real girlfriend, a bluestocking, and I begin to think that the road to romance is too slippery and that I prefer the road to study; no doubt I am destined to be an old maid. I find that idea very funny, and the talk about my debut in Havana this winter even funnier. Don't make fun: I feel a great disdain for the intellect of the young gentlemen with whom I am obliged to dance . . .

July 25. Marraine[1] arrived today, and although the day was damp and misty it seemed as if the sun were shining. We went to the docks to watch the ship come in, and the whole scene made a deep impression on me. Marraine gave me a letter from Eduardo as soon as she came, and my eagerness, my joy, in opening it made me thoughtful for the rest of the day, although I was happy. What is going to become of Mlle. Linotte if such a portion (I dare not think how much) of her happiness depends on a mere boy and a cousin. The fact remains, cold, unalterable, unchangeable, that it was my duty, nay, a necessity, to answer Marcus's letter today and yet I deliberately wrote 12 pages to Eduardo instead. Oh, fickleness! But I am so ashamed, and angry at myself also for such lack of will power. I wish I were good and determined and *true*. Eduardo's letter stirs all my happier feelings, but all the charm of it exists, I suppose, in my imagination only. That deceitful fancy of mine! No, I don't believe it. This time it is true, this friendship at least is perfect.

July 26. I have made it a habit now to wait until the blessed little household is asleep to then steal to the little sewing room to write. In a few moments I go back to my own room, cover my beloved birds, stand a few minutes near my wide-open window to feel the

1 *Godmother—Tia Juana.*

breath of the fields. A queer .picture I make as I sit scribbling away. My kimono is blue, my boudoir cap is rose, my slippers a flowered pink—most of it is inherited from my cousins and cannot be criticized. My hair is loosely braided, which reminds me of school days and my grande passion for a violinist, long, long ago. But today I am so happy that my exultant mood does not fit in myself alone; it spreads, it spreads, until people begin to wonder. How can they guess? It comes from Marraine's conversations. She has often spoken to me of Eduardo, unconsciously telling me how one of the first things he told his family was that I would be a great success in Havana society and when they asked him why, he told them that I had become pretty. And then something far lovelier and which I hold more precious: he has said that I was the most womanly woman he had ever met. As I write the severe criticisms of myself—the self condemnation and reproaches — I joyously write also the little rays of sunshine which penetrate mysteriously and bring such warmth to my icy heart. To think that these little things, so useless in themselves, sometimes are the substance of my daydreams—and how unreasonable is that little source of happiness in my life: to be liked and loved! But now I must retire, as my dear Walter Scott writes. Night brings good counsel and perhaps it will bring me good sense and reason.

July 27. I behaved like a foolish girl today and I'm ashamed. For punishment I will tell you of my misdoings. Marraine's trunks came this afternoon and out of them began to walk Cuca's[1] old dresses, new to me, and I was gay! I tried them all on, parading before all the family, and wasting hours and hours, lost in the admiration of the pink organdy, the brown silk dress, the peach-colored evening dress, the white skirt and middy blouse, just like any other plain, ordinary girl. Marraine finished for me an Alice-blue organdy dress which Mother was trying to make—darling, busy, brave little Mother—and the dress is like a dream. It makes me look strange, unfamiliar. Mother gave me a pink hat, delicately covered with light-pink feathers. Standing before my mirror I exclaimed foolishly, "I wish Eduardo were here." Oh, the shame of it, the shame of it! How unexpectedly my frivolous nature peeps out of me, and how unwelcome it is! Nobody suspects it or condemns it. My exclamations, my enthusiasm, my agitation, brought only benevolent smiles from my family—no reproach.

[1] *Caridad Sánchez, a cousin; Eduardo's sister.*

Nevertheless, the picture of my trousseau already installed in my otherwise not too full closet makes me smile happily.

I have thrown away sorrowfully the blue georgette dancing dress I wore at my first dance, second dance, Emilia's reception, and many other times, but had to cut off a tiny little piece because its history is so long and thrilling. The piece is hidden away because if anyone knew, I would be termed romantic. This is the end not of a perfect but of a futile day. May they not all be thus, Amen.

July 28. I am very unhappy today. For the twentieth time I have begun to answer Marcus's letter, struggling as I have never struggled in all my life to write a letter, and finally I pushed everything aside. Oh, I can't write. It seems like a masquerade, and it hurts. What has happened to me? Is there anything I can do to completely estrange Marcus from me? Otherwise I am so lighthearted; these days linger in my memory with a fragrance all their own, and I love them. In the evening only, when the sunshine is gone, then I experience the troubled longings and the loneliness which in me are asleep only, never truly gone.

9:30. Marraine and I went for a walk through the fields . . . how fresh and how soothing the smell of the fields! And farther on, the trees of the woods loom in complete darkness; what a myriad of mysterious sounds; what a blessed, beautiful memory these peaceful days will be when I advance in life and plunge deeper into troubles. I forget human beings, I lose myself in this new emotion, this realization of the presence of beauty.

July 31. Thursday I visited Tia Coco in Boonton, New Jersey, with Marraine. I was so deeply impressed by the scenery that while the train tore through the shadows on the way home, I impulsively scribbled the thoughts that crowded into my head. It is difficult to read the scribbled pages, but I wrote what I saw with a fresher impression than I have now and will copy it.

Tia Coco's house, an English cottage, dainty and simple, lies bounded on one side by a large road and on the other by wonderful woods and fields. The ferns grew in immense quantities. I saw a cherry tree, and an apple tree. I had never seen an apple tree in my life! We visited a little brook, a secluded, mysterious little spot overshadowed by trees through which the sun never shone; it flowed so evenly, so deliciously cool, that I thought of Tennyson's lines: "Men may come, and men may go, But I go on forever." How well the world is made if that little brook does go on forever. What matter men?

The silence of the woods was broken when we arrived at the waterfall. At first it seemed like a lake, where flowers, trees and bushes reflected their beauty; then the roaring, foaming water fell in heavy ripples down the walls of a rock, rushing onward on its splendid journey, eddying, dashing against the rocks below and losing itself in a dark, dangerous whirlpool. Ivy and wild flowers clung to the bridge that spanned the cascade. I noticed a very fragile flower, lovelier than all the rest, clinging to a rock, and at her feet the surging waters eddied, leaving her untouched. She seemed the queen of the majestic spectacle to me. Oh, what power, what incredible beauty and perfection were mingled there. How mighty the voice seemed to human ears! One could have watched forever under the spell of such perfection. We followed the path until the roar became a murmur and was finally lost. Then the woods began to whisper again; the breeze rustled through the leaves, carrying its mysterious messages. It was now the spell of solitude and silence, but the memory of the other spell lingered. Suddenly we came upon the town, and a factory, with its tall red-brick chimneys smoking; panting machinery, the workers' grimy faces, the strained cares and tasks, the hustle. Oh, how the contrast burst upon my understanding. This was the work of man, and the other the work of God.

August 3. Sometimes words fail me. I can only copy the letter I received this morning which is the cause of my happiness. Behold! from the Delineator: "My dear Miss Nin: I am so glad you did send us another poem and I hope you will be glad when you hear that this time we are going to consider it as we should consider a poem from an adult contributor to the magazine. This means not only that the check will be bigger but, what is more important, the poem will appear not in the youthful column but in the body of the magazine wherever we have space for it. I wonder if you wouldn't like to come in and see us someday when you are in New York? I noticed you live in Richmond Hill but you probably do occasionally come to the city. Sincerely: L. Myra Harbeson, Verse Editor." This morning my ecstasy was childish. I waved the letter and read it a thousand times while choking down my breakfast, fearing each minute that it would vanish like a vision. I want to tell the whole world. I could laugh with all my heart. One of the sweetest sides of it, to my eyes, is that it should be Mother who inspired my first little success. Mother, little Mother of mine! I am thinking now how happy Father will be, my aunts, my cousins, and Eduardo, if they knew, because of course I can't tell them all. I have been polishing my other scribblings for the great day.

Today was one of the most beautiful days of the summer. We all watched the glorious sunset, twilight—half shadows, half lights. I will remember this day for a long, long time, for the dreams I dreamed in the swing, watching on one side my dear little house with its lit-up windows in the darkness, on the other the woods, with the beautiful sky for a roof. And beyond that, life, life. Tonight my heart overflows.

The thought came to me tonight that I want to sketch my house, it looked so pretty and lovable, just like a person who has a heart. It does need new clothes, but in the evening you can't see it, only the little windows full of light and the shadow of the roof and chimney looming against the sky. I love it, my house, and all the things that happen to me now. I almost wish to remain seventeen always and just live in this manner, except for the care of the house and dishes.

August 4. Today I worked on business all day long, letters, bills, for Mother; cooked the luncheon and tidied the house and kitchen —in short, not a poetical moment for myself—and so I felt like a practical, sensible little housekeeper after the day was done, ready to fill my diary with recipes and advice.

I long to write. I feel that if I were left alone for a long time, I could do something, I could discover the source of the voice which calls me night and day. I wish for tranquillity, for solitude, and I wish for a letter from Eduardo also.

Mrs. Norman[1] gave me a photograph of my mother at the age of 19 or 20. I could not take my eyes away from it and I have it now on my dressing table. I want to be like her, I want to look like her. And the photograph lies there, whispering to me of Mother's youth while I resolve to imitate her. Nevertheless, I look so different. I fear sometimes that I am terribly plain, and that I seem just made to be a learned bluestocking. A plain cotton bluestocking. Who knows? But, somehow, even as an old maid, an author, an unnoticed individual, I am going to be useful and do something worthwhile during my life.

[1] *Rosetta Norman, a friend of Mrs. Nin's.*

August 11. I just received a very beautiful letter from Marcus, whom I had finally answered with a short letter. I don't understand how I can admire the way he thinks and yet like his character so very little. He is jealous of my cousin Eduardo. The mere idea seemed so absurd to me that I reread the words in which he expressed it twenty times and then I felt sad. As if Eduardo admired me the least bit, I who am so "queer" and far from beautiful. And my cousin, to boot! I despise the idea—it's so impossible. However, I don't always despise things that are impossible, like certain people, for example, and kindness, which Charles pretends doesn't exist.[1]

Oh, little Diary, how undeniably the French peeps out of me. I was writing French unconsciously, although it makes little difference. I wanted to tell you how during lunchtime we discovered and defined love. "Please don't ask me," I said. "I am in love, that is all I know, and it is the most wonderful feeling in the world." Each one gave a different definition. We argued, gave examples and proofs. Charles is a heathen. Thorvald a know-nothing. Joaquin's heart for romance is an unknown quantity. Tia Juana, the experienced, said little, and so it happened that all those who wished to discuss love could not explain it, either because of not having felt it or having felt it too much. Later I wondered about my own self. I said I was in love, and I am. I think I have always loved, and am loving and will love forever. Who? I do not know. A shadow, a fancy, smoke, a vision, no tangible person yet, but someone. Sometimes it is true I have given a name to my shadow, one boy after another, believing I would die of sorrow when the boy vanished from my life. I did it often long ago; as I grow wiser, or I think I am growing wiser, I adhere longer and more tenaciously to each of my idols, until their fall awakes me . . . to begin all over again. Had I been a man, I would have been an eternal lover. Being a woman, what am I? The future will tell. Only, I am in love, because my heart is awake to every vibration, to every touch of nature and humanity. I *feel*, always, from day to day, sorrow and joy. I *live* and *dream* love.

Charles, lately, like all children who know a great deal and know that they know, has become slightly pedantic. I almost lose my head each day with indignation caused by his views. While he remains with us (a few days) we have had time to talk. His

[1] *Translated from the French.*

cynicism is horrible, his "mépris"[1] of womanly qualities detestable. He says intelligent men seldom marry and that Diogenes, who searched for an honest man, never even attempted to search for an honest woman; that goodness is hypocrisy; experience of life is knowing the bad in it; the good in it is missing. Romance to him is nonexistent; in slang, rot. Love is a weakness, a mere passion. Humanity is worth nothing to him; he does not care what happens to him if he is healthy, well and safe. Oh, the horror of it! And yet mingled with these inhuman creeds he has a wonderful memory, a mind for logic, absorbs Plato with marvelous facility, and is a scholar. I wish he were more human. Does he believe what he says? Or is it the pedantry of his age? The love of bombastic effects accompanying the realization of one's knowledge? I hope his conceit will melt with the years, full of lessons that follow infantile, comparatively calm periods of existence. Wait until he loves others besides himself and loves love. How quickly he will change. I am sure I will like him better. Just now he awakens all my curiosity, then my indignation. If he continues, he will awaken my disapproval.

August 15. Today Mother and I saw Mary Pickford in *Suds*. A myriad of times the moving pictures are detestably stupid; they are a disgrace to the romance lovers. And so this time we enjoyed greatly Mary Pickford's true acting in a pretty, human story; how we sympathized and were thrilled. touched, at so many different times.

On the way home we greeted the tailor, smiled pleasantly at the butcher (all in Sunday clothes), spoke with the train man who watches all day at the crossing, answered the vegetable man's muddled English, bowed now to the fish man, now to the florist's wife. Such are the charms of rural life.

Thorvald and Charles have been in Edgemere all these days with Tia Antolina, who has our bungalow for several weeks. I am going there tomorrow to take care of Antolinita while her mother is in the city. Before Charles went, we took a memorable walk in the evening. I say memorable because of many things. At first, four of us started, Charles and I immediately indulging in a conversation all of our own. Then Thorvald was bored and fled home. We marched on, we spoke on. Then Joaquin retreated. We marched on, with the wise moon. enthroned in the clouds above

[1] *Contempt.*

us, left to listen. The subject was love. I was trying to convince an egotist, a self-centered and yet lonely boy, that my creed was true. I told him that love was not in our hands and that we all needed it, and he listened intently and half-believed me. He explained that he was always lonesome, and yet that books and games could make him forget it. "Forget it, yes, but not cure it!" I said.

"Love always brings troubles, worries, unhappiness, Anaïs, while if I remain a bachelor, I will have no one to think of but myself."

"And no one to love you but yourself, Charles. You only think of the troubles love brings you, but there is a reward, there is the companionship and many other things. When you are older, if you are only interested in yourself, you will be disenchanted because we really never know ourselves and you may find your own self uninteresting. Self-love is built on sand. Anyway, bachelor life is not life; it is mere existence, like that of cats and dogs."

"Very queer, very queer, your ideas," said Charles. "And do you think anyone loves willingly?"

"Oh, yes, there are people who long for love, who want it with all their hearts. I want it, and I will have it. It's an ideal like any other, only it comes at a certain age."

"Your ideal is a vision," said Charles gravely. "I doubt romance more than ever if you call it an ideal."

"No, romance is not an ideal, it is life, life, yours, mine and everybody's—only you do not wish to see it thus. You are blind."

"How do you feel when you are in love?" asked Charles. "I have never felt it."

"I can't explain it, but you will know when you feel it, I promise you. Besides, I am in love, yes, but in love with a shadow, no tangible person, and you could not understand how I feel. You love only yourself, and I have enough to love people *and* shadows *and* every beautiful thing I see. Men are very different, I know that."

For the first time in his life Charles complimented me, and I was happy to have wasted such a long walk and so many long pages on such a hackneyed subject as this odd little thing called love.

August 21. Monday and Tuesday I spent in great unhappiness in Edgemere. The riotous gaiety, the glare of the beach and then in the evening the *cards,* the flirtations. Ethel, a light-headed gossipy Cuban, Luis Rey, Charles in his masquerade outfit, sham admiration of Ethel's wiles—everything became so repulsive to me that for one moment I felt I was going to scream and vanish, perhaps to fly home toward Peace. In the train coming home I soliloquized severely, condemning my cranky temper and savage impulses. Home soothed me and instantly I became myself again, singing, speaking with my bird, watering my plants, whom I call my children, and altogether enjoying myself with all my heart in the big lonely house. I was happy to be with my typewriter once more. I wrote, I read, and chased out of my life the hateful moments spent in Edgemere.

Wednesday I visited Miss Harbeson. It was an adventure, neither more nor less. The bus left me in Washington Square, a bewildered stranger to the neighborhood. I asked passers-by for the Butterick building and finally someone directed me with the very comforting remark that it was a very, very bad street. My heart fluttered with expectation. I imagined myself brutally attacked by a sinister band of bad men, and saved by some gallant young knight of the twentieth century. "Oh, thrill, I called thee loudly, and ye listeneth not!" For I walked a half an hour from MacDougal St. to Spring St. absolutely undisturbed and unthrilled. I was accompanied by the lamentable music of a street organ, little ragamuffins, and Italians selling pears; and I saw only corpulent maidens breathing the dusty air on their unclean doorsteps; working men; crying, uncared-for babies; homely little girls; groups of colored individuals, probably discussing politics; and the only thing I could see, even with my large imagination, that was somewhat nearer to a thrill was the curious and fixed stare of all those I passed on the street. Reaching Spring St., I saw the Butterick building. An elevator took me to the twelfth floor while I noticed the names on the doors. We passed the Editorial Department, Printing Department, Subscription Department. It was the machinery behind the ordinary-looking Delineator I had been reading so unconcernedly each month with never a thought of the immense amount of work it represented. My surprise continued as I met Miss Harbeson, who really shattered all my conceptions (no, I should say misconceptions) of an editor. She was young and pleasant, interesting and human. She showed me the work she was doing, preparations for the December issue of the Delineator; we spoke on different subjects, and I finally left her, to wonder all the way home. Probably my verses will be published in December. This seems to be the list of necessities for a would-be author: Imagination, Industry, Perseverance, Patience.

August 22. Oh, how I enjoyed myself last night. At the Kew Gardens Inn, dances are given each Saturday night, and we arranged to go with the de Solas.[1] Mother, Marraine, and I, only; Thorvald being in bed with bronchitis. I wore my fairy dress of turquoise tulle and a happy expression of foolish joy. When we arrived there at nine the de Solas appeared by slices. I had no one to dance with and began to watch others philosophically. Just then Mother met a Mrs. Waterbury, whom we once knew when living with Tia Coco. "Well, Mrs. Nin, how are you? What are you doing here?"

"I am bringing my daughter to the dance," answered Mother.

Then later Mother told me how Mrs. Waterbury's nephew, Mr. Sanford, had been asking who the girl in blue was, wanting to meet her, and also a Mr. Blackwood, and we were finally introduced. I danced until midnight. Mr. Sanford was my age and very courteous and nice. With Mr. Blackwood I danced the most beautiful waltz in my life. He was older and very pleasant too. And so at the end, Mrs. Norman, Captain Norman, Marraine and Mother, who watched me sometimes and had conversed the rest of the evening on the veranda, complimented me on my good luck. We walked home very gaily. Marraine had danced several times and felt very youthful.

But, oh, how I liked this morning's Mass, with Mother's voice floating with the organ's prayer. And now we are going in a hired automobile to ride for two hours.

To Eduardo:

Don't you think, Eduardo, that life would be very monotonous if we knew everything? Fortunately each day we learn and find out how little we know. Oh, it is just like flying in an airplane, with endless stretches of unseen lands and oceans yet beyond, always beyond, beyond. Only, the unhappy people who have no imagination have no airplane and must walk.

I visited again Washington Irving's nook in the public library, the display of his letters, his diary, his penciled notes of the things from which he wrote his essays. And people gaze at those relics

---

[1] *Family friends; Candelaria de Sola and her son and daughter, Vicente and Elsie.*

reverently, a myriad of people who pass in and out, all day, with their hearts full of admiration. Look, what an abysm there is between Fame and the common life we lead. Can you ever fancy your letters, your diary, your poems thus displayed—or mine? Perhaps people will say when we die: "Era muy bueno, el pobre."[1] And that is all!

August 24. The family of Mr. Sanford, with whom I danced so much on Saturday, invited me to the vaudeville tonight. They are coming for me at 8 o'clock. I played all day long with Thorvald, who is sick in bed with a bad cold. When I stop playing with him, he picks up his violin, with which he has suddenly fallen in love again. I do a lot of work for Mother, but I do it all impatiently.[2]

August 27. Tuesday I had a very good time. Mr. Sanford is very complimentary and I laughed continually like a silly little girl. Then yesterday, oh, the mystery of my first bouquet of flowers! They came in the afternoon with a little card which said: "From an admirer." Imagine, someone *really, truly* and *honestly* sent me flowers! Who is it? I dreamed about them after taking them to my church to adorn the altar. I prayed heaven not to make me conceited.

It was a very little thing, to take flowers to church, and yet it has a great, wonderful meaning. It means that I have somehow banished that horrible coolness, that doubt, that cynicism, which entered my heart with each word in the books of [Christian] Science I had been reading lately. It means that exactly like a lost sheep I have returned where I belong. It means that through an unfortunate happening in our family, Tia Juana's betrayal of her religion through weakness, I have heard and seen things which bewildered and hurt me deeply, and yet afterward, by contrast, I understood the purity, the nobleness of the Roman Catholic religion, intelligently understood. On Sundays I pray fervently as I have never prayed, perhaps for many years, that I should never be entangled in the web of Christian Science doctrines. If I could tell you all the things Tia Juana has said, endeavoring to win my belief, you would understand, and yet I can't explain myself.

I have grown to hate with all my heart that *so-called* religion, founded by an immoral woman appealing only to our lowest in-

[1] *"He was very good, poor thing."*
[2] *Translated from the French.*

stincts: those of cowardice, or in other words, fear of living, fear of struggling, which is "in itself real living," fear of physical pain. A stupid, weak-minded blindness and hypocritical idealization; a total lack of love and emotion, although they pretend to love *everybody*. How can they when sympathy is frozen in their veins, when the red blood in their bodies tingles no more than if they were jellyfish. Is utter coldness spirituality? Is constant communication with heaven, constant appeal to heaven, constant expectation of heaven's help on every microscopic occasion religion? Pray but act. To ignore humanity and all things suffering or needy around you, to contemplate the infinite, is only selfishness disguised.

And thus Tia Juana, having abandoned such a beautiful religion for such a weak, repulsive invention, has wounded my love for her to death. Last year her faults shattered my illusions; this year, when I believed my love reborn through earnest efforts to see it live again, I find it dead, dead. And then how the thoughts have hurt me. Oh, sometimes I wish I had been spared some sad experiences for later years.

September 3. It seems ages since I have written in your pages, and yet in reality a few days. I have been living the life of Miss Anaïs Nin, not Linotte. One time I was invited by Mr. Sanford to the moving pictures at Richmond Hill, and on returning at ten o'clock, we conversed until midnight, while little Mother stole to her room to sleep. The next day, Saturday, I went with Mr. Sanford, his sister, a friend and Marraine to the Forest Hills Inn, and we danced until midnight. One of the dances I kept for Jimmy.[1] I think one time I told you I was going to examine Jimmy,[2] and since then we have been indifferent and cordial. At times his tongue was a flame, sometimes ice cold, so that I believed he didn't like me at all; and he believed I was too proud! But Saturday I discovered he liked me, because he sat next to Marraine, not knowing her, and spoke of me to his friend. When I heard what he said, I was so happy that, then and there, I discovered that I liked him . . . et voilà!

Mother brought home for a week's visit Miguel Jorrín and his friend Alberto Bequer. Miguel is a brother of Tio Enrique's wife. Ouf, I'm out of breath with this family gossip. But I must

[1] *Jimmy Forgie, a neighbor.*
[2] *See* Linotte: The Early Diary of Anaïs Nin, 1914–1920, p. 458.

become accustomed to it or else become a Japanese citizen and deny Cuba as my so-called motherland.

Wednesday I saw the famous *Ziegfeld Follies* with Antolinita; yesterday, *Gold Diggers*, with Antolinita and Charles. I liked both very much.

And, oh, the books I read in my stolen (not spare) moments. *Mary Marie* by Eleanor Porter. This little girl of crosscurrents and contradictions, the child of two unlikes, her parents . . . it was her diary. At first, finding in the pages echoes of my own thoughts, I felt hurt to see them printed there by someone else— my thoughts, my conceptions, and then I forgot this and read on and on till the very end. Then I grew to love Mary Marie and wish that I could write the English she writes, plain, ordinary words, the words I use when I speak but never use in my Diary because I love the other English, Scott's English, Washington Irving's English. I feel also the double person in me: Miss Nin and Linotte. Linotte is impossible and must be hidden, hidden. Miss Nin is not so bad. I thought of my father absorbed in his art; Mary Marie's father absorbed in his stars. Her parents are divorced, my parents are separated. But, oh, there all similarity ends: Her father and mother fall in love again! And mine? The end of *Mary Marie* was long ago the end for my dreams, but why should I think of this today? I don't know. Father's loneliness haunts my dreams sometimes, but I have never spoken of it. It is so strange to grow up without a father, and so sad.

September 7. Sunday Joaquin reached the respectable age of twelve. Mother and I gave him money; Mr. Reilly,[1] two books; and Mrs. Norman, candy. He seemed very happy, and yet grave, as if he were seeing new responsibilities and new tasks ahead of him. We all went as usual to our little church. Joaquin, with glowing eyes and the oddest of expressions, placed one dollar of his own into the collection basket. (When Mrs. Norman heard the story, she placed one dollar in an envelope and secretly put it under his plate at lunchtime, with the words: From St. Anthony for Joaquin. Address Gates of Heaven.)

And then in the afternoon—oh, little Diary, what an adventure. It was a glorious, cheerful day and we set out in an old hired automobile bound for Brentwood, Long Island, Mother's

[1] *Mrs. Norman's brother.*

convent, to visit her teacher. The party consisted of Mother, Mr. Reilly, Miguel Jorrín, Thorvald, Joaquin, Alberto Bequer and Linotte. It was two o'clock when we began. After two hours of lovely riding along beautiful roads and sometimes near enough to the sea to feel the salty breeze, we arrived at the Convent of Brentwood in the Pines. It was not school time, and the great, beautiful buildings were very silent.

We entered and were led by a very old sister through the long, still corridors. While waiting for Mother's teacher, we met a young sister. I believe I will never forget her face. She told us her name, Maria de la Concepción. She had great beautiful blue eyes as calm as lakes but far lovelier; they were full of soft lights and shadows with little ripples when she smiled; they seemed to have seen ethereal loveliness unknown to us. I felt I wanted to kneel at her feet; how pure, how good and gentle she must have been! I could fancy angels watching her asleep; I could fancy her at her prayers, and heaven listening to her perfect voice. When she left us I retained a strange emotion, as if in her presence I had been bathed in a flood of light. The perfect serenity of her thoughts, reflected in her eyes, mingled with the purity of her heart. Those things I want to remember whenever I am troubled and wicked.

Later I met Sister de Paul. It seemed she held great expectations as to the characteristics of Rosita Culmell's daughter! I loved her as soon as I saw how she kissed Mother, how she led her to some chairs, sat by her side and, looking into her eyes, whispered something. Mother blushed and became embarrassed and humble. It was the first time I had seen Mother like that. She answered but turned her face away: "Oh, about a month!" She told me later how Sister de Paul had asked her how long since she had been to communion. And Mother knew how hurt she would be if she knew the truth, the dear, dear sister.

Then she turned to me and held my face between her hands and kissed me, telling me that I looked like a *good, lovable* little daughter. She was Mother's French teacher, a French woman herself from the famous family of de Guise, and so she called me a little Parisienne and held my hand in hers all during the visit, exclaiming something lovely each time her blue eyes met mine. She was so simple, so motherly, remembering Mother's father, Mother's sisters, after a separation of more than thirty years. She had been told of Tia Juana's unfortunate change and charged me with the task of bringing Tia Juana to her.

"Petit ange du foyer,"[1] she murmured continually, and I felt that however wicked I might have been in the past, I could never be anything in the future that could betray Sister de Paul's faith in Rosita Culmell's daughter. She told me she would pray for us and that I should pray for her.

We rode back a different way; it was a still-lovelier road, belonging to the Vanderbilts, and we had to pay at the beginning of it for the right to use it. How quickly we traveled. How thrilled we were! How soon we would be home! Then—plaff! A puncture. After an intermission of 40 minutes we were once more ready. Meanwhile the sun had disappeared and the drowsy twilight succeeded the glorious afternoon. How quickly we traveled! How thrilled we were! How soon we would be home! And the shadows traveled with us, falling, falling over the sleepy fields, enveloping the trees in their misty embrace. Suddenly—the automobile, while climbing a hill, stopped. It was growing colder, and all of us, without food since one o'clock, began to murmur and mumble about being hungry. People stopped to help us; we had no lights, lacking kerosene or something like that. The word carburetor popped up often in the conversation; it seemed that if we could somehow get up the hill, the rest would be easier. We waited on the road in complete darkness now, and suddenly the machine began to go, up, up, up the hill and all of us had to run after it. When it reached the top of the hill we took our places once more and the voyage was resumed for a few yards. It was another hill we had to conquer or die. Thorvald was sent to the nearest telephone while the chauffeur struggled vainly with the complicated machinery. He said continually that if we could get up the hill, we could get home. Then a queer, unusual thing took place: Mlle. Linotte had an idea. Perhaps the reason was that Linotte was enjoying the situation immensely, thrilled although hungry. "Let us get out and push," I exclaimed. No sooner said than done. We pushed. It was very difficult and strenuous, and so, pushing, we reached the top of the hill. There the chauffeur fumbled with his tools for a while, and suddenly the thing began to crawl. We lost a half an hour looking for Thorvald. Part of the time he was running after us, endeavoring to reach us. At twelve o'clock the moon and the stars witnessed a strange sight. The automobile had somehow struggled until it reached Richmond Hill, a block away from home.

[1] *"Little angel of the hearth."*

There it remained. We marched to our house and to our supper. We slept until ten o'clock.

Monday morning Mr. Sanford, or Waldo, as I must now call him, telephoned, asking permission to come and see me. He came at four and we talked and laughed and danced together. He remained for dinner, and after dinner the rest of the family joined us to play games. At nine Joaquin went to bed. At nine-thirty Thorvald made his exit, then Alberto. At eleven Miguel yawned and departed. And so Waldo remained until a few minutes before twelve, when he was to take his train to New York. He made me promise to answer his letters and finally shook hands with me the way Doctor Murray does, painfully, forcibly and emphatically. And today at dinnertime he called up just to talk. Well, well, said Mlle. Linotte, this is an eventful life. Add to this a cold letter from Marcus—not a word from Eduardo.

September 10. I can't explain my mood today. I ought not to write and yet I am all alone in the house and sad . . . Then see if you can endure me for a little while, until I reform. I imagine it is because Thorvald and Joaquin have quarreled and I almost lost my head; and yet I should not have wasted so much time separating them, having so much work to do for Mother. When Thorvald went to play tennis with Miguel and Bequer, Joaquin became as quiet as a mouse, and I worked until my typewriter broke down, then I wrote to Jack, and here I am, a very moody individual to console. I will tell you what, little Diary: sometimes I feel very wicked. Many things make me think so, and then I grow calm and grave, calmer and graver, till I look like a sour old maid with a sorry-to-have-missed-so-much expression.

Then I read this book from the very beginning and find it ever so queer. I seem to change every day and so quickly that I have no time to understand myself. But this is not what matters so much; it's the realization that everybody changes also. The thought seems strange to me as I read Marcus's last letter, in which he tells me he is coming to New York Friday, and I realize I would give a great deal never to see him again—never. Yes, you see, here it is I who have changed. Another instance is Frances's correspondence, once with such short periods elapsing between each letter, and now when I write, she does not answer. She has changed. Somehow, instead of getting wiser I am growing more like a child who is afraid of darkness and shadows. Little things haunt my dreams at night and my thoughts by day, particularly questions which are never answered. And all this is folly, because it is true that we hold the greatest part of our own happiness in our own hands and what I am doing now is seeking shadows instead of sunshine. And yet I do so want to be good. It is true that Mlle. Linotte belongs to herself and to you, but Miss Nin must concentrate on her tasks and be useful. Only it is so much easier to be Mlle. Linotte. I am going to see Eduardo and Cuca very soon. They left Cuba today. And yet I imagine it will be a starchy meeting on Cuca's side. And heaven knows how changed Eduardo may be. Perhaps it will be impossible to live again that week of harmony, as I have termed it in my imaginary conversations.

Dear Frances:

A rainy day is a day of memories, and today seemed far lovelier than many glorious days put together. Can you guess why? I knelt by the side of my drawer, and seeking some papers, I found all your old letters, which I read one by one. Oh, if you knew how each brought such pictures before my eyes that I could not tell which I loved best. That is why I am writing today although I have not heard from you for a long, long time—because I am thinking of you. I read the problems. Do you remember when we tried to discover the bottom of little happenings? I read about your book, your diary, your stories, your poems, everything in short which made ours conversations instead of plain, ordinary letters. One letter you wrote in pencil I can't read. One by one I opened them and felt their fragrance chase away my loneliness (because you know I was lonely when I knelt by the drawer, not now). I read them all and wished the last ones would not grow so short and scarce. But Mother says very few people can waste as much time writing as I do! Well, now I have finished them—only *you* still stand in front of me. I suppose you will go when I close this letter and so I want to make it long; I don't want to break the charm. Perhaps you think I am a leetle off? No, it is just because I really have woven a charm around you so as to bring you here in spite of yourself. There are many things I would like to tell you, because I have been reading Socrates and Plato. And if you knew, Frances, how they make you think and wonder! Do you remember one time when you wrote that you were not sure whether you had a soul? In a long dialogue one book explains how there are a myriad of things we know which we have never been taught *on the earth*. It seems (I say it seems because I have not formed a decision of my own yet) well, it seems that long before we existed óur souls were living and learning in other worlds, then they come to us, and leave us again when we die. Everything they say is proved by logic; sometimes I dislike logic very very much, but it appears that no statement can be made without proofs! I am reading these books in preparation for my philosophy course. I would not like to be taken by surprise by the sudden discovery of so many strange beliefs. I have already on my own found out many things which haunt my dreams at night and my thoughts all day. Sometimes I wonder if I will like philosophy, and can I remain a poet and a philosopher in one? Don't you think that if I discover philosophy to be unfit for a poet, I could just let Miss Nin learn it? You know Miss Nin is the sensible side of me, Frances, the little housekeeper and sister and obedient (ahem) daughter. Linotte is the side which is always in a state of confusion and alarm, the impossible side which must be hidden or else endured—the moody and cranky individual and also the verse scribbler, etc. Which do you like best? It is easier to be Linotte. If you love me at all, write, Frances.

Anaïs & Linotte

The table is set, and culinary perfumes rise from the kitchen, to Thorvald's great joy and general satisfaction. I wanted to tell you how happily our Sunday had begun, and now . . . oh, how hard it is to be gay! Thorvald and Joaquin are quarreling, and poor little Mother is angry. Only a while ago Joaquin was playing on his beloved piano and Thorvald was reading. Can't boys ever control themselves? Must they always quarrel and shout and tear around the house? I don't know but I think sometimes . . . No, I won't write what I think because I fear my cranky disposition is having a good wicked laugh about me, boasting of how easily I fall under its influence.

I have thought a great deal about the Sánchez family, particularly about seeing Cuca and Eduardo again. Miss Nin is extremely frivolous and was given a new hat, partly because of her cousins' coming. Miss Nin likes it a great, great deal. It is all lace and feathery fluffiness and black, which makes me look dignified, pale, interesting—you know, little Diary, hats and other things change one's appearance, even though the inward appearance may be so-so.

I am watching this book as it grows, grows. What a gossipy little woman I am! Whether it be in English or French, did you notice how abundantly my thoughts settle themselves on your pages? It is horrible. The next little book will be in French again because this one was begun in English for Eduardo's sake, and I suspect he will not ask to read it—fortunately, because really, I would be ashamed to have the windows of my secret chambers opened like that by anyone . . . except Mother and my husband.

September 13. Eduardo came! Last night they arrived at the Hotel Waldorf, and this morning he came with my little cousin Anaïs. They had lunch with us, and Joaquin and Anaïs went off by themselves to play. So Eduardo and I held a Harmony meeting. It truly did not seem he had gone away for two months. He read some of your pages, facts and fancies, and we talked. Good heavens, how easy it is to speak when one has things to say. It was like reading a book . . . preface, contents and end, listening to each other's words. Then I asked myself why I was sleepless and thoughtful and sad; the answer did not come, and while I lay there with my eyes wide open, I lived once again the events of the day. I had gone to New York on a very early train. Cuca was sleeping, and Eduardo and Anaïs were at breakfast, so Tia Anaïs and I stole out for an hour, I think, to shop.

At 11:30 we were ready for the Tarrytown train and for the adventure. On the train Anaïs read and Eduardo and I held another Harmony meeting. I hardly know what we spoke of, but it seems that the trip lasted three-quarters of an hour, although I could not have told the length of it myself. Suddenly I know that the train jerked and the conductor shouted: "Tarrytown!" An ordinary station, an ordinary train, but our destination . . . Washington Irving's home. However our enthusiasm did not extend so far as to do away with our human weakness. We unanimously entered a store and purchased provisions for a picnic. Then, and only then, we set out for Sunnyside, which was about a mile away. We left the ordinary town behind us and walked at times by fields and by long stretches of tall hedges through which we often peeped to meet with beautiful, stately mansions and a little glimpse of the calm Hudson, the celebrated and beloved river. When we reached a field where cows grazed (do cows graze?), Anaïs and Eduardo decided we would have our lunch there, to the great consternation of Mlle. Linotte, the child of the city, afraid of cows! Shame, shame. The fearful beasts were, on the contrary, cruelly indifferent to us, staring sometimes with their fixed look and turning away disdainfully the next moment—also running

away if we merely waved our hands. The lunch was really perfect. We picked flowers and placed them in the empty olive bottle
as a centerpiece on the loveliest dinner table ever imagined, fresh
green grass under tall friendly trees. I thought of many things,
pleasant things, and, finally, that there were no dishes to wash!
You know, little Diary, how that would please.

After "the sated gourmands' finest repast," we resumed our
march. If I remember well, the conversation consisted mostly of
unreasonable laughter and exclamatory sentences. Had I been
alone I would have been grave and would perhaps have moralized
and wondered, soliloquized and dreamed. But Anaïs and Eduardo's
influence made me what I ought to be and can't be—a light-
hearted and sunny little lady. But what is that to me? It was a
very beautiful road with taller trees than I had ever seen. Some
parts of it were familiar to me, as if I had dreamed of them, particularly one house, for which either nature or man had built a
lake as smooth as a mirror with a tiny island in the center, from
which a lovely, eloquent weeping willow tree sprang. Tied to the
shore was a graceful canoe, and then as far as the eye could
reach, stretches of woods and hills. And yet this was the more
civilized section. When we reached a rustic, rugged lane, we
turned, until the gate of Sunnyside stood before us. "Wherefore a
gate if it be closed?" I was tempted to ask. Not closed literally,
but guarded by a forceful sign: "No trespassers. Punishable by
law." We had been told the house was closed, but how could we
abandon our wished for glimpse of Sunnyside so soon? We did not.
We skirted the forbidding hedge until we reached the river and
what we believed still to be Sunnyside. We crawled miraculously
under the iron railing, we followed a lovely little brook, we
climbed again and slid and whispered and laughed. Heaven
knows where he came from, that man! But he came to us from
somewhere, with his austere face and the great shadow of the
Law looming behind him. I could almost see the shadow. In his
own kind of English he told us to leave the place. And we de-
camped most unsolemnly through the gate we had feared to
force. Poor Eduardo stood disconsolately in front of the shut gate
of paradise and sketched it. We rambled all afternoon, always
over and under hedges and along strange paths and lanes. We
drank some water from a small waterfall, and discovered bird nests
in the trees. I wondered if Irving could possibly have rambled as
we did, and understood why he had come to that section at the
autumn of his life. A bus took us to the field where we had left

part of our lunch, and afterward we walked to the station and took the five-o'clock train home.

Eduardo was going to visit today, but I was left all alone and so Mother told him not to come. Silly conventions! I spent a lonely, lonely day working for Mother, a very sad day also. I am sure you will hardly believe me when I tell you that I think I will never see or hear of Marcus Anderson again if I send the answer to his letter that I want to send if Mother lets me. So you can understand my anger and the rebellion of all my pride, I will copy his letter here. Listen: "I had expected to be able to see you on Monday and was somewhat surprised to find that you were away. In view of the uncertainty of telephonic communications I think that it would perhaps be best for you to write me, stating when you would be at home or, if you prefer, when I could meet you in New York. I shall go to Boston to take some examinations on Sunday but shall be back by the middle of next week. If, however, I am to infer that you are angry with me or have, for some reason, ceased to take pleasure in my society, it would be well for you to frankly inform me so, and I shall try to pass out of your sight as gracefully as I can. Frankness is always valuable and in this case might obviate the necessity of painful concealment on the part of both of us . . . Of course, I may be merely imagining these things, but your absence on Monday has made me wonder. Hoping to hear from you soon, and if you so wish it to see you, I remain, my dear Anaïs, your affectionate friend."

What arrogance! I feel a thousand years older than this angry and conceited child. I believe I almost pity his nasty temper, but I will never like him again. Oh, what a life this is for masks and shame! Now, how on earth will I ever believe someone who tells me, "I love you," and then does not hesitate to wound my pride, my friendship, for the merest whim? The cruellest thought is of my blindness, my blindness. How I can pile illusions upon illusions, curtain upon curtain of self-deceit, and then watch my work be torn and crushed and laid bare before my very eyes.

I have blessed my solitude at times. At other times I have wanted Eduardo here, with the belief that if I could look into his kindly, honest eyes, I would not be so horribly alone with my thoughts. I wanted Mother for a different reason. She would make everything seem a mere trifle, something to laugh away and forget. I want Marcus here to tell him I hate him, to fling his gifts miles away from me, and to burn his letters.

I walked bareheaded and blessed the wind blowing my hair

against my burning cheeks, carrying a few dead leaves away. Could but my dreams be carried away as easily. But dead dreams are heavy. And yet now I am calmer. I am thinking of lovelier things, of nature, of fame, of sacrifice, and charity, and youth. Of make-believe love I won't think again. What is it to me? A boy, only a silly boy, will not hurt Mlle. Linotte very much. Now let us be reasonable and forget quickly. Am I weeping? No. It is not worth weeping for a dead dream, is it?

September 14. How could I live without Mother? What would I be without Mother? Last night I was Nin, the melodramatic, bombastic, word-loving and sentimental fool, nothing else. But Mother laughed everything away, opened the eyes of reason and showed me how Marcus was not a criminal, nor I an old woman on the last step of the ladder. I laughed too, but was still angry. I wrote a different letter, which I will send away today. "Spanish blood," said Mother, moralizing, and that was all. Oh, I forget, she said also that were I *another* girl, I would do everything in my power to *keep* Marcus, for the sake of being popular, to go to the theatre, to receive books, etc. I was very indignant. The very idea! Fortunately I am not *another* girl. I prefer being the loneliest girl in the world rather than welcoming people I do not admire.

The word loneliest reminds me of this morning's sadness. I went with Mother to see Cuca. Tia Anaïs[1] was ill, and so Cuca could not go out, and Mother was going to take Anaïsita and Graziella[2] shopping. The only thing left for me to do was to come home again. I felt as if no one liked me or wanted me; a strange and unreasonable feeling, I know, but I told you Mlle. Linotte was queer, and she is!

So I came home disconsolately. I soon forgot my loneliness, however, typewriting bills and letters, washing a dress for Sunday, mending, walking to the village to market. Oh, if you could see the wind bending the lovely trees and tearing off a few leaves —how near the autumn we are!

I washed my hair and then let the wind blow through it, much longer than really necessary because I enjoyed myself immensely. While doing that I thought of Frances and how she did not answer my last letter. Just then Joaquin came home from school whistling. He kissed me before he went away again, and

---

[1] *Anaïs de Culmell de Sánchez.*
[2] *Anaïs and Graziella Sánchez, A.N.'s cousins.*

so I fell into a pleasant reverie on all the things I had to be happy about. There is one thing I have decided after much soliloquizing and that is that my romanticism is assuming terrible proportions and must instantly stop. It is selfish. I am not really doing all the things I ought to do to help Mother, thinking continuously of Romance—and at my age! I almost long to be old and wrinkled so as to cease being silly.

September 16. Last night as I was writing, Mother awoke and said: "Put out your light, fifille."[1] And I lay in darkness again just as I was going to chat with you for a few moments.

September 18. Fancy my room as it was a little while ago, all in darkness except where the moon peeped in to hold consultations with my books and to caress the Kewpie doll on the chimney; and then, on the white bed, a restless Linotte who could not sleep. So now I have just lit my lamp on tiptoes so Mother will not hear me and I am scribbling away until some sandman closes my eyes. I can see myself in the mirror, my plain face but very troubled eyes and my hair floating all over the pillow. I feel like a white, white ghost at work while the world sleeps. Why? I can't tell. No great adventure has really taken place, but I suppose I am sleepless and troubled just because I have been very happy lately and it is not good for one to be happy too often.

September 19. A calm, beautiful Sunday, which makes me feel completely out of tune with my surroundings, and if you knew what a tempest there is in my heart! All day long I think and wander restlessly, and I believe that I suffered a great deal to-day—even if sometimes I am inclined to suffer for little things. Oh, today I can never forget. It seems like a punishment, this confession I am going to make. Fortunately I know that you won't hate me for that or for anything. I need a little help so much.

Yesterday, I think I awoke with a sigh. I did not know what the day would bring, but I could neither sing nor speak with myself while making the beds. Very quietly I wrote letters for Mother. I watered my plants, tended my birds, tidied everywhere until the telephone rang. It was Eduardo: "Cuca and I want you

---

[1] *An affectionate nickname for A.N., meaning "little girl."*

to come to the theatre with us, cuisine."[1] Mlle. Linotte said yes
and then she flew to her room and dressed. I wore my lovely hat
and Alice-blue dress, which does not seem important and yet
makes all the difference in the world, as it made the lady in the
mirror look just as well as any other lady, and feel foolishly
proud. Remember, I am writing a confession.

Well, the train was late and at Pennsylvania Station a boy
made me stop to ask me if I remembered him from Dorothy's
dance, and because I remembered him he kept me there 15
minutes, talking, writing down my name, telling me to remember
his (which I have forgotten). "But I must go," I said twenty times.
"Oh, just a minute, you know, etc., etc."

It was a very foolish incident, but after that, everybody and
everything seemed just to get in my way while I walked wildly
to the hotel. A blind man stood ready to cross the street and
asked me to help him, so I crossed with him, slowly, slowly. Instead of 1:30, I arrived at Cuca's room at 2:15. They were waiting for me and I lost my head. The real excuses seemed stupidly
impossible and my imagination was there—my poor father's greatest fault and my heritage, usually conquered, but this time the
conqueror. What made me do it? I don't know. I told a deliberate
and horrible falsehood. I invented a train stopped by strikers,
broken windows. Did I stop there? I described vividly the
wounded train conductor! The satanic power possessing me pre-
vented me from blushing when I met Cuca's gray-blue eyes, and
Eduardo's. At 2:30 we took our places at the theatre to see *The
Bad Man*. We were not one minute late! And, oh, if you knew
how indifferent Eduardo was, as he had been the day before too.
And I felt further away from Cuca than ever. The play was full
of laughter, and I thought of Pagliacci laughing when his heart
was breaking.

The day before, Eduardo had told Mother that he would come
to Richmond Hill after the theatre. In the evening we were to go
together to a little informal dance given by Elsie de Sola. But
Eduardo did not want to come. I am very foolish, and imagine,
when I reached Pennsylvania Station, I telephoned to tell Eduardo
that he could still change his mind and come after dinner. He
said he would try, but when I reached home he telephoned with
an excuse. I could hardly believe that Eduardo had changed so

[1] Cousine —"*cousin*"; *a private joke.*

much, because the day he came from Cuba he said that he had missed Mlle. Linotte immensely. I told little Mother everything, and about Eduardo she said that she was only hoping I would discover in time the characteristics of a Sánchez. It reminded me of all the meaning implied in the words: "You are a Nin."

I dressed in the most desolate mood imaginable. Each moment I thought I would lie on my bed and weep. Oh, it hurts to be disappointed—will I ever be brave?

Miguel was here from school and he came with Thorvald to Elsie's dance. It was just a shadow dance, little Diary. I mean that I could distinguish no one from the other, I did not care what they did, I heard the music, I know I danced with many, I heard myself laughing. Miguel was very complimentary, but everyone seemed just shadows, and I the strangest shadow of all. I was neither Linotte nor Miss Nin, but the most wicked and unlovable girl I have ever known. At last it ended. We came home at one o'clock.

The next day Tia Anaïs was to come for lunch with all her family. In the morning she telephoned that she could not come because Graziella was ill. "Can't Cuca and Eduardo come?" asked Mother, and I heard the answer: Cuca was afraid of the train after what I had witnessed. They spoke of other things, and when she finished Mother turned to me with a reproachful and angry look. I had to tell her everything, but I suffered so much I could not weep. We walked to church. I found myself kneeling and listening to the softest, loveliest, most touching music—my real punishment had come, because suddenly the burning shame sent all the blood to my cheeks and the hot bitter tears fell. The music seemed to tell me: shame, shame!

Mother had said she was going to tell my aunt about my falsehood, and I could see myself running away from home, to live away, away from everybody, alone in the world. But if it happened, I would sooner die. The more I thought of the horrid thing that was going to spoil my entire life, the more desperately I wept. And Mother was so cold and firm, never even turning her eyes toward me. Joaquin seemed to understand.

There is nothing as boundless in the world as a mother's heart, and her forgiveness. An hour later Mother was kissing me and promising to help me to make my falsehood as small as possible. She said she knew how I checked myself continually and tried. Oh, what a terrible lesson. Does all this pain prepare me for greater sorrows? You know that sometimes they seem to come all together, and oftener than not; my heart is heavy. Is it because I don't know how to be happy and forget little troubles quickly? I am afraid it is, because tonight I sat in the darkness of my room, sobbing again uncontrollably, and when Mother discovered me she said: "Comme tu es bête, fifille."[1]

Well, it is written. It was more difficult to write than to think about. Lately I find many things I cannot write at all, and many which hurt me to write. Someday, in a few years perhaps, I will close one of these books forever with End. Not the end of my life but of my girlhood, with its simple problems and little sorrows. If my pen fails me now, what will it be in womanhood?

And now I am going to sleep if I can, for I have asked myself a thousand times whether *they* know what I am. And Eduardo, am I destroying his illusions as others destroy mine. And all through the night I will dream, I know. Only I can't weep any more, oh, not for a long time!

If you could see me now as I see myself in my mirror, with troubled, wild eyes, dark circles beneath them, a white face, you would perhaps feel a little bit sorry for me even though I do not even deserve that.

La Nuit Blanche.[2] Darkness, darkness, all around me, and all those I love calmly sleeping and dreaming of pleasant things. Not a sound but the beating of my heart. What is burning my cheeks? Bitter tears. Then suddenly I hear the tinkling clock on the stairs —it is midnight. Ghosts and shadows come and go—they are the thoughts I am trying to forget, the people who make me unhappy. They whisper, they conspire, then they point at me, and I bury my face in my pillow.

I hear the clock strike one. One, two, three. Will I ever, ever sleep? Now I am thinking of Eduardo, now of Cuca. How it hurts! Why did Eduardo ever write to me. How far away he seems from me now, from the happy week of companionship of long ago! It is four o'clock. A lovely picture stands before me—the long, beautiful days without a thought of anyone but my little family, when I work, and read, and write, happy, alone; when I mend, and cook, and sweep, when I watch for Mother's coming behind the windows; when I watch the sunset from the porch; when I sit by this desk in my kimono to write of perfect days; when I am sleeping at half past nine, to wake early for the first

[1] *"How silly you are, fifille."*
[2] *Sleepless night.*

task of yet another perfect day; I am thinking of the marketing, of the lovely walks, of the great trees in our garden, of my home, and my ideals, encircling only Mother, Joaquin and Thorvald. I am thinking that none of this is changed and that I still have it all to dream about and work for; this is life, and happiness. What is the rest of the world to me? If I am wicked for once, and they despise me for it—what is that to me? What matter if Eduardo never looks at me again? If Cuca calls me queer and crazy; and what matter if no one loves me if Mother does? Tomorrow there is a great deal to do—if I do it, I make Mother happy. I am not going to weep; I must try to be myself again.

It is five o'clock. All the shadows go. The sun shines on another day and fills a white, white room. It wakes Mlle. Linotte, who opens one eye and smiles at nothing. Happiness is foolish, but sorrow is inexcusable.

The bird peeps. All the sadness of the night melts away into the sunbeams. New day, new hopes; the eternal gift of the One who never sleeps.

September 20. I wrote the last pages while the memory of the night was fresh in my mind. Now it is one o'clock and all my work is done. I can read all afternoon and wait for Mother. Everything in me is very, very still; I am as calm as the day itself, a cold day without the faintest whisper of the wind or the trace of a dark cloud.

Eduardo must be going to school today, I think. I received a letter from Waldo which is exactly like Jack [Cosgrove's] letters. Fancy how queer it is. Marcus writes—or wrote, I should say— letters containing all of my favorite subjects and thoughts, and Eduardo's letters contained all the charm. Then Jack and Waldo write commonplace, boyish letters. Yet both Marcus and Eduardo have hurt me. Marcus very much, Eduardo only a little. Letter writing is another of my great, big problems. No philosophy will ever solve it, but experience may. Enough moralizing!

September 24. I did not hear from Eduardo until Wednesday afternoon. I was in the midst of pots and pans, my hands in the hot soapy water, meditating on the ups and downs of life, when the telephone rang. "Hello, Anaïs, me voy al colegio esta tarde. No te he podido ver, chica."[1]

---

[1] *"I'm leaving for school this afternoon. I couldn't manage to see you, chica."*

"That's all right, Eduardo."

"Tu sabes, mis amigos me han llevado al teatro.[1] I'm sorry."

"That's all right."

"Te escribiré.[2] Don't worry."

I laughed: "Goodbye!"

"Goodbye!"

I went back to my dishes, singing. At least he had remembered me, of course.

Since then I have behaved very well. That same morning I had been at Columbia. I sat there waiting for my turn to come and dreamed about my studies, never doubting that something in me was going to prevent me from entering the great college. When my turn did come, I found myself speaking to a motherly and intelligent woman, Dr. Glass. I told her what I wanted, and she asked me questions. All the while I felt as if she were taking an inventory of me, as you might say, and her eyes twinkled with a mysterious opinion she formed of me. "Why, my dear," she said at last, "you are only a mere child. If you were my daughter, I would never let you enter this college at your age."

"But I am seventeen," pleaded Mlle. Linotte.

"Yes, I know, but you are a mere child, and you are not able to take care of yourself among such grown-up and experienced students, in such a free and large school where there is so much in and out."

I forget what else she said, but I realized she thought I was a mother's-baby sort of a girl, petted and spoiled and inexperienced and innocent, which made me tremendously indignant. She gave me an address—"the school where you belong"—and there I went directly. Well, "the school where I belonged," according to the dear adviser, was neither more nor less than a private school, The Veltin School, where Mother would have to spend $200 for a special course in my favorite subjects. I hurried home and fled to my mirror. There I stood, a seventeen-year-old young lady and yet a *child*. I stared at myself. Yes, of course, my eyes are odd and large, and what on earth makes them seem like two big question marks? And not a drop of rouge—how silly of me. I should have painted my lips a little too. Add to this my tam-o'-shanter, my velvet jacket with its immaculate white, round collar—how schoollike, and unladylike! I should have worn a silk dress with my small French shoes and my lace hat.

[1] *"You know, my friends have taken me to the theatre."*
[2] *"I'll write to you."*

A child! Of course, by the way I look and dress. Why didn't she ask me to tell her about Pascal, about Socrates? Why indeed! I stared at my mirror and wondered if I would ever look wise and sophisticated. A mere child! Well, well. And an aristocratic child at that, if I *belong* in an extravagant school instead of a plain ordinary public school.

Now I plan to study two whole hours a day. I have done it yesterday and today. I spend all my days alone in the house. Monsita[1] comes from New York in the afternoon. Today was almost ideal. I woke early and made beds and tidied. Fortunately the working girl came and so I took my books, pencil and paper on the little roof of the entrance hall, which can be reached by window climbing. From ten to twelve I studied. Oh, how I loved those two hours. I read from my *History of English Literature*, taking notes, then plunged into French verbs and exercises. Then I read French out loud to myself. I memorized poetry. I read Bossuet's[2] beautiful and marvelous reasonings. Sometimes I caught myself dreaming, awed by the lovely stillness and the nearness of the treetops, but at such times I would rap the book with my ruler to dispel all the mist enfolding my thoughts, and continue gravely with my self-instruction. I won't struggle again with Columbia until the Winter season, after my projected trip to Cuba, on which Mother's heart is set.

At about five-thirty I begin to watch for Mother behind the curtains of the parlor window, playing the phonograph and dreaming by the window until I see her through the branches, coming down the hill. Then I run to her, but today Mother had dinner with a friend, and so I sat at the head of the table, and the dinner calmly passed away, as a thousand other dinners have during all these years. Not always calmly, I must admit. And now I am in my room, alone.

Cuca, I think, is coming tomorrow to dance at the inn with Thorvald, and I with Miguel Jorrín perhaps. I don't care. I feel miles away from dancing and frivolity just now. Sometimes I really hate that side of life, and yet nearly each time I have gone to a dance, some little adventure has taken place—but always to bring trouble and confusion and sad days afterward. I love the calm one has while studying, the lasting serenity and inward contentment derived from books. I suppose the times I enjoy dancing and theatres is when youth just bubbles over, as you might

[1] *Montserrat, the maid, who had been a schoolteacher in Puerto Rico.*
[2] *Jacques Bénigne Bossuet, author of* Oraisons Funèbres.

say. Sometimes I can even endure tennis for half an hour or less —but none of those things are as near to my heart and my dreams as the other, serious friends.

September 26. One word is often the key to a thousand other words, which, blended, bring forth a complete picture in our minds. If it be only such things as moonlight, stars—I am plunged into a delicious reverie; sometimes dance brings forth the thrilling picture of anticipation, but oh, Sunday!

Forever and forever when I say Sunday I will think of the hurried breakfast, the hurried dressing, with Joaquin at the tail end of hurry (the nearest one to slowness), of Mother's voice rising above all others as, one by one, she discovers unwashed ears, missing buttons, torn stockings, untidy hair and whatnot.

Somehow we are always angry with one another on the way to church, whether because Joaquin is later than ever, Thorvald's shoes are dirty and Mother tells him so irritably, or just because there is no reason but we invent some, I cannot tell. With Sunday I will always think of the church music, which stirs me so until I wish to die, and of the great change that comes to me when the music ceases; how cold I become, and the horrible little details into which my mind wanders instead of praying. How I watch the back of people's hats until I recognize them Sunday after Sunday.

Today it was raining, and so a gentleman, in placing his hat on the bench with the drops of water still fresh on top of it, unconsciously helped a thirsty fly, who drank from the odd glass— or lake! Mediocrities? Yes. I will think of the return home, with all quarrels forgotten, of the conference in the kitchen, to be followed by an appetizing lunch. And then of the long, sleepy hours. I cannot write because I don't like to leave Mother alone. The boys are away playing, and so I must read with Mother. I cannot read serious books because we often stop and chat pleasantly.

Somehow the afternoon crawls away, and melts away into the quiet evening. I will think of the cold supper, and the biscuits we are in the habit of making, and I will think, too, of my dislike for that great, inevitable inaction. Sunday has that jellyfish consistency which I dislike both in people and in days.

September 27. I received a letter from Charles, to my great surprise. Indeed, to make the smallest dent in Charles's interest seemed to me as difficult as to make one in marble. Appearances are deceitful. It was the sort of letter I enjoy so much, although I would have wished it a little more human. It was full of philosophy, of opinions on books, and yet brief and just like Charles.

I lived in the kitchen for part of the day and for the rest in ecstasy while dusting my books downstairs (for I have books in my room also). I would be ashamed to tell you how many hours it took me to finish the lovely task. Shall I? No, I shan't. I know how well you can picture me, kneeling beside a Babel tower of literature, dust rag in hand, but not always in action, absorbed— well, I leave you to guess. I can truthfully say I did not control my passions today!

I studied my lessons; I have finished an extract from Bossuet's Reflections. It is perfectly wonderful, and I want to read more of Bossuet. How I long to find myself in an Olde Booke Shoppe whenever I discover a new treasure, a new unexplored land!

Eureka! Eureka! Would to heaven you could read the book I am reveling in. It is the journal of Eugénie de Guérin. At first, on reading it, I felt very unhappy. Many of the things I have wanted to express, or have expressed so diffidently, Eugénie has in her diary. And now I am contented. She writes so beautifully and sweetly. Listen to *her:* "While I was writing, the clouds and wind all returned. Nothing more variable than the sky and one's own soul." "Mud, rain, a wintry sky—inconvenient weather for a Sunday; but it is all one to me, just the same as sunshine. Not through indifference, though: I prefer fine weather; but all weather is good. When there is serenity within, what matters the rest?" "This has been one of my happy days: of those days that begin and end sweet as a cup of milk. God be praised for this day, spent without any sadness! Such are so rare in life, and my soul, more than any other, afflicts itself about the least thing." "I don't know why I have put down nothing for four days: I return to it now that I find myself alone in my room. Solitude leads to writing because it leads to thought. One enters into conversation with one's own soul. I ask mine what it has seen today, what it has learnt; what it has loved—for every day it loves something. This morning I saw a beautiful sky, and . . . etc, etc. But is it worth while to take ink out of the inkstand to write thee all these inutilities?"

How I wish I could write like her. I often feel I am not mistress of my pen and that myriad of thoughts I can never explain. How I love her words about the soul. It is a different object she has in her mind while writing, of course. She echoes many of my thoughts, and yet I am not one whit like Eugénie. How could I be? She is too fervent a Catholic, too angelical and pure. I cannot see God continually, or feel His presence or love Him as she does. I suppose I am not worthy of it, but in that lies the greatest contrast between this wonderful woman's journal and my own modest diary: her fervor and my usual coldness in regard to religion. What would she have thought in this city, in this century? The same? I doubt it.

I am happy that the Journal consists of two volumes, as my new friend's visit will last longer. If Catholicism were not so expanded in those pages, I know Eduardo would like to read them.

Apropos of Eduardo, I am always thinking of him while discovering fine books, and before falling asleep. That hour, I devote to imaginary conversations with those I have no time to think of during the daytime. While washing dishes and cleaning and dusting and cooking, I think of my family, Mother, Thorvald and Joaquin. The days seem very short after all those things are done. And slowly, slowly I begin to forgive myself for the horrid story I told and for many other things, because I feel I am controlling myself continually, incessantly and so firmly that it really hurts at night when I finally tell myself: Do what you wish to do.

I want to forget all the times I have done what I hated to do. I notice that I forgot to tell you about Saturday night. It denotes my normal state in reference to social life. Miguel Jorrín is now a part of the Saturday and Sunday tableau. He always comes from school on Saturday afternoon and leaves Sunday afternoon. Last Saturday, Thorvald, Miguel and I went to dance at the inn. I felt so sarcastic that I could have strangled the grinning musicians and all the silly-faced dancers. I do believe that even if my materialized Shadow of Romance had been there, I would not have recognized him and would have called him, like the others: un âne.[1]

What can you expect from a *child* trying to assimilate Bossuet, struggling against Darwinism, accepting doses of Plato, sprinkled with everyday experience and housekeeping avocations? What indeed! Were I to be made into a pie, I know that at the time to be eaten, blackbirds would fly out of me, and bluebirds, and catbirds, and doves, all confused in their personalities and species, because my mind is indeed in a sad state of contradictions and ecstasies and doubts.

[1] *An ass.*

September 28. I have been thinking a great part of the day of the dream I had last night. Dreams are the silliest things in the world, usually, and yet this one has saddened me, just like a prediction, it seemed. It was that Eduardo did not like me any more, and in my dream he told me so. I heard myself saying, "I don't care." "Oh, yes you do, cuisine," and he shrugged his shoulders as Thorvald does whenever I say something that does not interest him. And just then Mother called me.

I have done many useful things today and have not had time to study, but it is only five o'clock. The delicate perfume of a cottage pudding is in the atmosphere, and Thorvald is playing on his violin downstairs, Joaquin reading. How cozy the house seems on a day like this, with storms of rain and wind outside. The elm tree is losing its leaves already. When I open my eyes in the morning I notice each day the change in the foliage's hues, because the branches are near my window—oh, so near, and friendly.

Whenever I dream I feel sadness creeping into my heart, and so I work all day long and it makes me contented. Besides, there is nothing sweeter than self-satisfaction to me, who am always so severely criticizing myself, and today I could not help smiling at my reflection in the mirror; what with my blue apron, and my dab of flour on one cheek, and my tumbling hair, I looked as if I had honestly and sincerely *worked*. And not for myself—think of it! Aren't you a little bit proud of Mlle. Linotte reforming?

After all, the other little disenchantments are just to make life more interesting. One of the most difficult things is to convince one's self. And particularly of optimism. I would make a horrible lady lawyer.

This is what I wrote today. It is not classified yet, being neither prose nor poetry. "Life is the strangest song ever played upon the heartstrings; with its melodies of sorrows taught by the world of reality, its melodies of the perfect happiness the dream world brings. All my heart is singing now with my longing for love, until someone stops to listen and his heart responds. But let me live now, happy in those longings, for when love comes, in its passionate glory, I know it will leave my heart still forever and all strings . . . broken."

Whether a voluminous Diary means that as I grow older, many of my thoughts struggling in vain to find expression have at least pierced their way to the light, or simply that I am wasting more time than ever, I cannot decide. Of course, this scribbling *is* a waste of time, but I could not give it up now for anything in the world. Did you know that whatever I do or think I am always forming into words so that I may be able to tell you about it as perfectly as possible? At times I cannot absolutely express my thoughts and emotions, and I *feel* that they are quarreling inside of me, laughing loudly, now sobbing, now striking the prison door of my head, claiming their freedom vehemently, but with one object always: to leave their birthplace and fly!

September 29. A dinner à la Nin. We all sit down. The soup is served.

Mother: "Did you wash your hands, Joaquin?"

Joaquin mumbles, rises and goes upstairs to wash his hands, banging all the doors in his rage. He comes back when we have finished with the soup. Meanwhile Mother and I had begun an interesting conversation about Eleanora Duse and d'Annunzio.

Anaïs: "She had done so much for him . . ."

Joaquin (interrupting): "Thorvald, you took one of my ties."

Thorvald: "I didn't."

Joaquin: "You did."

Thorvald: "I didn't, you stupid XXX! ! ?? ! ! X X X X ! !"

Joaquin: "You did."

Mother: "This is what I get after working hard all day."

Anaïs (boiling inside): "Both of you keep still now this is too much."

The vegetables and meat arrive.

Mother: "Pass me your plate, Joaquin."

Joaquin: "I don't want any meat."

Mother: "Why not?"

Joaquin (crying suddenly): "A boy hit me."

Mother (indignant): "A boy hit you? Where? Why? When?"

Thorvald (calmly): "He is not telling the truth." (Only, Thorvald uses more forcible language.)

Anaïs (also calmly): "What did you do to him?"

Joaquin: "Nothing, of course."

Anaïs (sarcastic): "Is that so! He just came up to you and hit you, I suppose."

Joaquin: "Yes."

Mother (excitedly): "Who is it? You'll see what I'm going to do to him. Where does he live?"

Joaquin (conscience-stricken): "Oh, never mind, it's nothing."

Mother (angrily): "Nothing! Who is it? Answer my questions."

Joaquin: "It's Lucy's brother."

Thorvald: "That big boy."

Joaquin: "Yes."

Mother leaves the table and walks to the street very angry. Joaquin runs after her and tells her to wait until after dinner. Mother returns. We all sit down. We eat everything, cold and stiff. Silence.

Mother: "Serve yourself some potatoes, Joaquin."

Joaquin: "I don't want any."

Thorvald: "I eat everything even if I don't like it."

Joaquin: "Keep still. Mind your own business."

Thorvald: "Crazy."

Joaquin: "Crazy yourself."

Mother: "Mon Dieu! Mon Dieu! Thorvald, open the doors; it is too warm here."

Thorvald tries to open the doors without leaving his chair. Anaïs rises and opens them, indignant at Thorvald's laziness.

Mother: "What would you do if I worked for you the way you work for me, Thorvald?"

Thorvald grunts. The dinner proceeds. Once in a while Thorvald says something and Joaquin retorts that it is not true. Mother feels ill and speaks little. The telephone rings. Nobody moves.

Anaïs: "Thorvald, are you going?"

Thorvald: "Naw!"

So Anaïs answers it. It's a wrong number. The dessert is brought to the table. Joaquin spills a glass of water. Silence.

Mother: "Did you write the letter to Mrs. So-and-so, Anaïs?"

Anaïs: "Oh, I'm sorry, I forgot . . ."

Mother: "Yes, of course. You always forget. Did you buy the soap for the kitchen? No. The matches? No. Did you tell the vegetable man about the bad pears? No. My home, the way it is managed, makes me sick. How can I be the wage earner and the housekeeper and the mother all in one? Oh, it is too much, too much!"

Anaïs: "I remembered the matches, and the soap, and the bad fruits, and everything else, Mother. And I do everything I can to take care of the house . . ."

Mother: "Come here, fifille, and kiss me. Those boys tire me so much that I don't know what I am saying. I know you try hard, but you have a bad reputation, you know . . ."

Anaïs: "Yes, I know, but it is different now, and . . ."

Joaquin: "Give me that napkin ring."

Thorvald: "No, it's mine."

Joaquin (louder): "Give it to me, I say."

Thorvald: "I won't."

Joaquin (still louder): "GIVE ME THAT RING!"

Thorvald: "I won't."

Mother: "Mon Dieu! You drive me mad."

Thorvald and Joaquin (together): "What are we doing?"

Anaïs (sarcastic): "Oh, nothing! Just saying darling and dearest to each other!"

Thorvald drops a fork. We leave the table.

Mother: "Your medicine, Joaquin. I almost forgot. Can't *you* ever think of it, and yet you are twelve years old!"

Joaquin: "Mother, if a man is to be shot at sunrise, and the soldiers forget, you don't expect the *man* to remind them, do you?"

Thorvald: "Oh, what a terrible . . . er . . . er . . ."

Anaïs: "I suppose you mean 'metaphor.' "

Thorvald: "Sure—what an awful metaphor!"

Joaquin: "Mind your own business."

Joaquin gulps down his medicine, drops the spoon. Then he rushes out to play, Mother leaves to read, Thorvald goes to his lessons. And Mlle. Linotte—well, it would be a shame to tell you the secret of my occupation.

This account might be one of two species of satire, which has as an object to instruct men by attacking their vices and their ridiculousness; or chasing away my anger—because of course I am angry to think that boys should so thoughtlessly make Mother and me unhappy. And yet I could be telling of such lovely things, because I went to New York this morning, just to buy a few books I needed for my studies. First I went to an old book shop, although Mother had given me license to buy as many new books as I needed. A miser in such things, I thought I could get many more if I bought them old, and therefore inexpensive. So I asked the bookseller if he had any of Bossuet's works: "What's *that?*" he asked deprecatingly. And I fled. In Scribner's I found the beloved books: *A History of English Literature* by Long (because the one I was studying from belongs to Mrs. Norman). Also: *The Journal of Eugénie de Guérin* (same reason), *Problems of Philosophy*, *Connaissance de Dieu et de Soi Même* and *Métaphysique* of Bossuet. I have read in the last already with great interest and with the happy realization that I understand it beautifully alone, with no need of phlegmatic, stern, unsympathetic teachers. One volume of the *Cahiers de Saint Denis* contains all the principles of literature, much inclined toward French literature. That, also, I do not know when to leave aside. Everything in me is now one great desire and determination: to learn, to learn, to learn. I know now why Mother always called me her little philosopher. Bossuet says: "To become a perfect philosopher, man need study nothing but himself, and without leafing through so many books, without making a tedious collection of what the philosophers have said nor going far afield looking for experience, in noticing only what he finds within himself, there will he recognize his Maker."[1]

I have received a shock as to my conception of a soul. I held the poetic notion that the soul was the thing inside of us that is sincerely and deeply stirred, and roused, and thrilled, and wounded, the nest of our passions, emotions, sentiments; of reason, understanding and will—never—and yet so it is: Bossuet again: The soul is what makes us think, understand, feel, reason, will, choose one thing over another and choose one direction over another, such as to move to the right rather than to the left.[1] I don't like that. I prefer my idealistic conception, with the belief that the mind is responsible for the functions Bossuet attributed to the soul —and so I blamed reason and common sense on the well-ordered, calm and correctly distributed mind. Imagination, its flights, passions and ecstasies, lives in the winged, free, immortal soul. But it is apparently all wrong.

I suppose each truth of philosophy will be a shock to my romanticism, my idealism, my self-created conceptions, my daydreams.

And now, whenever I dream, I will suddenly ask myself: Am I imagining? Well, then this being a thing which continues after the exterior senses cease to act, it belongs naturally to the interior sense, etc., etc. For reference, read Bossuet, but please do not ask me any more questions: I am quite bewildered.

September 30. The last day of a month and the last pages of a diary! I suppose each day the sun sets on many ends . . . the end of life, or of hope sometimes, of illusions . . . who knows?

All my tears have fallen on your pages, all my smiles have beamed upon you, till you have swelled, and leave me to join the other books, to melt into one Book—my Life! Your strength will

[1] *Quotation translated from the French.*

be the wave that will sweep me, carry me to the pinnacle of my life's task, whatever it may yet be.

I love you. You are the treasure box of the things dearest to me—the images of someone who will never live again, the girl of today, older tomorrow. Time is the greatest thief of all; it carries away things that are never replaced or reborn. Tomorrow I will have lost something, the thoughts of today, but I will be learning other things, developing, crystallizing.

So keep here for me all the things I have given you—the unsolved mysteries, the broken enchantments, the reflections of a storm-tossed soul, the reflections of a girl's simple exterior and complicated, perplexing interior life. They do not belong to me any more; they are yours. I love them in you because a creator always loves his creations, like a mother her children. But I part with you for the very love of them: you will keep them for me, unsoiled, while I travel through strange, perilous lands. And when I return, if I return, I will claim my children and carry them away to my House of Sleep.

September 30. On the first page of the Diary I have just parted with I had to write: "One of the swiftest flights of my pen through the chronicle of the hours," as it was filled in an unbelievably short time. It was a very frivolous chapter of my life, also, and that is why it ended so quickly. But you are destined for a different thing. We are studying and discovering things, you and I. Stretching before me I see an unbroken series of serene days, well regulated and useful. All Autumn, perhaps I will be left alone to my studies. The Winter may bring a great revolution, with its visit to Cuba, but that will be another book yet. I want you to be serious—to share my absorbing voyages into the world of science, to doubt and learn and discover and wonder with me, share all the charms of such a contemplative life, the serenity that comes when contact with the world ceases, for I will not see many people if I can help it. All my longings for romance are hushed—not dead, you know, but dormant. I will not think of boys or silly dances; or of the Great Adventure and the Phantom—no, just learn, learn, learn.

This life has begun already. In the morning my bird wakes me up early. I do not trouble with my hair—would-be philosophers must not think of such things—I just wind it around my head and fasten it in the back. It makes me look dignified. Then I proceed to the house-tidying and make the beds, etc. The rest of the morning is devoted to my secretarial tasks. My typewriter and my fingers (when I add) are busy until lunchtime. Afterward I have given myself one hour of mending, which I hate, and as a reward, two hours of study. My books have not come yet, and I have only Bossuet to read and my French grammar. But just now Bossuet is enough to plunge me into abstraction. Then there is the marketing to do, and the dessert to be made for dinner, a cake or a pudding. I can read all evening. I put my books away only when Mother asks me to come and talk to her. She is always in bed at that time, reading and resting. Thorvald is doing his homework, Joaquin, playing. Are you pleased? Can you picture the old, cozy house in the evening?

While going to the village, where I did not really need to go but the weather tempted me, I thought each moment that the wind would carry me away. How it bent the trees and swept the rain round and round with the leaves in its iron grasp! The water trickled in my shoes and whipped my cheeks, and the wind almost carried me to the village with no more respect for my weight than if I had been a leaf. I was enjoying myself with all my soul and wished the wind would carry me away, away. What a glorious voyage it would be, away from the round-faced, grinning, platonic little world, to the moon . . . anywhere. The epitaph-writers would say that I died as I had lived, for am I not always swept off my feet by my enthusiasms, by my imagination, my fancy, my dreams?

October 2. Imagine, when I came home yesterday from New York, I found a letter from . . . Marcus!

It made me think of all the unexpected things life is made of, of all the buried, forgotten actors. And now, just contrary to all my plans, contrary to all I had imagined, Marcus appears again. I had already woven a picture of my old, gray-haired self, reading my worn, old-fashioned Diary and pausing at the passage where Marcus vanishes from my young life. I pictured myself shaking my head and saying in a cracked voice: I wonder what on earth became of that foolish little boy!

But that only happens in books. In life, enter Marcus again, and the act drags on indefinitely and most unromantically. He is neither broken-hearted nor humbled nor gloriously, resplendently haughty! Just a boy expressing his regret and trying to "impress upon your mind" the fact that whatever he wrote in that letter was only a petulant expression of his annoyance at not being able to see me, being so fond of me. In short, it was really not his fault, you know, but the bonds by which I hold him are too potent and far too charming to be severed by any temporary dispute. I believe I am quoting his letter word for word, and it is not surprising, as I have read it four or five times. No, I am not sarcastic—not at all. I am just plagued, and not one whit happy. Good gracious, I will never find another opportunity to rid myself of Marcus now, if the angry letter I sent him bore such small effect. Poor Marcus! What a dislike Mlle. Linotte feels for him now! And yet I feel so sorry for him that I must be kind and try to make the best of a forlorn adventure.

I suppose at the root of it all is my power as a coquette. Heaven knows what I did at the Christmas dance that Mr. Anderson should stoop down to bestow his fondness on me.

Yesterday I went to New York to visit Ana María,[1] my little cousin who had asked for me. She had undergone an operation on the throat and lay there in her little bed, the dark-eyed darling, a living doll in a Japanese robe. Oh, I love little people a thousand times more than grownups. How they trust you and love everybody and how clear and limpid their eyes are. You can read their tiny hearts like a fairy-tale book, and their laughter is lovely beyond description. Ana María slipped her tender little hand in mine and made me sit by her bedside. "I want you to stay here all day. I like you," she said, saucily. I began to tell her stories from my own head, and as soon as I finished she wanted more and more. And there I sat, pouring all my queer ideas into tales for Ana María. She would not take a glass of milk ordained by the doctor, so I invented a fantastic kingdom in a glass of milk, and then suddenly I stopped: "Now, you see, I can't explain to you how the princess felt until you drink the whole glass." She drank it so quickly that I had to ask her not to hurry so. We had the merriest time imaginable with paper dolls. I made them walk and talk and bow, and now lambs changed into princes, now into witches and goblins. I was so happy to hear her laugh that I remained with her all afternoon. "You are very queer, Anaïs," she said thoughtfully. "Me cuentas cuentos que nadie me dijo antes."[2]

[1] *Ana María Sánchez.*
[2] *"You tell me tales that no one has told me before."*

"And you are so nice I could tell you stories forever and for-ever."

The sad part came when she would not let me go, and I had to make believe I was coming right back. "Oh, I know you are going home. Come here and kiss me!"

I made believe I was a prince and I bowed deeply and kissed her hand, which she liked very much. And then I left her and found myself in the serious world of grownups once more.

Today was such a busy day that I could not study. I swept and dusted and tidied. Writing letters for Mother in between, I cooked and washed and mended; then we went marketing, and I wrote more for Mother.

In my bird's cage I found three of his little tail feathers. One of them I painted red with my water colors and pasted on the corner of a blank page of writing paper, then I drew an inkstand. The spider web and the pen and ink I call the Weavers. Can you divine for whom this odd little work is destined? For Eduardo, although he has not even written yet. Sometimes I wish Eduardo could feel the ardor Marcus feels for me. What has estranged him from me now? I always fall asleep thinking of him and wonder-ing; wondering also if I would do *that* if I were the "other girl" Mother so often speaks of when she says: "Another girl would do this and that to be popular and have a great many friends."

October 3. It is Sunday again. Mother is reading in her rocking chair and I, to keep her company, was reading also. Only, being installed on the porch is not at all beneficial to the study of Bossuet, as passers-by are numerous and I cannot help following them with my eyes. That is why I brought you down with me and placed the inkstand in a most perilous position for the sake of chatting. And I can see Mother look up once in a while, throw a questioning glance at the inkstand and return to her reading, probably wondering what on earth sustains the dangerous im-plement where it remains. I am sure it is the fairy godmother of all the bluestockings, who know that while there is ink . . . there is hope.

Of course, we went to church. I love the singing, and the thing that stirs me most is the Agnus Dei. You cannot imagine, dearest Diary, how deeply one can be stirred sometimes by music. While listening to those voices and the word "Miserere," I felt things that I am unable to describe. I will try to tell you when I know myself.

After a hearty and undisturbed dinner, Thorvald and Joaquin went to play tennis, Mother and I to the moving pictures. That reminds me of one thing I saw many weeks ago: *Humoresque*. I notice that I wrote nothing about it, and yet I often thought of its beauty. But how can I speak of a thing which has thrilled all New Yorkers, which the critics praised to the very skies, and which throng after throng have seen and been touched by? It brings to the stage a lovely, lifelike picture of the Jewish home, family, and simply crystallizes the emotions one feels while listening to Dvorák's *Humoresque*. Now the tear, now the smile to hide the tear—the lifelong struggle of humanity, the eternal play upon the heartstrings by all emotions until they snap. It was so human, so appealing! I could not keep back my tears and yet I heard myself sincerely laughing when all others laughed, which so rarely happens to me. Mother was deeply thrilled also, and Joaquin's soul could be read in his great brilliant eyes. Thorvald's callousness was pierced through and through, although he did not admit it. I was puzzled by the way it appealed to the crowd. I had never credited an American crowd with understanding of such things. It seemed way beyond them and so vivid and forcible a contrast to the vulgar, unartistic things generally offered them. It was a great lesson to me and yet a revelation also. Had it been all Art and Beauty and Reality and Pathos, it would have failed. But it was a melting pot of Art, Beauty, Pathos, Reality and *Humor*, so cleverly mingled that no one, however prejudiced, could resist its charm. I even forgot that its authoress, Fannie Hurst, is a woman whose personality I despise and whose morals I abhor. In the recent publicity she obtained, through her opinions on married life, she showed all her lack of womanliness and ideals. I can't imagine how such a story could flow from the pen of such a callous woman.

And as I write, my watch's needles work toward supper-time. In a little while we will be eating again. Mother has ceased looking at the inkstand. No wonder. She is reading the book of short stories by William Locke Eduardo gave me, and she has forgotten me. Apropos (I cannot say that in English) of Eduardo, I have added more to his will-be letter. There is a sprite in the corner of the page dressed in the colors of the autumn leaves, dancing and throwing away leaves, which fly down the side of the letter. Held from afar it is very pretty, but from near—well, I am no great painter, you know. I might be wasting precious time, for . . . will he write?

October 4. To Antolinita, who sometimes asks me what to write to her friends:

I hope you don't ask anybody what to write to me! I'll tell you what I do when I want to write you, and you can memorize the recipe: 1. Look out of the window and you see the treetops and the gloriously tinted leaves coquetting with the wind. You see the squirrels executing a toe dance on the electric wires and the Fall clouds flying. Write a page about that (it could be made into a book). 2. Look into your inkstand. See in the black, black ink a picture of all the things which have happened and all the ideas which are passing through your head. Dip your pen in quickly, fish out all those things and scatter them all over the letter. Then pass the blotting paper over them, and now they can't evaporate. 3. Look up at the ceiling and down at the pattern of the rug and it will make you think of all the things you *wish* would happen. Write them all down before you forget them. 4. Now blow some kisses into the envelope, place the heavy letter in it, and there you are! You see how easy it is! Now, suppose I had asked Thorvald what to say to you; he would tell you that the baseball scores were 4 to 2, and the cook (we have none) would tell you what we are going to have for dinner. It would not be very interesting, would it? Of course, perhaps you see palm trees and monkeys instead, and your ink may be red, but here you can use your imagination and make your letter more original than mine. And now I must go because I spilled the inkstand and I must take the cobwebs from the windows and the dust from the ceiling and the carpets. This letter proves to you that poets don't always tell the truth, for you see I did none of the things I told you to do and yet I wrote you a letter. P.S. Please don't show this letter to Charles, as I am supposed to be studying philosophy.

After Antolinita's letter I wrote an essay, and then as I finished it, the postman came, bringing only one of the books I bought the other day, but no letter. To console myself I read Eugénie de Guérin until I found this, which I want to quote: "But I observe that I hardly make any mention of others and that my egotism always occupies the stage. I keep saying I do this; I have seen that, have thought so and so, leaving the public in the background after the manner of self-love; but mine is that of the heart which knows only how to speak of itself. The inferior painter can but give his own portrait to his friends; the great painter has pictures to offer. So I go on with the portrait."

Thus things that I never say, because I am not able to and yet which I have thought and vaguely explained, Eugénie expresses so charmingly; and half-sorrowful, half-enchanted, I read her journal each day.

October 5. The autumn has entered into my heart, and as each day goes by, more leaves are carried away from the trees and from my tree of hope. For the postman, whom I watch from behind the parlor curtains, brings business letters and letters from everybody except Eduardo. He will never write. And yet I never think of him while working; it is just when I want to dream a little that Eduardo and his indifference stand before me. That is why I am never still now, and the days are so glorious all around me. There is nothing but beauty, beauty I have never so deeply felt before, and so I sing while I make the beds, I sing all morning and all afternoon, with my eyes turned as often as possible to the trees and the flying clouds. I love life, only life does not love *me*. It wants to disenchant me, but my dreams and I will never part.

October 6. What a strange day! Usually I twist Duty inside out and upside down, mixing it up with my joys, my studies, my singing and my meditations, and Duty lets me play with her. Today it was Duty who twisted me around her finger, inexorable, unbending, iron-handed, from the time I opened my eyes till now, when they should be closed in sleep. I ache all over, not only physically but mentally. It is because my darling mother remained home, the Chief Executor and Director among her mountain of letters and bills. She sat all day before her desk, and I before my typewriter. She dictated letters first, then the long list of things purchased by Tia Antolina and Tia Anaïs and Mrs. Thayer,[1] whose accounts are never clear—and on and on until lunchtime, of which Joaquin reminded us. We cook, we eat, we wash and we sit again before our work.

The afternoon wore away. We worked so much that dinner was a recreation. Thorvald had been playing football, and he was red-faced and exultant. Joaquin had been playing too. Just to watch them was to feel the thrill of the great outdoors. And now Mother is reading and resting.

My fingers hurt from the typewriter. How gratefully I greet

[1] *Jack Cosgrove's mother, Helen Thayer, whom A.N. sometimes called "Aunt Helen."*

my old-fashioned pen! And yet I have not written the great news! Thorvald has shown me his Algebra examination papers, on which he received 100 percent! Just imagine anyone understanding those perplexing problems as well as I understand my Walter Scott. What on earth is there in his normal-looking head? How I suffered with those Greek puzzles while in school. To think that *to my own brother* that instrument of torture is an open book of fascination, for he likes it and smilingly admits it. The 100 percent took me by surprise. I was proud, at Wadley, when my grade was a little above zero. What a contrast. It seems that my thoughts could be easily read in my expression, for Mother, after watching me for a little while said: "Viens ici, fifille—t'a pas besoin de tout ça pour aider ta Maman et faire des gateaux."[1] Whereupon she kissed me. Mother always kisses me when she cannot express in eloquent phrases what she is thinking, and when she kisses me . . . I understand.

No letter. Frances saddens me also. Suddenly idle, I feel the great loneliness in my heart again. I feel friendless, companionless. Wherever I turn for sunshine there is a cloud in between, a heavy, dark and lasting cloud. Do sunflowers fade when the sun is gone? And there, facing me, two post cards from Marcus, received many days ago. I have no courage to write. Can you guess what I am doing? What I see in my mirror? Weary eyes full of tears and nothing big enough to explain myself. I wish there were no postmen in the world, no cousins, no boys and no hearts.

October 7. I never realized there was as much work on Mother's papers as during these last two days. I have given up my regular study hours, my mending, house-tidying, and sit all day before my typewriter at work. I had scarcely time to read Waldo's letter when it came this morning.

Toward 5:30 I needed Mother's decision to continue, so I stopped and enjoyed myself baking a ginger cake. And now I am waiting for her, jumping up now and then to stand before the window. Oh, if you could see the trees. Sometimes I am so fascinated that I pick up the leaves and kiss them.

I study at night, and instead of dreaming now of Eduardo, I find myself lost in a labyrinth of wild questions and talking gravely with myself about things that have impressed me in the

---

[1] *"Come here, fifille, you don't need all that to help your Maman and bake cakes."*

chapters of my Problems of Philosophy, for instance. I do not awake any the wiser, nevertheless, from my scholarly dreams!

October 9. The descriptions of today's happenings would seem like one long nightmare, and I am not awake yet. Poor Mother works so incessantly all week that sometimes she breaks down on her rest day—then she becomes so irritable and unjust that all day long I hear nothing but quarrels and complaints. If you only understood—I can't write a line on Mother's faults without feeling that they are justified, and this idea that there is a reason for them drives me mad. It is always Work, Work, Work—the grinding wheel to which Mother is tied and which crushes slowly all her youth, her energy. If there is anything in the world that makes me doubt God, it is *money*, and my mother is suffering to earn it just because a hateful law I do not understand wills it so—giving to some so much and to others so little. What bitterness there is in the words "Earn your *living*," and what cruelty. As if a living were worth earning if your earning it kills your very soul midway! Rebellion, a fierce, burning, passionate rebellion, that is all I feel tonight.

I have been trying to sleep since I wrote these lines but could only sob. And now that a cold, strange feeling has crept into my heart, I feel so far away from my home, my life, and myself that I fear this terrible stillness as much as the burning despair. I am wondering if each time I see the darkest sides of life, whether in little things or great happenings, I will suffer so terribly and then suddenly grow so cold and queer, in such a way, it seems, that each sorrow leaves a deeper mark, and that slowly, slowly I am being taught the Great Lesson—that lesson that kills dreams and fancies and every blossoming hope and illusion and leaves nothing but the great weary, indifferent cynicism of man and woman.

Oh, I feel it, I feel it in my darker moods! I feel I am leaving my girlhood behind me; I feel the woman in me, the knowledge, the experience. I am losing my insouciance; perhaps I am losing the enthusiasm that bubbles over when I am happy, and that is so seldom. I think too much, I seek too much, I expect the impossible. I rebel and doubt. Am I still a young girl? Oh, no. In a few months I have wept more than during all my life. If only it would come slowly, that growing, dark, heavy reality, but sometimes it seems to destroy the work of a lifetime in one day!

Papa Chéri: [1]

   . . . Summer went by so fast. The leaves are already turning. A year ago we were living in our little house. A year ago, on a beautiful day like today, we came to visit this big empty house where we were going to build our nest. And everything goes, never to return. Fortunately, if I want to relive those happy days, I can go to my Diary and each day passes again before my eyes. I find it all in there: a faithful picture, the dreams that I will dream no more, and that age, which is now past. My Diary and I go around the world, so to speak. When one is a bit too much of an idealist, sometimes it isn't very gay, but then! When we get tired, you see, we are laid beneath a white stone, and then the people who never gave us a thought discover all our virtues. . . . No, I am not being sarcastic. We have to think like Henri Murger,[2] who in spite of everything is ready to clap his hands about life! Oh! But I haven't told you yet about Murger, nor about my studies, nor about— No, we must be systematic, we must begin at the beginning. I shall begin:

   Visit to Columbia University. Result? Well, it's quite unusual to be able to complain about being too *young*. It's not done, it's not acceptable, it's even unbelievable. But that's what happened to me.

   My studies—E. de Guérin's Diary—the struggle to express my ideas.

   Same thing with *Scènes de la Vie de Bohème*, which someone lent me. I was vaguely disenchanted with it. I understand the charm of the book, all its beauty, the author's talent, everything, everything that makes the French love the book so much. And yet I have been immersed for such a long time in classical literature that in spite of myself, my heart and head are full of "antiquities." That is to say, I have old-fashioned ideas about life, I am idealistic about love, about honor, about the conventions—centuries past, the age of chivalry, etc. So when I read a book like that, I bump into things the existence of which I had never suspected, even in my conception of bohemian life. It's the way love is portrayed by Mimi and Musette, for instance—all those things which surprise me, I must say. I really seem to have slept 100 years, as in the fairy tales, and to have awakened in 1920 in modern times. And so here I am at 17, with eyes like question marks because I read a book by Henri Murger. Here's a picture for you, little Papa, if you like! Personally, I don't admire that type. I don't like people who sleep

[1] *Letter translated from the French.*
[2] *Author of* Scènes de la Vie de Bohème.

100 years. Just think of being able to dream all that time without the day's events to destroy your dreams!! Deplorable!

Joaquin's birthday—piano, good health, good behavior, school.

Thorvald wants to be a doctor—but what's more, he got 100 in algebra!!!

Letter from Grandmother about her trip that fell through. Mother came home. Daydream about how to deal with a student who wrote me a letter.

Say anything, do anything, be untrue to anyone, but—write me, will you please?

Tenderly, etc.

Anaïs

October 11. I notice that I forgot to tell you about Friday's [October 8] dinner because Saturday I experienced another fit of rebellion. Mother and I had been invited by Madame Sorel. It was a social dinner for a business end, for Mme. Sorel and her husband own the loveliest shop in New York where gowns are sold for 250 dollars or more. In the same house where they live, Mme. Sorel creates her dresses with much art, her husband holds the business end of the thing, the gowns are executed and gorgeously presented to the exclusive public. I had time to study the French woman, her fascination, her charming coquetry, her undefined and inimitable attraction. She was not beautiful, barely pretty, but was dressed so becomingly and yet so artlessly, with an artistic sense of pose, with childish mannerisms, and worldly-wise tact and wit and gaiety. While M. Sorel and Mother discussed business, Mme. Sorel, a male friend and I played the phonograph and discussed books and laughed. They asked me what kind of life I wanted and I told them one very full of tremendous adventures. M. Sorel said I looked like a princess and wished I could wear some of their dresses, but Mother refused. Madame Sorel's friend looked at me a great deal and was teased for it.

I went home with more experience and a book loaned to me called *Scènes de la Vie de Bohème* by H. Murger, of which I spoke in father's letter. The book is simply witchcraft, and I have been spellbound from the first to the last pages. My admiration, nevertheless, is mingled with wonder and a faint disenchantment (as I told Father) because, of course, the women are strangers to me in a sense, and I distrust my opinion of them because they bewilder me.

And now the book is finished and I must return it. And yet I

retain its memory until that time when I will find myself surrounded by the books I love; up to the ceiling my library will rise,
into the clouds if necessary. Perhaps gray-haired, I will read it
again and love the entire story and understand it better, being
more accustomed, perhaps, to what shocks me now.

Sunday was quite perfect. But I was exceptionally still because I had gone horseback riding and felt like a tiny porcelain
statue at the point of breaking into a thousand pieces any minute.
I went with Elsie de Sola, but I made believe it was someone else.
And during the two-hour ride I was happy and contented, although my horse, Johnny, did not experience all the love of excitement his mistress did—which proves that enthusiasm is not
contagious between man and beast! Bossuet could have employed
this fact to advantage in his "Reflections," but I do not know what
to make of it.

Mother is so happy to see me appear interested in some outdoor occupation that she would let me do it often, and yet it is an
extravagance which troubles my conscience.

No letter. I wish I could understand myself. Do you know, it
is not all sadness I feel—it seems to be mingled somehow with
anger at myself. At times like this I remember that Tia Lolita[1]
said one could never write *everything* in a diary. I can tell you
everything I think and feel and love and hate. I can write of the
world, my home, my family and myself, but *explain* myself, I
cannot do. I don't know, nor ever will know, why I want a letter
so much. I know Eduardo's faults, I know I am older than he is,
I know he is my cousin, but all that seems to melt away before
one perfect dream of the perfect companionship I had conceived,
perhaps created and entirely imagined. And yet now it can't be
all a fancy. Eduardo realized it, too, he felt how well we understood each other, he knew that all the family called him a madman
and that to me alone he could tell all his wild ambitions and his
dreams. And if you only knew how extraordinary our letters were!
It seemed as if this perfect friendship would last all our lives. Few
people can dream without sharing their dreams, and of all people,
Eduardo, who was discouraged in every way and who *cannot*
dream alone because he is not *strong* enough. What has happened?
What has changed him? I know he understands his "cuisine" so
well that he must realize that I am hurt. And he would not hurt

---

[1] *Dolores Culmell, first wife of A.N.'s uncle Thorvald Culmell.*

without a very great reason. There are only two reasons I can imagine. One is his fault, the other mine. The Cubans are the most cynical, callous people in the world. I know that all the Sánchezes have ridiculed Eduardo's feeling for me. I heard that he carried my letters and my pictures in his pocket and that his little sister told his friends Eduardo had a sweetheart. Graziella said that before both of us one day and I tried to laugh it away. Perhaps his mother has reprimanded him about me; they all believe I am "queer," I suppose. And perhaps Eduardo was ashamed. And now he regrets it and thinks friendship is not worth the struggle to make his family understand a thing that is too fine for them, too idealistic. And yet, if Eduardo were the person I describe, I would not like him ever again. But he is not, and I am sure of it.

The other reason is the one that would, if it were true, hurt me far more because it would be my own fault.

Perhaps during his trip to Havana he idealized me too much. When I read his diary it was full of . . . me . . . *then*. And on seeing me again, I was not what he believed me to be, and that is all.

Oh, you cannot imagine how seriously I think of this. It is just like clinging to a cloud so that it will not vanish forever.

October 12. Such a rainy, rainy day! I can scarcely behave myself on days such as these, for I love to stand by the windows and watch the raindrops, dreaming. I have been rummaging in my "memories of infancy." And what strange things I found in that long-abandoned drawer. Stories written when I was 9 years old, books and books filled with terrible tales written in such language! My goodness! Plans for the future, at ten years of age, a mania for charity and ambitions then to erect orphanages, asylums, convents, all this with the money I would earn as a *painter*. Also childishly and passionately religious, writing prayers and hymns. And such poetry! I could die of shame if I had not almost expired laughing! A notebook in which I wrote down all the compliments I received, with dates! What a lot of things I burned today. I had a mania for confessions, and long articles describing Father and Mother. I began many poetical dictionaries, I coined words, I wasted piles of paper with only the *titles* of all the books I was going to write, such as *Life, A Philosopher's Thoughts, Essay on Human Nature, A Mother's Duty*. And dreaming of becoming a member of the French Academy.

October 13. Today was one of the happiest days from the time I opened my eyes until I jumped into bed. Not one moment wasted in reverie. I worked all day and I am satisfied. It was in preparation for Tia Anaïs's visit tomorrow. I don't believe either Tia Anaïs or Cuca cared to visit their poor relations, but when they asked Anaïsita and Graziella what they wished to do on Thursday, their day out of the convent, they both asked to visit us. And so Mother and I tidied and dusted and made a beautiful French caramel custard, and with the leftover white of egg, an enchanting meringue. I made a chocolate layer cake for the afternoon tea.

I heard a few days ago that Eduardo had a holiday and came to New York. He went skating with Ana Maria Maciá (the girl of the roses). Mother's opinions are priceless, and today I understood the value of balanced judgment. Mother knows all that is passing through her Linotte's head . . . and heart, so she spoke to me quietly and sensibly. Somehow all the *hurt* has fled from me, and all the anger and the regrets. I don't think I would care now if Eduardo turned his very back on me!—tonight, at least, when I am bubbling over with songs and optimism and a strange, new, genteel self-satisfaction.

Mother told me how Monsieur Sorel had spoken of me after his inventory on that famous visit. "Votre fille a une vrai petite frimousse Parisienne." Mlle. Linotte chuckled. "Vous savez, cette petite là va épouser un millionaire. Elle a un air!"[1] He complimented Mother on my way of dressing, of holding myself, of walking, of talking like a princess!

Mlle. Linotte laughed and laughed! And she laughed more when Mother told me the following story. Early in her marriage, Mother loved to read and would read most of the day. Then Father would thunder and exclaim: "That's why the stockings aren't mended! No wonder the whole house is like a madhouse and nothing is ever well done. You read all day and do nothing else!" I could almost see Father. His eyes must have blazed like Joaquin's, glittered steellike in Thorvald's way, burned and pierced like mine. Poor little Mother then would busy herself all day and read secretly at night when Father slept (just as I do while Mother sleeps). Well, a few weeks later Father was telling all the neighbors: "It is *horrible* to think that such an *intellectual, book-loving* gentlemen as I am should marry a woman who *never*

---

[1] *"Your daughter has a real little Parisian face."* . . . *"That girl is going to marry a millionaire, you know. She has a way about her!"*

reads!" And all the neighbors would echo: "How horrible! Such an intellectual man! Such an ignorant wife! Poor Monsieur Nin!"

"Well, well," said the Man in the Moon, "I have heard worse stories than that!"

But, of course, although the Man in the Moon is my sweetheart, he must see that I can't gather all experience in one lesson. It must come little by little.

But wait, you did not know that the Man in the Moon was my sweetheart? I will tell you how. There is printed in New York an abominably vulgar newspaper called the New York Journal. Well, in it there is one thing that atones for everything else. It is a series of drawings which appear now and then, the work of Nell Brinkly. It is really a clever reproduction of all the fancies the mere word Romance can create. I like them. Some tell how all the girls in the world, in looking at the moon, imagine their ideal to exist up there. And to the question When did you love me first? some men answer: "When I first saw you making bread." I admit it is all a little commonplace, perhaps, but I like the sketches, and when my crisis of nonsense comes, I often dream of the Man in the Moon.

Yet—hark! I hear the voice of my conscience, or in other words, the first pages of this volume; they speak to me. Did I not promise to make this a sensible and serious little book, devoted to knowledge and the confidences of an old spinster with profound design on worldly superficialities?

No one but me could look so distracted and yet have made a layer cake. I wish tomorrow could be skipped. It is an invasion of my dream home by people who do not understand beauty where paint is lacking and you can see through the curtains, which are not made of velvet. Also, we have no maid, and you know, Joaquin is another one of *those artists*, and of course I am quite crazy. I love them in my own way. But if life were a garden separated by an iron fence, the Sánchezes would be on one side and we on the other. And if we had to live near together, I would hang myself up on the fence. Eduardo came over on our side for a little while and then went home again. But that has nothing to do with my suicide. I hope you realize that.

October 14. I have read the last pages again and they do not harmonize with my light-heartedness today! I have no sarcasm and am reconciled with the world in general, as usual because I feel sorry for the world! Wednesday's banter covered a sinking heart.

Thursday passed off very charmingly. With Cuca, there is a veil between us, lack of common interests, lack of understanding. I do not yet understand coolness, even if it is mingled with sadness. Anaïs and I are more companionable. She seems to want love, and I have love, more than plentiful, to give away! The dinner was a success. Afterward we sang and played the piano. Anaïs was attracted to my tiny typewriter, and she wrote a letter for Eduardo on my own paper with my typewriter and signed Anaïs and yet not from me. But since then I have forgotten Eduardo, contented and dreaming other dreams. In a few months, I will not think of him at all. Saturday I enjoyed myself like a sensible, normal little girl, with Miguel and Thorvald, dancing at the inn. Miguel is pleasant and handsome, besides loving books, and we are becoming good friends. I was strangely stirred that night by many little incidents and things said to me. To you I can say without blushing that hence and forever Linotte, writing in your pages, is considered pretty and seductive by the world in general! I have been changing and changing since the last time I described myself. I am sure that the Diary of a person who isn't absolutely homely will be more interesting by and by.

And now you see all I have in the balance, my faults and my qualities. And the way the world treats me will show in the way the scales are tending.

I answered a letter from Waldo [Sanford], who was anxious because I did not answer his other letter. How boyish he is, how enthusiastic! He counted the days between our letters with so much eagerness and impatience. And I felt wickedly happy, because I was sure it was not my fault that Eduardo does not write any more. I know now that I have not changed in any way, that it must be true I am "seductive" if two boys can fall in love with me just after seeing me once at a dance. But enough conceit. I am only trying to reason myself into indifference, but reason is not succeeding, while time is! I am afraid I have chosen a very complicated book of philosophy. My favorite subject and my forte has always been a vocabulary, but now I find myself lost in a maze of strange words, which all placed together are supposed to be the definition of a stranger word! Such words as noumenon, feticism, norm, atomism, qualitatively, substractum, sensory, stimulus, postulate, epigrammatical, are the reasons why, although I am grappling very well with the meaning of the book, I cannot say I understand it completely.

I have just kissed Mother into submission, which means I may buy 2 books with part of Tia Anaïs's present! Two books! Two books! The words sound like music, celestial music! I know already what I want. Oh, joy of joys, two books!

October 19. The story of a moderately good girl's day. 7:30 Early rising with canary. 8:00 Breakfast and wild toast making. Breakfast carried up to Joaquin, who has suffered indigestion. 9:00 Heartache while watching for the postman. 9:30 More heartache when he brings only business letters. Housework. Secretarial work. Singing. 12:00 Lunch is cooked and served—dishes washed. 12:30 More bills and letters. Studies overdone. Knitting. One hour mending. Knitting. Marketing. Lonesome for a minute—I play the phonograph. 5:00 Beginning dinner. I am deeply perplexed by the scraping of carrots—it seems terribly difficult. Nevertheless, the last carrot is rather presentable—but my fingers are *not*. 6:30 Dinner successful, considering the fact. 7:00 Knitting and thinking. 7:15 Tia Coco telephones that she is coming to stay with us for many days. Mlle. Linotte gets cross inside, because it seems that we can never lead a peaceful life for more than a few days—and then more work when I am longing with all my heart to read. How selfish I am—oh, how selfish!

Imagine, Tia Anaïs gave me a present of $100, which Mother wants to use for a fur coat. When I said books, Mother was not pleased, and I did not insist, for I realize books are not exactly practical—and yet, how I dreamed and dreamed of all the books I could have bought.

The knitting I have mentioned is the beginning of a sweater for Joaquin. I can sing while I knit and sang all day so that I would not think too much, for whenever I think, I ask myself too many questions!

October 22. How very quiet the world seems now! My life is all sunshine and housekeeping, studies, songs and dreams. Mother leaves me at nine o'clock. Tia Coco goes to N.Y. all morning, and so I am left mistress of the great, still house. My bird, my plants are comfortably mothered first. Each wave of wind sweeps thousands of leaves away and strips the trees, and yet the sun is warm and dazzling. People say this early fall of leaves is a sign of a mild Winter. I grow ecstatic when I watch this supernatural beauty.

October 24. Tia Coco left us yesterday, and speaking of her reminds me that the day we celebrated Nuna's[1] birthday Mother had her hair cut short, what is now called bobbed hair and a great fad of Dame Fashion, and yet as clean, wholesome and sensible a fad as was ever invented. It makes Mother look years and years younger, independent somehow, even if at first it shocked and troubled me because of its extremely modernized appearance. I felt as if I were Mother's old-fashioned mother with my long hair sedately piled up upon my head and hers bewitchingly flying around her merry face.

Today we received holy communion. Most of the time my prayers were a cry of despair: "I want to believe, Jesus—I love you—I want to believe, but sometimes I can't, oh, I can't!"

Before my mind rose two pictures—the unbeliever, the doubter, the atheist, with all his unhappiness and his troubles, his uncertainties and despair; and, on the other hand, the good, faithful Roman Catholic with his childish confidence, his beautiful faith, his pure conceptions, enjoying that calm inward life, that serenity of soul and unbroken happiness of clear conscience and pious thoughts. Oh, that I could pray now as when a little child. I remember long ago, when sent to bed unkissed because I had been bad, I would pray and fall asleep, comforted and consoled. I prayed when I hurt myself. I had a little altar next to my bed with my crucifix, statues, a rosary and holy pictures. I would burn small candles before the Virgin and bring fresh flowers every day. Such a blind, beautiful faith. And now I am cynical and cold. I *think* until all my faith goes. Yet, no, my faith is not gone, it sleeps sometimes, but I can still pray with burning fervor occasionally.

October 27. Mother has been in bed all day with an abscess under her arm. I have taken a great deal of care of her, and nothing seemed to discourage me as long as it could please Mother. And yet what a coward I am and how ashamed I am! I could hardly bear to look at *it*, and Mother had to cure the abscess herself while Mlle. Linotte shivered by her side and looked as ill as Mother herself, or more, because Mother's spirits are something to wonder at, she is always so undaunted and patient. Several times the same operation took place, and I suffered so much I thought I would faint. And so tonight the mere thought of the day's happenings

[1] *Maria Teresa Chase, a cousin.*

make me shiver. I have tried to amend for my contemptible weakness by working with all my strength in the house. In the evening the craving for reading comes to me and I read until late in the night.

Whenever the postman comes I try to forget to watch for mail because Eduardo's neglect distresses me more than words can tell. Speaking of Eduardo reminds me that Sunday afternoon Thorvald and I visited Anaïs and Graziella in their convent. Anaïs showed me a *long* letter she had received from her brother because now, she tells me, he writes her all his secrets. It was really half the length of the letters he wrote me. I saw Rita Allie also, and her beauty left a deep impression on me, for she is lovelier than ever, although conscious of it now, and this lessens her charm a little, but ever so little.

I confided to Mother half-jestingly that I feared I was falling in love with my cousin, however strange the thought may seem, because I could not otherwise explain why I thought of him so much. "Nonsense, fifille, you will soon discover that Eduardo is only a very young boy, and you are much older than he is in every way." It was not exactly what I expected Mother to say, but then I saw the thought troubled her and I tried to make her forget it. Still, the other night I was knitting, with my legs tucked under me, at the foot of her bed, and suddenly I thought to myself: "I don't care." Only I whispered the words instead of thinking them and Mother asked: "What are you thinking about, fifille?" I blushed deeply and tried to laugh. "Of Eduardo, I suppose?"

"Yes, Mother."

"Cela te passera, chérie, ne soit pas bête."[1]

Dear little Mother with her practical advice! Where would I be, left to my own dramatic impulses and black despairs? Heaven knows. But certainly not writing in my calm blue nest as I am now; little blue nest of a young lady's secrets, what thoughts will I think, protected from the stormy weather by your four blue-papered walls? What will I see reflected in your fickle mirrors? Will the everlastingly curious moon always peep through the fragile curtains and lie across the soft feather quilt, where I can watch it during my many restless nights? Or will I be happy and sleepy and light-hearted again soon?

How the wind does blow and whistle! It means more leaves gone tomorrow. Oh, how my thoughts wander far on a night like

[1] *"You will get over it, my dear, don't be silly."*

this—how I love to sit alone thus, adding a chapter to the story of my great adventure.

October 28.
Dearest Dick [Frances Schiff]:

All the anxiety I felt at your long silence made me realize that just because my life is an eternal vacation I forget that you have countless things to do. I forget that you can't sit before your desk and scribble away whenever the impulse takes you, as I can do, for you have studies and earnest, real work all day long, while I—well I could not begin to tell you how I am spending what I call the loveliest years of my life. And besides, I want to tell you what I think of your letter. When you write that you believe school is going to ruin you, I know that you are feeling now what I felt during all my school life and yet could not express then— that crushed, hurt feeling, as if all school were but an inevitable wheel trampling each day on every lovable atom in us and leaving only some sort of commonplace skeleton stuffed with "education" and not the tiniest *spark* of the freedom we need to create and weave and dream our dreams. Oh, Frances, it does not seem kind to say this, but you know that I was always a horrid scholar and have proved it. But I think too that if one is brave enough to go through school (as I was not) and still not want to be ruined, it can be done, you know. You can study, study and yet not give up your creative self. And most of all don't give up your pen, if you can, and before you know it school will step suddenly into the background and you will be facing life—alone, free—free to worship the beauty that you feel so keenly and free to express it.

No, I don't believe you write because you are young, Dick, not at all. I earnestly believe heaven has given us life and a world to live it in, thoughts and reasons to understand it, and ways to express your feelings, and as by some this is done by acting, or singing, etc., or mere existence, by others it is through writing, etc., and none of these things are learned but they are born within us and, Frances, things that are deeply rooted into ourselves do not change with mere fancy or time, or at least this is what I think, and I know so very little. Yet I know that circumstances, and of these the world is full, can force a person to put aside their favorite inclination and accept some ordinary task. Nevertheless, they never change completely. *"Un artiste, née artiste, en est un jusqu'à la morte."*[1] Don't stifle those crazy dreams of yours.

[1] *"A born artist is an artist until death."*

How wonderful that ecstasy that enters one's heart when you have expressed your innermost thought and can watch the other being stirred by it! How wonderful, Frances, how a pen can lead and sway and command and plead and touch. It is a blessing and a *consolation*. I would not exchange the confidences and intimacy of my journal for any human friendship in the world, however strange this thought may seem to you . . .

Frances's letter pleased me very much, and as soon as it came this morning I longed to answer it. Perhaps you are surprised I tell her that these are the happiest years of my life, and yet to you I have seemed distressed and sad—but this is because I realize that the little sorrows that come to me now are in reality very, very little when compared with those that will come, and I love these years and feel I will cling to their memory when real life begins to play with me. And I want it to play roughly with me.

I have dressed the Kewpie doll Eduardo gave me in black tulle above the pink costume! The queer doll will mourn for the broken friendship. Mother laughed, and I with her.

I notice that in the beginning I had only a few books in my room and now the glorious enemy has invaded my blue nest. I have books on the mantelpiece, books on the stool beside my bed, books on the small table, and the joy I feel when I look at them is greater than my heart can hold.

Think of the things I am expecting. Saturday, a masquerade ball with the girls next door and Miguel, and today a seamstress fixed one of Cuca's dancing frocks, which is almost coming to pieces and yet makes me look—strange. I cannot write "pretty" yet—it makes me feel ashamed. It is peach-colored and odd in shape, which rather pleases me.

October 29. Sometimes my heart overflows with a queer happiness. And yet no one is the cause of it, no incident, no alteration in my life, nothing outside of my very own self. Happiness of the kind I love seems to emanate from the depths of my own self. Just as I create the greatest portion of my sorrows, sometimes I create a happy day and it rises resplendently from my hands and stands before me, dazzling me.

Thus today in one half-hour I lived a life of stirring emotions and infinite joys. It was when I left the house for a walk—a day of gray, swiftly moving clouds, of wind and flying leaves and Autumn cold. I had my cape on and as the wind tossed it now away from me, now suddenly against me like a whip, I felt so light —I felt like a leaf that the wind carried along. I saw the silver-gray sky through dark bowed tree limbs; I felt the moss beneath me, and just like a leaf I felt the great stirring soul of the forest. Still a leaf and not to be feared, I could fancy the bushes whispering to one another as I passed, the wind talking to the trees. Elves danced on the dead twigs—that was why they creaked so slightly when I passed. And I felt young and free and happy, happy because I loved the forest and the forest loved me.

It was only when I stepped into Mother's room and she asked me to mend some socks for Thorvald that I ceased being a leaf.

To love nature seems to me the greatest consolation for human woes that heaven ever gave us. Though I may long for stranger gifts, like the love of man, of home and children—or, rather, fame instead of these two—I realize with deep gratitude that I have already been given the greatest gifts—the love of nature and of books!

November 1. Fortunately I refrained from describing Saturday's events until today because in the hours following the masquerade dance I suffered from an acute attack of melancholic cynicism and was overpowered by a strange repulsion for frivolities, which is now cured. I had been preparing myself all week, inviting the Forgie girls and praying that Miguel would not get himself into trouble in school so that he might be free on Saturday. And so in the evening this is the group that waited in our salon for the taxi: Mother, who felt better and was full of enthusiasm; Thorvald in an ordinary suit but wearing a mask; Miguel, ditto; Jimmy, ditto. Jimmy's coming was a triumph, as he had been acting perfect indifference to the invitation all week. Martha Forgie looked like the Queen of Spain, blonde and blue-eyed, wearing the mantilla I loaned her. Wilhelmina, the Titian-haired, looked bewitching in a yellow clown costume. I felt quite myself in a black velvet skirt and cherry-colored blouse under a velvet bodice, a cherry-colored handkerchief around my head, two long and odd black jet earrings, a few bracelets and a jet necklace. And there I stood, half-Catalonian, half-gypsy. All my expectation and excitement flamed in my eyes and made them so dangerously large that I feared they were going to pop out . . . but they did not. Instead, like everyone else's eyes, they were hidden behind the black mask to keep the strangers guessing. My first real masquerade dance had begun.

It was not exactly like Dumas's descriptions, of course, which was what I expected every masquerade dance to be like. But *enfin!* It was the merriest dance I had ever seen. Spanish girls and toreadors, Russian brides and Russian soldiers, Arabs, Spanish peasants, clowns, dominoes, gypsies, Italians, painters and poets, fairies and Sing Sing prisoners, country bumpkins and Louis XVI, all of them masked, laughing figures, danced all night under red, green and blue lights in a strange serpentine confusion and showers of confetti. Now and then there were games which threw together people who did not know one another, and the laughter almost drowned the music. One man stole a kiss on my neck. I danced now with Thorvald, now with Miguel, who got sentimental, now with Fraser,[1] now with Jimmy; but with Jimmy himself, who is a consummate dancer, I enjoyed myself because the frivolous mood was on the surface and each dance seemed to me something like my dream of being a windblown leaf. I seemed so happy that Miguel asked me how on earth I could enjoy philosophy and yet love *mere* dancing.

I do not know myself. Perhaps it is because I am seventeen, who knows?

I was tempted to write in your pages but oh, how cynically and disdainfully I would have written. The words, insipid and stupid, danced in my head side by side with fragments of dance music and warm compliments. Today they are reconciled, they are on friendly terms, and I have signed my peace with the normal world. I am looking forward with normal complacency to Eleanor's[2] visit tomorrow. Miguel is still with us because of these holidays. I am studying with him and find that, like most Cuban boys, he has a polished surface of eternal "choteo"[3] and bantering, but beneath it I find that he is very intelligent and loves literature. We have many interesting conversations together. He is finer than the average boys; he is a gentleman, a courteous and cultured boy, and I like him for those qualities.

November 2. At times when I sit thus, seemingly alone in the great, still house, I wonder if the life I am leading is a dream or a reality. I feel far away from everything and everybody, ever so far away, and I feel as if all the adventures which succeed one another incessantly were unfolding themselves like a play in a

[1] *A friend who lived in Forest Hills.*
[2] *Eleanor Flynn, a former schoolmate.*
[3] *Teasing chatter.*

theatre—and I, miles and miles away, watching. For a long time tonight I have stood absolutely still, lost in an odd introspection, watching with an inward eye the progress of these years in our life.

It was Eleanor's visit which carried me back to the days of 158 West 75th St., our school life, the walks, and the homework together—the modest, simple, unchanged Eleanor. Unchanged, yes, for I could detect no sign of vanity, or self-consciousness, or any of the faults which all my friends and I myself have because we think ourselves old enough to have them. Her eyes, just as when we talked together of simpler things, are always astonishingly pure and true and untroubled. I felt today exactly as I felt when a little girl, that from Eleanor there emanates a contagious calmness and simplicity of heart. And I was happy to realize that I could not have changed much, since I loved Eleanor for the same qualities that attracted me four or five years ago when I chose her for a friend. What a strange contrast Eleanor and Frances are! These two school friends represent the two tendencies of my own heart. With Eleanor I can share only the simpler things of life, and I am attracted by her modesty and gentle, smiling outlook on life. On Frances's side, there is much more to my liking—the creative, imaginative, fantastic and poetic traits—the eccentricities, the changeful moods, the impulses, the complex and bewildering mind, the bohemian heart, which is neither faithful nor fickle. Thus I wandered from one friend to another, now perplexed, now soothed. Nobody understands why I love either of them, nobody understands how I can love both. But I know why.

I have told you their characteristics but not what their surface is. Outsiders (like Miguel today) form a poor opinion of Eleanor. She does not seem intelligent, or vivacious, or clever. And she is not pretty (Miguel again), but I have read the things beneath, the pages between the covers. Frances is not pretty; her personality is impossible to strangers. Her face has a common expression, which does great injustice to the thoughts behind it, but here again I laugh in my sleeve, for I see more than Miguel. And I have proved my faithfulness. I have had no other girlfriends. Bobby Foerster, the odd, boyish little Girl Scout from whom I still receive affectionate letters, and Dorothy Eddins come next in my ridiculously short list. And I do not seem ready to elongate it, do I?

In a few days it is the anniversary of our coming to Richmond Hill.

The world, that is to say, the United States, is waiting breathlessly for the election returns. We also have caught some of the interest. Had Mother been an American citizeness, she would have voted and voted for the Democrats. What is the world coming to!

November 3. This morning we were told that the Democrats had been defeated, which means that Warren Harding is elected. The newspapers are filled with descriptions of the "women's influence at the polls." It seems that it quieted the men who otherwise would have been riotous and "rough," and many other things are said, too, about women voters. I am not enough a politician or a patriot to realize the tremendous meaning of this new order of things—and yet everyone around me speaks of woman's suffrage with great happiness and enthusiasm. Mother, particularly, is very proud, and tries to cure me of my great indifference toward the solved problem of suffrage. I turn to a volume of Eugénie de Guérin's Journal and find: ". . . A woman's heart is talkative, and does not require much; it is able of itself to extend to infinity . . . It rains; I was watching it rain, and then I proposed to myself to let my thoughts too fall drop by drop on this paper."

And here is Mlle. Linotte, a mere girl, with a heart full of nonsense, attempting the same journal of life as this experienced and clever woman I have quoted above; it makes me feel very small indeed. And powerless, *yet bold,* for I have no intention of abandoning you, now, or ever, however pale and lifeless you appear when compared to Eugénie's wonderful pages.

Today while trotting around the great city, catching my reflection now and then in the show windows, and noticing the many glances directed to me, I felt suddenly like an antiquated shadow girl rising from the worn and yellow pages of a world of books—just a queer, inexplicable being who had lost itself by stepping out of some old-fashioned storybook. And the perplexing things that happen to me! A little thing I had to do for Mother was to leave a package at the hotel, and as the lady was not home, I took my message and the package to the desk, where a Spanish interpreter presided. A Cuban stood waiting for his turn and overheard me speaking Spanish. And then imagine my confusion when, as soon as I moved away, I heard the gentleman exclaim loudly: "¡Que simpática la Francesita! ¡Que bonita!"[1]

The other night Miguel interested me for a long time with

[1] *"How charming the little French girl is! How pretty!"*

the stories of *Don Juan Tenorio*[1] and *El estudiante de Salamanca*.[2] He is a good storyteller and has a fine memory so that I grasped a vivid and charming view of Spanish literature. I was enchanted to find that he loves belles lettres devotedly, enchanted and surprised, because I did not expect it in any boy and still less in a Cuban.

Slowly, very slowly I am forgetting Eduardo as he has forgotten me. At times when I think of him, I do so with less poignancy and pain—with only a calm little sadness all my own, which falls gently like a mist between me and my sunshine, but no storms of questions and distress and anger as I experienced in the beginning. Perhaps the only reason I regret it has happened is because it has lessened much of my sympathy and admiration. Oh, Eduardo, Eduardo, you said once that you understood me better than I myself, and that it was cruel to willfully shatter someone's else's illusions—and yet you were the first one to do so! I often wonder what he will say when he sees me, for, being cousins, we are bound to be thrown in each other's way someday. But let it rest, just like my little canary bird, buried under a lilac tree. I will keep all my affections centered on my Diary, I who wish to love passionately so many things and so many people! Let us pretend you at least are my faithful admirer and my best friend. My *human* friends' *hearts* are quicksand and question marks. Boys—let us consider them all like the people at the club dance, masked and costumed.

November 5. I am in such a black mood, such a black, black mood! Since Friday, when I wandered again in the woods and felt the same intoxication of the heart, I became suddenly wicked and cynical. Saturday night Thorvald, Miguel and I danced at the Kew Gardens Inn and betweentimes talked nonsense. I wore one of Cuca's old dancing frocks, remodeled, a peach-colored picture which made everyone turn around and stare at me and rush for dances with me, but nothing would change the cold, hushed heart beneath the frock. And I went to sleep sobbing with not a reason in the world.

I have compared a thousand times the great pure happiness I felt during my wanderings in the woods with the disgust I felt

[1] *A play by José Zorilla that was immensely popular in nineteenth-century Spain.*
[2] *A novella by José de Espronceda, nineteenth-century Spanish writer.*

Saturday for the wild music, the lights, the staring eyes, the sticky boys and compliments, the silly laughter and the great, stupendous waste of words. Intuitively I knew Miguel was, in his own way, in the same state of mind, although he enjoyed the dancing. He teased me with Cuban "choteo" all night.

November 8. I have just finished the third volume of Eugénie de Guérin's Journal. Few books have so deeply impressed me and no other book has ever impressed me in such a peculiar manner. I have never read anything so pure and beautiful, and all those pages into which this incomparable woman has poured her soul stand out from all the books I have read like a vision of some bluebird I have been seeking and find between my hands. I held all that purity and womanliness, that charm and goodness, against my heart, and Mother, Joaquin and Thorvald wondered at my conduct. Holding a book against one's heart as if it were a person, indeed! Yet no human being I know has ever done me so much good.

And so tonight, in contrast with my terrible mood of yesterday, I have been blessed with that delicious, inward serenity. And outside, the world, the November world, is gray and damp. It does not matter. Oh, nothing outside matters. I have worked all day, all alone in the house, with no one to speak to but myself. I sang. And all along I felt thankful for life, this life of books, songs, freedom, work, solitude, thankful for everything and anything. You know, even a common stocking to be mended can be interesting on such a day as today. Just like Eugénie, I want to underline the rare words: *I am happy today.* As to my journal, no, I do not want to and *cannot* make it the same.

And Mother says I have been "born writing." You and I, even if we are placed in the very midst of Mother's business papers (to her great distress), I seated in her executive's chair, using her business pen, we can still forget the entire world and travel faster than the Autumn clouds, faster than the windblown leaves, toward new thoughts and new hopes.

November 9. We found out that Manén, the great violinist and Father's lifelong friend, will give a concert soon. Mother is going to visit him for "auld time's sake," and he is going to tell her why he quarreled with Father. Manén is one of the players in the early acts of my life, theatrically speaking. Someday I will speak to you of my life as far back as I can remember and I am sure you will love it more than this chronicle of 1920. Nineteen twenty is a queer year, you know, and it may be true that "to live on, to see further, is to leave the fairest things behind us."

The Fairest Things. When does a life begin? Is it at the time one opens one's eyes to the light of the world? Somehow I believe it begins long before that . . . the golden years of Mother and Father; romance must have something to do with it, as if the Invisible Being were drawing together the separate threads of two lives, and from this union three other lives are woven in the same act. Of how Mother and Father met and loved each other and married I have spoken before in my Diary. In Mother's closet there is a box filled with old letters tied with a faded ribbon, which makes me dream of the days when Mother was perhaps my age and dreamed my dreams, and saw my visions and knew each thought, each impulse, each hope that I am only learning now. I can imagine the tenderness, the womanliness, the charm emanating from Mother's letters to Father, as I can see, if I dared, the passion, the vows, the eloquence of Father's letters to the woman he desired to win. The first year of Mother's married life was spent in the rue du Four in the midst of the quartier Latin, the Parisian world of poets and madmen. Perhaps that is why I was born a poet. This atmosphere, this environment, shaped the most important fact in my destiny, for were I not a poet, the whole world would seem altogether the reverse of what it seems to me now. Mlle. Linotte, then, was born in an apartment of a white stone house on the rue Henrion Berthier, Neuilly, on the twenty-first of February, 1903, at eight P.M. By asking Mother again, I find that it was a fair day, probably cold, but this did not affect my temperament very much. I would have thought the weather *important* if Mother had told me it was dark, stormy, with lightning and thunder tearing the skies. As it is, the fiercer elements took no notice of my birth. Poor Father, according to Mother, was sorely disappointed: he wanted a boy. He had no use for a crying, bad-tempered baby girl. A boy would not have cried. Fortunately, Mother was (according to Mother) supremely happy. I do not suppose anyone tried to decide which one I resembled. Poor Father thought that, by my hands, he could divine a pianist in the family; he did not divine they were meant to hold a pen most of the time. I was christened Rosa Juana Anaïs Edelmira Antolina Angela Nin!

Naturally I remember nothing of Thorvald's birth day. I have tired Mother with questions so that I can tell my story, because there are so many gaps in my memory. Only at times, when Mother's help fails me, I will be forced to use my imagination. For instance, Mother tells me that my brother was born when she went to Cuba to witness Tia Coco's wedding, on the twelfth of March, and the rest I deduce: Thorvald, who is the least aristocratic in the family, was born in Grandfather's house, which was a palace! I have found an explanation for his supreme laziness and love of sleeping: he was born at 5 A.M., and this early waking has tired him for life. Father must have been wildly happy (imagination). He wanted a boy and here it was. He must have bent over Thorvald's blessed cradle and kissed the microscopic fingers, for Thorvald was not only a boy, but his eyes were blue, the blue of the proud Father's eyes! Since then, I know Thorvald was Father's favorite child (imagination), and for many years, Mother's also, until I almost died before my parents' eyes and then, by remaining with them, was rewarded by being equally loved.

(Here I was interrupted by Thorvald, for whom I had to mend some socks. At first I wanted to be angry, but then I thought it was more useful to mend his socks than to write about him.)

St. Cloud. Today I am going to tell you about a period in my life when I began to remember things, places and persons. This little house in St. Cloud, which Father rented when we returned from Havana, was old and in great need of painting and repairs, and yet this made little difference to either Mother or Father because it was the most picturesque and poetical home you could imagine for a family that was not rich. It was covered with ivy and completely hidden from the world by beautiful trees. I recollect the garden faintly as a place filled with flowers, fruits and bushes. Tia Juana, the Fairy Godmother, was with us then and has told me many stories about those years. Thorvald was still too much of a baby and took no part in them as he did later. At that time I was a very lively little girl, trotting forever behind either Mother or Marraine. I am told that I used to lift the hem of my dress to cross the street after the manner of the ladies in those times who wore trains. You see how soon I began to want to be elegant. My favorite toys were old hats and feathers, which I pinned together and wore around the house. This, if you examine the fact closely, is the beginning of one of the most important faults in my nature: my liking for hats and dresses and costuming, because I even pinned whole packages of pins on Mother's dresses to imitate the dressmaker.

It seems that one time Thorvald and I narrowly escaped death. At the railroad crossing our nurse became frightened at the coming of an express train and fled, leaving the carriage in which Thorvald slept and me, standing by his side, in the middle of the tracks. The gateman, who was the father of a large family, risked his life and rushed to carry me away in his arms after kicking Thorvald's carriage out of danger. I remember seeing Father counting many dolls and several boxes of soldiers for the gateman's children.

Then one day I recollect that Mother left us, and when she returned months afterward she was dressed in black and her beautiful face was hidden behind a long black veil. Grandfather had just died in Havana. I little realized then what a great sorrow Mother had had to bear. It is very strange how, when I look back to those years, I cannot remember Father. Just Mother and her touch and her kisses and eyes. Somehow here my memory fails me. I can only recollect a scene in Switzerland with Mother bathing in a very blue lake and Thorvald and me sobbing with all our hearts because we thought she would drown.

From there we went to Berlin to a very neat and beautiful apartment, where the windows were adorned with geraniums. I only remember a severe governess and seeing less of Mother. This was because, as she told me, she had taken her place in the society life of Berlin, and Father and she were invited everywhere. Mother was admired and spoiled and feted. We were rich, it seems to me, and comfortable. All the fat, ungraceful German ladies admired Mother's way of dressing, her dancing. The years spent in Berlin must have been some of the happiest in Mother's life, although I know that there, more than ever, Father continued to spend much more than he could afford. During these years I can place Father dimly. I know he was always grave and strict and absorbed. He used to experiment with a cage of white mice (he was studying medicine, etc.), and I remember the mice so very well.

One day Mother did not leave her room and a great stillness fell upon the house, and for many days we were not allowed to see her. We had to walk on tiptoes and talk softly, and our poor literary father did not know what to do with us. I know he loved his books better and thought us troublesome. He was about to have another boy, and the day the news spread we were given permission to look at the newcomer. Thorvald and I entered Mother's room as softly as little mice, and after kissing her we peeped into Joaquin's cradle. I will never forget the first impression I received of my new brother: he was horribly dark and ugly and he greeted us with a fearful howl. His dark face and irritated eyes haunted my dreams for a long time. This was September 5, 1908. After that day the whole family watched Joaquin's every movement with adoration, how he grasped his bottle earlier than most babies, how he laughed and slept. The nurse, a German woman, was horrified at his bad temper and said he would make a good German soldier.

It was in Berlin that I got angry one day and decided to run away. I asked a little boy of about my age to wait for me at the corner of the street. I packed a croissant and my dresses. Mother and Father were watching me but I did not know it. I walked down the stairs with my bundle and out in the street. But before I had gone very far Father brought me back.

Brussels. After Joaquin's birth I remember nothing else until the time we found ourselves living at the rue Beau Séjour, Uccles, Brussels in a dear little house. Our home was four flights high, and each detail of its construction I can remember distinctly and with much regret. Here Father's personality becomes more distinct. He lived chiefly in his study or by his piano. His study had books to the very ceiling and a big imposing-looking desk near the window. I stole into the study when he went out and read books I could not understand. I sat on top of the ladder reading and trembling that I should be found out. Father moved from his study into the parlor where his piano was, and ever since I can remember he sat for hours playing. Mother, Joaquin, Thorvald and I lived mostly in the bedrooms or in the garden. The garden was a little larger than our backyard in New York, but Father had it filled with sand so that we could play there all day without shoes and stockings. During those days Joaquin began to demonstrate the characteristic wildness and love of mischief that he still has. Thorvald and I would play, but Joaquin would be breaking up things, until Father would have to catch him and spank him. Father was fond of spanking us anyway. Joaquin grew dreadfully afraid of Father, but he did not cease to get into mischief, though he would manage to keep it a secret. Most of the time he had to be locked up in his room where there was no furniture left that he could ruin, just his toys, with which he never played, and what he loved to do was to break them with a hammer. Meanwhile, Mother taught

Thorvald and me to read and write, read music and play the violin and piano. Thorvald studied his violin with great care, but I detested the piano and would sob and stamp my feet and get in a rage each time the lesson was to begin, until Mother gave up, and to console her I told her I had decided to become a painter.

At that time Thorvald and I were inseparable. He was then as gentle as a lamb and followed me everywhere. We used to play house under the great library table—can you imagine how small we were? Half was Thorvald's house, and half mine, and the trailing red tablecloth played the part of door and windows. We had a doormat made out of a leftover piece of linoleum. I have never forgotten the doormat. Often we would suddenly crawl out of our house and surprise Mother and Father talking. I was too little to realize what was going on, but I was fully aware of the great battles, the violent scenes which terrified us. I remember once Father and Mother were quarreling so violently that I threw myself on the floor in a fit of hysterics to distract their attention and because I feared Father was going to kill Mother. That time I frightened my parents into silence.

Father would read during meal times, only interrupting himself to scold about the microbes on the silverware, which he passed over an alcohol lamp before using. He never ate the piece of biscuit his fingers had touched. He believed in vegetarianism. We were taught to fear all but filtered water.

He was a strict father to us, and it was only through a great deal of acting that I escaped punishments, for I was a capable actress and could move Father very easily when, slipping to my knees and clasping my hands, I would whisper, "Please, please don't" through my tears. I would do anything to keep him from lifting my dress and beating me. Joaquin was the one most often punished, and Mother was always trying to save him from a whipping. Father once killed a cat with a broom. How well I understand my poor father through knowing Joaquin. He was impulsive, quick-tempered, hasty in words to wound, scathing in judgment, and almost childishly irresponsible for his actions.

Aside from these scenes, they seemed happy years. We had many little friends, jolly Christmases, friends of Father and Mother who filled the house with music. Ysaÿe, the great violinist, came there. Mother was studying singing for concert work. Thorvald and I were sent to German school. I liked best a little devil, Henri, a freckled boy, not of our class and whom we were forbidden to play with. Henri and I went to church one day during Mass, knelt before the altar and considered ourselves "married."

Then came my illness, which brought with it so many changes. For a long time I lay still and frightened in my bed because the ignorant doctor had said I was developing tuberculosis of the spine. What thoughts I had when I was told I would never walk again! Father suddenly abandoned all the things which kept him busy and away from me, and thought all day of the things which would please me. He bought me books, a compass set and drawing pencils, and Mother watched me all day long with such anxiety on her face as I have never seen since. All the neighbors called on me with books. I began to read voraciously, and to write stories. Each day I grew worse. Once or twice Mother was obliged to go out all day, and Father would bring his writing to my room and work while watching me. I was terribly happy then. I will never forget how he drank all my medicines with me to show me that they were not bad. It was the only time Father showed his love. Thus, through my illness, I was blessed with Father and Mother's quiet, *united* love. And now that this great love that helped me to bear so much is gone from my life, I like to think of it as a perfect dream beyond my reach. Father and Mother! How dear those two words were to me. How often I have asked God why he has given me this great sorrow to bear. And to some girls, who do not love their parents as I do, He gives both Father and Mother.

To me, "Father" is a mystery, a vision, a dream. What infinitely beautiful stories I have wound around the magic name, what a place I have given to it in my home and my heart. Father! Father! All my life has been one great longing for you. A longing for you as I want you to be. Alas, not as you have been, not as others believe you to be. Oh, dearly beloved shadow, what a great emptiness your absence has created in my life!

I did not think it would be so difficult to tell you about my childhood. I had forgotten that during those years, so happy for other children, for us there hung a continuous dark threat of misfortune.

After I had many months of terrible suffering, one night the doctor, whom Father was beginning to doubt, came and said less than usual. No one but he knew that I was dying. It was one of Father's nights by my side, and I watched him with a strange, detached feeling, as if I were so very tired of living and would soon be sleeping . . . forever. Then later Father was called down-stairs by a visitor. It was the father of one of my playmates, Clairette, who had met the doctor in the street. The doctor had said to him: "Monsieur Nin's daughter will die in the night." Mr. Hostelé felt it was his duty to warn Father. A few hours later three of the best Belgian doctors from Brussels were consulting among themselves. If I were not operated on for appendicitis in one hour, I would be dead. One doctor bent over me gruffly: "Are you afraid?" "Oh, no," I answered and closed my eyes. I was tired of pain. I was carried, as I was, into the car of a neighbor. It was one o'clock at night, and he got out of bed to drive me himself to the hospital, fortunately only a few minutes away from the house.

I was laid on a very white table. I kissed a nun's crucifix. I felt the mask placed over my face and fell asleep.

After the operation I suffered three months more. One day Mother ordered dozens of oranges and chocolates to celebrate my convalescence. I was wheeled around in a chair while I distributed the fruit and candy among the poor of the hospital. Then I came home. The little street was adorned with flags and all the neighbors were at the windows. The house was full of flowers and presents.

Arcachon. Villa Les Ruines. For my convalescence we went to Arcachon, where Father was already staying. We arrived there on my tenth birthday. It was a superb imitation of a ruined castle, gloomy, stately, cold. Strange forebodings caused me to weep uncontrollably the greater part of the night when I arrived. Nobody could understand me. But we spent a few happy months there, playing in the immense and beautiful garden, playing at the beach; and the "castle" appealed to me because of its strangeness and gloom. I did not know then what meaning "Les Ruines" would have. A few months later Father left us, apparently on another concert tour, but having planned never to return. He had often left us for concert tours and I did not weep. Was it a premonition? An instinct? This time when Father walked away he was obliged to come back several times while I kissed him wildly and called for him, weeping hysterically and clinging to him, a scene nobody but he could understand. He went to Brussels and took everything away from the house that he prized. Then Mother had to go and seal what remained. We were left in the care of a rich Cuban family, in the care of Father's young mistress! When Mother returned, we set out by third class for Barcelona, to Grandmother's house.

Barcelona. At first we lived with Grandfather, who was very strict and cold. I will never forget this quaint man with all his pride and severity. And sweet, submissive, crushed Grandmother! We lived with them only while Mother looked for an apartment. There in Barcelona for a year she gave singing lessons. Tia Antolina came to visit us and talked to Mother about New York. All during this time I wrote strange poetry and descriptions of things I saw and felt. When I left Barcelona for New York, I began the first book of this Journal.

November 15. So many little things have happened since I began to write about the past that toward the end I grew impatient and longed to finish it. Imagine, since Nov. 9 I have seen Enric Madriguera.[1] It was at a concert given by a young Cuban pianist, Pepito Echaniz, and Mother and I were occupying a box. Enric entered, and I watched him take his seat, terribly confused, although all morning I had known that it would be the most natural thing in the world for Enric to be at a young pianist's concert. Mother sent for him, and the rest of the concert I quite forgot that he was sitting by my side. Would you believe it? After the first excitement I realized that Enric did not thrill me any more! Perhaps it was different when I was very young. And so I noticed how wonderfully Pepito Echaniz played, although Mother said that in his interpretation of Chopin he had lost his rhythm, due to the impetuosity of youth. After the concert we congratulated him in the artists' reception room. He was very interested in Joaquin, having heard so much about Monsieur Nin. Suddenly I was introduced to an old pupil and friend of Mrs. [Emilia] Quintero, who said, laughing: "I know an admirer of yours, Anaïs."

"Who?" I asked innocently, while Enric opened his ears and eyes.

"A young American boy who writes poetry, Mr. Anderson."

"Mr. Anderson!" echoed Mlle. Linotte, blushing and bewildered. The next thing I did was to laugh and recover my worldly-wise poise. Enric walked with us to Penn Station. Tomorrow I am going to Manén's concert. There I am going to see one of Father's friends, who wrote to Mother a few days ago that he had just returned from Paris with Father's request to have him visit us and describe us. The lady who spoke to me of Marcus (and who knows him because she has a house in Greenwich, Con-

[1] *A young violinist who for a time lived with the Nin family.*

necticut, too) will be there, and so will Enric and Vicente [de Sola] and a young Frenchman friend of Tia Juana, who wants to meet me.

Mother says we are returning to the old life—the intellectual friends, the musicians, the social world. What a contrast to American life! Mother belongs among these people, artists and society; then she is brilliant and fascinating. I notice how people circle around her, how her opinion is asked, how well she appears against the background of the cosmopolitan and artistic world.

Returning to the old life! To think that for her children Mother has sacrificed the admiration of the world, her career as a singer, and her pleasure; for now as I see her I understand how she loves the old life, and yet it will only last a few days. After the concert by Manén, when he departs, when all the musical life sinks gently away from us, drowned in the noises of work and trade and American business, then the old life will be gone.

We have heard so much about Father lately. He is part of the old life, naturally. Social friends we seldom see and who know Mother as Madame Nin ask her when Father is coming back, or if he is here with us, or where is he.

And, from each voyage into the real living world I always return with heartaches and troubled thoughts. I am getting to fear contact with the outside and love my quiet home. After a day with the world I shrink back into my oyster shell and contemplate the incidents with sadness. Then the serenity of my shell soothes me and I am happy again, happy with my solitude, silence, books. I hear the buzz of the life outside and it seems very distant. And yet it is so near and I must live it now and then, I must step into reality and return to my shell, bruised and disconsolate. I was happy when I visited Anaïs and Graziella Sunday until Anaïs began to tell me how well Eduardo was studying in school and how long his letters were. Then suddenly I felt very hurt.

Miguel, as usual, was here Saturday and Sunday. He says that he knows of no one else made of such contrasting things as I am. He cannot understand how: I *feel* like a poet and I talk like a philosopher, how I like to dance and laugh and yet I like books and earnestness, how I can love my home and care for it and yet love eccentric things and act thrillingly, strangely. That is a picture of Mlle. Linotte according to Miguel.

I told him he perplexed me a little also. "You are a Cuban," I said, "And yet you are not an ignoramus."

He hardly knew whether to be flattered or offended, so he laughed.

What a Christmas this will be. So many of us united. I suppose Eduardo will be here also. How will he act? What will he say? I am glad I am not in his place, for I know I would feel terribly *ashamed*. But he is a *boy* and that is different.

How quickly I will have to put you away. You are almost filled in less than two months. It will take a library to hold your volumes. "A woman's heart has so much to say," wrote Eugénie, but I am not a real woman yet and mine overflows.

It is terrible! When I die, just as people say of a woman who talks too much, they will say: "My dear, when that woman began to write, she never knew when to stop. Think of all the paper she has wasted!"

And yet, the day I will have to burn you will hurt me, oh, so much! It would be lovelier to let you be read by my grandchildren. They will all wonder how on earth I could be so "old-fashioned" in my ideas. "What queer times our grandmother lived in," they will say. "Can it really be that at 18 she never used an airplane. Good gracious!" Really, I will chuckle in my grave if they say such things! Just as I have wondered how on earth Mother can live without automobiles.

Thorvald, who has just watched me writing, tells me I should use only one page for my Diary and erase each day what I wrote before. "Save paper!" says he.

November 16. I come to you tonight with my heart full of new emotions. Oh, I have heard Juan Manén, the violinist of violinists! There is no pen or tongue eloquent enough for the subtle and undefinable sensations showered upon the listener's ears. It was heavenly music. One of the things I loved most was his own composition. The American audience, usually so correct and undemonstrative, was wild with enthusiasm. So much applause, and encores. Suddenly the lights went out, the concert was ended, but the audience wanted more magic. The artists' room was so full, and Mother was in the very heart of it, laughing with Manén. All of us were recognized by him, and he said I had changed very little. He was interested in Enric Madriguera, and Enric could find no words to thank Mother for introducing him. Pepito Echaniz was there and Vicente. Father's friend, Mr. Velasco, sat by our side during the concert and afterward he spoke with us, asking us questions and answering those we asked him about Father. Manén is coming to dinner tomorrow, and later in the afternoon, Pepito and Enric are coming.

Later. And now all the glamour of the day's happenings has gone. Once more I notice with what happiness I sink back again into thought. No, I cannot deny it, and with what pain I realize it, I am not like Mother. I am like Father. Today I was told that I look exactly like him and at the same time I was told he lives quite alone. Why? Oh, I know why. He is proud and haughty. And yet I am like him, and I, too, seem distant. It is the blood, the blood in me that makes me act so strangely and shrink from people. Compared with Mother, who loves that brilliant, noisy life, who speaks so well, who laughs and talks so much, compared with Mother I . . . I am different. Yet this can't be. Oh, if I must be like Father, if I have his expressions, his gestures, his passionate temper, his disdain for those who surround him, I want that expression softened by my different outlook on life, I want my gestures tempered by Mother's desire to please, I want that passionate temper curbed and that disdain softened. Perhaps it will be, through my love of adventure and romance, for I will not be able to find my husband-to-be if I act like a savage. And I do so long for him. It seems that since heaven gave me a Father only to deprive me of him, it has also cursed me with a strange dream, one I dare not dream too often. I want, when I feel weak and discouraged, I want to lay my head on my husband's shoulder.

Shall I scratch this page out? No, I have promised to tell you all my thoughts and this is one of them. Am I ashamed? No, I am puzzled. Perhaps Miguel is right. I am a queer mixture of incompatible substances.

November 17. Many people would have given much to be in my place today. To hear Manén play is one thing, and the privilege of the public, but not many can hear him talk and can sit by his side during a dinner en famille and can be shown his violin box, with two beautiful violins lying on the blue velvet. He told us how he had played yesterday with a cracked violin, and then so many other things about himself and his travels around the world. Enric was hypnotized and Pepito was delighted. This has been in truth one of the most interesting days in my life.

I was just thinking now, with a smile, of what Pepito Echaniz said to me when he left. Perhaps when he is older and very famous, as I am sure he will be someday, I will remember his visit with still more smiles and how the well-known pianist said to Mlle. Linotte, "No lo beso porque tengo catarro."[1] You should have seen Enric look at me, only it did not thrill me at all. And to think that years ago I thought I would die of sorrow when he went to Spain. Do you know, I wonder sometimes if I will forget Eduardo as easily. Perhaps I am *naturally* fickle, yet I abhor fickleness in *others*.

10 P.M. How the wind howls in the night and shakes my windowpanes. Perhaps because of the tempest raging outside or perhaps because I have just read Edgar Allan Poe's poems, I feel indescribably desolate. Everybody else is sleeping, and I tried to bury my face in my pillow and forget, but after a long while the thoughts that passed through my head were so dreary and sad that I jumped out of bed, lit my lamp and sat by my dressing table to talk with you. I see such a queer reflection of myself in my three mirrors. If anyone looked at me now, they would faint, for I know many people think I am sweet and gentle, but there facing me sits a girl with a very haunted, stern, dramatic expression on her face. My eyes are long and narrow like Madame Butterfly's and that means trouble inside—a storm-tossed heart. My hair falling over my shoulders in wild, reddish ripples reminds me that I am not a philosopher battling with some great questions but an ordinary girl battling with her somber temper. Among the weird and desolate poetry of Poe's are these lines: "From childhood's hour I have not been / As others were—I have not seen / As others saw—I could not bring / My passion from a common spring— / From the same source I have not taken / My sorrow—I could not awaken / My heart to joy at the same tone— / And all I loved I loved alone—"

All the loneliness is expressed in them, the realization of the "difference." That is why I am so changed tonight, for just as when I read Shelley's life, I have lived again all the sorrows of other people's souls. I have not seen as others saw, or drawn my sorrows from the same sources, and I know the great, great loneliness of thoughts and dreams. Even when I sit thus, like tonight, while others sleep so calmly, I think and dream strange things all alone, all alone.

November 21. I have been so deeply impressed by so many things that I wanted to see if the time would come when I would be able

---

[1] *"I don't kiss you because I have a cold."*

to write calmly and coolly about them. But as I find that instead of effacing itself slowly from my memory, the thought of the dinner on Friday appears clearer, I have filled the ink bottle and sat at Mother's desk, and here I am. Thursday Enric telephoned. We were invited to dine Friday with Mr. Carl Hamilton, his protector, whom I have mentioned before in other diaries, as he had visited us in the city and later during Emilia's recital. Enric asked to speak with me particularly and called me "sweetheart" so that I would be sure to come. It was a dinner in honor of Manén. I wore the rose dress Mother bought me when I went to Lake Placid.

At first we were a little awed by the grandeur of the apartment house and its liveried attendants. And yet somehow that awe I felt was quickly replaced by a different feeling, for it is remarkable how quickly I find myself at ease in the midst of luxury, as if it were a natural part of my life instead of an adventure. You cannot picture a simpler, more unaffected man than Mr. Hamilton. His eyes are the kindest and the frankest I have ever seen; his smile is boyish; and yet his hair is turning silver—silver with sorrow, because he is young. He has a voice which even in its manliness is kind. And then behind that marvelous simplicity stands a great fortune and the story of how it is being spent. He has 26 or 27 young boys under his protection, paying for their education in the best colleges, and for their careers; one adopted son, and Enric; and many other charities. And I watched him talk and act so simply in his palatial home, filled with beautiful, rare paintings, antiques and ancient furniture. Perhaps the only fault I could find in that seemingly flawless luxury was the absence of the woman's touch, the woman's presence. The beautiful palace was cold and even gloomy. The man had not thought of flowers or anything but the great stateliness. I wonder if he knows that there is a great absence in his entire life when he shuts out women from his heart and house. He scarcely looked at me or at Mother, and I liked him all the more for it, because when I did meet his eyes, they were so respectful and yet so interested and kind. If ever I am able to write a book, I will paint Mr. Hamilton's portrait with infinite care, for I am sure he is an unusual figure. He and Manén and Mother made plans for Enric. You cannot picture Enric's joy. He kissed his benefactor, he kissed his teacher, he kissed Mother, and last he wanted to kiss me, but everyone cried out, and the talented violinist was only able to kiss both my hands. Then we decided he would come here to Richmond Hill for the three months preceding Manén's return to Europe. The memorable evening ended. I began to be aware again of Manén's presence, which I had felt little, being so absorbed in my study of Mr. Hamilton. I became conscious, too, of Enric and his great happiness. Manén and Enric took us to the station, and it was only on the way home that Mother and I could talk together. Mother often lets me explain sensations and thoughts we both have felt, because she says I know their names. This time I asked her if she had not felt elevated in the atmosphere we had just left. We remembered the solemn prayer Mr. Hamilton made before the sumptuous meal and the quiet way he expressed his wishes about telling Auer[1] that Enric was abandoning him, so as to hurt the old master as little as possible.

The next morning I visited Tia Anaïs dutifully, and Cuca, and suddenly, while listening to their outlook on Mother's actions lately, on her mixing with artists, etc., hearing their stupid fears that Mother would go back to the "old life," their bad opinions on artists and the world of art, I felt a sweeping wave of disgust for the *narrowness* of their minds and hearts. Perhaps because of the manner in which we had been treated the night before, I felt more keenly the arrogance of the Sánchezes towards us because Mother works so hard and cuts her hair in an independent fashion, because we are poor, because my father is an artist, because we love art, because I write. Oh, I was so angry, so hurt and indignant. I listened to complaints about other things, and not a kind word. And then that wave of anger and resentment rose higher and higher and caught at my throat, and I left that unhappy wealthy family hurriedly and spent the most miserable day at home. What I am struggling against is the fear of hating them, and I do not want to hate anyone, still less my family, my *poor* cousins, my *poor* aunt, poor in every way but the most useless of ways. Perhaps Eduardo was ashamed because the world thinks *I* am poor. But I am all *but* poor. Perhaps I have written bitter words. I did not mean them to be bitter. There will come a time when I will cease feeling so easily bruised and confused, and then I will not be so passionate and perhaps unjust.

Do you know how Manén explained Mr. Hamilton's extraordinary goodness of heart? "He must have suffered a great deal." And Manén knows. So now I am suffering so that I may be wonderful to others.

[1] *Leopold Auer, the great violin teacher of his day.*

I see that this is the end of another book. It has been stormier than I expected it to be, but it matters little as long as they all continue to be so faithfully filled. Tomorrow Enric is coming here, and my Diary may become slightly frivolous.

November 22. I had been knitting all evening, listening to the wind, and then as my thoughts became desolate and unreasonable, I decided to write the first pages of my new diary. I did not expect to continue writing it in English, but I have discovered that I can express myself a thousand times better in English, and until I can teach myself some of my beloved French, I will continue in the language I have used in two volumes already. How anxiously I watch for the postman, not because of any cousin, mind you, but for a far better reason—When will I hear from the editors? I am working now on a short story. Sometimes I feel a great, great longing to accomplish something by my pen, and at others, I feel I could easily lay it down in exchange for a mysterious wish there is in my heart now and which each day becomes clearer and lovelier. It is a very great secret, difficult to explain. I realized it only a few days ago when I caught myself watching the happy mothers with babies in their arms—and, instead of admiring dresses, or candy, or jewels in the show windows, I love to watch those that are filled with cradles and tiny baby boots. Oh! How I love little children.

Perhaps Mother guesses it. It is a very different way of looking at life. Many things lately have made me feel that romance or love is not the greatest thing in the world. I told Mother, days ago, that I was beginning to dislike boys and that I wished I knew what a man was like. "Give the boys time to grow," answered Mother, laughing, and I hardly knew whether to laugh or grow indignant. I am almost sure that in this volume, I will show you the results of my dislike for boys, because of my adventures with them. You will see how I will not lose my head, or heart, ever again—and how the dance we are going to give during the Christmas vacation is not going to thrill me at all. Oh! I feel I am growing so sedate and cynical.

November 23. I have lived another day in the Outside World—and with real, human beings. When will I find myself in my Inside World with all the personages of the World of Books? I long more for the latter's company, I fear. And yet, I acted today as only a true Linotte could. It was in the city, on a messy, miserable day—and would you believe it, I walked, or rather trotted, up and down Fifth Avenue, for business purposes, humming, solita,[1] tempted to smile at everyone, and smiling at my own thought, philosophizing in front of luxurious displays of fairylike and unattainable gowns. And discreetly endeavoring to walk under other peoples' umbrellas, as I had none of my own. I felt so happy that somehow I became a contagious element. After I selected a few things in a shop, it seems that the saleslady became a victim to my mood, for she exclaimed, as soon as I turned my back, "What a sweet little girl!" How can you explain my mood? It is just as unreasonable as my black crisis of despair, and the only difference is that my happy moods make others happy. I wish I could remember this oftener.

Mother and I had lunch with Tia Anaïs and Cuca at the Waldorf. Cuca was nicer to me. It seems that they all had noticed how quickly I ran away after accomplishing whatever I had to with their shopping. There are few things I notice as quickly and feel as keenly as being not wanted, and it is enough to make me fly to the end of the world. Tia Anaïs has always been very generous to me, and Cuca, too. I know that they want me, but they do not show it; their thoughtlessness hurts me to the quick. Mother has noticed it, and it has happened to her, but she says that we must try to realize that the minds of the wealthy are full of a thousand thoughts for *themselves*—in such a way that Cuca almost loses her head about choosing the color of a dress, where I would lose mine only about a problem of philosophy. Cuca has to choose many dresses, while I can study when I please. The results are that I am altogether happier than she is.

Out of 5 editors to whom I sent contributions, I have already been rejected by two. I still have three to dream about. Please admire my mathematics.

November 26. I had to laugh Wednesday when I was shown one of the dresses Cuca had bought: no less a personage hung in her closet than the "unattainable dress" I had admired in the shopwindow the day before. So it might still come down to me, in a year or so, and with just a little mending, I might still wear it!

Today the postman brought a letter from Father and one from Emilia Quintero (the sweet, dear soul). Everyone was away, so I enjoyed myself with housecleaning and cooking, sprinkled

[1] *Alone.*

with songs and happy thoughts. I discovered that being half a poet affects one's views of housework. I was combing and brushing the fringes of my carpets when I heard a great burst of laughter and turned to see the working woman who helps us out several days a week; she was laughing at me, needless to say. Mother saw Eduardo, who is having his Thanksgiving vacation. He simply asked Mother what I was doing and sent me "recuerdos."[1] I laughed. When I am bubbling over with self-made happiness, what is Eduardo to me?

I answer Father's letter in Spanish, for he asks me to do so; he says it is my language. Indeed, it is the language of my ancestors, but French is the language of my heart, and English of my intellect; and I regret to say, Spanish does not appeal to me one whit.

I suppose it is very good to clean, and cook and mend, but I fear it stops the flow of my ideas.

November 27. I suffered an attack of bibliomania today when I discovered a sale of books at $.25. Yet I was contented with only one little volume of Tennyson's *Princess,* whose leaves had not been cut yet, and resisted *John Halifax, Gentleman,*[2] and *Les Misérables,*[3] because I had read them.

This extravagance took place because I went to the city for a little while. I passed by the Waldorf and yet did not go in. It was very thrilling, for I could have suddenly found myself face to face with Eduardo. Had it been so, I would have laughed most merrily, as I have been all day in the wildest and happiest mood imaginable.

The editors are still silent. I dream each night of impossible glory and renown, and wealth for Mother's Christmas present. Poetlike again, I only wish for money at Christmas time!

Two little ragamuffins, or little newsboys, as you like, asked me for pennies. At such times, too, I long for fabulous wealth, to buy them shoes and warm coats and give them a cartload of pennies—nay, dimes—but what is the use of wishing? I am such a bad business woman, such a poor writer, such a terrible housekeeper—and money does not fall from the sky like raindrops.

I would love to visit Anaïs tomorrow. I long to see her and yet I have not the courage to go, knowing all the Sánchez family will

[1] *Regards.*
[2] *By Dinah Maria Craik.*
[3] *By Victor Hugo.*

be there. Did you ever wonder how it must feel to be buried in snow and ice? That is just the sensation I experience with the Sánchezes. What I can't imagine is why, if snow and ice melt a little at the touch of fire, I can't melt my aunts and cousins just a little.

November 30. I have just finished a most bewildering book. Perhaps I should not have read it—I have never read that sort of book before; still, it fell into my hands, as you might say, because I found it in Mrs. Norman's bookcase, and once I had begun it, I read it from cover to cover. I wonder if I can tell you its main characteristic, and incidentally, its one great fault. It is too "modern." It is called "The Real Adventure," written by Henry Kitchell Webster.[1] Perhaps the strangest thing about it is that I did not understand it. Why strange? Because all the books I read I understand perfectly well, or at least I interpret them to the complete satisfaction of my intelligence. People call that "understanding." I am afraid that even as I try to describe the manner in which it has impressed me, I am writing incoherently. How can I express why, in one book alone, I have found things to admire, things that revolted, things that elevated; and pages that shocked, and baffled, and dazzled; others which expressed magnificent ideals, original conceptions; characters admirably drawn; pages that were blank to me, others that opened the door to a new world of thoughts.

Enric now forms part of our daily life, just as of yore. Yesterday while I accomplished my morning duties, Enric's violin bathed the house in enchanting waves of song. I was delighted, and my little bird, so long silent and cheerless, began suddenly to sing with all the might of his throbbing soft, feathery throat. And now, to turn from sentiment and melody to the more common spheres, I will speak of Mother's gift. Mlle. Linotte found herself last night parading before her mirrors and the exclamatory family in an adorable gray squirrel coat. If I were to describe it, I should choose to say that it was something soft, beautiful, clinging, warm and queenly, which consequently belongs to Woman. I actually believe the possession of it changed my expression until, as I walked up and down Fifth Avenue, I became conscious of queer, cool stares.

Mother and I went to see Tia Anaïs and Cuca, partly to

[1] *American novelist.*

thank my aunt for the share that she had in my happiness. Little Mother was very proud of her gift. Every once in a while she stole sidelong glances at me, until my foolish contentment brought forth a melodious laughter.

Isn't it strange sometimes to discover other people's names for certain actions that you have often committed? To a person whose heart is full of bruises, for instance, and who is ready to speak out her woes, another says: "Now don't get tragic!" Tragic! I suppose that is what some other human being would call me during one of my inexplicable moods. Now, you see, I have learned things, and one of them is what to call myself when in a certain state of mind. By learning to know myself, I will begin to know others. At the end of this experiment I may aspire to be an author.

From each book I read, I draw some lesson, some purity, as from a fountain, leaving the rest, and eagerly storing away the precious preparations for a secret, beloved, uncertain dream. At times, I believe I have created this dream of authorship from my doubts as to the possibilities in the other dreams. "The wheels of Fate" may trample upon my dreams of home, womanhood, wife-hood, motherhood; then I will turn toward authorship. Do I seem to believe that fate may not trample upon the last? Oh! No, yet I believe that fate will have a harder time doing away with that ambition, somehow. It's stronger, because it emanates from your-self alone and does not depend for its existence on anyone else but its creator.

December 2. The scene of my chats has changed from Mother's business desk to my bed. I have a cold, one of those silly and lasting colds. Nevertheless I am enjoying myself immensely. I am bathed in the afternoon sunlight, and only half-awake from a wonderful voyage into Stevenson's world. I have read, with only trivial interruptions (such as breakfast and lunch), *New Arabian Nights* and *The Dynamiter.* And, in between, Mark Twain's *Christian Science,* which has lifted me, elated and satisfied. Do you wonder that I contemplate the setting sun with languid eyes and drowsy mind? And not till now have I become conscious that the wind is howling and shaking the windowpanes with furious strength. While I wrote these lines the sky behind the woods has become blood-red and purple. I want to write a great deal, and yet it seems that all my reading has paralyzed my own thoughts to a certain extent.

I should be sleeping, but oh, how tormented and restless I am, after the delicious serenity of the day. Mother was so happy, too, when she came from the city, until she opened her correspondence. Father, Father wants us back, or divorce. Oh, if you only knew how awful it is for little Mother, and for me, who understands, to read the letter that means our life, our home, is in the hands of the Law! I have never seen Mother as bitter, or as indignant. While she wept and spoke, I felt a dull, crushing pain. My hands were clenched, I was unable to speak for a long while, and besides, the violin upstairs, with its very sad, strange melody, almost drove me frantic! Oh, Mother, Mother, how she has suffered.

Still, now she is completely calmed; she says it was the unexpectedness that startled her into despondency, but now she only sees a struggle to be conquered, and Mother's spirit is indomitable. Her goodnight kiss imparted to me a little of her strength.

December 3.

Dearest Frances,

Still, your letter opened my eyes! How on earth could I expect you to divine everything! No wonder sensible people live in comical terror of bibliomaniacs, bookworms, poets and such things. Nevertheless, I think a poet once composed verses to tell the world that those madnesses were the sweetest and loveliest infirmities of creation. Oh, Pic, I fear I am getting unbearable. When you tell me you are having what is called a "good time," I see that you manage to do everything well, but I . . . someone ought to shake me. Shall I confess? Well, each day I retire further into the recess of my shell. That is to say, I have to be dragged out into the outside world, and once there I act like Rip Van Winkle. That means, in short, that the comparison between people, adventures and the world in general, and the other things—books, studies, meditations, soliloquies, etc.—has proved fatal to the first. When you ask me about the boys I liked so much last year, well, what shall I say? There is nothing to say, just shrug my shoulders. Any book, any tramp through the woods, can replace them and their inexplicable silliness. Amen. I did not mean to be so critical, Dear Pic, I understand now why it is said that comparison is so cruel, particularly one between books and boys. . . .

December 5. Last night Thorvald, Enric and I went to the Kew Gardens Club dance. I believe we all enjoyed ourselves. Still, had there been a shadow following me everywhere, I would not have been surprised, because of my two personalities. In spite of all, my sociable self seemed quite dominant. I discovered I had been so agreeable to a boy that he asked me if he could walk home with me. The other self longed to go home, and wondered why people in general seemed so, so silly; wondered what was the use of hopping around to some awful music, what was the use of all the senseless talk, of smiling—of being there at all. Oh, it is terrible to think that at seventeen I am ready to turn my back to the entire world and live a hermit's life.

December 6. Sunday I would have written more but for Manén's visit—he came for dinner and remained until 9:30. Mother sang for him while he accompanied her. He teased us about "going to Paris." Again I noticed how pleasing his personality was and how simply it unfolded itself. I wrote some business letters for him on my typewriter, a thing I was proud to do when I thought of how godlike he seemed the day of his triumph. This impression lasts but a second when one speaks to Manén; he dispels all but the realization that he is human, and ordinary, and lovable.

And now, here I am today—a gloomy, unreasonable Mlle. Linotte, who sobs because the wind is whistling and the sky is gray and dull.

It seems unbelievable that I still should have so many long years before me, for I act like a weary traveler nearing the end of his journey. It is especially when I am reminded by preparations for the great festive season of the year that I become keenly conscious that my heart is asleep, and not following the rest of the world. And I do so want to seem sunny and cheerful, for the sake of those around me. What habit is this I am falling in of allowing sadness to conquer me each day? It makes me so ashamed.

I believe it is only when you grow older that you realize the charm of plain, common friendship, without imaginary thrills and fairy tales woven around each word or act. Thus Enric and I are now good friends. We have very little in common; but he is very nice to me, bringing a necklace and candy, and I, on my side, try to make him forget that he is very "bored" when he is not studying.

He is not accustomed to our normal and unruffled life, and seeks to chat and play with everybody. He has changed a great deal since the days of 158 W. 75th Street. If I should try to tell you how, it would be something like "settled down." Or perhaps he has not changed much, but I have, and I see him differently. Who knows?

Mother is reading her old love letters, and below, Vicente and Enric are playing the song "Sweetheart." Oh, perhaps no one else would feel burning tears just because of these things, but I can't help it. And now the music changes, but music always stirs me and saddens me more than words can tell. There is no one I can speak to now. I could not explain, they would think me mad. But then you—I can just write, even if I have to stop to cover my eyes with my hand and listen to the great tempest roaring inside of me. Oh, I want to go away, away. Why does it seem so hard to "just live" sometimes? I want to be happy and careless and thoughtless, like the other girls of my age, and I can't. It does not seem as if I had ever been like them.

Joaquin is laughing, poor child. He only cries when he hurts himself with stones and such things. I hope he will never sit, as I do tonight, and feel his heart crushed in some inexplicable way, listening to music which expresses all the wordless sorrows. Yes, and that is music—tears and laughter. Just like life—and still, "life" does not sound as lovely. How I have tried with all my heart to believe this life to be glorious, how I have woven dream after dream around the ugly parts of it, and then gazed at my work with admiration and called it beautiful names, and how the veil is brutally torn, time after time—forever, perhaps I hardly know if it is the music speaking these words or I. The notes melt into one another, they all rise, then vanish, to give place to more tears, more thoughts. Poor *selfish* Linotte that I am. Have I no courage?

December 7. Have I no courage? Very little, but I have shame, and that is courage's shadow. That is why today I have conquered all my weakness, and hum while I work, and read the last lines I wrote last night with a critical, severe little smile. But enough self-condemnation, I am going to be good. I still have the entire day before me, to be good and useful. I am only scribbling a little between the time for "stockings mended" and some other little duty. I like to see my resolutions in black and white; it makes them more irrevocable.

December 9. I do not really know what is the trouble with me. Sometimes I wonder if my character is developing into that of a morbid, fearful person, and beyond my control. All these days, I have not been myself. Perhaps it is because I have been ill again, and pass each night in broken sleep. Then when the sunshine appears, I feel the contrast more keenly, and it saddens me. And at times I stand very still like one in a dream, and wonder if something in me will "break." It does not seem as if I were living. Just my body moves, but inside, oh, the terrible sleep of feelings! And yet, during these days, so many little things have happened which I like and appreciate. Surely, I cannot remain as I am; please, heaven, make me good again!

I know that this crisis will pass. If I could just for a little while cease to think of Father and Mother, Father and Mother—ever, ever. That I believe, is the great cause of all my struggles.

My little joys were letters from Frances and Miguel—the latter with an invitation for a dance on the 22nd of December—and a lovely, sincere and long conversation with Enric. You cannot imagine what a revelation this intimacy with Enric has been. I have never known Enric, and the boy I know now is far better than I have ever imagined him. I am glad that all our foolishness has vanished. Now that we understand each other in a far lovelier manner, we have serious, purposeful talks, which are like peeps into each other's mind.

Sometimes I was reminded of the talks I had with Eduardo, and I thought that we are all like "ships that pass in the night" and, hailing each other, are lost in the darkness. I realize now that it must be like that, and I do not mind giving Enric a little companionship while he needs it even if we lose each other later during the voyage. And now that I have named Eduardo, it will be for the last time, because I want to tell you my secret! I believe it to be a lesson—just to show me that we are in this queer world to make it better, and then pass on. I was very foolish, very, very childish, in clinging to things that always flit and change. It is true, as I have told Mother, that the thought of Eduardo and the terribly serious way I accepted his little entrance and exit now fills me with a great, wonderful mirth!

What is continually surprising me, and gives me perhaps more courage than I could have myself, is the opinion that others hold of me. Compare my "confessions," my self-censure, my doubts, etc. with the opinion of those who know me. I seem to be telling falsehood after falsehood. It is a glorious gift, that. Last night, Enric unconsciously repeated many things that have been said to me directly or indirectly. He must have wondered why I smiled when he told me I was womanly—or something about my eyes. They seemed like echoes.

The only thing which Enric said which bewildered and embarrassed me was that I was very cheerful but that my eyes were always sad. "I believe you are always just trying to be gay." I would rather tell you all the things he told me about himself, because I made *him* talk and enjoyed watching him—but then, I am so afraid of making a distorted picture of Enric and spoiling a personality which eludes mere words. That is why I stupidly confine my Diary to myself—I do not care how distortedly I present my foolish girlhood to you. You can always redress it, knowing me so well. Besides, I am only creating you for the sake of the day you will perish in the flames with all my relics, letters, etc. And now, to another nuit blanche—with the nightmares and the restlessness. Can my life have just begun?

December 13. I often wonder if, in our life, there are ever two or three days similar to each other. Even Sunday is transformed. Enric had two of his friends here yesterday—a violinist of 16 years, Joseph Lamkin, and an 18-year-old pianist, William Shaeffer. And all afternoon we heard music and laughter, wonderful music and boyish laughter, for Thorvald's friends were here also, Jimmie, Jerry and Edward. Belica [Tallet] came for a little while. At suppertime Enric's friends returned to N.Y., and the reception was considerably calmer with Mrs. Norman and Belica only.

After supper, Thorvald, Enric and I played and talked together. Then Thorvald went up to his room, and Enric and I had a short, queer talk, as we frequently have now. Enric tells me he likes the young pianist and asked me what I thought of him. And I told Enric how I had liked him a great deal, for his talent, his pleasant and sunny ways, his love of books. To Lamkin, the Russian boy, I spoke little. He was a very handsome, silent person but with a twinkle in his eyes, which puzzled me and which I afterward was told was the only trace of his personality. Enric says he is a great hypocrite. Thus I learn to read people through others' eyes, never with my own. How strange it seems. Still, it is safer than to judge completely wrong, as I invariably do.

I am invited to a "club meeting" for this coming Friday. This means that I am to become a member of the Kew Gardens club of young people. Half of me is willing to belong—the other half shrinks from the contact with "foolishness," but then, I must belong or else remain friendless.

When I read my old diaries, I find that I write a little too impulsively and elaborately. It is almost comical how I love the music of words and unconsciously clothe the simplest thoughts in foolishly bright arrays. It is not untruth or exaggeration—it is just a queer, inexplicable flaw in my sight, which doubles each little thing in value and importance, sorrow as well as happiness, friendships and dislikes. Therefore, the reflection in my Diary is wild and fantastic. I hope I will outgrow this.

Enric told me he did not realize until yesterday how changed I was. He told me my black velvet dress (the Princess dress) is the most beautiful dress he has ever seen. (He does not know how *old* it is.) I was not surprised at the "transformation." How well I remember the scraggy-legged, timid, peasantlike person of 158 W. 75th St., but what bewildered me again was the way Enric expressed it. He says *all* of me is changed—the way I speak and greet people, the ease with which I act my social duties. But he does not seem to regret it. I believe he likes me better, because I can tell by thousands of little things. He holds my chair at meal-time, he always wants me to win games, he is indignant when Thorvald teases me, and he always asks my opinion about everything. I never, never imagined while in Edgemere, writing his name in the sand, what was going to take place in the future.

December 16. My crisis of sadness has passed, and these last days I have been good. I believe it is the spirit of Christmas which has transformed me; all day I prepare and think only for others, and it makes me very happy. Mother and I have been shopping together—and how she has spoiled me! I have been given three new dresses. One of them is for the dance on the 22nd, another for tomorrow's club meeting, the third because Mother is terribly extravagant when my eyes begin to shine like a baby girl's. Standing in the midst of a thousand reflections of myself, I could only clap my hands and gasp and wonder. Do you mind if I tell you about them? My dance frock is coral-pink with an undefinable touch of the old-fashioned charm—yet very simple. It makes me look like—like—I don't know. The second seems like me—a dark-blue, clinging, very plain dress. It makes me look like a poet and a person with a very original character. The third melts into the color of my hair and eyes. You can scarcely tell what the shape of it is—just the brown of the dress and the white of my neck and hands and face can be distinguished. But enough frivolity. Today I was left at home, all alone. Even Enric, who seldom goes to

N.Y., is still away. And so I have sung, and spoken with myself, and tried my dresses on, and wondered about all the things that will happen to me while I wear them. At one time, I was enjoying myself so much that I laughed out loud. Just laughed—and then—I sat down and mended stockings, for shame.

Jimmy has suddenly taken a great fancy to me again. For one reason or another, he calls every evening and fills my ears with nonsense. Miguel writes to me again—a wonderful letter by which I can tell that he understands me as well as any boy could. And then, if you could just hear what Enric says to me. Somehow, what with one thing and another, I have peeped into another little corner of the world and found it very, very funny. For Christmas day I believe we are all going to be united, the Sánchez, Chase and Culmell families—and Eduardo. Now, it seems so comical and cheery that I wonder if some fairy has touched me with her wand.

One evening I asked Mother if all the things that happened to me happened to her at my age.

"Indeed yes," said Mother, laughing. "I fell in love with a different person every week."

"Then it is natural to be so foolish?" asked Mlle. Linotte.

Mother laughed again and said, "Naturellement."

December 18. I am still good. Last night was the date of our memorable entrance into the Sans Souci Club—Thorvald, Enric and I. It was at Peggy Jones's house, and it began with a business meeting, followed by a dance. Enric was blasé—he did not enjoy himself and I could read that in his eyes. Thorvald was just the opposite and laughed like a child with everybody. For my part, I knew it was silly and that I was ready to return home before I arrived there, but nevertheless I behaved myself beautifully. There is some lucky star always shining now for me as far as dances are concerned, and although before and after them I grow serious and sarcastic, while I am dancing I cannot help enjoying myself. You see, the boys are so exceptionally nice to me, everywhere and always. I cannot sit apart for one dance.

A very queer thing happened, which made me happy. (You must remember that, foolishly enough, certain compliments do me good, like sunshine.) There is an atrociously nonsensical dance now in favor called "tottling." Last night I found myself unexpectedly called upon to tottle for the first time in my life. I could do it with Jimmy, who is very strong and just forced me to follow him exactly as he pleased, but with other boys I made mistakes, chiefly because I did not like it and felt conscious of it. With one boy, who told me he had just learned to tottle, it was disastrous. Did he evade dancing with me? I felt sure he would—I was terribly ashamed. Imagine my surprise when he came to me as often as he could, cutting in continually, following me, bringing me cakes and punch. Goodness, how patient he was, and instead of dancing differently, he continued to tottle, and I to cling and laugh and repeat: "Oh, I am sorry."

Could any philosophically inclined personage resist the temptation of being the heroine of such a phenomenon as a young gentleman persisting in having his toes stepped on? What happened to him? Did he like my new dress (which even Thorvald liked), the one which clung and seemed "artistic"? I wish I could tell Miguel about this because his last letter was filled with apprehensions and misgivings about my presence at his class dance. He elaborately presents me both sides of the affair, the frivolous and the philosophical—and seemingly finding the latter's cause considerably weak, he surrenders and simply begs me to be there. He does not know I have discovered such a thing as psychology problems in a mere dance.

Oh, the Delineator editor has answered: "My dear Miss Nin, I like the idea of your love letters enormously, but I do think it needs more polishing. Won't you let me see it again? Sincerely, Verse Editor." Here is my greatest fault—the rendering of my thoughts into the proper form.

December 20. A glorious morning with the house to myself, pen, ink, a Diary and a merry heart. Perhaps what influenced this rare mood of supreme contentment is a dream I had. Perhaps the calendar, whispering dates of future adventure. Perhaps the manner in which we spent Sunday. Perhaps the spirit of mystery roving in the drawers full of little red-ribboned packages. Perhaps the Xmas tree which came, and now the holly. Still, perhaps, Mother's goodbye kiss, which was very long, and Joaquin's, which was very passionate. Oh, I cannot say.

Yesterday, Willie Shaeffer came again, and another of Enric's friends, Mr. Figueroa. We had music; and conversation which bordered on witchcraft, so spontaneous its nature was, so sincere, so full of sentiment and art. Not one moment did I feel strange and out of place, except when compliments suddenly sprang up. I felt in my own sphere, as I listened to the well-expressed opinions, and I calmly heard myself speaking out my own ideas, even leading sometimes. It was a glorious feeling, that of realizing the charm of the world which was Father's and Mother's and which is now mine also. I keenly felt the contrast, too, between the other world, of foolish talk and no ideals—Jimmy's world and Mary's[1] and Mrs. Thayer's (for examples)—and the one which by heritage may be mine. Although I write nothing of what was said for fear of marring and distorting, I will never forget all I hear—it enters to the very depths of my shell and forms part of my Inside World. Many things bewilder me, and I remain silent after I hear them. They have a surface meaning. When Mr. Figueroa asked what I was, Mother answered laughingly "American."

"Oh," retorted Mr. Figueroa quickly, "Una persona tan spirituelle no *puede* ser *Americana.*"[2]

There is the European speaking—lightly pointing to the great chasm existing between the two continents. Not the ocean alone holds them wide apart; it is the essential difference in ideals, in the intellectual lives of each. Europe is the native land of art, in the greatest, widest sense of the word; and for this land, you can almost picture a gigantic idol—the dollar.

You learn much each day, and the greatest lesson is that you cannot learn anything, or very little, in your own company. It is when I forget myself and plunge into mere existence, *without* self-analysis, that I am healthier in mind and body. Besides, I realize at times the egotistical side of my behavior. It is said that to know one's own faults is to have them half conquered. What will this Diary be when I am 40 years older a miracle of perfection? I doubt it.

December 23. Yesterday, at 9 o'clock Mother and I met Miguel at the [Hotel] Commodore. A little while before, I had seen myself in my new dress—and oh, it looked so pretty. I had a feather fan also, tulle around my shoulders and a little bag for my handkerchief, all in turquoise-blue, which made a lovely and very Frenchie contrast. A little while before, also, Enric had given me a large, beautiful set of perfume, sachet, lotion, powder, etc. in a Djer Kiss Box. Do you wonder that I should be quite excited and light-hearted? The dance began late, in a very brilliantly lighted and stately dance hall; the floor seemed like an immense mirror; it was almost regretfully that I stepped on it with Miguel. I was given my second dance card, which Miguel filled, halfway refus-

[1] *The maid.*
[2] *"Such a soulful person cannot be an American."*

ing to introduce me until it could not be helped. Then I danced with a Puerto Rican boy and a few of Miguel's classmates, while Mother watched and smiled at me. The dance ended just as Mother told me we were obliged to go if we wished to catch the last train to Kew Gardens. And we hurriedly said goodbye to Miguel, who had to return to his school to be freed again today. At 2 o'clock I turned off my light with a queer sigh, because all the while I was brushing my hair I was wondering how it could be that I liked my dress, my fan, my little bag, the music, the pretty picture reflected in the mirrors at the dance, the brilliance of the entire scene, the excitement of the small dance card, all except the "Boys!"

If I had not danced with Miguel, whose society I like and sincerely enjoy, I would have made now a very grave description of last night's dance. This morning I awoke at 10 and under my breakfast plate I found a note scribbled by Enric: "Did you dream with Miguel?" Can you imagine Mlle. Linotte in the midst of such nonsense? I believe I long for complete solitude again. Strangely enough, I laugh while these things happen and then afterward I realize that I do not like them. You would understand how I feel if you could watch how Enric acts and speaks. When I wrote that all foolishness was gone from me, I should not have included Enric, because he is too much of a Spaniard to be otherwise. And yet I have just begun this frivolous era. I still have Xmas day and Peggy's dance and the club's dance. I am tired of wasting time. "Without women the beginning of our life would be helpless; the middle devoid of pleasure; and the end of consolation." —Jouy.[1]

December 26. Oh, the wonder of this Christmas day. It began very early, at seven o'clock, because we had to go to Mass. Perhaps an hour later we were all united around the tree. The tree touched the ceiling and was heavy with tinsel and snow and candles— but who can describe a Christmas tree? The scent of pine, the cheery mystery of the packages below, the charm of the very top star, the flickering little candles. We sang, "Venite Adoremus," and then Thorvald and Joaquin rushed to the unfolding of the Mystery. Mother, on Christmas day as well as on every day of the year, forgot herself until I opened the boxes containing the little things I had made for her, and then she was very happy.

[1] *Victor de Jouy.*

We were all very spoiled. For me there was perfume, bags, hand-kerchiefs—all frivolous things. I was not saddened, nevertheless, for I probably deserved them, and still I longed for a book. The two rooms had been made cheerful and tidy and cozy—cheerful because of holly and the season's flowers and mistletoe. The lamps were clothed in red. In the dining room our table had been joined to Mrs. Norman's and beautifully set with candles in the center and big trays filled with fruit. In the kitchen there was an uproar; Tia Anaïs's maid was helping Monsita and the new maid, Petra. Somehow Mother and I found time to dress. No sooner were we dressed than Tia Juana appeared. Half an hour later entered the Sánchez family—and Eduardo, whose first look was for Mlle. Linotte, and such a look that since that moment I forgot every-thing except that he liked me and I liked him. Then followed laughter and dancing. The Xmas dinner lasted a long time. I had seated everyone according to Mother's and Tia Juana's advice, all except putting Eduardo by my side—this, I refused, and put him far away, so that I could see him and still not feel confused by his presence. Before the dinner we exchanged our little gifts. Eduardo gave me a small picture with printed verses, beginning, "I was thinking of you," and he labeled the package "Para cuisine de un admirador."[1] It was all very foolish, very fickle, very charm-ing, very boyish and still much in harmony with my happy mood. After the dinner I was made to recite *Love Letters* (by myself) and then we all rose and invaded the parlor once more. And danced. Thorvald Sánchez[2] and Rita Allie were much together. No words can describe her beauty or her sweetness. She makes me think of the Lily Maid who pined away for love of a great warrior in olden times, not of a modern girl who can breathe in this world today.

Eduardo and I seemed to be living again those days of har-mony, except that I felt how much older I was in every way and realized that if our fairy-tale friendship was very beautiful, it was nevertheless very fragile, very storm-tossed. Jimmy and Jerry appeared later and separated us. Jimmy and I shocked Tia Anaïs and Cuca with the new way of dancing; it was very funny. It made me think that, after all, I am old-fashioned but moderately so. Later Mr. Figueroa and Willy Shaeffer came, and then we had a concert, and the audience was increased by the arrival of Elsie de Sola, her brothers and cousins. Eduardo sat by my side. Their

[1] *"For cuisine from an admirer."*
[2] *A cousin, also called "Billin."*

merriment was hushed now and then by waves of emotion called forth now by Enric's violin or Figueroa's beautiful voice or Shaeffer's talent for the piano. Ana Maria asked her Mother if Figueroa was Caruso! After one of his great successes, Mr. Figueroa chose the seat nearest to me, and noticing I had somehow placed myself in a corner, spoke a graceful, gallant and charming compliment about the "scent of the violet and her modesty." And Eduardo looked at me! Just *looked!* Oh, it seemed as if I had read it all in a book! I could hardly realize that all those wonderful little adventures were happening to me. Very late, the Sánchezes departed; Eduardo told me he had sent me a Christmas card with an important message, and asked me to let him know when I received it. The de Solas said goodbye a little later, and then we served a bohemian supper to the remaining guests, heard more music, conversed, complimented, laughed and—separated. It was midnight. Tia Juana slept with me.

Somehow, we found courage to attend Mass. Christmas Day was gloriously beautiful in a cold, icy fashion, without snow.

December 28. Yesterday Tia Anaïs invited me to the opera. My first impulse, as always, was to shrink away, but then I was told it was to be Maeterlinck's "Blue Bird," and it was Eduardo's voice asking me, so I reluctantly accepted. I had lunch with them all, except Cuca, who was not well. At the opera Eduardo sat by my side, and we held long conferences between the acts; strange, half-uttered thoughts were exchanged, which, on my side, I knew puzzled him, for I was making believe I had thought little about his silence and attributed it to very natural and literary reasons. The strangest thing of all was that he allowed me to read his diary, and I came to a description of a wishing game we had played with cards one time. His wish had been that I should "love him!" I asked him with bewildered eyes if he knew what he had just given me to read. Graziella and Anaïs were there, and I did not understand what he said, except a vague "Ya todo eso pasó,"[1] and an embarrassed smile. I wondered if all this was happening to me. It almost struck my sense of humor, but this last characteristic is always difficult to strike in me. Therefore, the events of the day struck my sense of tragedy, and all my spirits drooped like the Blue Bird's whose death was so lamented.

With all this nonsense, I forget to speak of the Blue Bird.

[1] *"That is all past."*

The music stirred me at times. I had read the book, and was conscious of the beauty of the scenery and the voices, but my thoughts wandered, no one knows where. In such a state, I came home to find Miguel, who had been ill in school on Christmas day, and with a sinking heart, I prepared for Peggy's dance. Jimmy, Jerry and Edward, Miguel, Enric and Thorvald formed my escort.

The dance was just a dance. Last night I liked Edward only because he was so quiet, and kind and soothing. When the girls had to choose their partners, I chose him, much to Miguel's surprise and Enric's disgust, but it was so nice to dance without speaking with a slightly old-fashioned boy who blushes whenever he looks at me. Several times I almost fled through the open door, but there was the first snow on the ground, and I thought it would make me colder and colder. At one o'clock I fell asleep, with two terribly hot tears on my lashes. I was tired of dancing, I was tired of laughing, of boys, of the *hustling* life. I wanted a book and a weeping willow tree and an island with You.

The boys, dancing and singing downstairs, have called me several times. They do not know that I am scribbling for a little courage. I received Christmas cards from friends. No card from Eduardo. And now the sunshine disappears behind a heavy cloud. With that gone, I have no light left, because inside of me it is all very dark and hushed and yet with trouble brooding beneath the calmness of the treacherous regions of my emotions. Dear Diary, what would I do without you! When I remember the manner in which Eduardo fills his, I realize why so many diaries are great failures. It is not with himself but with his surroundings and outside happenings that he fills page after page. While here, I find the comfort of confession, the consolation of self-reproach or self-approval. What will I think of these divagations tomorrow?

December 29. There is almost as much charm about a fireplace devoid of fire as when it is filled with the crackling winter log, because of the memories which fill the hushed and gloomy place. It is thus with people too, those whose youth and brilliancy are gone, and still have charm, because of the memories which haunt their faded eyes. That is why now I have chosen, from all the cozy corners of the house, the one by the chimney, which is said to belong to old women and, I add, belongs also to poets.

The memories that haunt me are of a few hours ago, when Miguel, Enric and I sat around the cheery warmth and talked. It was Enric, I think, who originated the idea that we should tell our opinion of one another, promising to tell the truth. We began very cheerfully and ended in an oppressive silence, brought about by Enric, whose expression unexpectedly clouded into a half-veiled bitterness. It was far beyond my understanding. Miguel expressed it by saying that "Enric has become tragic." I fear that now I will avoid the odd experiment. Nevertheless, it made me happy, and Miguel was glad also. He had been the first to begin and spoke of me until I stopped him by saying, "What a hypocrite I am!" It made him laugh. Then I told him many things, and among them that he was in the finest sense of the word a "gentleman." This I meant, and he realized it, and was grateful. Then Enric spoke of me—in his usual way, and I was very much confused. Here the trouble followed, when my turn came to give my opinion of Enric. He fixed his eyes on me so earnestly that I lost my calmness and spoke nonsense, and Miguel helped me out, until I said what I was afraid to think: that I did not understand Enric's personality. Since the beginning, when Miguel judged me, Enric wore the expression I know so well, of annoyance. A few minutes before he had said something very queer, that there were days when he hated me. No sooner did he say this than I realized that a change in him had taken place, and I knew when. I asked him if he hated me on Christmas day, and he said yes. What he asked me afterward explained his statement—why I treated *all* the boys so nicely, so equally. Why didn't I choose my boyfriends more carefully? He did not like Eduardo! And then everything seemed so terribly, so marvelously *foolish* that I laughed, in Mother's rippling way, and looked up to see Enric's frowning face and Miguel's expression of mingled surprise and amusement.

Of course, I did not waste all these pages without knowing that I was wasting them. Only, I want to write of these terribly nonsensical happenings to laugh at them later on, and because they are part of my life now. You see, all the trouble comes from the queer fact that Miguel and I are good friends. Enric and I are good friends; Miguel and Enric, perhaps, also; each "duo" separates one from the other, but together we clash. I am in deadly fear of another "conference."

December 31. Yesterday Jack and I saw *Mary*, a sweet, agreeable musical comedy; then we had an ice-cream soda at the [Hotel] McAlpin, and I came home without a trace of excitement. You see, this is a new development in the process of my civilization. All morning was devoted to a tempestuous housecleaning, partly for the sake of health, partly because we are going to make merry in honor of the New Year. While endeavoring to polish until I could catch my reflection in the furniture, I thought of yesterday morning. First, the dear old postman brought me Eduardo's Christmas card, inscribed: "From your forgetful cousin who will soon write to thee as in days of old, (perhaps I have some reason for my forgetfulness, worthy to be told!)" And later Eduardo came himself. I had to hurry my preparations for the matinee because I forgot the time, conversing. Then we had a merry lunch. Eduardo accompanied me to the station, while Thorvald and Enric attacked us with snowballs. I asked my "forgetful cousin" why he had not written, and he answered that it was a thing difficult to explain, that perhaps he would write it. Then we spoke of lighter things and laughed, until the train arrived and carried me away, to Jack.

I fell asleep that night with confused thoughts about the varied personalities invading the peace of my shell life. Eduardo in the morning, Jack all afternoon, Miguel and Enric all evening. Miguel is changing a little (by watching Enric, who is very gallant when he is happy), and he is becoming wonderfully conscious of my presence. Enric continues to reveal himself to me, but now the discoveries trouble me. He is very moody, at times more temperamental than anyone I have ever known. At such times, it is to me that he does not speak. He avoids looking at me, and the corner of his lips curl in a bitter little smile, which hurts me all through because I realize how much he must have suffered to be so deeply unhappy with his own thoughts and memories. When we play games, Miguel is always helping me to win; Enric completely ignores me, except now and then, when I ask a question, which he answers with exaggerated politeness. I feel very sorry for him and wish I could help him, but his own excessive sensitiveness and my awkwardness and fear of misconceptions form a great barrier between us. How he must hate me today.

I do so long to read and scribble and dream again that I contemplate with a tinge of sadness the jollification which is going to take place tonight. Mother is marketing with Joaquin. Miguel is writing letters. Enric is in New York. And so, while the house is hushed, I scribble of my changed life—the Outside Life, which keeps me so far away from the things I most love. I contemplate with curiosity the future, as one is wont to do each time the old year fades. I contemplate the past also, and find that however powerful time is in the changes it brings, it has not changed yet the greatest thing in the heart of Mlle. Linotte. Year after year, I record in my Diary my adventures in the world of men and women and my longings for the other things. I am growing older, perhaps more civilized, less timid, prettier (who knows), but my heart is true to the dreams of my girlhood.

❧ 1 9 2 1 ❧

January 1. "Life is not all plays and poems." —G. B. Shaw. "Talent is that which is in a man's power; genius is that in whose power man is." —Lowell. Happy New Year, Little Diary! You need not say it to me, as I am certain of *making* it happy in spite of all that may happen, because I have been thinking until the weird resolution became fixed in my mind and heart. By happiness, of course, I mean the inward calm of my shell, and therefore, the banishment of all outside and superficial troubles. This philosophical state of mind began when the celebration of the new year proved a great failure, and while we clasped hands and consumed punch and sandwiches as the clock struck twelve, I felt keenly the magnificent contrast between my two worlds. Such was my first thought this year, a strange title perhaps for the story which is to follow.

January 2. Yesterday morning we attended Mass. In the afternoon we went to the Richmond Hill theatre. At night I refused an invitation to a "reunión" in spite of Mother's advice, Enric's pleading and a charming, gallant, beautiful request from Eduardo Figueroa by telephone. Why? Just because I wanted my "home," the shelter of my nest and its blue charm; just because I did not want music and dance and laughter and compliments that night —just that and nothing else. It was not very reasonable; it was just Mlle. Linotte's doings, which are often beyond my own understanding.

Now Enric is playing downstairs, accompanied by Willy Shaeffer, and wave upon wave of melody reaches me. I fear I have heard too much music today, because Mother took Joaquin and me to a concert by the Philharmonic Society, conducted by Josef Stransky. Enric was by my side, and I delighted in his enthusiasm for Manén, who was the "assisting artist." It is only now that I realize how stirred I was and how saddened in consequence. There are certain dreams which music wakes; that I cannot describe—and yet now, as I listen to his violin, I listen to Enric's heart. I sit here to dream about one of its secrets, which I *can* describe to you. Enric loves me. I have become conscious of it very slowly, after vainly seeking to laugh at all his words. Now when he says certain things, his eyes are so sincere, his meaning so simple, I can only listen and wonder. I have written this tonight because, before I came upstairs to my nest, Enric told me he was going to play *to me*, for me. Oh, how often he does it now, and tonight, as if the words were written to the magic music. I write: Enric loves me. It is good to be alive, to feel what one has read, to feel Life, to feel Love, to feel Youth. Just to feel, as I tonight, swept off this world by storms, adventures. No, I cannot write as I want to write. I am ashamed of the limits of my pen.

January 3. Do you remember when I read *Scènes de la Vie de Bohème?* Well, just imagine, I know someone who reminds me of one of the wonderful characters—was it Colline? Nay, I have forgotten the name of the one who always carried books in his pockets. In 1921 someone I know does it also. Oh, Willy Shaeffer, you have made me believe for once that the world of books resembles the world of men. When I made the discovery, I clapped my hands and asked question after question. My literary joy was complete when I found that it was shared by Miguel, who understood my madness and seemed to delight in it.

Eduardo is returning to his school in a few days—nay, tomorrow, I think, and I have to severely reprimand my own queer self each time I realize that of all the boys I know, I still like Eduardo best. Unconsciously, I have betrayed this favoritism, which is as unreasonable as it is incurable, and Enric has composed a song for me, thus: "Me gustan todos, me gustan todos. ¡Pero hay un rubio que me gusta más!"[1] I choose to write this as a punishment. Do you think it a facile task to write things which make my blood rise to my cheek?

Willy Shaeffer has begun a diary without knowing of mine. For one reason or another, we always have a myriad of things to speak of. I wish I could put Willy in a book. He was born on the

[1] *The well-known song goes, "I like them all, I like them all, but there is a blonde I like even better." Enric changed the gender of "them all" and "blonde" from feminine to masculine.*

lower East Side, the poorest region of the city, of Russian parents. Through his speech, you can trace at times the place of his birth, where he probably spent the best years of his childhood. What distinguished him from his surroundings? "Talent," the great "divider." Nowadays he is Manén's accomplished accompanist. He has a wonderful laughter, one of those laughters which spring from heart and head, peep through the eyes, transform the entire expression, and a boyish humor. He is only eighteen! It is difficult to fancy Willy bending over books of poetry and philosophy— and yet it happens. His conversation, although sprinkled with merriment and humor, is rich in knowledge of the classics, in understanding, in thoughtful conceptions and ideals, but it all simply peeps from behind his eternal gaiety, and it plays hide-and-seek with my mania for observation and discovery. But I have discovered that he carries books in his pockets! And it all goes to prove that, although I have revolved a long time around a description of Willy Shaeffer, I have returned to the point of my departure: He carries books in his pockets like one of Murger's heroes!

I am in the mood for descriptions. It seems suddenly as if I had grown dissatisfied with my personality and therefore turn to those around me. But there is no one else I could pin down on these pages, for they carry no books in their pockets, merely marbles, love letters, strings and whistles.

January 4. I am happy that last night has passed. There is a whole night of unbroken sleep and unfinished dreams between it and this cheery winter morning, which resembles Spring, and I can look backward and smile. It was a pretty dance. At 9 o'clock Thorvald, Enric, Miguel and I arrived at the Kew Gardens Club, after calling for Peggy, and we came home at half past one. I received my third dance card and danced every dance. Miguel and Enric enjoyed themselves, I am certain—there were so many pretty and vivacious girls. I love to watch them; they are as light as butterflies, with such sparkling eyes and a merry laughter, which fills me with strange longing. Oh, girls are very wonderful, and at such ages it is for a dance they seem most fitted. Last night, my very mood for watching betrayed my supreme loneliness, a loneliness without cause, for Enric followed all my movements with his eyes and stood always ready to ask me for a dance. Miguel sought dances also, and we always have pleasant, short talks because we understand each other's moods. To talk thus, we went downstairs once, and when we heard the music for another dance, we returned to find Enric with a strange expression in his eyes, which Miguel understood. I was happy when the musicians bowed and folded their tents! I almost fled downstairs to obtain my coat, and clapped my hands when we stepped into the ballroom of the shadows. (I mean Night.) I raised my soft fur collar very high, plunged my hands into my pockets, shivered a little, and laughing, I tripped home.

January 5. Miguel left us today. When I look back on these past days of vacations, I realize that his presence gave them much charm. He is like some indescribably pleasant influence which one misses very much when deprived of it. The last evening was the finest of all, when Enric, Miguel and I set out for the village, more for the sake of the walk (and the conversation) in the cool, crisp evening than anything else. Enric was in a mood which frequently reminded me of Murger's book, and Miguel and I, although far less versed in bohemian ways, felt just enough of the contagious spirit to complete the perfect trio, and so, in a manner which would deeply astonish mere followers of Common Sense, we transformed a walk into some chapter of a bohemian adventure. The reigning fact was that Enric was penniless—and had passed the day without lunch. Then he told us of all the times he had gone hungry and how often he had found his pockets empty. The realization that a story which seemed to exist in books alone, that an artist, a bohemian, one of those persons whose madnesses, eccentricities, weaknesses, are the property of all the Holders of a Pen, stood there among us, made us open our eyes and wonder. The evening had begun thus, and naturally it was followed by fantastic flights of our three imaginations. And so, watched by the moon, stars and majestic trees, with here and there a little light burning through the half-closed shutters of a house, we walked and talked, like bubbling fountains of—nonsense. Only a while ago Enric ceased to study his violin, wrote a message on a piece of paper, which he tied to a string and swung before my window. He wanted to know if I love him, and I answered for the thousandth time, "I like you." As I write, I discover that he has just come down and is speaking with Mother only a few yards away from me. It is so thrilling to just write all I please, so near to my victim, and yet without his knowledge.

January 6. "It is when most humanly alone that I feel the sweetest form of companionship." Thus today, I went to the village with a little piece of paper (filled with prosaic errands) in my pocket, and I returned transformed by a thousand things which I had seen and heard on my way—the long, silent country road, bordered by trees, and the cozy houses, which seem to lie so contented and placidly in the midst of their gardens that I could almost see them sleep. I was tempted to tiptoe as I passed them by, with the sun caressing their roofs ever so gently. I paused to listen to all the little sounds which reached me. I delighted, too, in the smell of the things which surrounded me, which even in Winter have a vague fragrance all their own, something nameless and lovely which made me stop to wonder and smile. It was about half past four when I looked back for the last time before entering the house. The sun was sinking behind the woods, a fiery copper ball. I lay my hand on my breast and listened to all the thoughts stirring inside of me, and felt all my heart going out toward that beauty, toward the witchcraft of that splendid scene.

January 7. Again I view the world from a promontory of pillows —fountain pen in hand and slightly humiliated by the vulgar character of my infirmity. I feel like a superfluous person, having just missed being interesting and on the verge of becoming a public nuisance, for I have a cold.

I have paused to listen to Enric's violin. He is "Le Violoniste Sous les Toits"[1] to me, and it is thus that I like him best. My mood today is like a leaf, which changes aspects with the wind. Suddenly it has changed from mockery to contemplation and sadness. And there it remains until the wind picks it up, plays with it and lets it fall to the ground, changed again. It is because I was thinking that much in my room reflects me. The Queen is Mother, whose portrait I have hung above my books, then there are my favorite books—half of them, books for study, reflection, meditation; the others, those around which I have woven the dreams I call life. Then there is a plant with a half-opened flower, a white, delicate dream flower, to which I give all the love I have for the woods and fields. And last, the Wastebasket into which all my literary efforts go, as the symbol of my efforts and my failures. I never thought a wastebasket could be so full of meaning, so human in the reprimands which emanate from its use as a piece of furniture! And here I end the enumeration of my regrets with a smile. I am

---

[1] *"A Garret Violinist"—a reference to the book title* A Garret Philosopher (Un Philosophe Sous les Toits).

spellbound by a sudden visit from the sunshine; it transforms all my nest; it lies at the bottom of my very wastebasket, and of my heart. It makes my reflection in the mirror very odd—my hair is gold and red; how cheery and blue my kimono is! Why was I sad? I forget. My bird is singing, my flower seems so happy; it has a way of speaking with the sunshine. It is the first one of 6 bulbs I brought from the city one day. I will call it Hope—because it is so tall and straight and strong—strong in the ways of flowers and women, which is the greatest strength of all!

All day my head ached more than anyone could guess. Finally the pain subsided and I lay very still, watching the shadows fall and wondering. without knowing why, as I often do now. Indeed, most of my questions I can never express. They simply lie in my heart and stir and shift until my restlessness finds relief in tears or, sometimes, in happiness, such as I experience in my walks through the woods but never among people.

January 9. Yesterday, in spite of coughs and a terrible longing to remain in bed, very still—for I felt weak and strange—I went to the city with Mother to say goodbye to Tia Anaïs and all my little cousins. I had seen so little of them, and then, even if they all hurt me at times, I love them: I came home with a sweet memory of Cuca, who opened the little door I knew so well in Lake Placid. To Tia Anaïs I gave "Hope," which pleased her very much. Anaïs and Graziella promised to write. Ana María clung to me till the last moment, and so I felt the warmth of their affectionate ways, which makes me so immensely happy and grateful. Eduardo was there. He was very pale, not being well at all. We spoke very little together.

Willy Shaeffer is now downstairs; in a little while he will give Joaquin a lesson. I have fled from all music, talk and laughter. I feel just like the dress I wear—my black velvet dress, which is so severe and serious. Still, I have only a few quiet minutes before dinnertime.

Now it is late; we have been to the movies. Mother threw herself on her bed, feeling very weak and nervous. I read while she rested, until the shadows fell, then I stood by the window and gazed fixedly and without thinking, at the half-veiled trees, standing against a sky the color of dense smoke. Then I sat to write, but I have left all my thoughts following the course of a lonely cloud, and there is nothing left for you but the reflection of a supreme and terrifying loneliness.

January 10. Mother is not well; you cannot imagine how little, in comparison, all else matters. I bear no other thought in mind than her condition. Now she is asleep; and I sit writing before a window, not so much because I want all these days shared with you, but because I need you. I feel helpless and friendless without Mother. Suppose the window facing me opened upon the future—the unfathomable mystery of it daunts me. Would I be writing as quietly, with only one small sorrow to contemplate, with so many expectations, so much curiosity, so much enthusiasm, eagerness, belief—aye, even confidence? I realize that it is better not to know. As it is, my gaze meets the neat simplicity of a pair of white curtains, which I have opened halfway; a little portion of the roof where I study in the summer; farther on, the leafless branches of one of our own trees; a glimpse of our neighbors' houses; more trees, more houses, then merely treetops and the horizon. And thus I am reminded that instead of questioning the future, I should be rendering thanks for the changes between the past and present. Is it not so? What had I to satisfy my longings for freedom to dream a year ago? If I used Mother's great, massive business desk, I could look upon the backyard, but if I raised my eyes, I was suffocated by a forbidding wall of houses, with bottles of milk on the window sills, yes, bottles of milk and cans of vegetables and perhaps bananas. If I wrote in my favorite site, the red velvet chair in the embrasure [bay] of the parlor window, I would be startled by the doorbell, by the thundering voice of the ice man, requesting a payment, by the passing newsboys, the numerous vehicles; in short, by all the voices of the street—and still imprisoned, guarded, closely watched by another formidable row of houses. If I chose to sit at the table in our room, I had to endure Joaquin's seraphic conduct, his sempiternal screeching, and Thorvald's explosions of indignation and the telephone. Oh, heaven be praised for the freedom to write, dream and wonder!

Days ago, while rummaging, in search "of some forgotten lore" I discovered a bit of paper on which I had written the faults most preeminent in my old diaries. I recognize the truth of the remarks now, and I wonder if I could begin today a more exacting regime in carrying out these chronicles of my life. I fear I am very egotistical. Indeed, I realize it is my Diary, my life, my self that I weave into a story, and yet my life is not made of "me." On the contrary. It all seems like a great circle to me; it is revolving around a central dot, I feel. I am it, thus. You notice how small I am? How insignificant? How uninteresting? I feel exactly like that, and the great circle represents all I love, all I live with—people, books, furniture, etc. Of course, it takes little intelligence to comprehend that the dot is the simplest thing to describe, analyze, dissect, pin upon a sheet of paper and expose to the multitude in some museum for criticism. By this I conclude that I am the central figure of these pages, much to my profound discontent surprise, discomfiture and horror. And now, what I propose to do is to offer you a wider view of the universe. In short, I will endeavor to write more of the circle. I will introduce you even as I am introduced. I have often described people to you, but in a most fantastic manner. I plunge directly, like an x-ray, into the profundities of their spiritual character; and I give never a thought to the outside. Oh, I have taken a long time to discover this great fault, but now I read of it, by coincidence, in 2 books, and it has filled me with good intentions. I speak of this today because I have seldom had the time before this to spread my resolution on your pages and watch the effects of it in black and white.

I should be writing to Father, but oh, how estranged we are in sentiments, ideals, in all! I love him; indeed, I love him more each day now that I cannot admire him. Oh, Father, Father—if I could have kept the dream I so faithfully held through childhood, and nearly all my girlhood, till death. I thought you were lost for a while and would return, but you are more than lost; you are not loved any more by anyone under this roof except me, and I love you only because you are my father.

January 11. I do not believe Eduardo is going to write. I thought of this while watching for the postman this morning. When he brought me a letter from Dorothy Eddins, inviting me to spend the greater part of Saturday with her, I read it with pleasure, slipped it into my pocket, and returned to the window, and to my thinking. "No, I do not believe Eduardo is going to write," I soliloquized; and if you knew Eduardo, you would think the same. Do you know the Prince Charming of all the fairy tales? Well, Eduardo resembles them. Oh, so much, except that he is not old enough to be staunch and true; he is seventeen! Indeed, all my aunts, cousins, distant relatives, etc., seem to have leagued themselves to convince me that my cousin is the reincarnation of fickleness. I soliloquized on this and wondered how fickleness could harmonize with Eduardo. I do not know. He is taller than I, broad-shouldered, lithe, well built, fleet of foot and graceful in all his movements. He holds his head proudly but at an angle, which saves it from arrogance. His face is very handsome, stamped with certain familiar expressions which reflect all his thoughts, a very fair face for a boy, with blond hair and eyes which can scarcely be described as wide apart, and a strange mixture of gray, blue and sea green. What lies in them is what I like—there are dreams, kindness, determination, ambition, boyish desires, wonder, surprise and, at times, something very gentle and lovely, which I always found there when he liked me so much. There are a thousand other things mingled in them of which I do not know the name. because the eyes change with the thoughts, with the feelings. They have ways of meditating, of sparkling, of hurting, of inflicting shame, or joy, or love, or strength. All eyes have, if they have a soul behind. Now and then you meet with soulless eyes; they are not eyes, they are optic nerves, etc. But I am wandering; I make a poor painter, indeed, beginning with Eduardo, finishing with moralizing. I wonder now if you like my cousin. Besides this sketch, I have told you many things; indirectly, by his acts, I am sure you know him well. That he is courteous, educated, intelligent—in short, a gentleman—is almost needless to write. You know me well enough to divine how eagerly I seek these characteristics in my friends—how tenaciously I cling to the belief that friendship is based on the intellect. although so much proves the contrary.

I am happy to have dedicated these pages to my "forgetful cousin." Surely, when old and faded and life-worn, I will read with pleasure my conception of Eduardo at seventeen. Even if time alters, and defaces, even if perhaps it divides our paths, or crosses them, or allows them to run side by side, smooth, or crooked, in spite of all, I will have this opinion untouched, unaltered. You see, I am old enough to realize the inestimable value of a "good opinion" of someone. I know that this state of mind, which is mine frequently these days, becomes rarer; one grows critical, severe, worldly-wise, and intolerant, like many people I know. Oh, Eduardo, if you knew all the pages I have scribbled in your name, you would laugh forever!

I wrote this before leaving for the city. I returned in time for lunch, read a book which sorely troubled me and then sat to write. What made me go to New York was the need of books, and also, perhaps, a subtle longing to hear that voice of the city again, a longing which has no excuse, no explanation, no remedy. It just steals into your heart and lies there until you find yourself in the midst of New York. When both my desires were satisfied, one through the medium of the Public Library, the other after having breathed the smoky air and the dust, after having felt the pressure of the crowd, heard the street organs, the slang, the newspaper boy, I persuaded myself to return home, and soon found myself plunged in a critical study of Stevenson by Frank Swinnerton. Why I should presume to judge criticism, even in the form of a confidence to my Diary, I do not know. But I love Stevenson. Lately I have devoted much of my time to the perusal of his books and have fallen under the spell of that charm which Swinnerton cannot deny. Of course, I know very little. And yet, to my reading I bring all I have—my intelligence, my enthusiasm, my curiosity, my understanding. My spirit never feels the lassitude which causes some to call certain books "dry." Therefore, to a certain extent, I know myself capable of judging a book, of forming an opinion. I have studied Stevenson very thoroughly, in my own way. I feel that I know him. Indeed, I recognize his faults, but I cannot help finding the critical study unjust and intolerant. It has even angered me at times; at others, I have recognized the truth of certain of its passages and passed them in silence.

It was a new emotion I felt this afternoon; the dangerous angles at which I set my little rocking chair spoke eloquently of the tempestuous nature of my thoughts. It was strange to see my preferences all calmly dissected and condemned; to watch the developments of opinions contradicting all of mine, in short, to see black called white. It was stranger still to realize this new aspect of a writer's life, of which I have been so serenely ignorant (or quasi). For, of course, I knew there existed Criticism, but I did not know a person could take someone else's life's task and dissect it, mangle it, turn it inside out and upside down, trail it in the dust, fling it to the four winds. And publish the whole results! And call it a critical study! But I forget myself. Even Stevenson, were he alive, would laugh at my Lilliputian outburst. And so I am forced "de faire la révérance"[1] to Mr. Swinnerton, having almost heard him say to me: "Go, dear child, and play in the garden. Leave Stevenson to me." Dear Stevenson, I am not a big friend for such a famous man as you, but my liking for you would fill a book— which you would surely prefer to a critical study! I will now go and play.

I am writing a chronicle of my garden of Narcissus in the last page of this Diary. I have now adopted 12 bulbs all together and

[1] *To curtsy.*

have christened them. Thus, you see, I can tell you that Opal Whitely and Joan of Arc are blossoming in a most charming manner. One, which persists in growing in a zigzag fashion, I have called Mark Twain. Sometimes, I get Walter Scott and Dickens confused. Colline, Rodolphe, and Schaunard are already showing bohemian inclinations; they are spreading and leaning over, without symmetry and order; they will soon fall out of the dish.

January 12.
I write to Father about Christmas day, Willy Shaeffer and Joaquin, Sans Souci Club dances:[1]

I find myself watching girls my age—they look like butterflies, so pretty, so lively, so full of gaiety—their eyes shine and their laughter is so constant, so fresh and light. Yes, I find myself wondering about a lot of things. I am not at all like them. Why, instead of being like a butterfly, am I like green moss, quiet and inexplicable? You must not think from that that I am always serious. Oh, no. These are the happiest years of my life, I am sure. I have a thousand reasons to be as happy as a lark—everything that a young girl can dream of, want, love. Often I fall asleep thinking about the many good things I have. Only, all my good humor, my happiness, gratitude and laughter end up on my little penpoint and are scattered over pages after pages. It's then that I am happiest—when I can write, read, study, meditate, dream. That's why I feel a bit removed from the "butterflies." One can't be good at everything . . . The sun has disappeared while I have been writing. Everything becomes gray and silent. There is just enough light left for me to give you a big kiss. Your little girl—

Anaïs

January 13. I have just returned from a walk to the village. As soon as I stepped into the sunlight, I felt a great, wonderful freedom and joy. Oh, you cannot imagine how well I love the touch of the cool, crisp, wintry air, when it whips my cheeks until the blood tingles, when it slightly pinches my chin and nose, plays with my hair, with the folds of my skirt. The road before me lies sunlit and dazzling and tempting. At times, the wind dies down; then I can hear the distinct, vibrating tones of a roadster. Another silence, and then suddenly, the air reverberates with the twittering

[1] *Letter translated from the French.*

of a thousand birds, who have come home from the North in great numbers, inseparable, and all perch in one tree. The shadows of the trees along the road lie across the sidewalk. They remind me of certain people, who are content to be the reflection of others and lie forever in the dust. In this way, I walk, and wander and soliloquize, and sometimes hum when I feel too happy to be philosophical, until the road makes a sharp turn and brings me face to face with the railroad tracks and the village. At certain times of the day, and particularly before the closing of schools, this view of Richmond Hill reminds me of a deserted village, and the illusion lasts until I hear the rumble of some carriage wheels, a cracked whip, a muttered injunction, which foretells the coming of Richmond Hill's chief way of delivery. I love to watch the train pass—long, heavy, accompanied by clanking chains, bells, thick smoke—and those men, who pour coal in the panting furnaces, with black, smiling faces; whose sinewy arms remind me of the "Village Blacksmith." Oh, there is a world of thoughts in such a simple walk.

Mother continues to lie in bed. She reads the greater part of the day, or else dictates letters to me which must necessarily be written.

Sadly, and with immense loneliness, I have watched the shadows creep into the woods. I have watched the flight of a flock of birds in the changing sky, changing from blue to purple, and then to gray—to the gray of a wintry twilight. I felt that great heavy gray curtain enfolding my heart as well as the trees. And one by one, the tears filled my eyes and fell in the palm of my hand—hot and bitter. I have displeased Mother, and angered her. I cannot beg her to forgive me, kiss me. Oh, I cannot; all my spirit rebels and conquers the girlish yearning, and so I— Can you guess what interrupted me? It was Mother's voice: "Fifille, what are you doing? Come here." And Mother took me in her arms. "You know I'm getting old. But why are you crying? What is it?"

"You used to be patient with me, but now you aren't. That's the difference."

"Well, fifille, one gets short of patience when one gets older. You hardly ever come for a talk with me, and I miss it, fifille."

"Oh, I didn't know you wanted me to. Why didn't you call me? All these days I have spent my time writing that I am lonely."

"Go tell those lies to your Diary." And Mother laughed.

"No, no, do you want to read it? I never tell lies. When you called me, I had just written that I wanted to ask your forgiveness but didn't dare to."[1]

Then Mother kisses me again, asks me to open the window and resumes her reading; and I, my scribbling, but I am so much happier! Thus little things make the world go round, just as big things do. But both little and big things make my world go topsy-turvy. What a calamity! What a catastrophe! But then, I was born a Mlle. Linotte and will die a Mlle. Linotte—unless someone will come who will send me red roses, who will love me in spite of my faults and, being strong, manly and full of convictions, will reform me. I doubt the existence of such a person. Besides, I should not waste time on this subject in the middle of the Winter. It can be explained in Spring when, indeed, all strong spirits wander. And now I go to give directions to the maid. She is a terribly distracting person—ill-fitted to be supervised by me. She has no imagination, requires orders with embarrassing details and sorely tries my patience and lack of skill. I learn to live or live to learn? So far, I am dying in the attempt to learn.

January 15. All these days, at moments I have felt very weak and spiritless. The healthy colors I had finally obtained have vanished again, and Mother anxiously watches my face growing thinner day by day. So I suppose it was natural that I should have suffered so much last night during the Sans Souci Club meeting. I was very cheerful and filled with good intentions when Fraser came to call for Enric and me—with his large, comfortable and luxurious car—and took us to Helena Ketchani's house in Forest Hills. From there we went to another house because our first hostess was invited to an important bridge party. It was only when I stood before my mirror, in my blue kimono, that all my spirits drooped, and I threw myself on the bed, with my eyes full of terribly hot tears.

Today I went to see Dorothy [Eddins], and the visit made me very happy, because her home breathes a very beautiful refinement of speech and thought that I yearn for so much and miss in so many people. Her mother is a typical Southern woman, beautiful, charming, sweet and wise in the management of her home. She has exquisite manners and presided over the delicious lunch with a certain indefinite charm and ease of the lady and mother. Dorothy herself is pretty and vivacious. Her blue eyes are always

1 *Dialogue translated from the French.*

dancing. She calls people either "pills" or "dear." We are friends very superficially, and still we are good friends and true to the promises we made each other during school days. She has a wonderful brother; I only wish he were a little older because our tastes and ideas harmonize very much. Homer has a great talent for drawing, and I was shown his sketches, and his paint box; we laughingly decided he was going to illustrate my books. "But I draw very fantastic things," said Homer, regretfully. I clapped my hands and answered that it was exactly what I needed. for I specialized in fantasy. After lunch and a chat, we simply walked through Riverside and down Broadway to 72nd St., where the subway took me to Penn Station. You cannot imagine with what placid, old-fashioned contentment I stepped from the train into the crisp, frosty twilight to face the realization of some sweet, mysterious dream, there, where little picture houses stood against a sky of pink rose petals and silver gray, there where, gracefully and slowly, smoke curled upward from many chimneys toward the clouds, where lights twinkled in the windows. Yes, it was a dream. How could the world be so still, so peaceful. My own footsteps were lost at times on the earth and grass. I felt like a shadow flitting across the fields, for as I walked, the darkness increased. Finally, I brought my illusions to the very door of my home, but they fell from me like a mantle when I heard Thorvald bellowing, "When do we eat?" Sometimes I thank heaven for the way it has balanced my family: Joaquin and I, afflicted with a common form of madness, due to excess of imaginative faculties; Mother and Thorvald, gifted with common sense—a certain cure for madness, and a good example. Such a question as When do we eat? recalls me to reality. So I rush to my room, I change my shoes, my dress; then to the culinary regions, where I make inquiries, give orders and supervise. Half an hour later we are seated before an appetizing dinner. Still later, I am seated before my patient Diary. And thus the years roll on!

January 17. I was very happy Sunday. Manén came for lunch and by coincidence Marraine came here also on the same train. Then later came Willy Shaeffer and Eduardo Figueroa. The conversation was so enthusiastic, the laughter so frequent and prolonged—with now and then a little singing—that the time was completely forgotten. Thorvald and I made a cheery fire in the old fireplace, and it was around it that Enric and Willy preferred to sit also. Meanwhile Mother, Manén and Tia Juana were listening to Mr. Figueroa's pleasant talk, until he left and thereby reminded us of supper, which we quickly arranged and served. Later, Mother, Manén and Tia Juana conversed in one corner of the salon while Enric, Willy and I drew our chairs in a small, intimate circle near the fireplace, where the fire had died, leaving only a fragrant memory. I will never forget the talks we had together, Willy, Enric and I. Few things outside of books have fascinated me as much as those peeps into the hearts and minds of artists. No words can describe the happiness I feel while listening to their opinions, their confidences, and the pride which creeps into my heart when I realize that they love to speak to me, and with me, because they know I understand them. And so we sit and chat, of their ideals, of their ambitions; of Willy's diary, of books, of life, of art, science, religion, philosophy; of little incidents in our lives, our opinion of one another, our memories, our tastes, our hobbies. We chat with shining eyes, filled with interest, enthusiasm, understanding and sympathy. One time we mentioned astronomy, which interests Willy enormously, and Manén heard us. In a few minutes we had drawn our chairs around the great musician and were listening. From astronomy and the discovery of Saturn, Manén turned to anthropology and told us about the discovery of the human skeleton in the mines of England.[1] I do not know how I remember what he spoke of because the display of another talent in this remarkable man had dazzled me. During supper he had told us he was planning to write a book on the life of a child prodigy. He also spoke of one of his operas, which was to be presented in Berlin this year, of one of his concertos, to be played by Kreisler for the first time soon, and of other things accomplished—by the man who sat in such simplicity at the head of our table. The charm of Manén's personality is still with me as I write these lines; it makes my pen seem very powerless.

Mother was already half-asleep. I was brushing my hair and wondering. Finally, my wondering shaped itself into words and I asked Mother why it was that I felt so unhappy in the company of the members of my club, for example, and so supremely contented in the company of Manén, Willy and Enric. "It is your blood, fifille. This is your world." Mother closed her eyes once more. And I returned to my brush, smiling. So today I had indeed much to think of while mending stockings. Sometimes it was Willy's wonderful laughter, which was echoed in my mind, some-

[1] A.N. probably means Piltdown man.

times I fell in deep reveries about Manén and his life. At others, it was Enric's face which appeared before me, with his sad eyes, until I pricked my finger or upset my rocking chair.

All night, all day, the wind has blown with fury, a beautiful but melancholy storm, which has shaken the house and accompanied all our actions with an angry roar. Indeed, when I went to the village this morning, I was almost torn to pieces, and returned with tumbling hair and filled with indignation.

January 19.

Cher Papa,[1]

Shortly after writing my last letter, I received one from you. I so wish that you hadn't written those things that I must answer now. You see, our letters could continue to portray our lives, like chats at the end of the day. But then you write things that, first of all, I don't understand—then when, after thinking about them, I understand them, they make me so very, very sad. You realize that all the things you write about the past—especially those things that caused the great misfortune that deprived me of a father—are things I have never known or even thought about? Oh, Papa, you don't know me! I should have told you, explained to you long ago how I felt when I saw the fathers of my little friends carrying their books to the schoolhouse door, kissing them, leaving them with regret, sometimes coming back to pick them up when school let out. I was 12 or 13 years old at the time. What did I think about? No, I didn't think. I wept! I cried myself to sleep, without asking anything of anyone or of myself! If I had been like other little girls, I would have been curious, unhappy, perhaps a little soured with envy. Good heavens, no—what saved me from that? What let me grow up calm, happy, supremely satisfied with my fate? It was that nothing touches me except beautiful things. I hear only the song of the birds, I see only flowers; the real world is far away. I don't hear people's voices (or hear them only in my own way). And all the rest goes on around me as though lost in a dense fog. I accept life like someone in a dream and realize only half or hardly any of what goes on around me. And for a girl, quite naturally, a mother's tenderness protects her from ugly things.

But if you could see Thorvald—his carefree ways, his gaiety, his innocence, the candor in his eyes, his spontaneous laughter, his

---

[1] *Letter translated from the French.*

frankness—you would realize the sublime isolation of our lives. You would see the calm, serene happiness with which our lives flow! That is why the years have gone by without our ever speaking of you. When I write you, I think of you as being alone, that you love us and that my letter will give you pleasure. Sometimes I dream you will come back one day—but the years have gone by! Suddenly you come to wake me from my dream. Among other things, you don't want me to blame your art, and I am forced to explain to you how that idea occurred to me all by itself. It was when I needed an image, when I began to want to understand almost everything, it was then I began to imagine that as you are a great artist, devoted to your art and only to your art, you didn't love us very much and that was why Mother went away one day, leaving you alone. Do you understand, Papa? If you knew me, you would see that only I could imagine such a thing. One has to be quite separated from reality, quite separated from other girls of my age and from the world in general to attribute to something ideal a misfortune that occurs every day and is caused by things so sadly human. And this, without ever having heard a word of accusation, a single thing against you, without having heard or asked or wanted to know anything, until the day I discovered a part of the truth. That came with age, with time, because of thinking and living. Especially living! And I love you just as much. Oh, Papa, pardon me for all that I have written . . . Yes, I love you just as much, but for me my mother is everything that is adorable, perfect, sublime. And now suddenly your letters have changed. You write as though you were defending yourself against a hostile influence that might change my love for you. Papa dearest, no one talks to me about you. If I alone love you, if my brothers don't share that love and don't write you, it's simply because they don't know you. We have a home without a father, but we are happy because we don't remember a home *with* a father. So as you say yourself, it was destiny that separated us. No, I will never blush for the name I carry. I have been taught to be proud of it. The thing you hide from me, I already know, alas. But nothing could be sadder than my despair as a child when first I discovered it. At present I know how to suffer. Forgive me, try to understand. I would like so much to share with you the peaceful life that you have disturbed for the first time. But since that is impossible, can't we remain united in our letters, without bitterness? And if you love me, don't write in a way that upsets me, hurts me, shocks me. Oh, that's terrible, Papa, don't you understand that? I will be waiting, then, and I leave you with a very sad, very tender kiss.

Your daughter,
Anaïs

Saperlotte![1] It is so cold! Today has indeed been a strange day, strange because of the varied emotions I have felt and what I have accomplished. At the first peep of day, I shivered, for it was icy and windy, and then I smiled because I often smile now in the mornings; my room is so cheery and neat. I was sitting at the breakfast table alone and very thoughtful when first Mother came down, then Thorvald and Enric, and suddenly Willy Shaeffer! Willy, smiling and dressed in a tuxedo! He had come home with Enric last night from Mr. Hamilton's house (where they had played for his guests). With laughter and dancing eyes, Willy and Enric told us how they had walked up the stairs in perfect harmony, soldierlike, so as not to attract attention. And to and fro in the room, which is above mine. Willy left us very early, because he had to study, and said with his characteristic laughter, "I'll see you suddenly again!"

The day had begun very gaily, but as soon as Willy went. each of us turned to his respective occupations. It was then I answered Father's letter; his letters now cause me so much sorrow, but I had never answered any of them in the tone I was forced to adopt today. I was so hurt by what I wrote that toward the end the pen fell from my trembling hand and I had to wait a long while before signing my name. How he will suffer when he reads this letter! It is so different from my habitual way of writing, it is so brutally truthful. But it was in Mother's defense. I could not bear to have Father write ill of her, even in a disguised or unconscious way. I wrote for a long time, with burning cheeks and sinking heart; and later, I walked to the village just for the sake of a touch of the frosty wind, and as I walked, gentle, tranquil thoughts came to me and a quiet happiness crept back into my heart.

The rest of the afternoon I spent with Mother. I made some tea for her, and we chatted over our cups. A stranger would have hesitated between the appellations mother and daughter or the best friends in the world! These days, I have felt oftener the rare privilege of Mother's dear companionship. All week she partly

[1] *Mild expletive, untranslatable.*

spent in bed, not always able to work, but cheerful and sweet; and these last days have been spent up and well, but resting—reading and pulling at the reins of housekeeping, which I hold too laxly.

January 20. Today I found myself in the city again, where I had lunch with Marraine and was afterward taken to see *Broken Wing.* I enjoyed this play like a child, while conversing with Marraine in a far from childlike manner during the intermissions. The happiest moment of the day was, nevertheless, during that short walk between the station and home, when I felt ecstatic because there were stars twinkling above me, because the field smelled in the ways of fields in winter, because it was so still, so cold, so friendly and soothing; because I was alone.

During dinner Thorvald asked me to go ice-skating, and I said yes, thinking of the stars. But he spoiled it all by adding that Jimmy and all the rest of the "crowd" were going. (Forgive me the word, it is Thorvald's.) Immediately there ejected a sentence I could not keep back: "I am not going." And my family adopted the familiar look of "She's crazy—leave her alone!"

Therefore Thorvald is gone, and I am devoting my first hour of self-inflicted imprisonment to you. I love my prison, I wonder why the charm of it is not reflected in my thoughts; I should be sweeter and finer when such long hours of my life are spent in it. So few girls are fortunate enough to have such a pretty little room. Just now, I hear the "tie, tie, tie" of my small watch. My bird is dozing. From my garden there emanates a lovely and delicate scent. My beloved books look so contented—did you know that books have character also?

Only one thing prevents me from speaking of my ambition tonight. It is my mirror. I am writing before my mirror, and as I pause to look up and into the reflection of my eyes, I sorrowfully shake my head. Oh, I do not look like someone capable of accomplishing very much. My head has a foolish way of appearing always ready to droop on someone else's strong, practical shoulders, or else, when set at an angle of determination, I seem barely fit to order a dinner or scold a little child, but never fit to command enough attention from the world while I pour the contents of my scribblings into its unwilling ears. Do I look wise? Do I look philosophical? Not even courageous enough to appear so.

January 21. If you knew how wicked and bad-tempered I have been today. Thorvald teased me beyond endurance, and suddenly all the Nin blood went to my head, and like lightning, I slapped his face. I slapped that great big, blue-eyed brother of mine, and he laughed! And when Mother angrily ordered him to his room, I pretended to look out of the window to hide the most bitter and silliest tears that have ever been shed. I regretted my action, my anger, my bad temper. Then he came down, his hands in his pockets, with twinkling eyes, "debonair," but no one could divine he was sorry. No one could resist his boyishness, his wonderful honest smile. Mother could not. She kissed him without resistance. And I by the window sobbed, "If I could only laugh like that—oh, Mother, ce grand bête-là."[1] And I laughed through my tears at the "grand bête." Mother forgave me also—because I wept—and forgave Thorvald because he laughed. Things such as these bewilder me. I ponder them, sadly and continually. All the rest of my surroundings, whatever takes place later during the day, remains clouded and misty—and I see this morning's scene everywhere at all times clearly and distinctly. It happened in Enric's presence. Later, I wondered what he thought of me. But we went to the theatre with Mother, and he seemed unchanged in his behavior. It matters very little, nevertheless. "Tú eres mi inspiración. ¡Si alguna vez he soñado con una persona ideal que creía no existía, esa eres tú!"[2]

January 23. I have pasted that strange little note up here for the sake of the memories it will bring back to me in my old age; memories of Enric's admiration for Mlle. Linotte; memories of an age when I believed that "to love and to be loved is the greatest happiness of existence." Enric scribbles many of those little messages, passes them to me during games. And once he wrote that there was no man worthy to become my husband! What often troubles me, when I speak with him, is his precocity. His impulses are boyish, but his moods are those of an old man who has suffered almost more than human nature can endure. Enric is bitter, disillusioned and terribly unhappy. Words which are beautiful to me bring a strange and mocking smile to his lips. He is a tired boy before being a man. Naturally, his character is stamped upon his face; in his eyes there is a curious, almost unnatural mingling of the boy and the man; there is the trace of sleepless nights, of

[1] *"That big brute."*
[2] *"You are my inspiration. If ever I dreamed of an ideal person I didn't believe existed, it is you!"*

passionate moods and brooding, of constant observation of those around him, with sorrowful results, of restlessness, of faded dreams —some of them like those flowers that die before blossoming— and then of a thing which haunts my thoughts of him: in his eyes there is a great thirst for friendship and companionship. He little realizes how difficult it is to be his friend, how difficult it is to understand and follow his moods, to receive his confidences, to give him companionship; he is all changes. all contrasts, all impressions and impulses. Just an Artist!

Last night Joaquin, Enric and I took a long walk because the temperature was almost as warm as a Spring evening, soft and balmy and beautiful. The smell of the earth rose in the stillness like a dream cloud. Our voices vibrated and almost trembled in that complete serenity, as if coming from frightened people who had forced their entrance into a strange world and feared to awake its inhabitants. And then this morning I waited in vain for the sunshine. Instead, I awoke to the "drip drip" of a characterless rain shower. But it little altered my cheery spirits. I perched myself here and there; I trotted up and down; I tittered now and then; I hummed and whistled, fled from Enric—and finally settled down most solemnly to the task of amiably wasting time. My definition of the words wasting time is this: "anything that is not done for anyone else's good."

Enter Miguel. Now the household is indeed complete. I do not regret having written a little, because this evening will not belong to me. It will be one of those evenings when I absorb myself in the study of Miguel and Enric and then retire, fall asleep and dream of . . . Eduardo!

I was thinking of Eduardo. I do not know why I think of my forgetful cousin; he deserves to be forgotten, but then, I do not know very much and still less about cousins and such things. That I dream of him at night, and sometimes during the day, is true. I feel no anger at his behavior, and wonder what will happen when I see him again, just as I wondered before Christmas. His inexplicable neglect will dissolve our friendship, the most charming, most dreamlike, finest, most perplexing and most fickle friendship of my girlhood. It lived exactly with the seasons: it was born in the Spring with the flowers, it bloomed all of one Summer, lingered through the Autumn—and at the first touch of Winter cold, it flashed once more, brilliantly, and died. Oh, Eduardo! Can you guess how I will revenge myself? I will put you in a book. You, and your charm, and your fickleness, and perhaps you will recognize yourself—the "forgetful cousin" of a Linotte who remembers all. And to think I still like you so. To think that if you wrote, I would reply with 20 pages as in the days of old. Yes, you said I was "womanly," but you do not know how foolish a girl I really am.

January 25. Eduardo's letter has come! It reached me yesterday when I was watching for the postman, as I watch for him daily. I had to eat my breakfast because Mother was there, but afterward I read the long and beautiful missive with a heart overflowing with the most childish joys. Heaven is so good to me! It fulfills all my desires, all my dreams, in its own mysterious way. Had it not been that for a long time I was deprived of Eduardo's companionship and letters, that I was given time to miss our little talks, time to long for them, I could never have felt the wonderful and sincere joy I experienced yesterday when Eduardo came back to me. His letter traveled in my pocket all day long, like a talisman. I snatched moments from my day's occupation to answer it. It is already written, but I want to mail it myself. I am so happy to think that I can close this Diary thus, for I have often allowed myself to write of Eduardo, and without his letter, the story of our tempestuous friendship would have been unfinished and incomplete. By a curious and unhappy coincidence, I must refuse Eduardo's invitation to a dance, because the date of it is the seventeenth of February—the date of Enric's birthday and his departure for Europe. Through Mother, Enric discovered the reason for my exuberance yesterday, and it made him so unhappy, so terribly unhappy, that I told him the story of Eduardo and Mlle. Linotte while we sat around a log fire in the evening—how we were friends, and friends only, because we liked the same things and were stirred by the same dreams. Today, also, I could not part with his letter (although I know it by heart) because the mere touch of it in the midst of any occupation would bring forth a host of memories. Sometimes I had to touch it to believe that it was not an illusion.

Tia Coco came to see us yesterday and left us only this afternoon. I accompanied her to the station, and then before returning home I posted my answer to Eduardo's letter. If you only knew the charm I find now in your pages, while reading my sketch of him, my talks to him, my reprimands, my little crises of sadness, my doubts and condemnations. It bewilders me to recognize so easily the times when I lost courage or faith, when my horizon clouded with tempests or when suddenly the sunshine filled my heart; tears, laughter, all the countless things which stir, bewitch, arouse, enchant, perplex or weary me, all I hear and see and feel and fancy—all, all flow into your pages. No human friend could be as faithful, as patient or discreet. I love you better each day. And sometimes, to people whom I hear telling of their lost friends, fickle friends, and wishing for a friend true and lasting, I am tempted to say, Write! Write! Friendship between a girl and a Diary is never broken or spoiled or dissolved by time and distance, as are those between men and women.

Tomorrow Mother will take me to the dusty and fascinating city, where I will look in some Olde Booke Shoppe for an edition of Maurice de Guérin's Journal, for the time has come to return the one I have just read to the library, and I long to have that book among my favorites forever. There also I must buy another diary. I truly wish I would never need to change books. I always regret the hour of parting. No sooner have I opened you, it seems, than you are filled and I must imprison you in one of my drawers. If I were to write a prayer at the end of this Diary, it would be one of thankfulness; when I look back to all that has happened, I am glad to be alive and glad, perhaps, that heaven should have made my life so different from the other girls', so wonderfully filled with fancies to supply all I lack in reality, and so wonderfully filled with tangible but often beautiful things. I am happy to be only seventeen, to resemble moss and not a butterfly, to make better friends with "books, and nature, than with people," to have that inward world for shelter and consolation.

January 28. I wish I could tell you of all the thoughts which have come to me while reading Marcus Aurelius. I felt all the emotions of the explorer, his difficulties, discouragements and doubts, as well as the joys of discovery, assimilation, understanding. The Meditations, a small and apparently lifeless book, has become a revelation and a comfort to me. After I had conquered the arid passages and certain oddities in expression and form, I became conscious of the great beauty and strength of the thought.

A thing which fills me with indescribable wonder is the immense and sublime kindness of God, who endows man with intelligence and understanding. I thought of this because after the time I devoted to this study, I felt thankfulness for understanding, thankfulness that as I read the great man's thought, my own—infinitesimal, invisible to all—followed his, merged into it at times; a vague, nameless, unformed thought of mine, which has long struggled for expression, found itself suddenly three thousand years old.

January 29. I have had the most agonizing experience, and now that it has passed I look back upon it with much bewilderment. So often after a series of placid, unruffled days there comes one filled with tangled emotions, and the tempest leaves me bruised and dreamless. All day I was drawn to my pen as if by a magnet. I have never felt so acutely that *suffocation of the spirit*. I sat down again and again to satisfy a passionate desire to write, just to write; it seemed as if all the thoughts that had so often found an outlet through verses, essays, half-finished stories, were now wildly seeking their liberty, beating against their prison door, calling in a nameless agony, palpitating—all in vain, for whenever I grasped my pen it seemed as if my faculties died.

I suffered the agonies of a man who receives an inspiration for an enchanting painting and does not know how to paint; of a man born with a marvelous flame of eloquence and who is deprived of a tongue. But then the transformation came; I pushed away the mass of half-written thoughts and arose.

I told myself that these insatiable longings would never ravage me again. I told myself that I would *learn* to express and then share with the world all that lies now in me, whispering in a language I understand but *cannot yet translate*—that I will learn to write of the thousand things I hear which others *have not heard*, and the things I see, and feel, and *create*. I will give names to all that is vague and nameless; I will give my visions to those who cannot visualize; I will share my fancies, dreams; I will describe all that is beautiful; I will make the *world listen to unseen and delicate music*, and listen to the stories of worlds which they have no time to discover and explore. Oh, dear vision, will your very frailty protect you from destruction?

January 30. Richmond Hill has been transformed at last by the magic touch of snow. Since dawn I have watched it fall, silent, smooth and dazzling. It is now so early that there are no footsteps on the virgin snow; since childhood I have felt so sorrowful when a human foot marred the purity of it.

Yesterday afternoon we visited a family Mother has long wanted me to know—the O'Kelleys. Mother, Enric, Thorvald and I met Willy and Mr. Figueroa at the station and soon found ourselves in a luxurious house near Riverside Drive with soft lights, music, enchanting and sparkling conversation and varied personalities. Mrs. O'Kelley is captivating; Mr. Alfaur, young and interestingly cynical, eluding description. Mr. Costa reminded me of a Wise Man. And just at the most dramatic moment, when I found myself surrounded by Figueroa, Enric, Willy and Mr. Alfaur, enter Germaine Sarlabous![1] She theatrically expressed her surprise, her admiration, etc. But she was only noticing the superficial changes. Little could she guess that a long time ago I used to feel an immense admiration for her boundless coquetry and jolliness and fall asleep weeping because of my own shyness, "sauvagerie." And Germaine was such a brilliant star in the world of laughter and compliments, which I watched from afar.

Imitate her? Never! Enric dislikes her intensely and mocks what time has done in augmenting her voluminousness. I only wanted to imitate the coquette when I wanted Enric to like me! None of her wiles could separate Enric from me yesterday, and I felt happy to have won at last a friendship I had idealized so much.

While waiting for the train to return home, I noticed an elderly man deeply absorbed in a book. He had a preoccupied and thoughtful air and was dressed with a certain distinguished carelessness that bespeaks the bibliomaniac. The lady by his side, probably his wife, was critically observing the passers-by, as women are wont to do. The man now and then would mark certain passages with his pencil and read them in a low voice to the lady. He was absolutely unconscious of his surroundings until suddenly she glanced at the clock, jumped up in an alarming manner and, seizing his arm, hurried with him to catch their train. His bewildered, faraway look was worthy of a study. The incident filled me with terror for the future. Reverse the sexes and you see me with my poor, poor husband. I in a daze and rapture, my husband with his wits about him, interrupting me, I refusing to awake completely, allowing him to drag me to the train, to push me into a seat and to place himself, resolute, panting, defiant at my side, to preserve and protect me while I am wondering *why* Marcus Aurelius said: "Life is a warfare and a pilgrim's sojourn."

I wonder if everyone feels the joy I feel when there is a letter in my pocket to be answered. I wonder if everyone appreciates

[1] *The daughter of Dr. Sarlabous, who treated Metropolitan Opera singers.*

letters as I do and looks forward to the moment that can be spared to answer them. The day has seemed brighter because the postman brought me a letter from Jack. Therefore, from one pocket there peeps the corner of Eduardo's letter, the very touch of which is like a talisman, and from the other the corner of Jack's letter, filled with humor and compliments of his own awkward making.

February 1. No one but you could endure me tonight. I despise myself for lacking the courage to shake off this unreasonable mood. I wonder even now if I should try and write of things I do not understand myself. But I must or I will go mad. Mother has said I am mad, and the word is still haunting me. Mother says I am tragic and foolish; she has scolded me with more harshness than she has ever shown. To think that all I feel is merely "being tragic." Does no one understand how it hurts and hurts to be branded by heritage, to have one's innermost impulses attributed to a parent's peculiarity, to hear again and again that it is the "Nin" in me which is the cause of all my inexplicable states. And then I am tormented by shame, by a perpetual effort of will to control my anger, the thoughtless words that Father used to say, the anger Father had. I cannot be *myself;* I am what Father is. Perhaps people love me now because I am a mere girl, but in a few years if I do not rise above the horrible chains, I will be left alone in the world. Mother tells me she *recognizes* my moods. How often I have struggled against the agonizing grip of unreasonable melancholy. It comes over me like a malignant influence. I often conquer it. I stand and defy it and shake it off; I make resolutions. It creeps, it creeps; it rises from little things or from nothing; it springs upon me from behind the most smiling faces. It terrifies me. It came last night after a long, fruitless struggle. Do you remember? I wrote of Germaine, of the snowstorm, of the incident in the station, and then I went coasting with Joaquin. I was so happy for a moment; I was breathing the crisp air of youth, and my blood tingled. The tinkling of the sleigh bells overjoyed me. Then Joaquin, unconsciously selfish, wanted to come home. He had no reason; it was just a whim. I felt a great desire to remain there, and I called Thorvald and pleaded with him. Thorvald turned his back on me, equally unconscious. I could not remain alone because there were many bold boys trying to kiss me. I had to return home sadly. This sadness, which was *not* caused by the thwarted desire, or my little brother's selfishness, angered Mother. Her words wounded me. When the storm of tears ceased, I walked to my mantelpiece and took the Imitation of Christ.[1] I opened it at hazard and read: "Nature has regard to temporal things, rejoices at earthly gains, is troubled at losses, and is provoked at every slight injurious word: But grace attends to things eternal, and cleaves not to those which pass with time; neither is she disturbed at the loss of things, nor exasperated with hard words for she places her treasure and her joy in heaven, where nothing is lost."

I clasped my hands very tightly and stood very still, awed, bewildered, fearing to breathe so that this wondrous eternity should not abandon me.

And then I undressed and I brushed my hair, proudly holding back fresh tears at the thought of what Mother thought of me.

February 2. After I had written of my wickedness last night I had no desire to write of anything else. I felt I had not deserved Eduardo's letter and was ashamed to speak of it. It came in the midst of my desolation, a long and characteristic letter. And can you guess what troubles him? He fears that I love Enric! He writes: "I pity those women who are so foolish as to marry them (artists) not because—as they think—they love him but because they love his art and therefore that art clothes, wraps him in a veil so pure, so divine, that they fall in love not with him but with the celestial veil. When marriage comes and that veil breaks— for it must, and I can prove it—then . . . annihilation! And that woman is doomed to suffering unless she has that practicability of life. But you, cuisine, you have not that practicability . . . I would give anything, my honor, and my life, to change the mind of my cuisine and give her happiness and joy: Cuisine, you do not love Enric, you only love his violin."

And today I answered hurriedly to accept the invitation to his dance because he had mistaken the date—and of Enric I wrote:

But to be serious, Eduardo, your letter did surprise me. I never thought the day would come when I should write to you about Enric and, what is more, when you should realize so perfectly the immense and bewildering difference there exists between the man and the artist. Oh, Eduardo, you need not sacrifice anything to change the mind of that "nameless thing" and give her happiness —first because she does not deserve much and also because it has been so willed that she should understand and know, oh, too well,

[1] *By Thomas à Kempis.*

what you so earnestly try to teach her today. Has not her entire life been influenced by artists? Oh, she knows, she knows the sublimity of the veil—and what lies behind it!

Do you remember Lake Placid? Oh, I know you could never forget it, but I mean, do you remember how, of all places, it seemed to *create* dreams—they arose like subtle charmers from everywhere and at all times, is it not true? Well, if to this place there came an impossible person suddenly transplanted from an ugly and sordid city, she could never keep her wits about her (particularly being a poet) and would naturally take the beautiful and inspiring scenery as the fittest stage one could possibly conceive to make believe. It was so easy to fancy in Lake Placid! So, I made believe Enric was the Knight and Prince of all the tales I had read, and during my walks I held fancied conversations with him. I could not talk to Cuca, who is such a wise and well-balanced little lady, and you seemed to make fun of me sometimes. And I have a habit of creating imaginary friends for fear of *boring* real people!

And that is all. Love? That is not love, is it, Eduardo? My love, if it will ever be awakened (for it exists and sometimes it stirs) will be the strongest and truest in all the whole wide world, a mingling of a sister's tenderest devotion with an eternal, gentle, tireless companionship and fidelity. How strange that we should speak of such things   it shows that we are growing up, or perhaps we are grown up! I love Enric's violin . . . (description of Enric) and I *used* to think a great deal about him . . . But that is not love.

February 4. Last night Joaquin, Enric and I took a long walk. It was not very cold and part of the snow was melting so that each moment the scenery assumed another aspect. We wandered a long while until we were facing a house which had always attracted me.

"It is Lhevinne's[1] house," whispered Joaquin.

Lhevinne, the well-known pianist! It was his house which harmonized so well with the trees and bushes. There was a light coming from the room on the ground floor. We listened intently and caught the faint sound of piano. Moved by curiosity, we crept to the window; in the snow our footsteps were scarcely audible. I do not think what we did was wrong. Being artists' children, we

---

[1] *Josef Lhevinne, Russian pianist.*

approached with veneration—to admire, not to mock! I will never forget with what wonder we stood there and listened to Lhevinne. Around us, the half-veiled trees and houses, rising like shadows from patches of snow; above, the dark-blue arch; and then inside, the pianist studying, his profile in relief, his lips moving. His eyes never wandered from his hands; he had a curious expression, determination mingled with abstraction; he seemed to have forgotten himself and his surroundings, all but his difficult task; he repeated again and again, intense and oblivious. And we listened, motionless, breathing as softly as possible. A cat suddenly jumped from somewhere, and the little bell tied around his neck jingled. We jumped—and smiled. I noticed Joaquin's eyes; they were so luminous and filled with softness and meditation. I am sure he was visualizing the future—his future. A whole life was framed like a picture in the window. The life of an artist who, contrary to the average belief, has a home, comfort and luxury, which he has earned by his art. We would have listened longer, perhaps, but that I broke the charm, for with a true bibliomaniac's intuition I soon discovered the library, and my interest wavered between the piano and the luxuriously bound books. "Oh, look at the books," I whispered to Enric, upon which he laughed, so that we had to run away as fast as possible for fear of causing a disturbance.

February 6. Today Enric is terribly moody. When I study him I wonder at the contrasts in him, but I study him little, for it is safer to run away from him. He is not one of those persons who merely sparkle, he explodes!!!!!! I don't love *him*, but I want passionately to marry an artist; *I want to marry a genius.* I am bursting with love. What Eduardo says does not worry me. I am not afraid of pain, of difficulties. I worship genius.

February 7. Mother had a great sorrow today. All through her unhappy married life and the period of the separation she had the consolation of being loved by Father's mother, an angelical and patient, devoted woman. My grandmother loves her son with the blindest, tenderest love, almost adoration, but she had always been marvelously just in her judgment of Mother as his wife. And now he has turned her against my poor mother, to whom she writes a passionate and sorrowful letter, accusing her of calumniating our father, of staining his honor, of depriving us of his presence through her resentment and prejudices. He has made her believe that his efforts to unite our lives have failed because Mother is unforgiving and cruel. She does not know that Father made his appeal a command through the law—in order to obtain a written refusal from Mother to be used against her in obtaining a divorce, and that Mother, with the advice of her lawyer, did not refuse to join Father in Paris but made conditions which would protect us from need. Oh, he wants his children now and expects them to abandon the mother who sacrificed her life, who toiled and suffered and endured for them, who had almost completed the task of educating them, of forming their hearts and thoughts. Thorvald and I are almost a man and woman, and for our mother we would die if we were asked. While Mother wept and I held her head in my arms, she repeated: "And now he will turn *you* against me too!" And at this all my nature rebelled, and while Mother suffered for the loss of Grandmother's love, I clenched my hands in nameless agony, for I felt my love for my father diminishing. I felt I could not love anyone who could hurt my Mother. Slowly, oh, so slowly, the father of my dreams has vanished, and now my real, unhappy father stands before me. Destiny has punished him in the strangest way: by heritage. No one but his own daughter, his own blood, could understand him so well, and I know him by intuition, I know the empty eloquence of his letters, his lack of sincerity, his actor's attitude in life. Oh, Father! It is you who have given me the traits I continually struggle to conquer, to up-root or at least control. You play with peoples' hearts, you move them and blind them. Oh, an actor, yes, an actor! A gifted and brilliant actor, and now you play the part of a martyr for your poor old mother. You tell her you have tried to do your duty, that you have appealed to your wife and tried to make her understand, but that she is too headstrong and replies with accusations! You forget that her heart would break if she knew that you are simply preparing for a divorce to *marry someone else!*

Is it just that Father should mar our happiness so? Mother strives to hide all the ugliness of life from us; she gives us a home and creates a life filled with ideals, teaches us to be useful, simple, contented, and through her constant care and love we finally have become straightforward, innocent, sincere. And then suddenly Father fills our life with struggles, lies and pain again. And the worst of it is that I love him, I love him in spite of all the things I find out about him. Yet all he may do will never, as she fears, estrange me from her. Her happiness comes first.

February 9. Do you know what I would answer to someone who asked me for a description of myself, in a hurry? This:

? ?   ! !

For indeed my life is a perpetual question mark—my thirst for books, my observations of people, all tend to satisfy a great, overwhelming desire to know, to understand, to find an answer to a million questions. And gradually the answers are revealed, many things are explained, and above all, many things are given *names* and *described*, and my restlessness is subdued. Then I become an *exclamatory* person, clapping my hands to the immense surprises the world holds for me, and falling from one ecstasy into another. I have the habit of peeping and prying and listening and seeking—passionate curiosity and expectation. But I have also the habit of *being surprised*, the habit of being filled with wonder and satisfaction *each time* I stumble on some wondrous thing. The first habit could make me a philosopher or a cynic or perhaps a humorist. But the other habit destroys all the delicate foundations, and I find each day that I am still . . . only a Woman!

This time I did not precisely fall into ecstasy, but I feel dazed, like a person whose thoughts have suddenly been scattered by a gust of wind. I am reading the most extraordinary book, *The Egoist*, by George Meredith. The book had the effect of a bombshell. My first impression was one of anger. I turned my eyes toward the unsympathetic sky and exclaimed, as if speaking to the gods of the writers: "Oh, has *everything, everything* been written already!" And for answer I fancied an endless procession of books mocking me, dancing around my bed. I saw *Un Philosophe Sous les Toits*, The *Journal* of Eugénie [de Guérin], *Walden* and a thousand others. Has everything been written? Yes. But . . . I can't stop writing.

To Eduardo:

I have been accepted at Columbia! The great college doors are opened to me on Monday! Only part of what I wanted to study, for the person in charge refused to let me take philosophy and psychology—said I was too young again. I fear everyone is misled by my appearance. Perhaps I do seem a featherhead and, figuratively speaking, a "fawn," whom it is a pity to startle and bewilder and bruise with cold philosophy. But I will show her that the "little French girl" (as she calls me) has gigantic ambitions, and that if people must smile at my *accent*, they will have to be serious when I write.

I have almost lost my head with delight. As you can see by this little sketch of my letter to Eduardo, I begin my studies Monday. It was yesterday that I suddenly determined to make my second effort to enter Columbia, and I went there in rain and snow. I spoke again with Dr. Glass. I realized that my accent, my lack of high school training, impressed her unfavorably; she did not believe me capable of the work I asked her to give me, and being responsible for failures, she planned a very reasonable and prudent course, comprising English composition and grammar, French reading, conversation and translation. The rest, philosophy and psychology, remain unattainable for the moment. And perhaps it is better so, for had I been allowed to pursue these studies, the fees would have been a great demand on Mother, who is having trouble now in her business. Thus the sacrifice is "forced," while otherwise I would have regretted it forever. How I long for Monday. Everyone is surprised that I should give up with so much ease the freedom I have had all this time—freedom and good times, they say—to study. Enric is absolutely perplexed. No one but my Diary knows that study is my favorite occupation.

February 15. Monday has passed. It was one of those days I will never forget. I was so impatient, so thrilled. I felt transplanted from a flowerpot to a garden, and it took me only a few hours to grow new roots. Who knows what fresh leaves and flowers might spring from this new earth, which otherwise would never have blossomed. Wind and the sunshine playing with the clouds. The curtain rises on a great mass of buildings which form the college. Girls and boys, men and women, walk from building to building with books under their arms. Before entering I looked with confidence at the face of Alma Mater. In a big sunlit class I assisted at the first session of English composition, my heart aching to be in the place of the pupils reading their stories to the young, humorous and tolerant teacher. Then followed an hour of inaction. I spent it visiting the Architectural Library and walking from building to building to familiarize myself with them. And speaking of friends, the first person who has helped and directed me in that great college filled with strangers is a young man. I don't know his name, but he is always by me. At six o'clock the curtain falls again. On my way to the subway I meet a host of students who invade the university for the evening sessions.

At home Mrs. Norman offered a dinner in honor of Enric.

We found valentines under our plates, which reminds me that I have received eight valentines, all anonymous but Jack's.

February 16. This new life makes the days pass like Autumn clouds. Several young men are keen on taking care of me. The name of the first one is Frank Holt. He travels on the subway with me, takes me to the book store, carries my books, opens the doors.

School life is a terribly quick friend-maker. In the grammar class my neighbor was distressingly attentive, but he was so boyishly gay that his sprightliness melted my determination to be freezingly indifferent to my classmates. I shall call him no. 1. I foresee a great struggle for the future. I wanted to be a stoic, and unapproachable, but I see I will have to be merely a woman and human.

February 18. There are moments in life of which one doubts the reality. Yesterday and today seemed an incredible dream. Can it be possible that Enric is gone, gone for a year? The days preceding his departure I watched him with anxiety. Marks of great suffering ravaged his face; he slept little, ate little and smiled only in a forced manner. Poor Enric! If I talked to him, endeavoring to soothe him he would rise suddenly and say with a passionate gesture: "Oh, Anaïs, do not play with fire!" Because of school I saw him little—fortunately, since my presence seemed to give him pain instead of pleasure. The last night, Joaquin proposed to go to the moving pictures, and I impulsively refused because I was very tired. Enric was silent, and I fancied that he did not wish to go. Much later I caught an expression of regret: "Did you want to go, Enric? It is not too late, and I am willing."

"If I had gone," he answered, "it would only have been to sit near you. I had something to tell you."

"Can't you tell me here and now?" He shook his head with a strange smile. Fate had not wished me to hear what Enric had to say, but it could not prevent me from understanding a thing which needs no words to be clear.

The next morning, while the sunshine filled the house, a strong contrast to the sadness we all felt, Enric made his last preparations, Mother was to accompany him to the ship, but she would not let me go. He said goodbye to his room, to everyone. I will never forget his face, the terrible paleness of it. All his soul was in his eyes, and the effort he made to control his suffering— suffering doubled in intensity by his frightful sensitiveness—were reflected in his drawn lips. He shook hands with me; his hand trembled. He brokenly reminded me to answer his letters. I tried to smile and said: "You will come back soon." And he shook his head. With a pang I realized what he feared. What has the world to offer to a passionately lonely, sensitive and storm-tossed boy? And his last words to Mother were: "Take good care of Anaïs. Don't let her marry!"

February 20. These days I have missed Enric very much. I miss his violin, his voice, his eyes watching me, his devotion, his impulsive confidences and moods. I do not think of him in the way Eduardo fears. Enric appeals strongly to my pity and makes me wish to be his sister, to comfort and cheer him. But it is impossible, I know, and Enric has often sorrowfully exclaimed that he wished I were a boy, for he could then confide all to me. It is terrible not to be able to love everyone who loves you. I wish I could.

This morning I prepared my first theme for Monday. It was to be a narrative introducing conversation, and I developed the incident of the branch cut down long ago, do you remember? I am very eager to hear the criticism. I also have lessons to study and self-imposed French, so that I may soon master my beloved native language.

February 22. At last a little moment for dreaming. My heart is tired and filled with sadness. Joaquin and I are alone before the fire. He is stretched at my feet, reading. I have been watching him for a few minutes while I wrote these lines. He has jumped to his feet in his characteristic way and kissed me goodnight. Thus I remain alone with the fire and my thoughts. My birthday has passed. I am eighteen. Only eighteen, and in supreme loneliness, for no one is really *close* to me, I wonder what life holds for me and look back to what it has given me. I am so happy to sit very still for a long while and rest and dream. If my heart were a hundred years old, it could not be wearier. The "friendships" offered me at Columbia only bring out the contrast between the people around me and those I imagine and want.

On Monday I went to school as usual but returned with Marraine. In the morning it had taken me a long time to reach the station—the snow was up to my knees—but on coming home I found the plow had been at work. At the door we stamped our feet to shake off the snow and found the cheery fire sparkling. Mother was preparing a pleasant dinner in my honor, and in my room I found five pots of hyacinths before my window and a bunch of roses on my dressing table. These marks of thoughtfulness touched me. After dinner we sat again around the fire and conversed. At 8:30 I said, "Now I am eighteen years old," and I kissed Mother. I talked very little for many reasons: I had little to say, much to think about and a great desire to be scribbling instead. All those things make me insufferably silent.

February 27. For a little while, at least, I will cease speaking of the word "adventure." I have had enough thrill and excitement to last me for a year and to make me quite disgusted. For many hours I sat wondering what on earth people would love in me if I remained the ridiculously homely person reflected in my mirror; for many hours, too, I bade goodbye to romance, to all of the opposite sex, and prepared to find consolation in science and study for my forced spinsterhood. And all because . . . well, let me begin at the beginning. I went coasting with Thorvald Wednesday night. We were having a wonderful, cheery time together, laughing, shouting, tumbling in the snow. Then the dramatic moment arrived, the unfolding of the plot, as my composition teacher would say. Thorvald *dared* me to go down a bumpity hill standing up on the sled. Dared me. He knows me well. Do you dare me, you say? Very well. Wait. One, two, three. A bump, a crash, a knock—a sudden stop; a little blood on the snow and a tear—and there I lay bruised and dazed. I stood up, I covered my face with my hands and I tottered into the house. Exclamations. running steps, ice, and hot water. No, I am not killed—none of my bones are broken, and even as I write, there are only a few traces left of my fall. I fell with my face on the sled, and barely escaped a broken nose and the loss of my left eye. The escape, therefore, consists of a terrible concussion, and a blue, yellow and red eye, with regions surrounding it matching in coloring. And "me voilà!" It is all. It was a blow to my vanity, and good punishment. It will make me more stoical. Tia Juana had no sympathy for me—it is part of her transformation. She was the one who said that about vanity, etc. She is trying vainly to reform me and shakes her head at my hopelessness.

The most comical part of it all is that Tia Juana and Tia Coco have come to visit. Thorvald brought Jack for the weekend, and Miguel appeared yesterday. And so the best I can do is to choose my place carefully so that I can watch the family with the right eye. I regret being forced to offer such an unartistic spectacle to the entire family, but they bore it well, and we have spent many long cheerful hours around the fire.

February 28. I received three letters, one from Eleanor, one from Frances and one containing an invitation to a dance at Edith Guiler's home in Forest Hills.

Eduardo is silent again but I am not saddened. Rather, I have a foreboding that soon we will be estranged again. You see, our correspondence is too idealistic and our intellectual friendship too delicate to survive the knocks and bruises of everyday realities.

I have not been able yet to return to school. This forced imprisonment makes me unhappy. But tomorrow I am going. How I long to *work* again, to study, to prepare homework. Mother says laughingly that the opportunity has come to test the interest of no. 1 and no. 2 at Columbia. Perhaps they will not carry my books any more, or open the doors, and pay my subway when they see the traces of my "adventure."

I have begun to attend daily Masses again. I try so earnestly not to be a "poor benighted heathen." And still, it is not while in church that my heart feels thankfulness and love. Oh, I am ashamed—but I feel nearer to God on my way to church, in the woods. Then I look up to the sky, and the beauty awes and inspires me; I pray, yes, I pray in that heathen way to the tune of twittering birds, or with the wind, dancing and skipping along without dignity or reverence.

I have been singing all day, now with the broom, now with the dish mop, as an accompaniment. The only time my heart stands still and hushed is when I hear the postman's whistle. But I watch in vain for Enric's letter. His passionate face haunts my daydreams persistently. I have never been able to describe or explain our friendship. We were *never* the same toward each other. Each day Enric seemed a different person, and he was always equally perplexed with me. How he could say just my name: "Anaïs!" It would give me chills to hear him. At times I remember him silent and moody, but before going to bed he would slip a note under my door, or some verses, or a drawing of me. Some days he watched me continually and sought to speak with me as often as possible. I did all in my power to prevent him from speaking of me. I grew frightened at the tone with which he began. He always finished sadly: "You will be married when I come back." Or: "No man on earth is worthy of you." His compliments sprang unexpectedly. No one, I believe, has observed me as Enric has, with such constancy, eagerness, sincerity and yet *blindness*. Each thing I wore he noticed and approved. He tried to fathom my moods, explain my impulses, and study the endless and continuous changes in me. And one day he told me he was going *mad* wondering and thinking and dreaming about me. Once he said I was cold and cruel and thoughtless, and other bitter things because I was not responsive when his feelings flowed uncontrollably in a torrent of words. "You will never understand, Anaïs; you will never know how I suffer, sometimes keeping things back." If I forgot myself and laughed and mocked or acted for him, or sang, or kissed Joaquin, Enric would suddenly say: "You are playing with me. You have no heart." This was like the lash of a whip when I first heard it. Since that day, I understood that I had to be incredibly thoughtful and reserved not to hurt that super-sensitiveness—for, of all things, I never want to willingly hurt anyone or anything. You see, if I am ever wicked or thoughtless, it is often because I do not *realize* many things. For example, I never imagined I was wounding Enric with certain foolish little actions, and when I discovered it, the revelation came in the form of a much needed *lesson*. I am, in truth, *ignorant of life*, and knowledge comes very gradually, very slowly and unexpectedly.

I learned much with Enric. I learned to think more of others. I learned to show my heart so that no one would doubt its existence! What a quaint, tempestuous friendship has grown in a few weeks between Enric and Mlle. Linotte. On his part, there is a delicate idealization and devotion which I little deserve—and on mine, alas, there is only a great sympathy, a sisterly interest and a desire to cheer, comfort and encourage.

March 3. My first day in school—a gray, sullen, wet day, ending with thunder and lightning and oppressive heat. All the snow has turned to mud.

Mother and I saw Mary Pickford in *The Love-Light*. Oh, it was a lovely story, which made me weep and laugh in spite of my attempts at stoicism!

In school I have found no. 3! He is not my friend, you know. He has scarcely looked at me, but I make believe, because I was struck by his intelligent, luminous eyes and curious smile. His theme was original and full of feeling, and he read it with a quaint accent. I have a foreboding that he is very interesting and that I will soon have the opportunity to discover what there is in his personality to awaken curiosity in such an indifferent person as I am.

In the same class there is someone who is always staring at me, and today I made a face at him. I could almost feel the Mephistophelean horns growing on my head. Such impudence! But I really do not regret it, for it will cure him forever, I hope. It was really for his own good because I noticed he was very inattentive and careless, and now that he will be afraid of staring, he may remember what he is there for.

To turn to frivolity, I have learned through Jimmy that the invitation to the Guiler dance is a great privilege (he has not been honored and neither has Thorvald, but his sisters are going). He knows of no one else invited; it appears to be rather for "grownups," a fact which tickles my sense of dignity!

March 4.
Letter to Frances:

. . . Before, all I did, I did alone, without purpose or discipline or criticism. And yet, you know what horror I have of discipline and routine. But Columbia is very different. There is a great deal of independence; we are trusted and left very much in the care of our honor and conscience. Now all I write must be complete, polished and definite, because before, my spirit was *vagrant;* I scribbled much but never finished or accomplished anything. We have themes to prepare twice a week, bits of narration, character sketches, descriptive essays; we study shades of suggestion in writing—in short, the things I was vainly seeking to learn alone. Do you know, this sounds as if coming from a sensible, practical, calculating and wise little woman. And I am none of those things. Not one! I do believe I have become a traitor. I have violated the sacred laws:

1. Madness is poetry.
2. A poet is a madman.

What you write of boys surprises me . . . we have not yet had the time to discover whether they are "creatures whose emotions are all of the senses" or strong, manly companions to make life useful and happy.

I have just finished studying *Rules for Punctuation.* I am terribly belittled by the discovery of all the laws of punctuation

I have violated, particularly in my poor, scribbled Diary! Just think how fortunate it is that no one should read it but myself! Who could tolerate my abominable grammar, my punctuation, my handwriting (including "ornaments"), my moralizing and sense-lessness? Who? I am, in the literary sense of the word, an outlaw. But I hope someday to be forgiven. People spending their lives in the woods may easily forget the etiquette of society. And persons with savage instincts, forced to retire from school and fleeing certain contacts, must naturally reflect the results in the . . . (sudden interruption)

March 13. To the tune of Joaquin's improvisations I will now try to describe a wonderful adventure. These last days scarcely left a mark of their passage; they have vanished, awed by the presence of the 12th of March. First, it was Thorvald's birthday. In his honor the supper was particularly well planned, ending with the presentation of the birthday cake surmounted with sixteen candles. And after that we separated. I rushed to my room to begin the mysterious preparations for the Guiler dance, heart afluttering with nameless expectations. After a long while I stood before my mirror and stared: dressed again with my beautiful rose dress and with the traces of excitement illuminating my face, I was ready. But I little knew what pleasure was reserved for me as I stepped into Mr. Guiler's automobile with Martha and Wilhelmina [Forgie]. I wonder what strange mood possessed me last night. I do believe I threw off all my resemblance to moss and stepped into Mrs. Guiler's home transformed into an imp—even perhaps with a dash of the devil. I know that somehow or other I was not "myself," and the "someone else" bore a heart that was lighter than a feather. Perhaps it *was* a feather, for surely *something* was tickling my throat to bring out that continuous laughter.

The mystery of all this is simply that the "someone else" managed to keep my love of literature, music, poetry, and to *share* it with others.

Oh, I only hope that those who like the "someone else" last night would like the real me, the plain, everyday Anaïs, without nameless *illumination*, without brilliancy or sprightliness or impish face! You see, it is all gone and it may never return.

Let me endeavor to be specific. Conversation is a perplexing thing when one pauses to contemplate its ways of shifting, of suddenly creating sympathy, interest, its power to surmount difficulties, of overcoming indifference or shyness; it is the bridge between strangers. I discovered that I could share many of my beloved "finer things" with Edith Guiler's older brother, Hugh[1] Guiler, also with Mr. Clapp; also a little with a painter. Because of these persons and because of everyone's attentiveness last night, I was bubbling over with joy. Do you wonder that I should remember each detail of that perfect dance? The pretty lights, the music, the laughter, the sparkling eyes, the compliments. I dreamed of Mr. Hugh Guiler and the "secret" we have (for he writes poetry) and of the painter. In short, I dreamed of the dance from beginning to end. I am going to hear from Mr. Clapp; he asked permission to take me to a concert. And I will certainly hear from Mr. Hugh Guiler. I was the first to dance last night, led by him, and the last on the polished floor with him also, because everyone else was tired and almost falling asleep. But during the last dance we almost *forgot to dance* in the excitement of the conversation.

March 14. I am tired in body and spirit. I feel the tyranny of school in spite of my love of it. It separates me from you. I live too quickly, without time for introspection, for my beloved meditations. I am strangely made: I am created to assimilate my surroundings slowly, gradually. I love to observe, to analyze, to write of this wonder world as it unfolds its phases to me, step by step. And now I struggle against *rushing*, the oppression of duty and routine.

Oh, how I need you now. I cling to you with a far better love than I have ever given you. You are my little lighthouse, constant and inspiring. I do not want to lose you, for I will lose myself!

After the turmoil of the day, I lie awake in bed for one long hour and talk with the shadows. Then, and only then, I feel the soothing touch of sleep—after dreaming the daydreams which must be shut out for so many long hours. No one can realize the great effort I make to concentrate in school. And because I must make this effort, I am thankful for the years of respite—when my heart could grow like a wild flower, unrestrained, free. I could not have endured school all these years; the very thought of it suffocates me.

[1] *Later referred to as "Hugo," as he was called by his family, since his father was also named Hugh.*

How strange it seems that it should always be Eduardo I dream of when I have time, in spite of the many types of boys I have been thrown into contact with lately.

March 20. For a few days I have lived again without introspection, and how full they have been. One of them brought a letter from Eduardo, an irresistible letter such as only Eduardo could write. but I had little time to dream about it.

Each day I have worked in the garden. The seeds I have planted in the cellar have begun to pierce through their brown earth, but they are so fragile I fear to look at them too long. I have nasturtiums, moonflowers, sweet peas, daisies and columbines.

I wrote to Eduardo last night because he seemed so desolate. He does not know why he has not written to me or to his sister. He says he forgets everyone and everything while he reads books. Mother gave me permission to invite him for the Easter vacation. And now I almost hope he will not accept. I like him *too much*. Miguel will also be here.

March 23. My composition teacher told me I was doing "mighty fine work."

"Do you read much Stevenson?" he asked me with a curious smile. Then he told me many things which I will never forget, and one of them was that writing nowadays was terse, direct, plain. "Your style is very beautiful, but . . ." He hesitated, and I understood.

"Is it old-fashioned, perhaps, Mr. Seitz?"

He advised me to read the *Atlantic Monthly* and *The Virginian*, by Owen Wister, also modern short stories. He told me to come to his private office every day so that he could watch my reading and give me extra guidance, because he was very interested in me. I was very happy. After all, what I must conquer is the influence of romanticism and poetry. Once more I felt like Rip Van Winkle. I have been traveling in old worlds of chivalry, elegant. elaborate speech, formality and pomp.

Letter to Frances:

Not even Spring makes me write poetry—all I feel flows in torrents into my Diary—mere prose—but, oh, Frances, each day I *feel* more—and the only reason I refrain from poetry is because I have been studying Tennyson, Wordsworth and Dryden, and I feel like a common city sparrow twittering in the presence of a thousand nightingales!

Jack came this morning to stay a few days. I do believe that he has not the slightest idea of what I really am. It is impossible that any boy should understand me. Perhaps Eduardo is the one who has come the nearest. Oh, I forgot to speak to you of his last letter. A few days before receiving the one in which he begged to be forgiven, having heard that he had been ill, I wrote pretending to be Mother's secretary, as though the invitation for Easter was a business transaction. He was waiting anxiously for my answer and disguised his anxiety in a business letter apparently written by *his* "secretary," Edgar Beverly. When it reached me, elaborate, and with its message easily read between the lines, I was filled with amusement. I was glad to be understood, glad that my fancies and games can be echoed somewhere, that someone should be able to "fly" with me. For often my spirits soar upward and leave all human friends on the way. Oh, yes, the great foundation of our friendship is harmony. Harmony so rarely exists. Will it last? Is it strong? I fear for it. I pray that it may not die yet, until I am strong enough to give it up, when I must.

March 25. Yesterday we froze, and today we fanned ourselves and puffed. These constant changes have a charm of their own. You have a glimpse of Spring, and then the door is shut violently upon your inquisitive face. Today was delicious. Mother bought me a red, red hat, which makes me look like an imp instead of a critical asparagus (asparagus stands for anything long and skinny and hopelessly colorless and plain). On returning, I dived into the regions of the cellar, where my hothouses are, and planted more mysterious seeds, because, being an egoist, I am thinking of all the pleasure they are going to give me while growing. To tell the truth, I thought of the *plants,* but Eduardo got mixed up with them. He is coming Tuesday.

March 26. Jack has gone—long, lanky, clear-eyed Jack, with his bashfulness before me, his Irish humor and contagious laughter. Now we expect Miguel, handsome egoist. My room is dainty and fresh. It seems ready for someone, for Eduardo, who used to love it, who used to caress my books and try to guess what dreams were held in my blue room. Has he changed?

I have read again an entire volume of my Diary—from July to September. There is no other word to express my emotion except absolute "surprise." I do not recognize my own writings! My old Diary is strange, impulsive, and seems to spring from me in *spite* of me. More than ever, I am resolved to continue writing—but why? I hardly know. I know I need you at all times. Perhaps you calm me, you soothe, you control. For after writing, I feel *reasonable*, and before acting, I pause to ask myself: Will I be ashamed to write this in my Diary?

I was contemplating the future, a fine *useful* future making brave resolutions. And then my thoughts turned to Eduardo . . . again Eduardo.

"Enough of this," I said to myself, "I must be reasonable. This is nonsense I am ashamed of." Eduardo barely likes me, and why must I act like a light-headed, silly girl. Once I was proud of being different from other girls; while they talked of boys, I was silent and longed for books. Have I changed? Have all these years of study, of concentration and thinking, years of solitude, created by myself by being "distant," and suffering to be called proud or cranky—have they been useless?

No! Today I despise my foolishness. Today the sun set on my last day of weakness, frailty, romanticism. Enough! I feel strong, almost invincible, unapproachable. I want to be distant, alone, abandoned. No one is going to enter my heart in the name of friendship. I will keep it pure for one great, supreme love of humanity, of nature. I hold the whip hand; I will conquer.

March 29. Every stranger's footsteps sound like a bombshell in my heart; I start and blush; then calm down when I discover it is the postman, the milkman, the gardener, but not my dear "forgetful cousin." The postman brought me a note from Enric; he is sick, bored, sad. I feel very sorry for him and will answer him soon. I am so afraid he will reenter his shell again as he did when he first came to our house.

It is freezing and the sunshine is dazzling. I fear for my tender buds and half-grown flowers. Only yesterday I worked and played in a gingham dress, and today we are glad to sit around the fire.

Miguel came in the afternoon. I should describe him superficially instead of continually prying in his inner nature. I might need him for a story. He is very tall, slender, distinguished in all his movements, with a touch of hauteur, which makes him very striking. He has jet-black expressive eyes, wavy black hair full of blue shadows, a high forehead. He is very winning and one of those persons one is glad to meet *socially*, but that is all, as he is such an egoist and demands all the sympathy, all the understanding, all the affection one can give but returns nothing.

March 30. Can my happiness be put into words? I snatch a few moments from this wonderful day, only half-lived, to tell you all. Eduardo came yesterday. He is not changed, unless I can say that each day he seems more lovable. In the evening we sit around the fire until bedtime. This morning we all walked to the village. And Eduardo bought me red, red roses. He does not know how I have dreamed of red roses until they became a myth. And then it is Eduardo who gives me my first red roses. Sometimes I turn away from the light of his eyes for fear he should guess how much I like him. Sometimes, too, I watch him and wonder if it is possible there should be someone in the world with so much charm in the form of a boy!

March 31. Yesterday afternoon Mother and Miguel went to the city, so that Eduardo and I sat by the fire and laughed and talked and teased each other and soared together far above the world of reality. Of people and incidents we spoke little, with metaphors. We also read each other's diaries. His is short but filled with reflections of his inner life and only here and there a fact, a picture of a human creature. I showed him my portrait of him, and he showed me mine—and more than he meant, I know, because as he handed me his diary, opened at a certain page, telling me that there was something in the others which he did not wish me to know, he made a mistake, and before I realized it I had read the wondrous something, his longings for "cuisine" while he was in Cuba and his struggle between two different loves. His love for a little Cuban girl, beautiful, with "two greenish Egyptian eyes," whose sight stirs what he calls "the lower passions and desires" and would drag him down, would merely satisfy his "love of Beauty"; and his love for his "cuisine," whom he describes as also beautiful (which is not true) and graceful and noble. *Between the lines* I read that when compared in beauty, I have naught to give. He says that I inspire him to do fine and great things, that I bring out his better self, satisfy his longings for intellectual companionship. He looks up to me almost as if I were unapproachable, not human. I felt all this and my heart was filled with a thousand questions—not regrets—but not pride either.

I understand him so well. It is foolish to think that heaven sent *him* to awaken my heart. I am older than he is, in age, experience, suffering! He will go to Perla or to some other beautiful lily girl later, and I will perhaps find Someone who believes, as I believe, that Love is merely a union of two hearts in one—giving each other what one lacks, sharing the fruits of the mingled natures, and then turning in common harmony toward some noble task. Oh, not Love without Ideals—useless—lasting only while youth and beauty last, fading when the bloom is fading. Not beauty but charm—the charm of a good woman, of a good mother, a good friend—I will strive to attain with all my heart!

I have never come so near to loving as during these days. But if my heart leaps up each time Eduardo calls me or turns his eyes toward me, it is only because ideals call to ideals, dreams to dreams, youth to youth; and harmony draws us together, a magnet in the crafty hands of Destiny.

It seems so difficult to remember Miguel is there. My half-uttered thoughts are echoed in Eduardo's heart and he responds to them in the mysterious language I alone can understand; and Miguel looks puzzled and critical.

I feel like exclaiming like Lamartine against the terrible, swift flight of time! The days are vanishing too quickly. Soon Eduardo will go. Most of the time I spent in school, eager to return home with the joyous news of a mark of 97 percent on my last theme.

All evening we sat around the fire while Mother talked of the past. Eduardo is now writing downstairs by the dying fire, in my place. I wonder what he is thinking, what he is dreaming and writing about. I fled upstairs with a heavy heart.

April 2. I went to the club dance, usually an ordinary and foolish dance, but not last night. I went with Eduardo, who looked so very handsome. I wore my rose dress, and Mrs. Norman loaned me a string of pearls. I would not have cared one whit if I had been dressed as a beggar maid because Eduardo in his new transformation was casting a spell. Just think, instead of studying the inner nature of Mlle. Linotte, he suddenly turned to the terribly human study of dimples, which he pretends I have, the color of my eyes, which are strange, he says, and of my hair, which is "dazzling." We sat on the stairs and he wrote a poem to me called "Our Dance." The blurred words on the preceding page are caused by his unexpected entrance in my room; I had to close my Diary in a hurry. We cannot stay five minutes without an explosion of enthusiasm in which we both take part, at the discovery of some beautiful page in a book, anything. Mother looks on with her own peculiar twinkling smile and calls us parrots, including Miguel. Speaking of Miguel, now he is worried and has come out of his egoism to buy me the *Vie de Bohème*, by Murger. I might go to the theatre with Jack this afternoon, a thing against which Miguel and Eduardo protested forcibly and eloquently.

April 4. The eve of the last day! And I am afraid to write. Eduardo is changed, but in a way I had never dreamed of. Oh, if you could see him. Somehow the time when he seemed lost to me has passed like a sad dream, and this one is so glad, so beautiful, that I am afraid to touch it. I doubted if he liked me, but now I am certain he wants my presence as much as I want his. We are drawn together in an irresistible way in spite of Miguel, who is always with us, in spite of Mother, who is always laughing at us. We never finish speaking, or, what is still more wonderful, we know how to be silent together.

Yesterday I did go to the theatre with Jack. Miguel and Eduardo took me to the station.

This afternoon Eduardo, Miguel and I walked through the woods and had the oddest conversation you could possibly imagine. The three of us together, how odd we are. We spoke of, among other things, our wives and husbands. Upon one thing we agreed —the wives must be intellectual and pretty. Eduardo's must be a companion. My husband is a person, as you know, who could never exist, but that does not prevent me from speaking of him. The rest of the afternoon we read and talked and laughed. The supper was simple. Neither Eduardo nor Miguel wishes to return to school. Last night they spoke of the inexplicable charm of this house, in which one does nothing and one is never bored, in which one speaks of all the things one loves.

"There is a spirit in this house," I said.

"It's *you*," said Eduardo. And Miguel echoed him. Always me in their talk. I never thought I occupied such a big place in the world. But I am tired. I am forever on tiptoes, reaching my hands to a divine shower of petals—petals from red, red roses. My heart leaps up a million times each day, and when bedtime comes, I fall asleep like a child who has played too much.

I write in Eduardo's new diary: "Write—and remember, if you hear a voice calling, it is someone who loves Daydreams and with whom you can share your own."

The red roses are withered, but I have the petals in a box with my cousin's letters. He has a few of them also in his diary.

Eduardo wrote in the diary book he gave me: "Write: let not Dante or Milton obstruct your path. They are the masters of the mind of humanity, you can be the mistress of the heart of humanity. Say not that all things have been written! Your heart has never been written. So whenever you falter in the path of your life, whenever you need words of comfort, words of friendship, words of love, there is someone waiting patiently to administer to thy wants—to eternity."

How we have liked each other these days, without discord, or estrangement, not a moment of boredom or weariness.

Are you surprised at the name of Mimi? Both Eduardo and Miguel call me Mimi without knowing that Enric was the first to say it. Mimi de Bohème.

An invisible chain links us vaguely together, Charles, Enric, Miguel, Eduardo and I. Mr. Guiler is a member in spite of himself. I am the only woman.

In the evening the house is silent, the hearth holds no fire, the chairs drawn around it are empty. This is the aftermath. I sit alone in my room and write without sadness because there is no place for sadness in my heart. It is full of memories, full of his laughter, of the looks in his eyes, his voice. I see him at the piano when he played "Sweetheart" and "Narcissus" and other things for me. I see him watching the fire and turning to me with his meditations; I see him reading, writing and dreaming, with his pipe. I see him everywhere. He is still speaking to me and laughing at me, still teasing gently and telling me what I am; he knows me well; he knows my better self and likes my thoughts as much as the rest in me. He has gone, but his spirit still hovers. I will never like a friend as much as I like my cousin.

We created, in perfect accord, an imaginary personage: his secretary, the writer of the formal, pompous letter with which he answered my own. I said I liked him far better than Eduardo himself, as I had read between the lines certain interesting traits of character which Eduardo did not have. We talked about the secretary and decided he would be informed of my preference for him and that we could correspond, since Eduardo so often forgot to write. We kept this up many days until whenever the secretary was mentioned we burst out laughing. Once I said I even suspected it was the secretary who had written *all* the letters; they were too beautiful to have been written by Eduardo. He was indignant. But nothing that I could ever write could portray this quaint relationship of ours in which the imagination plays such a big part. Mother said, in the middle of our impulsive repartees, that she hoped all this would give us bread and butter someday. "Why not?" I answered. "You, for example, are a tired business woman; don't we entertain and amuse you all day? We will do that for a living." Mother could not deny that she had been amused.

April 6. I seem deprived of all sensibilities. In school my attention wanders; I turn away with supreme indifference from my over-ardent classmates. They bore me. I want to be alone. At home I sit for hours with idle hands and eyes which see nothing at all. A vague torpor seizes me like a malignant poison. Even nature, each day more splendidly arrayed, does not touch me. I gaze without joy or sorrow. Am I suffering? I cannot tell. The silence that has crept into me is terrible; is it an eternal silence? Will I hear again the whispering of my thoughts? Will my heart ever stir or leap and thrill to a touch, a call, a scene? Nothing betrays the supreme desolation in me but eyes, which have ceased to sparkle; they are wistful, long and narrow like Madame Butterfly's. If I look inside I can almost visualize a tiny cemetery; on one white tomb there is inscribed:

Here lies my Youth.

On another:

Here lie my Impulses and Quaint Thoughts.

And again:

Here lie my Imagination,
My love of Nature.
Here lie my Heart—my Dreams.

In school I often meet the creatures whom the Spring has touched. They walk in in pairs; they look into each other's eyes; she has a bunch of sweet peas or violets, which he has given her; he holds her books. I pass them by and say to myself: "They love." But it does not stir me. Perhaps the only thing I love these days are little children. I see them everywhere and something in me goes out to them. They understand because they smile into my face, always. They are the only little rays of sunshine which can penetrate the cold austerity of my inexplicable mood.

The whip hand? I cannot use it. I do not know the name of

what I must conquer! The deep, black shadows gather closer; my spirit suffocates.

One of my greatest agonies comes from this great restlessness of mine, which leads me into all the tangled paths of life, paths obstructed by questions, paths without a single light sometimes.

And yet, how simple it is to listen; then and then alone comes the happiness accompanying a serene, unruffled life. Still, I cannot always listen. My nature is inquisitive. Even Eduardo said that my eyes were too *big* and too *inquisitive!* They are the "windows of my soul"!

This makes me think of what a poet said about women's eyes: ". . . the beauty that lies in them . . ."

Whereupon a cynic spoke: "Yes, and how it lies and lies and lies . . ."

My thoughts have turned to Eduardo once more. They circle and circle around him. I want him near me.

Will I have much to write of Eduardo in my Diary? Or will Someone, my Shadow, my Mysterious Stranger, step into my life? He will only be a little different from Eduardo. Different in his love for me, different in age, with more strength, more fidelity, and without admiration for beauty (of which I have so little). It must be someone to whom I can say: "I possess nothing. Do you want me in spite of this?"

My poor, impossible husband!

My breakfast becomes a thing of no importance when I find myself in possession of a letter from Eduardo. "My chère, chère Mimi. Instead of studying, I am conjecturing what you are doing, thinking, writing. I want you to know I am not fickle and I am thinking of you, remembering you . . ."

I go to school with the talisman in my pocket. I can watch the others without sadness. They love, but that talisman in my pocket, though a message of a *different* love, is wonderful. Sometimes my whole being cries out: enough, enough! *I feel too much,* more than I can bear. Nothing happened today on the surface, but in a mysterious way the gray dampness of the day pierced my heart. I shrank from my surroundings, I longed to shut out the grim invader.

April 7. I am suffering still, suffering with the fear of suffocation, for my heart cannot breathe. Someday the long-pent-up emotions will break forth in some furious, dangerous rebellion. Music doubles the pain.

I answer Eduardo's letter so that he may receive mine on his birthday. I do not hide my mood from him. I tell him I want to run away. Eduardo is sad also. Is it the reaction after bliss? Did we pour forth so much light, throw around us so much radiance, that like weary lamps, the flame in us trembles, almost dies out?

The relief came while I walked to the station with the raindrops dancing merrily on top of my umbrella. Then my heart stirred and responded once more to the glistening beauty of nature. In school I laughed secretly at my "admirers," who can never guess how tangled my heart is behind the face they like. How strange life seems sometimes. What makes a person suffer intensely one moment and rejoice the next? Is every human creature subject to these changes? Or am I the only one with queer, queer ways and tangled heart?

Evening. The raindrops lash the windowpanes. I hear the wind moaning and spending itself in gusts and quavers. Joaquin plays a slow Venetian melody. And I sit here tonight as I have done so many times to talk with you—our last talk, because you need a rest; your binding has become loose, as if symbolical of your tempestuous contents. I have opened and closed you too often, and I have torn out some pages. You see, I am really a very plain and ordinary person, wicked, moody, selfish, thoughtless— but there is only one reason why I have created you and ask you to have patience, only one reason why I come to you each night: I have dreams, dreams which are finer than anything I have ever done or said, and I do not want them to die. It is my better self, the self of my ideals and resolutions struggling against the dreamless self with its faults and defilings, and they struggle in your pages. Your mere power of reflecting is worth more to me than all the sermons and advice in the world. You are the strongest help I have to fulfill my vision to achieve womanhood.

April 9. I watched the shadows creep over the country. Standing on the porch, awed and silent, I saw the gold-and-purple glow fade gradually; then there followed a breathless suspense, when my soul seemed to have flown from me to become a part of that mysterious transformation. A mist hung over the fields, over the roads, and veiled the woods in an unearthly, almost mystical way. After the gold and purple vanished, the shadows became bolder, turning a world which seemed simple by day into weird scenery fit for fantastic creatures of mystery and magic. I watched, scarcely breathing, spellbound and ecstatic. I heard music which did not exist in reality, soft, low and delicate, expressing sadness, passion, and something else I could not understand. Then suddenly I started, my heart leaped. I knew, I knew! There, while I dreamed and watched the twilight, someone had called me. I understood. I knew. It was a longing, a desire of some stranger's heart, which reached me across a long, long distance, perhaps, and which I heard because all my being was listening for it. Who is it? Has he ever called before in vain? Is this the cause of all my restlessness, my longings? Call me again, my Stranger. I will always listen now. Are you real? I wonder. I heard you call, but how can I answer you?

I am not mad, beloved Diary. I write this in all sincerity. Perhaps my constant dreaming has carried me away. All of today, each hour of it, has been half-real, half-dream. What am I but a creature of dreams? My life is made of them; they are my Reality. Please believe in them as I believe in them. We shall have too many years afterward to dissect and doubt them. Love them with me while we have the right, the privilege.

April 10. Thorvald is ill, and Thorvald ill is the most irresistible thing imaginable. His good humor, his roguishness and perpetual mood for jokes and "bon mots" are more than I can fathom.

I should write a lot about Thorvald, because he is much more lovable then I am. But he is the sort of person you are contented merely to have near you, without studying him. He is so miraculously simple. Sunny-tempered. There is nothing to write about. He is just like a wide blue lake with a clear, transparent bottom. Strong, healthy, spirited, secretly loving and affectionate, faithful and iron-willed: that is Thorvald, that and one more thing. He is an incurable, irresistible and maddening tease. I do believe Thorvald would tease an angel to exasperation. How on earth he is going to woo a wife for himself I do not know. Thorvald and compliments have always been mortal enemies. He will never tell a maiden: "Oh, your hair is like etc. Your eyes are like etc." And neither will he sigh and pine. No. Thorvald will look once and. having decided, will lift her up, as he lifts me up (unless she is of the class that cannot be lifted up by one man alone, and in this case he will ask Jack, his bosom friend, to help him), and having lifted her up, he will carry her to the church, where he will marry her without asking her if it suits her. And who, I ask you, would not be suited?

Evening. I read *Hypatia*[1] all day long, interrupted often for things which I did like a person in a dream, once to receive some characterless visitors whom Tia Juana brought us, but always returning to my book and finding myself soon unconscious of my surroundings. I read it slowly, thoughtfully, pausing when I could not control the rush of my own feelings. There is so much in that book which is tragic, true and terrible. It awakened a million doubts which I thought I had put away forever during my researches into philosophy a few months ago: it conjured old dreams; it gave birth to contradictions, regrets, sympathy, repulsion, admiration; all sentiments clashed against reasoning, and I seemed to be fighting a great and mysterious battle of my own through each of these living pages, until the last.

I will never forget the unfortunate Hypatia, who seemed real to me until I awoke from the awful dream. Nor will I forget Philammon, or Pelagia, Miriam and Raphael.

This has been a restless Sunday indeed. But I have seen much of the world with Philammon and I am satisfied to feel that, in spirit at least, one can visit other lands, know other people and live with them the life of other centuries, become familiar with their doubts, which are ours also, their sufferings, their heroism or cowardice, all of which makes humanity ever the same in spite of all philosophies and religions.

Do you like this: "A woman's heart must never weary of loving; it is made to help, to forgive, to comfort, and encourage, to be brave, patient and charitable. It must be constant, tender, sincere, full of the love of home, nature, humanity. It must be ever awake, devoted, unselfish, and tolerant, pure, and full of gentleness and understanding. A young girl's heart must be all that and more. It must be womanly."

April 11. I have finished my theme on a "Perfect Gentleman." I began unwillingly and unfeelingly, and then warmed to the "heat of composition," and finished triumphantly. And now for the period of suspense to follow. How I want to know if I have redeemed my failure!

A few minutes after the homecoming, which means that I have kissed Mother, and gladly dropped my heavy books, and pulled off my coat and hat, I am already scribbling. I cannot

[1] *By Charles Kingsley.*

control my thoughts. I am so glad to be alive! I just want to write, write, write. Fortunately, I do not lavish all my madness on you. It flows into voluminous essays, fragments, poetry, and all of that I scribble away on the train, and in the classrooms, besides spending the greater part of my mornings attached to my desk. From now on I wish to reform my writing, and today I learned a very important thing, which we might call the first chapter in the process of reformation. It is the use of dashes, which, as you can see, I sprinkle generously and profusely in your pages—a most abominable habit! Mr. Seitz said something vague about it being too aesthetic, and that it betrayed lack of *true thinking*. It seems people use it when they wish to write all their thoughts down without troubling about coordination and harmony. I will give you an example taken from my own experience. If I come to you without my wits about me, which I usually do, I will say: "Oh, I am so happy (dash) the day is beautiful (dash) and my heart (etc. dash) dash etc." Probably, if I used my reasoning, I could have written: "The beauty of the day made my heart very happy." How practical and sensible. Not a dash, not a sign of that state of being which is called not having your wits about you!

Evening. When I compare the littleness of what I know with the immense quantity of things I have still to learn, I stand aghast and become sorrowful. Today in class Mr. Seitz was announcing the homework. Make an outline of *The Deserted Village*.

I knew it was a work by [Oliver] Goldsmith. How well I thought I knew my Goldsmith. I have read about his character, his strange, wayward life and finally his very best work, *The Vicar of Wakefield*. But I thought *The Deserted Village* was a book and I asked, "Shall we divide it according to chapters?"

"It has no chapters," answered Mr. Seitz with a curious smile, which I now understand too well, having just read the poem in the *Book of Knowledge*.

How little I know. How infinitesimal is my knowledge of literature in spite of my perpetual reading. And how I thirst for knowledge. Such a thirst which is never satisfied, never soothed or calmed, what will it make of me? The more I study and observe, the more inquisitive I become. My inquisitiveness is becoming a pedantic mania. I am always looking up words in the dictionary, and prying into my own heart, looking for its most secret contents, and peeping curiously into other creatures' characters. And yet, I never read quickly and forget one book at the coming of another. No. Shall I tell you how I read? It is laughable and absurd, but it has become a part of my queer nature. A book, in whatever form, of whatever origin, is in itself sacred to me. And there my folly begins, for I am drawn to it, and if it falls into my hands, I almost lose my head for joy. Then I begin to read. I pause to copy passages from it because I know this book will not belong to me for long. I have many books filled with notes. From note taking I plunge into the refreshing discovery of new words. and when I become familiar with them, I feel happier, many times happier, and long for an opportunity to use them. They are mine! And I love them for the sake of the thoughts they express, the pictures they bring forth, the heartstrings they touch. And thus I read, I write, I overflow with enthusiasm, with satisfaction. My own opinions, my own criticisms, I hold back with difficulty. I have no right to judge as yet, but the time will come. Do you understand why the very word Book is sacred to me? It is always a long, complete voyage followed by the discovery of some new world. Each time, if the book is good, all my mind responds to it. I think, I feel, I laugh and cry with it. They are nearly always good, fine old books, those books I read. Have they not made me the old-fashioned girl I am?

Now and then, I timidly, fearfully stretch forth a hand toward modern literature, and my good fortune guides me. Then I read James Allen's books, and the *Diary of Opal Whiteley*, and *The Country Interlude*, by [Hildegarde] Hawthorne. Opal Whiteley lives. I have read her article on book reviews in The Times. She is alive and writing, an authoress who loves the things I love. Just think, if these people she has pictured, Kendrik and Imogen, exist in someone else's mind besides Eduardo's and my own, then they *can* be real.

After days of happy, useless doings, with the futile and foolish thoughts accompanying them, I have begun once more to retire into my Inward World, and succeeded. The Easter vacations drew me away from my serious self. I always said I could not be a good philosopher when with Eduardo. We do speak of serious things, but somehow not for their sake so much as for the pleasure of speaking together. Eduardo does not know it, being a boy, but I have found it out intuitively. Suppose I were very, very ugly, and awkward, suppose . . . Would he like me for the sake of my thoughts, my intellect? Nay, it could not be. He is too young. That is why I wonder sometimes how I am going to find someone who will love me for what I am inwardly. Is my stranger very young? But such are not the thoughts of a creature who has decided to shut out most of the world and open her secret door to science, literature and philosophy and self-improvement. Stand back, you silly failings of youth. Away, I say, from this temple of study. And yet, they say the Spring is here, and they are selling violets on the street corner, and the world is full of "whispering lovers." Can I resist?

April 12. I was wondering yesterday if someone would think of giving me violets or red roses, but nothing, nothing can equal the lovely gift which came to me this morning. In a box, lying on a patch of soft damp moss, a bunch of wild flowers. I think they are trailing arbutus, from the woods. And who could think of sending them? Who but a person who knows me well, and knows my love of flowers, and my love of thoughtfulness? Eduardo.

And not the flowers alone, but a letter came this morning too, such a letter as I would like to answer a minute after reading it. His family did not remember his birthday on time and he writes sadly: "Your letter was like a pearly dew to a thirsty soul, yes, cuisine, even if it had been only a word! This morning I waited for seven letters, cuisine; I found only one, but what a treasure. You were the only being who showed remembrance in words, and I am thankful." Another letter came from Jack, one such as Mark Twain would have written. How I laughed. Letters, letters, you are as full of contrasts, of revelations, as people themselves. And how much people miss who never receive them. Do I deserve so much kindness from the world?

While traveling homeward I read a remarkable book called *The Rubáiyát of Omar Khayyám.* In it I recognized the famous lines:

> A Book of Verses underneath the Bough,
> A Jug of Wine, a Loaf of Bread—and Thou.

They call Omar Khayyám the Astronomer-Poet of Persia, and I have no doubt that he is very wise, but at first I was unpleasantly struck by the sensuality of the lines; it took me some time to discover the fine thoughts veiled in them. But now I realize well what has made the little book immortal and I am glad to know it. I owe it to Mr. Jones, who belongs to my English class. He has intuitively discovered my taste in books, and we sometimes have short talks before class in which we simply exchange opinions—short, formal talks, because unfortunately, though intelligent, refined, and with the education of a gentleman, a wide gulf separates us: he is a Negro.

There is a bold person in the same class who unconsciously disturbs my philosophical attitude. He pounces on me as soon as I enter the class, and begins to dazzle me with long, complimentary discourses. I make fun of each thing he says, which seems to discourage him little. Sometimes he embarrasses me, and that seems to enchant him all the more. It is terrible, and I wonder how I can get rid of him. He is one of those man creatures who thinks himself irresistibly handsome and charming, believing that sooner or later I will fall under his spell. He never heard of Hypatia; how can he understand?

April 13. I have discovered two things today; one, a thing which many people have discovered before me, the incomparable book of *Essays* by [Ralph Waldo] Emerson; the other, an idea of my own, which came to me while I was talking with Frances. I met her today in the city, by appointment, and we walked while talking, as we so often did in the past. And while we exchanged confidences and impressions, I was comparing the friendship between girls and the friendship between girl and boy, man and woman. I was thinking how much I valued the friendship Frances has given me since the first day we met in school; I was happy to notice how constant, how sincere and helpful it has been always. But friendship between women seems so natural: it is usually smooth, gentle, understanding and sympathetic, and it seems taken for granted, so to speak.

What difference is there between that and the other friendship? The other is full of mystery, full of spontaneity and yet reserve; the man and woman seem to be always standing on the brink of revelation; the heart is awake, expectant, perplexed; it trembles at the call of the unknown! Yes, mystery, and the sweet steps of revelation are climbed one by one. The man's heart wonders and the woman's heart thrills at the wonder of being "wondered about." Is it vanity again? Then that makes the friendship of man valued perhaps more. It cannot be. Woman is not all vanity. If secretly I prize Eduardo's friendship more than Frances's, it must be because it is rarer, it is more difficult to win, to keep. And then, I understand a young girl's heart like Frances's so well, while a boy's . . . It is the call of the unknown. It is again my inquisitiveness which guides me. I want to know what a boy's heart is made of. And it is through friendship that I can study their hearts; and perhaps above that, I would like to study their minds. I know they possess hearts, but I wonder if they possess minds.

April 14. For the first time today I could not study. If I went to the porch my eyes wandered and my thoughts carried me to other worlds. If I remained indoors, the sunshine beckoned at my window.

In school I found that I had received 87 percent on my "gentleman." I know of no one who received a higher mark, and I was happy to have earned it.

While feeding squirrels this morning I noticed the furnace man passing by and I smiled at him. He smiled back and said: "Dat's right. Feeda da squirra and den he skiddoo." And I was left to ponder on the ingratitude of squirrels and on Italian accents. In class there was much dissatisfaction about the outline of "The Deserted Village." No one could do it. One boy said he did not know, anyway, why "those people deserted that old village; if they had stayed there, the poem would not have been written and our lesson would not have been so hard." My classmates are surprised at my good work. For the first time I have heard Mr. Seitz laugh, laugh with all his heart. He has a very good face, but his laughter alone reveals what I fancy to be a splendid character. There is something undefinable about him which sometimes holds my attention so completely that I forget that I am there to learn, not to study. Often his matter-of-fact questions startle me from a reverie, perhaps when I am wondering what he thinks, and whether he dreams. Teachers always have two natures; their teaching in itself imposes a heavy responsibility and care on them, which I am sure they must shake off as soon as they cease teaching. And then, what is the human being like? Does Mr. Seitz like to ramble through the woods, or does he prefer the grimy city? Does he read the new books and admire the world of today? Is he practical, commonplace and ordinary? Or a dreamer who controls his dreams while he works? I cannot tell yet. I only know he is young, but can penetrate into characters unerringly; that he has a sense of humor, that he is tolerant sometimes, and exacting with certain people, nevertheless without showing favoritism. I can see no more than that because he is my teacher, and I have no other time to study him except while he teaches, and that is when I believe a person is less like his real self. Of one thing I am certain.

I could never have a better teacher. The very thought of some-one else makes me tremble.

I wrote to Eduardo: I want to tell you what I think of what you wrote in your diary. Eduardo, I do not believe in this: the need of exposing your vital, irrevocable, invariable faults and weak-nesses to your friends. Does it seem strange? Tell me, then, don't you think that certain friends inspire you? Is it not true that some draw out your better self, call forth your best impulses, kindle ideals, inspire your finest thoughts? Such as your good friends make you, you *are*. All faults, weaknesses or weak impulses which you may have while in the presence of someone else, a friend who is perhaps not fine enough to bring out your better self, such faults, I say, disappear, fall off like an impure mantle as soon as you return to the other, the one whose companionship purifies and ennobles you. Unconsciously you give me an example. Lad-die,[1] when he is with you, loses his affectations, his absurdities. Poor cousin, what made you write me the first letter? You little knew all the trouble it would bring you!

April 15. I had been happy in school until today. I hope I will forget today soon, but meanwhile I might as well tell you of it. It was all because of a certain person who came into the grammar class to see how we were doing, apparently an Authority, but (the important but) to my mind, a Monster. Half the class was sent to the blackboard to analyze some sentences (fortunately I was not, as I sit in the back of the room). He stood there before each of them to criticize and mark, but not as Mrs. Charleson always does, in her calm, just way; no, he pounded on the blackboard with his clenched fist, he pointed violently to the shivering victim, and his questions sprang up like devils from their boxes. He turned mistakes into coarse jokes, and pointed them out to the class with clownish gestures. And the class laughed. The boy or girl thus taunted and mocked would stand there with red face and a hurt look. One boy with a fine, proud face and lovable blue eyes held his temper until the last with great effort. Anger, shame and contempt were clearly stamped upon his face. Contempt, yes, it was contemptible, and many of us felt it because we did not laugh. But I felt it so violently, it pierced me through and through and

[1] *A classmate of Eduardo's.*

isolated me in a loneliness of opinion. Why am I so foolishly sensitive to the way the class is treated? Canterbury[1] came with me. We agreed that we had been treated like trained clowns in a circus. He had been poked fun at but was facing it good-humoredly, and I could not help laughing with him while at the same time burning with indignation.

A few days ago I wrote briefly about Emerson's *Essays*, but now my enthusiasm knows no bounds. I could not part with the little book for all the gold in the world. Mother gave it to me; that is to say, she gave me permission to buy two or three French books, but instead I chose the *Essays*, first and second series, in a small, soft leather book with light, transparent paper which they call India paper, I think. The very appearance of the book, apart from the contents, gives me a little thrill of pride and satisfaction. I do believe I am developing bibliomania. I read the Essay on Friendship, which is magnificent although austere, the one on Self-Reliance, a masterpiece of revelation, and finally, the Essay on Love, which is sublime, as befits the subject. Still, to read and admire does not mean that I take Emerson's philosophy as my own. Several times I absolutely disagreed with him, even with a courage he himself has taught me in the wonderful Essay on Self-Reliance. It is in this very essay I find a great fault, which I am going to discuss with Eduardo, for we have decided to discuss subjects in our letters, as much to find out our points of view as to teach each other. Again I circle and return to Eduardo. I cannot separate him from Nature or from Books, and to tell the truth, he is entangled in all my life, whether at school, or at home, or in the garden.

And yet, no one could call him an intruder. He does not force his way into your thoughts; merely glides like a shadow and melts into them. Never harrying or wearing, a quiet companion shadow, almost a part of my imaginary world. I wonder what he feels. That question reminds me that he is real, for if he were an imaginary friend, I could imagine what he thought of me, but my cousin is real and human, and therefore secretive. And yet, no, not secretive. He reveals himself in his letters, reveals his attitude toward life, toward books, toward nature, but not his thoughts of me. He veils them in mystic dreams, and when he does express them, vaguely, indefinitely, then I fear he is thinking of someone else.

[1] *A classmate.*

Fortunately I am the only one destined to read these pages, and I do believe I write them in the contemplation of a lonely old age. For suppose I do not marry, and suppose I read all the good books that have been written, then I will have nothing else to do but read my old diaries, and ponder over the "frailty and failings of human nature."

I hear Mrs. Norman and her husband discussing religion. Yes, perhaps I will marry, and in the evening my husband and I will sit and talk about books, or read our diaries to each other, for of course, my husband will have to begin his Diary as soon as he marries me. Do you pity him?

April 17. I have just awakened from the spell of *Thelma*, by Marie Corelli. It is a beautiful, touching story, and Thelma is a glorious woman. It droops a little toward the middle, but before I had time to dislike it, the story shifted once more to the Land of the Midnight Sun and radiated inspiration. I love Sigurd, with his strange, weird fancies, his secret sorrows, his frailty. Poor, pathetic little creature, who dies because his beloved Thelma is taken from him. Love, love, love is the song which all these pages sing to me, sad love, noble love, happy love, love which elevates. Oh, love in all its forms and aspects.

April 18. It rains, drearily, continuously, a noiseless shower of very fine, light raindrops. The sky is gray and oppressing. All the light, the coloring, the beauty and cheerfulness of the world seem to have found refuge in the tender new leaves, for they alone radiate life. They alone speak of Spring, of hope. I have finished my lessons, and I sit here very cold and brooding. Flora has just left me and expressed in the quaint way of her country her thankfulness for my addressing of some envelopes for her.

"May heaven grant you all your wishes, Señorita."

I look up at the desolate sky and wonder. Do I wish for anything? Ah, yes, but what do I deserve? Nothing, nothing. It is a wonder that people love me; they cannot see my heart; my heart is wicked, wicked. I have so many dreams, so many ideals. I know so well what is fine and noble. Why is it that I cannot be like the people in my dreams, like my ideals? Why am I not fine and noble like Hypatia, like Thelma? I am not beautiful, I am not good. Compared with them, I am filled with faults.

Last night I fell asleep wondering what I was doing for Love. Love, the inevitable, the greatest gift of God. Books, thousands of them, tell me that Love is Everything. Is it more than fame, than study, than philosophy or science? Books, some of them, answer yes, but others shut love out. Slowly, gradually, I have learned to believe that, for my part at least, I need love. With my studies, my constant digging and questioning, my work, am I making myself worthy of Love when it comes to me? What a lovely ideal to live up to. Not the Love for beauty, of which I have none, but a Love like Browning's, Love for all the intangible and self-created things. And I will wait, and work, to make myself worthy. Not by studying alone, for what is knowledge by itself? No, I am going to fix my eyes on my ideal of a Woman and strive to come as near as I can, with all my faults and wickedness.

I am growing almost frightened at my thirst for books, and what is worse, my intense forgetfulness of all the world while reading them. I feel like one entering a temple, for there is so much sacredness in my worship, like one in a mystic trance. From one book grows the longing for another book, and from the last a new longing, more desires, a greater restlessness. In reading *Thelma* I have found quotations from a book called *Love-Letters of a Violinist*, by Eric Mackay, and I am all curiosity. Each Sunday now I watch for the name of Hildegarde Hawthorne in the book reviews, and smile when I find it, as if it were the name of an acquaintance. I know her well, though she has never heard of me, and I have called her my friend, without her permission. It is a pity we cannot see each other. What a wonderful woman she must be. If I ever grow famous (ahem), I shall go and see her and tell her how I wanted to write her about her book but did not dare, nor knew where she lived. I hope she will wait till I grow up completely. If she dies, like all my favorite authors, I will feel terribly alone in the world of writers. I do believe I would not be afraid to let her read my Diary. I am becoming familiar, too, with the names of modern authors like William Locke, Ethel Dell, Irvin S. Cobb, [Joseph] Conrad, [Marie] Corelli, [Gene Stratton] Porter, [James] Oppenheim and Jack London, which means that I am drifting away from the queer, antiquated sensation of resembling Rip Van Winkle.

My poor trailing arbutus has withered, but I could not bring myself to throw it out, the thoughtful symbol of my forgetful cousin's return to me, and so I emptied my little jewel basket of its insignificant trinkets and placed the bunch of dead wild flowers in it. One of my faults is this habit of living so much in the past. I have a reverence and love of memories which only my love of

Anaïs Nin, c. *1922*

The Nin house in Richmond Hill

A. N.'s brother Joaquin

Rosa Culmell Nin

*A. N.'s brother Thorvald (right)
with his cousins
Charles Cárdenas (left)
and Gilbert Chase*

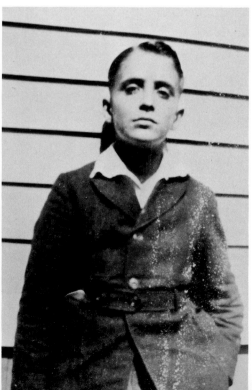

Joaquin Nin-Culmell

Miguel Jorrín

Enric Madriguera

Eduardo Sánchez

Hugo (Hugh) Guiler, Fort Monroe, Virginia, 1920

A. N. as a model, 1922

A. N. as a cover girl

A. N. modeling as Cleopatra, 1922

building for the future can surpass. And I see everything so *vividly*. A stranger would take me for a visionary, a madwoman. Thus, that little basket with its mysterious contents would be called rubbish by a sensible person. I can almost hear my mother telling me to throw it out. And yet each time I see it, it brings up a lovely picture, half-imaginary, half-true. I see Eduardo in some glorious woods, kneeling to pick the fresh scented flowers and thinking of Mimi with a curious smile and the soft, approving look in his fine eyes which I always found there when I had pleased him.

I notice I write nothing of Miguel's visit Saturday and Sunday. He came, he talked, he went, and I was hardly conscious. Is this another fault of mine? I do not know its name, but I suppose it is a grave fault. And yet, how on earth could one think of Miguel while reading *Thelma?* This is, indeed, a psychological problem. 'Tis better so, however, for my philosophical peace of mind.

April 19. A few days ago I wrote of a bold and handsome person in the class whom I was planning to get rid of. His name is Carnival, and a very strange thing is happening. I am learning to like him a little, not exactly what he is now as much as what I expect to make of him. It is, in some ways, a perilous experiment. I know him to be merely playing with me, momentarily attracted by a new face, and still I want to try to make him respect me, not for my own sake or for what I am, and, in me, girlhood. I feel as if I could make him good, and take away his boldness, insincerity and disrespect. The thought rouses all my fighting spirit. I only hope he will be attracted long enough for me to accomplish the transformation. But I do not know how to go about it. I will not preach. I wonder if my own behavior will be enough. I know already that it attracts his curiosity. He would be such a fine boy otherwise. He seems like someone who has breathed "bad air" which has dulled all his ideals, but perhaps not through his own fault. If only I could awake them, once more rouse in him chivalry and honor. I have been warned against him by boys and girls, and today when he accompanied me to the corner of the street, I caught glances of disapproval from one girl. And yet it might be jealousy. Do you know that to walk with me meant he would be late for his next session, and yet he chose unhesitatingly? Thus I am blending nonsense with a lofty purpose. I am so in earnest that I hope my experiment will not fail. Can it be so very hard to bring out the best in people? Can it be so very dangerous to deal with people as if they were noble? Hafiz[1] says: "She believed that by dealing nobly with all, all would show themselves nobly." Time will tell, and I will tell my Diary.

April 20. I went to see a play today with Tia Juana. It is called *The Green Goddess.* Its chief actor, George Arliss, is very famous, and I now understand why. The play in itself was very thrilling, and remarkably clever. Home, I found that Tia Coco had come for a few days; but she has a sick headache and I had to steal softly into my darkened room, feeling my way into drawers and closets to find my books for study, and to find you. And so now, instead of sitting before my dressing table, I am installed before Mother's business desk. Somehow, this change of atmosphere, as it were, disturbs my flow of observations and moralizings. It cools my enthusiasm to work side by side with business papers, bills, receipts, checkbooks, etc. I stare persistently at the pale-yellow wallpaper, or at the menacing telephone, and return to the blank page before me without inspiration. In truth, this is only one of the many changes in me these days, changes without reasonable cause and which disturb me deeply. I do not feel like studying. I merely want to dream and laugh and sing. As in the days of long ago, in class, I feel like a spiritless prisoner, and as soon as I am out, I could dance my way home. Tonight I had to talk to myself a long while; I pleaded, I commanded, I entreated and scolded; and then, with a comforting vision of austere resolution before me, I slowly, awkwardly prepared my lesson: a book review for Mr. Seitz. I chose *Thelma* and felt ashamed to speak with so little spirit of a story I love. I must conquer that impudent little devil who prompts me to rebellion whenever I am *forced* to do a thing. I must remember that the wild flower is free because it deserves it, being beautiful and fragrant; I must remember that everything and everyone who wishes to do exactly as he pleases must first show himself worthy of it, capable of it. I must learn, unless I choose to live like Thoreau, in the solitude of the woods. But then I could not carry out my ideal of being useful in the world, for a hermit's life is selfish; though how contented and happy one must be quite, quite alone.

I could not pin down on these pages my longings for Eduardo's letter. They are as elusive as butterflies, now here, now there (which means now in my heart, now in my head). And I have

[1] *Fourteenth-century Persian lyric poet.*

not the heart to give them a good shaking, as they deserve, for fear of spoiling their delicate wings. I sometimes wonder about the future, wonder who on earth Eduardo's wife is going to be. And how will I feel when he marries? As soon as he finds her (she may be like Thelma), he will completely forget me. Or perhaps long before he finds her. How will I feel when I lose his friendship? It will hurt a great deal, for nothing could equal or surpass it except Love. I will be left alone with my memories, with letters tied with blue ribbons, with faded rose petals pressed in the leaves of a book, and withered arbutus in a basket. Alone. Alone, yes, if love does not come to me.

Oh, what queer, happy thoughts came to me tonight. They now fill the little room, which was so cold and empty a few minutes ago. And who, pray tell me, brought them here? Eduardo, of course. He always glides into whatever place I choose for dreaming, and the very sound of his name opens a secret door to a world of memories and joyous thoughts. He is the Prince of Magicians, but fortunately he cannot, with all his power, guess what I think of him. Someday, indeed, before I die, I will have to bury my thoughts, one by one, in the cold sea so that no one may discover them.

April 21. Tonight I felt the strong and powerful call of the out doors. No, it was not a call; it was more like a loving arm stretching out from the shadows to carry me away. I slipped on a light jacket and glided almost unnoticed from the house. To walk. I walked all alone, dreaming and pondering. I walked under a roof, half sky, half branches, which sometimes reminded me of a great silent cathedral, with the streetlights twinkling here and there among the new leaves like candles. And then the wonderful stillness of the country in the evening.

Dream: A cathedral, white, empty and silent, without statues or altar or organ. And then I enter and walk up the aisle: to pray? A strange prayer comes to my lips, yes. Dear God, I thank you for the trees, and the sweet air, the sky. I thank you for this beautiful life. And then silence again. The lights twinkle, but are they not candles? Silence and darkness. When will the music begin, the angel voices, the majestic roll of the organ? I am alone in the great cathedral. I walk slowly, like a phantom. Finally I am home, and the voices, the steady lights, awaken me from this mystic dream. The cathedral has vanished, but I shall find my way to it again, for I understand God there and I can pray there better than in church.

April 22. Suppose you were going to the theatre with your brother. and suppose you wished for a new hat for the occasion—know what to do? I shall tell you: turn one of your old hats inside out and upside down. I have just made a very pretty one which no new hat could surpass.

April 23. It was *Macbeth* Thorvald and I saw last night, and my dreams were haunted by Macbeth's haggard and bloody face, the witches' shrieks and horrible laughter, the rush of wind, the lightning, each scene of blood and fear stamped upon my memory by that inexplicable trait in my character which makes me so impressionable. Behind us sat a group of schoolgirls tittering and whispering. They laughed softly when someone was supposed to lie dead and yet betrayed the "staging" by the regular rise and fall of his breathing, and they criticized so-and-so's wig, which was *"really* too red," and made other remarks of this kind, to which Thorvald and I listened, sometimes with suppressed mirth. There are really two things of great interest in a theatre: the play itself and the small talk of the audience.

Walter Hampden is an admirable actor: he puts all his heart and soul in his work, and I am certain that at the end he sinks exhausted by this vivid display of the strangest passions of humankind. I felt as if he *suffered* truly, sincerely and deeply whatever he intended to represent. I remember seeing him in *Hamlet* and experiencing the same sensation.

What a life it must be! Night after night to stand upon that stage and pour one's soul into words and actions which are not one's own. Night after night to lose one's self in another character, to be completely and absolutely not Walter Hampden but Macbeth, Macbeth in glory, in temptation, in a torment of indecision and of fear. Macbeth the murderer, the sleepless king, the visionary madman; Macbeth in death. I shuddered when he lay there, his face besmirched in blood, and felt intensely happy to watch him rise and bow to the audience, although he did not smile. How could he? He was still Macbeth; he was still breathing in that world of tragedy created by Shakespeare.

Shakespeare. I am thinking now of that boy, Carnival, I wished to transform. Alas, what a senseless dream. Will I ever read natures with accuracy? I can make nothing of Mr. Carnival.

Yesterday in class I saw what I had secretly feared to see: the absolute, complete, hopeless emptiness and shallowness in him. He said to me, speaking of Shakespeare, that they bored him, those silly plays.

Mother was trying to explain to me how I could not always expect to find intellectual companionship in everyone I met; that there were thousands of plain people with whom I could enjoy myself plainly. "If you are always judging people as if they were going to be bound to you by eternal ties, you will never be popular, my dear," said Mother. "You could be merely nice to Carnival." I know she fears I am going to scare him away by my visions and then I will soon be left alone and neglected. I shall be merely "nice" to please my mother, but for this I must brush aside all my impulses and ideals. It will be difficult, for I am not *naturally* nice. My natural qualities tend more to crankiness, seriousness and pedantry. Poor Carnival does not know what stormy and yet philosophical thoughts lie behind that face of mine, which he happens to think attractive. If he knew, he would turn away disgustedly and classify me with Shakespeare's tragedies.

He calls me the prettiest girl in the class and never fails to turn around fifty times during the session to look at Mlle. Linotte. But beware, poor boy, the queer thoughts of a queer girl are bottomless but very elastic, and they have a way of springing unexpectedly upon some people: in short, I might be tempted some day to make fun of you. Take care!

What is it like to be "nice"? Must one be shy, or bold? Funny or dramatic? Be nice. Be nice. I fear I don't know how. You can be called nice by flattering a little, or by laughing a lot. Sometimes people say you are nice because you agree with everything they say; or because you have a nice dress on, or because you have a pretty face. How shall I be nice? I will try, but I know I will be tempted to be tragic instead.

April 25. I am sitting out on the upper porch, the one that can be reached only by actually jumping out of the window. It is here I used to sit last year, while studying, and this morning when I felt the warm breeze and soft, comforting sunshine I longed to sit again near the treetops and apparently isolated from the rest of the house. I could call this my studio, for it is the fashion now to boast of one's studio. I am certain no studio could be better than this plain porch, with the sky arched overhead for roof, treetops for walls, to save me from inquisitive neighbors. Add to this a stool, freedom to breathe, to sing, to smell the earth and flowers, to hear the birds, to watch the clouds with nothing in your way (for I have no windows to open, no curtains to push aside). What more could a human creature desire?

As to the housekeeping, I have nothing to do. It does not need sweeping, this quaint studio—the rain and wind take care of that—and I need not worry about its appearance in general, for there is nothing I could put out of its place. When I want to leave my studio I pick up my stool and jump in through the window. What use will I make of it? I shall study and read, and write and dream in it.

Yesterday, Sunday, we simply existed, without accomplishing more than that. This morning the postman brought a letter from Father, and I pondered on it while I worked in the garden.

I have had such a terrible dream of Enric, and I feel as if something had happened to him. I think it was two nights ago, he was bruised and covered with blood, and his face, distorted with pain, has haunted me ever since. I remember that I laid my hands on his shoulder and called his name reproachfully. Instantly he became calm, and the terrific anguish left his face, leaving it pale and indescribably sad. "You are too late, Anaïs, too late." How I hope he will soon contradict these evil forebodings. Poor Enrique!

April 26.
Eduardo writes:

Ah, cuisine, I knew you would understand, appreciate, be delighted with, those trailing arbutus. I was pleased to hear you speak of them as a poem—ah, yes, a poem indeed. Did you not find within their fragrance a silent message for thee, written in fragrance not by Nature this time but by someone called "poor cousin?" Alas, I meant to send a eulogy with them, but I forgot, so I have kept it in my diary as a remembrance of Spring and a Princess. I thank you for the pictures. I was delighted with the one of Our house, caressingly covered with a velvet mantle of shadows: everything saturated with romance, the ideal home of a simple Princess, or an angel.

Is it *me* Eduardo calls a Princess or an angel? On a day like this, beautiful beyond description, Eduardo's letter comes to me like the translation of what the trees whisper to one another, of what birds chatter about in the branches. How strange it is! Are these the transports and ecstasies of true friendship? Oh, may the illusion last if it be but an illusion. I have won Eduardo's friendship at last; but I had won it last year also and it was taken away from me, perhaps by a Cuban girl. Will I lose it again? The friendship has proved itself finer than I had ever dreamed, but the ideal shall be shattered if it cannot stand the test of time and absence. And the test will come soon, when Eduardo goes to Cuba, where the lily girl lives. Then, will he forget me? I am so plain, even though he may call me a Princess today.

Eduardo tells me that John Burroughs says of Emerson's work: "He is the philosopher of young men . . . Emerson appeals to youth and genius."

Appeals to youth and to genius! Then in me he has appealed to youth. How strange it is how one finds less when alone, less of books, I mean. With Eduardo I have read Hildegarde Hawthorne, Kingsley's *Hypatia*, and *Journal of Opal Whiteley*, and soon I am to read John Burroughs. But of course, to explore together, one must have the same taste and feeling. We are roused by more or less the same sentiments, guided by the same impulses, influenced by almost the same surroundings, the same persons. And yet, in all our relationships there are always the wonderful contrasts of man and woman. Thus I do believe that I am more constant than Eduardo. I cling to fancies or facts with more tenacity, and although I have not his strength, the strength of manhood, I have a greater power in me, which is that of the woman: her very weakness is her greatest strength. In life I sometimes wonder which of us will accomplish more.

April 27. With Marraine I saw today *The Four Horsemen of the Apocalypse*, staged from Blasco-Ibáñez's famous book. It impressed me so deeply that tears came down my cheeks, foolish, irrepressible tears. I was not the only one, for the tragic horror of the war was brought so vividly, so touchingly before us that it stirred many besides myself. I felt how little of the tragedy I had realized while knitting for the soldiers. How comparatively happy and calm our life was while the Old World bled and struggled fiercely. To me it meant merely Red Cross work and prayer. I worked a great deal, it is true, for my age, but how infinitesimal was my simple work compared to the supreme sacrifices, the heroism, the magnificent daring and recklessness of our beloved soldiers, their families, wives, children, sisters.

When I walked out of the theatre into the dazzling daylight, into the bristling life, into the chattering, laughing crowd animated by the spirit of the season, I was dazed and ashamed of my tear-stained face. All I had just seen passed long ago; it belonged to history. Now I was in another world, one full of sunshine and happiness. My spirits rose quickly.

Love was in that story too. Love, which now makes my blood tingle, my heart vibrate and respond, which brings leaping flames into my cheeks; a great desire to understand it comes to me, which had *never* been there before. And so whenever people love in books, in stories, everywhere, I read and listen. I see them love all around me; I know how they look at each other; no one can hide the look of love. I watch, and I feel a great loneliness. Ibáñez's story is very striking and thrilling, but perhaps the finest quality of it is its tense reality. If it had not seemed so real, my world today would not have been veiled in tears.

Evening. I was thinking now of what Mother and I heard at mission[1] night a few days ago. The preacher was answering written questions from parishioners. One of them was: "Where is Hell? Is it on this earth?"

"I do not know where it is," answered the preacher.

What a terrible life the person who asked it must be enduring to ask such a question. I do not believe in hell at all, however, and still less in hell on this earth of ours. I do believe in something vastly different: that we expiate our faults on earth, by sacrifice and suffering; that we atone for our great weaknesses every day; but that is not the hell of superstitions, the site of flames and physical torture. Such a place does not exist. God could not have created it. He is too infinitely good and forgiving. Yet these are merely my beliefs on a subject which great thinkers, theologians, philosophers and even poets have probed in vain. I only dare to speak of such things in my Diary.

April 29.

Papa Chéri:[2]

. . . As for Thorvald, he reads only books that are necessary for his studies. I have never understood how Thorvald can know everything when he reads so little. He knows a thousand times more than I about history, science, current events, politics—it's unbelievable! I attribute this as much to his intelligence as to the wonderful way he has of judging everything logically. He doesn't

[1] *In Catholicism, a series of religious services to stimulate faith.*
[2] *Letter translated from the French.*

lose his head, and his reasoning gives a quiet balance to everything he learns. I can spend a day reading philosophy (which I like enormously) and Thorvald can spend it playing tennis, yet if we get into a discussion, he immediately throws me off balance. At present he talks to anyone he can corner about Einstein's theory of relativity, and I listen without understanding one word.

I tell you this because you might think you should be sad about Thorvald's attitude toward reading, but you see, there are people who can get along without it. On this point he is not at all like Mlle. Linotte . . . A course in English composition has filled me with hope. It is only in class, where you are surrounded by rivals and severely corrected by a teacher who doesn't know you, that you can tell whether you are good at something. Do you remember my childish aspirations? How I wanted to belong to the Académie française? Think what an earful those venerable gentlemen would give me if they knew! You mustn't tell them! . . . I have to study—above all, I have the complicated task of becoming absolutely natural in a language that is not my own.

About Joaquin: it isn't so much what he plays (Clementi's sonatinas, arrangements of the Bach *Preludes*) as his interpretation of the easiest pieces. The boy has magic in his fingers.

I shall never forget one evening when I was in my room writing down my dreams and impressions, as I do every day. Thorvald was studying in his room, Mother was reading. Downstairs in the living room, Joaquin was at the piano. Suddenly I heard a melody —infinitely sweet, delicate, touching—which filled the house with wonderful sounds. One felt oneself carried away on the wing of a dream, which that child poured like a perfume into the notes.

I thought it was one of the most beautiful pieces of music I had ever heard. I went downstairs without a sound just at the moment his little hands, tanned by the sun and outdoor games, played the final notes. Only the hands of a little boy, not those of a great pianist, and the piece a simple barcarole which could hardly be called a classic, and yet the miracle had happened—we had felt it, experienced it, recognized it. . . .

Anaïs

P.S. Thorvald never takes a good picture; he is much handsomer than he looks in these. I suppose it's because the pictures don't capture the gaiety that sparkles in his blue eyes, the character and frankness in his face, his look of health and happiness. . . . He always looks like a Spring day.

April 30.
To Eduardo:

There is something so fantastic and unreal in our letters that I wonder if someday I will awake to find it was all a dream. Emerson says: "If you are noble, I will love; if you are not, I will not hurt you and myself by hypocritical attentions." What does this mean? I take "noble" to mean lovable, good. Does Emerson mean that it is not right to conquer one's dislike of a person who is not noble? Suppose someone near me is harsh, bitter, cynical, unkind; in short, possessing any of these faults which are so repulsive to me; is it hypocrisy not to openly show my repulsion for the sake of not *hurting* or wounding? Emerson is a great thinker, but this thought is not charitable. Who can tell if this creature may need my "attention" to *make* her noble? Is it kind and thoughtful to turn away from a person because she has no virtues? Are we in this world to think of *ourselves*, our likes, our dislikes, or to help others? And to endure, to make an *effort* to *make* other people noble is not, cannot be, hypocrisy but a way of helping the world, a way of improving it perhaps? What do you think? Do you not think philosophy is sometimes uncharitable? One must not always think, but feel a little too. And it is so cruel to say: "You are not noble, I will not love you." I believe love must not only be given away to those it is easy to love because they are good, or beautiful; no, love is for *whoever needs* it, or at least, that is what Mimi thinks . . .

In a way this has something to do with what you say of people who fly off like a butterfly from a flower devoid of honey. Do you know, Eduardo, I have come to the conclusion that it is selfishness to idealize a person and then turn away because he has fallen short of our ideal. An idealist should first ask himself if he has a right to expect too much from another creature. Is *he* living up to his ideal? Is he himself as good as he wishes the other to be? You can guess what I am thinking of. I idealized someone, then turned away sadly because that someone was full of faults. And suddenly I asked myself: Well, am *I* not full of faults, am I not perhaps far more wicked than that someone? Then I have no right to idealize! I must forgive, I must be tolerant, to expiate for all the times I may have shattered *someone else's dream* of me. I must atone for my own faults by bearing those of other people.

I was thinking of Marcus. Are you surprised? I sometimes do think of Marcus and wonder what has become of him. Will I ever see him again? Does he ever think of me? And what on earth does he think? I feel that I have learned much since we quarreled and I would like to talk to him. At that time I was so awed, so bewildered at the thought that someone could possibly be in *love* with *me* that I was a little afraid of him, so to speak. Now I know that love is natural, possible, and, like lightning, it can strike anyone. I have more self-reliance these days; if he called me "dear child," I would laugh. And I would not be intimidated by his self-assertive manner, his strange conceit. I could endure him better and I would not try to make him into what he is not (to remember what *I* am not). Now that I am so practical, I would simply admire him for the talent which he undeniably possesses. But the humorous side of this short-lived adventure is the fact that Marcus never loved me. Oh, I know the different qualities of love by intuition: fanciful love, selfish love and fickle love, which, compared with true and noble love, should not even bear the name. They are simply results of whims, vanity, self-love and selfishness! All this sounds quite dramatic, and yet while writing I have been laughing to myself. Time heals many troubles and love affairs and gives you a little sense of humor.

Eduardo wrote four words on each petal of a lovely white flower: "Faith, Hope, Love, Charity." And a few nights ago during one of my solitary rambles, I stood on tiptoes to smell the drooping branch of a tree and recognized the flowers. Today I sallied out under a threatening sky and returned with an armful of the delicate dogwood sprays. Now it rains, but I have all the cheeriness imprisoned in the house. White sprays in tall vases, and in the center of the dinner table, a green Japanese bowl full of pansies and daisies. My pansies are specially lovely; they have grown large and have the most beautiful colors imaginable. I love all flowers, but in pansies I find a strange, appealing character. They are thoughtful, reflective flowers, it seems to me. Those that are tinted with purple are plunged in a sad, continuous pensiveness, with a blue that looks dreamy and faraway. When I kneel by them to pick them, I hold them in the palm of my hand, gazing in ecstatic silence at their colors, and then I kiss them softly. It rains; perhaps that is what has suddenly made my spirits droop. I read somewhere of a musician who said he was affected by all the changes in the weather like a barometer. But he was a musician, and had a reason, while I . . .

Later. I believe I have often named Mr. Canterbury. He is going to play a part in one of my school adventures, so I better introduce him to you. Canterbury is one of my classmates in grammar class (he sits next to Carnival). I could not tell precisely how the acquaintance began, but before I knew it he was always accompanying me to the subway as far as 42nd St. We talked of a great many things. He is very much like Jack, a good boy with plain manners and honest ways. I have found out now the way to know when a boy likes you. He will talk about his hobby. And Canterbury told me that he had tamed snakes, small ones, for pets. At first I was horrified. All girls pretend to be afraid of snakes and mice. I pretend sometimes, but I saw that I was not really frightened when he brought one of them to class in his pocket. He held it in the palm of his hand, a smooth, speckled little snake neatly coiled and quiet. I saw how inoffensive it was, at least in his hands, and I believe I am cured of the foolish fear of little snakes. Mind you, *little* ones. I dare not say what I should do if I met a large one in the woods.

Now that you know him a little, I shall tell you that he asked me to go to a dance next Friday, and when I asked Mother's permission, she assented. Thorvald is to bring me back home. The dance is given by the club of Columbia students returned from the war. Holt[1] had told me he would ask me, but he has been sick lately. I have not said yes, yet; but it appeals to my love of adventure. Who knows what may happen? Of one thing I am sure: I shall not meet my Stranger at a dance. Perhaps in some strange, wild place in the mountains, somewhere in the heart of nature. People who like me at dances do not like the real me, and I always want to laugh for the terrible mistake they make. They take me for a butterfly, when I am really a little blade of grass swinging in the breeze! And if I told them this, they would be shocked. The best I can do is to behave myself in a civilized manner, and wait until I come home to you to let my observations flow freely. Thus, if someone talks to me about the weather (and you know that everyone has something to say about this antiquated subject) and says: "It's a nice day," I shall *not* answer: "My dear sir, your power of description is unfortunately excessively poor. This is indeed an enchanting day, such as poets continually praise and mere people admire profoundly. It is a day of exquisite charm which inspires the beholder with sublime thoughts and infinitely noble emotions." No, I shall say: "Oh, my! Yes! Isn't

[1] *A classmate.*

it!" and smile stupidly. Then that person will turn to the other person and whisper in his ear: "She's a 'nice' girl, isn't she?"

Evening. Once in a while I change the position of all the pictures in my room. I call it visiting day; that is to say, I make Stevenson come to visit Mark Twain by placing them near each other, and they have great talks together. Or I shift Mark Twain to the region of a Girl's Face, and I am sure he admires the lovely drawing, etc. I have sketched the spray of dogwood and placed it beneath my Ideal of a Woman and a Young Girl. Now my pictures look down on me from their new abode. I do not give them time to bore each other. In a few weeks I shall change everything once more.

If some fairy godmother appeared before me to ask me what I wished for, and gave me little time to think, I should instantly answer: a little sketch of Walter Scott, and a new cage for my bird. Of course, if she gave me time to think, I would ask for more practical things, and not for myself but for Mother. That is why one must always think before speaking. It would be very queer and lovely if we were rich (I mean if we become rich now, for I am glad we have been poor all these years); then my bird should have a new cage, and I would buy a million books, and plants, and a Japanese garden in a bowl. Mother would have the house painted and roofed and improved. Joaquin would . . . But what's the use? We are happy as we are, united, contented, drawn close to one another by dreams of things we do not have. We love each other and all else is little in comparison.

May 2. It is ten o'clock, and I should be preparing my Argument for school. It was with this idea in mind that I dragged out onto the big porch a ponderous, comfortable chair and nestled in it like a lazy cat. But how on earth is one expected to study or work on such a morning? I cannot collect my thoughts. They are fluttering in the breeze like the leaves themselves. Besides, no one can argue to the tune of an incessant concert: the birds are chattering over their breakfast, and now and then are seen against the cloudless May sky little black-winged specks whom everyone longs to follow. Squirrels trot up and down the trees, waving their tails with more grace and charm than ladies wave their luxurious fans. I throw my notes and issues to one side. Deductions, inductions, propositions and decisions do not harmonize with an illogical mood.

And as I sit here nestled in this big armchair, I look out into the world and think of all my friendships, things and people I love so much that I wish I could hold them to my heart. Eduardo steals softly into my daydream. There he stands now, before me. Oh, I love Eduardo as I love nature and books. There is no one I could ever love in the same way: it is like the love of a sister, a friend, a cousin and a companion blended with the love of nature. I thought of this as I wondered about the joys I take in his letters. Suddenly I told myself: Eduardo, I love you. I love you in a way no creature can understand. It is not the love that real people feel.

A long time ago, do you remember, it was his wish in a game that I should love him. It has come true, but I could never tell him for fear he might misunderstand, for it is not what his family feared when they looked disfavorably upon our friendship. It is something I have created, it belongs to me, and will forever lie a beautiful dream sacred and secret in my heart and in the pages of my Diary.

Canterbury was so curious to know my answer on the matter of the dance that he waited for me at the entrance door of the Journalism Building, where I take my composition class. He could not wait until tomorrow. Tonight I contemplate the prospect with indifference. It does not appeal to me one whit. Beware of my tragic moods. I feel one stealing softly over me. I shall spend the evening reading from Descartes' *Discours de la Méthode* and *Méditations Métaphysiques*.

May 7. Alone in the quiet parlor, curled up on a sofa, with loose hair and a big sweater, I am ready to carry you back to last night's adventure. I could hardly wait to begin dressing, because Wednesday Mother bought me a new dress, and there it hung, little knowing all it was going to see. At last came the time to slip it on. It is made of Copenhagen-blue chiffon, very fragile and light, stirring at each step I took until it made me think of a fairy dancing with veils. Here and there peeped small pink roses. The thought came to me that it resembled a cloud that had fallen from heaven. Add to this the fact that I was illuminated with happiness, radiating from the tip of my curls to the tip of my toes. I met Mr. Canterbury at Pennsylvania Station, and a while later I found myself stepping on the well-polished floor of an immense room with a ceiling arching far over our heads; with nooks in the walls for solemn statues of great men, and a few grave portraits. But they were the only solemn things there, for the music, the lights, the rhythm of the dance, soon set everyone's heart beating to the tune of Foolishness. And of all people, I was the most foolish. My laughter broke out quietly but continuously; and after all, the secret of a happy dance is to have a pretty dress and a happy face: it makes everyone want to dance with you. I danced every time except when Canterbury seemed to prefer a little talk before an empty fireplace, though this corner soon became a group of laughing chatterers, for several boys surrounded me. I was told many bewildering things, such as: "I didn't think you could dance so wonderfully because in class you were so shy that I thought you were a minister's daughter . . ." (Ahem ahem ahem.) But what interested me most was not Canterbury and the dance in itself. I fear it was Carnival. Mr. Carnival was in a mood I had not observed before. At first when he saw me (I was dancing with Mr. Canterbury) he was surprised and admiring, which made all my philosophical resolutions vanish. No one can be philosophical with Mr. Carnival. He watched me as if he had never known this phase of Miss Nin before. When he joined the group around the fireplace, he took my hand and bowed before me with a princely gesture (I do believe he thought me someone else because of my cloudy dress!). Then terribly seriously, respectful, emphatic and *apparently* sincere, he said: "You dance *divinely*." Now where did he obtain that word? Half of me was chatting and laughing, the other half wondering, Does he read poetry? He cannot be very, very ignorant if he can translate his opinions with such elegance. How much does he know? Canterbury later made fun of the word, and said he thought I danced like *that* too. Of course, I had little time to wonder, for the music began to play "Bright Eyes" and Mr. Carnival begged for a dance. And we danced. Or did we fly? I never thought I could dance so well with someone who disdained Shakespeare! And then, oh, the sad interruption, someone "cut in" (please forgive me this terrible modernism). Carnival was greatly displeased. Then Canterbury cut in on the thoughtless person who had spoiled my dance with Carnival, this last one cut in on Canterbury, but was soon driven away by a Mr. McLean, who in turn was replaced by a nonentity. At midnight the lights went out. Of the last dance Mr. Carnival tried to snatch a part, but Canterbury refused and Carnival said he was very mean. Then we rushed to Pennsylvania Station in the subway and there I met Thorvald, who took me home. While brushing my hair before my mirror, I smiled at myself and pondered.

I notice that a few days ago I prophesied a tragic mood, but it was blown away by three days of strong north winds. Hats blown off, and umbrellas turned inside out, ladies holding on to their skirts (in vain, for they puffed out with each gust of wind, fluttered far above the ground and behaved very disrespectfully), hairpins blown away and hair flying on cheeks pink with cold; and all these sights made you feel like a gust of wind yourself, much too light-headed and light-hearted to bear the weight of unreasonable sadness. Strange weather for May, but today warmth and sunshine are slowly, timidly returning. And oh, only the flutter and excitement of these last hours has momentarily effaced the memory of one of my happy moments. Eduardo sent me more flowers, violets and others resembling wild tulips. Of all signs of boyish admiration, his are those I prize most. Is not each addressed to a different thing in me? What makes my present classmates like me? They do not know me. Their liking is based on things that do not count. (They think I am pretty.) Eduardo knows me as I am, inwardly and outwardly, and the inward me does not displease him. There is the miracle.

May 8. I have a literary triumph to share with you. I feel as if you have the right to know that you are not destined to be the Diary of a frivolous, scatterbrained girl. No, rejoice, my patient confidant! I have made a wonderful discovery about Mlle. Linotte's literary possibilities. And this is the way it came about: Even in my Rip Van Winkle world, as far as modern books are concerned, I could not help being rendered deaf by the name of the most-talked-of book of the season, *Main Street*, by Sinclair Lewis. The book stared at me from every bookstall and library; its name was in every mouth. I reached the conclusion that not to read *Main Street* was an offense to Literature. So I bought it with a beating heart, read it and, filled with horror and dislike, paced up and down my room, saying to myself in plain colloquial language: "Now *what* is the *matter* with *me?* Here is a book everybody likes. Why on earth should I be so 'fussy' and old-fashioned? Am I going to be a 'highbrow,' a pedant?" Then sadly I sat by my writing table and scribbled this opinion on scraps of paper: "*Main Street* has given me a thorough, merciless mental shock. But the reaction is a terrible discouragement and sadness: that such a book should be so acclaimed, so popularly received by the American Public. For my part, I confess I do not like it. I confess quietly. I feel so alone in this strange opinion that it must be because of my own stupidity. It pulls you down, drags your spirit into vulgarism, down, down,

down into a black existence in a bleak world. That side of life of which I had never dreamed seemed more like a nightmare. It cannot be true. It is not true, such plainness, terseness, ugliness of style, lack of ideal, of poetry. Taken as a whole, the book stifled me, bored me and saddened me. What has discouragement to do with this severe criticism? The public Sinclair Lewis has pleased is the one I hope to please someday to earn my living. I had never thought of it before, that American public, and there it is, and *Main Street* is the book it wants. Then I can never write. My things would bore them to death. I can write, but not for them. I must seek some other way to live . . . Heaven help me!"

Of course, this was the most pessimistic outlook imaginable. I almost always plunge into despair first: it is a habit. Fortunately, the same thing which pulls me down into the depths, too much imagination, quickly pulls me upward. In a few hours I found myself talking to Frances, and I asked her, "Is *Main Street* typical?"

"It's a type," answered Frances, "but not typical."

"Why has it been so popular?"

"It fell in the hands of good publishers who advertised it widely. The American public does not know what it likes and is glad to be told. It was told that it would like *Main Street*, and so it swallowed it up, merely a fad."

I came home in high spirits. And here comes the climax. Today I read in the Times Book Review a criticism called "A Belated Promenade on Main Street," by Catherine Beach Ely: "Pursued at every turn by echoes of *Main Street* I became the last inhabitant to make its acquaintance. Some presentiment of my own idiosyncrasy must have led me to postpone the ordeal . . . a loan of a friend's copy goaded me to an attempted perusal of the season's wonderwork—attempted is used deliberately, for the writer of this sketch must admit an out-of-tunedness with the infinite of psycho Sinclairism. *Main Street* bored me to extinction. I hated it as one hates stale bread seven days a week . . . murkiness of *Main Street* . . . *Main Street*'s lack of style hurt at every step the reader who is susceptible to ill-written stuff. If these *Main Street* writers would only pick themselves up out of the oozy commonplace and air their souls . . . Such a mud puddle of sordid tattle is *Main Street* . . . Better never write a line than create stuff in which man abandons his struggle for character growth to watch his reflection in a mud puddle."

I have two dances to look forward to, one Tuesday, a charity affair, and the other at Frances's house the 4th of June. Frances coupled me with a young man who, according to her description, is 27 years old, tall, handsome, and a good dancer. After all, a young girl's life is certainly made up of a great variety of things. From literary criticism to dances, and apropos of frivolity, I am wondering how Carnival is going to behave, because he was disappointed at the last dance, and I did not see him after it. There are two psychological questions to be studied here: he may have forgotten all about it, or it may have increased his interest in the minister's daughter who can dance divinely.

May. 9. Quiet, well regulated days are the most difficult to write of. There is a vague serenity, a sweet contentment, in this side of life which no one can understand but he who has led it. I awake early to study and read and sew. Then in the afternoon I go to school with my black schoolbag, neat dress and well-ordered mind. At half past five I am home, and I quickly abandon my books, slip into a gingham dress and allow my poor thoughts to wander as they please. After dinner I steal away into the woods, to walk, to drink all the loveliness of May, its scents, its freshness, its soft, warm breezes, infinitely blue sky and glorious evening. Last night Mother and I went to church in Forest Hills for a short service. The sun was setting while we were walking, and we returned through the darkened forest path with only tiny glimpses of the new moon through the tall, dark trees. My soul seems changed into a leaf, trembling at the slightest touch of air, a leaf which turns always toward the sky, toward the sunshine, toward the stars. And the leaf ponders night and day: Which do I need most? Mine is the problem of the leaf, if the sky were Knowledge, if the stars were Fame, and the sun, Love.

May 11. This is a repetition of: "alone in the quiet parlor, curled up on a sofa, with loose hair and a big sweater." I am ready to tell you about another dance. I do believe there is witchery in this blue dress of mine, and I felt this as soon as I stepped with Mother into the large, brilliantly lit rooms of the handsome Pouch Mansion in Brooklyn, for just think, we went completely alone, and before the evening was half over Mother had danced a waltz with a friend from her youth, and I . . . but let me tell you gradually, methodically. I was waiting with Mother near the entrance for Belica and her escort, Mr. Hernandez, when I noticed two young men wandering through the crowded rooms and staring at me while they wandered. No rude staring, you know, but just a succession of stolen glances. Thorvald had refused to come, so after dancing once with Mr. Hernandez, I sat next to Mother, philosophically prepared to watch the dancers. Across the Blue Room sat the two young men, equally occupied. Once I noticed they were whispering together and before I divined the cause, one of them had wound his way through the dancers and with a mixture of boyish timidity and boldness asked me if I danced. I turned to Mother for advice at this critical stage of affairs; she laughed and nodded, and I was soon dancing my first dance with Mr. Herbert Orces of Ecuador. Of course, the next was with his friend, Mr. Garcia. I danced all night. A few hours had flitted by since we came: my blue dress was casting a spell. It would have been a perfect adventure except that the young men were not very fitted for the part. Mr. Garcia reminded me of Enric, small of stature, with black eyes, and glossy black hair. I could not dislike him because he had pleading eyes and gentle, courteous ways, but I could not like him because he was so young and frail-looking. There is something in me stronger than any judgment or reasoning; it is an admiration of virility, of noble, strong, dominating manhood in man. I abhor a virago, a masculine woman, but I feel just motherly toward a half-developed boy. You see, I am not a little girl any more. Mr. Orces was very nice, more Americanized and more light-hearted than Mr. Garcia, a good dancer, but also extremely boyish (and not much taller than I). He was the first who had asked me to dance. Both asked for my telephone number, and wish to take me to the theatre. I felt so sorry at all the mischief caused by my blue dress that I was glad to escape at midnight though the dance was not finished. I hope they will forget me quickly.

I am having trouble with Canterbury just now. Yesterday he invited me enthusiastically to another dance at the Hotel Pennsylvania on the 26th, and I said I would ask Mother, knowing, nevertheless, that I cannot accept. I cannot continue, or rather increase, a friendship for which I care very little. It is not fair, and I love fairness in my dealings with men. It is so cowardly to take advantage of what heaven has given woman to please and charm. Cowardly and contemptible. I have observed that it is very easy to please men and boys. It is a pity to demolish these illusions, and I, who cherish my own ideals, I, at least, shall try not to destroy theirs.

May 13. Mr. Orces did not forget. He telephoned yesterday. He could not understand me very well so I asked him to write, and in my answer I shall tell him what Mother decided I could do: ask him to come to visit me. He wanted to invite me to the theatre. an idea Mother emphatically condemned. I can still hear him say: "I have been dreaming of you all these days." Oh, that terrible blue dress. I shall tremble at wearing it from now on, but it might bring my Stranger to me.

I do not know if I told you about the last task imposed upon us for English composition: an argument of about 2,000 words. I have struggled long over it, but toward the end my pen caught fire, figuratively speaking, and spread flames all over the pages. I terminated with a flourish and contemplated this unique feat of a poet's life: that of somehow finding a way to appear logical for ten minutes. Truly, while my argument lasts, there is spread before you a clear enough field of debatable issues, proofs by inductions and deductions, appeals to feeling and reason, psychological and abstract theories, heated and reasonable refutations and finally a practical, almost balanced summary. We discussed the Honor System, a modern method of discipline, for our modern schools. Naturally, I took the conservative side of the argument and pleaded for my old-fashioned principles. Mrs. Norman's criticism of it is that it betrays my "visionary character."

May 14. Behold the world under a shower. Behold the postman approaching under his umbrella. What brings he for the phantom-like person watching behind the curtains? Not a letter from Eduardo, whose silence cannot be forgetfulness because it has been twice broken by the gift of wild flowers. No. It is Herbert Orces, who writes: "Every minute since I met you I have been thinking of the wonderful girl you are . . ." etc., etc. No one will ever understand the contradictory sides of my nature. At a dance all my seriousness and pedantry vanish. I become someone which part of me observes with wonder and surprise and does not recognize. And whoever watches me believes that I am wonderful and nice. But afterward, when I leave aside my frivolous dress, when I dress simply and sit by my desk to write, then the transformation has come. I retreat far into my shell and remain sadly brooding there for hours. And who could like me thus? Yet it is my true self who sits apart from the world, and who thinks painful thoughts. Deep down in my heart, for instance, I do not like boys. And lately so many of them have invaded my serenity of mind.

I studied them while they were my classmates, and now in a few days I shall see no more of them, for my course of studies ends. I can truthfully say I have studied four subjects at Columbia University: Composition, Grammar, French and Boys. I am glad to rid myself of both grammar and boys. Still, I try with all my heart to resemble other girls, to get interested. And then what happens? Boys, like Herbert Orces, believe me to be like other girls. If my acquaintance with him is to continue, he will, at some time or other, discover how I am made or realize that I am impossible. With all my faults, there is another which makes me suffer greatly; it is my absent-mindedness. I have always known it, felt it and tried to conquer it. However it towers far above my other traits and becomes more marked each day. Soon I shall become unbearable and will have to hide in the woods.

Do you think I was kind yesterday when I refused to let Canterbury accompany me on a visit I was to make? I felt I could not bear his company, while feeling grave and inexplicable. He was puzzled and slightly disturbed, but I did not care and I almost fled from him. Oh, no one can understand, and I hope no one will try, for to examine me closely is the beginning of a succession of sad discoveries. One thing I must add. Speaking of boys excludes Eduardo completely. He is not quite real, I often find, because he resembles so greatly some dream of mine who breathes and moves; and dreams come and go. Eduardo cannot be a part of my real life, for in reality, almost always, people meet naturally and simply in real places. We two meet on mountaintops, are brought together by gusts of wind, and our thoughts melt into one another like passing clouds.

May 15. Such a Sunday as this is like a whisper of some other world, a foretaste of a life which must exist somewhere: all serenity, peacefulness and piety. We began today by receiving holy communion at the little chapel of Forest Hills, returning under a pale sunshine which had finally decided to appear, brushing aside a tender mistiness which hung above us and soon gave way to all the triumphant brilliancy of a perfect May day. For a while Miguel's sparkling personality troubled a scene set for dreaming, but he left us after dinner, and Mother and I soon found ourselves absorbed in our books, rocking softly on little rocking chairs on the porch. Mother plodded her weary way through the irksome pages of *Main Street*, while I forgot all the world in the company of Oliver Goldsmith, [David] Garrick and [Samuel] Johnson.

framed in a story called *The Jessamy Bride,* by [Frank] Frankfort Moore. Oliver Goldsmith was idealized in the kindly pages, and this alone made me love the book as one loves someone who loves one's friends.

We interrupted ourselves only to take a long, beautiful walk through the woods. The benches, the solitary trails, were full of lovers. I felt no desire to be in their place. I long for something loftier than those clasped hands and whisperings. A love both free and wild. I cannot define the hazy idea which has penetrated into my mind. Perhaps it is a mere illusion I have about my love —that if it comes to me, it should be vastly different from all loves, great and strange, undescribably pure, magnificent, indestructible. It should be blended also with my treasured Books and my worship of Nature. Can anything be greater than such a perfect union—of things that endure forever and of which no one could ever tire? When I hear of people who weary of each other, I believe it is because they have sought virtues in themselves alone, attractions of physical beauty. Have they based their love on each other's thoughts? Who can weary of thoughts which change every day?

Miguel was bragging that he would marry late, that he would conserve his liberty, his peace, as long as possible; that women were made to amuse and that to love one continually was impossible, as if marriage were a sad imprisonment, as if constancy were a heavy, unbearable chain. Did not Charles speak in nearly the same way? Poor young boys who know not the infinite charm of companionship. To amuse? We were not made for that alone. Heaven knows what burdens Woman bears in this world. Heaven also knows the tenderness of Woman's heart, which makes it capable of more kindliness than man's. I wish almost that it were not so, for few men, I believe, understand. They think we are romantic. Miguel and Charles will probably feel someday the need of a woman to complete their lives, though they may now feel quite satisfied with their own selves for friend and playmate.

Mr. Garcia telephoned while I was not home. Alas, this little book, which I desired to dedicate to study and seclusion, to seriousness and thought, is filled with things further away from my heart and true liking. Before I part with you, you are destined to endure the description of two dances. Something else, too, has been planned that greatly troubles me. I long for solitude, for the regulated and calm intimacy of our family life, but Miguel will spend the month of June with us. Solitude! Solitude! All my heart cries out for it. My physical endurance seems to end with the end of my studies. I have done little in reality and it is appalling to notice what changes have come over me lately. My face is white and transparent, my eyes, wide and tired. Mother worries, which makes me long for good health. Otherwise I do believe I should not care a whit. There is only one little pleasure gleaming afar in my plans for the future, a true and deep pleasure which may come to me if Eduardo spends a few days here before going to Cuba. But nothing has been said. If he were here all June, instead of Miguel, would I long to escape?

May 16. I have taken my final examination in English composition and French literature. Both were incredibly simple. However I made a terrible mistake which makes me blush whenever I think of it. After I had successfully answered all the questions, I found myself confronting my Waterloo. For a while I knitted my brows in deep thinking, but of what use is thinking to me? I was to give the definition of "syllogism" and "induction." I wrote stupidly about both and particularly about induction, of which I completely reversed the meaning.

When I left that class I felt regret at the thought of leaving Mr. Seitz. He has been one of my kindliest teachers, and although he made little distinction between the class and Mlle. Linotte, I felt helpfulness and interest in his very silence since the day he spoke to me of my "style."

"I shall try to come back to you in the Fall," I said.

"I will not be here then, Miss Nin, but I hope we'll meet again somewhere."

Suddenly I became my old self again. My tongue refused to move and I wanted to fly. And so I left Mr. Seitz without thanks, awkwardly and frightened at the boldness which made me approach his desk. I thought I had conquered the absurd reserve of long ago, but it has come back often lately during my school life.

After the examination in English, I took half of the required questions in French. The other part follows on Thursday. Here also I found myself pleased with the familiar sound of questions I did not fear. I wrote about Voltaire, Victor Hugo, Lamartine, Alfred de Vigny, giving a quotation from each, an opinion and review of Zadig.[1] I returned early, contented and joyful, to find that my answer to Mr. Orces's letter had traveled in the depth of my pocket, forgotten and neglected during a whole day. To-

[1] Zadig or Destiny, *by Voltaire.*

morrow it is the turn of grammar, and I bid farewell to Canterbury, Carnival, and the rest of my honored classmates.

Evening. I was taking notes from *The Jessamy Bride;* all my interest centered on its lovable pages. Gradually a strange thought came to me as I sat here reading and writing. That story was like a story in my own life, one of my love stories, and I knew someone once who resembled Oliver Goldsmith vaguely. Who can explain the changes which come over people as time goes by? For my part, I know that now I judge the same things in a vastly different way than I did years ago.

I have not forgotten Marcus, but my way of thinking has changed immensely. I remember him as I saw him first, at Dorothy's dance. I was blind to all things that night except to that gleam of intelligence I had caught in his eyes and the contrast of his speech with that of other boys.

Then came his fine, eloquent letters. They appealed to all my preferences for talent, for poetical emotions, poetical understanding of life. Together we loved literature and poetry. How well Marcus wrote. And how well he wrote of Love!

We met seldom. I was still blind and I did not see *him* but his talent. I was hurt because Mother and Mrs. Thayer made jest of his outward traits. I remember being obliged to wear low-heeled shoes. Marcus was not as tall as I. One day we did stand, like Oliver Goldsmith and Mary Horneck, before a mirror together. But here lies the great contrast. Marcus did not think of the pathetic comparison Oliver Goldsmith made. He looked at himself *complacently*. He, with his frail body, his ungraceful movements and unattractive face. Still I admired him. I believed his physique was not well developed because he studied too much. I did not feel his lack of manhood, I dwelt on his knowledge of books. He was not strong enough to protect me, but he was eloquent enough to stir me. His poems to me seemed to replace well the qualities of other boys who excelled in sports, in feats of strength and agility. We passed hours together when I visited his school. I felt something then which I did not write in my Diary, for I was trying to like Marcus in return for his love. His classmates mocked him and thought little of me because I was his friend. His aunt had gestures of contempt for the friendship I showed the unhappy boy. But I soon knew the true, true Marcus. The last hours spent together stifled me. Besides, Eduardo was here then, saw him, and talked earnestly against him. Still, I clung faithfully to my poet. I brushed aside all comparisons of Marcus with my cousin, my cousin whom I began then to love.

I struggled with all feelings of repulsion for the defects I had refused to see. Then Marcus himself freed me from the painful ties by an act of sadly ridiculous and presumptuous jealousy. I do not mean to compare Marcus with Oliver Goldsmith. Heaven forbid! It was simply a few chance lines which reminded me of him, an allusion to how the poet makes songs of man's passions, thoughts sprinkled here and there in a story in which a Poet is the Lover. Merely this and nothing else, for I love Goldsmith, a man "of such sweet simplicity that every word he spoke came from his heart," while for Marcus I have only the faded remains of a girlish admiration.

May 18. This day marks the beginning of a new life. When I returned from school yesterday, after having taken my examination in grammar, I employed my time thus: in tying all my papers together with red ribbons, my themes in blue ribbons, and burying them at the bottom of a drawer with other manuscripts. Then I sat by what I call my desk and sketched the books and authors I intend to study during the summer.

After dinner I sallied out for a walk in the twilight, and there in the solitary roads skirting the shadowy woods, I made many plans and dreamed many dreams.

At first I asked myself what I had learned in the university. I placed all the answers to this question in a corner of my mind. Then for a few minutes I dwelt on the number of things I did not know. Then I compared, and became perplexed. Still, as I walked with my face upturned toward the sky, I thought of all I had to say, of all the things stirring within me. Inexperience, youth, all seem things which I must conquer, alone, and only one comforting thought remains, that I have learned the rudiments of my art and that I shall spend the summer writing. I know the first laws of the trade. Why should I shrink and stand back and doubt myself? All around me people are writing my thoughts, my ideals, my observations. I read books of which I might have written a few pages. I thought of the Essay on Self-Reliance, and, tramping through dusty roads at twilight, I formed many resolutions.

All winter I have sat by my desk and filled numberless pages, but each time my work did not satisfy me I tore it into fragments, all except my themes for school and my Diary. I have in reality spent half my life at my desk when not studying or in college. I say that today marks the beginning of a new life because it marks the end of my studies and of those hours spent in my room. From now on I begin new studies without teachers, and I shall live on the porch. Maytime, sunshine, balmy evenings and cool dawns, and with them comes the great longing to live outdoors. Therefore I have abandoned my blue nest for this porch, where I shall spend many hours and on which I shall write a great, great deal. I shall write all things which come into my head, while the rest of me goes about not knowing what it is doing, to the great despair of all the family. It is a fact that when I do not seem to have a head for anything, when my absent-mindedness draws indignation from all quarters, it is a fact that this is the time when a thousand thoughts are rushing into it, into a head which apparently contradicts all human notions held about a head. But ah, there are heads and heads. Mine is an unpractical head, therefore practical people think I have none. That is the way of the world.

The porch itself I will describe to show you whether the writer draws his inspiration from his surroundings or from within. It is a very long and wide enough porch which runs alongside of the house and a little along the front, not like the "broad smile" of the heroine's porch I have been reading about, but resembling a half-suppressed smile because the house knows it needs painting. The color of my porch is nondescript. It might have been white in the days of the spinning wheel, it might have been gray, or cream-color, or yellow, or green a few years ago. Now it is some mellow and restful tone of which historians alone can trace the origin. As a protection against intruders (whether tramps or mosquitoes), it is enclosed in a screen. Surrounding it stand many tall trees, with wide-spreading branches nearly touching the edge of the roof. If I look away my gaze loses itself where the road, after climbing upward, takes a sudden downhill turn, and as far as I can see, trees and trees and trees in rows and groups stand all around me, with here and there a patch of blue sky or a cloud peeping between the branches. And that is all. The neighbors are shut off by trees; my porch seems almost like a nook in the middle of a vast forest, with its tranquil, secluded appearance, its simple homeliness and comfort. Here I can attack the world or praise it. I can paint human nature or distort it. I can philosophize, or chatter without intelligence. I can reason like a poet or versify no better than a woman of affairs. I can use all the ink I wish, I can try your patience, I can waste time and paper. I can do nothing. I can do *everything*. Did you ever ask yourself why I, like everyone, do not use contractions in writing my Diary? Such as "I'll," for I will, or "hasn't" for has not, etc. I have often asked myself. It seems pedantic to use such chosen English to speak of everyday life. I want you to know another fault of mine. The English I use to chatter with you is *not chosen*; it is the one which comes to me most naturally, and the kind I love best; though all the world may say the contrary, it seems to me that in using "I can't," or "I ain't" continually is to fall gradually into the use of another language—call it colloquialism, slang, whatever you wish, but not English. And yet this is not my most important reason. I also do not use colloquialisms because I do not know how to spell their contractions! Laugh if you will; if you have learned to spell "presumptuous" and forgotten the spelling of "fresh," is it not better to use the former? And oh, how seldom I approve of slang. Some of its phrases I know to be forcible and direct, but they sound to me like an argument won by blows instead of reasoning. Of course, I admit good English would seem out of place in the mouth of a tramp or newsboy; slang is well fitted for those who use it. But colloquialism is only a little step above it, and I do not believe those who love Stevenson, Walter Scott and Washington Irving can love colloquialism. Can those who have tasted the choicest delicacies of food imaginable accustom themselves to a jug of water and a dusty piece of dry bread?

Evening. I have always thought of my mother as the woman nearest perfection in the world. I have admired thousands and thousands of things in her: her optimism, her courage, her unselfishness. It would take books to speak of her as she deserves. But this time it is Mother's philosophy I admire. Today I come to you with a surprise, a thing I had never dreamed of looking for in my busy little mother, whose head I thought to be always filled with business propositions and schemes. I come to you so spellbound by my discovery that although it would take me hours to set down on paper properly the long conversation we held while walking through the woods, I shall tell you all I am capable of transferring on paper.

Of course, I did the questioning. I am so full of questions that sometimes they overflow, and this time the flood almost drowned Mother. Millions of questions poured upon her, quickly, voluminously, deafeningly. I asked and asked and asked, often unreasonably, at other times plunging into depths which somewhat startled her. I railed against Destiny, against Injustice, against the continuous struggle we undergo for existence. I asked the use of suffering, of vicissitude, the use of living, the use of learning. I asked first if man *was* useful, if all things were useful. Why live, and study, and struggle to be good, virtuous, unselfish; why seek the answer to problems; why suffer so much—to then die? All for what? Mother answered that vicissitudes and all the sufferings were imposed upon us in order to teach us. Teach us! For a while I listened to Mother, Mother who has suffered immensely, tell me that all things had a purpose and that all things were created for some use; suffering taught us endurance, unselfishness, courage, a thousand things. I agreed. Then we learn by suffering.

And why do we study, and read, etc.? To learn. Then the purpose of life is to learn? But what is the purpose of learning? To help those coming after us. Then the purpose of life is doing as much as possible for others, to give your best to the world. I pondered.

Then I returned to my first question: "You say all created things are useful?"

"Yes."

"Of what use is the criminal?"

"To show us the contrast between the bad and the good. As an example, you would not know what is bad unless you saw it."

I pondered again and talked awhile about this. "Why are we given intelligence to ask questions which are not soluble by human intelligence?"

"All these things we do not know keep us busy thinking. We must have something to do during all these years of life. That is why we are puzzled, and why we must work to earn a living. Do you think I could be happy if I did not have this perpetual going and coming, the ups and downs of my business, the difficulties of bringing up children, to keep me from brooding on little sorrows of no consequence?"

To myself I imagined God looking down upon this world as I would look upon a doll house. How small our passions seem to Him. We, in his hands, railing against the invisible, the inevitable, are not worthy to be pitied but are in need of help.

Sometimes I wonder if, after all, the answer to all these feverish questions lies in the blessed resignation taught by the Catholic faith. Resignation, to realize our littleness and know that whatever befalls us is planned by an infinite Mind. How beautiful it is to believe, to smile, to confide, and hope! Sometimes it is good to fly from too much pondering and find refuge in Christian faith.

Mother answered all my questions, and unconsciously laid bare before my eyes the selfishness of my doubts. Cease asking human reasons for things not made by man. Yes, I must only remember we are here to give to the world. If others had not thought so before, they would not have left us the very books I treasure, paintings, sculptures, music, inventions, all the products of genius.

Mother has been a glorious mother. All she has done alone, with her fine mind and plucky body, stands as the best of her philosophy, the philosophy of action. What a lesson for me. I, with all my presumptuous demands, my Lilliputian indignations and expectations, I do not deserve a noble, clever mother who can explain my puzzles, soothe me, teach me, set order in my chaotic mind and calm my ruffled spirit. I deserve to learn by painful years of severe experience. Indeed, the entire world gives me more than I deserve, and if I could only keep my own faults in mind, I would be more charitable, more tolerant of others and not so alarmingly inquisitive and critical. And now that I have preached to myself, by way of penance, I shall go to bed and give myself a good scolding instead of thinking about Eduardo.

May 20. Many strange moods have followed my outburst of cynicism of the other night, and I do believe I have learned a lesson. Dear Diary, you were chosen to be the confidant of the oddest girl in the world, and a very wicked one besides. And yet these days I have understood myself perhaps better than during all the years that have gone by. For a while I have stood completely revealed, to be judged not by the standards of the world but according to my own laws and ideals. This revelation caused me great suffering. It showed me my absolute worthlessness, my contemptible subjection to moods and my distorted understanding of life.

How well it has been said of Emerson that he is the champion of the secret and suppressed heart. He is also one who teaches you sane thinking, calm contemplation and self-control. I shall tell you how I came to find him when I needed him most. When I talked with Mother I felt a great admiration for her sturdy, practical sanity and balanced judgment. I admired the way she stood far above the shameful slavery of feeling—uncontrolled feelings, I mean. I admired also the way she told me to live simply and trustfully without prying and questioning. I looked up to her glorious smile, to the smile of optimism, of confidence, of action, then down upon my ungratefulness and stupidity, feeling that her philosophy was above my understanding.

I was plunged in a fathomless abyss, tortured by a continuous self-study which I now realize to be the basest act of egoism. An egoist! I began life with a thirst for knowledge, I traveled on with my questions and observations, but accomplished nothing, nothing. Somewhere I took a wrong turn in the road, and all this time I was trying simply to disguise the clearest signs of egoism, calling them studies of the world! For hours I dwelt upon these thoughts and ended always by saying: I have done nothing, nothing. I must retrace my steps. I must begin at the beginning, and with my new understanding, I must face life once more. What blinded me all these years was the constant brooding on my own self. I will forget myself. I must forget myself. For hours I suffered more than words can tell.

I attended school for the last time, as one in a trance. Then came my salvation. On the train I opened Emerson's *Essays* listlessly, and my eyes fell on the first line of the Essay on Experience. How thankful I was for these pages. I took refuge in their serene sturdiness with all the eagerness of one caught in a great storm who has found a shelter.

Emerson says: "To fill the hours, that is happiness: to fill the hour and leave no crevice for repentance or approval . . ."

Each day I have filled my hours, but I have voluntarily set aside a crevice for repentance or approval. In your pages I have done my thinking. That is why I suffer more in you. I used to think that thinking was pleasant. Thinking hurts. And the greatest fault of my thinking is that it is influenced by my changing moods, by my vast capacity for courting suffering, by my intense sensitiveness. Emerson says, "There are moods in which we court suffering, in the hope that here, at last, we shall find reality, peaks and edges of truth . . ." Such thinking as I do makes a pessimist, a cynic or a madman. But I have realized it in time. I have my idealism to help me struggle against those horrible masters, who shall never get the better of me while I live and while I have Emerson for a friend. Emerson! Emerson! Perhaps you understand the great malady in my spirit better than anyone in the world, for you have written as a great doctor writes when he has humanity in mind. Or perhaps only youth. Youth who knows so little and wants so much, youth who gives nothing and expects everything.

These days of suffering, then, of turning around thoughts which are circles and have no end, have changed me greatly. They may mark a change in my Diary. If, before, I lived one hour, then quickly fled to you in order to analyze that hour, I shall now always live, forget myself, forget my worthlessness instead of brooding on it and accomplishing nothing toward atoning for it.

This constant introspection, this constant dissection and analysis, has come to an end. I thought to derive happiness from this watchfulness. By keeping a mental judgment court before which all my being stood forever explaining itself, by prying into the most secret recesses of my heart, by approving or doubting, by brooding on the past and contemplating the future, I have almost killed the flame of life. I have watched it tremble, stifled by darkness and lack of air. I have called it bad health, as the color left my cheeks.

No. It shall not be killed. I am going to fill every hour; I shall sew and read and walk and dance. I shall never sit idle, with head thrown back wearily, with hands clasped, brooding, brooding, brooding. To live! To live like other girls, to have a light heart and a happy face and for a while to shun my own company, to forget myself, to cease being different, and queer, and serious. Even in school I have stood apart and distant. Pride and reserve stamped upon my attitude, until, as I look back now to days which shall never return, I see that though I have received proofs of admiration, of respect, and boyish desires for a word, a kind look, I have not been treated as a girl, as a plain, friendly girl, but as a queenly, distant oddity whom it is dangerous to approach and whom no one would care to speak to if I were not pretty enough to encourage them. This confession comes at the end of another volume.

May 24. I went to a club dance and suffered intense longings for my books and isolation. This, only a few hours after promising myself to be like other girls. I cannot change myself in one day, alas! As I have always done, I shall continue to pour all the reflections of my follies in your pages, freely, sincerely, impulsively. As to my attempts at sociability and frivolousness, you and I shall laugh together at the pathetic results, as we have always done in the shelter of my room in the evening.

Let me examine my conscience: I have not done so for 4 days because you were not there to help me. I had not bought you yet! You may laugh at today's extravagance. I spent the entire morning book-hunting in the city and came back with Thoreau's *Walden* and Carlyle's *Hero Worship* (which cost me 60 cents). And I brought you back, but it would be a shame to tell what I paid for you. The world does not know your value; they look at your blank pages, your simple cover, and decide your worth in weight and appearance. If I told the shopkeeper that your pages have the magic gift of listening, he would laugh in my face.

May 25. I have lived this day in memories, because suddenly I decided that I would put some order in my papers. I knelt before my manuscript drawer and threw its contents on the floor. At the bottom of the drawer I replaced in neat mountains some stories and sketches whose very stupidity saved them from destruction. I want them to remind me of my girlhood—infancy, I should say, since some of them were written when I was nine. The greatest part of everything, I tore into fragments and dashed into my scrap basket. I could scarcely suppress my mirth at those foolish attempts. There was even a story I wrote when I had just learned enough English for everyday use—when I forgot or missed the word in English, I simply said it in French. And what English! What stories! Even my latest fragments of poetry, my unfinished attempts, breathe only inexperience and lack of talent.

My mocking and critical attitude was tinged with sadness. When I rose I looked thoughtfully at my little heaps of ink and paper and soliloquized: "I shall never make any practical use of my writing. It is all rubbish!" At my age I have done nothing to be proud of, while Mother works all day. These days I have turned many thoughts in my head and come to the conclusion that in my case writing is not sensible. It would be selfishness to pursue such an illusion. Were I exceptionally talented, it would be different. As it is, I have merely the facility for expression and the love of writing, which comes to me by inheritance. Grandfather was a scholar, although rather a poor one. Father is a critic and a champion of musical opinions and is accustomed to using his pen when he is not at the piano. I have ink in my blood. But must I take it for granted that I possess their talent? It is true that in school I have done good work and quickly learned the rudiments of the craft. But Columbia has taught me, in a way I cannot explain, that whatever power I possess, it is not that of pleasing and entertaining. No one has told me, but I know that my style is tedious, stilted, voluminous. I know that I have a tendency toward moralizing, which, at my age, is a thing that sorely tries older people's patience.

Therefore I shut all my ambitions in that drawer, for a little while, and I went with my troubles to Mrs. Norman.

"I want to work, to help Mother, to act usefully and seriously."

Mrs. Norman says I do many of the things (sensible and foolish) that she did at my age, so she sympathizes readily. I had to speak with her because whenever I broached the subject with Mother, she has emphatically condemned the idea. Mother is too kind and does not think me strong enough, but I am determined not to be useless. In talking, we found that I can do either of two things: I can care for little children, teach them French and tell them stories; or I can pose for head and hands. Are you surprised at the latter? It is because I never told you of one of my adventures at Columbia. It was too—too—complimentary! I met a painter, a young, handsome and intelligent-looking boy in my composition class. He was very attentive and filled his sketch book with pictures of Mlle. Linotte. On the last day I was running up the stairway and collided with him. He looked so absolutely pleased that I will always think of him as a study of manly contradiction. Imagine anyone being pleased at such a time. However, he gave me his card and said very seriously: "If someday you would condescend to visit my studio, I would convince you that there is no face in the world so fitted to inspire a picture as yours —your madonna face." I suppose I looked so frightened that he added very earnestly, "Please, please don't be angry. I am only telling you this for the sake of art. Goodbye!" He extended his hand with so much gentlemanliness that somehow I found courage to smile and place mine into it. Instead of pressing it, he began to examine it! "A dreamer's hand, a poet's hand." This time all my shyness vanished. It was so funny to have anyone praise my hands, little knowing all the dishes they have washed! How did he not guess? But I kept my mirth to myself, and with a quick movement I fled, while my painter watched me with a curious smile. Halfway home I glanced at his name on the card and tore it into shreds. And that was the end of the adventure.

Still, when I told it to Mrs. Norman, to whom Mother had already spoken of [Francisco] Pausas, the Catalonian painter who wanted me to pose for him, she caught the idea and said it could be truly carried out. She knows an Art Alliance where I can register and wait until needed. Earn money! Bring whatever I can earn to Mother! Help her with her burden. Just think, for a few days we have lived in the dreadful fear of losing our home. Mother could not pay, and the Kew Gardens Corporation threatened and barked. She feared, besides, the loss of her credit. But during the crisis her marvelous mind has wrought a plan—a new way to earn money—and it has all the signs of proving successful. The idea is growing gradually into the cleverest of Mother's attempts. Oh, I wish to be rich only for her sake. Whatever little I do is for her, and we need money for our home, for Joaquin's school, his piano lessons, for Thorvald. Supposing I alone could earn enough for Joaquin's piano lessons, I would be so happy! I can see my face in the mirror—my curious, old-fashioned face. I can fancy myself telling stories to little children.

There is little pride in the thought of using the features heaven has given me or my love for children as ways of earning money. How I wish I could use my *mind*, my thoughts, my pen; perish the thought! I am not clever enough, and in this case the means *do* justify the end!

Evening. I fear I have lost myself; I have lost myself since the day I told about my longing to shun my thoughts; they tormented me until I grew to fear them. I have lost myself since I promised myself that I would "live," that I would "fill the hour," and leave no crevices for repentance or approval. My attempts failed a few hours later. Alas! I suffered more at the club dance than during all my hours of meditation. I shall try something between the two extremes, between continuous brooding and solitude and frivolous hours of social activities. I want to find myself again —my queer self, any self, but I cannot remain as I am tonight.

Eduardo has again broken his inexplicable silence by a token of remembrance. He sent me a telegram: "Ever am, Eduardo." I realize now that he is one of the causes of my sadness. In my conversations with Mrs. Norman, somehow his name came up, and because of a phrase she let fall I asked her what she thought of him, wonderingly.

"He is very attractive, very handsome, but something in his eyes, his expression, leads me to believe he rather 'likes the girls,' that he is somewhat fickle, what you might term a 'lover' by nature."

"Do you think he is spiritual in his ways?" I asked.

"No. I rather fancy he is inclined toward the contrary. He is indolent by nature, and I fancy, too, fond of being loved and spoiled."

We talked of other things, but it was of this alone I thought, standing by the window and listening to the heavily falling raindrops.

"Do not take him seriously," added Mrs. Norman, laughing.

Mother told me, "Do not believe him."

Marraine has told me, "Do not take him too seriously."

And I am giving him the best in me, confiding in him, trusting him with my secrets, my opinions, my dreams. In my letters I give him proofs of the most sacred friendship. And with all this, will he prove fickle and forgetful? He is a rich man's son. With all that wealth can give, with beauty and charm and intelligence, will his life be a mere satisfaction of all the desires of the senses? His father's life has been thus.

Inheritance—do I not know its awful power? And still, to see Eduardo now, to compare him with the hard, unfeeling man his Father is—Eduardo, the only one in the family with artistic temperament; the only one with an understanding of books, nature, and music; loving, unselfish. Can the lower instincts triumph over all these? I suffer with the problem because it is my desire, my sincerest longing, to see Eduardo happy, to see him develop into the finest, noblest example of manhood. I know that real, true, lasting happiness does not come from the senses but from the intellect—the spirit. No one could understand the ambitions I have for him, for what he may achieve. I feel in a strange way that he, too, has deposited the best in his nature in my hands, has entrusted his ideals to me, and I am responsible for him. I must be ready to help him, rise above the doubts which all others entertain of him. I believe in him. I believe in him—until he himself tells me with his own tongue: "I am a sensualist." Only a boy! And I shall be his big sister while his fancy for me lasts. While his liking for Mimi lives, I can conquer his weaker self. I shall only surrender him the day he marries Perla or some other lily girl of Cuba.

May 26. I have found myself again, but it was not until I returned from the city in the afternoon, until I took my hat off and sat on the edge of my bed, wondering how I could fill the hours to come. And suddenly I forgot myself, my imaginary troubles, my sorrowful musings, and with a beautiful piece of old lace, a bunch of tiny roses, a frame, I made a beautiful hat for Mother. That finished, I transformed the porch; ordered Flora to bring a little wicker table from the attic; placed pillows on the rocking chair, books and magazines on the tables; flitted in and out of the garden and picked pansies with which I made a center-piece for the dining table and another for the porch table. In a few minutes I gave the house an air of care. And then, smiling, contented, I brought you down to the porch to tell you my secret: to find yourself, work for others, forget yourself.

I am so happy. Each minute I jump up to see if Mother is coming home. The surprise I have for her doubles my desire to see her; my pleasure is increased at the thought of the one I have reserved for her. When I contemplate how selfish I have been all this time, I shudder—but wait, I shall atone for it.

I went to the city because Mother wanted me to meet Georgina Menocal, the daughter of Cuba's ex-president. We found her asleep, and after waiting a long time I finally found myself shaking the hand of a pleasant and affectionate girl of about my age and yet with far greater ease of speech and manner than I ever dreamed of possessing. I saw her briefly, for she was hurry-ing off with her grandmother to the services at the cathedral. To-day is Corpus Christi, one of Spain's lovely and picturesque holi-days, the details of which I could never forget. Do you know, the sitting room where I waited was like a garden of red roses. Bunches far greater than my arms could hold were scattered in big vases. They represented so much money (Mother works so hard to earn a little) that I could not enjoy them. not as I enjoyed the few given to me once.

"What do you think of them?" Mother asked.

"I would not like so many at a time," I answered.

For hours afterward the scent of roses followed me, and I pondered on the unhappiness which sometimes comes with wealth —to have too much of lovely things until you lose the love you have for them; for is not half the pleasure of life *wishing, desiring?*

May 30. We had visitors Sunday and I was quite sociable. The day before, Mother and I had gone to an absurd musical tea at the Waldorf, to the moving pictures in Richmond Hill in the evening. Today Miguel and Marraine are here, and after dinner we are going out again. I have just stolen a few minutes for myself be-cause I noticed that Mother and Marraine are talking of business and therefore will probably not disagree.

Oh, I am so unhappy! There is no apparent reason for this mood, and yet perhaps the one cause is Herbert Orces. You see, he came Sunday and I had the opportunity to observe him. I only wish I could say something about him; the people there is nothing to say of are the most uninteresting, and in this case Herbert Orces is a nonentity. He is a good boy, yes, of course, but what else? Had he been talking to me from China I could not have felt a greater abysm between us. His attentions, his silly boy talk, his compliments, his admiration, were simply torture. We went out for a walk and talked. I thought the time would never come for him to go home. The worst part of this is that I did not blame him for the situation—poor blind boy!—but myself. Why on earth should I seem agreeable to *boys*, half-developed, simple-minded, awkward-mannered *boys*—I, with all my seriousness, my old-fashioned thoughts? Would you believe it, I was absolutely humiliated, when I looked at Herbert Orces, to think of myself as the embodiment of his "wonderful girl." Call it conceit, call it any wicked word, but it cannot be that I am destined to be judged merely as a pretty doll to play with. Has not all my girlhood been spent in creating my ideal of womanhood and in trying to live up to it—an ideal which is made of all the intangible charms of education, intellect, knowledge? And *last* of its charms I count beauty. It is the irony of fate that I should be made love to for my eyes, mouth, etc. I could really scream when listening to his talk; and all the indignation it stirred, indignation he may take for passion!

"I believe you love someone else," he said, despairing of my ever sharing his ardent curiosity for the future.

"Perhaps I do," I said, laughing wickedly. And I thought of Eduardo, strong, manly, intelligent and full of understanding. I thought of my Stranger, my Wise Man, my future husband! I should have answered, "I love *several* others!"

He is coming again next Sunday, hoping to obtain from Mother permission to take me to the theatre. If Herbert Orces had the tiniest idea of what I am writing in my Diary—if he had, in short, any idea of what I am made of—he would not come back. And we should celebrate!

May 31. Today was a day of dreams. I shall live all of it in company with my thoughts and my books; I shall live all of it within myself, in my shell—I shall, in short, be my true self.

Mother is gone to the city; Thorvald and Joaquin are in school. Miguel is here but he is reading downstairs. How often I have sat thus alone with my thoughts. How often I have filled the big, quiet house with shadows and pictures of past and future.

And then because my thoughts grew sad and I brooded too much, I suddenly expressed the wish to escape from them, to be free, to live lightly. For a few days I found myself listening to other people's thoughts (or you might call them thoughtlessnesses) and talking when I had naught to say, according to the laws of society. I found the house full of real people, the silence was broken by visitors' voices, I was even made love to. What a contrast! If I thought I suffered before, now the pain was excruciating. Alas, it takes experience to teach a fool. I now know better than ever what life I am destined to live. I am happier thinking, dreaming, soliloquizing, than chattering and laughing and bowing. I am content to watch the fluttering of my dreams' wings; content to listen, to talk only to the clouds and leaves—to myself, when I need scolding. But above all else just now, I wish to keep as far away from me as possible real people, lightly filled hours, thoughtless and dreamless dents made in the smooth course of time.

Two questions have sprung to my head these days: Why does Woman believe more than Man in God and in religion? Do we do more good in the world through reasoning than through feeling?

How will Eduardo explain his strange silence? I fear that he is ill. I am trying to understand why he has sent me proofs of remembrance and yet has not written the letter he knows I am expecting. Is there only one quality lacking in Eduardo which I am to be convinced that he does not possess: steadfastness?

All my pride rebels at the thought that so much of my happiness depends on Eduardo's friendship and that his heart should change continually like clouds. It is in this very changeableness I have been seeking not to believe—and I believe in Eduardo, as long as he wishes me to believe, perhaps *forever*. You see, perhaps it is my fault: I may not be *worthy* of a steadfast friendship. And something in me may *make* Eduardo fickle. If this is true, then Eduardo is steadfast; Eduardo is true to those who *deserve it*.

Miguel was sad and homesick and begged me to talk to him, so we sat on the porch and chatted for a long time, trying not to be serious. I was wondering at his longing for "something exciting" to do, and why he felt the weight of silence and sought to escape his own society. When he was gone I asked Mrs. Norman about this, and her answer set me thinking. She says I am comparing all young people with myself, and yet, she added, she knew none other at my age as contented to remain home alone, quietly busying myself with books or writing. It surprises her to see that I have no companionship but Mother's and that I do not express the need of any other, of amusements, of the "good times" all girls crave.

Miguel expressed only the normal wishes of a young boy, who, although fond of books and serious studies, enjoys equally friends and entertainment. I remember playing with Thorvald when I was very little, but most of my girlhood, from ten to fifteen and even sixteen, was grave and full of cares; that is why I have become the serious person I am now.

What do most girls do at eleven? I do not know. I used to take Joaquin to the park and sit on a bench. mending stockings and watching over his frolics. Thorvald's too. Marraine had told me that Mother was working to earn money to feed us. To me food became even distasteful and I thought that the less I ate of it, the better for my little mother.

At sixteen, when not in school, I had housework to do and I could hardly read or study because the doorbell rang fifty times a day for each boarder and the telephone was equally tyrannical. Mother went twice to Cuba in her brave attempts at moneymaking, leaving the house apparently in care of certain persons but with all the true weight of it on Monsita's little shoulders and on my own, not little but very inexperienced. As to "fun" I did not miss it much. Mother spoiled me greatly as she gave me more love than I deserved. I remember feeling abandoned and not wanted only when there were many people about, all carefully dressed, talking lightly, laughing brightly and dancing. Those were the parties at which Germaine Sarlabous was the most brilliant star. I preferred, after sadly watching things I could not understand, to steal away into some corner to read, and no one missed me ever.

Thus I grew up into an Impossibility. Thus I grew up so that I am set pondering because Miguel tells me he wishes for something exciting to do. Do I wish for excitement? Perhaps once in a great while, strange, wild longings for boisterous freedom stir me, stir my heart. I long to run, to shout, to race the wind, to reach up to the stars, to fly after a bluebird, to laugh. Instead I steal softly upstairs to fetch the ink bottle; I drag out a queer book and sit somewhere to write gently, thoughtfully. My heart is made of odds and ends—mostly oddities. How anyone could love me is more than I can fathom. And yet, though I say nothing, oh, how I long to be loved like other girls—yet who would endure my seriousness? Eduardo would. Yes, now and then I do feel like an imp, and become full of fun, and I want to be happy in the light way of civilized persons, but then people whom I cannot endure in my natural mood fall in love with me. Here I have turned all my sorrowful musings into a theme for jest, for it is a laughable predicament to be in, to be loved only when I am not *myself*.

June 1. How strange my life is. Last night Mrs. Norman and I took a long walk and talked. Among other things she told me she did not approve of my friendship for Eduardo. You see, my likings and feelings are very transparent, and Mrs. Norman knows everything and guesses the rest. This makes her speak to me simply and sincerely like another mother, and I listen to her with pleasure. I listened then while she told me that intimacy between cousins was not right because all traits, sentiments and likings were intensified in such companionship. I knew instantly that she did not understand and told her the purpose of it all. I told her how I knew I could bring forth the best in Eduardo and that I wanted him to be the finest of all my cousins, possessing as he does the sort of qualities one can mold. I told her how I knew that a woman's influence could "make or break" a man's life and that I wanted to be Eduardo's good influence as long as he valued my opinions.

"Well, my dear, of course this is a lofty ideal and purpose, and it is fine that you should think in this manner, but we are all terribly human, and if I were you, I would remember the risks."

"Do you fear that Eduardo should fall in love with a plain-looking cousin when he can choose among all the lovely Cuban girls of his own rank and fortune?" I interrupted with fire. "No, you will see, Mrs. Norman, how this friendship will do nothing but good to him and make a useful, great-hearted man of him."

We continued, always speaking of him, then changed the subject and returned slowly homeward.

And then today I took out my sewing and mended all my dresses one by one. I sang as I stitched and soliloquized gaily. I finished a gingham dress and took out my dancing frock, my beautiful old-fashioned rose gown. All my gaiety vanished. I held the brilliant fabric in my arms and dreamed of the club dance to which Eduardo took me; dreamed of the time we sat on the stairs and he wrote me a poem, watching me curiously, and telling me things he had never said before. I dreamed of the dances we danced together. My heart ached and ached and ached for *him*. I wanted him, I wanted to hear his voice again, to see him. The longing was so great, so unexpected, that frightened and bewildered, I looked into my heart and sought to understand. We are terribly human . . . but shall I be the first to shatter the spiritual relationship? Am I so feeble of purpose that I cannot finish an unselfish task without breaking down and surrendering to selfish desires? Mrs. Norman knew there was a risk, but we both thought of him falling in love first, and not of *my* unworthiness. Oh, it cannot be true. I thought myself so strong, so above human failings. I never dreamed that my desire to do good would bring such a great sorrow upon myself. If I cannot conquer myself, life holds so very little for me—unrequited love, an impossible love, nothing but to waste myself on a being I cannot, should not, love. No, this is madness. It will pass. It is only because I am young, and too much within myself, seeing few people able to respond to my desires for intellectual companionship, and thinking that because I have found one he is necessary to my human life. Oh, it is only a momentary blindness—soon I shall see again through the eyes of my Ideal and feel shame, unspeakable shame, for this waywardness.

And now, calmly, thoughtfully, I contemplate the memories which have stolen into my mind—memories of the most lovable young boy in all the world, who could not be destined for a plain, serious Linotte such as I am. Of course, I shall continue to do all I can for him, and stifle each desire which is not worthy of the trust he places in me. I, to whom he looks up because he thinks me the symbol of the ideal he wants to attain. I will be worthy of his faith and not stoop to the very things I despise and condemn, weakness, human frailty, subjection to the senses, forgetfulness of spirit and intellect.

Evening. I come to you tonight because I can speak to no one —I need a friend. Oh, I can hardly see what I am writing! I stopped because the tears blinded me. All my being is consumed by a terrible rebellion; no one can guess the bitterness there is in my silent fits of passion. And then exhausted, ashamed, spiritless, I cease to feel or think and seem to sink into a state of lethargy. when I do not care and wonder why I do not die. Oh, what is the use of putting these things into words! I am growing into woman-hood and only pain can mold my character. It is only just, there-fore, that I should suffer the sorrows of girlhood.

June 2. By a curious coincidence I found a long article in a maga-zine discussing the friendship between men and women. It is called: "Can We Be Comrades?" With Mrs. Norman's warnings and counsels in mind, I studied the question seriously and begin to find that they all know more than I do—Mother, Mrs. Norman and Mr. W. L. George, the author. I shall tell you some of the things which struck me most, and you and I shall then be ready to discover the truth by ourselves: "It (Europe) is ready to admit that it would be very good, both for men and women, to have frank and simple relations, but Europe considers this to be im-possible because we puzzle one another, because we are inevitably curious of one another, and because we cannot help being attracted by one another's strangeness, by the discoveries our curiosity makes. There is another name for that attraction, and that is 'love.' A cynical comment was made on the subject by Tolstoy when saying: 'I am told that between a man and woman there can exist companionship, community of interest, fellowship of the soul, but it is strange that young men should so seldom enjoy the companionship, the common tastes, or discover fellowship of soul with a woman who happens to be old and ugly.' (In parenthesis, this seems very true to me, although I seldom approve of cyn-icism.) 'Without going so far as to say that comradeship is pos-sible only between men and women who are incapable of experi-encing love, I do suggest that it cannot exist between people of ardent dispositions.' "

I am afraid I must be one of those, "people of ardent dis-positions." Here I sit, then, facing grave truths, the wisdom of older people. Have I not experienced the dreadful waverings of my idealism, become feeble and allowed my sentiments to over-rule my mind? Should I write Eduardo today in such a way that I should tear myself away from his companionship, too dangerous now? Have I the courage to destroy a friendship which is price-less to me? If I reason, if I weigh my human frailty against my self-taught worship of the ideal, I tremble and doubt the strength of my spirit. What if my spirit fails? It means heart hunger, pain and shame. What if my spirit conquers? It will mean the continua-tion of the sweetest experience of my life. Shall I trust my spirit? Yes, I will dare against the opinion of the entire world. Alone, defiant, convinced, I shall prove that true intellectual fellowship *can* exist. My love for Eduardo is a hunger of the spirit. I have no one my age now as companion. Is it not natural that my longings should turn to him? His silence now perplexes me. He had been writing me such enthusiastic, spontaneous letters; they expressed more depths of feeling and thought than ever before; they were more personal, more conscious of the one to whom they were addressed, written with more tenderness and a greater understanding, and yet always reflecting a sense of freedom, of impulse and absolute sincerity, such as no one feels except when realizing the attitudes of responsiveness and accord in the other. There is one thing in which he betrays a boy's thoughtlessness; he is only vaguely, if at all, conscious of the sensitiveness and delicacy in me in regard to proofs of friendship. During his first estrangement, he wrote in his diary that if he lost my friendship he could never replace or regain it. This realization spurred him to write the letter he knew I would answer. Not once, I believe, did he think I could *suffer* from his neglect—willful or accidental. I did not know the cause then; and perhaps now, in spite of his repeated proofs of remembrance, I may not hear from him until he goes to Cuba. But enough brooding. Let time bring its own joys and sorrows to us without our going forward to meet them.

June 3. Time brought its own joys and sorrows. Two great events have marked this day in my life with unforgettable strength. The joy was a visit Mother and I made to Father McLaughlin[1] last night, from whose house I returned with five books under my arms and the promise that he would teach me, direct me, in the study of Catholic philosophy. This morning I received holy communion, and kneeling at the feet of the cross, I promised to stand by my faith until death. Carried away by the sincerity of my prayer, I became suddenly conscious of a great peace so unearthly that the realization of possessing God flashed upon my mind like a vision. I feel protected against a thousand evils, defended, strengthened. This afternoon I shall begin my studies of Father McLaughlin's books.

Compare with this uplifted state of mind the sorrow which awaited me at home. I found a letter from Eduardo, a revelation of his instability, his lack of steadfastness. It was the only thing

---

[1] *Father Joseph McLaughlin, pastor of Our Lady Queen of Martyrs in Forest Hills.*

which could help me to decide. It showed me that I was risking my happiness and taking his friendship too seriously. My pride rebelled against such slavery, and today I made the supreme effort to tear myself away from Eduardo. He writes: "Cuisine, here at school I am a solitary dog; I want no one, I wish no one! At times I want companionship but this is not often. I wander alone, I think alone, I act alone. Cuisine, when I am with you, I think always about you, I ask for you, I am happy with you, for you, I am sorrowful for you, in short, I live and only live for you, your life is entangled with mine. And when I leave you, you are no longer present, so gradually that magnetism draws off and I cease to be the person I used to be. I think of you, yes, but only like a dream. Alas . . . Mimi, I am as a flame that needs constantly to be kindled. I receive your letter and I am kindled, I am set aflame again, and I immediately answer it—but alas—if I cannot answer then, if three or four days pass, I lose interest, my hand becomes cold and I seem to lose the power of even writing letters. If you feel like writing, if your heart beats in the affirmative, then I beg you write to someone unworthy and who knows it. Adieu, ou à bientôt. P.S. Cuisine, you might as well know it, it is prohibited me to see you. I was not supposed—I did not know it then—to have seen you at Easter. They do not know what you are to me!"

Alas, for a moment I was tempted to forgive him. Is it so wrong that he should be one of those persons whose lives are ruled by impressions? One moment he is drawn to me, the other he wanders away; the indolence of his nature prevents him from being constant. It is indolence which prevents him from writing, indolence of spirit, and also perhaps the fact that I have shown him that he could count on my understanding always. Even today all that is loving, forgiving, tender, in me is stirred by the appealing tone of his letter—the tenderness with which he uses my names, "Mimi," "cuisine." It is my nature at times to try to appreciate others, but in so doing I depreciate myself. That is why part of me could forgive again. But all that is proud and sensitive in me is roused to terrible indignation at the thought that Eduardo's family, because they are rich, powerful, use their arrogance and disdain and *forbid* their son to be in my society, to see me. Here at last my eyes are opened. Not good enough to be Eduardo's friend? Yes, because I am poor, because my father is only an artist. Despicable advantages that worldly riches have over the rest! I would defy his entire family, laugh at them, ignore their opinion —if Eduardo's friendship were worth it. But alas, in his last letter he reveals to me what others said but I refused to believe. I, who am so exaggeratedly earnest, serious, tenacious, would be tossed to and fro at each change of his whims and impressions. Oh, Eduardo, Eduardo, I have filled my life with you, but you have not proved yourself what I believed you to be!

When Mother came home, she was deeply offended and hurt by the action of Eduardo's family. For a moment we realized bitterly the injustices of fortune—felt the piercing agony of being insulted and having to bear it. Little Mother only thought of me, telling me I had not deserved this humiliation. She was thinking of the past, of all the little things I did, my efforts to be helpful—thinking only of the good in me. Weighed against all these, the others have only *money*—no charity, no ideals, but narrow minds and little hearts. Had Eduardo's friendship been all in my life, they would not have hesitated to tear it from me—fearing I might do him harm because I am poor. Oh, God, how thankful I am that you have opened my eyes in time—that you have shown me the unworthiness of the object for whom I might have ruined my life! It is with difficulty I can conquer the rising wave of resentment and bitterness. Of all things, hate must never enter my heart. Heaven will punish arrogance and meanness and give *us* happiness later. It will crown Mother's untiring efforts. It seems to me that already we have a thousand blessings more than the Sánchezes. We know the joys of work, of suffering; we have more contentment; and above all we love one another with a love not one of them has ever felt—unselfish love, helpful love, devoted love. The pages I tore out are the things I wanted to say in answer to Eduardo's letter, but Mother forbids me to write and I obey. Had I obeyed her long before, I would have been spared this disillusion and humiliation. Silence on my part forever!

June 5. At about nine o'clock yesterday I found myself in Frances's apartment. The dance had begun. First I was introduced to my partner, Richard Jeffrey, and a few boys, but suddenly I found myself surrounded by a group of school friends, kissed and talked to without finding time to answer their questions. We were very curious about one another, curious to notice the transformations of schoolgirls into butterflies. But my surprise was far greater than theirs. First there was Natalie Lederer, whom I admired a great deal when she was in my class. I thought her original and intelligent. She was my only rival in composition and I expected she would become a wonderful woman later on. We separated for two or three years, during which we wrote to each other spasmodically. Then last night I received a great shock. She stood before me unchanged physically, but the Natalie Lederer of long ago is gone forever. Her dress was some heavy silver fabric into which scissors had cut so hopelessly that there was nothing left. It had no sleeves, no back, just a tiny piece in the front and then it followed each curve of her little body and terminated abruptly over the knees. The expression of her face startled me, brazen, a vacant laughter. Her speech was vulgar, her humor coarse, her manners undescribably audacious. The boys handled her like a toy. There was also Lois Jacoby, with her hair cut short, and others, all wise now in the art of chattering and flirting and make-up. There was Albert Rosett, who a year ago at my first dance took a great fancy to me and then wearied of my seriousness. Last night he looked blasé, dulled. As to the impression I made on the others, I could read it clearly in their eyes. Once a pale-faced, thin schoolgirl with stupid reserve, I suddenly came upon them in a beautiful dress fit for a queen, with a face illuminated by expectation, with a lovely fan in one hand, and the other hand fingering a pearl necklace (Mrs. Norman's). I even wore a tiny crown of pearls set in a comb worn by Mother long ago. They all looked at me with admiration. There was nothing lacking to permit me to join them, be one with them, except an undefinable touch of "sauvagerie," unapproachableness, in me.

Once I caught Frances alone and she leaned toward me. "You look wonderful, dear," she said.

"I don't feel wonderful, I feel countrified," I answered, laughing. I danced until one o'clock, when Mother came for me. I made particular friends with one boy whose name I do not remember.

June 6. I am ready for a survey of my universe. I shall first tell you what took place in it yesterday. Herbert Orces and Jacinto Garcia had arranged to come in the afternoon. I observed many things: that I cannot endure Orces; that Garcia I rather like, and Miguel also. You see, Orces monopolized me, and Miguel and Garcia were thrown into each other's company. I heard them converse pleasantly and easily while I sustained the ordeal of Orces's conversation, which is either nonsense or nothing. He is an absolute nonentity and has, besides, a very disagreeable forwardness of speech and manner. He is one of those persons with evasive eyes. He is stupid and extremely conceited. Of Garcia I gathered a better opinion. His large black eyes are gentle and honest; he has quiet and unobtrusive ways, a respectful tongue and, I believe, a small share of intelligence. It seems that he is returning to Spain soon so that I will not see him very much. I shall find some way of frightening Orces away. Miguel was profoundly amused by their long visit, and I, indignant. I would rather be left completely alone for life than to stoop to such company and such admirers. But the evening effaced the disagreeable impression; Mother, Joaquin, Miguel and I went to the Richmond Hill theatre. Miguel is such a fine companion, with his brilliant personality, his intelligence, his refinement. With all my head full of Eduardo, I have done little justice to my other friends. Even at Easter time, I thought Miguel "de trop" when my conversations with Eduardo became intimate and fanciful. But now that I have lost Eduardo, I can judge with more consideration, with my head, since it again belongs to me.

Afternoon. It is said that Time is the greatest Doctor for heart troubles. I long for the time when I will have forgotten the things which hurt me deeply today. I sat sewing a little while ago, making myself a dress out of old goods, odds and ends. They always turn out pretty and original, and everybody likes them. I made one a few weeks ago which somehow reflected a mood. It was red and white trimmed with small strips of black velvet— dignity and seriousness blended with much joyousness. A strange fancy came to me and I promised I would wear it when Eduardo came. What is the use of sewing pretty things to wear now? I shall never see Eduardo again because his family has forbidden it. Oh, no one knows what pain this separation causes me. Each little thing, frivolous or serious, with which my days are filled reminds me of Eduardo. I think of him when I hear the postman's whistle. He shall never again bring the envelope with the familiar writing. I see Eduardo sitting by the fireside, reading, writing, smoking thoughtfully. I meet him going up the stairs, because once, when we almost collided, we each thought of the same thing: he bowed deeply and I curtsied in the old-fashioned style. I see him by the piano; I can still hear the tune of "Sweetheart" and "Narcissus." He did not play classics because there was no one to tell him, to direct him, but his family. Even the woods are full of him, the walks around the house. And upstairs in my closet, buried in a little box, tied with black ribbons, a package of letters. There is a handful of faded red roses too. There is one sweet light in all my desolation; this did not happen because he forgot. He did not forget, but his family succeeded in extinguishing the little flame we had lit and fed.

The night Mother and I were walking home after our visit to Father McLaughlin, we were talking seriously of Tia Juana's religion, of faith in general, when I caught the sound of laughter from a nearby porch where several young boys and girls sat playing and chatting. I wondered at the contrast. While others of my age enjoyed themselves, I was preparing for a new study: I was pondering on solemn subjects, entertaining serious thoughts. Did I long to exchange places? I was learning, they were playing; which of us would receive a greater share of happiness later on? We all desire happiness (though sometimes we obtain it by selfish means). Is there happiness in study? It seems to me that the world is divided into two great classes: those who believe life is short—"Amuse yourself as much as you can"—and the students. I want to be a student, whatever I may be now, and I often ask myself if it means that I shall give up the pleasures of my age— give up happiness for the sake of knowledge. Ah, but are the other things *happiness?* Or is true happiness found in the intellect and spirit? I would like to know. I will know someday.

Meanwhile, I am certain that I did not wish to exchange places with those laughing and chatting. My visit to Father Mc-Laughlin I will remember all my life. He is the most remarkable priest I have ever known. I remember the first time I heard him speak. I have always had a dread of sermons; they gave me all the strange feelings they gave David Copperfield (all except sleepiness, of course, because I am much older). But when he began, I was forced to raise my head and listen. Instantly I felt the magnetism of sincerity and simplicity. Mother was also impressed. Since that day, although his little church is twice as far, we walk to it each Sunday. Father McLaughlin has the forehead of a dreamer and a visionary. His large blue eyes are candid, indescribably pure and confident, earnest and intelligent. The curves of his mouth and chin show a grave determination, and one knows his life is not made of visions alone but actions, achievements. There is something in the "ensemble" of his features, his expression, which is almost unearthly—such spirituality, uprightness as one seldom sees now in man or woman. And yet none of these qualities, as it would seem, render him unapproachable.

In the neat room where he received us he sat conversing simply but unable to veil his profound knowledge, not only of religion but of people. Among other things, I asked him if he thought curiosity to be wrong. I told him of my love of philosophy, my natural tendency for exploration. He answered that, particularly at my age, the mind was naturally flexible. If I loved philosophy, why did I not study Catholic philosophy? Then he left us for a moment. He returned with five books. "I have a whole library for you," he exclaimed, laughing. I am to come back in a month.

Face to face with Father McLaughlin's intelligent understanding of faith, I felt ashamed of my vacillations and grave doubts. I felt that if I could understand my religion as he does and possess as much faith, I would never seek light in other philosophies; but I need a philosophy. What have all the other books I have read done to me? Those theories and beliefs, each in turn, have only planted doubts in my heart, despair, and have crazed me with thinking and pondering, have left me without solution or understanding, offering what in return? Nothing but to be able to boast of knowledge that is not knowledge, a knowledge of questions to which there are no answers, contradictions and obscurities.

I am a Roman Catholic by birth, by habit, by obedience, but now I shall be one by reasoning. I want to satisfy my *intelligence*. I want to understand.

Evening. Joaquin is at the piano, improvising in his own strange way. He is playing sadly, softly, and all the longings of my heart melt into the tender notes. I long for Eduardo. I cannot uproot the things in me as lightly as others. It is because I have few friends, allow few friendships to grow in my heart, that I love each more and care for each with all my strength and power. My affection for Eduardo has grown into something strong, quiet and enduring, and even the very fact that I was often expected to forgive him appealed to me. I love to give. And now suddenly he is forbidden to see me as if I were wicked and harmful, as if I could not be trusted—I who want to trust everyone and be trusted. Oh, tonight, if I continue writing it will be like looking into a deep, deep well. To look too long would be to fall into it. And who, pray, would take the trouble to look for me?

June 7. These last days it seems to me that my spirit was dragged downward into the world of sensation and impressions alone. I was passing a crisis such as so often comes to those who are not strong enough to crush the domineering Feeling and listen to Reason. I was tossed and ballotted mercilessly by each gust of wind, now happy I found a little light, now sorrowful because it was gone. Emerson tells us not to allow ourselves to fall into these extremes. There is a medium state of mind, of quiet self-control, when one is not swayed by each mood and is yet keenly living and conscious and sensitive. It must be wrong to allow myself to fall into a life of mere sensation, and today I freed myself from this. I have fallen into the deep well I wrote of, by looking too much into it, but this morning someone did take the trouble to look for me, found me, and is gently carrying me upward, upward to a higher, purer realm of thought. I have almost reached the end of my voyage; there is no obscurity, no confusion, no pain and desolation where I am now. The change in me came when I brought down one of Father McLaughlin's books. Oh, I had forgotten, in my ignorance, that books give the tenderest and truest consolation. I can hardly describe what influence study seems to have over pain. It seems as if something far above human passions and impulses had come down to guide me away from them, as if some voice had told me to forget all but that there was knowledge, art and science waiting there for me to consecrate my life to. I feel strong, morally proud and invincible—and yet I have only *looked* into the avenue stretching before me invitingly. I have not begun my studies, and already I feel that the joy they give surpasses all others. How strange that at times I should become so blind as to turn to human nature for companionship.

Truly, I know that human understanding is imperfect. I know that I am surrounded by false theories, by false principles. Young, inexperienced perhaps, with a flexible mind, I may think for years, study, speculate and then find my thinking inaccurate, my studies stained and rendered useless by some false step, my speculations terminating in maddening circles. Then, as a woman and as a scholar I will have failed. Failed as a woman because I will have abandoned society, the love of home, the duties of wifehood and motherhood, in the pursuit of truths; and failed as a scholar because of my misconceptions and distorted results. But then I may succeed in one thing. Supposing that I can grasp the Catholic philosophy intelligently, supposing that I should succeed in indicating my achievements in agreeable, perfect English, I could perhaps convince or guide and elevate others, as I have been myself.

I have just finished *Walden*. The book being my own, I took joy in marking each passage, and in some instances I even scribble an observation on the margin of the page. Thoreau's way of dealing with his life in the woods startled me. I can hardly say what I expected, but I know the book fell short of my expectations. Something in my own nature is keenly averse to discord, and the great contrasts between certain pages is jarring. I would like to cut up the book, leaving only those pages that are filled with beauty, feeling and charm. Why should Thoreau appear so calculating, so practical, stoical, arrogant, cold in chapters such as "Economy," the latter part of "Solitude" and others, when he proves himself a poet, a naturalist, a kind-hearted sagacious man in others? However, I can truthfully say that although I cannot love Thoreau, there are a thousand qualities in him which inspire admiration and liking. Perhaps when I am older, less idealistic, more humane and practical, I may pay a just tribute to the great Thoreau.

June 8. Every hour since I wrote of the great change which came to me, I have remained happy—as if I had been lifted far above earth's passions and hurts and could see only the joy and contentment in it. Eduardo seems far away, like someone who was lost a long, long time ago, and when I think of him it is with pleasure and tenderness and not regret and longing.

Yesterday Mother took me to the city for shopping. While I was wandering up and down Fifth Avenue, humming and pausing before the attractive windows, Mother was visiting Mrs. Menocal. It seems that her daughter, Georgina, expressed the wish to see me and asked Mother to telephone Richmond Hill and tell me to come immediately. She was told I was already in the city, and a few hours later I found myself lunching in the Ritz Carlton Hotel with her, her fiancé, Mrs. Ortega and Ester Gonzales, a strange, talented and erratic poor relation of the family. We went to the theatre and laughed a good deal because the play was *Snapshots of 1921*, with Nora Bayes. On returning we found the room filled with visitors. I met Guillermo de Blanc,[1] a diplomat and a friend of both Father and Mother, and others whose names I forget. Later I met the ex-president of Cuba, Mario Menocal. He has a kindly, intelligent face. All the family is affectionate, unaffected and generous. Georgina has given me a lovely dance frock of pale-blue tulle. I was entertained by all these distinguished people and so interested in observing their ways, their kindness, in sitting face to face with persons bearing names I hear constantly,

[1] *Better known as Willy de Blanck.*

that when I came home I fell asleep thinking that the world was a very interesting place after all!

Just a few minutes ago Orces telephoned—for the last time, I hope. I told him I was going away for the summer; he asked me if I would answer his letters; I answered that I did not promise. He told me that he loved me; I answered that I did not care. He said I was cruel, and I answered I was not enough so. He said I was born to be his sweetheart, and I almost fainted with rage. Then, after recovering, I said goodbye cheerfully, pretending Mother was calling me. Of course this means I will not see Garcia again either.

June 13. Outside, the rain falls in torrents and I can hear the thunder rolling. At such a time my thoughts come quickly and in great numbers. I want my pen to fly instead of crawl along the lines. Perhaps I may pin a few of them down before they melt like raindrops in the ground.

I was so happy for a few days that I made everyone else happy. Miguel says that he has never seen me so light-hearted, so impish.

Thorvald took me to a dance given by his fraternity at the Hotel Pennsylvania, and we both had the most enjoyable, the merriest, time imaginable. The grand ballroom was magnificent; the floor seemed like one wide mirror and each dancer, as if he had been given wings. My program was quickly filled, and all night you would have heard me laugh and chatter, spreading merriment everywhere and making many friends. I had forgotten myself and, in doing so, was pleasing others and tasting a few hours of frolic and joy. Two of Thorvald's friends are coming to visit me tonight. I had many things to be happy about Friday night, but among them the best was that I was making Thorvald proud of me! I did not realize this until we walked homeward and he expressed his satisfaction in a few brief phrases. I do believe this is the first compliment Thorvald ever gave me in his life! He never stoops to flattery or approbation; it is not in him. This doubles the sincerity of whatever he might say.

Saturday and Sunday I flitted about the house, took long walks with Miguel, who is very gallant, read little and thought nothing at all. Miguel demands all my time and interest. He is sailing for Havana this coming Saturday. He has nothing to do meanwhile and enjoys company, entreating me to sit and talk with him. He is one of the most agreeable companions I have ever known whenever he forgets himself a little. But even if he does remember himself or talk uniquely of himself, his "self" is pleasing enough and you do not get tired or sleepy as you do in the presence of certain egoists! Intelligence and culture in a person always attract me. I hope that when I am a woman I shall always have such friends as I am seeking now.

Although everyone notices the change in me, no one knows how it has come about. I promised I would be good and I am fulfilling my promise. Contentment radiates in my face. I want to make everyone happy, cease to brood on the sorrow which came to me days ago. I seldom dream; yesterday at twilight, only for a moment, a great wave of loneliness came upon me, a feeling of heart hunger. I was passing by the station and noticed the roses in bloom. A year ago Eduardo and I had walked by them and he had picked one for me. Our friendship had begun before this, in our letters, but that night we seemed to have sealed it, a sacred treaty, while walking in the twilight and talking about books and the world. But that was only one memory of Eduardo in many days, and as time goes by, he seems further and further away, a blurred, vague picture which it is my duty to forget completely.

June 14. Last night Mother was very ill. Overwork, constant strain on all her faculties, trials and cares cause great ravages on her health; and sometimes she breaks down into a heap of sensitive nerves, nearing hysteria, which so frightens me that for days I feel like someone who is bending under a heavy burden. It is only my love for Mother that makes me fear illness so greatly; her health is always in my mind like a terrible menace. When she felt better and Thorvald and I had carried her up to her room, and when finally she lay on her bed, quiet and resting, I wanted with all my heart to run away, far away, where I could think alone and allow all my pent-up feelings to flow freely, and perhaps I wanted to pray.

Instead I had to pull myself together and prepare myself for Thorvald's friends. When they came we all sat on the porch and talked and laughed. I gave them orangeade and cake and tried to be a pleasant hostess. Now and then I forgot that they were there and listened to the wind, dreaming . . . then a word would bring me back to earth, and with my accent, my peculiar inflections, my gestures, I turned commonplace phrases into things that made them laugh. I hope they had a good time. Both were refined, agreeable boys, only a little older than Thorvald, but I could not observe them as I do other boys; my thoughts wandered to Mother's room too often.

Today she is much better. The house is full of sunshine and of the sound of the wind, which continues to blow with strength. It makes me think of an ocean, the tide retreating and advancing, whispering sea shells and foam and seaweeds. The house is full of Miguel, of Thorvald, who has no school today. They tramp heavily up and down the stairs, shout and talk, then suddenly decide to play tennis, and go, for a few hours only. In the kitchen Flora is washing dishes for the last time. She is leaving (culinary warfare, housekeeping statistics). I sit here alone, listening and taking notes as I so often do; that is my life now, irregular, but on the whole natural. I might say, like the life of other girls, for once. I am still behaving myself and trying to control all the things in me which are constantly stirring and bursting into flames like a volcano. I am a volcanic person, but just now my volcano is corked.

June 16. I fear I am growing disgusted with boys, even as Frances has been for a long time. For a few days I sincerely enjoyed Miguel's company. When we did not discourse on philosophy and literature, we became humorous and foolish, but in a peculiar way of our own; that is, with the humor and playfulness of poets, book-worms and would-be philosophers. I took pleasure in watching the varied panorama of his mind, and, being masculine, he took still greater pleasure in demonstrating it to me, pointing to each thing I might pass over unnoticed, and attaching the letter *I* here and there so that I might not forget it was his mind I was examining. Then suddenly, when I thought I had formed an opinion of him, thinking him out of the ordinary, a "different" boy, Miguel turns out to be like any other boy, with any other boy's conception of "pleasure," admiration of "pretty faces" in girls and disdain for whatever those pretty heads may *contain*. Sometimes one boy knows more than another, appears to love books, to have other things in his head except pretty girls, dancing, sports, but in the end, what? Sometimes one boy seems more in-telligent than another, more serious, more settled, but in the end, what? They are *all* alike. They are all young, inexperienced, ignorant, vacillating. They all have the self-satisfaction of eigh-teen-year-old manhood; think they know everything and that they have learned the goal of life; think that they understand Woman;

that one must make the most of life. They therefore set out to dance, to make love to every girl they meet, to deliver pretty speeches, to discuss their victories; in short, set out to act like men when they should be learning the ABCs of manhood.

Perhaps while I am writing this, Miguel is comparing *me* with other girls, telling himself we are all alike. I am eighteen also. I have all of eighteen's absurdities—yet no, not all. I have the seriousness of older girls, though I may not have their knowledge.

And still I have not yet reached the stage of dislike Frances has reached. Even while I write I am thinking of a new specimen I am to meet Saturday. It is another *boy*, alas, but he *might* be interesting. He has telephoned Thorvald often, and by coincidence, never when Thorvald is home. Hence, by taking and giving messages we became friendly. He liked my voice and now he invites Thorvald to a dance at his home and begs him to bring his sister. Marsh McCurdy is his name; he is one of the fraternity boys, and I shall meet again those whom I danced with Friday night. All this sounds comical, and yet I am writing without a smile. 'Tis sad indeed to know that half the world is filled with men and that they should be so feather-headed.

June 19. Let me write this date as one of my happiest adventures. I am so eager, so impatient, to tell you of it that I shall skip the story of last night. Do you remember the pleasure the Guiler dance gave me? I came to you filled with enthusiasm for Hugo Guiler and interested in the likeness between our tastes. I thought that I would meet him again, but forgot the customs of this country and took no step to make this come true. As days passed, I believed he had forgotten me. Now his family has gone to Europe, and each weekend he spends with Mrs. and Mr. Parker,[1] who own a beautiful house on our corner; that is to say, there are two houses between us, and a few trees. Behold me, therefore (in your mind's eyes), reading on the porch and Hugo Guiler passing now and then. Each time, the words remained in my throat and I lost my poise. If I did not stutter, it was because I said no more than, "How do you do?" I dare not think or imagine what he thought of me for being so stupid and rude. However, Mother saved the situation, and this afternoon, before I realized what had taken place, Hugo Guiler was sitting near me and we were talking,

[1] *His aunt and uncle.*

oblivious of Martha Forgie and the other visitors who had been walking with him when Mother kidnapped them all. Mr. Guiler carries Emerson in his pocket, loves Stevenson, and writes a journal! As we talked, I wished he would like me well enough to let me be his friend. Do you know, it seems as if all the things I loved in Eduardo had come back to me in someone else, in an older person, and mixed with still more seriousness and *wisdom*. This is the impression I have of Mr. Guiler, that he *knows*, that he is strong, reliable, manly and yet with a poet's heart and mind. Oh, what may come of this stranger who has knocked at the door of my Inward World in the name of Poetry, Books? He has knocked, and I am thrilled, almost ready to open my door wide and exclaim: Welcome! Welcome!

June 20. Alas, there is as much stoicism in me as there is wisdom in a fly. I read, I write, I think myself prepared, therefore, to meet the unexpected turns in my life's path calmly, serenely, wisely. And then, because I meet Hugh Guiler, I lose my head and am filled with joy, wonder, expectation, one excitement after another playing a merry tune on the strings of my imagination. It is difficult to tell you what happened. It seems as if we were both two rivers—our thoughts, I should say—and they had been flowing in a different direction until a big storm came, a decree of fate, and the wall between crumbled, was swept away. Then with great strength, eddying, whirling, the waters were joined and continued to flow, doubled in power and might. All in one day! When he came in the afternoon, the words we exchanged were like the rush of a strong, uncontrollable wind through the trees, filling the world with a thousand new harmonies, and it seemed as if by this magic, a thousand little doors had been opened, not one by one, but almost in unison, softly and smoothly.

In the evening Mother and I had gone for a walk through the woods. We returned to find Hugo Guiler and a friend wandering away after discovering I was not home. Mr. Guiler was bringing me a book of essays by John Erskine, Professor of English at Columbia University, whom he admires deeply. We walked again for a little while, Mother conversing with the stranger and I with Mr. Guiler. Once we paused on top of a hill to watch the moon. We had never seen it so beautiful. It was suspended against a clear, absolutely cloudless sky, a bright round world of mystery, which seemed very near at that moment because its purity made it stand detached, as it were, from the rest of the infinite space.

At last we separated. I almost sang my way to bed, and when the lights were out I lay there wide awake for a long time, my eyes fixed on the little patch of sky framed by my blue curtains, dreaming, dreaming, dreaming. I thought that after my deep, strong friendship with Eduardo and its sudden end, I would make friends slowly, cautiously, fearfully, but Hugh Guiler is one of those persons one likes instantly, like a flash of lightning. How I hope he will like me as well.

An evening with my Books. No, there is nothing equal to those lovable friends. For hours I peeped into each one's heart, and set them in order, and dusted them, and pressed them close to my heart, my little book of Emerson's *Essays*, my *Philosophe Sous les Toits*, the *Journal* of Eugénie de Guérin (which I have finally found), Shelley's lyrical poems, Tennyson's, Browning's, Musset and Keats's works; there are many more. I love them so. My imagination dilates after such an occupation. I feel the world to be larger, and I myself am changed. I am all tenderness and worship for each precious page and forget all else in this true, enduring love.

June 23. I hardly know what has happened to me. For I have been living quickly, busily, unthinkingly. Marraine came; there were seamstresses in the house, new maids, Monsita to help; I had not a moment to myself, and even at night when I lay in bed I could not dream and ponder because Marraine and Mother talked until I fell asleep. No wonder I could not write in my Diary. I notice that I have even forgotten to tell you that Miguel sailed Saturday for Cuba. Thorvald and I accompanied him to the docks. I will never forget the last study I made of him, for it was of a very different person. A Miguel whose boastfulness had fallen entirely away, suddenly sincerely touched and forgetful of self. I was very sorry to see him go, and yet happy to know he was leaving New York to face a very brilliant and pleasant future in Cuba, as the new president, Alfredo Zayas, is a relative of Miguel's sister and a very good friend of Miguel's father, who showed Zayas proofs of devotion on several occasions for which he is grateful. And yet, not with influence and help, but through his own fine qualities, his intelligence, his personality, his education, Miguel is certain to become one of Cuba's most remarkable men. At eighteen he shows all the signs of becoming a thinker and a clever orator.

I notice also that I have said nothing about Marsh McCurdy's dance. It was just foolishness—music, ice cream and cake. Indeed, this is my first moment of retrospection for many days. The house is silent, almost uninhabited, and when all is silent around me, when I am left alone with my thoughts, my pen, my Diary, it is not Miguel I think of, nor of dances. Suddenly, whatever loneliness or longing or sadness I have brushed aside during my days of housekeeping returns in one great, overpowering wave. I think of Eduardo. He telephoned this morning to tell Mother he was coming to New York tomorrow night. I think of him in spite of all that has happened to obliterate his memory. Most of all, I would like to know what he thinks. I was so accustomed to knowing all that took place in his heart, or nearly all, through his diary. Now his life, his thoughts, everything pertaining to him is like a closed book—a book in which there was so much sweetness and charm. I will perhaps often be told what he is doing, never what he truly thinks and feels. And how actions belie one's feelings sometimes, how people distort one's actions! I am never to know the true Eduardo again, the cousin I still believe so good and lovable.

It is on this porch I thought I would accomplish so much. Then came the days I thought it necessary to work. And now? Now Flora is gone and I am the maid. I can neither work outside nor devote myself to things I love. I have the marketing to do; I must cook and sweep and dust and mend. Fortunately the days have grown longer. After a busy day we all sit on the porch until the night comes. The sky changes, the world becomes filled with mystery. I could dream forever at such a time. Of what? Who can tell what dreams are made of? Only poets with their magic pen, only those who can weave precious pictures out of words—and even then, only half is said, only half is whispered. We each have our dreams, and no one else's pen can speak truthfully of them.

June 25. For a moment yesterday it seemed as if my life had come to a sudden stop—for a moment only, and then all feelings and thoughts rushed onward once more at their usual pace. It was when I read to Mother a letter Eduardo had written her. He says: "You have done your duty, Tia Rosa, but you forget your nephew is doing it too. Bonds cannot be broken so easily, especially in time of youth. Now if you have a little pride for your nephew, a little love for your nephew, and a little thought for your nephew's welfare and future, allow him to write to Anaïs even if she does not wish to receive my letters. If not, I shall become the

Prince and kill the 'dragon.' Hoping that hearts will melt, etc., etc. Eduardo." You cannot imagine what impression this letter made on me. I never expected Eduardo to *plead*. But what a boyish, impulsive letter this is! It shows how deeply rooted is his devotion to me now, but it also reminds me how much younger he is than I—and surely at such an age he will soon forget.

However strong is my desire to see him, and to receive his letters, to continue sharing his thoughts and emotions, I must not, I cannot, ever do so again. Eduardo does not realize fully the reason for his father's opposition; it has never occurred to his idealistic nature that his father dreads the consequences of his son's friendship with the *penniless* daughter of a musician. He dreads my influence over Eduardo. It never occurred to me either, but I have little Mother to guide and help me. At this very moment Mother is with Eduardo at the Hotel Pennsylvania, only a few minutes' trip from here, and yet I am condemned to sit here alone and not to see him. Tomorrow he is going to Cuba to his family, in which no one appreciates him as he deserves. What will be the destiny of such a boy? Unless he emancipates himself from his father's hardness and calculating tyranny, he will have to give up every inclination and inborn love of art. Alone, will he have the courage? Eduardo had an uncle whose life began thus, a rich young boy with a great talent for painting. He met only opposition and criticism; he was literally suffocated in a life he abhorred, forced to marry against his will, tyrannized, misunderstood—he killed himself!

Oh, Eduardo, how it pains me to think of all the suffering that will come to you! How I want to be your true friend always, to help you. To think that you shall never know that every thought you had for me was returned, perhaps doubled and intensified.

Oh, the beautiful, beautiful ending to our story. Mother brought me back two books I had loaned Eduardo and a mysterious package. I opened it and found a leather book, heavy with blank pages, for a journal. Its brown covers with gilt edges are fastened with a little lock, the key hanging on a string, the key to my heart. On the flyleaf Eduardo has written: "To My Lost Princess: When my wings shall cease to be clipped—then shall I stretch my pinions and fly to thee with all my joy, all the fervor, all the ardor of Youth. Time can never crumble a true Devotion!! E. S."

I had not dreamed of this, that Eduardo could be my friend only when he is old enough to be his own master. Someday, then, unless he forgets me, we shall be united again. Thus, this separation which so deeply saddened me is only temporary. Meanwhile, he will become a man, know his own heart and know his own mind in such a way that he will be a truer, better friend, even as I will be a woman, with more understanding, more to give in return.

I will often look forward to this reunion in the future. How thankful I am to possess such wondrous memories to keep me company while I wait, to replace Eduardo until he flies back to me, free. Only one thing may keep us apart forever. During the period of waiting, we may find Love.

Evening. What peace comes at times when the shadows have fallen over the country; the soul seems a shadow itself, stealing softly along deserted roads until it finds a grove of trees and there nestles and stands very still.

It is late. I sit alone in my room and my pen moves almost of its own accord. I did not know I had anything to say tonight, but suddenly I felt that I wanted to express this magic of a summer night, this wonderful detachment from the rest of the world which I now feel. I fear that I am becoming very strange. Each day I tell you less and less what I *do;* it is always what I think and dream. Thus I have forgotten to tell you that Thursday I went to the beach with Joaquin; that yesterday I visited the French ship "Paris" with Uncle Gilbert and Gilbert, Jr. Why? Because as soon as I am home I forget all about these things and plunge again into introspection.

June 26. Last night the Parkers had a Maypole dance for the children of the neighborhood. Hugh Guiler could not leave their house, of course, but he came a little while after we returned from church this morning. He has invited me to the theatre Friday, and Mother arranged that he should come for dinner first. Oh, I was glad to think I shall have him as a friend. When I see him I am so interested in what he says that I cannot yet describe him to you.

June 27. I have spent a long time with Alan Seeger.[1] I have the porch all to myself, I am free to dream, to fly to whatever sphere of thought attracts me; at such times Alan Seeger's poetry transfigures my universe. All barriers fall; I am a prisoner no longer.

[1] *World War I poet.*

With his book on my lap, with one finger on a word, my spirit is instantly transported. It was an hour devoted to the worship of beauty with incantations not my own. From this I passed to Carlyle's *Heroes and Hero Worship* and read "The Hero as Man of Letters." I found not fanciful imagery and melody but austerity of thought; what a contrast. And yet I take great pleasure in both things. I love to unite passion and reflection; I cannot bear to have them separated and made, as it were, two essentially different states. In the book of essays Hugh Guiler loaned me, I found many things said concerning nearly the same question: "The tendency to neglect as unpoetical all writers who are given to vigorous intellectual processes, who really think, and to praise exclusively those who appeal to our emotions has largely destroyed the ability to read."

Lately I have given much thought to this tendency of mine toward study and contemplation. It is curious to notice the things which help to mold our natures, which influence our character and habits. I began writing poetry when I was a child because whatever was beautiful or pure, or in any way inspiring, touched me very deeply, and I had to express this, unconscious that my childish language was inadequate to translate feelings which were not childish. Then because I was frail and sickly and because I had to spend so many hours of my time in bed, I returned to books for companionship, for *delectation*. I say delectation only because I want to show you a certain observation I have drawn. As the years pass, I read continually, widely, and without guidance. Slowly I have wandered away from the first purpose of my reading. I have grown into this love of books, seeing not only *pleasure* but knowledge. Then it must be that Literature *is* Knowledge. In my case it has developed into knowledge, seeking, without interference or suggestion, without teaching or guidance. When I contemplate the possibilities, what may be brought forth from this communion with books, my spirit feels a million times more freedom; it soars into such infinite distance that what is left behind can only sit and marvel. Mine is a double joy—the pleasure I find in the flight of fancy and the pleasure I find in this mind which has been given us to see into something; the mind that asks, doubts and proceeds in its own way to seek the truth, the answer—philosophy; the mind which makes us reflect, meditate, ponder, inquire and find.

How I wish my control of language were adequate enough

to make intelligible the never-ending train of ideas which pass through my head. At this very moment I see everything so clearly, as if my own thoughts themselves were thrown on the ground before me instead of their reflection, as so often happens. I can truly see them, strongly defined, not phantoms, shadows, clouded and vague reproductions of thoughts, and therefore misleading. Could I but set them down as I see them!

Somewhere I have read of a universe expanded, enlarged by poetry, by reading. No one can grasp the truth in such words who has not spent a few hours alone with books, pen and paper. It is at such a time that one does feel this expansion of the universe, this dilation of the imagination and the soul. It is such a great, great feeling that one's heart does not hold it; it overflows, and one wonders if human beings were made to receive such strong emotions.

June 30. From my easy chair on the porch I can observe all that goes on in my universe. Whatever I cannot see I divine, such as what is taking place in the house, by the vague sounds that reach me—Joaquin at his piano, Mother and Belica in the business room, Monsita in the kitchen, Thorvald whistling from somewhere. And now that I have looked around, I am ready to look into my own heart. What do I see? Behold, no deep thoughts cutting one another's throat, no loneliness knocking and tearing its hands against an iron door, no elusive feelings pursued by relentless reason. Instead, peace, contentment, joy. My heart is like one great white room which the spirits are preparing for a visitor. Tomorrow, you ask? Yes, it is tomorrow that Hugh Guiler is coming and tomorrow that we shall, for the first time, be together for several hours, free to speak of poetry, of books, of the world, of all we please. I want to be ready. When we shall talk and discover each other's ways, Hugh Guiler will knock at the door of the great white room, the door will be flung open, and I will say: "Welcome into my Kingdom of Friends."

July 5. There are certain things of which one hesitates to write. Write of sorrow, and sorrow creeps into the words, but will happiness let itself be imprisoned in your pages? Today I am awed by the thought that I am to speak to you of Hugo, and I realize fully the littleness of whatever I might write. Hugo's infinite wisdom and goodness, his deep, fine qualities, silence me. I am content to listen, to wonder, and do not wish to describe yet.

Friday night we attended an open-air concert at Columbia. Sometimes instead of listening we whispered of those things which are part of music. Later we danced at a roof garden, at the Bossert [Hotel],[1] in Brooklyn. Above us the sky was dark and starless; it seemed as if all its little lights had fallen on the world below, on the river which stretched at our feet and on us. On parting, Hugo recited:

"O lac! rochers muets! grottes! forêt obscure!
Vous, que le temps épargne ou qu'il peut rajeunir,
Gardez de cette nuit, gardez, belle nature,
Au moins le souvenir!"[2]

Then came last night. What shall I say of last night? It was the hot Fourth of July night of tradition. The open square at Forest Hills was decorated with flags and soft lights; the center thickly carpeted for dancing; and the band, from its imposing stand, filled the air with the joyous strains of dance music. Hugo came with Martha and another girl, whose name I forget. We soon made other friends, and among them two young boys from Columbia, with whom we are going to the inn this coming Saturday. Hugo danced with me often, and then we slipped away between dances and walked, talking as brooks flow to the river. It was one of the happiest nights of my life. Hugo enjoys dancing immensely, and I also. Other boys came, and I danced with many but was always looking forward to my dances with Hugo, and never in vain! For the greatest wonder of it all is that Hugo, with all his wisdom, likes me.

Oh, my happiness is too great. It fills not my heart alone but all the universe. That I should be worthy to possess such a priceless friendship! Hugo is a little more than 20 years old; he knows his own heart and mind, and nothing he does is vacillating, uncertain. He inspires the utmost trust and confidence. I had heard from Martha that he was unsociable, took little or no interest in girls, and I am proud of his interest when I realize the rarity of it. Little by little, perhaps touch by touch, line by line, I may be able to paint my portrait of him, or at least to sketch him.

[1] *Later known as the St. George Hotel.*
[2] *From "Le Lac," by Lamartine:*

"O lake! silent rocks! dark forest!
You whom time spares or can rejuvenate,
Keep this night, keep, fair nature,
At least the memory."

We talked of Erskine's book, of *Walden*, of Carlyle's *Heroes and Hero Worship*, of Dryden and Shelley, of our diaries, of all the thoughts that came to us, sometimes meditatively, at other times with laughter lurking in the corners of our eyes, or still oftener laughing merrily in the rippled way people laugh, not so much because of witticisms but because of happiness. And now I count the days until his return.

July 6. I have spent the day singing, singing while mending and sewing. Of what? Of Hugo. There was no other way to express the joy in my heart, and my thoughts of him were so perfect, so like a fairy tale that they turned into song as naturally as . . . (Mother was reading over my shoulder and while she laughed at me, my inspiration fled!)

July 7. Heat, heat, heat. All day the sun pours burning rays upon the world. The roads are parched, the plants are thirsty. I cannot even find my thoughts; I suppose they are fanning themselves in some cool, secluded corner of my mind. My day resembled somewhat the life of a normal girl, for I worked in the garden with Thorvald, and played *tennis* for an hour, slept, played other things, never opened a book or drew one drop of ink from my ink bottle, until now. I received an invitation to go to the beach with the young college boys we met the other night and refused it. However, we shall go to the inn this Saturday—the two boys, Martha and I, perhaps Thorvald.

How seldom I write like this, so matter-of-fact and about facts. It is like taking a photograph of my actions. Usually I dip into a paint box with a little brush, taking some color from here, from there, mixing them, scattering them, touching and retouching—and making, in short, a queer, half-real, half-fancied sketch of a life which is half-mortal, half-impish. The photograph would never reflect the coloring, the intangible, the wild and free beauty of my world, my life, as I see them through my moods and with a paint box.

July 10. I saw Hugo a little while yesterday, another little while this morning, and finally, with Martha, we took a long walk through the woods. Martha and I made him laugh with the stories of our adventure with the two college boys, how we went to the inn with them, danced until midnight, and returned firmly convinced of their . . . ahem . . . stupidity!

July 11. Yesterday, I would have liked the woods to belong simply to Hugo and me. Instead, the three of us filled the air with merry chatter and irresistible laughter and were very happy, but then I could not watch and study him. Those many little doors opened the first night we spent together showed me only little glimpses of him and make me want to know more. Yet I do not often see him alone. For one minute I wondered if I would *ever* be his friend; it seems as if a great white cloud descended from above to whisper to a tree, or to something still smaller, a blade of grass. But meanwhile the cloud is very kind to the blade of grass (he came last night to bring me a book), but when I remember that I must wait 5 long days before seeing him, I wish that Hugo would not be so wise and good.

Mother is not well and therefore I left the porch, where I had been singing softly to myself, to keep her company. She says she likes to hear my pen scratching on—would that this scratching meant useful work and not, as it does, simply one more pleasure added to those which crowd my existence. What have I done that I should live like a wild flower, free in such a wondrous world?

July 12. Strange that I should study and read, and write continuously and yet be so deeply ignorant of life's simplest experiences. For hours today I played tennis with Thorvald and Martha. At one moment I was so surprised to find myself playing in a flood of sunshine, so surprised to be breathing the fresh, pure air, to be outdoors, free, wildly active, with tingling blood, and eager to *win*, that I forgot to send back the ball when it came to me. Now, since that moment, a new love has grown into my heart, a love for that strange life of sport and health, which all others around me know so well. I feel that I have opened a new book and read the first page; it spells Youth. And I am young, although when I look back on all these years and my quiet, contemplative ways I wonder how I have not grown *rusty*. I still have time, however, and in some strange way, I know that my pen shall not suffer because of my frivolousness—nay, sunshine and breezes and exciting games will give new life to my spirits and prevent stagnation.

Cher Papa,[1]

I am going to take advantage of a cool, quiet day to write you a long letter. When it is very hot (and it has been very, very hot these last few days) and when many little adventures happen to me at the same time, my ideas fly away—and without ideas, how can I write you?

Since my last letter, our life has changed a lot because we are on vacation. Thorvald passed all his examinations and furthermore was second in his school in Algebra! Joaquin did well too, and as for me, I had the easiest tests in the world. You will be glad to know that in French I got an A, which is the best grade. My test was in literature. I read a little of Voltaire, Victor Hugo, Lamartine, Alfred de Vigny, and learned a few things by heart—poems like "The Lake" and the "Préludes" by Lamartine. Do you know them? How beautiful is French poetry! And to think that in spite of my French heart, I can express myself better, as far as literature goes, in English. I have even had to change the language of my Diary and now my whole life is expressed in English. When this happened, I began to love English with all my heart, almost as much as French. This love is as natural as the love of a musician for his instrument, of a painter for his brush. Whatever can translate our ideas, our feelings, our philosophy, should be dear and sacred to us. Toward French I feel only a deep love mingled with an exile's regret, but for English I feel the tenderness of an artist.

If you only knew, Papa, how often we speak of how we miss Europe! Our dearest wish is to see Europe again, to live there again, perhaps never to leave. It's strange, isn't it, the admiration that children of the Old World have for her—an admiration that remains intact, eternal, after so many years. We are like birds whose wings tremble, who can hardly keep from flying away to the sunny lands from which they came.

And yet we aren't blind—we feel an immense gratitude toward this great and generous country. No one can understand that unless he has experienced its benefits, the education, the living that America gives so generously. Here, one learns to struggle, to defend oneself, to be practical and strong. If we have missed certain things, *it's too late* to make up for them. Thorvald and Joaquin are American in every sense of the word, especially Thorvald.

[1] *Letter translated from the French.*

Joaquin will always be ready to understand and assimilate that *other life* because the blood of Europe is in his veins. We must remember that we can't have everything in this world. One always has to choose—choose between two mystiques. Circumstances forced us to choose the New World, and perhaps it's for the best. Sometimes, Papa, I have a premonition that if I marry, I will marry an American.

With all these digressions, I have told you nothing of what you want to know—what Thorvald and Joaquin are doing. Since the doors of Thorvald's school closed (to his great joy), he plays a lot and works occasionally. He looked a long time for a job, but the situation is not favorable. There is no work right now, business is bad, the streets are full of unemployed men, and it's even more difficult for a boy to find something when he has to go back to school in September. So now he sleeps late in the morning and when he wakes up, his loud voice makes the whole house shake and we have to send him outside. He cuts the grass, works a little while in the garden, eats, plays tennis all afternoon, eats again and goes out to play or walk with his friends until bedtime. Sometimes he goes to the cinema, to a dance or to the theatre, and that's it! Joaquin does about the same things, except that he also practices the piano every morning. He has just composed something he calls "The Devil's Dance," a fantastic and grandiose thing, with wonderful chords for a boy of his age. He plays tennis quite well, but outdoor life doesn't make him gain weight—he is tanned, thin, agile and strong—and as lively as a grasshopper. Devilish? Rather—but here he has more room, he has woods and fields, and all his little friends and enemies to amuse him and keep him busy. And the secret of making Joaquin behave is to keep him busy! . .

I would like to tell you about the dances we go to, about our friends, and other things too, Papa, but this letter is getting very long. Also it's a little sad to write letters that you don't answer. I never know what you think of the things I write you or whether I bore you. When I put my letter in the mailbox, I feel as though I am putting it in a bottomless hole and that all those pages, so full of news, will never be read or answered.

So I shall stop, hoping you will find a moment to tie a little thread of your life to mine, as I try to do with my letters. But it takes two threads to tie a knot, Papa!

With tenderness and a thousand kisses from your daughter, who loves you,

Anaïs

July 14. This is the hour I love best, the hour when so often I write my Diary. Twilight. At twilight my heart melts into the heart of nature. The calmness, the softness, the mystic beauty of it penetrate into my very being like the sweet notes of a poem or a song. Perhaps in life also I like twilight. I turn more naturally toward the shadows, the sadness, the vague, uncertain dream world of visions and memories. I can dream now, but it is only in preparation for the future. Perhaps soon I will face a great dawn, the day of revelation and decision. I shall take my first faltering steps toward my Achievement, whether it be Authorship or Wifehood.

July 17. Yesterday I watched the road for hours, expecting Hugo, but he did not pass, and when the evening came I sat on the porch thinking of him while Mother, Belica and her friend Mr. Hernandez talked, and suddenly I heard him calling me from the garden. He had come with a friend, Mr. Hazin, to invite me to the moving pictures. Thus again we almost forgot where we were and whispered. Hugo made me laugh often, I who thought myself so hopelessly serious. And there we sat in the open air, under the sky, very far away from the story of troubles, hatred and profane love unfolding before us, although now and then Hugo would pretend to be ashamed and sit tense and rigid and silent, trying to appear interested in the story—in vain. You see, we ourselves were building up a story much more to our liking, the story of our friendship, which seems to grow every minute we are together, and those minutes are scarce indeed, but we make the most of them. Later, Hugo accepted refreshments, and we offered him among other things a piece of chocolate cake which I had made. I gave him Musset's poems to read and my notebooks with extracts from my readings, and I returned regretfully Erskine's *Essays*. I do believe that it is time for me to describe Hugo as well as I can so that you may know as much of him as I do; and not so much by being with him do I know him, as by *intuition*.

Hugo is very tall, of slight build and perfect symmetry. My first impression of him, the night of his dance, was that he possessed the ease and grace belonging to the gentleman, mingled with great simplicity and frankness, the touchstone of his character, I was afterward to find out. His face is oval, the oval of the idealist and the dreamer; his features very regular and clearly defined. All his strength lies in his broad forehead, in his intelligent, clear and expressive eyes. His lips are delicate and sensitive, but firmly, resolutely controlled. The nostrils are delicately chiseled, tender, mobile, but the chin is strong and firm. This ensemble is characteristic of his nature—that mixture of strength and decision with feeling and depth and tenderness. I see goodness, sincerity and genuineness in his smile, which is open, frank and simple. I see kindness and understanding and delicacy in his eyes, and concentrated thought and wisdom are stamped on his forehead.

And not a gesture that is not spontaneous and natural, not a word that does not come from the heart. Outwardly he is all manliness, splendid, resolute. Inwardly he has the poet's wondrous fancies, balanced judgment, clear perceptions, practicability and wisdom. And then, as far as I can see, unselfishness, not a trace of egoism or conceit. His flashes of humor, his quiet optimism and yet keen understanding of the pathetic, his confidence and trust in people, his love of nature and music and poetry, his idealism, make of Hugo's character a thing incredibly harmonious and complete.

I can compare him with no one. Eduardo was my equal; he was younger and not half as strong and firm of purpose. Although it seems strange that I should say this, that I should think Hugo greater and finer than all my friends when in reality I have seen little of him. I seem to have known Hugo a long time, although I never dreamed of one who could possess at once all the best and finest qualities and those I most prize.

This morning Hugo telephoned to arrange a game of tennis with Thorvald next Saturday, then he asked for me and told me he did not think he would see me today, as the Parkers had company. I asked him if he had read a little of my notebook.

"I read it all."

"Did you like many things in it?"

"I liked *everything*."

"Even my own criticisms?"

And he answered, "They were the best of all."

It seems, too, that we may go out during the week, and later Hugo wants me to meet his best friend, Eugene Graves, who loves what we love, and perhaps more devotedly, because he does not share his heart with other things; he is fond of solitude, of the hermit's life, and is said to be unsociable, according to the standards of the world. Hugo believes him a genius.

Oh, that the world were filled with friends like these! And yet the very rarity of reasonable conversation, of spiritual relationships, makes them dearer and sweeter when they come to us. One of my fondest dreams is to find myself someday in a home with a husband and children, and with friends with whom one can share the love of books and music, talented, intellectual friends, not gossipers, vain women and idle men, social butterflies expecting to be amused, unable to think or to speak their thoughts and whose purpose in life is to fill the hour, caring not a whit whether they are accomplishing *something*, helping someone, embellishing the world or serving humanity. Here I have spoken of two kinds of people, those I admire, those I abhor. And I know that I am in the right; I know that my choice is made forever, that I will remain unchanged through the years—for this worship of mine for the things of the mind is rooted within my very nature.

Evening. I have come to the end of another volume. My last words to each one are usually of thoughts that come to me as I look back. But tonight my heart holds naught but thankfulness— as it did once before, upon musing on all the good that comes to me.

Above all things, my thoughts are with Hugo, and I am thankful that he has come into my life. It is an Ideal that has come to life, a breathing, living dream, and it all happened because I believed, trusted and hoped.

July 19. A proof of my appreciation of the immediate present is the use I am making of this book [from Eduardo] when I might have kept it to record a greater or more important period of my life. It is because I sometimes think that the preparations one makes for the future, for the Adventure, are more difficult to write of than the Thing itself, that today I do not hesitate to unlock this strange, luxurious book, to fill it with the story of a heart which does not draw inspiration from unusual events and odd environments but from the contemplation of a simple life with the daily cares and sorrows, with hours of sunshine and play, hours of twilight. And besides, even if I do not write better in this book than in others, it matters little. No book's outward beauty need translate the contents. Each page may be ugly in its very self, but it will always be my Diary, the Diary I have never written with a thought of composition or selected style. If each night, when I lock you I can say to myself, My heart was sincere, as is what I have written, then the beautiful book need not be ashamed of its pages, nor I of my heart—and of my pen.

I have just read pages from Stevenson's *Memories and Portraits*, etc. Stevenson's attitude in "Virginibus Puerisque" I do not like, but if his ideas on marriage did not appeal to me in the least, he quickly set me aflame again with his "Walking Tour." How well he paints the benefits of a good walk.

I love both Stevenson and Emerson because they are great givers-of-freedom, as it were, givers-of-names to all that is too often mute or inadequately spoken of in other hearts. It seems strange that I should unite their names, for this gift of theirs is the only one they have in common—in all else they are vastly different and incomparable; nor is Stevenson as great perhaps as Emerson, but I love them both dearly and devotedly. Do you know, I have come to feel Emerson's presence at all hours of the day. He is linked irrevocably with all my theories of life, although most of my thoughts follow their own paths. Sometimes I pause before an essay of his; I let the book lie open on my knees, but do not read. I want my own ideas to shape themselves; from a confused mass they emerge at last, clear, intelligible, concise. It is then I read—but alas, Emerson speaks! It has all been said, and better said. The spirit hangs upon his every word, humbled by the greatness of its teacher. The heart swells with thankfulness and love for being so kindly understood—and explained. But Emerson, however great and wise, has never tempted me to lay down my pen. No. His philosophy is alive and active; through it the message of the man is easily read: Emerson tells us, commands us, entreats us, to *speak*. To speak if we are able, and if we are unable, to learn. In this, he is greater than many great men. Many know how to create, how to raise with their own hands great and solid towers of philosophy. Their theories, explanations and descriptions are like gigantic pyramids which tower above the desert sands for centuries and to which little men look up with reverence, awe and fear. Yes, many can create, but few can speak to the human heart and bring forth all that is good in it without frightening it. Move with noise, and the terrified oyster will enter its shell. But Emerson takes pains; he seeks lovingly, he speaks simply—man to man, heart to heart—and then heals and reconstructs, and leads with a strong, firm, yet kindly hand whatever spirit is in need of him. Thus it happens that as each day passes and I understand Emerson more and more, I am drawn even with greater strength, to my pen.

July 22. Oh, I am so happy, so happy that the world seems too little for me. I awoke singing and I am still singing—for it is easier to sing of joy than to write of it. Each incident of the day was like another drop added to a brimming cup. Joaquin poured into his notes the reflection of one of his rarest moods; elfish, whimsical and merry melodies flood the house, together with the sunshine. I should not be writing. Certain moods, like certain people, need not be named; they are part of . . .

My idea was violently extinguished when Mother asked me to help her mend stockings. Now my head is full of other things. How varied and contrasting are women's tasks—to let go a pen for a needle, to change the needle for a broom, the broom for a book, and this last for the pen once more. Which do I love best? All alike, it should be, although I cannot tell how this is possible. The womanly part of me realizes fully the duty of woman; the other, nameless part can master the pen as well as the needle, and wonders if it can always master both. Am I clever enough to be a woman and a writer? Is such a thing possible? Or will I make a bad woman, a useless woman, because I love books? If will power exists in me, I will blend duty and inclination until one cannot be distinguished from the other. There is no merit in doing one thing well; no, all things you can do—all others, learn to do— in such a way that you are never idle, useless. This sounds like a recipe or a prescription, but if I do not give myself advice and if I do not preach incessantly, who will? No one ever scolds me as I deserve; Mother forgives me in the same breath. And I am so often tempted to do only the things I like—I mean, the things Mimi the writer, the scribbler, likes and not what a good daughter and good sister should do in her house.

Last night Mother and I saw a picture called *Sentimental Tommy*, as adapted from the book by Sir James Barrie. It is one of the most beautiful stories I have seen. Tommy's "passion for make-believe," his whimsical ways, his vivid imagination and fickleness touched responsive and sensitive chords in me; and Grizel's love for him, her unrequited love, her madness, how he redeems himself and brings her back from the "shadows"—all this touched in some inexplicable way and charmed. Joaquin's sentiments were deeply stirred also. One could see it in his wide, luminous eyes. How easily we are (both of us) touched and stirred. How quickly our imaginations are kindled. Alas, I fear for this, more for him than for myself, for Joaquin, being a man, will have to rely on himself, protect himself, struggle alone. He seems to be made of flames, constantly kindled, consuming himself in passionate outbursts of all kinds—anger, desires, sympathy, loneliness.

Sentimental Tommy reminded me strongly of Eduardo. I thought so much of this last night that I dreamed of my cousin, dreamed that he was changing. Alas, this is not the first time I have thought of Eduardo, although I never write of him. Often I wonder if he is true to his ideals—our ideals—and I pray that his family may not completely extinguish in him his love of art. You see, I fear for his strength. Eduardo was my favorite companion, a good friend, but throughout our relationship I noticed this lack of moral strength and endurance—his only fault. Fickleness, they call it, those who do not understand him, fickleness of heart. Perhaps, but if hopes count in the hands of fate, then Eduardo will be victorious—and return to me unchanged, or if changed, then for the better.

July 25. I was not left to myself long Saturday night, for Elsie came with a young man and the evening was devoted to conversation. We talked about books, but there are varied ways of conversing on books and we employed "le moyen banal."[1] Sunday dawned only to bring heat and brilliancy. I longed to hide my sad thoughts from the whole world. Hugo came in the afternoon, however, and we walked for a few minutes, accompanied by Joaquin and Eric Parker—both of the same age and unconsciously hurting me by their teasing and with their glances full of malice and mockery. You see, how could they understand the deep interest Hugo and I hold for each other's ideas? I wanted to listen to Hugo, I had so much to say to him and yet—I wanted to run away. It was simply my old instinct to fly which possessed me, the ancient shyness which I believed conquered. When Hugo returned in the evening I had conquered myself, but he only remained a little while, leaving me a book of fairy tales. We showed him a woodpecker with a broken wing which Jimmy had found in his garden and given me to care for. A strange thought entered my head. I told myself that if the bird lived, Hugo would remain my friend. The bird was found dead this morning. I fear Hugo guessed my wicked mood of yesterday. I do not deserve friends. And today, one long, long week to face, and then Hugo's last weekend here, because the Parkers are leaving for the rest of the summer.

Evening. Again I have looked for consolation in books, and what I sought I found. Hurt by inexplicable things, thirsty for unattainable friends, I opened my *Heroes and Hero Worship* and forgot my pain and found my friends. I sometimes believe books should answer all our needs, satisfy all our desires. I remember

[1] *The ordinary way.*

asking Hugo if he thought this possible. He did not think so: "After we read a book, discover an ideal, a character, we naturally long to find this ideal in the people around us. We seek living characters such as we have been reading of." We talked of this at the open-air [moving picture], Hugo merely whispering so that I do not remember what he said word for word, although I am certain that this was his thought. It was not of this I meant to write, however; I wanted to tell you that I found a strange truth in my *Heroes and Hero Worship*. Carlyle speaks of the "Divine Idea in Man"—that all things which we see or work with on this earth, especially ourselves and all other persons, are like a kind of vesture or sensuous Appearance, that under all, there lies, as the essence of them, what he calls the "Divine Idea of the World." This is the reality which lies at the bottom of all Appearance. To the mass of men, no such Divine Idea is recognizable in the world; they live, says Fichte,[1] merely among the superficialities, practicalities and [appearances] of the world, not dreaming that there is anything divine under them.

Does this Divine Idea explain the supreme longings, the things that call to us, the things that stir in us? Sometimes when I have been stirred too deeply, when my entire being trembles in the agony of revelations which cannot be spoken, I have exclaimed against the littleness of our bodies in which souls, like prisoners, suffer and rejoice with an intensity we seem incapable of resisting. Was this only a spark from the Divine in us?

"The Hero is he who lives in the inward sphere of Things, in the True, Divine, and Eternal, which exist always, unseen to most, under the Temporary Trivial!" This appeals to me because of its loftiness and purity. It seems to explain many things, and above all it makes clear the reason for peace and contentment entering a human heart when it turns away from the trivial, and the vexations and anguish attending the trivial. But it takes a hero to accomplish this; it takes a brave, strong heart to turn away from the trivial. No wonder the great man who succeeds in living in the inward sphere of things can complete those masterful tasks, write the immortal books, prophesy—kings, men of letters, prophets, poets, they are all moved by the True, the Divine, the Eternal, and are inspired by the light within, a light Fichte and Carlyle apparently believe to be possessed by every man, although seldom recognized.

[1] *Johann Gottlieb Fichte.*

It reminds me of something Hugo told me; that there is poetry in every human being but it lies hidden sometimes because the person is ashamed of it and believes it to be a weakness. I could not believe this. I thought of Eduardo's father—a hard, unfeeling man. There could not be a grain of poetical outlook in him. Nor in others like him. To this Hugo replied that the poetry, in such a case, may have died, but that it was there when the man was a child. "All children are poetical," Hugo said. "You see this in their love of fairy tales, of beautiful things, in their love of make-believe. Afterward they lose this, some entirely, some partly, burying it under a rough exterior. Many never lose it." And poetry, after all, being divine, is another name for the Divine Idea.

July 26. This is almost a continuation of yesterday's musings. Since I closed and locked you last night I have not ceased to ponder and dream of what I wrote. In my sleep the Divine Idea took the shape of a bird. I dreamed that there was no Divine Idea in me and that I was condemned to wander in the world until I found it. I followed the bird unceasingly, through the strangest lands and for many weary years. Then one day I told myself that I had no strength left; I returned home and found the bird in my room. It was like the pursuit of happiness in Maeterlinck's *Blue Bird*. Hugo has a theory of life and he wishes to convert me. I have seldom been influenced by the people surrounding me. Most of my character, I believe, has been molded by Mother, but my theories, my mind, are consecrated to books. And yet this time I find myself half-convinced, not by a book but, what is rarer, by a man with an idea! But Hugo and his idea would not impress me as deeply were it not that he is masterful in his expression of it—so masterful that you must prepare yourself for changes in my attitude. This, of course, if the legend of the bird with the broken wing proves untrue. Oh, my books have always answered all my needs, but now, in some inexplicable way, I long for good, wise and true friends. I long for them with all my heart. Friendship cannot be trivial. It is the most beautiful thing in the world, next to love!

Evening. I am to see Hugo Thursday night, as he accepted Mother's invitation to come and hear Rafaelo Diaz.[1] Mr. Hamilton is coming also, Vicente de Sola, as Rafaelo's accompanist, Tia Juana and other people of whom we are not quite certain. I am

---

[1] *American tenor.*

divided between joy and expectation and—the longing to fly. Never has a thing been so great a mystery to me as Hugo's opinion of me. And on it does not our friendship depend? But I shall not think or ponder. Let time once more bring its own joys or sorrows.

I have been reading Montaigne's *Essais sur la Tristesse*. It does not satisfy me. Someday I would like to write of "tristesse" myself. And yet, it would do little good to the world. It would be better to write of glad things. Think how beautiful these books would be if I tore every sad page in them and only preserved those filled with contentment and joy. How beautiful and—how empty!

July 27. I have been reading Stevenson's essay "Talk and Talkers." Good talks are very rare, but I suppose each person has a different idea as to what constitutes a good talk. It is because I have such a horror of conventional talks, polite and forced interests and careless chatter that I enjoy a good talk with all my heart. Indeed, I have been spoiled in this. I have known so many people possessing intelligence, talent and education that when I am thrown in the company of just girls and boys of my age, such as the members of the Sans Souci Club, I am very unhappy and feel completely out of my element. I remember the night Manén was here with Enric and Willy Shaeffer. I was afraid to breathe for fear I would miss a word, and although my own tongue ached to speak a million things, I was silent for fear of interrupting someone or chasing away thoughts better than my own. I remember my talks with Enric alone, my talks with Miguel, not always of serious things, because his moods changed often from seriousness to frivolousness. My talks with Eduardo—oh, how beautiful they were! I remember when Miguel, Eduardo and I were together, or Miguel, Enric and I. In all these, the best that was in each was drawn out—knowledge, personality, experience—and whether we walked through the woods, or sat around the fire, the whole scene was transformed by the magic of conversation. We learned; we shared; we gave and took; and unthinkingly stored away the richest treasures on earth for ourselves—the stuff of which memories are made. Another benefit also to be had from this kind of intercourse is that we inspire each other, we give each other the benefit of our discoveries, as it were. This, I believe, happened to us all, and I sometimes wonder if all these people I have named will remember in later life the things we said and thought when "we were young." Or shall we laugh at everything and pretend to be much wiser?

July 30. Someday I shall be swept off my feet and carried so far away that I will never find the path that leads back to earth. What will bring me back today? Where am I? Is it possible to sit calmly and write of things which have suddenly crowded my life in such a way that I wish I could be divided into three persons? One thing might have happened to each and I would not have to think and feel for all of them. Alas, only one mind and one heart is very little!

First I must speak of Thursday night, which turned out as perfect as one could wish—a brilliant, interesting evening consecrated to music and the conversation so dear to my heart. Diaz came for dinner, and later, Thorvald brought Mr. Hamilton, with whom he had been playing tennis. About 9 o'clock the remaining guests arrived: Vicente, his mother and sister; Madame Lhevinne and her son; Paul Fox, the writer; Leopold and Frank de Sola; Brewster Board, a painter—none of these are named in order of importance, mind you. On the contrary, I name last the person I liked best: Hugo. Marraine, Mrs. Norman, Captain Norman and Charles were part of the household. How useless words seem at times when one longs to translate the spirit, the intangible charms of an event. People get together: the atmosphere grows warm and intimate, the talk increases, each one turns to the one who understands his language. You hear phrases exchanged on many topics, in French, English and Spanish. You catch smiles, and glances and expressive gestures. The room glows with interest and enthusiasm. It is the most unselfish time in men's lives, when good, worthwhile things are discussed into which each pours his best possessions for the sake of others—wit, intelligence, knowledge or kindness—"in search of progress." And then, silence. The conversation is hushed, the gestures cease; the people sit calm, ready to listen; the faces become contemplative, absorbed in the one personality that rises like a god above the little audience. Diaz singing! Once his voice is heard, it is unforgettable.

Hugo and I sat on the stairs, from which we could see everything—a little observation tower. From there we drank deeply of the indescribable magic of the hour, and talked and were silent, together. It was a great happiness for me to share his enthusiasm, his opinion. He is so sincere that I wish I were not so afraid of him—then I could be more like my true self. As is it, I am always myself with him but ready to fly if he should ever attempt to observe me. Fortunately he does not! Once Diaz turned to me and said: "Ceci est pour toi, Anaïs, tout à fait pour toi."[1] And he sang: "Tes yeux, tes jolis yeux,"[2] etc. Hugo pretended to be displeased, saying laughingly that it seemed Diaz did not know that he understood French. Diaz sang "Tes Yeux" twice during the evening. It was my song, he repeated, and I was grateful and happy. At midnight the people slowly dispersed. How short the evening had seemed! How often my memories will linger on each incident, each personality. Diaz is incredibly simple, with all his talent, loquacious and open-hearted. Madame Lhevinne was interesting also.

If this alone had happened, it would have been enough food for the thoughts of one person. But the night before, we met Tia Antolina, Antolinita and Charles at the station. I found Antolinita as tall as I! Yesterday I spent the day with her and renewed my old debates with Charles, who is staying with us. To talk with Charles is enough to upset the most stoical person. But oh, the letter which reached me this morning was a thousand times more bewildering. Eduardo writes! Eduardo writes and again my world stands still for a moment. My thoughts are confused, my sentiments inexplicable. I have found a better friend. It is true that Hugo cannot even be compared with Eduardo, but I have enough room in my heart for both. Alas, Eduardo little knows how my hands are tied, little knows how strongly I am forbidden to write— although I want to. He writes: "Cuisine, my family did not prohibit me to see you. I was only a victim of my own conscience. I wish with all my heart to shout this. Cuisine, how can I expiate? Do you remember when I sent the trailing arbutus? I thought you would answer immediately." (He tells me then how he believed I had been forbidden to write, how when at Easter his father, thinking he was coming here to go to dances, theatres, etc., forbade him to come, he misunderstood the reason, as the fear had been in his mind for long. When he saw his father, the misunderstanding was cleared.) "Do you see it now, cuisine? *Would you think of forgiveness*, chère cuisine? Cuisine, it has been my great fortune to have found you so soon in my life! They say women are the stimulus and the inspiration of man's heart and ambition, but you are more, cuisine, you are my goddess, my angel, at

[1] *"This is for you, Anaïs, entirely for you."*
[2] *"Your eyes, your pretty eyes."*

whose feet I shall lay the fruits of my ambition and my pains, and from whom I draw hope, fervor, and take courage for the future. Other men have found their inspiration in their prime of life, but I, like Dante, have found mine in my youth. And without you, what would have become of me, 'ere now, sweet inspiration?"

August 1. How I have suffered during these three days. No one can guess how I long to answer Eduardo's letter. Whenever I have been left alone to dream, whenever I have heard music, my thoughts turned to Eduardo and his letter. Mother's warning rings in my ear: "Remember, Eduardo's friendship will ruin your life!" And yet the tone of the letter, the thousand memories rushing on me of Eduardo's wonderful companionship, fill me with a great, great longing. And above all, the thought that he needs me, that he also feels the loneliness of spirit, the realization that he has not forgotten either the ideals we created or me, give impulses to my pen. I have written, but I fear to send the letter, for it is written against Mother's wishes. His face haunts me. Alas, I could have forgotten—if he had. What shall I do? Obey Mother or my impulse? I cannot reason in this—everything pertaining to Eduardo touches a sensitive chord in me; the music that is brought forth is beautiful and sad, but the agony leaves the chord lifeless.

August 2. The struggle continues. The letter is there; if I send it, Eduardo will realize how easy it is to touch me, to make me believe in him. There lies all the pain, for his letter convinces me that I have achieved my purpose, that Eduardo's sentiments have ceased to waver, but Mother is not convinced; she believes him fickle and accuses him of pretending. "Do as you please, but I wash my hands of the results. You will remember my advice later," Mother tells me. How well I know my incapability to judge persons. How I doubt myself. How I fear to be led astray by my feeling, my pity for his loneliness, my infinite trust in his words. Always the great chasm between Mother and me: she tells me not to believe, and I believe. "He does not mean what he says, he is only a dreamer, a romantic boy." The words fall on me, icy, austere and unkind. I ask Mother if she will not try to feel a little bit sorry for Eduardo. She answers that she will not, that she thinks only of *my* happiness and *my* future; she begs me to remember the times I have been neglected, the silences between his letters, his unkindness while his family was here. "But he has changed. His remembrance today is a proof of his constancy. Why should he write if he did not need me?" "He has not changed, no Sánchez ever changes. You can do nothing for him without being hated and ill-judged by his entire family. And not only that, but in helping Eduardo, in demonstrating your interest in him, you will lose all your other friends and chances for happiness. No one will understand or interpret in your way this interest for your cousin. It will be said that you sought his money, etc."

Oh, incurable idealism of mine. What rude lessons I receive at times; they seem more than I can bear. I can do nothing for Eduardo without sacrificing my happiness. My happiness counts next to nothing in my own eyes, but Mother is guarding and watching it. Mother looks deep into the future. She foresees what I cannot divine; she is wiser, and what seems unkind, nay, almost cruel, to me is only her defense against the world to preserve the very things I make light of tonight. Yes, no one would understand. Why should they not believe that I am a fortune-chaser? Is it not the usual way of judging actions? Who knows of my ideal; who will believe that I want to make a fine man of a lovable boy who needs love, and comfort and cheer, and companionship? Oh. I believe, I trust, but reality is harsh and unrelenting. It is destructive. It kills the spirit.

"Lose all my friends." Which friends? I would lose Hugo. Like a thunderbolt, this realization bursts upon my consciousness. I cannot bear to lose him! Thus I am torn between duty and sentiment, between the thought of Eduardo's happiness and my own. What greater friendship is this which prompts me to think of my own happiness? Can it be even nobler than my friendship for Eduardo? One name, one friend, is enough to help me decide. And in some mysterious way, I believe that if Eduardo knew, he would understand and approve. He would not let me sacrifice anything. God grant him strength to fight this battle alone, the courage to remain firm in face of the scorn and disdain shown by his family for the things which are sacred and divine. God grant him light and understanding of what he himself calls the "divine law," calling to him to follow. It is the Divine Idea stirring in Eduardo. Oh, if they should kill it as they have killed it in themselves!

August 3. Last night my mind was so full of Eduardo that I wrote of nothing else, but an hour or so before I began to plead with Mother, Hugo telephoned. We are going to have dinner at Long Beach—Hugo, Eugene Graves and I—tomorrow night. Hugo calls it a "literary evening," and we are each expected to bring something from our writings. For the first time in my life I am heartily ashamed of the little I have done, so ashamed, in fact, that I shall take nothing. You know, it seems as if heaven has finally answered my prayer, for often I have pondered and asked myself if I stood quite alone in my ideas and tastes. When I looked around me, I found all those of my age engrossed in pleasure. No one could respond to any of my serious thoughts. No one could answer the thousand questions in my mind, nor satisfy the desires of my heart. I grew to doubt myself, and to doubt my understanding of actual life. I wondered if I was merely a visionary and therefore gazing upon the impossible and seeking the unattainable. Also, I termed myself "queer" and unreasonable, and impossible. All this in one person—how charming, how sweet, how lovable a picture I made of the Ego. However, as soon as these thoughts came to me, there came also a prayer for friends like the friends in books. Suddenly my universe was peopled only with imaginative creatures from the world of make-believe, with phantasms, with shadows. Into it stepped real, living friends: Eduardo and his whimsical ways; Enric, who brought vivid reflections from the *Vie de Bohème;* Frances and her originality and frankness; and others—some, friends indeed; many, simply visitors; and again others whom I mistook for friends. And now enters Hugo, and I am bewildered by the pleasure I take in the company of my friends, and above all, in his. I love them like my books and trust them like my books, although in the deepest corner of my heart I fear them a little. Why? Friends change, and hurt—books are faithful and consoling. Friends inspire, but they also disenchant. Books inspire and teach the same eternal truths. Still, I believe in friendship and shall trust my friends until the last.

August 5. I have never hesitated as long to dip my pen into my ink bottle, but there are times when one wonders how, with a mere pen dipped in a mere bottle, one dares to approach things so incredibly unreal and wonderful; and so it happened last night.

At about half past six Hugo appeared with Eugene Graves. When I had told Hugo I would not bring anything, he protested, and I simply took my Diary and my notebook of quotations. Almost as if we had been carried on a flying carpet from the Arabian

Nights, we found ourselves at Long Beach, and facing, from the boardwalk, a sea so beautiful in coloring that it made me think of Spain. Nature was celebrating with us. For days we had had nothing but rain, but yesterday, as if to add to our happiness, we were given sunshine, a glorious sea and, later, stars. The sun was setting while we walked to the end of the boardwalk and into a hotel, where we had dinner. Afterward we sought a place where we could read and talk. We found enough light on the boardwalk, where we dragged three rocking chairs, and there, to the sound of the waves breaking at our feet, Hugo and Eugene opened their journals, and we discussed and read, compared experiences, agreed and disagreed, to our hearts' content.

Eugene is indeed a genius. What a privilege it was to listen to him as he read his thoughts. No one could form a false opinion of him; there he stood revealed and transfigured. I marveled at his talent, his sincerity and genuineness. He expressed his thoughts, his philosophy, in a strange way. There was never a superfluous word or a deviation—briefness, compactness, always—until I was set wondering by this manner of concentrating on the subject, for I know it to be a proof of true talent.

Eugene is continually in pain. It seems that he suffers from pain in his head without hope of being cured. This tinges his character with sadness. The expression which most often crosses his face is one of forgetfulness of surroundings. He seems absorbed in other things, far away sometimes from the actual life about him. Hugo's devotion to him, their opinion of each other, the quality of their friendship is something which only the nobleness in each can explain. They are often together, friends since their schooldays at Columbia. Sometimes their conversation brings forth such strange thoughts or facts that they began to write what each says on envelopes, and this they transferred into their diaries.

I have spoken of the privilege of knowing Eugene, of listening to him. And yet much more than that was given to me last night, for there was Hugo, his journal, his character. He writes as he is. I understood him better than I understood Eugene, although Hugo's philosophy is vastly different from anything I have ever known, and Eugene has a way of thinking a little more like my own. Eugene is the one who prefers to shrink from close contact with actual existence and people; he likes solitude. Hugo's philosophy strongly recalls to one's mind the lines: "Life is real, Life is earnest." His fearlessness of it—no, more than that, the willful challenge and confidence in his attitude—is admirable.

He brings idealism down to earth, by our very side; he makes it part of life itself, and not what I often thought—that here was reality, and far up there, winged, elusive idealism, to help us bear it. I can hear Hugo now: "Wrong, wrong, absolutely wrong!" I do not remember what it was of Eugene's that Hugo strongly condemned in his journal. When he finished he said, laughing, "Eugene is crushed, finished." It was one of my ideas, too, so I said: "Not Eugene alone, but I also!" We are different enough to offer different thoughts and yet not different enough to jar upon each other; we harmonize in some vague way, and nothing Hugo or Eugene says sounds discordant to me, nor what I say, to them. It seems to be natural that I should know less. I am better fitted, in my ignorance, to listen to them. I pray only that they should always consider me worthy to listen.

On the train coming home, I had a glimpse of Eugene's selections from his readings. He has compiled the greatest amount of worthwhile and beautiful quotations one could dream of and says that there is one thought binding them together. Published, it would be one of those books which become part of one's life and an inspiration. In one night I have come to feel with Hugo that we should do all we can for Eugene. If he could be relieved from pain, what would he not do, or write? It was also on the train that I showed Hugo and Eugene a few lines from my journal, in connection with the things we had discussed.

The evening had been too short. We had just begun to understand each other, and I to appreciate. Halfway, Eugene left us to take a different train. Before we had time to realize it, Hugo and I were stepping off at our own station and walking slowly home. Hugo did not turn toward Audley Street by the shortest way; he made the way a little longer. I suddenly wished my house would vanish, that it might take us a little longer to find it, but all beautiful things have endings, and our Literary Evening came to a close in spite of the wicked wish. A mist had settled over the country, and in the great, great stillness of the night we walked like people from some other world. When we reached my door, with just a few words and a clasp of the hand, we parted—for only two weeks, if Hugo remembers. He says we shall get together again when he returns. Will such a perfect night ever repeat itself?

August 7. Well, the scenery has changed. I am neither at my desk nor on the porch but in bed, and shall remain in it several days.

I am an invalid, condemned to lie still and almost without change of position while I am cured of something which followed a ride on horseback with Antolinita this morning—a strange pain, but not the stiffness which usually follows strong exercise. No one who knows anything would think Spartans remain in bed out of weariness. No. It is something a little more serious, and yet not enough to affect my cheerfulness. I have been singing to myself very softly and have thought a great deal while inspecting the ceiling. This cheeriness is not a product of a natural state of satisfaction. Quite the contrary—deep, deep down in my heart I have been very sad all these days, but I heard, the night of our Literary Evening, that moods could be controlled and need not control us. Whereupon I decided to conquer my reflective and regretful mood. But it rains, and with each pattering of raindrops my cheerfulness melts away. Rain wakes many memories, many smoldering sentiments, many strange thoughts.

August 8. I have had long hours to readjust my thoughts, long hours to dream, to look back upon past incidents and to question the future. "No hay mal que por bien no venga."[1] Had it not been for this accident, I would not have been left to myself; and I wanted to think of the things I heard the other night, I wanted to ponder on them. Ever since I talked with Hugo and Eugene I longed to escape for a moment and to fix all my attention on this new phase of my universe, this illumination which their thoughts have brought about. Instead I was with Antolinita, trying to understand this restlessness and "ennui" which forever pushes her toward excitement—the movies, followed by rowing on the lake in Central Park and by a visit to the animals the next day; a dance at the inn with Thorvald, Luis Rey (an absolute nonentity) and Charles; and finally the ride on horseback Sunday morning. None of these things are necessary to my happiness, but Antolinita cannot do without them. This attitude toward life is a perpetual problem to me. I have observed it in many people. "Is there nothing to do? Nothing exciting?" And if not, they are plunged in a sea of despondency and boredom. With such people I am ill at ease and uncongenial. I feel as if they were blind; they miss all the beauty in the world, and they truly go through life without knowing themselves, escaping their thoughts like wanderers pursued by a curse. Of course, with Antolinita it is very different. She

[1] *"Every cloud has a silver lining."*

is irresponsible; she has drifted into this purposeless and shallow life unconsciously. But I love her all the same, for she is all sunshine and exuberance, and her heart is made of gold. No serious thought ever entered her head; she laughs in church because the altar boy's cassock is too short, and laughs at the theatre when the players are depicting a deep and passionate love scene; she is glad when music comes to an end, for it bores her; picks up a book only to pass the time away; smiles sarcastically if you speak of friendship between man and woman, or of an ideal, or of art and artists, of marriage and love. Light-hearted, light-headed; in her, the Spiritual in Womanhood is yet asleep. True, she is only fourteen, although as tall as I, and much wiser than I am in the "ways of the social world." She has yet time to blossom in the ways of the other world.

My love of Walter Scott, not supplanted in any way by my love of other writers but hidden in some deep corner of my being, was suddenly brought most vividly to the surface today when I read a thing he seems to have written for me: "I fear you have some very young ideas in your head. Are you not too apt to measure things by some reference to literature—to disbelieve that anybody can be worth much care who has no knowledge of that sort of thing, or taste for it? God help us! What a poor world this would be if that were the true doctrine! . . . We shall never learn to feel and respect our real calling and destiny, unless we have taught ourselves to consider everything as moonshine compared with the education of the heart."

The realization and understanding of the truth Scott expresses in this characteristic fragment has always been one of my favorite subjects. I have written about it in my Description of a Gentleman, I have thought about it, I have sought for it in people. And today I can only add that I pray God that He should never allow me to forget that kindness is greater than wisdom. In seeking knowledge one is easily tempted to commit many errors. There is pedantry, there is conceit, arrogance and false conceptions. As Father McLaughlin said: "At eighteen or twenty, the tools are put into our hands to seek Truth, and we think, when we have but the tools, that we know a great deal, that we can create, that we are wise and educated." Eighteen I know to be a dangerous age, the age of false triumphs, when one believes that one has found something new and discovers it to be universally known, when one, in seeking to understand, believes to be explaining. The little knowledge one has seems to turn one's head. I, who am so deeply plunged in this desire for utility, realize how quickly I can transform myself into a superfluity, but oh, let me remember that what I hold in my hands are only tools.

August 9. How can I expect so much from my very own self? With my eyes fixed on my ideal, I see nothing else, I forget my faults, my frailties, all but that bright light leading me. What of the obstacles? What of the faltering footsteps, the wrong turnings, the discouragements? A strange creed this, that I should expect no more from others than what I obtain from myself, and expect nothing until I have earned the right by possession of the very same qualities! Is it presumptuous? Is it impossible? Is it ridiculous? People so far seemed to have judged human nature by three things: books, observation and conversation. My idea is to first train myself by introspection, by analysis, until I have a perfect control of my sentiments, moods, impulses and temper, a firm hold on my reason and understanding. Then what follows? The self-condemned, self-judged, self-controlled and self-made creature shall be ready to judge others with equality and justice, kindly and truthfully. I may be wrong. Meanwhile, I have an example that seems convincing.

Charles is incredulous of good, not so much for what he sees around him and reads, but because he finds no good in himself. I find no good in myself. In this we agree. The contrast begins where Charles has no dreams of goodness, while I have. Believing in good, I shall struggle until I find it in Self. Once I can feel it, know it, recognize it, I will look at the world through the eyes of goodness and feel it, know it, recognize it everywhere. I will have taught my heart to believe. Is this utterly unreasonable? Can one see goodness without being good? And by goodness, of course, I mean the ideal. This thought seems clear and direct. But who knows if in writing it I have distorted it beyond recognition.

You may ask me what I am doing meanwhile if I am only preparing myself now. Why all this writing, these scattered thoughts, these descriptions? It is still the preparation; it is the first brown seed timidly opening itself in the moist earth, it is the attempt, the struggle for light, the desire to grow, to blossom, it is the thirst for completeness, the great, great longing to act.

I wonder how often I contradict myself. But I am not ashamed, for in no other way can I hope to attain, at least *practice*, the cultivation of clear thinking. I wonder, too, how often, in thinking, I wander to the left and right for long hours, groping for the direct path and reaching it only once or twice out of a thousand trials. What matter. All this ink and paper will harm no one, and it keeps me out of mischief. Never bored, never restless or in need of amusement, never (or seldom) lonely while I am with you, and Mother watching me contentedly. Isn't this a pleasant picture for a summer's day? Just think how interesting it would be if I came to you and, instead of all my collection of thoughts without head or tails, instead of my endless wanderings and annotations of their results, I began: "What can I do? I am bored to extinction. Everybody is busy, and I can talk with no one. There is not an exciting novel in the house. How I wish I were well! I could go to see *Sally*, which is quite a favorite comedy. I want to dance, too; I cannot live another week without a dance. And I haven't seen a boy for 5 days. They are such nice things, you know. I really do need a new dress and a hat, or I'm sure Jimmy or Bill or Tom or Dick and Harry will get tired of me," etc. It is said that "of two evils, choose the lesser." Mostly everyone can be simple and balanced. Few can be queer and impossible, so I shall continue to confess my queer thoughts and impossibilities. I choose the greater evil. There is more of the unexpected in it.

In two days I have read five books, and three of them are like three heavy chests of gold added to my treasure island—three chests of valuable ideas, of fine thoughts, of knowledge. They have kindled my imagination and fired my enthusiasm to such a degree that henceforward these three books shall stand side by side on my mantelpiece, and, as you know, up there I only allow the noblest and best, and the place is crowded, each space a privilege granted only to new arrivals who are considered equals. They are: Longfellow's Poetical Works, *Compendium of English Literature* (nineteenth century) and *Talks to Writers*, by Lafcadio Hearn. The *English Literature* belongs to Captain Norman, and I will not rest until I can find another like it. You have no idea what I have found in those yellowed pages, almost torn from their binding, whether by time or usage I cannot tell. Essays, fragments from books, poems, all preceded by a sketch of the life of each author, abounding in annotations and valuable criticisms, and with all this, such precision of details, such "charm through the entire book that each page I turned only increased my joy and my desire for possession." Possession! Half the books I most dearly love are not yet my own, to cherish and touch and read again. But I sometimes think it is this very fact which has sharpened my appreciation and doubled my love for books. But I want to tell you of a wonderful thing I read. Sydney Smith,[1] a "most accomplished scholar and very original writer" says, on "Female Education": "A great many of the lesser and more obscure duties of life necessarily devolve upon the female sex. The arrangement of all household matters, and the care of children in their early infancy, must of course depend upon them. Now, there is a very general notion that the moment you put the education of women upon a better footing than it is at present, at that moment there will be an end of all domestic economy; and that if you once suffer women to eat of the tree of knowledge, the rest of the family will very soon be reduced to the same kind of aerial and unsatisfactory diet." He goes on to say that this "general notion is referable to a great and common cause of error," explaining this error, pointing to its absurdity, and then: "The instruction of women improves the stock of national talents, and employs more minds for the instruction and amusement of the world; it increases the pleasure of society by multiplying the topics upon which the two sexes take a common interest, and makes marriage an intercourse of understanding as well as of affection by giving dignity and importance to the female character," etc. All this is much more than I ask. The "general notion" only troubled me because it seemed to mean but one thing: Choose between your home and domestic happiness—and your pen and your books. The choice seemed unbearable. One moment I thought I could banish all thoughts of love and retire in absolute loneliness into the life of study and labor; one moment I was overwhelmed by longings for human companionship, for a hearth and its warmth, comfort, cheeriness. I saw children's faces everywhere. In the street my heart flew out to them. Compared to a baby's smile, I thought my books dull and dusty. And then, ashamed of my weakness, I returned to my books, piled them around me so that they might stand between me and that vision of a home and love, which so tenderly beckoned to the womanly side of me. My love of literature or anything I cultivate with care and sacredness will add nothing "to the stock of national talent," nor do I want it for society's pleasure or to give my character greater importance and dignity; I am not talented or sociable or dignified or, still less, marriageable. It is only because I believe that the cultivation of such things will broaden my understanding of those very "lesser and obscure duties" of woman, will fit me better as a companion and helpmate

[1] *Early-nineteenth-century English essayist.*

to whoever wants me. To what Sydney Smith says, I could add Dr. Hugh Blair's[1] lines on the "Cultivation of Taste." Oh, nothing has been left unsaid. I would quote all of it if it were not so long, to show you the boundless treasures hid in mere yellowed pages. You need encouragement? Read. You need advice? Read. You need enlightenment? Read. You shall find everything but—love! Tonight I have conquered the fear of the "general notion" because Sydney Smith agrees with me that it is an error!

August 11. I have returned to the normal life. Whatever thoughts or meditations I indulge in from now on will have to be interrupted and put aside for other things. Distractions of all kinds will again throw obscurity and confusion upon an understanding which seems to broaden as soon as I am left alone. I sometimes think I could write something worthwhile if I could stand apart from the busy world. This may sound foolish. It looks unreasonable on paper, but it is the only explanation I can give to the things calling to me incessantly. Look, in a few days I was lifted far away from the scene of my daily thoughts. The sensation that I was at least near to grasping the Vision, forever pursued and so often lost, was so strange that no shadow of it could be reflected in my Diary. One who could read between the lines would catch perhaps some faint echo of the indescribable. In me, there is nothing left but a vague memory, as one has of a place visited in dreams, and nothing more. It will take another period of solitude and peace to find my way again to that world where understanding is poured upon the soul like sunshine over the flowers. Saints and martyrs whose souls were steeped in prayer saw things which no other eyes could see; I believe it is the same with any human being, no matter what it is he worships, whether the soul be steeped in beauty, in joy, or sorrow; any state that is absolute and sincere will bring some result, some *flash of understanding.*

That is why no one who feels only the little things is great. Only the great soul is capable of great suffering and great joy; great thoughts and, therefore, great beauty are the results, and through them—and only through them—understanding. This explains how it is that only the man who is greatly moved by his idea is capable of accomplishing great things.

I believe, too, that it is mostly in solitude that great men have approached the sacred fires which kindled and awakened

1 *Eighteenth-century Scottish author of* Lectures on Rhetoric.

their own. It is in silence most have heard the murmurings which gave fire and eloquence to their own tongues. I do not mean that this is always so. How often genius has risen from warfare, crowded cities, or from misery and obscurity. No noise is too great to silence it, no incident or circumstance can discourage it. This is genius of *action*—a king, a general, an orator, a prophet, etc. But I am thinking of men of letters.

All this I have written in spite of myself, a poor effort at a translation of some of the thoughts with which these hours were filled. Hours too swiftly passed, of which there remains no record but what my frightened pen dares capture. If I but dared! But I must wait; indeed, in writing I only seem to be playing with paintbrushes and water. I need gold and red and all the colors of the rainbow.

I count the days of Hugo's vacation. Here is a friendship that must be earned. Hugo's judgment of people, as far as I can see, is based on many substantial qualities. He uses more of his head, and what he gives of his heart you know, therefore, to be as true and as sincere as all the rest of him. No pretense, no blindness, no vacillations. He makes me think of Emerson: "If you are noble, I will love you." It is said of women that they distract attention from their faults by the spell of their femininities. I hoped it would not be true. It is true! It has happened to me. The different loves offered to me did not belong to me. That is why I prize friendship more than words can tell. It is based on merit. Marcus idealized me until he thought me beautiful. How far I am from this; how plain I really am. Boys flirted with me because they thought me pretty and sweet and angelical. All wrong again. Enric endowed me with virtues because I gave him sympathy, which he termed inspiration. Miguel would never have been such a pleasant companion nor talked to me if I had been truly and really *ugly*. What kind of admiration is that? Eduardo knew me and was my friend. Even if he does idealize too much, it is in a way nearer to the truth.

Hugo is above all this. There is so little exaggeration in his sentiments that now he never thinks of writing. If I did not know that he acts almost always only when he is certain of himself, I should judge this by ordinary standards and call it indifference. Do you know, I believe Hugo controls and forces back much that is impulsive in him. If I did not notice his eyes, their depth and the delicate, yet firmly pressed lips, and if I had not heard pages from his journal, I might have thought him the very incarnation of the Respectable, Commonsense, Practical, Phlegmatic, Cold-blooded Man of the Age—horrors! But then, because his sentiments do not get the better of him, because they do not shine in his whole attitude or overflow from him in torrents of words and acts, because he does not make a display of them, I feel that they are rarer and finer, like some hidden pearl in a shell. If Hugo tells me: "I like this," I know so well that he does that I could defy the whole world to prove the contrary. If little things could make you see his character, I could fill pages with them. But you have to *see* them and feel them; they are too difficult to write.

The joys and sorrows of a bookworm! Here I come upon a poem by Longfellow which he ought not to have written. Think of it, some time ago in your very pages I said the very same thing in my own awkward, one-legged, turtle-paced way.[1] But I said it! And now listen to this and ask yourself whether I had a right to imitate Longfellow, or Longfellow to have preceded me.

My Cathedral

Like two cathedral towers there stately pines
Uplift their fretted summits tipped with cones;
The arch beneath them is not built with stones,
Not Art but Nature traced these lovely lines;
And carved this graceful arabesque of vines;
No organ but the wind here sighs and moans
Enter! The pavement, carpeted with leaves
Gives back a softened echo to thy tread!
Listen! The choir is singing; all the birds,
In leafy galleries beneath the eaves,
Are singing! Listen, 'ere the sound be fled,
And learn there may be worship without words.

Well, I will console myself with the thought that Longfellow wrote of pines and I of Audley St. He forgot to speak of the lights; his cathedral was dark, mine had candles. Oh, he may have entered in the daytime, but a cathedral is not complete without candles or something to give the illusion of them. At Easter time Longfellow's poems were brought to the house from the public library, and ever since, I have longed for the book. Now it is in my hands again, but my own, and how I love it!

Sweet day of dreams and little duties. Yes, I have returned to the normal life; I sew, I mend, I tidy and I watch over the meals.

[1] *See page 179.*

and yet share the hours with my books and musings. But I have a happy heart and happiness transforms every duty into a simple pleasure. Nothing seems too dull or too long. I love life and its little cares. I see poetry in everything. One tiny happy day among so many that are sad and desolate. But the happy man has no history. So after all, it is better for you and it is better for me—as it is.

August 13. I sometimes wish I could cease dreaming and lay my fingers on the actual life about me. I wish that I could feel nearer, draw closer, to the real world, and see things as everyone else sees them. And sometimes, too, I wish I could turn my eyes away from the "inward sphere of things, the abstract, the visionary." I am tired of my constant brooding.

Last night I went to the open-air with Thorvald, Charles and two other boys. They laughed all night, sang, talked nonsense—in short, did what is called "cutting up," and although I could not help laughing, I secretly longed to run away, to hide. I felt so far away from them. For this I scolded myself without pity. I promised to control these foolish moods, to brush aside these unreasonable longings. I must remember that if I am not like other girls, I should at least try to be like them when I am with people. Alone, I can be as I please—it harms no one—but at other times, oh, my heart, be gay. Be light, be simple and accessible.

Evening. You are truly the only friend I have tonight. I have been scolded by Mother, and without reason, but before words of rebellion or anger could rise to my lips, I fled, a coward. Afraid of myself and the strong feelings which I have been holding back all day.

What is the trouble with me? I have forbidden myself many things—thinking of Eduardo, too—but what is the use of writing these resolutions? Thoughts cannot be controlled like actions, and there are moments when mine turn naturally and inevitably to the persons I long to have near me. But are these thoughts the cause of my desolation? Or Mother's injustice? I fear there is little cause. My sorrows seem to come from nowhere, like dark and heavy clouds which fall upon me, and I am wrapped in them so completely that I cannot see the smallest gleam of light. If I had courage to break away . . .

August 15. I have found the key to contentment, the charm which dispels my "dark clouds." It can be described in a few words:

"Work for others. Never cease working for others. Do not think of yourself!"

Work! This is my first day of work only and work alone. I awoke early and attended Mass in honor of the Blessed Virgin's Feast, receiving communion with the ancient spirit of childish devotion and fervor which so often animated me in Spain.

Once home, I covered my head with a red gypsy handkerchief and began my housecleaning. For hours I dusted, and swept, and shook everything. I carried scrap baskets up and down the stairs, I tidied, made beds, set order in the closets, rubbed the furniture until I could see myself in it. You should have seen the dust fly out of the window, and the cobwebs abandon their strongholds. You should have heard the noise of brooms and brushes and dustpans clattering up and down the stairs, the creaking of the beds I tried to push. And you should have seen the face under that red gypsy handkerchief. I was proud of my soiled hands—the long fingers, so often coiled round a pen, could well hold a broom; it was more useful. And all the time, I sang. I sang to the sunshine, and sang about Hugo, and all my friends—after exhausting my repertoire, of course. At three o'clock I had cleaned the house from top to bottom, excluding the attic and the cellar but including the porch and the sidewalk and the garden path and the kitchen stairs.

At this time, I took my gypsy headdress off and went amarketing. I gave the train watchman a pear, and everybody a dozen or so smiles—unnecessary but uncontrollable smiles—and then, once home, I mended stockings and set the dinner going. When Mother came, of course, her satisfaction increased my joy. A perfect day, a useful day, a happy day. If I could only remember that the greatest and most beautiful thing in the world is to labor for those you love. I might have sat for hours brooding on my faults. I might have filled many of your pages with laments, with the description of sad moods which are the effect of idleness. Instead, with broom and dustpan I cleared the cobwebs from the house and from my mind. It simplifies life so much—to live more of it and to write less.

August 16.

To Dick [Frances]:

It is because my ideas have suddenly awakened—they do not crawl, they bounce. I have never discovered as many things nor thought as many things as during these last days—and the result was that for some time I was heartily ashamed of myself and only wrote in my Diary. I always begin by being ashamed—it's a habit—then slowly I grow accustomed to my new attitude, read Emerson's essay on Self-Reliance and come forth, if not satisfied, at least resigned! . . .

August 18. Just one little stolen moment for myself in the midst of another busy day. Alas, what little courage there is in me. The first day of housework I sang, the second day, after dusting my books, I ceased singing and became thoughtful. Yesterday I could not sing at all. The dishwater, the smell of kitchen soap, the dust— choke me! Once I remember wondering if heaven had meant woman for this kind of work. Joaquin was playing his compositions and I was cooking, having just finished ironing his shirts and handkerchiefs and mending his socks—in short, attending to his physical comfort. If I had been writing upstairs, he would not have been fed and clothed, and fit to play and compose. His work on the piano is worth a thousand times more than mine at my desk, is it not? Well there, Mimi, stay in the kitchen; genius must be served. But oh, today when a cleaning woman came I could have hugged her. She is the queen of the brooms and dust rags for the day. I'll be the humblest subject of her kingdom—willingly and gaily.

Not a day has passed that I have not thought of Hugo. His two weeks of vacation end Saturday, but he will probably return Sunday night or Monday morning. And then? I cannot tell. Will he remember? Will he want to see me again? I have knelt every night and prayed heaven to bring Hugo back to me, prayed with all my heart. If his friendship fails me, I fear my trust in friendship will not pass its severest test. Oh, the sadness of uncertainty— and about people I seem to know so little, so terribly little. When will I be able to discern, to judge, to place my trust in trustworthy hands. I am always giving myself away in some strange way. People know all that is in my heart; they read my face, my eyes. I can hold no secret likes and dislikes. No. Foolishly, childishly, stupidly, I show all I feel, the blood rushes to my cheeks; it comes quickly and goes, only to return. This has happened particularly with Hugo. If my impulse prompts me to jump from my chair when I see him come, I forget that conventions expect me to sit still and look indifferent. *One* mistake! It would take all day to count them!

Of course, few people could want me for a friend. People expect you to have manners, to know precisely what to do and say on every occasion. I am always blundering, and saying queer things—I ought to be exiled from the polite world and abandoned on an island with my books and my ink bottle.

August 19. Dorothy [Eddins] is coming this afternoon. The house is ready; there is another substantial-looking maid in the kitchen washing and ironing, and I have only the cooking to do, and the supervision, directing and planning. Never has my Diary heard the details of "woman's obscure and humble duties," but I like to write in out-of-the-ordinary terms, such as belong to housekeeping, to see how they look in black and white! On close observation, they look quite respectable and matter-of-fact. But whatever I might do, however I might control my impulses, a broom will never be just a broom to me, nor pots and pans just pots and pans. I always endow them with powers of understanding. Make-believe so often makes me do things with pleasure which I otherwise would do without enthusiasm.

Am I afraid to tell you what is truly passing in my heart? I have not an ounce of courage left. There is something in the beauty of the day, its softness, its caressing breezes, its lovely sunshine, that offers a great contrast to my own feelings. I would like to hide somewhere, to be left alone with my "dark cloud." Can I conquer this time as I conquered days ago?

I will probably write nothing until Monday. These will be the kind of days that all girls have and like and enjoy. I know so little about them and fear them. You will lie quietly at the bottom of my desk drawer, meanwhile, and let us hope, you and I, that I will take you out to write: "I have heard from Hugo!"

August 22. I have heard from Hugo! I have heard from Hugo! It is almost like a fairy tale, that I should close my Diary hoping for something and that it should come true. He sends me post cards and writes: "Dear Anaïs: I thought I could just follow this lovely road forever but have found 'compañia de Dios.' So I am going back to get my two friends and resume the journey with them. Hugo." He alludes to the Spanish proverb "Compañia de uno, compañia ninguna; compañia de dos, compañia de Dios; compañia de tres, compañia es! Compañia de cuatro, compañia del Diablo."[1]

[1] *"Company of one, no company at all; company of two, company of God; company of three is real company; company of four, company of the Devil."*

And besides this to gladden the day, I had a thousand things. They were chiefly memories of the weekend, which turned into the most pleasant and amusing little house party imaginable. Thorvald was bewitched by Dorothy, and they became great friends. Homer [Eddins], although only fifteen, but tall, witty, talkative and flirtatious, made quite a charming partner for me. The four of us danced at the inn Saturday night, took long walks, and chatted from daybreak till daybreak, almost. Sunday afternoon, Mr. Eddins came to see Mother, and we finally accompanied them all to the station in the evening. And then today I spent the afternoon with Antolinita, so that my head is quite empty and my heart light. This is the price you pay for so many frivolous hours. After such a long absence from my books, I feel like one who has traveled for long in foreign lands and is eager to return to his cozy home and hearth.

Homer put flowers in my hair, drew my profile, showered compliments and insisted that he had never given them to anyone else (I did not believe him!) and finally kissed my hand when we parted—but tell me, is not all this a waste of time? I might have read three books meanwhile. But of course you cannot do the same thing continually, and I must learn to resign myself to the destiny of woman, which makes her a victim of compliments and impossible, unbelievable and worn-out tricks, which might succeed with some, but with Mimi—oh, well, Mimi is a skeptic.

In this first bit of writing from Hugo I find many characteristic traits. It gives the impression of frankness and "squareness" and simplicity, with an undefinable thing which might be called "matter-of-fact" without too much emphasis on "fact." Hugo betrays little of the fanciful—I should say none—in his writing; the capital letters are attached so directly and briefly. Compare them with mine. Oh, I hope the contrast does not mean that I am not fit to make him a good friend. We could not very well be exactly the same. I would not want him to be like me at all; how could he be without being impossible and full of faults? No, Hugo is himself. That is why he is a thousand times better.

August 27. The week has passed, and I have lost myself. I will try to tell you why I am bewildered by my own doings—so bewildered that I do not recognize them. I have not opened a book, I have not dreamed or thought deeply or written. Each day has been thrown away, just lived and well-filled with action and conversation. I have played tennis with Antolinita, Charles and Thorvald;

I have been now the cook, the housekeeper, now the sociable and communicative young lady Mother wishes me to be, the athlete Thorvald admires, and a thousand other unexpected persons, to the great joy and satisfaction of the family. At night I am tired, not of brooding and reading and writing, but tired like Thorvald, or like the maid. I fall asleep instantly and dream of Hugo. He has not telephoned, and although I count the days, I am not saddened, because while he does not know it, he is talking with me nearly each night. No earthly power can take my dreams away from me, and they give me enough joy to last me the whole day.

And so the week has passed, empty if judged by my usual standards, filled according to the standards of those around me. And I am not sad, because I am looking at life in the manner of others, complacently, simply—but I am not happy, because I am a stranger in this new world, and I am homesick. I long for my books and my solitudes, my dreams, my thoughts. What I am doing now is flying over the surface of things—it is all polished, and smooth, and simple. Usually I plunge into the depths, I dig and search in these intricate, rugged depths, I am storm-tossed and bruised, yes, but only by this can I find the treasures hidden *below the surface.*

Today for the first time I have felt the sweetness of nature, I have heard its sounds and am conscious of its reign over my heart—because I am alone. Today for the first time I have felt the yearning for my pen and the true joy of speaking with my own heart—because I am alone. Today, also, for the first time I realize the great, great empty space Hugo's forgetfulness creates in my life—because I am alone. I am alone, and the great waves of feeling sweep down all barriers, uncontrolled, recognized. I am carried away by emotions too long asleep, and my thoughts have broken loose and are scattered like autumn leaves. I have found myself.

There is so much to do that I must try to travel on the surface a little longer. My explorations in the depths will be only between you and me, if I can find time. You see, I have the house on my shoulders, for Mother is passing a serious crisis in her affairs. Perhaps, after all, I can help her more when I deny myself books. Then I seem always on the alert for work and more work. I forget myself completely. In the evening I share her doubts and hopes, and we speculate on the future and its possibilities. The question of money is always hanging over our heads. Days ago I exclaimed that I wished myself nearer to actual life, and these days this is what has taken place. I have been brought face to face with practicalities, facts. And then I lose my head and wonder where I am, and who I am. There is something wrong, totally wrong, in this attitude, though what it is I cannot tell. Actual, practical life lies beneath my fingers. Why should I fear to touch it, to grasp it firmly? Lose myself? No, I should only lose some of my foolish and useless notions. Well, I am ready. No hesitations, no outcry, no laments. I do believe what I call the "surface" is in reality the hard things I have long evaded; the depths are the abstract, the shadows, the ghostly in life, in which I take a selfish pleasure. If I can do more for Mother by my understanding and practice of the hard things, then I begin today. I begin to brush aside my tender reveries on nature, my longings for writing, my futile desires for friendship and companionship. Be strong, oh, my heart—at least for another week. Should I despise these delicate and tender sentiments which seem to make one unfit for a life of successful actions? Can there be an understanding of the harder things, the sterner discipline of everyday duties, where there are visions, ideals, constant dreaming? Hugo seems to unite these in a way I do not yet grasp—as if they were all part of one life, and necessary to one life, equally useful, and equally shared.

August 29. For days I have controlled myself, thinking always that I could be more useful, more thoughtful of the good of others, if I concentrated on my work and on my work alone. Everywhere you hear: Anaïs remembered this, she thought of that—how good, how wonderful! Oh, and I am going to be thoughtful forever. At last I have found the way to help and please. What if I hear music, am thrilled by a scene in nature? All my thoughts and feelings are immediately awakened, but they are only for myself, and it is not right to be always living for one's self. Thus tonight, if I allowed myself to dream, I should end sorrowfully, I should think of the Friend who is forgetting, and lose courage . . . But I am leaving you to mend stockings.

August 31. Heaven takes away a little of my happiness by allowing Hugo to remain silent, but in return it has made one of my dearest and most cherished dreams come true. Eduardo writes! And by what he writes I see that at last he understands the *purpose* of my friendship. I have succeeded, succeeded in all ways. Apparently, it would seem that I am doing him harm, strengthening him in an attitude which endangers his happiness as far as his family and his father's wealth are concerned. But I *know* that now he possesses the only true and worthwhile sources of happiness. The secret is his forever, no one can wrench it from him, no earthly powers can touch him. His spirit and his heart *are awake and strong*. There is no greater gift to be obtained; he is in reality a thousand times richer than all his family!

This is the joy I derived from his letter, but there is much sadness in it. Listen: "Ah, indeed, sadness! Why should I not be sad since the thought has come to my mind that perhaps you may have lost the ideal I stood for? I well know, cuisine, that you cannot but idealize your friends, as I do! I well know I had an ideal— and then—that deed!! If you knew, cuisine, how hard I tried, and am trying to live up to that ideal! And I wish you to know it. I wish you to know how you have inspired me to see goodness, honesty, nobleness and truthfulness. Having perceived all these, I try my utmost to keep to that ideal—at times, cuisine, I turn to find myself successful. Then the consciousness of having done good gives me peacefulness and hope. Mimi, my devotion to you will be forever in my heart as well as your endeared image . . . You shall see how true, how firm, I shall stand till the end! Oh, cuisine, if I could tell you what you have been to me—but forgive these wild utterances; they come from a heart that finds it hard to part with you!! Tout à vous, Eduardo. P.S. I ask only one boon which you ought to grant me, cuisine: think of me sometimes."

To think of him *sometimes*. I, who think of him each day! What if he knew, when he speaks of "the dreams of a lonely heart," that all of my lonely heart leaps up, ready to fly to him with all the sympathy I have strength to give, and the desire to give? Alas, what keeps my hand from tracing the words which would unite us? Mother, who says it is all nonsense from a romantic and exalted boy—all words, as frail as rose petals and as long-lived as butterflies. But I do not believe her! No, it is not what she *says*, it is that she *forbids* me to answer Eduardo's letter, and I would not make Mother unhappy. Perhaps some day I will understand *her* point of view, *her* reasoning. Now I can only bow my head in submission. Last time I had more courage, for the thought of Hugo helped me, but today it offers only a great contrast and is emphasized by his indifference, and Eduardo's sincerity . . . until I am strongly tempted to turn away from the former and seek refuge in the true friendship of "mon cousin."

September 1. Voltaire says that ideas are like beards; women and young men have none! Well, well. I shall have to find another name for all the odd evolutions continually taking place in my head. Even today while I was sweeping, dusting and tidying, so many of what I call *ideas* came to me that it took all my strength and long conversations with myself to keep me from flying to you. And now that my work is done, I fear I mixed the dust and ideas and shook both out of the window, for there is nothing left of either. Both the house and head are immaculately clean. Perhaps that is why tradition has never separated cobwebs from a true author's room (unless he had a wife who was not literary). There is something cheerful and placid about housekeeping, and also an almost miraculous simplicity about such problems as food and cleanliness and comfort. I fear that I am far from being the typical "bluestocking," so often defined and classified as someone out of place in a home. Sometimes my taste grows really prosaic, as plain as the tastes of a born housekeeper. I find fun in the making of a cake, I grow enthusiastic when my dinners are gobbled down, I cannot sit in a room which needs sweeping. And still I am not yet entirely or hopelessly domesticated. No sooner are my duties finished than I creep up to my room, where I find Carlyle or Emerson waiting for me.

September 2. I have forbidden my family to name Hugo and to tease me. Mother suggests I answer: "Where there's a will, there's a way." One might think that there is a great difference in race between Hugo and me. He might be thought simply undemonstrative because he is Scottish, and I, too impatient, too impulsive, because of my quick-fire Spanish blood. But with me Hugo has shown equal enthusiasm; I have seen his eyes flash, I have seen the blood rise to cover his cheeks; his gestures are all quick and spontaneous, his emotions just as strong, perhaps stronger, than mine. As from an open book I could read the pleasure he took in my company. Then *why, why, why* is there not the smallest word from him now? I am so perplexed, so surprised, by this that I am beginning to be angry with myself for being so sensitive and so impatient. I wish I were one of those cold-blooded, phlegmatic persons who stand like rocks under any circumstance. I wish I were cynical and sarcastic so that I should expect nothing. But no, I am still full of hopes and trust. Oh, is it right to hope and trust so untiringly? Does heaven wish to teach me the lesson that one must not look to others for happiness? Friends! How I love the very sound of the word, and all it implies, all it stands for. Dear friends! I do not understand your ways, but I love you. It must be my fault that I do not understand. I shall wait another week before I cease to hope.

September 4. After days of intolerable heat when the thermometer reached 100 degrees at times, there followed a great, sweeping storm. Today the streets are covered with leaves and branches torn by the wind and hail; the sun, after appearing through the mist which envelops the entire country, has vanished and left the world gray, humid and sad. Sunday!—its placid charm, its placid contentments, its placid hours, today mean only one thing: this is the end of an interminable week. Not an hour of it has been wasted, and still it has seemed long. When one expects something, even if it be a little thing, how large it seems to grow in proportion with our faith and constancy. The little thing is like a great cloud above one's head from the first hour of waking until night, and sometimes throughout the night, when one dreams of it. You lift your eyes to pray and you see It. You work or read or write, and you feel It.

Mother's common sense, her cheery judgment, are my greatest comfort and only source of strength. If I could only see the world through her eyes, I would be laughing now instead of wasting ink. But what can you expect from a creature who sleeps 100 years and then walks into the world with hands stretched out to receive rose petals and love and kindness? Among these things there certainly must be a little casket full of thorns with this message: "What you deserve!"

The sunshine reappeared and some of the warmth and cheeriness of the day has pierced the mists surrounding my own heart. Mother and I have taken possession of the porch. Her face is hidden behind a newspaper; mine turns from the sky to the end of the road and back toward my Diary. The sky is serene and cloudless, the road is silent and empty.

Later. Recipe for gladness: Make biscuits and watch Thorvald eat them!

September 6. After another interminable day of great sadness I sat with Mother on the porch, incapable of shaking off the heavy shadows. There were times when the aching grew almost intolerable. Then suddenly, the telephone rang. I flew upstairs and could hardly believe my own ears when Hugo's voice reached me. "This is a surprise!" I exclaimed. Surprise! After all the pain I have undergone, I had the courage to appear merely surprised. Hugo explained lightly that he had been very busy, that the time had fled, etc., and that he would come tomorrow night if I were home. He has not guessed one inkling of the things that have passed in my head, and how can I not forgive him for a thing he knows nothing of? I fear, in spite of my happiness tonight that this incident denotes a flaw in our friendship. Hugo does not understand me very well, and yet, do I understand him? Do I understand "lightness" in anyone for that matter? Am I not too serious, too unbearably serious, not to be daily hurt and brushed aside by all those I love? I make little things large; I count the hours carefully, I analyze, and brood, and question continually. I have few friends, and I give them all I have, and study them, and feel hunger for them. One little contrariety, one little indifference, one harsh word or one unreasonable action upsets my whole life and inflicts such great pain that I long to die. And around me people pass me by, rushing onward with aspirations I cannot fathom, active, light-hearted, brave, unfailing. *Strong*. They almost trample on me, while I stand there wondering, asking questions, trying to understand so that I may follow them. No one can pause to help me or to teach me; they have not the patience, nor the love. I must do my thinking alone, and *discover* alone.

September 9. Many things are mysteries to me; the thousand things that pass my comprehension would fill a book, and among them, if I were to write that book, I should put down Hugo's name in large letters. It is also a mystery to me how one can be glad and suffer at the same time. This happened to me Wednesday night. I was infinitely happy because Hugo came, and yet hurt and distressed by many things which I dare not write. Hugo had brought Eugene with him, and Mother and Joaquin joined us, so that it was indeed "Compañia de cuatro, compañia del Diablo." I, the fifth, was the observer who detected the "Diablo." We talked of general things, and Hugo and Mother sang by turn. There was a formal air about the evening which smothered all my impulses. Whatever I wanted to say to Hugo literally stuck in my throat. Eugene talked little; we had wandered so far from his favorite topics. That night I fell asleep telling myself that it seemed as if all I knew of Hugo he was by intention trying to hide. I was looking beyond all outward appearances, beyond words and gesture directly at the very heart and spirit in him. Can I be totally wrong? If I were given just one more evening with Hugo alone, I could unravel the mystery. There was truly understanding and harmony between us the first fairylike night of the concert and dance, and during Diaz's concert and at Long Beach. But the other night, too, there was understanding in his eyes, but not a word or act to prove it.

Fortunately Antolinita put a stop to my broodings by inviting me to her house. We went to the moving pictures yesterday afternoon and to the theatre in the evening, the Century Theatre, where they were presenting *The Last Waltz*. It is gorgeous and festive-looking. There are moments when one is glad to be surrounded by strange faces, glad to follow those people who seek pleasure in frivolousness, glad to be where life bubbles over, light, shallow and brilliant. No serious thoughts, no mysteries, no torturing analyses and wondering. Of course, you miss the joys of the other life also; you miss the satisfaction of discovery, the lovable hours of solitude and silence, the dreams, the meditations, which belong to the deeper kind of life and never appear on its surface. You miss, in short, the things which are happiness, the only happiness given us on earth. Not everybody knows how to glide or dance through life, forever on the gay surface of things. I am one of them.

September 10. The leaves have begun to fall. When I go to the village I hear the wind passing through the trees, claiming a little of their foliage each day. Some leaves fell on my hair and were entangled in it. Oh, if they would all fall on me, I would stand very still and straight and I might be changed into a tree, a silent, watchful tree by the roadside, incapable of suffering, incapable of thinking. That so much beauty should pass away, and yet return. Are all things made only to cause us pain, regret and then infinite joy, more than a creature seems able to bear? Is there not pain in nature, and yet a power far greater than our own drawing us nearer to it? Is there not pain in love? And yet the same power wills that we cannot live without it; makes our hearts hunger for it and fear it; we die for want of love and are killed by its cruelties and changefulness. To dwell on such things is enough to make one believe in Fatality. Yes, a Fatal Power, not a Godly Power, rules over us. A Power which takes pleasure in destruction, in inflicting pain and discouragement, a Power that crushes the rebellious spirit, and that answers questions by another manifestation of its indomitable strength.

What daring pushes me to write these words? Have I become an atheist? Is life, only just begun for me, already proving itself unbearable? Only an understanding of the things which are happening to us can explain why today I rail against Destiny and refuse to pray. Why should I pray? Would a beggar who had been kicked by a passer-by follow him and beg again? Why should I humiliate myself before a power that gives as much to a sinner as to one who has believed for years? Oh, Mother! It is your tired face which makes me say these things. You work each day, bravely, cheerfully, and then it is willed that things should change, that all your hopes should dissolve.

Obstacles which no human being could foresee have arisen on Mother's path. The struggle for a living has become harder, each day harder. Efforts fail, the debts grow larger, the political situation in Cuba[1] bears terrible effects on business. I have struggled against Mother's pride and mother love to obtain permission to work. She refuses absolutely. I can only care for the house, and spend the greater part of the night pondering and asking myself what I can do. We sometimes sit on the porch at night, Mother and I, and talk of selling the house and going back to Europe, where we would earn money, Mother says, by her singing lessons or anything. To begin a new life, far away from the relatives to whom we owe much help and kindness and also much of our unhappiness and troubles. I would regret nothing. One of Mother's fondest dreams seems further away from realization each day. She wanted to take me to Havana, but in our position we can do nothing, and the only ones who might have made this possible do not want to do it. The Sánchezes have never known what it is to give to others a little of what they have. Oh, why should we not go and leave all these shattered hopes behind us? At night sometimes I lay awake for hours asking myself the *Why* of *everything*.

Much later. Hugo is again coming here during weekends. I shall call him my Favorite Mystery and observe his unfathomable ways. I shall write here everything I gather from these observations, and then you and I will put them together on a large page and read them off without interruption to see if they make sense. I will number them. Would it not be amusing if the subject of my study did not appear on the scene at all?

[1] *Following the collapse of the sugar market in World War I.*

September 11. 1. I watched the road for hours. 2. My Favorite Mystery passed by, paused for a few minutes while we exchanged trifles and walked away. (I said everything except what I had *wanted* to say.) And that is all. From my window this morning I saw him in his garden. After this, another long week, another weekend, a glimpse of him now and then—rien de plus, hélas![1] for in true life friendship n'est qu'un autre chagrin![2]

Afternoon. A gray, cold, sad day with showers of leaves each time the wind sighs. I have been reading the book reviews and my mind is full of fresh ideas and valuable information. There are times when my thoughts circle around one solitary object, and for days they are enchained and tortured by a dominant reality, an incident, a sorrow. This happened because of Mother's unhappiness and discouragement. Nothing could draw my attention away from the terrible future; I thought day and night about all kinds of things, and silently created a world of protest and rebellion against injustices which seemed more like a vast fire consuming all my strength and faith.

Fortunately this cannot last long. All that I have learned from books, all that I have created in my happy hours, my cherished ideals—nameless voices coming from everywhere—call out to me. I am lifted far above the sorrowful present and forget all that must be forgotten in order to advance and continue laboring and building. Others forget in joyous company at the theatre, at the dance.

Mother works about the house or sits in her armchair with a pleasant book. I read, or walk, and my thoughts cease to revolve around one hopeless pain and set out to wander with the leaves. They travel to England and circle round Vanessa's letters to Jonathan Swift, about which the Literary Review gives many details. Or they circle about things Hugo said to me; but here I scold myself for nonsense and return to literature, always to literature, the well beloved of many but I doubt if ever as deeply loved as by this lonely girl's heart.

Evening. It seems strange to leave the porch and settle in the parlor, but we could not bear the humid and cold air of a truly autumnal evening. For my part, I am satisfied because I can sit near the lamplight and employ my time in scribbling. There was almost always a touch of a sadness in the weird dreams I had

[1] *Nothing more, alas.*
[2] *Is only another sorrow.*

while we sat in the darkness, waiting for bedtime. I will often remember these days, I will think of the porch and the moonlight, and the incessant buzz of insects. I will remember the faint light of other homes trembling through the branches, and I will remember the reveries which came to me at these hours. In spite of this I have always disliked sitting with idle hands for any long period and I prefer to be near the light where I may write.

Tonight my heart is very full. If I wrote bitter words yesterday, I want to tell you now that I am sorry for them. Indeed, it is only the wicked and blinded fool who would rail against things beyond his understanding. No mortal mind will ever understand the ways of God. When I cry out against oppression, misfortune, injustice, I am doing so because things are unjust and unkind when judged from my point of view. In God's mind these selfsame things may be only good for us. Adversity may be sent to strengthen and broaden us although it may seem incredibly cruel and undeserved punishment.

I first began to understand how blinded I was by bitterness when I thought of all we had to be *thankful* for, when I looked around and took notice of all we had in comparison to others: health, love and devotion to one another. We have Joaquin's genius to be thankful for, Thorvald's fine character and manliness. See tonight how we sit together. Joaquin is at the piano and it sounds like an organ; the notes roll upon one another, wavelike, brilliant, liquid; I cannot tell just how it sounds, but the world is transformed as if under the touch of some magician's wand. Thorvald is in great despair, thinking that school will begin tomorrow. He is contemplating long evenings of studies, early rising, enough to make even Thorvald honestly serious—for five minutes. Mother's face alone makes my heart sink (I have been trying to recover my gaiety). How furrowed it is, how full of troubles and cares. Tomorrow I will read something of Emerson's. I long to feel again the touch of his powerful yet gentle and healing hand. I feel that his sane philosophy will set my own on its feet again. His counsels are like sunshine, or pure air, the truest medium for the distressed heart. I am going to work for Mother, but I might steal a moment while waiting for the train.

September 12. Nothing can take away from me the happiness that has nestled in my heart. I have a talisman to dispel all sadness for many days. Oh, I did not deserve it. I had just returned from a walk with Mother and Charles when the telephone rang. It was

Hugo's voice; I cannot describe the pleasure it gave me. For a little while, he was not my Favorite Mystery but my Dearest Friend. We talked of many things, and he told me (when I asked him if he would like to come again as he did the other evening) that he could not do it this week and would let me know as soon as it would be possible. I tried to express a little of my joy and toward the end I said that I was glad he had called. Wouldn't people think you quite insane if you told the *exact truth* always, in spite of "convenance"? I should have said: I am *so glad, so glad* that you telephoned that I have forgotten all I wanted to say to you! I sometimes feel that Hugo understands me when I cannot say something. I am so often intimidated or startled by the unexpected that I can never count on finding my head in precisely the proper place at the critical moment. Let us hope (here we are supposed to clasp our hands and turn our eyes to heaven) that time will cure me of all these impossibilities!

Well, I did read Emerson, but I must admit that a little talk with Hugo did far more to increase my optimism than all the philosophies in the world. This is indeed a shameful confession for a bookworm to make. It sounds as if it came from someone else. I am being corrupted by my worldly environment. Where, pray tell me, have my hermit's instincts gone? Where is my ancient disdain for my fellow creatures? Where is . . . Oh, rejoice with me, and ask no questions. "L'homme heureux n'a pas d'histoire."[1]

September 13. Nothing less than a poem should be written about a day like this. It seems an act of daring and irreverence to be writing prose, or, what is more, to be writing at all. In spite of this I know I may write as long as I please, and as stupidly as I am capable of without attracting the least attention. There is no one to censure me. This is an encouraging thought, and therefore prepare yourself to follow all the usual antics of a pen under the influence of a hopeless malady commonly termed: talkativeness.

At times I wonder how it is that your pages do not absorb colors. You lie open under gray skies, you lie open in the most glorious floods of sunshine (such as today, for instance), and yet when I reopen you it is always to find a white page with closely written lines of black ink. What have you done with my beloved twilights? Where is the sun's beautiful gold? Where is the deep rose of the lamplight? No answer. Always the black and white be-

---

[1] *"A happy man has no history."*

fore my eyes. To your smooth surface nothing clings. All that is sweet, beautiful, joyous, slips off your pages like the waves which pass over rocks and are carried back with the tide. The essence of things and all that I cannot describe in black and white passes away to take its place in the kingdom of the past. It is the same today—I would not want today to vanish, to be lost forever, but it will soon slip between my fingers like a dream. I paused because one of my bird's feathers came flying down, ending its aerial voyage on the arm of my chair. With the tip of my pen stuck in the heart of it, I carried it to the little basket I have for all the captive feathers. I wish happy days would turn into feathers.

The other day I bitterly denounced calamity as unjust and useless. Emerson gives the reason for it and partly answers my questions. I still think that calamity in general is an obstacle to the growth of character. Does not sorrow cause bitterness, harshness and envy in individuals? This does not mean that I totally disregard calamity as having its compensations. We can alone be strong by learning to master pain; sorrow often ennobles and inspires. But what I cannot see is to what *purpose* we are made to undergo all this. Of what good is this growth attained by privations? We are asked to sacrifice our all, to build temporary homes, to adopt temporary beliefs, because we are incessantly ordered to leave all this and, without looking backward, step again into a new transformation, "that of the man of today who does not recognize the man of yesterday." Does this not give a sense of futility? Of being the smallest part of the universe, puppets of relentless laws? Growth? Toward what? Sacrifice and labor—then death and darkness. I believe there is only one kind of compensation, and only one. It might be the happiness we derive from our moral achievements, the satisfaction of our consciences, the certain freedom allowed to the spirit—and even here there is a limit to our understanding, there is a limit to our *faith*. There is something desolate in the contemplation of so much transition, so much wearing away of things we would wish fixed and everlasting. Perhaps it is easier for the happier mind to put off "dead circumstances day by day" without lingering in the ruins of the old tent, without looking backward. But there are minds who attach themselves to things they have loved once and find something sacred in being true and faithful to them. Idolaters of the old! Is that essentially the cause of literature, and the cause of almost every written thing? Is it the instinct of preservation against the ravages of time, the preservation of history, of sentiments and thought; and in individuals, is it the preservation of the "man of yesterday"?

The more I think and ponder on these things, the more I realize the truth of Lafcadio Hearn's words: "The mystery of the universe is now weighing upon us, becoming heavier and heavier, more and more awful as our knowledge expands, and it is a specially ghostly mystery." I say this because all the little mysteries of which the world is full seem to lead only to the One Mystery. All my questions lead to the one great question, all my ideas circle around the important subject, and though I may read and wonder for ages, I will never know any more than all the others who had the same experience. Most probably even now I know less because I waste much of my time supplying you with landscapes as I go along, flourishing my pen continuously and making of my journey not a matter of pressing business but a casual stroll. I am enjoying the walk, as it were, stopping often on the roadside to sketch a stone or a primrose. I should add that although I am enjoying myself, I would like to know *where* I am going. Am I too inquisitive?

They cry out against literary women because they are unfit for home, or domestic life. While scribbling down these divagations I have interrupted myself three times. Primero: to make a cake for dinner. Segundo: To make the beds and cook the lunch. Tercero: To mend stockings. Here are the facts for you who turn up your noses at bluestockings.

September 14. The days of busy people seem short, so short that there is no time to write about them. Hugo says that we have more ideas when we are active but that we have not the time to write them down. It is no wonder then that it should appear as if all our ideas come only while we are alone and calm. We pretend to desire solitude to think, and it is only a secret longing to write or set our ideas in order when our heads become crowded. I thought of this today while I ran errands for Mother, addressed envelopes and answered the telephone at her office. Ideas came so quickly, and such humorous ideas, that I wondered if I would ever find myself alone with you so that we might laugh together. Now the time has come, but I am so sleepy. What if I should write something that I could regret tomorrow on awakening completely? Besides, really, as a humorist I would be stoned to death. To feel absurdly happy is one thing. To make others feel absurdly happy is another thing—it's a gift. And I bow in profound submission to the gods who forgot me on the day of distribution!

September 17. Tearing pages? Well, well, here is another mystery to be solved. What did I write on them? (One the other day and another today.) Nothing to be ashamed of, that alone I can promise. I often think that I should tear many pages off these little books. They would be lighter. And yet at other times I do believe one needs much space to set down one's ideas, and still more space if one has the habit of cutting off their heads now and then, as I do. You are really like a garden in which all things grow, including weeds; should not weeds be torn out? Yes, of course, but if I took out the weeds in my garden, there would be nothing left.

Evening. Hugo paused a long while today when he passed and we talked of many things. I wish I could give a name to the feeling I have when we talk in this way, even for a short time. Hugo never turns his eyes away, and I would like to do the same but then I forget what I am going to say. When he leaves, I want to call him back just for a moment more, and when there is no excuse I begin wondering why it is that I did not tell him a word of what I most wanted to tell him. What would he think if he knew that I have long conversations with him each day in preparation for the moment that I will see him? But in spite of all, I am always caught at the unexpected moment; I almost always lose my head and the blood rises quickly to my cheeks. If Mother could read over my shoulders she would say: "Que tu es bête, fifille!"[1] With all this I forget to tell you that I saw a fine play with Antolinita; Henri Bataille's[2] version of *Don Juan*. Then yesterday with Charles I saw the beautiful and touching *Way Down East*. I will not forget either one for a long, long time, and especially *Way Down East*, upholding the very ideal I cherish. One heart for one heart, one love for one love, one man for one woman. Its sincere appeal to faithfulness and nobleness and the spiritual offered a strange contrast to *Don Juan*. Don Juan, beloved for his very changefulness, reckless and splendid in his love-making, so ardent, yet heartless and false—the legendary hero of Spain, fine enough on the stage but who would like him in real life?

September 18. A day made to worship blue skies and sunshine, but a worship without words, for the wind is boisterous and strong

[1] *"How silly you are, fifille."*
[2] *French poet and playwright.*

and drowns all sounds. To beautiful days I usually offer up chants of my own making, but on this Sunday, for warm and glowing magic I am content to listen. All night the branches swayed to and fro before my window. Twice I tiptoed to the window and found the country buried in mist. How I longed to go out and walk through the fields instead of sleep. The mysterious loveliness vanished at the coming of dawn.

Hugo's brother, John, is arriving from Europe today. Probably I will not see my Favorite Mystery, then, until he telephones and arranges to come during the week.

Later. I was thinking of a little incident which brightened my whole day some time ago. I was in a trolley car which was taking me to Mother's office. In front of me sat a little boy about three or four years old and his mother. He turned his head back often, looking at me with a mixture of coyness and roguishness, which was really adorable. His eyes were large and clear, of the most brilliant brown I have ever seen; and some of his little brown curls had escaped from under his sailor hat. Just to see the beautiful baby face turned trustingly toward me, just to meet those pure baby eyes, filled my heart with a pleasure I cannot describe. It was more than looking up at the sky, it was better than dreaming, it was sweeter than even the pleasure of reading . . . But the little sorcerer was casting a spell on someone else at the same time. The conductor, hereto gruff and irritable, suddenly dissolved in smiles. His eyes followed every movement of the boy, he talked to him as one does to a king, he was absurdly happy and desirous to serve and please. Then finally, with his strong arms, he lifted him off his seat and set him down gently on the street beside the waiting mother. The child waved his hand—and the car started off. The conductor's enthusiasm was so great that he sought someone with whom he could share it. His beaming face was a study. When his eyes fell on my face, something in it told him I understood. He beamed more emphatically, but this time his smile was directed to me: "Cute little fellow, ain't he?" I smiled back. Mutual admiration for a baby boy had filled the great distance between a conductor and a queer girl—in one thing at least, we were equally human.

4:30. I saw Hugo when he passed by with John. Since Hugo has come here on weekends, I have discovered that footsteps have a wonderful significance. Nowadays my eyes are often sweeping up and down the road. The sound of approaching steps makes me jump up or else sit very still, while inwardly are heard strange sounds and flutterings of which I never guessed the existence. Footsteps, footsteps—how much they promise, and how much they carry away. At first far away and faint, then louder and still louder, until they pause before the house. And all the time between the first sound of those footsteps and the last is spent in anticipation.

Evening. You are not a mere book. I have made of you a thing alive and comforting and faithful. I fancy that you reproach me for silences and neglect. I fancy that you are angry when I am wicked, that you always know everything that happens to me and laugh when I describe poorly or wander from the exact truth. Tonight I am doing something which is very much like what human friends would do. I have nothing to say to you, but I want you near me. It is as if we were walking in the quiet of a Sunday evening, just you and I, silent, thoughtful, and yet understanding, and glad to be with each other. It might be foolish to think of you as Someone. You are really my shadow, a reflection one sees in a mirror—nothing else. And yet when I need company, you fill my room with cheery pictures and cheery words. I wonder why I ever want other friends besides my books and my ink bottle and you. I have so wondered all evening. And all evening too I have wished for Hugo.

September 20. Another wish came true. Hugo passed by today. I was taking the bread from the baker at the kitchen door and suddenly I saw him, became very pleased and embarrassed and fled inside with my armful of loaves and flew out again because he had a book for me. We talked just a little, and when he walked away I could have danced for joy. It seems that he comes to be with John, and I will see them both often until the rest of the family returns from Europe. He just telephoned to ask me for a Columbia catalogue—the pretext Wilhelmina used to come the night of his visit here. And as I took it to her the following day, he will have to borrow it from her. The name of Wilhelmina makes me think of many things. Though you may not know it, Hugo's friendship for me is a matter of much antagonism and unkindness on the part of my next-door neighbors;[1] I am the intruder, the tricky foreigner, the cause of trouble and envy and discussions. I had often heard about the so-called cattiness of women, but did not believe in it. The thought never entered my head that I was doing

[1] *The Forgie family.*

something wicked by enthusiastically returning Hugo's friendly advances. It took a hammer and brass tacks to push the thought into my clouded understanding. While Martha and Wilhelmina hinted and mocked, I smiled sweetly and was no more conscious of the truth than if I had been deaf and blind. And it was only after everyone else in my family discovered it that I began to wonder and consider the possibility of their being correct in their surmises. But then hostilities and tricks began to be too frequent and my faith was shaken. They have done and said all they could to place me in a false position simply because they have known Hugo a long time, while I, only a few months. And in these few months I know that I have been nearer the true Hugo than they will ever be. Instead of being happy because I am happy, they want their friend for themselves alone. Fortunately I do not need to use any tricks and plots to make Hugo pause when he passes by, or comes to see me, or telephones. I always remember this when I am almost growing angry about something that is done to me. I remember how much I must be thankful for, how much is given me, and then I do not feel hurt at anything; I also have tried to realize that I might have acted in the same manner if I were in their place.

It is no wonder that Charles says I have no experience of life. What is more, he says I do not know life and human nature as it truly is. Is it this great fault which prevents me from making any practical use of my writings? I am incapable of writing short stories, incapable of describing action and the ways of people. I cannot imagine what they would do under certain circumstances, what they would say or think. If I put myself in their place, I would be sure to do some impossible thing, in the peculiar way of no one else in this world but me. And I do not want myself in a story. Oh, far from that, I would like to know others; and yet whenever I look at or study any particular creature, I do it with a strange-colored lens.

September 22. A new friend or a new book sometimes marks a new epoch in a human's life history. With me, it happens oftener with books. I receive a shock and from the violent clash the sparks come forth, illuminating many things in a short moment—and dying out too quickly. But I am given time to recognize what has been brought to light. I have received two such mental shocks lately, and the effects almost blinded me. I grope for words, I hesitate, simply because I am so bewildered that I hardly know if I am in a real world or in one of my own making. But no. Here is my faithful little ink bottle, my blue blotting paper, the reflection of myself in the mirror—all that I see each night when I sit here to write. And if I stretch my hand, I can touch the first cause of my shock—only a small, simply bound book which reached me from France this morning: *Journal de Marie Bashkirtsev*.[1] Long ago I was enraptured by the *Journal d'Eugénie de Guérin*. I loved it for its simplicity, its purity, its *goodness*. It was delicately written and by an angelical woman. This journal is vastly different; Marie Bashkirtsev is not good, she is not simple, and she writes with a frankness that borders on coarseness. And yet I was fascinated from the very beginning; at first by the picture of her as a young girl, and then by her opening words: "À quoi bon mentir et poser?"[2] What I felt throughout was an amazement no words can reproduce. Amazement at her boldness, her sincerity, her vanity, her conceit, her arrogance, her cleverness. Amazement at her exaggerations, her flashes of wisdom, her skepticism, her folly. But I could write all night and you would not know this impossible and yet admirable creature. She has a thousand faults, and yet she captivates by her intelligence and originality. I have never been so divided between like and dislike, admiration and disapproval, but this time I am forced to admit that I cannot for the life of me concentrate my judgment of this book in one phrase. There are too many sides to it, too many phases and points of view. Some would begin to find it ridiculous and then there would be no end to the ridiculous. If you read with sympathy and a desire to understand, you are carried away by the good in each page and convinced that the entire book is marvelous. It depends on how you open the book, as it were. I opened it in the same way I look at people for the first time. I am ready to like and admire and idealize. I am willing to sympathize and confide always. (Later on, of course, I may be brought to grief by this stupid trust in miracles, but meanwhile I am happier than the skeptics.)

September 23. It's useless to try to analyze Marie's Journal in English.[3] I want to be free to feel indignant, to be angry, to discuss her opinions with her, contradict her, blame her, and with the heat of battle ahead of me, I find that French (the language of my heart) has more vigor and brilliance. No doubt a member of the

[1] *Russian painter and diarist.*
[2] *"Why lie and pose?"*
[3] *Entry translated from the French.*

Académie would find my French a little rusty. Haven't I been in exile a long time, without books to read and French friends to listen to me? But no matter. I am not writing for the Académie!

To tell the truth, I don't know where to begin. I think it's because I keep a diary myself that Marie's diary made such an impression on me. I understand her so well that sometimes I wonder if I am like her. There are things she says that are reflected word for word here in my own diary. It's enough to make me think I am mad and that I copied them—or else that Marie's soul has been reincarnated in me!

I write about religion and human nature, as she does; I talk about my surroundings, as she does about hers; also, we both have written down ideas that come to us about anything and every-thing, things great and profound as well as things small and trivial. And in spite of that, the difference between us is absolutely incredible!

What food for thought it is to be able to look into the heart of another human being! To put one's finger on the forces that move a soul! To explore and analyze a whole life without taking part in it, without suffering, and without losing one's own self! I don't believe Marie Bashkirtsev realized the extent of the task she set for herself, so that she might not be forgotten. Her diary is a priceless human document. One can forgive her every-thing because of the sincerity and warmth with which she revealed even the most sacred and intimate things, which someone else would have hidden or disguised.

I speak of forgiveness. I would do well to add here that I am speaking for myself. I speak of things I see from the promontory I have chosen for my observations; that is, one that agrees with my own point of view. If I were placed differently, I would prob-ably say something else, and I would think I was right. But since I am trying to talk to you about how things look from the view-point I have chosen, it's because it's impossible for me to move elsewhere. Everything holds me back. I have built my house, my nest, my observatory (I leave the choice of term to you), and here I stay because my point of view has taken root where I first planted it and I want only to pick the flowers (or thorns?).

First of all, see what Marie writes that makes me love her like a sister. A hundred times I have written the same way, using other words. It's sad to think I do nothing but repeat her, like an echo! "Oh, no! People won't understand what I mean, because they haven't had the same experiences." No, that isn't it; it's that I despair each time I try to express what I feel! It's like a nightmare, when one hasn't the strength to cry out!

Also, writing can never give the slightest idea of real life. How can you express that freshness, that fragrance, of memory? You can invent ways, you can cry out, but you cannot copy. Whatever you feel when you write, the result is only ordinary words: woods, mountain, sky, moon—everyone says the same things.

At a time like this, I could lay down my pen forever. I could say, sadly, that by letting others speak for me, everything in my soul could be identified and explained—all my thoughts could be described, and better than I can do myself. But no. I admit there are many similarities, many repetitions, many things already written, and written very well—almost everything, all but one. I believe that every living creature has been endowed with a mystery to unveil, which no one else can touch and understand. One's self. In spite of all that has been said, done, thought and felt in this old world, each of us is different. Certainly there are reflections, surprising similarities, comparisons, resemblances. But oh, I am sure, absolutely sure, that deep, deep within each of us there are new things to be discovered. And as long as there is a mystery, however small, there must be someone to explore it, to experiment. Each one of us has a mystery, each his own. We all have immeasurable depths; we undergo evolution, and on the ruins grow other chimeras and other new impulses. For all of this, words are needed. In brief, as long as man lives, literature cannot perish. Will it grow? Who knows!

When I think of this, I take up my pen again. I stop reading Marie's Journal and look deep within myself. What I see surprises me. I am quite different, not an echo of another soul, another personality. I am myself. I am different. Oh, how sweet to think that poor though one may be, there are great riches in each of us. Possessing something that no one can take away but that one can *give* freely. To give, one must write, and I shall. I think I understand better why we have to bear the humiliation of seeing others carry off something we thought we ourselves had created. It gives us courage and the desire to climb higher, closer to the Ideal—so high that no one can outdo us.

But I am getting away from my study, from my effort. Marie's pride is incomprehensible. I have never understood people who are self-satisfied. When there are so many virtues to acquire, so many things to learn, so many fine things to do, how can one find time for self-admiration? She sits in front of a mirror and admires her hands! On almost every page she drops a word that is flattering to herself, and she never fails to show toward others a disdain that is neither charitable nor *reasonable*.

One has to have Eugénie's charming Journal to realize what a fault such lack of humility is. Eugénie never posed, nor lied either, but she was modest. It's when you don't look up to yourself that others look up to you—at least that's what I think. He who thinks well of himself leaves no room for the good opinion of others. Why say: Don't you think I'm witty, pretty, sweet, good and nice? They answer yes, politely, but the Devil alone knows the truth! And he won't tell. All this is meant to prove that it's pretty stupid to think yourself better than others.

But suddenly Marie writes: "The more I read, the more I want to read; and the more I learn, the more I have to learn. I don't say that in imitation of the wise men of old. I say what I feel." There I understand her. I feel her very close to me—perhaps writing at the same little table, dipping her pen in the same inkwell. And I feel that our ideas are in tune, that we are kindred spirits.

Alas, there she goes again! She writes about men: "Man is like a cave. In the depths we find dampness and dirt, or else an exit; in other words, there are no depths there at all."

To that I say no, no, no. She can go to Russia and leave me my little inkwell and table. She makes me angry sitting close to me with an idea like that!

Here I must stop. I have read only half the book. I shall return.

Evening. What a day! Oh, what a day! In the first place I awoke in a state of "talkativeness" (Marie Bashkirtsev would call it eloquence) and I was drawn to my pen with an irresistible force. In the second place I had a million things to do and was expected in the city at 1:30. What a predicament! I managed in this manner: I opened my Diary and laid it on the table with my pen and ink ready to use. I would make a bed and write five lines; I would wash dishes and write 10 lines—the compensation according to size of task! This is the way I wrote about Marie's Journal and took care of my house. There are days when I write very badly and simply repeat and borrow thoughts. There are others when I write perhaps as badly, but, in spite of myself, guided by an inexplicable impulse and heat, the things come smoothly and naturally, and I feel that at least they are my own (or seem to be my own). It is at such times that I love most to write. This happened today and I wrote on the train, going and coming. Near me there is now a little heap of scraps of paper filled with notes, and someday, if I have time, these notes will serve as material for essays. You may ask now why I called today an extraordinary one. "What," you say, "merely writing a great deal and getting excited over it?" There is much more than excitement, and it is not because I have written so much. Today I have felt strange things and all I write will only be a pale reflection of those things. Oh, this life of study and observation I love for its very own sake. How it changes the meaning and aspect of my actions. How it metamorphoses the world. After reading a book I see new things with clearer eyes. I believe also that following the reading of books, experiences in life are magnified. The meaning of each adventure is deeper and stronger; you take pleasure in little things which may pass by because their minds have been trained to be perpetually busy. A new book might be compared to a new pair of glasses—it fortifies and increases the power of perception. Fancy my mind with glasses! Or my heart?

Oh, I cannot write as quickly as I want tonight. Words fly by before I can catch them. Never fear, the loss is not great, but it is vexing to think that some faculties cannot work in unison.

I have talked to Eduardo over the telephone. I was so bewildered at the sound of his voice that I lost my head, hurriedly took his message for Mother and hung up abruptly. He is leaving for school on Sunday.

September 26. Saturday was my last day with Antolinita and her family. They left for New York early Sunday morning. My cousins Charles and Eduardo I did not see, although I thought I might meet them in the streets, by chance, for I often passed by the Waldorf. If I could have talked with Eduardo! I wanted to tell him that my opinion of him has not changed and also that I do not want him to think of me as being sad. I am so happy. Of course, happy in certain ways. You see, it does not seem fair that Eduardo should think me longing for his friendship, because he is apt to feel pity and believe it to be longing, too. And I am hoping that he will always like me but in a sincere and steadfast manner, as I like him and always will.

Hugo came to see me Sunday morning. We had a long, long talk about John Erskine's book and his philosophy of life, which has formed Hugo's own and explains his character and ideals. Something in Hugo's ways, which I cannot yet name, inspires so much confidence that I found myself telling him the true reason why I cannot study at Columbia this fall—economics. We had a discussion about the life of a poet. Hugo said he needed to lead the normal life of others to gather ideas and experiences and emotions. I reminded him that the poet had time to lead only half of a normal life because he needed the other part to retire within himself in order to describe, recognize and record these ideas, experiences and emotions. Here we agreed that the ideal would be this then—equal division of action and reaction's results.

The ideal! But alas, it is mostly one-sided and unbalanced, this life of a poet. (We say poet and include the prose writer.) I believe Hugo is carrying out this ideal in a very admirable way. He is a business man; he turns from his work to tennis or golf—from these to books and his writing. Compare this life with mine. On one side work, on the other reading and writing. You see, mine is not as well balanced.

October 1. Work, work, work. I often thought of these three words repeated so wearily and sadly in the "Song of the Shirt."[1] This does not mean that this week was as sad as the poem, but I felt a little of the sorrow painted in those lines. Mother had so much work to do that she took me with her every morning. Her office is a cheery little room, and there we sat from 9 o'clock to 5—sewing. I thought many things while I stitched, and worked faster with my mind than with my needle. I made flowers and covered buttons, sold dresses and served as model, as errand girl and secretary. I love to work, but I only wish I were stronger. If you knew how my bones ached from bending over my sewing, you would understand why sometimes I lose courage.

Once home, Mother and I had to cook the dinner and wash the dishes. At 8 o'clock each night, instead of sitting at my writing table to write, I was so tired that I could only curl myself at the foot of Mother's bed and dream.

Today I feel that I am not thoroughly awake. My head seems heavy, and I look in vain for the quick, flashing thoughts that come to me almost every day. But no. My horizon goes no further than my work; the whole world is revolving around a little room where

[1] *A poem by Thomas Hood.*

one must sew and sew, for bread and butter! I am ashamed of the littleness of my heart. I will come back to you when it has ceased to complain.

No, it is not my heart which is small. My heart is strong and willing, but my body is not. And that is why today I do not sit still to rest but am working harder than ever to teach it strength. Is it not stupid to think that my bones should ache from sewing, from sweeping a house? I feel not pity but anger at such weakness and will control it and crush it as one does a terrible fault.

Oh, I promised to write both the bad and the good about myself, and I have heard a very agreeable thing, which does not sound true, but who cares? I have been told by a painter, a friend of the young woman with whom Mother shares her office, that I have a face like the pictures of Persian princesses. Persian princesses! He said also (after seeing me for 5 to 10 minutes) that I was "fine, spirituelle," etc. Fiddlesticks and humbug!

Evening. It seems a long time since I have settled in my room for a whole evening with my books and thoughts. Whatever happens and however long the period which takes me away from the calm solitude and meditations I love so much, I return to my shell with greater joy. I take part in active life, but it seems to be a more natural tendency in my nature to contemplate and to wonder, to question and to find the answers in silence and in solitude. And yet how can I say such a thing? Daily I thirst for life, for adventure, for love. Oh, above all things, for love! Although this may appear to be inconsistent, it is the keystone of my attitude toward life. I yearn for the things which all girls of my age want, natural, normal desires. I look up to friendship and love as life's greatest blessings. And when they come to me, perhaps because I have expected such nobleness and beauty in each, I am disappointed. Then it is I return to my hermit's life. Then it is I read and study, and find a perfect joy in nature. In this state of mind I feel an exaltation which is almost incredible and unnatural. I become pedantic, grave, impossible!

Then enter an Ordinary Person. I drop my book and my pen. I open my eyes (there are eyes that seeth not). I stretch forth my hand and offer my heart. I begin once again to trust implicitly, to love sincerely, to weave fairy tales around an imaginary personality which I fancy the Ordinary Person to possess. There follows the tragic revelations, one by one, or sometimes in a bulk. I gather all the fragments and place them away in another drawer with an inscription. (I have 1,000 drawers with inscriptions). And then richer, with a new experience, wiser (a wisdom which evaporates at the end of five minutes), I return to my former occupation. And so on until eternity.

It is of no use making resolutions to devote all my time to study. My foolishness always makes me break them. Even tonight I know that although I have planned to continue my study of Marie's journal, if Hugo should come I would run downstairs like a wild bird, blushing, laughing and talking as any other girl would who is in the habit of expecting young men every evening. But no, Hugo is not coming.

You should see my face in the mirror! It bears none of the expression you would expect in a philosopher's features. My hair is dancing under the electric light in a most frivolous and coquettish manner. My eyes are dancing; nothing will make them brooding and grave and deep tonight. My nose looks impudent and challenging. I see the dimples which so fascinated Eduardo. Alas, what a terrible and foolish head confronts me this minute. How can any reasonable thought enter it? And to think I began meditatively. What mischievous spirit possesses me tonight, I do not know. If I were a bird, I would twitter and chirp merrily. If I were a man, I would certainly make love to someone, like Don Juan.

October 2. Each day my universe grows larger, and with it my enthusiasm increases, and my boldness. I travel continually onward, I peep and pry into all manner of mysteries, my reading illuminates a million new fathoms, and I am surprised that no one should shut the door of this wonder world upon my inquisitive face. No, nothing happens. I am allowed to wander as far and as long as I please, discovering, exclaiming, taking notes as if I had a right to understand and know all I wish. Someone in a fairy tale had a pair of boots with which he could travel seven leagues in one step. Sometimes I seem to have boots very much like those. Indeed, today my ideas have taken such a leap that I cannot follow with my pen.

October 3. Sunday I was preparing myself to write about a book— at that moment the most important object on my horizon. But Hugo came and scattered all my thoughts to the four winds—that is to say, all thoughts of books and literature. He came to ask me to walk with him to Forest Hills, where I could watch him play a tennis match. Before I realized what was happening, I found my-self walking by the side of an ideal friend, talking in a much more wonderful way than can ever be dreamed of or imagined. I was so surprised that I wondered if suddenly Hugo would vanish and I would find myself in my rocking chair, mending stockings. But no. He began the story of a play he had seen, *The Return of Peter Grim*, and when he was half-finished we found ourselves at the door of the Forest Hills Club. Hugo's opponent won out of pure good luck. I cannot describe the feeling I had while I sat there watching Hugo's every movement. He is all agility and grace and swiftness. He lost because in the beginning, for some inexplicable reason, he was nervous—but he lost *smiling*.

We returned while the sun was setting. I had often wished that someday I might walk with Hugo through the silent country roads and fresh fields at twilight. I wondered if he would experi-ence the same contentment and blessed joy, the same feeling of living in a dream. How fortunate I was to see this wish realized. I will always remember this walk, which made me see that Hugo understood everything. You must not think that we talk of this; neither one spoke one word, but we knew. Hugo was finishing the story of Peter Grim and his voice had sunk to a deep, tender note. I had never heard a voice as warm and as vibrant, so much in harmony with our surroundings and the mystic twilight that at times I could not tell precisely what he was saying but only knew that I was stirred—as one is stirred by strange music. By the time we reached my house it was completely dark. While we shook hands he told me he would try to telephone during the week. Only yesterday we were together for several long hours, but Wednesday he wants to go to the theatre with me. We are going to see *Blossom Time*. Oh, I hope he likes to talk with me as much as I with him! Last night I could not sleep, musing on all that is happening to me. Again and again I told myself that I was very fortunate and that I had to prove myself worthy of Hugo's fine friendship. His face was constantly before my eyes, and for hours I pondered and wished. Yes, I am going to wish for many things because they come true—when Hugo is concerned.

October 4. There are days when I do not appear grown-up in the least, and what is more, I do not think anyone ever thinks me grown-up but myself. I am going to write things which are diffi-cult to write, just to punish myself.

I have thought of nothing else all day but Hugo. It is terrible.

No *serious* thoughts, no philosophy or psychology—oh, no, just *nonsense*, and such happy nonsense that joy radiated from me and everybody looked at me in the streets. I never knew before how people love a happy face. You can wear strange and beautiful clothes, and passers-by will stare. If you are beautiful yourself, they also stare. But walk lightly with the feeling that you have wings, and allow your joy to be seen in your eyes and entire carriage, and people will not stare but look on with a pleasure and understanding, which makes you feel that the whole world is full of friends rejoicing and celebrating with you! But if they had known the cause of my gladness! I was glad (let me clear my throat, this is a most tragic confession)—I was glad because I will see Hugo tomorrow; I was glad because I have an exquisite dress to wear, which I know will please him. (In parentheses, it is only a new transformation of my old black velvet dress.) It has a tight old-fashioned bodice and full skirt, very simple and yet original. Mrs. Norman says there is something chaste about it, and I add that, being velvet, it has a touch of royalty besides. With it I will wear a cerise hat, my coral necklace and earrings and my ermine scarf. No one could guess that I am only the penniless daughter of a pianist. And no one could guess that I can wash dishes and handle a broom and order a steak. No. Dressed in this manner, I could truly make believe almost anything, even being a Persian Princess!

The other reasons for my gladness are purely imaginary. I have begun to be happy about a thing which has not yet taken place. I have imaginary conversations with Hugo. I walk up and down the house as if he were holding my arm in the way he does to help me across the streets.

I stand before the mirror and wish that I were beautiful (in vain). Then I sit down and call myself bad names. Then I get up in order to make amends and begin working about the house. I put the milk in the oven instead of the icebox. I sweep the clean rooms and forget those that truly need cleaning. I make the beds in reverse ways. I hang up pictures, after dusting them, with their faces against the wall. And now, as a climax, I am writing instead of beginning the preparations for dinner.

Later (at peace with my conscience). I was thinking of the happy contrast existing between Hugo's character and my own. He seems to possess all I lack, and if this were so in his case, I believe we would have the firmest and best foundation for friendship. I cannot think of anything I possess to give in return except just my femininity. This is specially true in the matter of strength. Some uncontrollable excess of sensitiveness in my nature causes the strange way I have of shrinking away from many things. It is like a sudden retreat, an instinctive search for protection in deeper recesses, in some secluded savage and hidden place. Compare this with the daring and confidence, whether moral or physical, of Hugo's nature. He is masterful, he is strong. I have learned to know the source of his moral strength. It comes of John Erskine's teaching.

It was in search of strength that I read Emerson, and I found much strength, but I also found that I could not put all of the great thinker's philosophy into practice now. I felt vaguely the need of fresh ideas, of practical guidance, something to cope with the life of today, of the immediate present. Then Hugo gave me Erskine's books to read. I have felt like one stepping into a new world—a world of independence and security. Some of Hugo's bravado has penetrated my own spirit. When he said: "I am my own master," I knew that soon I would *learn* to be my own master also. I want to free myself from that sensitiveness, from all thoughts which tie me down like one enslaved. I am certain that I will be incapable from now on of writing as I wrote some time ago: "A Fatal Power, not a Godly Power, rules over us." I read somewhere that the belief in fatality comes from either laziness or despair. Mine was despair then, but despair can be overcome, and to continue in such a stupid belief would indeed make me guilty of laziness.

I have never heard of a mind as active as my own—for mischief-making and nonsensical notions. Fortunately, to know one's faults is to half conquer them. I do not intend to plunge into details tonight because Mother is keeping a watchful and unforgiving eye on the clock. And how quickly the minutes fly when you are writing to please your heart. I pity those who write for money or for fame. Money is debasing, and fame transitory and exacting. But for your own heart . . . Oh, what a difference!

October 6. I have tried to control this impatience of mine to write so quickly after an adventure. Perhaps I should still wait until my enthusiasm calms down—but I can't, I can't. Think of being alone in a great, silent house with a heart so full that it almost aches! Yes, I must write, and write a great deal, for I want my happiness to last always, at least in these pages.

At 7:30 I tripped down the stairs to greet Hugo, and the evening began, the curtain rose. We walked briskly to the station, and later, fom Pennsylvania Station to the theatre. The first times that we were out together, Hugo simply held my arm at crossings, but last night he did so continually and I could follow his pace. We were no longer two strangers walking each in his own way, but two friends moving in such common accord and with so much harmony that words seemed useless. But we talked and laughed a great deal and even our voices harmonized. You must not laugh. No one knows how true this can be until one has been with a person who responds to everything as if moved and touched by the same hand and animated by the same spirit. And *Blossom Time*, with its exquisite music, its old-fashioned scenes, its color, its mixture of humor and pathos, completed the magic as nothing else could have done. I made many wonderful discoveries. Hugo had begun to tell me things about myself. We were watching a young girl dance to one of Schubert's melodies, gliding lightly on her toes with marvelous grace and charm. Hugo told me he thought I could do that also, as if he had known that I often dance about the house when I am alone. I asked him how he knew, and he reminded me of the day we went to the woods, Martha, he and I. There was a tree broken in half which had fallen across the path, and while Martha exclaimed and laughed, Hugo and I climbed it. He had noticed how I kept my balance. And I thought him unobservant of what concerns me. Hugo liked my dress and my coral necklace, and told me—but no, it is one thing to be proud of what he tells me and another to write it down. As soon as I find my critical self, I will begin to be ashamed and tear pages out. Let us spare the pages. They are beginning to become scarce.

Well, the evening did not terminate after the theatre. It was only 11:30, and Hugo proposed we go to Greenwich Village to dance. I opened my eyes wide—and accepted. A little later we entered a little place bearing the sign: "Dinner—Dancing." It was quaint and dimly lighted. The walls were decorated with pictures from Alice in Wonderland. The tables were of plain wood and set by the walls so that one could dance in the middle of the large room. The music said as clearly as possible—Dance! Dance! To this description add that there was no one else there, and then you have the beginning of the second part of my story. We danced. And when we saw that we were alone, we began to improvise. Hugo can do that also, just invent according to one's fancy. We had to leave at 12:30 because the musicians folded their tents.

It was too early for our train, and we walked part of the way to the station, talking seriously and earnestly. We felt as if we could have begun all over again. We were not tired, we were not sleepy. At 2 o'clock, when we stood before the two roads leading to our destination, Hugo asked which was the shortest way. I pointed to the left—and he turned to the right! He told me he wanted to make the most of our night because the days to follow would be very full and he was not coming home this weekend. He has singing and guitar lessons and a course at City College, so that I will not see him again for a long time.

Only one thing troubled me last night, and I do not know what to think of it. It was when we were dancing. Hugo had said that he has been studying character—reading the hand, its shape and lines, and he watched my hands often. While we danced he suddenly looked at the hand he felt in his and laughingly exclaimed: "Oh! I see many things!" In fun I tried to draw it away and he gripped it tightly. I am certain he was not conscious of his strength. But something like an electric shock passed through my whole being. For one minute I did not know what was happening to me. He made a remark, and I answered in an uncertain voice. But he did not notice, fortunately. Often I have been drawn to people because of similarity in tastes and ideals—to Eduardo, for instance—but there is something in Hugo which is pure magnetism. He shakes your hand masterfully, frankly. Every little thing assumes a character of strength—things which most people do vaguely, uncertainly. I am awed sometimes, and it is not strange that I should feel a thrill merely because he grips my hand tightly without thinking. He has the superiority which I have sought for a long time, the quality of manhood which I have not found in anyone and the lack of which was the cause of my turning away from many; I did not know what I wanted. To feel the mastery of a character like Hugo's is one of the rare privileges of life, I believe. No relation between man and woman, no comradeship, no companionship, can be complete without at least the qualities in each which sustain, uphold and foster the other. Thus, with Hugo, because of what he is himself, I can be nothing else but truthful, straightforward. I cannot say that my habitual shyness has entirely left me. It is better so, however, because then I listen and Hugo speaks well, better than I. With him I have discovered that although I thought myself conservative in my views, I am in certain cases a radical. They say a woman who meddles with theories loses her womanliness—whatever that is nowadays.

It may be so when she is not truly a woman, possessing only the envelope, as it were. In this case, well and good. She becomes coarse, she becomes argumentative, strong-headed; she trades her elusive charms for a higher post in the Chamber of Debates. She might be clever, famous and unwomanly, but if this happens, then she was not a real woman in the beginning or else she would have remained one throughout.

Hugo and I feel our way with words until we reach a palpable fact. When we discover that we agree about the question of religion, that we have radical views on certain other subjects, I keep by his side, yes, but I do not lose myself nor my womanliness—how? I think that I have found the secret. My so-called shyness is a certain amount of reserve, a small amount. A woman must listen. It is only the woman who makes the man feel that he is breathing a charged atmosphere, who smothers him with her self-assurance, who is fond of display, of being the center of interest—it is only this type of woman who has made herself detestable. When I realized that I had *found my place*, one that requires no effort because I *know it to be my natural place*, I felt a joy no words can describe. Oh, I am fortunate, fortunate even in my faults. I turn those faults to advantage, I control them until they serve me as ends to reach the things to which they would appear as obstacles.

Hugo and I have discussed Individuality. All this time we were journeying by widely different roads, only to reach the same end. And now we seem to stand on a hilltop, telling each other what happened while we traveled, and drawing inspiration from each other to pursue the new paths, which run parallel. We find that we have decided ideas about living our own lives in our own way. I was struggling for my individuality at Wadleigh [High School], I have sacrificed common pleasures and everyday friends to the same purpose. If I wanted to assume another character, I would have silly boys call, I would have excitement, invitations, so-called fun and good times. But no. I am myself and it is worth all the little sacrifices. In no other way could I have won Hugo's friendship, Eduardo's devotion. Enric's love and even Marcus's passionate admiration, although of this last I am not proud, though he was a talented poet.

Oh! Oh! I believe Marie has corrupted me. All this sounds as if I were pleased with myself, and it sounds abominable. I might scratch it out, but if I leave it here, it will serve as a reminder to beware of being kind and forgiving with yourself. Or, I might say, to beware of seeking excuses, for they are very easily found—like weeds. I was excusing my not resembling other girls.

One more thing. Hugo said that he liked going to the theatre with me better than with anyone else because I was appreciative and he felt that I understood. "I am afraid I do not say very much," I answered, thinking guiltily of the time I forgot to clap because the song was so beautiful, and kept silent. "But that is just it, I know," said Hugo. At the theatre he was telling me that such music and such a story ought to be enjoyed in beautiful surroundings with beautiful persons to look at. "Do you like to share things with people?" I asked. "With certain persons. I would never have come to see this alone, but, for instance, with you I get a double pleasure because I know that you appreciate all these things." We try to distinguish between true sentiment and sentimentality. Hugo asked me if I could remember something sentimental in the play. I did not remember but agreed with him completely when he retold the part where Schubert repeats a phrase of his beloved's: "Into the moonlight you and I . . ." And his voice quavered. This, Hugo said, was not convincing because it was not true, it was not sincere. In life, would we speak of the moonlight with a quavering voice, as if our whole soul were deeply enthralled by the very word? No.

Hugo is not always critical. He uses his intelligence to *discriminate*, and when it came to a part where Schubert was inspired and a song seemed to softly come from nowhere, we both felt our hearts carried away.

The memory of last night is still so warm and near that I seem to be living again through every phase and mood of it. I feel. like Marie, a degree of anger at words which do not carry the color and heat they are meant to carry. I would want to coin new words for these new feelings . . . to say exactly what I experienced while we walked. It was crisp and windy and dark, but we ourselves were full of light and warmth, like two metamorphosed creatures. We literally shone and beamed upon each other. There, I have boldly written what I felt and it sounds ungrammatical. But who cares? How my pen talks this morning. I am almost dizzy. Over my happiness there passes now and then a mist—it is when I think that last night will not repeat itself for a long time. I am so strangely made that now I feel a vast emptiness where before there was so much contentment. I wonder if Hugo feels that desire, and if his thoughts are as full of me—no, it's impossible. I fear I am unreasonable. I would give a great deal, however, just to know, to know.

October 7. I waited until today to record an impression I thought would diminish with time, but it is still as strong as in the beginning, and I must write of it; why should I fear as a weakness my facility to receive impressions? It seems now a long time ago that I was in Lake Placid. I remember this one particular day as clearly, however, as I remember Wednesday night. Anaïs [Sánchez], Eduardo and I had gone to one of the afternoon concerts at the Lakeside Music House. We sat in the warm concert room completely forgetful of everything else except the music. They were playing Schubert's Unfinished Symphony. Without, the rain was falling monotonously—sadly. The branches of pine trees swung gently before the windows as if set in motion by the music. I was conscious of the desolate scene; of being completely alone; of an insatiable longing for a thing I could not name—and gradually the music seemed to enter my own heart as it had never done before. The melody echoed every nameless sentiment I held most secret. I was listening not only to the notes and their beauty but for something it was trying to say. Then suddenly I felt a great pang, and through the pain I heard distinctly: Love, love, love.

It meant love! I knew it was that I longed for, and it had taken music to tell me so on a desolate afternoon at Lake Placid.

No one could tell me the name of the melody, but I never forgot it and have sung snatches of it since. And then Wednesday night I heard it again. The very first notes stirred the same feelings and brought back the vivid memory. If all that the entire audience felt at that moment had been united, it could not have equaled either in depth or in strength what I experienced for a fleeting minute. I had never dreamed that I would hear my beloved melody again, and still less, with Hugo. I was happy because it had come at such a perfect time. I know its name, and will hear it often for it has become dearer to me now.

Hugo and I talked about the love of art. "It seems to make you stand apart, does it not?" I asked. "Yes, and yet, strangely enough, in our love of art we are trying to draw nearer to life." We were both thinking of the poets who have wanted love in vain after singing of it as no ordinary man could and therefore helping that man to win his love. I had told him the story of Oliver Goldsmith, who resembles François [Franz] Schubert in many ways.

Hugo says that I am in an Anglo-Saxon mood when I depreciate the beauty of woman and extol virtue and intelligence. He says that I cannot mean this, that it is not an inborn but acquired theory which does not seem a possible part of such a temperament as mine. I was profoundly shocked by his views on this question. It was the Spanish in him speaking and for a moment I felt that I *recognized* his sentiments; they were mine long ago until I had so much imbibed the spirit of English literature that I began to write, in all sincerity, what he does not believe natural on my part.

By speaking of this, Hugo has rekindled a thousand questions and doubts I believed extinguished. I feel again the constant battle in my nature I have so long puzzled over. I am one person when I hear frivolous music. My blood is fired, I can dance with the wild, fantastic spirit of a gypsy, I am all laughter and lightness and fickleness. If I had hearts around me, I would break them carelessly and without regret. If Don Juan appeared before me, I would accept his kind of love as a thing which completes this attitude of wickedness. Wine, song, a mocking and tantalizing spirit in effervescence, giving full play to passion and impetuous desires—these are the ingredients out of which springs the eternal romance of Spain, the inflammable Spanish hearts. And I feel all this when my Spanish comes to the surface.

But I am not carried away. Something in me stands far above the reach of such things and finally lays a powerful hold on my entire self as soon as silence and solitude return. I may be standing at that moment before my mirror, playing. How often it has happened in this way. I am dressed in fantastic clothes of vivid colors, old shawls, full skirts and red bedroom slippers. I leave my shoulders uncovered, clasping the shawl loosely with a tiny pin. I wear my hair in one high bunch of curls, with a large comb on the side and flowers. Earrings dangle, and bracelets and necklaces. I have perhaps a fan and I am walking about majestically, or, if the whim comes, I lift my skirt like the ladies of old and dance around the room. My eyes grow full of mischief, my thoughts are inexplicable, nonsensical, frivolous.

Suddenly my eyes fall on the books on the mantelpiece. I fancy I feel like Cinderella when her beautiful dress and tiara turned into rags, for my mood drops from me in the same manner. The transformation is incredible. I can plunge into philosophy and find sincere and absolute pleasure in this deliberate analysis, weighing, comparing and reasoning. Or I read a thoughtful story, some stirring poetry. If I write, I speak of intelligence, I describe lofty ideals, I simply pursue this worship of all that is spiritual, and pure and brave, or useful. And I mean what I write, even if it is acquired. As to woman's beauty, if I rebel against its supreme power in the world, against the admiration and praise it receives, against its seeming superiority when compared with intellect and virtue—it is *because I am a woman, because I have been angered by certain forms of devotion offered to what I know will only belong to me for a limited time.* It is my way of rebelling against a weakness and my way of praying for a nobler love—one that would comprise at least what lies beneath the face and deeper than the surface anyone can notice. Alas, I am indeed rebelling against a thing which is part of nature. God knows if I myself, were I a man, would feel unhappy and unsatisfied in the presence of a homely person, and joyful, ecstatic, in the way of poets or painters, when my eyes fell on a beautiful face. Even as a woman I realize that I have felt disdain for boys of small, fragile stature. But if they had been geniuses? Could I love a great mind or a great heart under an unfortunate exterior? I feel that I could. I might have loved Oliver Goldsmith! I still maintain that it should not be as it is, but I have begun to believe that it *is*. We are indeed strange creatures, born with such a one-sided love of the beautiful that we can worship it in our fellow creatures in spite of the shallowness or wickedness it may cover. What a deplorable attempt to reach forward to catch a living spark of the Divine. We must give it a shape and color, a body—we are not noble enough to love what we cannot see and can only feel.

The contrast I picture here between the very opposite manners of acting, feeling and thinking explains my character somewhat. It tells you how I can understand and sympathize with what I term the lovable weakness of humankind, and why, in spite of this, a little portion of me condemns and despises that weakness and struggles to rise above it. And to think these are not the only opposing influences I have within me! You can trace some of the practical Frenchwoman in my sewing, my housekeeping, my way of dressing. It is almost laughable! I belittle beauty, and yet I feel it my duty to look my best in order to give pleasure to others. Is this not trying to appear beautiful? Oh, I can catch myself in many of its contradictions. It is no wonder that Enric should have said he was going mad trying to fathom me. It is no wonder Miguel should have said that I was the most complex creature he had ever known.

But Hugo, on one side Anglo-Saxon, on the other, Spanish, must feel strange things too, and be a strange person. What a great deal we have to discover about each other! How interesting it will be to compare experiences, moods, thoughts, ideals. Even if I were to try tonight to tell you what he seemed each time I have seen him, I would be deeply puzzled. He has changed each time. Whenever I thought I had formed an estimate of his character, he took a sharp turn and offered another side to study. But this does not mean I have made any change in my first description of him. All I said the first day still stands untouched, but I am going deeper than all that now.

Evening. Often I wonder if I deserve what is given me. To think that of all the persons I have known here, I found only Hugo exceptional, and that he should become my friend! A young man whose personality fascinates as his does could choose as he pleased. I always remember the strange ideas which crossed my head when a long time passed and I heard nothing of him. I told Mother it was impossible that he should not be betrothed at 23 (to me, 23 seems quite a grave affair), and that this being the case, he would never notice any other young person even if we agreed on many things from the first.

It sounded almost incredible when I heard him say: "You know, Anaïs, I have just three good friends—Eugene, Gillette and you." He has just as many as I have. Frances and Eduardo—perhaps Enric and Miguel in the past. But Hugo is incomparable. Do not laugh, for I am very serious. You know how my enthusiasm is set aflame about a book. Should it not be more so about a person who is better than a book? And I am certain that I am not making a mistake. Oh, so certain that if I ever misjudge Hugo, it will be by omission of some new quality. And meanwhile, what on earth is he thinking and writing—about me?

This English mood of mine is indeed causing much nonsense to be written. I act like a modern author in a hurry to finish his book and sell it. (The quicker and more carelessly it is written, the nearer it sounds to the modern realism, etc.) And yet, heaven knows, I am in no hurry to finish this book and still less to sell it; I would be hung for causing public disturbance. I feel the Spanish coming—coming. Here it is. Now I cease to be dignified and edifying. Most likely I shall go to bed.

October 8. This is a day of repentance. I realize how far I have wandered from my daily self-discipline, how I have allowed my-

self not only to entertain foolish thoughts but to write them. I
suppose Hugo would laugh at all this, a big, broad laugh—a broad-
minded laugh—but I cannot change myself in one day and I
have always been persistently severe and critical toward myself.
I have never felt any tenderness toward the wild impulses guiding
so many of my actions and have always kept a rigorous watch over
my excesses of romanticism and imagination. Of course, all this is
simply wasted eloquence. No amount of preaching will ever instill
the qualities of phlegm, composure, insensibility and stoicism in
a creature who is perpetually in a state of turbulence and who is
susceptible to every form of influence—whether real or imaginary,
it does not matter. Someone will have to use a hammer and
brass tacks.

I laughed a great deal with Mrs. Norman last night when
she told me of her ideas about marriage at the age of fourteen.
She thought it a species of slavery and lived in dreadful fear
lest someone should want to marry her. Sometimes I wonder if
marriage will domesticate me. I may become deliberate and calculating and well ordered inwardly—results of the constant tyranny imposed upon me. Will anything bring back the state of
moderation I had finally acquired by reading Marcus Aurelius?

Even in my hours of seriousness and melancholy the thoughts
of Hugo never leave me. Then I fancy him serious too, and tender
and deep. He might dispel my cloud with a flash of humor, but
he would never laugh at me, I know. More often I think he divines
my sentiments too well, but he does not like to meddle with them.
But I must not write of Hugo so continually. I will have many days
to add to my store of classified and analyzed characters, and it is
better I should write a little each day, for when I have exhausted
my supply I will begin longing for a fresh view of him in order
to resume my study! Meanwhile Hugo thinks and dreams of what?
Business, perhaps!

We made the first log fire tonight. What memories it brought
me! Memories of all the nights we sat around it a year ago. It made
me think of Mother's stories of her past, of Eduardo. Eduardo
smoking his pipe and telling stories, and looking into my eyes
dreamily. Of Miguel and his pipe and his brilliant talk, of Enric
and his moods, his passionate outbursts, his intimate confidences,
which always came when the family went to bed and we remained
alone a few minutes more. It was around the fire that Miguel,
Enric and I told our opinions of one another. It was by the fire
Eduardo and I spent a long afternoon talking. And more often it

was by the fire I would sit alone, seeing things in the flames no one has ever seen, writing, writing. Alas, as everybody writes.

October 9. I am writing by the rose lamplight of the parlor table. Near me the fire sends out bright, cheery little flames. The house is still except for the faint sound of Mother's voice as she talks with Joaquin upstairs. My heart expands in this atmosphere of warmth and cheer, and not alone does my heart expand, but my mind. This has been one of my happiest days although I have seen no one outside of my own family and nothing extraordinary has happened. I found all my happiness within myself. I have had fresh and provoking ideas following the reading of certain portions of the newspapers, I have made a discovery, I have experienced new feelings. Is not all that enough to fill a day?

First and foremost I will tell you about my discovery. It is Hugo's fault. It was sufficient for him to express his love of dancing to set me wondering how I could please him. If you knew him, you would understand this. He is the kind of person one finds delight in pleasing without being certain why. Well, I have always danced when absolutely alone, thinking it a foolish waste of time. Suddenly my dancing assumes a new character, a dignified character simply because it has a purpose, an excuse, as it were (I am always looking for excuses in order to please my conscience!). And today the miracle took place. I began dancing for Hugo and found that I could do all I pleased. I was so bewildered by my own doings that I wondered if I had unexpectedly become someone else. But no, it was "me"—I whirled and whirled, swung, and slid and tiptoed, carried away by the rhythm, unconscious of my feet and arms and knowing only that I could sway my body with the merest whim and fancy of my will, a will in turn guided by each mood in the music. Oh, it is a glorious feeling, that almost dreamlike motion in harmony with melody. I had never known the charm of it, all the poetry one can express in this manner. Henceforward if there is a mood or a dream I cannot write, they will find outlets in my dancing and in my singing. Because I can sing! Mother told me today. These two things are essentially rooted in my nature, inborn but discovered only lately. It gives me greater joy to find them there than to be told that I am beautiful. I have always been thankful for being able to write, however simply or unwisely. I sometimes wonder what I would do if I could neither write nor sing. I do not believe I could bear such a desolate silence. No, there is too much enthusiasm, too much amazement, too much rebellion, too much of everything in me, and it must flow out toward something.

October 11. I am happy, happy, happy, so happy that I could simply write the word again and again. I have met Cuba's great poet, Gustavo Galarraga. We had a very wonderful conversation, or, rather, he talked to me for a long while in Mother's studio. He likes Byron and Shelley. His own poetry is chiefly lyrical, but he has written a play satirizing the Cuban society. (We are going to see it Sunday.) I found myself saying things to which he responded instantly. Unwittingly I made him talk about himself—and afterward I realized what a privilege I had been granted, for he told me things I shall never forget. He is the poet of *strength* and of action. He did not rest after writing but struggled until he made all Havana listen to him. The Cubans as a rule hold no respect for art, and still less for poetry. Galarraga has suffered immensely, he has been ridiculed, tyrannized by his father, but, as he says himself, he persevered—and he won. Today he is the Idol. And yet he is still at work. His ideals for Cuba he will teach and spread not by his poetry alone but by satire, which is the stronger tool, and in his case necessary. The Cuban's intellect needs a rude awakening. I was deeply impressed by his personality. I had the feeling of standing before one truly inspired, a great man in the sense of all that is spiritual and ennobling. When he recites poetry, his face is transfigured. His eyes grow resplendent, almost more than one can bear to watch steadily, and the entire expression conveys but one meaning: it reflects the intensity of the light burning within. The Sunday following the presentation of his play he is coming to see us with Thomas Walsh, the translator of his poems and a notable figure himself. It is merely in the contemplation of these things that I have found my joy today. It would be perfect if I could share it with Hugo.

Evening. At the close of this happy day all my feelings have become subdued and tempered. Softly and gradually a veil of sadness has stolen around my heart. I think Eduardo is the cause of it. He has written to Mother on business, but at the end, as if he could not control himself, he reminds her of a promise she made him to let him write to whoever he pleased when he reached the age of independence. And then, resolutely, he writes these two simple words: "Semper Fidelis." If it is true, if he still thinks of me, if I am still a part of his dream world, his fragile, tender but infinitely lovable dream world, oh, then I ought to answer him and write: Semper Fidelis! Yes, I have been faithful to my cousin in my thoughts at least. If ever he should come to read these lines, they will show him that I am not only true to our friendship but to all that this friendship is based on. He has risen far above all the doubts others entertained of him; he has proved ideally constant when all believed him incurably fickle and uncertain—even I sometimes feared that I was doing wrong in trusting him. And see, he has been victorious. He is what I wanted him to be. It is only just that I should remain what he believes me to be and repay his trust.

Later. I wish sometimes you would absorb scenery—that things should photograph themselves on your pages. Alas, color, freshness, things that are beautiful to look at, to feel, to touch because they are soft, all seem to turn into a mass of marble when I grasp my pen. Tonight I would like to translate a song of color. With needle and thread and pieces of rose silk I have acted the part of magician with my lamps. I have covered each light with the silk, to which I gave the shape of a Moorish bit of architecture. On my desk there is a little reading lamp with lampshade of the same color, a gift of Mother's. When night came (and I could hardly wait for it) I was enchanted by the effect. The deep rich rose of the lamplight works magic. It makes the room soft and warm. It tints the birdcage with a semblance of firelight, it plays on the surface of my perfume bottle and hairbrush, it hovers quietly about my white bed. It makes the mirrors deep and mysterious so that when I look into them I seem very much part of a faraway dream, of some Arabian Night fantasy. In this subdued, delicate and fanciful setting I dream still-stranger dreams. I wonder why it is that I am so easily impressed by little things. I am always keenly conscious of the lights everywhere I go, of sounds, of scents. I often like to fancy my home as it will be in the future. In it, just as in everything else, I want art—lights will be full of charm and meaning and harmony. They are like the moods and fancies of a creature—they need gentle, tender handling. I am not like Marie Bashkirtsev. I believe that I will be happy and that all my wishes will come true in the future.

I have wished for knowledge, but it does not satisfy the heart. I fear I am made to love and to be loved. Who am I tonight? Can it be the one Mother calls her "little philosopher," sending a call out into the night, a call for mere love? Oh, it is the Spanish blood! It is the romance throbbing in my pulse. I would like to step out of my shell, to see more of the world.

What? Lose the peace and joy of my books and studies? Give up the silence of my room, this almost complete solitude? Exchange the quietness and comparative loneliness of my life for excitement and gaiety and company? Alas, how can I tell which of these will bring me Love? As I am now, I see few people; I make one friend now and then; I am truly in a cage, a golden cage. What if I should move forward to meet an adventure at least half-way? Would I be pursuing a bluebird and leaving my true happiness at home? Who knows? Oh, the mysteries which hover round the lamplight. It would be wiser to go to bed.

I was thinking of Fame, of that mysterious and sublime power which raises one man above his fellow creatures and stamps him as an individual, a personality and an extraordinary being. And he is not always famous in the general sense of the word, but simply extraordinary, superior. There is Manén, Diaz, and my own father and Granados. Now I have known Gustavo Galarraga. I feel that Mr. Hamilton is also exceptional, and Joaquin's godmother, Teresa Carreño,[1] whom I should have named among the first. I remember Gabriele d'Annunzio—a childhood memory, and with this period I associate father's friends Blanco Recio and Mathieu Crickboom,[2] Joseph Bonnet, the organist, and last, our dear old friend, Emilia Quintero. All of them men and women who probably think me a child.

I often wonder if among those of my age or thereabouts there are any destined to become as extraordinary as those I have named above. There is often so much obscurity about the first efforts of genius and talent—they burst into flower before one can realize their greatness. How strange it must seem to be a friend of such people! I sometimes love to pry into the future to fancy all my friends [famous]—men and women. I imagine Enric as great as Manén, I think of Willy Shaeffer and of the good fortune he deserves for his industry and perseverance. I ask myself if Frances Schiff will make something out of her genius for original creation, her keen power of observation, her modern directness and abruptness of style. I wonder what is to become of Miguel Jorrín, of Eduardo, even of Marcus! From unimportant and unnoticed childhood and youth spring later the musicians, writers, lawyers, architects, etc., of the future.

And I? Is there anything in me which distinguishes me from the other girls? Oh, there is a charm about these speculations—

1 *Venezuelan concert pianist.*
2 *Famous violinists of their day.*

the charm of unfathomable mysteries which speak to the heart. Yes, I will know the answer to all my questions if I wait, and work while waiting. Indeed, Emerson was writing truth when he said that the happier mind saw no tragedy in these perpetual evolutions. Today I understand and approve. But tomorrow?

October 12. Alone by the fire for a few minutes. The day has been all quietness, with Mother and Isabel Duarte talking over old times. I felt very far away from them, far away from Thorvald's exuberance, in tune with Joaquin alone—Joaquin, who has sat for hours at his piano composing beautiful things and playing my song: "J'ai Pardonné," by Schumann. Joaquin and the fire alone seem to act in accord with the longings of my heart. All else gives me pain—the cold outside, the harsh, bitter wind, and another little thing which sounds terribly unreasonable, and which I shall not write.

And yet I must be truthful, I will write it. It is Hugo. I believe he will make me suffer a great deal. Je trouve qu'il a beaucoup trop de sang froid.[1] Is it possible? Yes, I find him too cold-blooded, too deliberate. The thought makes me shiver. I say this because I have been thinking about his ways. When I like someone, I like him greatly, intensely. I want to see that person often. I am all enthusiasm and impetus and fire. Hugo likes me, or he would not have come to see me and invited me to go out with him. He likes me sincerely because he has said things to me with feeling and sincerity, and impulse. He also is enthusiastic and full of fire— sometimes. And that is what drives me to despair. Something in his nature cries out "Beware!" and he suddenly stops, controls himself. He changes. He becomes English, and what is incredible, he becomes actually cold, incomprehensible.

I could not let the days slip by with so much patience after the pleasure we had the other night if it were in my power to repeat the experiment. No, I am not laughing, I am serious. Alas, I wish I could be careless and mocking. But a week has passed and I have heard nothing. What is worse, I *know* that I am not to hear—he *told* me that it was to be so—but in spite of all, I *expect* the unexpected, I long for a contradiction. I do not want things to happen according to law and order and plan. No, I want the impulse to burst the chains of habit, convention, carefully laid-out tactics. Simply because I cannot wait is no reason why

[1] *I find that he is too cold-blooded.*

Hugo should feel the same. That is exactly what troubles me: his wisdom, his calmness! I am neither wise nor calm, and I fear I am spoiled because I have never been treated in this deliberate and wise way. I hope he will do something extremely reckless some day, something so absolutely and completely spontaneous that I will lose this feeling which strongly resembles indignation!

October 14. How cold it is! My fingers are quite frozen but I hope to warm them in the "heat of composition." I have watched Sunday come nearer and nearer with a thrill which passes all description. Hugo is coming with us [to the play by Galarraga]! Mother telephoned him yesterday and he was "delighted" (I know this is the word he used because I made Mother repeat the conversation word for word), and in order to be original I decided that I would become ill, so here you have me today coughing for dear life with bandages around my throat, a spoon in one hand and a medicine bottle in the other—a charming tableau. No one else in the world would have found time to be ill in the middle of so much excitement. Sometimes it is very inconvenient to be so original, is it not? Every five minutes I pray fervently that I might be well tomorrow at about 5:30, when Hugo is coming for a few minutes to know more details as to what is taking place on Sunday.

We were invited to hear Mr. Lhevinne at his own home—Sunday. When Mrs. Lhevinne talked with Mother, she added: "Bring Joaquin and Anaïs." I went mad with joy. And yet we cannot go. How I love the world of musicians and poets. I think I could ask no more of life than to be allowed to mingle with them, and already because of Mother I have been granted the privilege many times. To the Lhevinnes' house! And no need of listening at the windows, shivering in the cold night. No, we would be near the pianist, we would talk with him, and breathe that air of art—of Europe. And to think we must choose between that and listening to a Great Poet. No, we did not even choose, for Mother had given her first promise to Galarraga. I have so much to tell Hugo.

Yesterday Mrs. Norman took me to the "Art Worker's Club for Women," where I registered, as a model in quest of work. There is almost witchcraft in my good fortune. It happens that just now all that is Spanish has become, in the words of Miss Foster, "quite the rage." My type is "à la mode"! In short, it is probable and possible that I should obtain work. Perhaps you did not know that my face is also a piece of antiquity—even like my ideas of what a woman should be. It has struck painters now as

Persian, now as Byzantine. I have always been told I reminded people of some old painting or of an old-fashioned portrait. Mrs. Lhevinne said I had a Parisian face, and so did Monsieur Sorel. You must not ask me what I think—I am dazzled and vexed. True, I would not like to be exactly like all other girls, but enough to live a little nearer to them and not to experience that feeling of total remoteness and uncongeniality—and sometimes hostility! I feel as if I have crossed the threshold of a new adventure and am infinitely grateful to Mrs. Norman, who is responsible for it. I am hoping for great things, and they all merge into one object—work, work, that I might help Mother.

Saturday evening. Hugo came. I had thought of nothing else all day but that, and yet when the moment arrived I behaved like—like a fool! To think that I know him so well, that I do not fear him at all and yet I lose all my balance the moment he is near me. It takes me time to find myself again (to regain my composure!), and that is why all is well when we have a whole evening to ourselves, but when for only a few minutes—then I must suffer the consequences of my stupidity. I do not want to imagine what he thinks of me. Do you know, it is one of the strangest feelings in the world, that which I experience when I get in such a state. And anyone who knows what it is to be timid and lost in the presence of someone will recognize this description. You sit facing a certain person—looking into this person's eyes in which understanding glows as clear as daylight. You are saying things with your eyes, or at least trying to, and perhaps the other person is trying to answer you. Meanwhile your tongue, simply because you cannot control it, is painfully going through the process of stringing off banalities. All your heart is crying out a million phrases in vain. And you wonder how it is that you have not the courage to stop in the very middle of it all and say quietly: "What is the *use of all this talk?* I have other things to tell you!" Does Hugo *know?* We say things with our eyes, but perhaps I imagine this weird manner of speech, and in reality he wonders what is the *trouble* with me. I feel very desolate after he is gone and want to call him back.

We were talking about Galarraga—Mother, Hugo and I. Mother was telling of the time he had such a great success in Havana that the ladies kissed him. And now he has said he hopes they will do the same tomorrow night, and Mother promised to give a good example. "There's a chance for Anaïs," added Mother. "She can stand behind me." "And I'll stand behind her with a club," said Hugo, laughing. The idea pleased me immensely, that and the great concern he showed when told that I might not be able to attend the play tomorrow because of my throat. It is incredibly thrilling to know that one is becoming a little bit important. Suddenly my self-reliance increased several inches. We forgot to shake hands. It does not seem a very necessary ritual, and yet I miss it tonight, for often I have come to you with the warmth and pain of his handshake, and I would be conscious of it all through my hour of writing.

He read Mother's character from her hand, pointing to the two fingers which end squarely and denote the practical in her. I looked at mine meanwhile and disconsolately slipped my hands into my pockets. All my fingers are pointed. My whole hand is long and slender; there is nothing square and strong about it. Hugo knows this, and probably he did not need to see my hands to know that I am an incurable idealist and a worshiper of artistic things. I wonder what he thinks of my character. Does he intend to convert and reform me? Does he like me as I am, or does he expect to change me, thinking me easy to mold?

October 16. It would take a million closely written pages to give you the vaguest idea of last night. I have thought of a better way, and that is by labeling it: Perfect. Where did last night truly begin? For Thorvald and Joaquin, probably when the curtain rose and the play began. For Mother, perhaps the same, but for me it began before that, from the first moment I caught sight of Hugo waiting for us at the entrance. We had a box near the stage itself. As soon as we had seated ourselves, Mother noticed Mr. Emilio Agramonte and pointed him out to Hugo. We then discovered he had taught Hugo Spanish at Columbia! Agramonte is a friend of Mother's, and when he finally came to speak with her he told her many things about his pupil. He says Hugo knows a great, great deal of Spanish, that he is one of the finest and most intelligent young men he has ever known, etc. And I was so proud! While he talked with Mother, Hugo and I talked also, and yet it seemed a very different thing. I felt as if we were all alone, and having lost all my timidity, I could look at him steadily. Hugo is so absorbing sometimes that I seem to lose all consciousness of Self, as if my ideas had melted into his! He was stroking my fur coat while we talked. These little and seemingly unimportant ways of his are full of charm for me. They tear that inexplicable veil of "distance" that appears to lie so persistently between some hearts and minds; they bring him very near where otherwise, because of that fault in my nature which causes that "veil," I would ever stand apart. I do not know precisely why, but the picture of that special moment stands out very distinctly from all others of last night. There are many such pictures in life which surpass those of our dreams. The trouble is that we are so absorbed in "living" them that we cannot judge or describe them from the point of view of an observer. I sat there in the dimly lighted box, dressed in black and rose, my coat of silver gray lying on the back of my chair, my hands folded on my lap, listening to Hugo and watching his face. He sat very near me, bending over a trifle in his enthusiasm, talking in a subdued and yet vibrant, thrilling tone and laughing in that peculiarly melodious manner I have never heard in anyone else. He was passing one hand gently and caressingly over the soft surface of my coat—that movement and the marvelous depth of his eyes were the only signs of tenderness about him. The rest—his carriage, his expression, his personality—was essentially manly, unwavering, absolute.

When the play began I found it difficult to transfer my interest—it seemed fixed upon Hugo! Galarraga preceded the story by an inspiring utterance, ending by begging for indulgence in such a simple, sincere manner that he left one without breath. The play itself was worthy of his talent and fame. It was undisguised satire, witty, clever and so deftly handled that all it touched upon was hit to the heart, as it were. He never missed his mark, he never exaggerated; he painted with so much justice, so much truth and wealth of language and spontaneity that you actually felt the double genius in a man capable of painting the bitterness and weaknesses in human nature with such an absolute understanding that it seemed as if he were subject to them himself, instead of hovering above—the idea that life is sorrowful and one must make it as pleasant as possible, by dancing and merrymaking, disdaining the ties of home life; the idea that life is like a glass of champagne, all lightness, gaiety, frivolousness, that one must not feel or think in order to be happy. How often I have heard this expressed and how often I have seen this lived. Drown your sentiments in excitement, but they come back. At the end the young girl who has sought happiness finds that nothing will fill the insatiable hunger of her heart but the true, serious love of Ricardo, who lives apart from "El Mundo de los Muñecos,"[1] because he both thinks and feels deeply.

At the end of the play Galarraga recited his poems. One cannot say in words the emotion he arouses. I believe Galarraga greater than Heredia.[2] His words were like fire. Ils jaillissaient des plus belles profondeurs de son âme, brûlants, étincellants, nous aveuglant presque avec tant d'éclat et d'intensité.[3] There, in such a man at such a time, you recognize the divine idea in full flame. Nothing less than the divine can make of man the resplendent, inspired and conquering poet embodied in Gustavo Galarraga. I was shocked at the applause, as I am each time it breaks the spell following such music as Manén's or such poetry as Galarraga's. Applause makes me shiver as one does upon awakening to something cruelly cold and misplaced. Will I ever conquer this unreasonable idea?

We visited Galarraga backstage and brought him back to our box to watch a little play by the Quintero brothers.[4] At the very end we met Thomas Walsh, and Galarraga asked Mother to join the little group of friends who were to celebrate at the Waldorf. Because of her children and because I felt ill, Mother refused.

Hugo placed us in a taxi and accompanied us to the station. Only by this quick action did we catch a train and were saved from waiting an entire hour. We parted so hurriedly that we had little to say, but I know Hugo was happy. Mother said that it was a pleasure to have him with us because he is so appreciative. He complimented her on her earrings and on her hat (which I made myself!). Mother looked so beautiful last night. I am all impatience for the day I will see Hugo again.

Evening. Tia Coco is here and we have talked the greater part of the day. She is suffering much, and all because she has married a man she does not love. She tells me many things about men; that they are all alike—but a likeness which is not flattering. And always when I am told such things I am set wondering and comparing. I would like to decide for myself, and that day I will set it down in large letters. Madame de Staël says that "Love is the history of woman's life; it is an episode in man's." I can truthfully

[1] *"The World of Puppets."*
[2] *Cuban-born French poet.*
[3] *They spring from the most beautiful depths of his soul, burning, sparkling, almost blinding us with so much brilliance and intensity.*
[4] *Spanish playwrights of the turn of the century.*

say that Man is a subject I have never studied. Boys, yes. They are impressionable and, with four or five exceptions, insipid.

October 18. I never dreamed I would come to the end of this book so quickly. I expected to fill it with a long period of incidents. I thought that it would stretch to Christmas, to the days of sleigh rides and councils around the fire. And what is more, I believe I expected to have found more answers to my incessant questionings. When I look back, I realize how little I have advanced, although at times I have written exultantly of the great leaps my mind appears to have taken. Occasionally, this has happened, and the proof lies in this quickly filled book. But more often I have simply stepped into a new web, or bruised myself against more walls, you might say. I must confess I have still little wisdom of the world and that it has many surprises in store for me. It is no wonder, after all, that I should have so much to write of in spite of my comparatively calm existence. I have time to study each adventure so minutely that I derive enough "food for thought" to last me for months. Add to that the books I read and my few friends and my impossibilities, and you have the explanation for all my talkativeness (not eloquence). I am at an age when thinking is considered a mere *attempt*. I know that older persons believe I am simply passing through a crisis of emulation; I feel that they doubt my *sincerity*. "What is the cause of all this excitement?" they seem to ask disdainfully. "Why are you so amazed, and so curious? It is only inevitable at your age, I suppose. Young ideas in young heads are mostly nonsense. You will get over taking yourself so seriously and all else so earnestly besides. You will soon calm down." And the speaker settles down comfortably in his armchair, probably puffing at his pipe, smiling sarcastically. Oh, the skepticism of my elders. I give them the shape of an old man preaching from an armchair while he smokes merely to give my imaginary person some appearance of reality, but what it represents I have often found in many varied men and women I know. I tell you this because it is one of the forms of discouragement I have met on my way. And sometimes it is the influence of such words which makes me doubt myself. I begin wondering: Can all this be a pose? Am I truly deceiving myself and others by my idealism? Is it conceit on my part to disbelieve all I am told until I discover myself and draw my own conclusions? Is it merely the hotheadedness of youth which pushes me into provoking and taunting fate? Is it the daring and recklessness of ignorance which makes me so defiant, so rebellious, so impatient under the tyranny of accepted traditions and ideas and conventions? I stand proudly shouting: "Let *me* think, let *me* decide, let *me* live." And I hear laughter with this answer: "She is so young. It will soon pass. It is always the same." What particularly sends the blood leaping to my face is the idea that woman should not think. I read everywhere that men despise those who do. Just as there is an eternal sarcasm and scoffing about marriage, there is scorn most clearly expressed concerning the woman whose mind is awake. Apart from this I have never found anything to criticize. My modernism stops here. It is with a great indifference that I have watched women fight their way into politics. I believe them to be ridiculously unfit for what they proudly call "Equality." Let us have equality in mentality and education but not in careers, in occupations. The woman who steps out of her home is not a woman any more. She is the pathetic product of an age of restlessness. She is not worthy of Love and Home unless she is capable and great enough and strong enough to carry out two distinctly opposite tasks to a successful end. There are gifted and extraordinary women in the world, but it is the women we meet everywhere, every day, who will attempt the impossible. One must feel infinitely sorry for them.

I hardly know how I have wandered into these explosive tirades. I intended to finish reflectively, to deliver a calm little sermon to myself in order to recall me from my waywardness and set my ideas traveling on a fresh, virtuous road. However, I do believe you have had quite enough of me, and it is time for you to join Carlyle and Erskine on my mantelpiece. And is it not better to leave you in suspense and wondering what kind of a person I am going to make of myself than to tell you right out?

October 19. "Ai-je le talent de décrire la vie sans le talent pour la vivre?"[1]

Being at an age when everything unfolds and grows, I find that the dawn of a new day is the dawn of fresh aspirations, hopes and ideas; and the opening of a book, the beginning of more evolutions, more crowded hours and startling discoveries. If this is to be a story of growth and unfolding, it is well therefore that I should open this book by planting a seed (figuratively speaking) so you and I can watch it germinate during the long winter

[1] *Do I have the talent to describe life without the talent to live it?*

months. To be explicit: I persist in writing because I persist in my pursuit of truth. And if I do not write today a thing I have long withheld from my other Diary book, I will be guilty of reserve (reserve in this case is an offense).

But to be brief: A change has been wrought in me during the last few days which I cannot explain. Lately everything speaks to me but of one thing. I hear music and my heart seems gripped in the strong hold of Love. Poetry, all poetry, is one long, endless song of Love. In books, in nature, I see Love and feel its inspiring presence ever by my side. At night sometimes I stand by my window and I experience a new restlessness, longings which are intensified by every moment of solitude and silence. I stretch forth my hand, and all my being calls out: Love! Love!

I try to laugh at myself and say that this is not the proper season of the year to feel such things—in vain. I feel as if this great Thing were coming nearer to me, as if *its approach were stirring all things about me as a warning*. Music and Poetry and Nature are the means Love employs to teach my heart without frightening it. But I do not fear Love.

October 20. Is there a world where our hearts will feel satisfied and at rest? Why must we always seek the unattainable, perfect happiness, complete *joy?* Suppose we could accept sorrow, be contented with *sorrow* instead. While you are sad, you long for nothing else.

Strange, by watching nature we attain a better understanding of ourselves. We are like nature in our mysteries, in our changes, in our growth, sorrows, joys and aspirations, in all except our imperfections.

Did the same Being who made nature perfect make us weak and yet with a love of the noble and perfect never to be satisfied?

We ask questions we cannot answer. Everywhere there is a limit set upon our achievements and no bound to our ideals and expectations. I am told God did not place our felicity in this world but holds it before us in the form of a promise, and a compromise: that is to say, we *must* be virtuous and pious in order to see this promise fulfilled.

However ashamed I am of these thoughts, they come persistently to the surface. I cannot silence them. In all my actions I am endeavoring to find a more reasonable cause. I would want a greater use applied to all we undergo now, in this actual world, than simply the test of our goodness and courage, a more satisfying reason for our existence than this talk of temporary station in a world of pomp, temptation and vanities. How can I act among people who insist on the futility of all earthly things?

The words seem written in fire, provoking a punishment, like nothing I have ever written. But I am only asking, supposing, not affirming. If I am mistaken, I will soon know. If I am stepping into the shadows of unbelief when I only wish to fortify my faith, God will help me and bring me back.

October 22. Oh, Hugo, how I envy those of your own family who see you every day, who can hear you laugh and talk, who are sure of your love.

If I were brave enough tonight, I would laugh away this sadness about such a little thing. Just because I expected Hugo to telephone, only to telephone. I have a thousand things to tell him, but of what use is it if he feels no need of talking to me?

I awake from dreams of him which bewilder and sadden me when I compare them with reality. And this restlessness does not spring from idleness or from solitude, for I have been incredibly busy about the house and nursing Joaquin, conversing with Tia Coco and Juanita [Tia Juana], and all the while I feel that impatience and perplexity tugging at my heart.

I count the hours sadly. If Hugo should not like me, the friendship of the rest of the world would not console me. It is his alone I want, *his* opinion, *his* companionship. Am I asking too much? He is so great, so good!

October 23. One thing which has given me a severe shock is using certain words seriously, earnestly and in all sincerity, to find them ridiculed in others' writing, as if their meaning had changed. Such words as understanding, ideals, illusion, sensitiveness, sometimes even art, are treated either with a sneer or apologetically. The first takes it for granted that these words and others such as these belong only to the vocabulary of the *young*, those at the age of ignorance and inexperience and exaggeration. The second, exceedingly self-conscious, acts as if he were sorely trying the reader's patience.

It seems exactly as if by using these names for our ideas they cease to be ideas and become caricatures. The first time I realized this I was startled; the second time, angered and distressed. Today I have made a resolution. I will employ these words whenever I need them. If I am serious and sincere when I write and unconscious of the foreign meaning attached to my familiar expressions, the expressions should convey my meaning, the meaning I give them. If there are those who can scoff at all the sacred things of life, there must naturally be some to scoff at words, and still more at words used by persons such as I who do not pretend to know but are merely groping and feeling their way toward truth.

I realize, of course, that in these efforts there is much that can be ridiculed. For those who want to find it, there is, in fact, a ridiculous side to everything. At eighteen, the world is full of interest and fascination. One finds life amazing and can think of nothing else but its changes, coincidences, mysteries. Everything is a pleasure: to dream about the future, to muse on the past, to dwell lovingly on memories, to suppose, to meditate, to discover, to talk and associate with those with whom you can compare experience. Curiosity, enthusiasm, satisfaction, succeed one another, each one stronger than the other.

Perhaps we do use words which deserve criticism from those whose curiosity and enthusiasm are no longer inflammable. We use—and with fire—words which should be treated with smiles and moderation. We laugh, I suppose, when we should be solemn and respectful. But all these are signs, good signs, that we are making efforts, that we are alive and working. Our very own mistakes, being the mistakes of the inexperienced, should disarm the most furious criticisms. But tolerance is a virtue of the past.

The present regime is severe, but it may be for our own good (as they say of whipping). I mean by this that to come forth victorious from the hands of such "faucheurs d'illusions"[1] will indeed test the strength of these illusions and increase our faith in them.

Whereupon I return to more prosaic subjects.

October 25. I will never forget Sunday. It was a day of so many impressions that I have not ceased to think about it for one moment. My pen was absolutely silenced, and even today I feel that I can give you only a simple sketch of Galarraga, a sketch where there is more between the lines than in them. But some day when my pen grows bolder and more capable, I will fill these empty pages with all the memories I store away and give you a finished portrait. A man who, when silent, gives the appearance of a mere dreamer, Galarraga has only to speak or raise his hand and

[1] *Kill-joys.*

the immense latent power in him is instantly felt, the power of the true poet, whose inspiration is consumed not in words alone but which spreads like a living flame throughout his actions. Whatever his mind conceives is carried out into achievements, labors of strength and purpose which mark the complete genius.

Above all I was deeply struck by the deep melancholy emanating from his voice, eyes and gestures. It is as if all his exaltation, his aspirations, were drawn from one secret source: sorrow. A sorrow which is not restlessness, not pettishness, or weakness, but a sorrow of understanding and resignation, firm, deep, eternal, from which his spirit rises purified and softened. He has suffered, but he does not rail; he sings. And because his poetry is born from the strife of life, from the universal pain and agony of disenchantments, it is always genuine, exquisitely touching and sad.

When he recites he is transfigured by the loftiness and fire of his emotions; his eyes grow resplendent, overflowing with passion and intelligence and expressing fully the intensity of his visions. More than once he has reached sublimity, and I felt it was a rare privilege to be present before so sacred an enthusiasm and so spontaneous a display of genuine sentiments. So often I have found genius absorbed in its own development, in its own greatness, but Galarraga is an admirable exception, an instance where egoism may be a pardonable failing of superior minds but not of superior hearts. He takes an interest in all those about him; he observes and listens with patience and simplicity that passes understanding, for how often those he listens to must try his intelligence with puerilities and shallowness.

This forebearance is stranger still in a man who, moreover, is gifted with an extraordinary insight into human nature. I had never attributed this particular gift to the poet, but to the novelist, and I believe even now that it is the playwright in Galarraga who possesses this sharp judgment and unerring intuition. What contradictions there must be between the tender heart of the poet, made to trust and idealize, and the mind of the playwright, who is observing so critically and cannot fail to meet with hypocrisy.

October 28. Galarraga brought Mother three volumes of his poetry. With dedications which perplexed me greatly. They were the first proofs I had of his insight, his consciousness of actual life. I opened one of them at hazard and read: "I am a man of sadness. My youth, believing and thoughtful, appears at the clear windows of my eyes only to weep. I am a man who has forgotten the facial expression of happiness, who has torn off the mask of joy in the midst of the crazed masquerade."[1]

These lines pierced my very heart; they might have been mine if I had known the names of these feelings, which in the great poet's soul are a song, and in mine, an echo. I could not refrain from turning to him and saying: "How beautiful this is!"

"Pero es demasiado triste,"[2] he answered.

"Por eso mismo lo comprendo mejor. Siempre he comprendido la tristeza,"[3] I said.

If for one moment I feared the impulse which guided these words, I was soon compensated for their truthfulness. Galarraga looked at me earnestly for a moment, as if considering whether I would understand him or not, and then "Yo creo que la tristeza es la cosa más bella en el mundo. Y sin embargo, todo el resto de la gente no buscan mas que la alegría, ¿porqué será?"[4] He shrugged his shoulders and smiled as if he knew the question well but could not answer it.

Since that moment he has talked with me with greater confidence. Of Schubert and Blossom Time he said: "One loves a man like Schubert because of his music, his works, and if you are going to stage his life it musn't be to make him appear grotesque. A genius like Schubert cannot be ridiculous. His limitations are sublime and not limitations at all but rather subtleties."[5]

He asked Mother to tell him all she knew of D'Annunzio. I asked him if he thought a little man, in the character sense, could be a great poet. He answered with uncertainty that often our ideals were greater than ourselves and that if our actions fell short of them, it was a matter of circumstances.

Mother asked him if he was fatalistic. For a moment I trembled in my chair. I remembered the definition of fatalism; in man it meant either despair or laziness. But Galarraga denied fatalism, admitting only that something more powerful than our character guided some great steps in our lives, not all.

He himself has had to struggle against his environment. He tells sadly of his parents stifling and enervating him. His father

---

[1] *Translated from the Spanish.*
[2] *"But it is too sad."*
[3] *"That is why I understand it better. I have always understood sadness."*
[4] *"I believe that sadness is the most beautiful thing in the world. Yet the rest of the people look only for joy. Why must it be thus?"*
[5] *Translated from the Spanish.*

had destined him for "business"; the word itself revolts him. His mother had dreamed of seeing him succeed in society, the type of shallow young man who devotes his life to social pleasures.

In his voice one divines great suffering, the sorrow so commonly the lot of the poet: indifference or violent disapproval and mockery from the world, misunderstanding by all those who ought to encourage him, coldness and condemnation everywhere. And in the shame, humiliation, of such attitude genius must strive, unloved, deprived of all warmth and sympathy. And it strives! It strives in his case, in many cases, but not all. Alas, that is the crime of it. It kills so many of them.

His generosity was revealed in these words which followed some questions he asked about Joaquin's future: "Si fuese rico, seria buen rico le aseguro. Me ocuparia de artistas pobres, de niños como Joaquinito, haciendo todo lo posible para que estudie, que su talento no se pierda al mundo. Pero no lo seré. No soy práctico."[1]

"Algún dia su padre . . ."[2] began Mother.

But he interrupted: "Ay, los millones de mi padre no los quiero heredar, y además, él es quien me va a enterrar a mí."[3]

At one time he said something so justly and aptly that I almost jumped from my chair. He was speaking of someone who visited a few minutes, out of pure curiosity, and left a very disagreeable impression on Galarraga. "No *vibró* más que cuando . . ."[4]

That is the word, I almost shouted, that is just the word I have been seeking for years. Vibrate! People vibrate and do not vibrate. It is vibration you secretly long for in your friends and acquaintances. It is a vibration which so quickly forms sympathies. It is constant vibration which makes the lasting friendships. How grateful, how boundlessly happy one is when someone *vibrates* at a word, a look, an unspoken thought. And that is too often what we find lacking and which makes us turn away sadly from people it is our duty to like. That is what makes it so difficult for me to enter easily into conventional talk. I like to step right into the intricate path leading to other people's souls.

[1] "*If I were wealthy, I would use my wealth for a good purpose. I would take care of struggling artists, of children like Joaquinito, doing all that is possible for his studies in order that his talent not be lost to the world. But I will not be [wealthy]. I am not practical.*"
[2] "*Someday your father . . .*"
[3] "*Alas, I do not wish to inherit my father's millions; besides, he is the one who will bury me.*"
[4] "*He only vibrated when . . .*"

Oh, I must learn the secret of making all those around me vibrate to *something*, even if it is, for example, talking about Charles Chaplin; or about housekeeping; or about one's neighbors. Perhaps in the crowd I will now and then find one who vibrates at the name of books, at the sound of music, at the charm of nature. Who knows—if many others are also seeking the same thing, I will not have to travel all the way alone!

Galarraga understood so well why I find so little pleasure in associating with the boys and girls of my age. We have such widely different ideas and ways. He did not think that I was queer but as all girls *should* be! It was a very comforting thought—too pleasant to be true—so that I believed it for a minute but soon returned to my former opinion of myself, which is not very flattering, as you well know.

He praised the Cuban woman for her evenness of temper, her sweetness and gentleness, her honesty and purity. He said that she was the true wife, faithful, extremely affectionate, virtuous, devoted and unselfish. He praised her goodness and her beauty. He knows of many instances where an American married a Cuban woman and was happy and satisfied, and compared the cases where a Cuban married an American woman and derived much unhappiness, being unaccustomed to her independence, her selfishness and domination. I was tempted here to hold up the intelligence of the "American woman" as a quality which in the Cuban woman does not exist at all. But in a wife, I suppose, it is far better to find affection and sweetness, flexibility and devotion, than intelligence. But why not have both, the culture of the American and the virtue of the Cuban woman?

About woman, as about everything else, I have ideas which seem to contradict one another. I would like to see combined in her submissiveness, gentleness, love of service, the qualities of affection and faithfulness together with intelligence. Why should this be said to be impossible? Why should a woman cease to be feminine because she cultivates her mind as well as her heart? No, I do not believe a word of it. It is possible, this ideal of mine; I feel that it exists somewhere. Galarraga, in praising goodness and beauty, seemed to have an unspoken thought in his mind. I was conscious that he did not lament the lack of intelligence because he does not expect it, and something which is not expected cannot be missed! He has written a new version of the French fable *La Cigale et la Fourmi*,[1] in which, when the singer begs for food from the laborer,

[1] *One of the fables of La Fontaine, known as "The Grasshopper and the Ant."*

instead of being repulsed with the words "You sang instead of working, now you shall go hungry as a punishment," the laborer welcomes him into his home and offers him food and comfort, saying, "You sang for me while I worked and made my burden lighter with your song, so now take from me all you need."

What a lesson, and what a beautiful, hopeless dream!

The morning of that memorable day a thing occurred which gave me as much pleasure as Galarraga's visit. We were coming out of our little church and bending our steps homeward when Hugo appeared. It was so unexpected that my heart leaped and I had to fix my eyes on the ground in order not to appear disturbed. It was clear, even to me, who is so blind about such things, that he had come purposely to walk home with us. I was so happy I hardly talked and forgot to laugh at the proper time. I could only watch his face and listen to his voice as if I had never known him before.

He was telling us about his family, who had returned from Europe, about his having had his Church while walking though the woods, little guessing how he had touched one of my most cherished ideals and how deeply it thrilled me to discover this similarity in our actions.

I do not know whether he is the realization of all my dreams or whether I am building my admiration upon the qualities I find in him, one by one.

The warmth of my esteem for Hugo sometimes frightens me. Friendship is defined as a quiet, enduring affection, but each day I find less quietness in my feelings and wonder whether it is merely because there is nothing quiet in my nature.

Later. I am all impatience and hope. I have had my photograph taken, and Mother is bringing the proofs tonight.

October 29. The result far surpassed my wildest expectations. Of eight poses one alone was bad, and there are four so good that we cannot choose among them. They were taken with so much care and artistry that they seem portraits not of what I believed myself to be but of what I dreamed and longed to look like.

The photographer was interested in my profile, so that of the best four there are three side views. In one I look upward as if watching lofty ideals and all ready to follow them. I look like Mother.

In another I look in front of me quite contentedly and with a mischievous ghost of a *smile.*

In the third, a three-quarter length (the others are just heads), my eyes are fixed on the ground, my head bowed, my arms curved, with the hands resting on my hips (Spanish fashion), and I look as if someone had whispered a compliment I did not deserve (but also as if I liked it!). And then the fourth: I face the world but not very bravely. Captain Norman said I looked "melancholic" and also as if saying, "go to . . ." which is terrible, but he is frank and a sailor.

Yes, I know why he says that. I do look a little proud and terribly sad. My eyes seem to tell everyone: "Leave me alone." But then my mouth contradicts it with a faint smile, the whole of my expression is a little defiant: "I don't care if you like me or not, but if you do, I am ready to love you."

From all the pictures you might be led to believe I am very sweet and very good, almost angelical. But beware of faces! No wonder the photographer asked Mother if I were as good a little girl as I looked. At this I laughed, and that is how I spoiled one picture. In all of them my hair is full of light; sometimes my profile is softly shadowed, in others, illuminated. It is a pleasure to be so artistically transformed. What a surprise it will be for the Cubans. Mother intends to send one to Havana to be published with those of other society girls. Some time ago we received a group of photographs published in an illustrated newspaper, which included one of Ana María Maciá, my future cousin, and Perlita Fowler, with whom I had the honor of sharing Eduardo's admiration and whom I finally unconsciously surpassed, and one of Mother, who has again begun to dream of taking me to Havana.

Later. I have news for you. And what news. The Forgies are giving a party tonight, and your friend Linotte is not invited! With all my blindness, my foolishness and almost stupid trust, the effort I make to believe the best, to find excuses for the bad, I cannot help seeing clearly this time and being slightly hurt by so mean a retaliation—for what? Because Hugo likes me. And Hugo will be there with his sister Edie, with whom I have just talked by telephone. Martha and Wilhelmina wish to prevent us from being together. They never gave a thought to sacrificing a little vanity to give me a little pleasure. Why should they? They only want pleasure for themselves. I had never dreamed of such pettiness in anyone. In one way I am glad because I feel that Hugo will miss me perhaps a tiny bit, and although he is too good to realize why

I am not invited, he might be sorry. What can my neighbors fear from me now? What more have I than they have? If they so eagerly desire to keep me hidden away, they are admitting that I am a dangerous creature to have about. It certainly is thrilling to be dangerous, and such a novelty. I look at myself in the mirror and smile—oh, so wickedly. Beware, gentlemen, I am quite a fascinating person. You see, I have an angelical-looking face so I can hide all my faults very cleverly. And besides, I am a foreigner. I know many tricks and charms which make me win friends by the thousand. Oh, yes, I have a million friends. Just look around. I do nothing but dance and flirt. I never open a book. I never think. I never care for my house. And so, I repeat, beware, gentlemen. Young ladies who are left out of parties are either nonentities or wicked specimens who have not succeeded in winning the approbation of their feminine judges. In other words, they are on their way to perdition.

Afternoon. As the evening approaches, the gaiety with which I welcomed my last adventure grows more and more subdued. I was exceedingly flattered, and still am, to be so greatly envied, but now while I arranged my velvet dress and French shoes for tonight's visitors, I experienced a little pang of regret remembering the night Hugo and I danced in Greenwich Village, thinking that while he dances with Martha and Wilhelmina, I am wearing something he liked. Thoughts unworthy of a would-be philosopher, thoughts very foolish indeed and girlish, but so true and natural. If I withheld them, I would be only partly confessing the wild ways of my nature.

But I have not the courage to continue. In a little while I will fall into a state of black despair simply because I cannot dance with Hugo tonight. Oh, Martha, oh, Wilhelmina, someday I will put you in a book. My first experience with the universally accepted theory of the cattiness of woman, First Chapter.

Evening. I gathered all my courage a moment ago and telephoned Hugo to tell him to come for a few minutes tomorrow so that I may give him Galarraga's poems and show him something (my pictures). He expected to see me tonight and was greatly surprised when I told him what happened.

No one will ever realize what an effort it cost me to make this advance. Mother told me my foolish pride and reserve would do me much harm, and I had to struggle against both. Twice I almost dropped the receiver, and when he answered, I longed to fly. I hardly know if he was glad I telephoned or shocked. But, of course, no one else would judge such a little thing in my way—what shocks me appears natural to others. Hugo is the first young man I have ever called! And girls do this ten or twenty times a day, unconcerned and perfectly at ease!

Now, of course, I have begun to feel the *pain* of it. In the middle of all the preparations for tonight, the hurry and bustle, I felt my hands trembling. Hugo's voice over the telephone was the climax to my excitement. I feel bruised. The thought that he is to be so near me, that I may hear him laugh and yet have no share in his merriment—oh, to be deprived of him is truly the only pain my neighbors have succeeded in inflicting upon me. I might have been so happy tonight.

7 o'clock. Just a few minutes before Galarraga's arrival with Belica [Tallet] and Manuela Simon. I tried to sing, and in the middle of a note my voice broke down. Writing here, I know not why, is my only comfort.

7:15. They are beginning to laugh—the party has begun. I have prayed that something would prevent our visitors' coming.

7:20. What is Hugo thinking? Even if he is absolutely happy, I feel that he misses me a little.

7:30. My guests are late. Heaven bless them. I have more time to control myself!

7:45. By an incredible effort I have conquered my spirits and they are rising now as quickly and as lightly as soap bubbles. Oh, my heart, what a troublesome portion of me you are!

8:00. You alone know how I truly feel. I have made everybody else believe that I am very gay—and inwardly I am all longing and loneliness.

His voice has just reached me from the Parkers' garden. He talks—I have not heard him laugh yet. He said he was coming tomorrow—but tomorrow is so far off.

Oh, they laugh! They laugh and it pierces me like the stab of a knife.

Why must they have Hugo for themselves when he is the only one among them all that I esteem? Why must my preference be disputed and made the cause of unkindness? I hope that I shall never be capable of such an act in all my life. Oh, God, help me to be kind and thoughtful and unselfish toward other girls, that I may never cause anyone as much sadness as I feel tonight.

They have just passed and walked into the Forgies' house, where the party is to end. I heard Hugo's voice again.

October 30. I am waiting for Hugo. My hands are cold, but this time it does not signify warmth of heart. My heart today is dead. It is very late and I fear he is not coming. Nothing, nothing matters. It is the reaction following last night's tense excitement. I think my feelings are worn out.

Edith just telephoned that her brother Hugo had forgotten an engagement and, having failed to reach me this morning, asked her to let me know he could come this evening instead. Tia Coco and my cousin Bernabé [Sánchez] are here. It will be a day of conversation. If I could hide somewhere . . .

It was extremely foolish of me to take all this so seriously. Now the hour of sense has come. It began when I stood before the window of my room and wondered *why* I was so sad. Because I regretted being deprived of Hugo's company one whole evening, knowing him to be dancing with girls bearing me ill will? But he is coming tonight, just for me. I repeated it to myself, and it became a talisman: "He is coming tonight, he is coming tonight"—and my sadness fled.

October 31. All that happened Saturday night appears now like a bad dream, from which I awakened last night. When Hugo came, it was the return of joy and faith. The sound of his voice dispelled all my sadness and doubts. At the end of his visit I felt sorry for Martha and Wilhelmina because they will never feel such happiness as I felt.

Of all the nights I have been with him, last night was the most perfect. I almost fear to write. It seems a thing too sacred for words. We were so happy together, we felt so near to each other, and the more we talked, the warmer our feelings grew, making our understanding of each other so complete that conversation was no longer conversation but an overflowing of all our hearts hold.

Hugo teases me because he says I always agree with him and we should find something to quarrel about, but it is his fault. I do not agree with him always, but when he expresses an opinion or a theory and then, smiling, asks me if I think it is right, his smile and his glance take me by surprise; all my ideas are scattered. I cannot find courage to squarely contradict him. He can easily persuade me, but very often not by the means of reason. His power comes from something else, a smile, a gesture, a swift change of expression. My mind says no, and my heart says yes.

Oh, that I should be so wrought up by such simple things, by just the ways of a person, when I thought nothing but a great superiority of intellect could hold my attention. Fortunately, in Hugo I find combined the intelligence which I look up to and the lovable traits which bring him near and which make him both a companion and a leader. He leads me—this is true—but how tenderly he leads!

I showed him the proofs of my photographs, and he was very enthusiastic, hesitating in his choice until at last we agreed he would give me one of his in exchange for one of my profiles. After this we talked of serious things, but not very seriously. At the least cause we would laugh gaily, and Mother afterward told me she had never heard people laugh so much in one evening alone in a quiet house.

Hugo said so many things I would like to write down. Oftentimes he placed his finger on the very problems I have been considering, but I find that his ideas on most subjects are more developed than mine, more positive, and also more practical. His judgment is older. He startled me when he said we should begin by perfecting ourselves before we seek for ideals in others. How can I disagree when so many of our aspirations are identical?

I would indeed like to write down everything, but I cannot do it yet. And it is not only what he said that I cannot write. I am always bolder with my pen than in my ways and talk, but there are times when my pen also feels the clutch of shyness. It is in this I differ so greatly from all the others whose journals I have read. I cannot bear to see certain things in black and white, infinite little shades of thoughts and feelings. They are like the perfume of flowers; if you stretch forth your hand, you can grasp the flower but the perfume eludes you. I would rather be guilty of shyness in writing than of an extremity in truthfulness. Such sacred things as I withhold are in truth very little things, but they are dear to my heart as only little things can be—glances, a word, a clasp of the hand at parting—almost nothing—but behind them there is friendship; there is the mystery of a thousand awakenings and a thousand joys, a thousand questions which only the soul knows and only the soul can name.

For hours afterward I lay awake, thinking and praying in my thankfulness. And when sleep finally came, it was only to bring me dreams of him. My first thought in the morning was of Hugo. My only thoughts today were of Hugo, and tonight, as you see, he is the subject of my confidences. He fills me with wonder, admiration and esteem to such a degree that I must scold myself for excess of enthusiasm. What a happy contrast there is between the night I wrote while they laughed and danced next door and tonight, while I remember Hugo's interest, his little compliments; the pleasure I take in his ideas, his sincerity, every phase of his companionship and every step we climb toward a better understanding.

November 1. It was raining when we walked to church, Joaquin and I, but when I returned alone, the country was bathed in soft light and freshness. I found myself walking under showers of glistening leaves which the wind set dancing and twirling about me. Now and then a flock of birds would darken the sky, filling the air with loud twittering, traveling as fast as the clouds.

I paused to drink in all this magic, and paused the longest when I came upon my own house rising from a soft, deep carpet of gold-brown leaves, the branches swinging to and fro before its windows. I entered into it with a feeling of worship. Old unpainted house, with your windows forever opening on scenes of incredible beauty, with your modest little roof smiling at the sky, and your chimney, its curling smoke ascending softly toward the clouds— every bit of you is poetry, the poetry of home and shelter, the poetry of life and memories. I love every nook and curve of you, every inch of wood. I love you in the morning when you are bathed in sunlight, in the evening when your lamp-lit windows keep watch in the darkness. I love you when the rain patters on your roof, and when you seem buried in Autumn leaves, in snow, or covered with icicles while inside a bright, cheery fire crackles in the fireplace. I love you when I return home at night and see your silhouette against the sky.

And what if someday I should not return? What if my Stranger should carry me off to another home?

To Dick [Frances]:
You are right in thinking I have grown older. I am changing so quickly that almost every day brings me a startling discovery. Instead of becoming more sociable, more frivolous, as time passes, I continue to find an incomparable joy in little things, in solitude, in dreaming, and reading and writing, and only now and then a friend, a letter. The result of this is that each day my curiosity and wonder increase. My world is crowded with a thousand new ideas, with new sentiments, new theories, new ideals and aspirations. In everything I find a meaning which gives me either a great

joy or a great sorrow. Everywhere little doors are opening upon more and more mysteries which fascinate me. I am all interest, enthusiasm, suspense and bewilderment. Transports succeed one another so quickly that sometimes I long for a little quietness, a moment of such placid contentment as you tell me you experience, a moment of rest. You see, Dick, I am awake to so many things that I want to reach forth toward them all in one hold, in one day. There is not an inch of my heart or my mind which is not at work, incessantly, intensely, eagerly and with so much fire and vigor that it gives the impression of a continual shock. In my diary I can only record half of these things; they are too numerous, vast and often nameless. I want to know what you are thinking and writing . . .

I would ask no more of life than to be allowed to sit by my desk writing from morning till night, with a few interruptions such as a walk in the woods, or a visit from Hugo. I believe I could never exhaust the supply of material lying within me. The deeper I plunge, the more I discover. There is no bottom to my heart and no limit to the acrobatic feats of my imagination.

If I did finish with myself, by chance, I could write of Hugo, which would be infinitely more interesting. But he is too good to suffer from the indiscretions of such a pen as mine.

With a mother such as mine, brothers and a friend like Hugo, I think the world admirable and complete. I have four tremendous reasons to be happy and only one to cause lament: Myself! But I will reform . . . someday.

Later. First effort on behalf of Reformation: Mending of Stockings. (Someday I will write a poem entitled: "The Atrocities Imposed Upon Blue Stockings.")

I have discovered a curious little book entitled *Pleasures of Life* by Lord Avebury. It is written in the style of school geographies or arithmetics but nevertheless contains valuable quotations. The first one which interested me was by Epictetus (I do not know who he is—that is what comes of self-teaching—but in my diary this will offend no one). I do not believe God made man to be happy, and I can prove it. We are taught in the Catholic religion *resignation*, that this is a "vale of tears" and not that we should expect happiness. The Stoics sought happiness in insensibility, thereby admitting that there were sorrows. God sends us our sorrows, and though we, with our human minds, cannot understand

His designs in doing so, we must know that they have a divine cause. If He sends us sorrows, He did not intend for us to be happy. And there is sorrow even in our happiest moments.

Hugo says that there is nothing that does as much harm as satisfaction and contentment. It prevents us from *growing*; it kills all the sources from which we obtain stimulus, inspiration and ambition. Hugo speaks of "growth" even as Emerson does. Everybody seems to agree that we must grow. But what I would like to know is the purpose of our growth, its object? Who will tell me?

Life is not full of suffering, but if it were, tonight I feel with Galarraga that sorrow is a very beautiful thing. If only I could feel the same when the sorrow does come to me, but at such a time it takes possession of me and leaves no space for thankfulness.

My way of being sad differs from all others'. I love sadness as well as joy. I do not think we can triumph over pain and sorrow but that we can enjoy them. Great suffering is the *privilege* of great hearts. In a few hours I may contradict myself. If I were to receive a harsh word now, I would pray passionately to God not to send me so much pain; I would fall asleep, sobbing perhaps, and longing for the return of happiness. These are the inconsistencies of my age, of my inexperience. I only ask for patience while I find my way in spite of a thousand opposing influences and opinions surrounding me. I must do my own thinking boldly, and though it may be radically wrong now, only by my own efforts can I correct my misconceptions.

This pleased me: "If we separate ourselves so much from the interest of those around us that we do not sympathize with their suffering, we shut ourselves from sharing their happiness and lose far more than we gain. If we avoid sympathy and wrap ourselves round in a cold chain armor of selfishness, we exclude ourselves from many of the greatest and purest joys of life. To render ourselves insensible to pain we must forfeit also the possibility of happiness." This is a summing up of Charles's philosophy and the key to his character. In order to preserve himself from any pain he shuts off friendship and coldly condemns love as if it were in his power to guide his heart as well as he does his mind. I have had long arguments with him, and in answer he tells me: "See how you suffer with *your* friends. And in the future how you will suffer in your love! While I . . . ."

"But you are not *living*," I answer furiously. "You are merely existing."

That is why I have written so little about Charles. His philosophy revolts me although I admire him sincerely where other things are concerned. Selfishness I abhor, so that in a person I can only see the fearful *It* and nothing else.

November 3. If I do not watch my pen tonight, my confidences will become a series of explosions, outbursts, exclamations and exaggerations. If you saw my face, you would think that something incredibly startling had changed the face of the world. You might also think I had been made a member of the French Academy. My expression is one vast expanse of beaming and glowing wonder and satisfaction; my eyes are a sea of amazement rising and falling like the tides, with dreams as fantastic as the moonlight dancing on its waves. Oh, never mind my metaphors; I am certain I have mixed them, there is so much confusion in my mind. But none of the things I have named are the cause of my excitement. I have been in the house all day, alone. I have written a poem in Spanish, three in French, without a moment's interruption, completely rewritten my sketch of Galarraga and filled thirty pages with "spacious nonsense." Add to this the reading of a remarkable book, Lafcadio Hearn's *Life,* and there you are. On the one hand, scattering my thoughts; on the other acquiring the knowledge of man's heart, which has stirred all my sympathy in the deepest and most piercing manner. What I have felt, thought and dreamed today passes description. It is at such a time that I feel my Vocation. I have been made to write. I have been made to sit by my desk day after day, pouring into a million pages the contents of my mind and heart, the results of my observations, the things I conceive, the things that are revealed to me, the things I *must speak.* How else can I explain this flow of ideas to which the words are attached almost miraculously? It comes from within me, something stronger than my will, at the times I least expect it. I am led, I am carried away by a thing which is beyond myself, beyond control and discipline.

As I write, when in such a state, it is as if all the *heat* in me increased and with it the clearness of my vision. I see vividly, without hesitation or doubt, and what I see I write without difficulty, and without hesitation.

Where this heat comes from I do not know. But what I have felt all day is something more than an inclination or a whim or a momentary exaltation. It is a fire which can never die, nor be subdued and quieted. It must be given freedom, and whatever restraint be imposed on it will only intensify its strength.

It seems absurd to write in this manner now when I have done nothing to distinguish myself from all the young people with the scribbling mania. Alas, I have done less perhaps than most of them. When I look down upon my work, it shrinks to almost nothing. One day I write poems and essays and the next I tear and burn them, to begin again, and in the same manner I have done this for years. Nothing satisfies me. The reading I do serves only to impress me with my inferiority of style and character. I write in a scattering fashion, always with a purpose in mind and yet never capable of reaching it. My works lack "roundness," concentration and clearness. I drift into vague visions and abstract forms and above all into superfluities. Although it is not so, it appears very much as if my mind wandered; when I most want to appear fixed upon my subject, I deviate and I miss my point. And above all what I cannot forgive myself is the unreliableness of my judgment because of my enthusiasm.

Against all these handicaps, I have only a few remedies. I know that I have application, a hard-headed kind of persistence. Where will all this lead me? Roundness, concentration and clearness can be acquired. Directness and the eloquent virtue of reserve equally so. As to my enthusiastic, explosive and exclamatory weaknesses, I maintain they are the infirmities of my age, and I will not always be eighteen. Probably in a year or so I will have exhausted these powers and a period of quiet will follow, a period of settled judgment, of moderate opinions, a more judicious reasoning, and instead of jumping to conclusions, I will *arrive* at them. What is more, in a year or so I hope to have acquired some experience, a greater wisdom of the world of which I am now so sadly lacking. It will give my writing an air of respectability, and I may go so far as to appear well balanced. Now, as I write today, it is only a succession of blunders—the undeniable reflection of a thousand experiments with ideas and words (a less charitable person might term it *juggling*).

Nevertheless, I am resolved to write, write and write. Nothing can turn me away from a path I have definitely set myself to follow. And the hope which is the sustenance of poets will lead me onward, if nothing else, for what can give me courage but the thought of what I aspire to reach, what I desire to make of myself? Oh, I must not look back or I will be frightened by what *I am*.

November 5. Twilight. Does twilight ever come without finding my heart so full that, like a plant, it bows gently to the ground?

When the shadows have gathered, it is time for me to retire within myself, to turn my gaze inward, to contemplate all the riches I have amassed, and like a miser counting his gold, I count my experiences. How lovingly, how tenderly I dwell upon each trifle. How minutely and impassionately I study the reaction of these trifles, the thoughts they give birth to, the theories they demonstrate, the opinions they confirm or disprove, the aspirations they arouse. Like a scientist I analyze, classify, separate, eager to get at the truth, eager to trace the cause, the effects, and determined to explain and to *describe* adequately the delicate laws of which I so keenly feel the pulsations, whose works I so clearly distinguish and so warmly admire. For in truth, I sometimes believe that hero worship, so natural to man, in me has taken a new form. I worship not so much the actions of men but what *moves* them to such actions. I am not satisfied with the actor's behavior. I want to know his soul. I want to know the inner self. I long to look deeper than the gestures and ways of those about me. I long to know the intention behind the action, the *misconception* which may be the cause of it. That is why I am fascinated by journals and biographies. Nothing holds so great an interest for me now than the study of a human heart seeking to express itself in life. I am interested in its failures, in its mistakes, in its deviations. I believe in its goodness in most cases, and I feel there is much that is misinterpreted and falsified. Descartes was wise when he decided to tear down everything and begin afresh on barren ground. In his philosophy he took nothing for granted, he accepted nothing. I, in my humble way, am working in an absolutely opposite manner. I have begun my constructive thinking where others have abandoned it. I expect everything which relates to the Ideal, and that Ideal is as much a part of me as life itself—and more necessary, more vital, than life. When I say that I discredit all I am told, it is because it does not conform with my convictions—my hard-headedness. Perhaps in a few days I will find all this in someone else's book—written, of course, faultlessly and backed by a reputation. This always happens, time after time. Discouraged? No indeed. Someday I might strike upon something unsaid before, original, unusual.

Hugo has given me a great surprise. And yet no, it is not a surprise, for I *expect* him capable of everything, and though he had never given me a tangible proof of his talents as a poet, I knew intuitively this and other things he quietly made a secret of.

Later. Of what use is it to write about Hugo when he himself just came to see me? My hand still thrills from his handclasp as

I write, and my heart is still beating wildly from infinite and indescribable joy.

He came only for an hour and we talked. We had a wonderful, wonderful talk. We are beginning to say more with our eyes than with words. Sometimes the light in his makes me tremble. I would like to believe that he likes me as much as I like him, and yet I dare not.

At one moment we were speaking of beauty and virtue in woman (one of our favorite topics), and as I had been teasing him, he pretended he had to *make* me understand once and for all what he really meant. And looking at me very piercingly, he said: "You *know* I, for instance, could not admire beauty without intelligence."

His gaze and the emphasis on the "know" made everything in me tingle and vibrate. He had touched such a sensitive chord unknowingly. In one question he had called for an answer which sums up his character, the thing in him I most admire, the trait in his nature for which I feel a boundless enthusiasm.

Yes, I *know* he wants *intelligence* as much as goodness and beauty. And that is what distinguishes him from the rest of men. Could I tell him that? I answered him as quietly as I could, tempted by an undefinable something in his eyes to give my enthusiasm freedom. How often I control my enthusiasms. And it is far better so. Hugo would understand but I cannot yet tell him what I think of him. He is incomparable. Think of him compared with Miguel, Enric, Charles, even Eduardo. Eduardo, who came so near to the ideal and yet lacks so many things. Hugo is better than anyone I have ever created in my most beautiful dreams.

Mother has just asked me if I intend to write all night.

November 6. When I asked Charles some time ago what he thought of Hugo, he answered: "He does not seem as serious as you take him to be." I know that Hugo gives this impression, but he never deceived me by it. I saw beyond the outward appearance from the first, not certain of depths in him, but already conscious of a nature infinitely different and superior. And last night as he talked, I realized how in earnest, how serious, and how perfectly sincere he is. His whole heart is always in his words and in his eyes, and that is why his voice awakens in my own being things I never felt before, and in his eyes I read the revelations on which my understanding is based. Where before I was perplexed by some of his ways, now they are no mystery to me, and after all, the only things I could not understand were those relating to me, whether he wanted to see me, whether he liked me. All this has vanished. He has conquered my shyness, my doubts, my hesitations, and now he stands by me, my friend of friends. We are so near to each other that we can look into each other's hearts as well as we look into our own.

It is as he says: "We know four languages."

"Four?" I repeated. "What is the fourth?"

"Poetry."

Knowing all these, can we ever misunderstand each other?

November 9.

To Eleanor:

I compare you too with the girls I meet every day everywhere, and I find none as sweet, nor half as good as you. Most of them have no hearts, Eleanor, none of the tenderness and gentleness I love in you. The expression of their faces, those looks of effrontery and mockery, their silly talk and silly ways, make me fly from them and prefer absolute solitude by far. How often my mind travels back to those days in school when you helped me with my lessons, when we walked home talking. You never laughed at things. One could trust you. You never changed, you were never angry, never impatient.

Evening. There is something volcanic in the way my mind works. Hidden fires smolder quietly in the heart of it, of which I am utterly ignorant, and I go about the rest of my life's business peaceably enough until the day of eruption, which comes to destroy all my tranquillity and spread misery and confusion, sometimes destruction.

One of these eruptions occurred during these last days and was caused by a mission week at our little church. Mother and I began attending the sermons and Mass and instructions.

All the ideas I entertained about my religion were stirred, all my old doubts reawakened, the same perplexities brought to light. Again I had to struggle against evil thoughts, again I was tortured and tormented by rebellion, by vain and powerful efforts at understanding. It was maddening.

The first night, the priest eloquently pictured the Christ crucified, the magnitude of his sacrifice. The description of the intense agonies he underwent for our sake, the thought of his blood, his sacred blood shed for the remission of our sins—all these I felt like the stab of a knife. Touched more deeply than words can tell, humbled, profoundly moved by this appeal, I fell upon my knees with my eyes full of tears. Through these tears I looked up at the Christ upon his cross and all my heart flowed to him in overwhelming gratitude, an immense and sweeping pity and love.

I was carried away by these sentiments. Kneeling there, I felt how deeply Catholicism was rooted in my soul. I felt the sublimity of my beloved religion, its spirituality, its nobility, its greatness. I murmured: "I believe, I believe, I believe." My dreams that night were haunted by the memory of incense, candlelight, organ music. The sublime face of Christ was ever before my eyes, his beautiful, sorrowful face so full of pain that I could not bear to look upon it long.

The following night I received a cruel shock. The priest threatened. He described hell, he violently attacked sin, he emphasized the punishment inflicted upon guilty souls. He appealed to our fear of torture, to our superstition. Where before, my better sentiments were aroused, I found myself thinking, thinking. I reasoned coldly, I anticipated the priest's thoughts and criticized them before he uttered them. His sermon was, like most sermons, incapable of satisfying the most ordinary thinking mind.

Hardness and coldness crept into my heart, with a sense of loss, disappointment and despair I had never felt before. I was wounded in my religion. Suddenly I found myself alone and abandoned, cheated of my faith, hurt in my trust and willingness to believe. Could it all be a gross deception? I asked myself. Perhaps *nothing is true*. There is no eternal punishment, no heaven, no eternity. For a moment the Church appeared to me like a theatre, a stage set for the Comedy of Religion. I gazed at the women around me. Could they possibly believe all *this?* Not a proof, not a manifestation of God, in the priest's words. He was delineating actions such as man would commit; he was threatening us with a vengeance such as man would plan and carry out. God, never. It could not be. Not that God whose presence I feel in the woods. Not that God so gloriously alive in Nature. Not the God of heaven, the Creator of stars, of the sun, the moon, the wondrous planet on which we now live, and the Creator of man with his mysterious and awe-inspiring Soul. Can it be that He, so great in nature, may be badly interpreted in his Churches?

And so, while the priest spoke, I thought and argued with myself. Restless, dissatisfied, disappointed, I knelt with the others when the time came, but I could not pray. The Church was small, the people seemed unreal, and above all I was far too frightened at what I saw in my own soul.

I partly explained these things to Mother. She thinks that these ideas are caused by my ignorance of sin. "If you knew how horrible sin really is, you would understand why these priests must of necessity speak in this manner. They know what these women are capable of, and it is their duty to recall them by the best of means. These means to some may appear unnecessary and exaggerated. Few have your sensitiveness, fifille, and the priest cannot heed them. You must bear this talk of hell and punishment for the sake of others who can be affected only in this way, whose reasoning is vague and dense."

Ignorant of sin! With Mother's care, of course I am ignorant of sin, and perhaps it does explain my impatience at the mention of it. It is a subject which leaves me totally untouched and unmoved. But what right have I to criticize, then, a form of address which is not meant for me?

Alas, it is always in search of the highest peaks that I fail. Of all things, I thought I would find them in my religion. And now must I believe that religion is not an aspiration toward God, not a communion in which the spirit can find fortitude and purity, but a painful battle against sin? I wonder what makes me balk at this talk of eternal punishment, what is the cause of this perversity of thought? Why does the mention of flames and torture make me indignant and revolted? I am expected to feel contrition, humility, repentance. But I feel, instead, defiance and doubts. Yes, there is perversity in such an attitude. But I am determined to be an intelligent Catholic or nothing at all. I have been called a renegade. I shall be called several things before I am certain of what I am myself.

But the day I know, beware—I will know so well no one will dare make a mistake.

Papa Chéri:[1]

I am very grateful to you when you send me a book that gives me an electric shock. Shocks like that shoot off the sparks that illuminate my own thoughts, and I go my way a thousand times braver than before, hotly brandishing my pen, emboldened by the example of others, or, as in the case of this last book, driven

[1] *Letter translated from the French.*

by a spirit of contradiction and love for the clash of ideas. Well, I can't talk about this throughout my whole letter. When one suffers from an excess of Enthusiasm (universal sickness at 18 years of age!), one has to know where to draw the line.

So I come back to earth and observe my surroundings. I can assure you that it is an interesting and varied landscape!

About Joaquin. After all, what Joaquin has is something for which there is a word in every language: he has a *soul*, he has feelings, impulses, deep and lofty aspirations, that are the principal source of his strength and power, and especially of his depth. His improvisations are serious, tragic, solemn. But his music is never heavy; it floats and penetrates, it surrounds you and carries you away. . . . Joaquin is an extraordinary child. He seems to be made of *springs*, and one has to find the secret of moving them. He has the kindness, gentleness, the patience of a saint . . . but he is hard-headed! What distinguishes him from children of talent in the Old World is his normal, healthy love for outdoor life and games. This is one of the strongest influences in American life. True happiness consists of developing oneself as much physically as intellectually and artistically. I know you approve of this. I took a long time to understand it myself. I have always felt a great disdain for the physical side of things. For a long time I tried to ignore the envelope completely and to fortify and ennoble only the spirit. It is only lately that I have accepted the fact that to be well balanced and truly as close to the ideal as possible, one must grow in every way. We owe that to the world.

As for Thorvald, the 100 percents in algebra keep coming, and I listen and marvel. I have never grown in that direction, but so far I seem to be flourishing and no one suspects my ignorance.

To prove to you the sincerity of my theory, imagine me—a failed poet, a mediocre philosopher and writer of prose—at a football game the other day with Thorvald. It was in a big college stadium, a thrilling, superb spectacle. A crowd! Shouts! Applause! And what enthusiasm, for goodness sake! I felt real pleasure in it. It wasn't what I had thought, a brutal and stupid game, an exhibition of animal talent. No, the players also had to be supple, daring and brave. My thoughts traveled backward in time to the Roman games. In my imagination I could see the great stadia of ancient times; I heard other shouts, I saw other crowds and other games.

I don't want you to take this as a sign that I am becoming American in the worst sense of the word. You have no idea how much I have kept of the feelings of my ancestry. I am the least American of the three of us. I have a feeling for art in my blood, and my heart beats only for poetry and beauty, the great, sublime and spiritual things. What I admire in the American national game is the poetry of skill, agility, strength and courage. Whatever it may have that is barbarous is lost in its heroic side! Amen. The proof that I am far from turning into an American is that if I had to choose between the football game and a concert—a good concert, naturally—I would choose the concert, so you have nothing to fear.

Thorvald and "college"—he is practical, well balanced, positive. Joaquin and I probably shall die like poets and musicians from trying to live on air and illusions, but not with Thorvald in the family.

I wish I knew from whom I inherited this chatty pen, since you say that my epistolary style puts you on edge! . . .

Petit Papa, your daughter has a voice. It's the kind of voice that goes nicely with twilight, moonlight, etc., because it isn't very loud or very splendid. It seems that I gargle about as much as I sing. (Thus the opinion that I would make a good actress.)

I am afraid that you may think from my letters that I am a little mad, but you see in truth I am a very accomplished creature. I could run a newspaper ad for a husband something like this: "I sing, I dance, I am a good cook. All I ask is peace, books and ink." But ink frightens gentlemen. It's the odious sign of activity in the cerebral region. And in a woman, that's unpardonable!

November 12. After writing 26 pages to Father, I experienced for the first time in my life the celebrated writer's cramp. My cheeks were deeply flushed, my hands ached, and my head seemed made of fire. And yet throughout these discomforts I felt a sharp, keen joy when my eyes fell on my work. It was only a letter, but I can say the same of all I write. This is only a journal. Most of my work is only fragments, attempts, only poems. But in some mysterious way I find that I pour my whole heart and soul into each of these "onlies." Who can say why?

So much of me, in a spiritual sense, goes into all my letters. Someday there will be nothing left. Still, it is better to invest trifles, little labors, with a certain amount of importance and sacredness. In doing this I am continually exacting the very best from myself and practicing.

Seeking coolness and freshness from my fever, I was standing by the window when the postman's whistle blew. Long ago this whistle used to make me jump. Lately I never move to greet the postman. The mail holds no charm for me. But Thursday something drew me to the door. There was a letter for me. "It looks like Hugo's writing, but it is *impossible*." I tore the letter open and sought the signature. It *was* Hugo.

During one of his visits he had teased me because I did not contradict him: "You are afraid of me," he said, laughing. The next time he came I told him that I agreed because I believed him in the right and not because I was afraid of him. We were neither of us in earnest, but Hugo takes the word "afraid" as the subject of his letter, calling it a soap bubble which he must prick before it floats too far. His letter is a poem. It is one of the most beautiful letters I have received. He told me that in his wildest thoughts he had never applied the word to me in connection with anyone, much less this "uncouth swain," himself. And he tells me why: "Because you seem to me the very soul of quiet courage, soft-spoken as the mountain streamlet that yet dares to choose to cranny through sheerest granite rocks its passage valleyward. And indeed this is no fiction, for I know you have made an individual way through the granite walls of the most rigid rules of thought and conduct known to man, over the barriers of sect and race. You have been true to yourself, and your eyes, Anaïs, are frank and clear with the consciousness that you have kept that most sacred faith. And it is such a faith as leaves no room for fear of man, God, or devil that I see in them. Won't you tell me that you understand?"

Someone said he knew of no greater joy than to make a good action in secret and to have it found out by stealth. I thought of this on reading Hugo's letter. One of life's greatest joys is to possess a quality unknown to yourself and to have it discovered by someone dear to you, by someone whose opinion you value. His letter was like a talisman. I answered him simply: "In writing, you are like the magician who, with each wave of his pen, can dispel mists and leave a clear, illumined path for true understanding to tread upon in its blessed and mysterious ways . . ."

I mailed my letter Friday night at Pennsylvania Station, and as we crossed the street toward the Hotel Waldorf we caught sight of Hugo waiting for a car. We exchanged a few words, clasped hands and separated. He was going to a guitar rehearsal, and

Mother, Joaquin and I, to meet Galarraga. I can write nothing of Galarraga's recitation of his poem at Columbia University. A veil had fallen between me and the world. My thoughts circled persistently about Hugo. I walked as one in a dream.

I know that we left the hotel in a taxi, Thomas Walsh, Pepito Echaniz, Galarraga and we three. Afterward I found myself in the midst of many people who were chattering, chattering, chattering. Then silence. Galarraga recited, was warmly applauded, the chatter continued, and in this confusion of talk, perfume, introductions, more talk and lights, I felt sorrowful and lost. This strange and unreasonable detachment from the world, this vague and dreamy forgetfulness of my actual surroundings, this veiled, misty outlook upon all things, I cannot explain. It has come now and then and I find people mean nothing to me; the world becomes ghostly and distressingly unreal. It is as if my soul had fled from me, and I were left abandoned, forlorn and confused in a world of which I am not a part.

It was the last time we were to see Galarraga. We parted regretfully. He was surrounded by admirers, and my last memory of him was that of a sad-eyed, frail man receiving compliments and shaking hands, with a courteous and gentle smile.

But soon I lost consciousness of him. Pepito Echaniz, with all his winning personality, left only a hazy impression on my mind. Fortunately he is coming to see us Monday night and I will atone for this inexplicable indifference.

November 13. I must remember to speak to you of my talk with Frances, but tonight I am obliged to keep my mind away from all serious subjects by way of preparation for a certain visitor. (This reveals that it is not Hugo I am expecting.) Do you remember Waldo Sanford? About a year ago he stepped into my life, became interested in me, following a dance at the inn, marched off to school, and we corresponded a little while; then exit Waldo. And I never thought of him again. But le voilà! He telephoned me some days ago, asked permission to visit me. It is another adventure, and besides, I must take advantage of all the varied specimens which fall under my eyes if I am to study human nature. I am praying that Hugo should not think of coming; he has once before taken me by surprise. I may be sorely tempted to laugh at the impossible contrast, or weep. And then how I should wish Waldo to disappear, for when Hugo is there, who, pray tell me, can move my attention? It would be disastrous.

November 14. Last night, you would have either laughed at me or pitied me. What happened was such a thing as could happen only to me. Perhaps, it is true, it might have happened to other girls, as far as the *facts* themselves are concerned, but never in that peculiar way things have of affecting me and of projecting themselves upon the tablets of my mind in a hard, photographic manner.

At about seven-thirty someone knocked on the door and sedately, reluctantly, I went downstairs to receive the visitor. It was Hugo! He called it a flying visit, as he was afterward to catch a train for the city. We sat down and talked for a while. Each minute that passed increased a strange pain in my heart. I hardly knew what he was saying. I was watching his face, and looking intently into his eyes, conscious of him, of his voice, his winning ways. And conscious, above all, that in a few minutes he would be gone. I had never known such feelings before. It was like holding something incredibly beautiful and priceless between your fingers and knowing it to be slipping away, knowing that you could not grasp it firmly or cling to it because it was not yours; you had no right to it.

In that desolate sense of loss I was insensitive to the pleasure of those few moments. Suffering in this unreasonable manner, simply in imagination, has no remedy. It is the most hopeless of pains. It is your own mind torturing your own heart.

He was reading me something from [Francis] Palgrave's *Golden Treasury*[1] when Waldo Sanford knocked. My heart sank. I wonder if Hugo realized this interruption, this cold breaking-off in an evening which might have been so joyful. I was in such a state of perturbation that I could not read *his* heart. I have never wanted so much to know a heart as I want to know Hugo's. Why this feeling of being drawn into the strong current of his life? What gives Hugo such a powerful hold on me? Why does all in him move me and touch me so deeply that I sometimes feel anger, burning anger, at *myself*, at my feebleness and sensitiveness? It is as if I were looking into a deep pool, fascinated, incapable of turning my eyes away, gazing and dreading some mysterious spell which will make me lose myself forever. Magic. I called him a magician in my letter. How well the name fits him. That is the secret of his power. He has drawn a circle of enchantment about

[1] Golden Treasury of the Best Songs and Lyrical Poems in the English Language.

me, and I am caught! But he is a good magician, one with an infinitely tender heart. What will he do to me? He does not wish to make me suffer, but why has he chosen me, of all girls to work his unfathomable spells upon?

Hugo remained a few minutes after meeting Waldo, creating conversation in a wise and clever way, for which I was immensely grateful. How on earth Hugo has managed to master all these accomplishments I do not know. He is never thrown off his balance; his tact, exquisite breeding and ease and poise leave me speechless. I, who am such a perfect and ridiculous savage! Picture a gypsy girl, a wanderer, wild, untamed in all the ways of the conventional world, and you have a portrait of me. There is something detestable in this failing when you consider the aristocratic traits of my ancestors. And what is worse, I do not seem truly wild, uncouth of speech, outlandish in my tastes and dress—no, time after time I have been called a "Princess." Think of it! A Princess I may seem when I remain quiet in my chair. But let anyone enter the room and then watch me. It is laughable and tragical—but it is also a conquerable fault, and heaven knows, though it takes me 10 years, I will trample upon this shortcoming without mercy!

It is no use writing about Waldo. He is a good, nice boy, but we have as much in common as Eskimos and Japanese. The minutes dragged by. And in the beginning I could think of nothing else but of Hugo walking away in the darkness while my heart cried out, "Come back! Come back! Oh, please come back!" This, inside. And on the surface, a painful stringing-off of light talk and an inhuman effort at interest and sympathy and agreeableness. At ten-thirty Waldo rushed away for his train.

For hours I lay awake, wondering, wondering. And Hugo? One more long week with an uncertain visit at the end. But he is taking me to a Thanksgiving dance. Poor Martha. Poor Wilhelmina. If you knew how little it pays to thrust yourself forward in the eyes of a Magician. He is all mystery, all secrets. He looks about him and chooses the girl who was dreaming and thinking quietly in a far-off corner of the world. He chooses the gypsy, the scribbler, the unwise and strange recluse, the girl of fantastic ways and impulses. Why should he do so, the all-wise and all-good, all-knowing Reader of Hearts? Magic, magic, magic. It is *all* magic. It is all blessed, joy-giving, glorious, unfathomable Magic!

Later. What would Hugo think of my courage if he knew that ten times today my heart paused, so to speak, and asked itself, panic-stricken: Does Hugo like me less since last night?

What a desolate day! It rains drearily and persistently; only a few dead leaves cling to the branches, those branches stretched for the rest of the winter in the sad, forlorn way of leafless things. All this and the nature of my reflections oppress my heart in an intolerable manner. If I look out the window, I see sadness. If I look in my own heart, I see sadness. The weight of silence gives me a sense of imprisonment, suffocation. I lie exposed to all impressions without means of defense. I know when I am touched, wounded, pleased. I recognize pain, joy and disenchantment, but I can shut none of these things off. I am penetrated by all things, pierced and tormented. The tide is ever incoming and never retreats. I do not know the secret of Control, of Indifference, of Escape. People ward off these invaders with one cold, proud glance of disbelief, or with the powerful lashing hand of Humor. They are on the defensive and no tricks of fancy, of imagination, of susceptibility, no impulse, ever upset their balanced, measured, wisely regulated lives.

Impressions! One short talk, a glance, an expression swiftly passing on someone's face and a thousand impressions are the result. The fact has passed; the tangible cause is removed, the friend is already far away, but the impression once born is vividly stamped on my memory. And long after the incident is lost in the current of fast-moving life, the impressions still surround you, enduring, clinging, tenacious, sometimes unforgettable. This is the ghostly side of life. Not the facts, the things that you touch, but the multitude of recollections, echoes, and vague recognitions that surround these things. They flow into your actions. They are walking dreams, and it is no wonder some of our actions, we find, resemble dreams. Are our dreams born from action, or our actions from our dreams? The two flow into each other, and no one can tell. What fills me with wonder is the great circle impressions trace, before you can capture them with one word and give them a name.

I have watched this in people. Hugo, each time I have been with him, has given birth to a thousand contradicting impressions. They changed meaning, color, shape and substance as I saw more and more of him. From a visit or an ordinary evening together, I would gather a certain attitude. It would last me until I saw him again, warm and fresh because I had written it down. Gradually I have outlined in my Diary whatever was revealed to me of his character. In his talk, his ways, and lately in his letters I found a constant source of admiration.

What bewilders me is my incapability of condensing these varied impressions in a few words. I have described him, I have noted his sayings, some of his ways, and always, always I feel the unknown, the intangible lurking in his eyes and in the changes of his voice and manner. I cannot catch these things; fundamentally he is the same, I know, but what he is I do not know yet. If I could but catch these shades of feelings, these changing impressions which remain with me so long after he has gone . . . All the essence, the frailty of these delineations, are endangered by the inexperience and crudeness of my pen.

In this, indeed, I differ so greatly from most people. I am not content with the feeling of all these things, not content in recognizing, knowing and understanding them. I want to name them, to speak them, to describe them. Why?

Today I understand far better what Enric meant when he said: "I will go mad trying to understand you." I laughed then, but I would not laugh now. Enric was serious, as I am now trying to understand Hugo. Miguel and Eduardo tried to explain me also, but in doing so did not suffer as Enric did. Poor Enric! I think heaven has sent me Hugo that I might know sentiments at which I used to laugh the laughter of the unknowing. Now as I experience it, I sympathize with all the people who are trying to read each other's hearts, with all the curiosity, wonder and perplexity that leaves no room for other thoughts during the day and no time for sleep at night.

As we grow older we should not grow skeptical. On the contrary. Should not our sympathy, pity and understanding increase when our eyes are opened by experience to the suffering and trouble of others?

November 15. Pure, glowing sunshine, and into my heart has descended a blessed peace. I look back to yesterday as one does at a day of fever and am filled with a childlike wonder at these great changes in Nature and in my own heart. Sometimes they seem reflections of each other; the worlds, one great and sublime, the other self-enclosed and only half-known, yet both moving to the same rhythm of joy and sorrow.

Today I feel brave and calm. All doubts, all criticisms of self, all pains, all uncertainties, are hushed in a mysterious sleep. I went about my work in the house singing softly, and doing all things quietly and tenderly, as if in awe of that supreme peace and fearing it should leave me.

And now the shadows fall. I feel that my thoughts are too sacred for words, that I can only show you the silence in my soul by silence here.

November 16. I am filling notebooks, covering envelopes, saturating all papers which fall into my hands. I write in the train, in streetcars, in Mother's office, in the kitchen—everywhere, anywhere, at any time. I cannot find a reason for this; things float in vast clouds around my head, settle, invade all my kingdoms, spread alarm, confusion and pleasure, arouse, inflame, inspire, exalt and, above all things, cry loudly, piercingly, Ink, ink. Give us ink!

Ink, pen and paper seem the greatest necessities of my existence. I could go without food, without friends, without home or books, but without ink and paper I should die.

And I write, oblivious of surroundings, forgetful of the hour, of my duties and obligations. If only I wrote worthwhile things. It is only the certainty that I *can* do something that fires me. In spite of the worthlessness of my present work, always on my visionary horizon remains fixed an eternal and unaccountable Faith. Why? I cannot tell. I will not be discouraged. I throw myself heart and soul into little works. In my inner consciousness has dawned the fact that I am in training, that I am practicing, experimenting and thereby moving closer to my heart's desire, to my life's task.

I am ready to sacrifice everything to answer this all-powerful call which, once heard, stamps itself upon the soul in letters of fire. I must not lose patience with myself and must keep forever in sight my aim and goal. Knowing I can reach someday what seems so far away now because of my faults and inexperiences, I must look upon these fruitless efforts not as discouragements but as the inevitable signs attending all ambitions, all desires, and all healthy activities in pursuit of the Ideal. Inevitable signs, also, of Youth.

Evening. Snow has fallen over the wide, burning expanse of my emotions. This is the feeling I experienced when, suddenly, I was brought violently face to face with hard, cold facts. It was the word "Money." Some time ago the same word caused a revolution in my life, and then by dwelling much on other things, I again wandered far off from it, and again became utterly unconscious of all that relates to life's practicalities. Alas, if I could learn what Mother knows so well. Food and shelter, and without these, no happiness. The all-important task lies in providing for these necessities. Perhaps afterward there will be time for other things. When the truth of things, the real and the sensible, penetrate me, they do so in a terrible way. I will never write until I have settled this disgusting business of life. And however great the effort, I *must*, I must keep my thoughts in the direct and plain path of utility. Oh, money, money! And whenever Mother talks of her debts, her difficulties, the whole foundation of my existence seems to shake on its fragile structure. Indeed, I build on sand, and Mother on granite. Mine is the worthless task, but watch me use the whip hand and instill in myself at least a respect for money and the acknowledgment of its importance.

November 19. If Humor had been looking for material to jot down in his notebook, he surely would have paused here this morning and written: "Have witnessed a laughable sight. A literary girl of eighteen at her housework." It was all I could do not to laugh at myself outright. And I do not pretend to any particular humor. I set out early in the morning for the great battle of dust and brooms. Throughout all this my thoughts revolved rapidly. Now and then I would drop everything and jot down a few words on a bit of paper, just key words to a multitude of discoveries. Then, earnestly conversing with myself, I would return to my work. (Here is a very dusty corner.) Addison is disappointing. He writes . . . (I wonder why Joaquin throws all his shoes about the room) he writes as a man talks after a good dinner . . . (Is the baker knocking? I must remember to ask him for . . .) refined nonsense, that is all. (What can I cook for dinner? We had cauliflower yesterday.) George Meredith should not play so much with his ideas. Oh, I must write something down. Whereupon I sketch a criticism of Meredith. (We shall have spinach. My cookbook says it is healthy. Well, Mother's room is clean now.) Addison does not enlighten in the least. I must read Hazlitt's essays. I wonder why Charles dislikes them. What kind of mind takes delight in essays? I would like to ask someone. It is a very fragmentary form of literature, but instructive in most cases. It teaches the habit of forming individual, condensed and definite ideas on things and men. Not always conclusive because it shifts according to the writer's personality and experience. If Montaigne, Stevenson, Addison and John Erskine were to write an essay on precisely the same theme, I would know only each one's point of view and find each work another face of the one subject. I could only choose which I like best. I could not tell if one had more truth and soundness than the other. Most probably none of them would satisfy me, but I would have been taught the manner of unearthing my own views. This is to the rhythm of brooms and dustpans. And now my work is finished.

I promised to write of my visit to Frances. It was a memorable talk we had, and both of us parted, I believe, with an increased faith in each other. By our words. we joined hands more firmly. I think we enlarged our vision, too, because we talked of the things we wanted to talk about. It is a curious failing of youth to place itself in false positions in regard to other people. We are blunderers with our tongues. We talk, and half of what we meant remains glued in our minds. Afterward we call ourselves donkeys. and wonder how anyone can love us. But our friends are having the same experience and are also calling themselves donkeys, and wondering why we love them. And friendship, if it is sincere, strives in spite of this awkwardness and is rewarded when the day comes and brings Revelation. Then it is we know why we have loved each other in the past and realize that we are going to love even more in the future. That is what happened with Frances. We had faith in each other. This faith subsisted on our letters, the most honest reflection of ourselves; the rest of the proofs were disadvantages which we ourselves created and suffered.

The other day we tore down all this and showed ourselves clearly and fairly to each other. Toward the end we felt exhilarated by our discoveries, proud of our friendship. There was not a phrase we would have taken back. We talked in a very satisfying manner, made things clear, with that sensation of ascending, of moving toward something. Too often talks have no purpose; they shift, shrink, elude and finally fade away, leaving no trace behind of their insipid, colorless passage.

And what makes a talk worthwhile? Such little qualities that I am surprised all people should not say things worth listening to: ideas and interest. Those who have no ideas could have sympathy and interest. Those who would cultivate interest would soon have ideas. How simple it is. Frances tears up all she writes. She will not have proofs of her foolishness, she says. She will not risk what I risk when I write clearly and hopelessly as I do here. But of course, she has more to fear than I have. Her life is made of *facts*. Facts are *destructive*. She is always criticizing, thus shattering things she has no time to form theories on. I read to her portions of my Diary in my effort to convince her that it is a joyful task, this, of recording all things. She was bewildered: "You have so many abstract thoughts, Anaïs." I am building, building, building, and destroying very little.

We set out to compare our lives. Now, she is a young girl in a great city. What is more, she is a schoolgirl. Half of the day her mind is busy with studies. If she finds time to read, she has not the courage to read a thoughtful book. Her head is dull and tired. Then she has dances, she goes out with boys, giddy, silly boys. It is such a life as would damage minds other than hers. I marvel at the thought that she has not yet lost *herself*. She has not lost her habit of observation, of gazing inward, of drawing judgment, of feeling, apart from the excitement and purposeless life of her friends. But she is often discouraged. Her mind travels back, not forward. She looks to the ideas she had when she was younger. She likes herself better then.

This is the sign of what her kind of life does to the spirit. It does not kill it because she is brave, and she is fond of writing, but it paralyzes it. While she writes, she will be true to herself, and that is why I implore her to keep a diary. No outside influence can interfere with inner growth while you are kindled by the necessity of *giving something* to those blank pages waiting there.

I gave her a picture of my life, its calmness, solitude, retirement. And how in my sunny room I sit for hours *feeling myself grow* and watching the process. Alone, undisturbed by social life, inspired by nature, untouched by the nervousness and excitement of city life, happily deprived of the contact with giddy boys, my thoughts naturally flow smoothly, and certainly upward. Nothing draws them away from their purpose. I look back to criticize and dream of what I am *going* to be, not of what I was. Constructive thinking—and only a fresh, unfettered mind can think constructively. I have the woods and the fields; I threw off the yoke of school. I risked ignorance, but I am free, free, free.

And today Frances, who travels on an opposite road, longs to change places with me. Our points of view are startlingly different. We kindle each other. I give her freshness and faith; she gives wisdom and advice. It is never good to know only one side of life. But as it is, we provoke each other, help each other, two contrasts walking hand in hand. If one inclines too much to the right, the other sets her straight. And wisdom is, after all, only a matter of balance and proportion. There is no need of arithmetic to know this.

I love Frances for many things, among them her wit. She

has the lightest and most comic touch about men, a flavoring of mockery. She shrinks from what she delicately describes as the demonstrativeness of boys. When I did this, I did not call it goodness. I scolded myself for being prudish and ridiculous. Yet I adhered to my foolish instinct, and now I am proud. To find it in Frances has turned it into a quality. I admire in Frances her human ways. She read me, with much shame, a wish she had made one day: to be small and pretty, above all things. There is no use deceiving one's self and pretending to a stoic indifference. The most human of failings is vanity, and if I am a mortal, let me admit frankly that I am *human*. I told this to Frances, and how I also had violently wished to be beautiful some time ago (to please Hugo). Philosophy mocks these things with undisguised disdain. I worship Philosophy, but when I fail to respond to one of its teachings, I will boldly write it. And I am glad Frances has done the same. Why pose? Why assume a virtue not your own? To cheat others? They are not interested. You only cheat yourself and degrade your soul with hypocrisy. I rejoiced at her honesty, and she was relieved.

Evening. If Hugo would only come tonight. It is terrible to think that my Magician has cast such a powerful enchantment over me that toward the end of the week I long as much for the sound of his voice and a glimpse of his face as an invalid does for a breath of fresh air. At the very thought that I may be deprived of this joy, I feel forlorn and lost.

Bed time. I spent the evening studying George Meredith. I have just closed the book sadly, unsatisfied, and wondering why my peace of mind should leave me altogether because of an unfulfilled expectation.

November 20. I think an interesting person has appeared on the horizon, untrumpeted, unannounced, unheralded. She stepped out of a background of which I know nothing, quietly captured my fancy and awakened my curiosity. She is just a girl, perhaps a little older than I, with a name and Ideas. That is all I know to identify her, and if she has no name, Ideas alone would satisfy me. We met in the most unconventional way, mutually attracted to each other at the station, smiling, with a word the third day, which set fire to a good talk. Where were my habitual reserve, my insufferable shyness? They had melted away. As soon as I saw Teddy Tolputt, I noticed she had none of the hardness in her eyes, the flippant, mocking ways, the impudent manners of nearly every young girl I have met lately. Her eyes are clear and thoughtful, her expression earnest, absorbed, reflecting a busy mind. She has an extremely pretty and artistic face, slightly veiled in dreaminess. Chance brought us together three times on the same train and finally today at three o'clock we are going to walk together and talk. I have a feeling that she is more than interesting, that she is lovable. She is still on the horizon line, unusual, original, mysterious. I cannot let her pass by. Shall I stretch forth a hand and call her Friend?

5:30. We walked two hours through the woods, Teddy and I. In one afternoon I had a clear revelation of her character, and I am altogether pleased. There is something childlike, simple, and unspoiled in her ways which appeal to me. Above all things I love nobility and faith in people, and when sincere feelings are united with high thinking, there is no room for smallness. Whatever faults she may have, they must be such as endear the tie of friendship. We like each other, and I believe it will grow into a friendship, but you know how delicate I am, how strange in my choices and how seldom I have called friend persons about me without hesitating longer than most. Friendship, like everything else, I take seriously, and I will not trifle with the word while it lies in my power to weaken its meaning in my own estimation.

November 21. Sunday evening, following dinner, I stole to my room with the intention of writing. I sat by my little table and tried to collect my thoughts, in vain. It seemed as if a storm had broken within me, and its strength frightened me. All the little streams which usually appeared to flow quietly, in all directions, merged into a whirling river. I could not think of my books, of my other friends, of anything else. No, it was just one great wish, one solitary longing, one powerful call above all others . . . for Hugo. "I must write," I repeated to myself. "This won't do." During all this time I had forgotten to light my lamp. Suddenly someone knocked downstairs, and it resounded throughout the house in an unreal manner. I heard Joaquin moving to open the door. My heart was quiet, as if it had flown away. Hello! The warm, vibrant voice of the Magician reached me and I caught my breath. I was so thrilled I could hardly move. "Ah, Linotte," I said to myself, "Don't be a fool!" And quickly picking up two books I had for him, I tripped downstairs, wondering if I would dazzle him because I felt illumined with joy and wonder.

Magicians can work spells from afar, as you know. As he walked toward my house, he must have whispered magic words which caused the magnificent confusion in my heart. In the future I will not be angered and will try to recognize the signs of the approaching enchantment.

His first words, following the greeting, were to the effect that he had to catch a train for New York. I instantly said to myself in the most perverse and unkind manner: I hope you will miss it.

We talked, and the Magician read me things from Palgrave's *Golden Treasury*. I love English poetry, but it has never sounded so beautiful to me as when Hugo recites or reads it. In reading English to myself, I have a foreign accent and intonations which completely change the language. Hugo, in addition to a beautiful voice, has the most expressive modulations, the most musical intonations, I have ever heard. And then his choice of poems reveals so much of himself. This to me is a constant source of interest and happiness.

Like lightning the hour came for him to go. We looked at the tall clock at the head of the stairs and its solemn pendulum swinging to and fro. "I have missed my train," said Hugo gaily. I fancied the clock paused a moment in its ticking to titter. We returned to our seats. I wonder now how I controlled the impulse to dance in my chair. Hugo had missed his train; it was my fault, and yet he was not angry. No, he was glad. We talked. Among other things Hugo pointed out to me the quality of restraint in English poetry.

A few yards away the clock ticked away her stupid time. My wishing had caused enough mischief already, and I did not dare repeat, as in the beginning, I hope you will miss your train. And so again we found ourselves standing by the door. We talked. We began to say goodbye. We clasped hands and Hugo rushed away. And that is how our evening ended. I was ready to face a whole week of earnest work, of calamities, of hard facts; nothing could have frightened me after this visit.

I fell asleep thinking of Hugo, and of Teddy Tolputt. Usually I dwell on philosophical truths, on my unphilosophical behavior and on plans of reform. Which proves? Am I growing worldly-minded? Call it by any name you please, but whatever it may be, this new state, it is extremely agreeable.

November 22. Life seems made of scenes, at times. One by one they are hung by an invisible hand in the galleries of our mind, strange pictures, indeed, to which memory imparts warmth and life, pictures that, as we look back at them, have the power to move us and sometimes to inspire us. But most often they awaken regrets. We tell ourselves that we did not love them enough when they were ours, and we are reminded that we are in the midst of another picture which is soon to fade away into the past. This realization, this sense of approaching loss, kindles in us a deeper love for the present moment.

Such a picture is the one I am living now each night as I sit here to write. I remember myself writing in my Diary in many places at odd times. The moments I have devoted to this task have grown into a ritual. If I look back into the past, I cannot separate any of my adventures from the habit of stealing away somewhere to write at the end of the day. I see myself on the ship bearing us away from Spain when I first began my journal. And after that, from place to place, very often in a room with all the family; at Mother's desk covered with business papers; at Lake Placid; at Edgemere; and back to the city house, dark and so unlike home, being filled with strangers; sometimes in school, or at the park, in bed; and finally in the dearest of houses. In this house I only move my journal from room to room. The summer evenings caught me dreaming on the dark porch, but I wrote during the day, in the sunshine. And in looking back to these days I shall see myself in my room, at my little desk, drenched in a magic rose light, surrounded by my favorite books, my bird, the blessed peace of it all penetrating to my heart and filling it with gratitude. How can I write of bitter things in such a house, in such a room?

Downstairs Joaquin plays, revealing his moods and fancies as I reveal mine here, pouring his soul into melodious notes even as I pour mine into these words. In the room next to mine Mother is resting. When she is not too tired she calls me and asks me to talk to her. We tell each other everything. Mother knows me as she knows herself, and the only things I do not wish to annoy her with are my little troubles, my little imaginary sorrows and my discouragements; all these I keep from her.

November 23. I have received a compliment which has given me more pleasure than anyone can guess. Mrs. Norman said yesterday that she had never seen anyone improve as quickly as I had this last year.

"In what way?" I asked, very much surprised.

"Your head. Why Anaïs, when I came here you had the most useless memory I have ever seen in a girl. And the way you have changed, the way you put your mind on your work now, is wonderful."

She was referring to my housekeeping. It is true I am improved, but what an effort of will it has cost me. It was so simple to forget things, to evade responsibilities and calm my conscience by reading. I did not do it purposely, knowingly.

I do not know when the change took place, but of one thing I am certain; I have changed. I believe this attitude, this willingness to work, this desire to spend my efforts not alone in studies and writing but in humbler and more menial duties, grew out of my ideal of a woman. This ideal, long ago forming itself in my mind, became clearer and stronger as time passed, kindling all my dreams of the future, imposed itself on the very present and demanded instant, practical proofs of my sincerity. Out of a girl who dreamed too much I made another who still dreams but *lives*, besides. And so you see me today, giving most of my time to little things, to work and housekeeping, thinking as much of Thorvald's socks and Joaquin's torn school trousers and dinner as of what I shall write in my journal about George Meredith or Pascal. There is something very humble and simple about such a life. And the pleasure I take in it shows only that I am a woman now and shall always be womanly. My worship of literature, of philosophy, of all that is knowledge and food for the mind, has not gone to my head and made me one of those persons it is good to talk to but impossible to live with. In short, a literary woman!

Here, I might end this book, having recorded at least one triumph. I have traced many plans of life for myself and taken pleasure in watching my progress as one examines the growth of a plant or the habits of a squirrel. Strangely enough, little Diary, I take pleasure, too, in my deviations and failures. I do not believe you would exist if I were perfect, for you have really grown out of my efforts and battles and imperfections, the most often reflected in your pages.

That is why I do not wish to end this journal flattering myself. I will not rest, but, spurred on by a thousand desires, shall continue at war with myself until death.

I am not only very much in earnest but very *positive*. Goethe says: "The art of living rightly is like all arts: the capacity alone is born with us; it must be learned and practiced with incessant care." This is the most sagacious answer to the question with which I opened this book: "Ai-je le talent de décrire la vie sans le talent pour la vivre?"

❦ 1 9 2 2 ❦

"To Anaïs from one who is economical in diaries,
Eduardo, *The Mysterious!*
I am presenting this diary to you, but I fervently hope that it will, when stored with your secrets, run away and come back to its original owner. Lo, I pray you, cuisine, not to clasp it in chains,— it may come back! ¿Quién sabe?"[1]

*   *   *

January 5. Not one of us can be said to be absolutely different from the other. There is a certain number of qualities in the world—and of faults. What constitutes the difference is the proportion in which these are distributed in each. We are compounds of the same ingredients and act according to the balance within us. (Some according to their lack of balance!) Hearn says: "We are compounds of innumerable lives, each a sum of an infinite addition—the dead are not dead, they live in all of us, stirring faintly in every heartbeat." Somewhere before, Eduardo's dreams and my own have known each other, for it is not possible that we should understand so well. Loves, friendships, admiration, inspiration from other times, other men and women, stirred in us the other night. And at the same time, I was keenly conscious of the differences between us, between Eduardo and Hugo, between Hugo and me, and yet of our being undeniably alike—the three of us. Mysteries of character! Mysteries of life! And we may ponder, "though we acomplish no more in our philosophy than the poor insect which momentarily illumines its wandering through the illimitable night by a flash from its own body."

When Eduardo came Tuesday night, we sat near the fire to talk and read from our journals. As I watched him, I remembered that Hugo had done the same thing. A thousand comparisons stamped themselves on my mind. Hugo represents the Present—

[1] *"Who knows?"*

Real and Earnest Life. He is the man of action whose dreams follow him like a shadow, whispering and kindling. Eduardo is the Past. His dreams have fallen like a veil between him and the world. They shroud him, they bear him away; they tinge his writing with a fragrance of old times, old books, old heroisms. His venerations and exaltations are echoes of bygone worlds. Hugo is the Possible, a curious and *trust*-inspiring mixture of fact and fancy. Eduardo's soul is still unconscious of Reality, of Utility, of Responsibility. It is in a trance, steeped in an unquestioning worship of the beautiful for its own sake—not as a source of inspiration for action. He is adoring life, not using it. He is praising the works of others and allows his own tools to lie idle. A friend has described his soul as rose-hued. And it glows in his delicate face— still a reflection of tender, ecstatic boyhood. How refreshing it is to watch him, to look into his soft, clear eyes. No disguise in them, no hardness, no suspicion. They look out into the world, wide, confident and loving, with boyhood's expansiveness, confidence and sparkling love of life. He may have his days of dark forebodings, grim despair, terrifying doubts—we all have. But they are merely the gray storm clouds in a sky that is certainly and unquestionably blue.

Hugo's eyes look out from a more settled nature. There is more decisiveness and force in him; he is certain of his ground; he has weighed and taken his choice of things. He is building, working, *creating*. To him life has revealed its more serious meaning, its purposes, its sacrifices. He is the man who has accepted his part and who has nobly and courageously set about to fulfill it. Courage, endurance, these he has, and with them kindness and an essentially human and sympathetic understanding of his fellow creatures, tinged with a lovable poetic faith—a touch so light, so carefully disguised, that it can scarcely escape from the effect of the whole, and I have only discovered it by anticipation (a little trick of mine by which I endow a person with a little virtue and watch and wait until I notice the signs of its existence). Both Hugo and Eduardo are impressionable and imaginative. But how they differ in their demonstration! Here Eduardo is unequaled and Hugo's appears in another light. Eduardo's voice, his eyes and manners correspond entirely to his sentiments. Warmth emanates from him. It is like a flood of light which draws one around him into a magic circle. He touches by an undefinable charm of appeal. Hugo's face is sometimes impenetrable. In him the poet is a prisoner, and of the man within the man one has but rare and flashing glimpses. I have long sought for outward signs. Now I have learned to watch incessantly for the rare flashes which unexpectedly reveal the depths of his soul. But often before I have time to look, the quiet veil falls once more over his eyes. And yet I know the ineffable beauty that is hidden there. And when my heart hangs upon his sensitive, delicately molded lips, I know too that they can form the most passionate, the tenderest and truest words ever spoken. If I could say to him: "Oh, Hugo, speak these intense and sacred sentiments! Speak to me! Your silence maddens me! I know you feel, but tell me, tell me! Do you love me?" I want to see him carried away—moved, angry, hurt or gloriously happy. I would not mind if he should hurt me, forget himself, strike me even! But that some emotion should shake his patient ways, his quiet words, his regulated machine life, shake his soul—set it aflame! And to think he has as many loves, ecstasies, reactions and capacities for joy and sorrow as I have! Have I not heard pages from his journal? He loves nature, he understands music, he is impressed by all manner of things, conscious of colors, sounds; he has beautiful ideals, beautiful principles, a warm, glowing imagination, tender sympathies, impulsive praises—everything! And yet throughout it all hovers the unmistakable "restraint of English poetry"! He is prudent, slow in carrying out— oh, I don't know how to say it, but my heart knows what it is I condemn, and fear. It would never have occurred to me to judge Hugo had it not been that I realized how near to each other we have been lately—and how much we would suffer together unless neither one made demands on the other of any nature but friendship. How could I ever compare Eduardo and Hugo? Each one is an ideal of its own kind—in its own sphere, and gulfs separate them. They are alike only in that they are both dear to me. In Eduardo, dreams call to dreams, spirit to spirit, and that is all. We were not meant to love each other in the ordinary way as men and women. In Hugo, but for one thing, every quality, every need, every impulse, correspond to mine. We were meant to know together the sublime love that binds two souls into one—the only completeness, the only strength, the only heavenly happiness known in this world. If I could forgive that one thing! If my love were strong enough to accept him as he is! Have I not got faults too? Have I not perhaps a thing that makes him suffer? Surely nothing is perfect in this world. Would it be right for me to say to him: "Give me the love you have to give. I will make myself be contented with it." Alas, no, not while I am conscious of a sacrifice in doing so! It would not be fair to him, for he might find someone who would take his love as the greatest blessing, a thing to complete a woman's life, and that may silence all her doubts. Is it possible that I should be mistaken, that later on I should find someone better than Hugo? All this, every word I have written concerning Hugo, he has yet the power to silence and extinguish forever. By one assertion of his power, one word that should make me believe in his love—that he should speak, and I would yield proudly.

Eduardo telephoned yesterday, sent me two diary books; witnessed with us Pepito Echaniz's triumphant concert at Town Hall in the evening of the same day. He telephoned me this morning; he wants to come this afternoon, begs me for my photograph. He is taking me to the opera Saturday. And the other night, just as Hugo did once, he missed his train because he hesitated too long at parting time. And meanwhile—Hugo? Hugo is silent, busy, absorbed. Tuesday night Eduardo read me nearly half of his journal. He has been strongly influenced by nature; his emotions are all interwoven with scenes of beauty and change. What a contrast between our diaries! I have been thinking objectively, intensely. I have been sifting ideas and weighing all things which fall under my eyes. He has been more of the poet, abandoning himself to influences, receiving impressions, not seeking results. There is a certain element of passivity in his attitude. Mine is questioning and curious. His reactions are natural consequences of quiet observations. Mine are forced down my throat, so to speak, by my voluntary prying and meddling with all things. His descriptive power is highly developed, so developed that it has endangered his conclusive and decisive powers. He tells me he has changed. I believe he has been revolving around a larger circle, but always the same circle. He has moved, figuratively speaking, as much as I, but he has not advanced. I did not realize that I had grown older until I compared myself with him. He is younger than I, in age and in thought. I recognize in his ideas a vagueness and a lack of purpose and decisiveness which I feel I have outgrown—only a little, perhaps, but enough to know what I am moving away from. At least we are equals. I may feel wiser simply because we all think ourselves wiser than our neighbor. Equals—I make no effort to follow him—sometimes I precede him. Not one of his feelings and ideas is a mystery to me, and if I love to know them, it is because they are stamped with his personality and his own peculiar charm. Here I am strongly tempted to compare again. Shall I? Yes. Why not? With Hugo I am eternally on tiptoes, striving to reach his heights and fascinated by his leadership. I came to him with my problems, and he solved them like a child's game. The last night we were together he solved my tormenting questioning of religion—by one deft, clear and marvelously just line of reasoning. I understood instantly and was convinced. I shall write of it someday.

January 6. I am oppressed by a sadness that has no name—and no bonds. And yet almost each morning I rise with a song on my lips. The tide of joy wells in my heart at the sight of the sunshine streaming through my window. At such moments my heart is fresh and light because it is conscious of only half of life. But how short is my thoughtlessness! I am like a man who has forgotten that he is in a prison and stretches his arms—they hit the wall and he suddenly remembers . . . I remember people, and instantly the song dies . . . A black and heavy cloud falls on me. I fight against it and then slowly surrender to its influence. Of what use is it to struggle? More than ever I love my books and solitude. I have long resisted the tendency to shrink from people. Today discouragement seemed to whisper in my ears: "Obey your inclination. See what unhappiness you have derived from your friends!" It is indeed as Charles said. All human ties serve but to inflict pain. I thought of this today because the weather was beautiful, and as I walked to the station I heard the chirping of birds, I felt the caress of the sun, the cool air. If I looked to the heavens, I saw but blue and gold, with here and there the fleeciest of white clouds. The trees, black and bare, pointed heavenward with their twisted dead branches. On the fields danced some dead leaves, and when the gust of wind tired, they lay quivering on the ground—still of that tarnished gold and faintly echoing the Autumn's long-past splendor. All this I had. The earth, the sky— all the calm, sad, dead beauty of winter. Could I not have been happy? Here was a thing to love and to admire, beauty ever changing, but undying. Enough to fill the loneliest life, and to satisfy the wildest dream. So I thought when my heart was virgin in earthly attachments; when people were but shadows to me— shadows coming and going, to which I paid no attention.

And today? Today a man's name embitters my taste of nature, nature that reveals its joys only to pure hearts. She had her shrine in mine, and I loved her alone until the day I sinned by linking his name to hers—by calling her voices the call of love—a human love! But for Hugo I would still feel that little child in me which was ever ready to dream and play with fancies, "the frank and simple" child who kept my heart young and my faith alive. Will I ever have these dreams and these fancies again? Alas, what seriousness has come to me. How incessantly I brood. How tormented I am by his conduct. He has indeed fallen like a black shadow over my life, and I long for the day when I shall be free of thoughts of him. That day will bring, too, a return of the life I knew before and which cannot be lost forever. I can still make believe. But it is too much make-believe and dreaming that has made this semblance of love all the harder to bear. How I admired Hugo! When I think of what I believed him to be . . .

Evening. I have been looking for work. I could not help remembering as I did so the strange expression that came over Eduardo's face yesterday when I told him. "Looking for work—you, Anaïs?" He echoed as if it *hurt* him. And indeed today I was often humiliated, not by work itself—no, of that I am proud—but of its uglier phases. I feel ridiculously out of place everywhere I go, and yet long to be initiated into the mysteries of ordinary life. Work for a living, be treated like everybody else. I revel in the very hardness of the words. I want to become hardened, to train my body to never cry out, for now I am always tired, and night finds me bruised in every way. I want to control my thoughts and live more of the other life, the active, animal life—machine life, too! I want to become, like others, dulled by physical exertions. It may be the secret of happiness, for happiness is balance; peace is rationality. Not to lose one's self in gulfs of speculation and fabrication, not to sink into a life of sensation after sensation, but to live so crowded and so complete a life that while moving from one occupation to the other I have no time to brood. This is the good I see in work. It may hurt the dream-loving self Eduardo would always want to see alive in me. But this self deserves to be hurt! And you, who reflect its sad influence over my life, you, I say, know why.

Eduardo came to see me yesterday. We spent the afternoon together. It passed like ten minutes. This time he read from my journal. I even read in fragments what I have written of him here. He objected to "sparkling love of life" and said I wrote nothing of the eternal sadness that haunts all his writings. Strange! I think it is because sadness to me seems the most natural thing. I might have observed and been surprised by much happiness perhaps. Yes, Eduardo broods, too, but not on human character, on active life. Sadness in him is like a perfume in a flower; it will always be there until the flower withers. He has begun to read Amiel's journal,[1] which he found by chance long before I obtained it at the library. He speaks already of his letters. We are going to begin again. Mother is willing because she trusts me and understands what I feel toward Eduardo. But one thing frightens me, and that is Eduardo's exalted praise of his Mimi and what I see in his eyes. I fear he believes he loves me. Half of his journal, or nearly half, is filled with thoughts of me, which he either passed over or read in fragments. "Will I ever know what you have written about me?" I asked him once. "When you are married," he answered teasingly. What happiness my letters have given him, it seems; what anxiety, my silences.

Words I once read return to me: "Except in the cases where the fountain of Romance has gone dry, no friendship exists between men and women without underlying love." No emotional natures can contain themselves, but turn to a "friend" with their need of devotion and warmth. How easily our emotions flow out toward an understanding heart. This innocent and unquestioned exchange of confidences seems as natural as the flow of rivers to the ocean—and as inevitable. In youth every tide sweeps us off our feet. Let people call it love, criticize it; we need it. We are poets, not lawyers or officers of the law. Conventions, fear of opinions, fear of misunderstanding—I laugh to think of it all. How magnificent it is to be *one's own law!*

Yet when I said I feared Eduardo's changing sentiments, from the quiet, enduring affection of friendship to love, I meant that I shrink from the thought of hurting him, being unable to return love for love—as people understand love. I will cease thinking. It does little good.

Oh, my heart, learn to wait and trust in all things. Questioning is but a useless torment, a thing to poison all your appreciation of the present. I love the present, as Eduardo makes it these days. I shall teach myself contentment.

Later. An answer to my secret wish for something that should help me to forget. We are invited to a soirée at the Sarlabouses' house, and Pepito Echaniz will be there. Tomorrow night, this is, after going to the opera with Eduardo. I am as happy looking forward as I was sorrowful looking backward.

[1] Journal Intime, *by Henri Frédéric Amiel.*

Hugo Guiler

A. N. and Rosa Nin
with the violinist Juan Manén

Finca La Generala—the ranch of A. N.'s Tia Antolina in Havana

A. N. in Havana,
1922

A. N. in Havana

A photograph of A. N. that appeared in a Cuban newspaper in 1922

A. N. as a Gibson girl; two drawings by Charles Dana Gibson, also published in a Cuban newspaper: "Preparing for graduation," "Little Mother"

A. N. in Havana

A. N. in Havana

Anaïs and Hugo Guiler at the time of their marriage in Havana,
1923

Anaïs and Hugo Guiler

January 10. I will never, never again live like other people. I am irrevocably borne on different currents—powerless to mingle the swiftly passing waters of my existence with theirs. These days I have lived their real life. For a moment I thought I had escaped mine. But no. I live, I act, I talk, I laugh with others, but in my inner self there wells constantly the most gigantic tides of sentiments.

At the opera Saturday we heard Martinelli and Farrar in *Madame Butterfly*. I was seated between Eduardo and his cousin, and by the way we talked during the intermissions we might have been taken for ordinary mortals. Even when now and then Eduardo and I bent our heads nearer to each other and whispered, we might have been thought to be talking of the music. But in the whispering lay all the difference. I talked to Eduardo of my other friend and wanted to know if he wanted my letters even while knowing that my friendship was divided. He had been looking off into space; he turned his face full upon mine and enveloped me in a gentle and tender flood of light from his eyes. "Yes, cuisine, I want your letters," and after a moment: "I hope your friend makes you happy." But our letters! Oh, our letters will mark the beginning of another dream. And again I place my fancies, my hopes, my faith in Eduardo's hands. He is chivalrous: he shall be my Knight and fight my Cause, which is the cause of Friendship. And I trust him. I trust his young and tender heart and our friendship shall be my star of guidance. He tells me he needs me. The thought of this is enough to help me be true to all my aspirations—for what I am is what shall encourage and inspire him. Without him to live for, my dreams would have turned to ashes. I owe him a great debt. He came Sunday morning to say goodbye. We talked but little, as Mother, Thorvald and Joaquin were with us. A firm handshake, a smile, one last melting of eyes into eyes, and that was all! And today, for the first time in years the postman's whistle has regained its magic meaning and its importance.

Saturday night *real* life again throbbed in my veins—for an hour! The soirée was animated and interesting. I was lost in admiration of three Spanish girls with black flashing eyes, flashing smiles, flashing gestures. What fire, what beauty there is in Spanish people! One of them took a red shawl, a comb and a red flower and sang two songs from Spain, one of which I know.

I was *Spanish*. My blood tingled at the rhythm of her feet. I longed to dance, to give those dangerous and fascinating glances. I longed, in short, to let the fire burn freely and naturally and expressively. I envied her her freedom and her charm. I caught a sight of myself in a large mirror. A frail creature in blue, wide-eyed, with soft brown hair shining in the light, quiet, so quiet and dreamy, unreal, looked at me. Am I real? I asked myself. *She* was real, she glowed, she was gloriously, resplendently real. The general dancing began. I plunged into it with joy. I reveled in the gaiety of the beautiful girls; I watched them admiringly. And I danced! I received compliments. I was grateful. I liked everybody. In a corner, alone, sat Mr. Alfaur, whom I had met at the Kellys' house with Enric. I noticed he did not dance, that he looked scornful. In the middle of my forgetfulness, I experienced curiosity. How different from *us* he looks, I thought. Already hidden forces were at work. He was watching me, and when we went upstairs for refreshments, he edged his way toward me and we fell into conversation. From that moment I was no longer part of the frivolous and the young. Three times young men dragged me downstairs to join them in their games. Three times I returned to Alfaur, and he was waiting for me. He was a symbol of my thought life, and I was wavering between it and the other life. The end of the evening found us deep in talk, far away from the merry chatter, the dancers. If I am not mistaken, our talk promised many others. "You are going to be bored with me," he told me, "I do not dance." Of what use is it to struggle? This life which does me so much harm has too strong a hold on me. I love it, though it hurts.

Sunday evening while waiting for Hugo, I began a book. He did not come—why should he?—and I finished it. That book is a landmark in the eternal pilgrimage of my understanding through desolate, unending voyages. It has shaken my whole life. It has opened my eyes to a thousand truths. I cannot tell now what it has meant to me, what it has done to me. Its nearness makes it a very part of me, its meaning is interwoven with the meaning of all things. How much of me unexpressed there is in Sanchia. How much of Eduardo is revealed in Senhouse.

Hugo is too late now, too late! He did not come, he did not save me from the reading of *Open Country*[1] and allowing it to speak to me of Eduardo. It was such a heroic man I had the vision of in Senhouse, and it is as such a man that I pictured Eduardo in

[1] *By Maurice Hewlett.*

the future. In reading *Open Country* I recognized true love. It has never come to me. It is love's nearness I have felt. Love itself, never. It lies all around me, part of nature, ideals, life itself, and simply because I am sensitive and conscious of everything around me, I was conscious of love's presence and power and mysteries.

But my heart is free. Free of Hugo, free of love, free of longings. I am strong because now I *know*. A vision of realization has slowly come upon me. Recognition. Courage and youth are quickening in my veins. I feel the wild pulsations of hope. And all because I can say to the Thing that has cast its shadow over my life: "I do not fear you. You are not what I want. You are only a Semblance of the Great Love I am waiting for. I have seen through your mask, and your face does not bear the expression of Love!"

And yet does this Great Love exist? It does not matter. I shall not accept the Semblance because I doubt the True. I am young. I am going to work. I shall be independent in every way. But how tired I am! I thought I had found the True—that my eternal pilgrimage was ended, that as a woman I had found my place, by Hugo's side. Eduardo's face is now before me. He trusts me to be true to what we created together. If not for my sake, at least for *his*, let me be strong.

Blessed sunshine. I walked out after writing, and it healed me. I feel ashamed of my despair and broodings. To live for others is the secret of happiness. To give, to write, to laugh, to work— all for the others. For Mother, my brothers and Eduardo. For Frances. I will, O God, and in thy blessings I shall find strength. Sunshine. Books. They are gifts and tools and inspirations. What right have I to use them for other things but Creation and Action? Sadness is an illness of the heart, and it should be conquered. Yesterday I spent looking for work. How well I shall work when the time comes!

I told you once that appreciation and compliments were like the sun, and I was a sunflower ever turning to them for warmth and food. Last year when Eduardo sent me the trailing arbutus he had written a little note which he forgot to enclose and which he gave me the other day. In it I found: "But I am sending you these that they might bring their message of all that is sweet and divine to one who is worthy—to one who is sweeter, more divine and nobler than they!" And throughout his diary it is the same, in all that he read me out of it. And I am proud and thankful. To be trusted, to be believed good, and noble and sweet—how it kindles you to strive to be in truth what you are thought to be. Saturday night, too, Alfaur in one moment gave me more compliments than Hugo ever did in months! And yet I was ready and willing to appreciate Hugo's reserve more than all the gallantry in the world. I never asked for things in him. I gloried in what I found and felt it to be enough. And now his ways pass my understanding. And too often what one does not understand one condemns.

Four days during which I did not write. And what in them made me most happy? Not the time I spent with Eduardo. Not the soirée at the Sarlabouses'. Nothing of what I wrote. No. I will never forget yesterday afternoon. All morning I had been in quest of work, in vain. Mother told me to return home. Instead I sallied out to the 15th St. bookshops. For hours I pored over the musty books, jingling a few pennies in my pocket. I had Mother's permission to buy Amiel's *Journal*, but I could not find it. I saw Voltaire's *Dictionnaire Philosophique*, which for a while I could not part with. Volumes of Rostand for twenty-five cents. Poe's *Poetical Works* for twenty cents. French novels, English literature, biographies. What treasures! The fever of the bibliomaniac was upon me. What matter the world—people? I forgot what I was and why I existed, forgot I wrote a journal, forgot my troubles, my age, all that can be forgotten. I was just a spirit in a world of volumes, a spirit unclassified, unidentified, unwanted and of no use to anyone. It is a happy state. All thoughts, feelings, center on one subject: books. The only desire: to melt into them, to become part of them. A book! I wish I were a book. I could have my heart read without the trouble of explaining myself. And I would not be responsible for my quality—this would revert to the author. What a relief it would be. But I am wandering. My happiness knew no bounds when I found Carlyle's *Sartor Resartus*. It was old, it was torn, it was soiled—it was a treasure. I asked its price. The saleslady looked at me scornfully: "You can have it for fifteen cents if it's of any use to you." "Of any use to me!" I echoed. The phrase would not penetrate. It jarred me. How on earth could anyone say such a thing? I opened my mouth and closed it. My surprise stifled my ordinary eloquence. I looked so distressed that the woman added: "This is the only copy I have now. I can get you a better one in a week." "Give me that," I interrupted, and almost tore it out of her hands. I did not breathe until I was out of the shop. I thought that certainly the book would vanish, or that they all would rush after me for a higher price. And so they would if they had known what the book was worth to me. How strangely we value things. There are as many standards as there are individuals. According to the fixed laws of Money, the value of things are enough to draw tears from poets and laughter from the just.

For once, however, I prized the folly of these laws, and sallied out once more (in search of Amiel's *Journal*) with a singing heart. Every sound, every face, increased my joy. The thousand and one voices of the city, the rumbling, the shuffling, the rolling, the chatter—all mixed, confused, not melodious as the sounds of the country, but thrilling and moving, giving a sense of energy, activity and ambition. And the faces! They are like a thousand books, a thousand stories flitting by, of which you catch but a glimpse. You read the preface, the introduction, only. And thus I walked, listening and looking, with Carlyle's book pressed close to my heart—happy because I was reading the universe in a city, and was soon to read an idea of the universe. And on I walked, asking everywhere for Amiel's *Journal* until I reached Macy's, where I found it at last. From there I tripped to the station, and from the station I stepped into the wintry twilight. Winged feet, winged spirit, how sunlit and happy are the lands into which they bear you! I had left black clouds behind me. How could they pursue me at such a pace? They did not—while I had wings. But once home I opened my drawer; a scrap of paper fell to the ground. I bent to pick it up and saw "Hugo" on it. My wings dropped from me as mysteriously as they had come, the black cloud settled once more, the sense of oppression returned.

Absent-mindedness is a gentle synonym for some cases of selfishness. Never does one experience the sense of the ghostliness of things as when one is too eager to grip them firmly. Elusiveness is felt by the writer above all. In his endeavor to find forms and names for all things, he often pursues a word until he loses track of the idea itself. He can only retrace his steps.

January 11. I begged Mother to let me go to the city with her. "If I stay home," I told her, "I write and read all day and when night comes I want to throw myself into a river." This I said half in earnest, but I meant it with all my heart. But there is a snowstorm and Mother answered that I should wait until it ceases. My room, my dear quiet soothing nest, has become a prison. My one longing is to escape from the weight of silence, from my thoughts, from myself. The life I loved has become intolerable.

It maddens me. Last night I could not sleep for hours. Finally I drifted into a state of semiconsciousness and had a dream of Hugo—cold, indifferent, impenetrable. I started, awoke and sprang out of bed. I stood by the window looking up at the sky but powerless to pray. The future stood before me, a grimacing monster. I trembled at the sight of it, and bitter, burning tears welled from my heart. It was madness, that struggle with myself in the middle of the night. It was the unreasonable fear of a child—not of a young girl who has all her life before her. The rest of the night was one long broken and fitful sleep, filled with nightmares. And now I wait for the end of the storm. What I cannot understand is what draws me to my pen when writing only doubles my suffering. Fatal tendency, indeed, and it may yet happen that I shall cease my Diary absolutely.

Evening. Through hail, snow and rain and wind I marched off to the city and then tramped for hours for a cause not worth recording, it was so trivial. The rest of the day I spent by Mother's side at her studio, glad to be among people, glad of the talk, the bustle, and now and then sallying forth in my quest for work. Wholesome, healing, absorbing life, which I may still adopt. for after all, I am very much like ordinary creatures when I am not writing and thinking. Watch for the progress of my reformation.

January 12. I never thought that the day would come when I should sit for hours before my open journal pondering on how to begin and hesitating. Both yesterday and today I tried to write— it is impossible for me to say what I feel. All these days I have written a great deal; it was the only relief I could find for the ever increasing pain I felt. I argued, I reasoned, I set down every hope, doubt, every light I could throw upon Hugo's conduct. What can I say tonight when I realize that every word I have written concerning Hugo since our walk in the woods comes from a *misunderstanding* of which I alone am guilty? I am a fool, a fool forever to be the dupe of a diabolical imagination. And what a lesson I have learned! But it shall never happen again. What I have suffered through my own fault is enough to help me conquer not this fault but all of them! I will not tear the pages out. I am going to read them every time I am tempted to misjudge Hugo again, as a punishment, a warning. I will read them and read this: Last night I sat by Mother's bedside, talking of Hugo— complaining, exclaiming. Mother tried by every means to cheer me, to give me courage. "If he would but give me a sign of life," I said sadly. The telephone rang. It was Hugo! Hugo and his warm voice, with a simple story of busy days, fatigue, which would extend over another week yet. Hugo looking forward to the 28th, when we are going to Erskine's lecture together. Hugo unchanged. My voice trembled as I answered him. I was ashamed, conquered, more shaken by the simplicity of his action than by all I had imagined. And heavens, what I had imagined— the saddest, the worst. And I, who pretend to love people well. See how small was my faith, how short my patience. And tolerance. I deserve to lose him. Hugo, whom I have misunderstood and condemned. But no, no, at the bottom of all this lies my ignorance of the world, the real world. And would heaven punish me for a thing like that?

Hugo in his journal praised my understanding. Alas, I do understand ideals, dreams, feelings, others' thoughts. I can respond to their silences, their longings, and give their actions always the noblest interpretation. I understand faithfulness, the truths, sacrifices, devotions of friendships, all things except actual, visible life. It seems to slip between my fingers. I cannot grasp it. I cannot realize its duties, its hold on those I love. To fail in this means to fail in all things. It means that time after time I shall blunder and expect the impossible. It means that I shall suffer. But were I alone to suffer, it would not matter. What I realize is that it makes others suffer, and that is unforgivable. Yes, after a time I would lose Hugo, for he has a right to expect perfect understanding because he gives perfect frankness and sincerity. But oh, to know one's fault is to half conquer it. I know what I must mistrust in myself. I shall be on my guard. I will never again go to extremes. And to Hugo, though he does not know it, I owe repentance. It shall be paid him in full. The rest of the year I will devote to doing him justice. I will train my understanding like a climbing ivy that is ever taught to grow upward instead of rambling vaguely about the ground in all directions. The most difficult thing of all will be to forgive myself, and it will take a long time. When I have given Hugo the best in me, the most reliable and comforting and satisfying companionship, then it will be time to ask myself: Have I given enough? Oh, Love. You are again whispering to my heart. I am not ready for you yet!

Later. I read this to Mother. I tell her I do not know what truly happens to me until I see it written. I cannot do my thinking in any other way. Once I see a thing in black and white, I know what I am to do, and what it has done to me, and what it means. Our talk terminated in this way: Mother said I spent half of my life doing foolish things and the other half being sorry for them. "Console yourself," I replied. "Some people spend all their lives doing foolish things and are never sorry!" At this point Mother sent me to bed. It may be that she thought I needed sleep to regain my equanimity—or it may be that she was bored. Strange, I am ashamed, I am humbled, I am sorry, and yet I am happy! Mysteries of character. Mysteries of womanly contradictions. For one, I shall let the mysteries alone and devote myself to the unusual occupation of being happy without knowing why.

January 14. It seems to me there is always some mysterious connection between a scene of nature and our moods. As if one were a reflection of the other, as if each mood had sprung not from itself but from nature. However it may be, I feel this kinship constantly, and I am so strongly drawn toward nature that its nearness seems the breath of life itself and I can imagine nothing more desolate or more terrible than being separated from it. I am bound closer to it than to men and women. Skies, trees, hills, snow and rain and winds are dearer to me than all the wonders of the human heart. To understand and love nature, one only needs a willing and trusting heart, but it takes a brave heart to understand and love human beings. Is this the secret of my shifting interest? One day I devote to the worship of trees, the other to men. One or two hours of men send me flying back to the woods for refreshment and a renewal of courage. And so on, ad infinitum! Today I am hovering between the two. I had a vision of the relationship between human moods and nature's. I merely used my own heart for experiment because it was the nearest at hand. As to the scenery, it is framed in a window to which I raise my eyes so often that my meditation stands in serious danger of becoming a poem.

Later. And so it did! A book! A book sent to me by my father and no less a wonder than Rostand's *Les Musardises*,[1] which I had read and loved years ago and longed to own! But I notice I am using exclamatory marks much too profusely. I must read a few pages of Descartes and study my grammar. That window is

[1] Idle Times.

the cause of it all. There is a curious name for this state in which it has thrown me. These are the symptoms: a fullness of the heart; a passion for the use of such adjectives as beautiful, glorious, radiant, indescribable and incomparable; a total lack of restraint along the lines of admiration, enthusiasm and praise expressed by Volubility; high tension of the nerves used in holding a pen. And the malady? Some call it rhapsodizing. It is held in great contempt by Men of Sense, and said to be incurable. Most blessed of infirmities; if I wished to be cured, I would need only to move away from the scene before my eyes. But I enjoy feeling nonsensical now and then—it breaks the monotony. The snow glitters like a field of diamonds, bathed in sunlight, in pale-blue shadows from the sky, smooth and dazzling and beautiful. Each hour brings a change of light and a transformation. At noon it is all white and blue and gold. At sunset, shafts of fire turn it rose and purple. At twilight the colors fade, the blue of the sky deepens and trees and snows are touched by gray until they appear to melt into one another. At night the radiance of the moon dispels all vagueness and grayness. From shadowy masses the trees emerge, boldly outlined against a snow so white and luminous that the sunlight might have hidden beneath it. And what calm, what dead and icy stillness. What transparency, what purity, what holiness. A human footstep is sacrilegious. A human voice—impiety. We should have wings to hover—and as to voice, if we must say something, let us write, for writing is silent and sacred; it does not break the spell, it deepens it.

I got a telegram from Eduardo: "Have destroyed letter. Will try to write again." Why is it difficult for him to write me? I cannot understand, and await his letter anxiously. In reading over Eduardo's old letters I found a note of tenderness which touches me more now, I know not why. I am proud, too, of what he tells me at times. The thought that we are again to have this heart-to-heart correspondence, that I am to share his confidences, know his sadnesses and hopes and aspirations, fills me with an emotion for which there is no name. To me his life seems like that of a rare flower which it is my privilege to watch and help unfold. Eduardo has great possibilities, a wonderful character, and I feel that I am made to give in full measure what it is woman's divine power to give and woman's alone: sympathy, understanding. With Eduardo I have a duty, a sacred task to fulfill. He has written to me: "You are my goddess, my angel, at whose feet I shall lay the fruits of my ambition and my pains, and from whom I draw hope, fervor, and take courage for the future." Oh, to be *worthy* of his faith!

January 16. At the end of a day which I passed in sadness I sat quietly in my room last night, dreaming, with an open book on my lap. I had not even courage enough to wish, though the longing I felt no room for any thoughts but of Hugo. Sometimes I pictured him in my mind's eye walking down the dark roads. I would listen eagerly for a sound at the door. The dead stillness throughout the house made this watch strange and fantastic. I expected Hugo to walk suddenly into my room, like a ghost, and then to disappear in a cloud of smoke. When a real knock came, I was so surprised that I could not move, and did not believe my ears. I rushed to the door. Yes, it was Hugo.

We sat around the lamplight and talked. At the beginning I was trembling from head to foot, and my lips quivered and my voice was unsteady. I wish I had more self-control and coolness. All the heat went to my head, my hands were frozen. I do not know what to make of all this. I write it to see if it makes sense. Hugo sang, too, accompanying himself on his guitar. I gave him Amiel's Journal to read and quoted some lines to this effect: "Go often to thy friend's house or the path will grow coarse with weeds."

Hugo laughed: "I'll bring the lawn mower next time!"

"You see what too much business does to you? Now you are calling a spade a spade," I replied, laughing.

Can you guess what he is looking forward to? When the Spring comes, we are to walk in the woods!

The key to Hugo's character can be summed up in this word: *Patience.* He has the most incredible, boundless, inimitable and exasperating patience in the world. He seems to think that all is well, that there is all the time in the world for all things, and all things come in time. There is only one way to put it: he takes it easily and reasonably; and while I am storming, and wondering, and seeking explanations, and writing books about him, and drowning Mother in passionate outbursts of indignation, and brooding, all because I do not see him often enough—he is patiently and quietly dreaming of the Spring Days, and the woods, content to be with me a little while whenever he can—now and then, content with the present and whatever it brings him. And between us, between Patience and Impatience, personified and typified by Hugo and Mandra[1]—pray, who is the better friend and the most devoted? For that, in the end, is the vital question! But what is undeniable, what stares me in the face day and night, is that all things, great and small, tend to demonstrate that Hugo is the best and wisest. And the best and wisest thing I can do is to imitate him as far as it is in my power. And so—perish the calendar, and all the various ways of counting the days. Perish the clock and all the countless ways of adding the hours. Perish time. We shall live with the seasons, watch for the Spring (forget how far away it is). We shall rejoice when the Magician can come, cease to lament if he cannot, cease to brood and think only of the day that some event or other brings us together, as for example, Erskine's lecture on the 28th. With my best and wisest I shall learn patience. And who can say if he cannot teach me how to be happy?

January 19. The world is the Sea. You are my Ship. I am the Sailor. Now and then I plunge into the depths, am ballotted and storm-tossed and wind-lashed, or gently carried on the crest of the waves and blessed by a vision of shores and harbors. My hands are tightly gripped around Experience's very hair; I go wherever it leads me until I tire of her strenuous company and swim back to my Ship. Once there, I rid myself of all the trinkets I have gathered during my expedition. Pearls, seaweeds, sea shells, foam. I place them all in my treasure chest. Then I stand by the steering wheel and gravely guide my Ship toward the shore of which I had a fleeting glimpse. The voyage is slow, because I am intent on noticing everything, and because I plunge so often. The flight of the sea gulls, the passing of a cloud, sunrises, sunsets, every phase, transformation, change of light, every mood of the sea, its anger, its calms, its heavings and rollings—all these attract my attention, force me to pause, and to record. Thus while I am meditating, dreaming, rhapsodizing and philosophizing, my ship is left to wander left and right, at the mercy of changing winds and capricious waves. Other ships pass mine by, pursuing a direct and well-charted course. They never pause. It never occurs to the man at the wheel to notice what I notice, and still less to record it. Yet which is the happier voyage? Which is the fortunate ship? Mine! Mine is the Errant Ship. It is guided by a poet. It has a treasure chest. Its sails are Hopes. It is Enchanted.

[1] *Another of A.N.'s nicknames for herself.*

Today I have returned from a plunge into the deeps. My hands are full of little things, which I spread before me and contemplate. There is a letter from Father, and two more books. There is a discovery about myself. There is Josef Lhevinne's concert last night; a telephone call from Hugo while I was out; a short note from Eduardo this morning; some newspaper cuttings and a quotation in an envelope from Hugo; the announcement of Cuca's engagement to Adolfo Ovies. Pearls, seaweeds, sea shells, foam! I do not pretend to classify or compare.

5 o'clock. How thankful, how unutterably grateful I am for a day like this in which all things please me and satisfy me, in which the kindness and thoughtfulness of my friends kindle me. I am so happy, so quiet, so filled with the love of little things that I let the hours slip by almost lost in the wonder of their perfection. And yet I have done nothing. I have wasted the day in dreams, in soft songs and make-believe. I have had long conversations with my ideas, but most of all, I have thought of Hugo, thought long and deeply and tenderly. I feel as if it were a spell cast on me. I did not write for fear of breaking it. Can I be the same person who many days ago wrote so tragically and desperately?

Grief, joy, contentment, hope or despair—every one seems immense, vast, universal. I only realize their actual size, true value and importance when I have moved away from them. Is it to be always thus? Even now happiness radiates from me, my heart is flooded in it. Yet outside there never was so dreary and dismal a day. And I am alone, idle, but so happy that I dare not trust myself and wonder: Why? Shall I always be swayed by nameless and inexplicable influences? I am always disconcerted when I endeavor to account for my ways and attitudes. Perhaps the best thing is to set the facts and truths down without explanations, as one takes notice of a phenomenon. Tendencies, environment, temperament, all mysteriously fused, leading me I know not where, though I have will to master them all. But it is not my business to stifle all natural "états d'âme"[1] while they do no harm. I like to drift into meditation and observation without being responsible for the action that has roused them. I like to wander through the intricate phraseology of things. The danger lies in such a crisis as I have passed some time ago—which is a state which I could have escaped by sheer force of will. Such is the

[1] *Moods.*

control I would like to find. And I know that by it alone, by this absolute mastery of Self, can peace be obtained and retained.

I did not want to write on all the subjects of interest I enumerated this morning. For once in the story of my journal I felt the dislike of what Frances aptly calls "raking up the past." I never knew it before, but it takes a certain kind of energy and courage to voluntarily take up every day the restless process of Explanation and Description. It seems to strain certain faculties which are seldom called upon in ordinary life. Every sense has a double work to do. After a while it becomes a habit and less of an effort. But now and then a mental laziness steals upon you and you shrink from the effort.

Evening. I had a long talk with Hugo over the telephone. He felt precisely as I did about Amiel and the throwing away of our own pens. If Hugo would but come or call every week, I would ask no more. What a joy his voice gives me. It is as if I had been very near him for a moment, and it is all I ask, for it is enough to set me dreaming for many days instead of tormenting myself with imaginary sorrows.

January 20.
Mon cher cousin:

We must write, Eduardo, as the rivers flow to the ocean. Sadnesses, fears, hopes, joys, you must let all things flow freely and have confidence in me, for I take pride in all you do, and in all your thoughts, dreams, sorrows. I believe in you and I believe you true to the great things calling you. All this is my answer to your three or four lines! Do you know, Eduardo, I feel as if neither you nor I am content to watch all things "unfold within us," as in a garden, and to keep the flowers that have blossomed only for our own selfish delight or edification. We like to cut all these flowers and send them—though we are extremely careful of addressing them thus: "to an understanding friend" (I fear you do not feel this always . . .) and it is because I feel this so earnestly, because I realized that the capacity for friendship is a blessing which does not come to all of us, because of these, I say, I ask you to lose no time. For you know that it is decreed that the Woman's Garden must be consecrated to One, and that its contents exist but for the pleasure (or despair) of the Master. Then she must close the garden door and no one else can ever peep into it but He who has its key—which is Love. Do you understand? So write, Cousin, and I shall send you all the flowers you ask. If now and then there appear some weeds between them, you send them back and tell me: this I did not like in your letter, or that. Remember, the "severest truth!" You ask me about *Open Country* . . . What are words when there is an inexplicable emotion moving within you? Alas, words cannot say the best! Had you been here, I believe I would have simply looked at you in silence . . . And you would have read my eyes in silence too. You would have read all I cannot explain. But you, what did you think when you read it? What did you feel? Tell me. Oh, did you know that the Woman's Art would so deeply stir me, and inspire me? Did you know, Eduardo, that in Sanchia there is much of me as I would like to be? As I would like to seem to others, and be to others? Did you know what pity, what admiration, what intense sympathy I would feel for Senhouse—so heroic, so utterly unselfish, so beautiful, so strange and rare a character! His oddities touched me, and his failures, for he failed in one thing, and do you know what? He failed to understand and realize that woman is willing to make all sacrifices, willing to do those humble duties, willing to waste herself, and give herself in return for a love that should forever keep her heart warm and satisfied by its steadiness, its strength and its beauty. For a love that should protect and shelter and keep her. Oh, more than willing if she is truly woman, for woman is made to give, to give always, eternally, and only when giving can she be happy. And love which comprises faithfulness, inspiration, helpfulness, all qualities, is her supreme gift. She finds glory in the sacrifices it exacts, she revels in the obscure duties imposed on her. That is what Senhouse did not know . . . I am waiting! Mimi.

I *believe* heart and soul what I have just written to Eduardo. I believed it when I wrote I feared marriage and told you why. For what I mean is that true love can transform all things, small and narrow, and sad and ugly, can change any life, and answer all our needs and repay tenfold all its demands on us.

I have written more to Eduardo than he deserves (and I tell him so) because I feel that he needs to be kindled, touched and set vibrating. My letter to him is like an appeal which I hope will rouse him. Now at least I understand him perfectly. It was while reading over his old letters that I noticed what I must struggle against. One moment he is infinitely poetic, passionate, eloquent— his soul, expanded, flows out into his letters and actually radiates. Then he pauses. A dead silence takes hold of him, a lethargy.

He does not write, he forces the words, and they are heavy, life-less, devoid of energy and enthusiasm. It is like his indolent mood, spiritually his hour of stagnation. To be reliable and truly a man, he must learn to conquer this state of mental collapse. He must be made to keep an even and steady flow of thoughts, with less fire perhaps, but more durability. He tells me I kindle him. I set him in motion, and he keeps pace with me, for a while. I was too sorrowful at what I called faithlessness then to understand that these deviations are part of his nature and character.

Have I the power now, knowing the truth, to constantly strive to touch him, to sacrifice vanity, all of my own feelings, in order that I may make him vibrate? While my influence lasts, I shall struggle to make every thought and every sentiment live in him always, burn high and steadily. I shall provoke him to a constant energy and straining of his faculties. For these indolent moods are signs of weakness. This short note he sent me after struggling to write a letter—I recognized. It was inarticulate, like the sound a man makes after being deprived of the use of his tongue for a long while. That he feels, that he thinks, I know. But he cannot ex-press it; it remains like a shapeless mass in his mind—and there is no harmony, no unity, between it and pen and ink. And is this not the sign which distinguishes the ordinary man from the writer? Eduardo cannot belong to the second class until he obtains a perfect control and reaches this harmony.

January 21. Mother has written to Tia Anaïs asking if I may go to Havana. Cuca's engagement has made a great change. How I have prayed for her happiness! And yet it seems to me her marriage is to be simply for marriage's sake, not for love. In a life as empty as hers, marriage is a necessity, an obligation. As a society girl she would have been considered a failure had she remained unmarried. I hope I am mistaken.

The world to me these days seems full of love. Or perhaps my eyes are full of love and they see love everywhere. First Bernabé and his young wife, then Cuca. Our own maid, Amparo, receives letters and visits and telephone messages which throw her into fits of abstraction. Belica, though secretive, has plans and smiles mysteriously at the mention of Hernandez. In books, in plays, in pictures, in the streets, in the parks—everywhere, I see love, romance, and it sets me wondering and longing. Havana to me means the . . .

3 o'clock. You shall never know what Havana means to me.

A telephone message from Eduardo interrupted me and sent all my speculations aflying. He came for lunch and remained nearly two hours. We had a short but wonderful talk, and I gave him my letter to him, which I had not mailed.

Tonight Mother and I are going to the Sarlabous soirée. Tomorrow night Willy Shaeffer and others are coming. (I hear Enric has signed a contract to tour Germany and Spain before he comes here for a debut.) [Renarto] Zanelli,[1] on being asked to be present tonight, asked if "la muchacha vaporosa"[2] was coming, that one feared to touch me lest I should break and that he had lost his heart to me. How I laughed when I heard it. I wonder if Alfaur will be there. And so I am the vaporous one, am I? That is interesting!

Later. Raindrops froze on the branches and hang like glistening diamonds. I stood by my window entranced, drinking color and harmony from the perfect scene. By chance, on turning away, my eyes fell on my own reflection in the mirror. Transfigured by ecstasy, I was startled by what I saw: a creature flooded in a mystic light, with eyes large and deep and luminous, a white, white skin, thin, delicate hands folded on her breast, dark hair like a shadow fallen over snow. *For the first time* in my life I realized that of woman's beauty, of which I had written, which had troubled and perplexed me, I have been given a share. A song forced itself to my lips, a song of unutterable joy and gratitude. And before I knew what I was singing, these words broke forth: "Ninon, Ninon, que fait tu de la vie?"[3] To live! To live! I have a right to live, a right to love, a right to all things. I am neither wicked nor homely. Que fais-je de la vie? Mon Dieu, elle s'écoule en encre![4] Beauty all around me. A ray of it within myself. Am I not fortunate? A heart and mind to appreciate and love nature, and the desire to give pleasure to others with what is my own. Strange ideas. They have never entered my head before. I want to live, to burn, and give out warmth and light before I become ashes.

January 23. I believe my last exclamation has died a natural death. It was my last struggle against the universal currents into which I find myself suddenly drawn. At last I am going to live

---

[1] *Metropolitan Opera singer.*
[2] *The ethereal girl.*
[3] *"Ninon, Ninon, what are you making of life?"*
[4] *What am I making of life? My Lord, it flows into ink.*

like others, and write besides. How long will I love this new life? I hardly know. It is in my character to interpret it differently than others, that is to say, I lose no sight of my purpose and my serious inclinations. I am still the collector of ideas, the receiver of impressions and the describer. But it does not interfere with my pleasure; it deepens it, it seems to make it richer and more lasting and useful. I live doubly. And the inner self I so carefully keep hidden from most is comfortably lodged under a surface that serves well enough to hold the attention of the object while I study it. (This sounds like a phrase of Marie Bashkirtsev's Journal. Horrors!)

At the Sarlabouses' house I almost lost my head for joy. Alfaur was not there, but there was a young American dancer who gave us a sample of his art and did so with marvelous grace. And you know I love dancing. I longed to cry out: Let me dance with you. But he might have laughed, so I simply watched and admired. I am beginning to make friends. With Zanelli I had a long, long talk and a dance. Cesar, who is short, extremely witty and good natured, followed me a great deal and calls me "angelito." Toward the end I receive astounding compliments from Galvan. Pepito Echaniz was there and played and danced, but I like him far better at the piano. Cesar said once: "¡Con estos aretes rojos está para comérsela!"[1] Also that I was more beautiful every time he saw me. And that he had dreamed of me three times. Fortunately I know that Spaniards are not to be believed in these matters. Do you know, at the end of the evening, I was tired of laughing. And adjectives buzzed in my head long after I heard them. That night, too, it was decided I would go to a ball at the Astor with Germaine and the young men—that is, Zanelli, Echaniz, Galvan, Cesar, etc. This was but the beginning. Willy Shaeffer and Xavier Cugat[2] came for lunch Sunday. Toward three o'clock Germaine appeared. She was to come with Galvan, but it seems that he is seriously ill. We had music and talk and laughter all afternoon. Cugat is a Catalonian violinist, 20 years old and talented. He is one of those persons one must know to appreciate, as his appearance does him little justice. He is small, frail and hungry-looking, like Enric, but Enric had an expressive and sad, appealing face. Willy is the same as a year ago. The same hearty and contagious laughter, the same effervescence and boyishness

[1] *"With those red earrings, you are good enough to eat."*
[2] *Later famous as the leader of a Latin-American band.*

and modesty. He is truly a marvelous character. As they played I sat there lost in the wonder of it all, my heart overflowing with memories. The sound of the violin brought Enric vividly back to me. I recognized the things he played, the *Hymn to the Sun* and *Mighty Like a Rose*, which Willy and Cugat played repeatedly. The *Jota Aragonesa* too. What memories! And how they saddened me, for in a serious talk I had with Willy about Enric, I discovered I had made him suffer greatly. Both Willy and I were touched as we talked, for Enric told Willy everything, and as I listened to Willy repeat it to me, I could see Enric and knew what gestures would accompany his words. "How I love that girl," he told Willy. "But she is very indifferent." Willy understood what I explained, and together we came to this conclusion: that Enric was incapable of grasping the Ideal though he had depth of feeling and a passionate, intense nature. The capacity for friendship, unselfish, unquestioning, with a mutual sympathy and interest, was not in him. He was too human in his longings; he would admit no compromise. His demand was: give me either everything or nothing. He knew I could not return his love; I offered him friendship, a friendship as warm and as sincere as anyone could ask. But it was an *ideal*, and he would have none of it. And so Willy and I closed our talk with an exchange of promises. He would write to Enric and then talk to him and tell him about me. My message is: always the same. Willy is to write to us and give us news. He wanted to take my photograph to Enric, but Mother . . . well, Mother objected.

Following dinner we danced a little. Germaine recited, and she is very gifted. Someday I will describe her, for she has many talents but a peculiar trick of appearing a light-headed coquette in the eyes of those who know her little. Mrs. Norman and Captain Norman joined us when the music began. And then Hugo came. My happiness was doubled when I heard his laughter mingling with ours. And he had his share of applause too, when he sang, accompanying himself on his guitar. We talked together whenever possible. Eugene is ill. Poor Eugene. He makes me think of Amiel sometimes, in his suffering.

At eleven o'clock I found myself in my room, alone. I was dazed. Melodies, voices, faces, danced in my head. It was so much of music, of talk after solitude and long days of writing, writing, thinking, brooding. My heart was filled with memories, and it overflowed at the thought of the future, for I shall have more of this life, I shall see more of these people whose ways and talents fascinate me. At last I am in my element! I hear my languages, Spanish and French. I am among artists, musicians, poets, gallant Spaniards. Everywhere conversations reveal ideas, interests, ambitions, cleverness. They are brilliant, sparkling, expressive, intelligent people, and I love them! What a contrast with the people with whom I have vainly tried to sympathize. It is no wonder I felt utterly unhappy and disgusted with Jimmy, Mary, Dorothy, Thorvald's friends, Peggy, the members of the Sans Souci Club, etc. We have as much in common as fishes and birds. The first class needs water, the second air and space. Try to make a fish live in the clouds, or a bird at the bottom of the ocean.

January 24. There are some persons devoted to collecting riches; others, books; still more, friends; in fact, all things under the sun. Old furniture, paintings, first editions, stamps, wines, antiques, oddities, rarities, curios of whatever kind, inspire in some creatures the desire to preserve, or arouses the sense of ownership, the sense of power over the masses. In place of all these things, which are innumerable and as varied as life itself, I do believe mine is a passion for collecting ideas and words to suit them. How I love to listen to people when they have something to say. How I love to set them thinking and watch the results. To turn to books for ideas happens to prove only that they are far more easily obtained there. That is to say, it requires no effort and but an ordinary intelligence. Because of this they are more easily loved. But are the ideas more reliable, more truthful, more exact and clarifying and convincing, than people's? It takes a braver heart to love people. It takes a superior understanding to comprehend them justly. It takes an extraordinary patience and faith to draw the least spark from beneath their surface; it takes the greatest wisdom and delicacy to penetrate into the workings of their spiritual life. But are the results worth our while? So long a worshiper of books, I find myself suddenly attracted toward human nature about me. Each person, each character, is indeed a book, a living, moving, active book. The only difference is that they are more difficult to read, and there lurks an unworthy suspicion in my mind as to their being equally interesting. If I count on my fingers the characters in literature that have inspired and edified, ennobled and influenced me, I am certain to lose count. Each has brought its little source of knowledge or experience, sincerely, freely, offered in all forms. Each book I read filled a need, spurred me to more questioning. How rare is such an occurrence among men and women. How few the friends I have. Yet how is it that I love them so deeply? I consider them a constant source of pride and joy. I exult in the knowledge of their minds and hearts. I love them, and yet I wonder which is nobler or loftier: these human ties, these companionships in which there is mingled the human share of great and small, divine and earthy—or the other, the unwavering, faultless teachers and revelators? It seems to me there is selfishness and cowardice in choosing the last to the exclusion of the former. Yes, the capacity for human friendship demands more nobleness—the willingness to give and to suffer. Does this quickening interest of mine mean that I have gradually realized this? And it is an interest which has cost me peace of mind and heartaches.

I spoke of ideas in the beginning, having in mind a sharp comparison. In a few days I gathered many ideas worth remembering, from Alfaur, Eduardo, Dr. Chambers, Willy, Germaine and Hugo. I have just read two books—[Leslie] Moore's *Jester* and *Love Letters of an Englishman*. I had a strange impression, as when one listens to a person talking and discovers suddenly a complete change of voice. And the first was incredibly warm, near and convincing; it did its work quietly, appealing but to the intellect. The second was more impersonal, less moving, and touched many confusing strings; it was disturbing. I will endeavor here to find harmony and unity by recording the working-out of both elements and establishing whatever connection might exist between the two.

It is chiefly with Hugo that I have experienced this doubt. Is it what he says and thinks—or just *himself* that wins me? His ideas! Some of them were distasteful to me before he expressed them. For example, his acknowledgment of the practical. Yet he gives me for each a good cause; he appeals to my reason and persuades me. Thus we are often clashing, though we do so without discord. He tells me a thing. I ponder over it before I answer. Days later I return to it. It has taken root, it has flowered. It is a flower, so to speak, though I once called it a weed and abhorred the very mention of it. Am I not to be thankful for this?

Later. I had no need of going very far to find what I sought. It is even distressing to find that I have been babbling my ABCs when I thought I was reaching out toward a problem of my own making. It is in a book Eduardo brought me: *Essays on Nature* by H. W. Mabie. Listen: "A man must be self-centered, self-sustained and complete in himself before he can carry any real power or character into specific relationship; a tree must have independent rootage before it can take to itself the elements of life and growth about it. . . . That which is individual in us and which makes us distinct and different from all other men is fostered and developed by solitude. In society one is constantly assailed by the influences, views, convictions, temperamental attitudes which are alien and often antagonistic. In solitude a man learns what is in him; he makes terms with the power about him; he comes into intelligent relations with the world which surrounds him. Solitude is essential to real thinking and it is only by thinking that we arrive at a knowledge of ourselves and at the significance of experience. After a day of intense activity, of deep emotion, of sudden or momentous happenings, one feels the necessity of being alone in order to get at the meaning of what has taken place."

Mabie's circle is larger. He was revolving around solitude and society—different subjects entirely than mine and differently treated. But he touched as he passed; he came near mine and there is a resemblance between the two problems. To his last words I subscribe ardently, though instead of: "One feels the necessity of being alone," I would have said: "One feels the necessity of writing in one's journal." Mabie speaks of readjustments. This is a word for which I am grateful. It describes accurately an occupation so frequent in me that it might be termed a mania. And until now I had no name for it. One word served for everything: writing. Writing to me means thinking, digging, pondering, creating, shattering. It means getting at the meaning of all things; it means reaching climaxes; it means moral and spiritual and physical life all in one. Writing implies manual labor, a strain on one's conscience and an exercise of the mind. Readjusting is but one of the things I do, and I disguised it under the name of writing until I found its true and proper title. Yes, my life flows into ink! And I am pleased. For I can live others' lives without incurring the danger of smothering my inner thought life. It undergoes a process of complete resuscitation, resurrection, rebirth, every time I sit by my desk to write. That is what I preached to Frances, Eduardo, to Eugene. One thing I seldom tell, and scarcely admit to myself for fear it may be too true, is that the process is painful. But it has its compensations. And pray, is anything of worth obtained without pain? And now that I speak of worth, I am reminded of a question: Is this a useful task? Have I a right to devote so much time to it? In my heart of hearts I believe with Gladstone that an honest biography is the best one can give to literature. Poor little Diary! You are an honest biography, but badly written and I fear someday you shall perish in the flames. And to appease my conscience I will say: Well, I have *done* something, but I did not *give* it. Heaven, perhaps, will consider the intention.

3 o'clock. I have spent the day by the fire reading, alone. When I tired of books, I wrote, and when I tired of writing, I gazed at Hugo's photograph, which he brought me Sunday. I dare not tell you how many times I have held it before me and dreamed. He faces me fully, so that I must face what I see; there is no disguising it. I read determination, firmness, strength. His eyes perplex me. They are intelligent, discerning, frank but critical. Kindliness, tenderness, softer things, lurk beneath the surface—possibilities. I would not like to see Hugo's treatment of sham, deception, or dishonesty. For forgiveness I turn to the curves of his lips, which he controls firmly and yet I have known to quiver and mold the softest words of poems. What a mingling of uprightness and compassion, justice and mercy, sharp criticism and human tolerance. Do you know, a wicked person could fear Hugo, and I feel dizzy at the thought of the heights to which I must rise with him. And yet the higher he goes, the higher I know I can go, too!

To Eduardo:

I have another cause for this delay, which is happiness. Too much happiness has come to me unexpectedly, dispersing the dark clouds of which I gave you a glimpse when you were here. . . . And happiness is a strange thing, Eduardo, it makes one sing and dream, but write—never! And today I was so happy that I became sad—do you know that happiness that lies close to tears? I felt it, and the flow of words returned. I can write and I will write about you. Eduardo, I do not think it is through writing you are to express yourself. And I say this after pondering much. . . . I believe you have the Idea within you, the desire, the talent. I have watched for them in you, and found them there. But I have also seen that you have not the signs of the one vocation you and I revere: creating with words. Writing implies manual labor as well as the strain on one's conscience and an exercise of the mind. One of these demands is distasteful to you, and to fail in one condition means that your vocation is imperfect unless you can conquer by practice and habit. See what happens to Joaquin—he possesses the gift of music without the application, industry and perseverance that makes the complete artist. What can he make of his gift? It lies in his own hands. He is fortunate enough because he has what cannot be obtained, acquired. What he lacks he can make his own by sheer force of will. It is the same with you. Question yourself. Are you willing to make the effort? Do you think it is worthwhile to struggle against writing "slowly, badly, imperfectly"? For my part there is not a demand of my writing to which I do not respond fully and completely. No labor is too strenuous, no rewriting too wearisome, no effort too unreasonable. I find joy even in the work of it, in mental and physical pain. My head burns, and my fingers ache, but I am satisfied, willing and proud. Do you feel this? Unless you do, you should not force yourself. Surely the day of revelation will come to you as it has come to me. And I believe implicitly that you will discover the tools that suit your character. Do not let that feeling of failure take hold of you. Throw it all off! Have confidence in yourself and for solace remember, as I remembered, that the workings of our spiritual life are infinitely subtle, delicate and mysterious. Its blossomings are as tender as the unfolding of flowers, and it has its reasons, its time for everything. Do not force it. Patience, care, watchfulness—above all, patience—are invaluable, for the outcome of our growth is very sacred. Remember, it is our place in the world we are deciding, our life's task that we are choosing. Oh, wait, and if the waiting and doubting cause you pain, think that a reckless, unwise choice will mean eternal sorrow and shame. Write when you can. Watch yourself work, and your conception will be slowly crystallized into some form, some visible and palpable result. I know your two predominant moods. Heat and Lethargy. And I dream of the power that should inspire you to an even and steady flow of thought. I dream of a harmony in you by which all faculties will be as One. For I know you think and *feel* always but etc., etc. . . . Dreams such as I have for you are like prayers. And I hope these dreams will make you read my foolish preaching patiently, and perhaps help you to believe me. . . . Mimi.

January 29. I sit to write with Hugo's photograph before me. How happy he has made me! Last night I loved best of all for many reasons. But I know it was his tenderness which moved me so deeply that I fell asleep with quiet tears in my eyes, those tears which are neither hot nor bitter and that flow when the heart is too full of joy. The snowstorm raged all night, whirlwinds, snowdrifts. The wind whipped the snow against our faces as we walked to the station; we were blinded by it and lashed. Yet we walked with pleasure, arm in arm, our even steps falling noiselessly on the soft carpet of a snow as fine as sand. Hugo described John Erskine's lecture as one of the high moments of life. And I can say no more. He read from his own poems, told their story, talked, and the memory I retained of his personality, his voice, his face will never leave me. I believe with Hugo that Erskine is a great man. To have read his books and then to meet him, hear and see him, was indeed as if we had seen Emerson. Hugo's admiration was contagious. Three times during the reading, we looked at each other in mute approval. He touched by chance on things Hugo and I had discussed on our way there, and we were thrilled. One poem, above all, I want to read again—Erskine said he had written it recently—the work of a man living now, and as we do, in the same crowded city. It seems strange, for I have come to associate the best with the past—in literature.

Afterward Hugo and I sallied out under the snowstorm and walked, hardly knowing what we were doing, lost in our talk, and Hugo almost said word for word what I once wrote: we had sunshine within us. We talked seriously at first, earnestly. I asked questions and he talked of himself—which he seldom does. He recited a love poem of Verlaine's to me, for me. I teased him. For a moment we drifted into nonsense, then dropped a thought that showed our minds were set on Erskine, and once more dived below the surface, and yet with laughter lurking in the corners of our eyes because our hearts were light. And we walked partway to Pennsylvania Station—rode, and waited for our train, and talked, and were lost again to the rest of the world. It was good to face the wind and snow again with *him*—with his strong arm under mine and his voice ringing in my ears. We walked slowly even, watching with pleasure the snow drifting across fields and circling around trees and playing about the roofs of the houses.

Thorvald's dance was still going on (a little dance Mother gave for him) and I asked Hugo if he wanted to steal inside by the back door, through my secret passageway, as I call it. I was to give him one of his books, and when I brought it down we stood there whispering and laughing until he had to leave in order to catch his train. I gave him my hand. Instead of clasping it he bent over and kissed it! I caught my breath and wondered if I would run. But no, I managed in some mysterious way to talk and say goodbye, and when I closed the door after him I kissed the hand his lips had touched. Oh, what foolish nonsense. But what enchanting, what wonderful, what precious nonsense! The picture of Hugo bending over my hand has been in my mind all day. How I have dreamed, recalled his words, his every look and gesture, all day, all day. Hugo, my wisest and best, kissed this hand I use in writing, as if I were a princess—his princess. Is it so? I feel he loves me. And yet I fear. I fear the Hugo I knew last night will be changed when I see him again, will become cold, and watch his words, and let the veil I dread fall over his eyes. If I could make him tender always. Last night he won my heart because he was himself, free from the restraint of English poetry. Yet it is better he should become cold and impenetrable, for if he ever kisses my hand again and reveals his lovable, expressive, spontaneous self, I shall be tempted to point to my cheek and say: "Kiss me here instead!" Then I'll throw myself in the ocean for shame.

January 30. I was tempted to tear the last page off. I am ashamed of my foolishness. I feel like a philosopher who has suddenly descended from his dignified position to that of a babbling child, and a sentimental one at that. And yet—I am happy. I smile all day at nothing, I dream from morning til night; and I feel Hugo's presence continually. Should I keep all this a secret? Write again of Saturday night more seriously, more coolly? But it would not be the truth. I felt and thought what I wrote under the first impression, though today I chide myself and call it nonsense. I want to tell the truth always, even if it should reveal my faults and my inconsistencies. Forgive me for being as I am and for feeling as I write. It is true that it matters little what we did together, Hugo and I, but being together alone made us happy. To hear Erskine only added to the perfection of our night, lifting it from the range of ordinary experiences. Erskine was an embodiment of a Divine Ideal and Hugo and I were brought closer to each other by the ties of common worship. All pleasures were mingled in those simple acts of ours, listening to a Poet, and walking, for our hearts were moved and our minds exalted. And they spoke to each other through glances and expressions, in silences, in flowing speeches, in gestures. More often, however, in ways we cannot account for.

Once Hugo said: "I can tell my thoughts better to you than to anyone else." But when I asked him why, he could not tell. Can I tell why I tell him mine? No. These are the mysteries Hearn wrote of: ". . . hearts are the supreme mysteries in life, people meet, touch each other's inner being with a shock and a feeling as if they had seen a ghost." And again: "To touch men's souls you must know all that those souls can be made to feel by words; and to know that, you must yourself have a ghost in you that can be touched in the same way." And Hugo wrote beside these lines: "Anaïs, have you a little ghost in you?" We both have! Hugo has been reading of the characteristics of French and Spaniards, endeavoring to pigeonhole me, to classify me. Naturally, he has failed. I cannot be said to belong to any nation, nor to resemble any creature under the sun. And I would dare anyone to describe me properly in a few coherent phrases. It would take a book, and when the book was written I would already be another person. Fortunately no one has given this many-sided problem a thought. You and I are waging our great battle for truth, secretly and quietly, but our purpose is not to describe Anaïs Nin; indeed not— what a waste of time that would be. We are here practicing in order to be able to write someone's life, someone who would be a character, a hero, for the edification and despair of the world. Someday, perhaps—who shall say?

Days ago I wrote: Is it what he says and thinks or just *himself* that wins me? Today I had another doubt concerning Hugo, one which sprang on me suddenly as I wrote a few lines to him, to enclose a poem he will love. Is it what he represents that touches me, or his character? Hugo is my ideal of Friend, fulfilled; my ideal of leader and counselor. He is my living Poetry, my books come to life through his lips. He bears the stamp of all things I love: wisdom, intelligence, knowledge, strength. He makes my conceptions certainties; he solves my problems; his thoughts inspire me and kindle my own, support, provoke and mend them. But *he* himself. Do I love his dreams, his ideals, his moods? Would I love him stripped of his utterances, of his understanding of me, his knowledge of music and poetry? Yes, a thousand times yes. I have had poetry and wisdom in others, have I not? And yet I did not love them. I bowed to their talents, yet I held it apart from the character. Enric is a genius. I do not love him. Marcus's poetry moved me, yet I despised the boy. Eduardo's perfect response where dreams are concerned thrilled and enchanted me and does so even now, but I do not love him as a man. In Hugo these outward forms in which he clothes his nature, his very self, are merely ways. What counts, what holds my attention is this Self, apart from whatever brilliant method he has chosen to express himself and reveal himself. Thus if Enric were to lose his gift of music, he would seem but a mere shadow. If Marcus had not been a poet, I would never have spoken to him. If Eduardo lost interest in the ideals we have created together, became an ordinary creature without inner life, it would never occur to me to call him friend. While with Hugo, it is Hugo always to me. As Senhouse said to Sanchia: "You are *You*." So I say to him: "You are you, always. That is all I know."

I often wish we had met in another way Outwardly how casual and how smooth runs the course of our friendship—or love? (I dare not use the word with certainty yet.) All the adventures take place in our own minds. It is all a matter of words, of a letter, glances, handclasps. We know each other by what we tell each other. There is little action. Our doings are microscopic. One act is sufficient to set us pondering and dreaming for a week. A world, indeed, of little things, details, quiet hours upon which we meditate. The romance of little things, truly, it lives in our imagination. There is never any quickening or climax. Our hearts unfold, like plants in the sunshine, slowly, gradually. We learn to watch each other, we hold our heads very near sometimes. Each is yet free to turn to another flower. Still, we do so only to compare and return to our favorite. I dream sometimes vague dreams of a day of change—when the great adventure crystallizes itself, for my life is yet all my own and I yearn to give it. But Hugo? It is not yet Blossom Time. Patience. "N'obligez pas le poème / Qui, mysterieusement / Voudrait s'ouvrir de lui même / À devancer le moment."[1] And love is a poem.

January 31. I have struggled to form an opinion of Maurice Hewlett. In his *Open Country* and *Rest Harrow* there is much to praise and much to blame. I am not certain that his characters are noble; they are mad, and yet there is a beauty and truth in them. It is Maurice Hewlett's painting of them which touches me. He has the signs of the visionary—yes, his head is in the clouds — but his feet are chained to the earth—earthy, heavy, leaden, hideous. I cannot understand how anyone can know the ideal, grasp it, describe it, sing of it in exalted words, and yet not rise with it above the foul world wherein hypocrisy, shallowness, selfishness, weaknesses, abound. Indeed, Hewlett's creatures are, taken from this point of view, monsters. They have distorted conceptions of all things. Sanchia is weak where she should be brave.

[1] Do not force the poem / Which, mysteriously / Wants to flower of itself / To open before its time. —*Edmond Rostand.*

She is described various times as deep and clear-sighted, yet proves at every turn that she is stupid. I mean that were she truly what she is said to be and believed to be, her conduct is inexplicable and unreasonable. The trouble is that she was idealized, and when made to act, she acted like the most ordinary woman. Had she been treated as an ordinary woman, her actions would have suited her place; she would have passed unnoticed and disappointed no one.

I have my own ideas on these things and therefore it may be that what I disliked in *Rest Harrow* was their being ignored. *Open Country* startled me, it is true. The charm of it baffled me. Let us say it aroused my curiosity. *Rest Harrow* irritated me. I could no longer hold back my disapproval. Why is it I am not certain of my reasons yet? I cannot tell. I shall write and study Hewlett better meanwhile. A positive opinion might come gradually, as I write perhaps. Throughout the books, what I find lacking is the true sense of the meaning of such words as ideal, poetry, love, happiness, even freedom. They seem all badly defined, badly interpreted. Of course, the meaning of words cannot be like a set law to which we all bow submissively. But there is a general standard by which the individual can judge. And to one who reads much, these meanings are incredibly clear and stable, or if they change, they change gradually, step by step with the history of progress, of evolution, influenced by many elements yet even then easily traced through the very same medium, for literature keeps abreast of the times; more than that, it is the Recorder of all these things. Thus while in touch with the "creators with words," the significance of all changes, small or great, deep or superficial, is in our hands. And so are the new ideals, the changes in love's forms, the modern demands implied by happiness, the modern interpretation of age-old freedom.

February 2. I know. I know what accusation I bring up against Hewlett's characters. After reading half of his *Mainswaring*, it became very clear in my mind that what most of them essentially lack in a sorrowfully large proportion is *nobility*. Therefore, on the whole I dislike Hewlett more than I admire him, and although I willingly praise his style for its originality and other qualities, I prefer to banish him altogether from my shelf of choice books. All is said; I shall not return to the subject. I might have been reading finer things had I known.

I no longer stand in danger of misjudging Hugo during his

spells of silence. I have originated a way to bring him nearer in spite of himself. The week is coming to an end and I have had no word from him concerning the visit to the Sarlabouses or my note to him, but last night I began writing him letters which he is never to read. In them I write all I cannot say to him, and more. Whatever burdens my heart flows out in the ever faithful, untiring old way: ink. Thus I speak to him, and dream of how he should take my words were he to hear them. Strange offerings on the altar of devotion, are they not? Merely letters that are never to be read and yet all his own. Imagination at times is truly a blessing. The happiness I find in these confidences is as real to me as what I feel when we talk together. What is more, it is a perfect happiness; no shadow lingers near it as it does in the other (for I suffer at the thought of parting) while in my letters to him I write as long as I wish. It is so with all dreams, all fancies. What the mind and heart conceive is always perfect, and while it looks to its own doings for happiness, it finds it. Yet why do we turn to other hearts and risk pain? Because the horizon that is the bounds of our dealings with Self is narrow and blinds us to the true purpose of existence, which is happiness with others. And our higher impulses lead us toward others, to live in the other and for others. So my letter writing is an act of selfishness! Yet let me be happy in this way: it is the only one. It helps me to be patient and reasonable. Since I have begun writing, not a word of complaint has passed my lips. Were he never again to speak to me, I would be satisfied with the image I have formed of him and to which I can speak when I please. Oh, but I pray it might not happen. It is simple to write stoically, but to be stoical is another thing.

February 3. In twelve hours I shall be dancing and chattering. I wish I could die before that, or become invisible and be suddenly forgotten by all. Why? I am again my old self, the incorrigible, the philosopher, the scribbler. I have no desire for music, and lights, and compliments. Dancing, yes, but alone. Instead, I shall have to look on faces long and round, pale and ruddy, stupid, cynical, foolish, admiring, insincere, bored, whatnot. And they recall by contrast the only face I do want to see, the frank lovable face of my silent one.

February 5. A joy so deep has penetrated into my heart that I am frightened. I am lost to the world and float between heaven and earth, entranced, spellbound, heart and soul afire, yet rendered speechless by the infinite beauty of the revelation that has set them aflame. And not a vision this, but truth, glorious truth! Oh, I love him! I love him!

Last night each time I looked into his face I had a glimpse of heaven; each time he spoke to me I knew the voice I have heard in dreams; I thrilled at his every touch, at his nearness. To see him far from me gave me strange pangs of longing and pain. And he bows before me. He bows to smile and to speak. And how? By a letter, which is in itself a poem. It was an answer to mine, and he slipped it into my pocket as we entered Germaine's house.

Evening. Now as I sit by the fire, after much thinking and pondering, I marvel that I should have been able to write a single line this morning, for how high welled the tide of sentiment! I could neither think nor ponder as I did tonight. I believe that I did not even know that I was writing. I know what I am doing now, however, but I do not write because I know what to say. I write because I am deeply shaken, and startled, and filled with wonder, and I need explanation. I have been looking in the fire again. I have nothing to say. I can but dream.

February 6. There is a rule I should have thought of in the very beginning of the Diary, and that is never to write in the very heat of the first emotion or impression. It never occurred to me, for the very simple reason that sensible things seldom occur to me, if ever. And the rule is sensible, extremely sensible, and the more I think of it the more sensible it appears, and therefore the less like me, so that I am driven to the belief that I am quoting someone else. The cause of this rule? It can be briefly told. It lies in the fact that when one is startled, or bewildered, or touched, or thrown out of balance by an extraordinary incident or unusual occurrence, there can be no coherence in one's utterances. The words literally tumble out of your heart in the most unliterary disorder. And instantly one exposes one's sacred feelings to the malignant influence of ridicule. So that I was forced to laugh at myself for the wildness of my writing lately—laugh through tears because I knew how sincere I was, and how foolish I seemed; know well what I meant and read between the lines to find the sacredness, the holiness, the beauty which my poor words so sadly deformed and belittled. Well, I waited until calm returned, and my thoughts became quiet, and my feelings intelligible, waited and now can vindicate myself.

I shall pass over quickly the dance on Friday night, gay and brilliant though it was. Zanelli, the singer, was remarkably good to me—such are the things my memory clings to. So was his cousin, and Cesar, and some others. But I missed Hugo, who had telephoned early in the evening and whose voice was still ringing in my ears. I was saddened, too, by a lesson inflicted on me. I wrote of a certain Galvan's astounding compliments. He rattled them off (there is no other way to describe what I mean) and no wonder! He has this repertoire well worn and makes continuous use of it—plays his part before every girl in turn as they catch his fancy. His is the type of which the world is full, to whom life is a farce, hearts are mere toys, and words a pastime. It does me worlds of good to strike upon such creatures occasionally, I who take all things so earnestly, so seriously, who hold the meaning of words sacred. From the shock I obtain a clearer view of things and a sense of balance. Yet strangely enough I become more obstinate in my own attitude, believe more firmly than ever that I am in the right.

Here is enough material for a cynic to ponder on. And enough to throw any composition teacher into a passion of indignation, for do they not preach, all of them, from morn till night. of the sin of digression? I am guilty, and will prove my contrition by returning to my point of departure.

February 8. Events have crowded upon one another so that they take my breath away and leave me, in consequence, unable to spread my ink in my usual abundant, profuse, inimitable and illimitable way. In short, I must be brief, use exclamation marks sparingly and adjectives only in the most critical passages. But Hugo's letter I shall not treat so ruthlessly. I will write of it when I have time to do it justice. Therefore the best and most loved thing I keep in my heart under lock and key. As to the rest? The soirée at the Sarlabouses' was more animated than ever. Mr de Oro taught me the tango, Cesar found more names for me; with Zanelli I had only a few words but a long talk with his cousin, a dance with Costa, etc. And with Hugo but a fragment of a dance. I tried to approach him at refreshment time, seeing he was edging his way toward me and calling me with his eyes, but Cesar and de Oro surrounded, captured and pulled me upstairs. Germaine and de Oro had originated a bohemian club of which you shall hear more by and by.

What I loved best of the evening was (do not laugh) the

coming home with Hugo sitting at my side. As we talked, each time he turned his face fully on mine, my heart leaped as if charged with electricity, the spring of which he held in his hands, and pressed far too often for my peace of mind. It was when he left us at Forest Hills that I read his letter. It filled me with that feeling one has when looking up at the sky at night, and at the stars—awe, wonder and joy mingled with one another, and the soul flowing out toward that vast, infinite mystery and beauty. Why I had such a feeling I cannot tell. But it seems to me I can say no more about a letter than that, for am I not comparing the reading of one to the reading of the heavens? Comparing what my eyes saw on paper to what they see in the skies. He writes these words, which I know by heart: "Would you call these things the stuff of poetry—the scent of rosy hours rising with swift memory from the dust of day; the music of sweet confidences uttered, echoing clearly after other sounds have died; the silent joy of feeling beauty at my arm, of walking as in a dream with loveliness long sought? Such a scene comes to me, such music vibrates within me, and such a dreamful joy have you breathed on me. If these are of the stuff of poetry—then, Anaïs, they have been in me long. But I would pick for you only perfect flowers in my garden, such as it is. And if flowers are to grow as the gardener wishes, they need his day-long care, which some day I shall be free to give them. Meanwhile their fragrance is rioting about me, and I give deep thanks that I am alive to see, and hear, and smell, and taste, and feel the selfsame mystery of beauty that awed great Plato in the dim far ages. Hugo."

This was in answer to a short note I sent him alluding to a poem he had promised me and which is still unfinished. I quoted Rostand: "N'obligez pas le poème / Qui, mysterieusement / Veux s'ouvrir de lui même / À devancer le moment." I wrote, I shall be more patient. He asked me to answer him in French if I liked his letter. My note in French had pleased him. I mailed my answer today, still under the spell of his beautiful letter and still too moved to find such words as I ought to find for him. But are any of my words worthy of him? No, nothing I do, or say, or write, or am is worthy of him. I can only give love to one who can bow before me in this kingly manner, with all his strength, his wisdom, his tenderness and exquisite appreciation. And if he wants the supreme gift, he shall indeed have it to its fullest measure.

Yesterday this thought filled my heart. I was with Mrs. Norman at the Woman's Art Club, where I was to be given a costume for the Review of Models. I was given a Watteau dress, the Shepherdess. It fitted me to perfection and when I looked at the mirror I gasped. I was undeniably French, French, French! The ladies exclaimed admiringly. They said the oval of my face reminded them of old prints. They approved my hair, my profile, my eyes, my feet, and as they talked, my heart swelled not with pride but with my thought. "Of course, of course," it sang softly, "one loved by Hugo must need be like this. All this is Hugo's doing. He loves this hair, these eyes, this profile, and by loving them made them beautiful." And again I looked at the mirror and yet not at myself. Not I was standing there, but the One he loves, his very own "loveliness long sought." So it was throughout the rehearsal. A lady sent for me in the middle of the evening. "Will you be free tomorrow?" she asked me bluntly. "Yes, certainly." "Then I want you to come to my studio at 9:30 to pose for me." And so it was done. She is Mrs. May Fairchild. I posed for her today from 9:30 to 12 and earned $2.50. What a happy omen. At a simple rehearsal to please not once, but twice, thrice, for there was a Mrs. Becker who promised to send for me, and someone else who observed me closely and approvingly, saying loudly to another lady: "She has more than prettiness, that child. Did you notice her expression?" I glowed, while my heart sang merrily: Hugo, Hugo, Hugo.

Well, it is done, I have found work, and a work which suits me, for as I sit there hour after hour, so quietly, so still, I can dream, dream, dream and dream to my heart's content. Assuredly I have only had one sitting, but tomorrow I hope to be given more work. It is the day of the Review and all the painters will be there. My costume is beautiful. My shoulders emerge from creamy lace. My bodice and pannier and train are of gold, old gold with a color such as one sees in paintings. The full skirt is of white satin. There is more drooping, graceful lace at the elbows. No sooner did I see myself in it than I knew precisely how to stand, how to walk, how to curtsy. It was the heart of a truly old-fashioned girl that fluttered under the tight gold bodice. I felt like a Queen, I longed for a King! I was born to move among those splendors of court life, born indeed to step with old-fashioned grace, to feel the soft swish of satin, the frills of lace, and to smell old perfumes, to know old courtesies, hand-kissing, and to dance minuets. Will any of the painters feel this, read it in my face, understand it? I pray that at least one might, and wish to paint me, dress, face, spirit and all. But this is a dream. It is enough they should see something worth studying in my face. To expect any of them to read my heart in it would be indeed too much.

I can hardly wait until tomorrow. Meanwhile, I pray, and pray fervently. And I dream of Hugo. If my letter could please him as much as his pleased me.

The telephone rings. I rush to it. It is Hugo. He is pleased with my letter. And my exclamation is answered as soon as it is uttered. Now I can sleep contentedly.

February 11. Success! Success! And such success as I never dreamed of! There are no words to describe my happiness. It is like the perfect contentment an old person might feel at the close of a life that has fulfilled every one of its expectations and realized every dream. Gratitude, tenderness, this is what I felt after the first moments of wild exultation passed. And such serenity of mind as I have not known for a long time. Why am I happy? Because I have found work to help my mother and because Hugo is thinking of me. My heart is full of these two things.

Hugo's thoughts of me reached me in the form of another telephone call. Two in one week. We talked much. We are each time more conscious of the You and I, and forgetting literature. I feel my love for him growing. Such a fine, strong man, and yet with a heart so tender, so delicate and kind. He is even shy, sometimes, like a boy, and I see the boy's chivalrous respect for woman lurking in his eyes, the boy's sweet faith and trust—and the man's tolerance. Mingle all good things, take the best in men and the noblest in poets—and you have Hugo as I see him today. Yet I am no reader of human hearts; in this art I am the eternal blunderer. But what I know of Hugo seems born in me, a thing of mystery, the age-old knowledge which is woman's very own gift and blessing and called by some: intuition.

As to the other thing—Thursday brought me fulfillment in a measure far greater than I had ever dreamed. My hair was pushed back completely, exposing fully every line of my face and head and my ears (which, according to the present-day fashion, had never seen the light of such publicity). A flat, flowered, ribboned little Watteau hat pinned on top of my head completed my costume. At first I was tempted to weep at the extraordinary figure I presented. It was certainly a severe test of real beauty I was undergoing, and I shook and shivered in my small silver slippers while my heart beat wildly under the tight gold bodice. The critical moment arrived. I saw Beatrice, the Dutch girl, the Indian girl, the Persian girl, the Old-Fashioned girl, pass before me. Then I—and all I remembered were the applause and the painters' curious, critical eyes.

But at the end! How the artists gathered around me! All the models had their names taken down according to the impression they had created. It was my good fortune to have a costume exactly suited to my type and setting it off in its own distinctive category. The artists compared me to Greuze and other painters. They talked very freely so that the humor of the situation overwhelmed me and I compared myself to a piece of furniture that was being sold at auction. This thought will always save me from conceit. Nothing in the world could ever change my estimation of my own self. For all the good strangers find, I know a fault; so that I am ever humbled by praise. I finally won over Mrs. Becker. She engaged me for three mornings next week. I am to see a Mr. Brown Monday afternoon, and Mr. Tolman Tuesday. An Italian, Arthur Lorenzani, and an Englishman, Mr. Eland, were also interested, and many others whose names I cannot remember. Miss Curtis, the President, added to my joy by voicing her pleasure at what she termed "my success." If ever a girl felt in a cloud of glory, for which she thanked all but herself, that girl was your Linotte, your scribbler, your philosopher. Strange, is it not, that I should have the means in my own hands to study the worthlessness of Woman's beauty, to test its power, to realize to what extent it covers the inner self, whose value alone is eternal and fixed. There is only one in the world who loves me apart from it, and that is the one who said once: "You know, I could not love beauty without intelligence." Oh, Hugo, of you I am sure, and you I can trust. Your praise alone I prize.

This was my answer to his letter. Last night he repeated that he had thought it beautiful and exactly what he expected of me. When I think of his letter, I wonder that I should not have written a poem instead of these simple lines:

My friend:[1]
If poetry springs from those precious moments when solitude is erased by the murmur of shared dreams, or from those furtive hours when thoughts melt into one another or bloom in the

[1] *Translated from the French.*

warmth of confidences exchanged, then my hands, like yours, are full of flowers.

With you, I cease to feel the painful isolation of ideas and feelings that I had thought was the fate of all who dare to penetrate beyond the world that surrounds us, or to plunge beneath the surfaces of life.

With you I have learned, too, that the ideal that separates one from the crowd brings one close to a person like you and inspires that rarest, sweetest harmony: the harmony of souls.

Doesn't that kind of harmony exist between us, overcoming all the obstacles that otherwise would seem to bar the way?

All this is very little. There are so many other flowers, my friend, that I shall pluck if you want them, and when I find them worthy.

Tell me that you understand. I love to hear you say it, although many times I can feel that you do, without needing words.

Anaïs

I could only partly explain my attitude in the letter which I have just written and which belongs to the class that is never to be read by him. In it I tell him: "When I see you, when I am with you, when we talk together, then I cannot write. You fill my heart with wonder and delight, and it can no longer make use of words. These letters shall only be signs of loneliness and longing; they fill those hollow hours I find so long between your visits or your letters. Your way of writing to me has set my poor pen quaking. My old careless, unconscious flow of words is quenched. Nothing I can say seems worthy of you, although I would not have hesitated to face all the editors in the country had the opportunity presented itself! What do you make of this? Oh, my dear one, it is a deep, deep mystery. I have no fear of you because I know you to be kind. It is rather a respect for your opinion. I feel so high an estimation of your judgment, so keen a realization of what it means to me, that nothing short of the ideal can satisfy me. Oftentimes, I long to be perfect, thinking you might love me more. For my very own self I ask no more than I have, but for you I want the noblest, the highest and the most beautiful. This wish has even penetrated my writing and rules it as it rules my simplest actions. . . ."

This is the note that rings the loudest throughout the theme of our companionship. The ideal! The ideal! We want to give it to each other, we want to be it to each other. I feel it when I realize he has written but two letters to me, and I to him. But they are the best and choicest he can give. I would not like it to be so much this way, though I would never tell him. Perhaps because I am woman, and therefore inconsistent, or because I am weak and too *human*. I sometimes wish he would write more often and be less exacting so that I might do the same. And yet what beauty there is in this restraint. Instead of a thousand feelings rushing forth headlong—instead, a calm, wise choice of the most perfect words, dropping one by one from a pen dipped in the same ardent flames that moved the great English poets I love so well. In Hugo I admire it; I know it does not exist in me, but I shall learn it from him. You know how little it takes to move me, to send all my emotions soaring on the highest peaks of ecstasy, or plunging into diabolical depths. And how quickly it all flows into reams of paper—miles of phrases. Indeed, I realize I cannot trust myself, or my feelings, above all. And he helps me, by his admirable control, to master my own self. I feel his strong hand holding back my own when I write those fiery, impetuous words, which too easily flow from my pen. The hours I spent in contemplation of his character, and writing of him, are like those hours I spend in the woods, on hilltops, gazing at the clear, pure sky or feeling the fresh, clean wind on my face.

With all this, I forsake Eduardo. I received a letter from him Wednesday. I almost believe we made a mistake by renewing our correspondence. In some way or other, we are changed to each other. It may be a simple trick of my fancy, but I feel sorrowfully far away from him, as if we no longer had the same interests, as if our dreams were no longer equal and suffered from being compared and thrown into each other's company. And it is no matter for mirth either. Indeed, I would no more write of it to him than I would willingly hurt Mother. I shall wait to see if he is experiencing the same thing. And then decide what is to be done.

Mother says I am fickle. Horrors! She laughs when I tell her I fear I am falling in love. All I can do is wait, with Hugo's boundless patience, for I do believe I have the heart of a little girl and am speaking of things I know nothing about. Is it possible? If I am still a little girl, then I can be Eduardo's friend. But if not, then I know I have grown too old and will be satisfied only with Hugo. And I know, too, that Eduardo will not like me any more if he discovers it.

February 12.
Cher Papa:[1]

I am very sad about my French. With all my heart I love the language that little by little is slipping away from me. In English, no sooner does an idea occur to me than the appropriate word for it comes to mind. It's almost miraculous. I live with words that were unknown to me only eight years ago!

This inclination toward analysis, criticism, observation, will bear fruit some day. It remains to be seen whether I shall be a better woman than a writer. . . .

If you have time, tell me about your visit to Italy, even if you send only post cards. My most fantastic, most cherished dreams will go with you on that trip. There are certain things that one keeps carefully locked in one's heart because they would only interfere with daily life, and one of those things is the dream of travel. The word sets one afire. You speak of Italy, and before my longing eyes there passes a vision of all I would like to see, all I would like to feel, touch and know.

But in the meantime, let's keep our desire secret—a secret that trembles like a little candle flame, yet never goes out.

You must take me for an owl perched in front of a writing desk (if owls write), forever lost in a kind of meditation that verges on sleepwalking or madness. I am mad about thinking and writing. What happens is that from time to time I fall into a well, so to speak, and grow weary of my indefatigable Why? How? Then I turn from an owl into a butterfly and fly off to Madame Sarlabous's house!

For you to understand our life, it would take a lot more than these few letters, which give you only a glimpse of the vast array of events, transformations and evolutions that make the man and woman, ready to take their place in the world, ready to look out for themselves, ready to live according to their own logic and to suffer.

But I shall write, *for I suffer because destiny has made our father almost a stranger, a distant and quite improbable being* . . .

Anaïs

February 13. I am forced to quote, and what is worse, quote myself. Do you remember: "I pray that at least one might wish to paint me, dress, face, spirit and all!" It was a dream, yet it was

[1] *Letter translated from the French.*

realized today. Mr. George Elmer Brown is to paint me in my Watteau costume. He made the engagement today when I went to see him, so that my mornings this week shall be devoted to Mrs. Becker and my afternoons to Mr. Brown, as long as he needs me, that is, until the painting is completed. It is to be exhibited within two weeks. Rejoice! Rejoice! And Hugo is coming tonight. Ah!

6:30. The hour is coming, coming. What will he say? Which of his moods shall I share tonight? He can be impenetrable, undemonstrative, matter-of-fact. He can be tender, full of revelations, fanciful, poetic . . .

7:10. I wait for the long-expected knock, and while waiting, dream of tomorrow. The thought of that painting fires me. I feel as if I were touching the hem of Art's garment, humble, adoring, although my share of the work is the lowliest. To be near artists, to see them every day, to talk and work with them—surely, I shall be initiated into the mysteries of their lives and its charms after a time. I revel in the idea, and am grateful for the privilege. I stand on the threshold of a new life, and whatever it brings to me I shall unfold in your pages. Could any work have been nearer to the things I love?

8:15. I fear he is not coming. Oh, to wait like this with your heart leaping at every footstep, every sound. Is it to be in vain?

February 17. It is done. I work now as others work; I go about the day's business with my mind set on what I am doing. All that once constituted my past life is now buried deep in my heart, locked, imprisoned, and is allowed to flow out only during the hour of rest. I have made a million discoveries. I have learned a thousand lessons. Phrases that once sounded unreal in my ears have now a deep meaning: "I am too busy." Or: "I am tired, too tired to read or write." What Mother, and Hugo, and all the others said to me while I wondered and wrote skeptically. It is all true, intensely true and real. Of course, you must not expect my descriptions to agree with my first conception of what this life would be. When I first wrote I was fired by my eternal idealism, and my ignorance. But now I speak of things I have *lived*. In a week, it is unbelievable what I have come to know of the world. I have learned that I must protect myself. The first thing Mr. Brown did was to try to kiss me, to make me dance with him. Mrs. Becker tried to pay me less than she owed me. Slowly my shyness is vanishing. I have a strong foothold upon the earth. My object is to make money for Mother. No more dreaming, no more wasting of time. I hold my head high, I look unwaveringly at people, I ignore my feelings, I refuse to be hurt by what I see and hear. The world is the world. I have long been sheltered from it, allowed to fashion it according to my pleasure. And now I have joined the tussle. I face facts, modifying my rosy ideas of this world and willing to accept.

Mother was at first unhappy to think of her "little girl running from studio to studio." She had dreamed of my passing from her hands and her care to the hands and watchfulness and protection of a husband, without the need of this that I am doing now. I answered her that there was only one man I would want to be "protected" by and that he did not want to do so. And besides, I want to work, I do not want others to work for me merely because they love me. I want to see the world too.

And now that I speak of Hugo, I want to write of him and let all other things sink into oblivion. He did come Sunday, and he read me from Browning's works. I told him about my work; we talked, but not as freely as we usually do. Something was preying on his mind. I could not tell whether it was the thought of my work for work's sake or for its *reputation*. A model! I know what most people think of the profession, but to me it means what all things mean: another place where I can be myself just as well as anywhere else. That is, I am always myself, whether in my own home, alone, or running from one studio to another. And Hugo trusts me implicitly. If he fears anything, it may be the opinion of his family, the Anglo-Saxon prejudices. He telephoned tonight. Our little talk has brightened my whole life, although I have had the joy of his presence throughout the week in the form of a short letter he gave me Sunday. It has been in my pocket ever since, and the very touch of it was like the touch of his hand. I hope he is proud of me, for it is only Mother's and Hugo's opinion that I value against that of the whole world.

February 24. My heart is full to overflowing. Last night I fell asleep in tears because I longed to write as I have never longed . . . and could not. My head would not work, my ideas were dulled, my fingers stiff. And now I am nineteen! No longer a writer and dreamer, oh, no, but a busy, thoughtful person who is continually storing away in the secret recesses of her being all her observations on a life of which she knew so little. It used to be that I took life in small doses, so to speak. One incident, one person, one change, sufficed me for months. I had time to meditate, and to take notes, to linger on the subject, to expand, to deepen, to amplify. I wrote copiously.

Now? Now it is an avalanche. Discoveries, disenchantments, joys, sorrows, doubts, hopes, follow one another, tumbling one over the other. Every hour is full. Impressions crowd in my mind. Thoughts swell, and feelings surge in such vast quantities that I am deeply startled. I gaze, wide-eyed, I listen, I speak little, and life passes me by, no longer a calm panorama unfolding, but a swirling, whirling river that bears me swiftly onward.

Nineteen! And to celebrate this day we had a dance. I shall never forget it. If I could write about it as much as I think about it during my long hours of posing. Work, work, work. I pose for Luis Mora, Miss Curtis, Mr. Tolman. During my days of dreaming I never imagined the possibilities of such an existence, such a world and such a life. Throughout it all, however, like some soft note vaguely heard through a loud, disturbing song, runs a silvery melody. And that is my love for Hugo. He is the only calm, glowing note in this half-barbaric chant I sing all day with the others, the song of work, struggle, of earnings, of weariness, a revolt. And at night, when the others die, it is he who remains by me, his song, his name, his face. For hours, sometimes, I dream of him until soothed and comforted.

If the gods were to ask me to make a wish today, I would beg them to grant me this: that things should not *hurt* me so. Everything hurts me, sorrow, and joy as well. I am always quivering and bleeding. In this manner my birthday was full of pain, and its joys moved me to tears. Those who came that evening were Renarto Zanelli, Carlos Zanelli, Germaine, two Besosa sisters, Mrs. Sarlabous, a painter, Cesar, de Oro, Costa, Alendad, Hugo and his brother John and two or three others. I have a strange recollection of much music, and laughter, and happy faces, as I had heard and seen them in a dream. The famous Zanelli of the Metropolitan sang. It was so beautiful that I felt myself tremble. Hugo was by my side, and I watched him— the artist, the poet, the boy, the man, all afire, at last, with face illumined, heart and soul revealed. How wonderful, how unutterably wonderful he is at such times. He was happy Tuesday night, happier than I because . . . Can I write why? I must, or you will never understand me in the future, for this sentiment is, I fear, to guide my life. I was happy only when Hugo complimented me—nothing the others said, although it was more flattering, seemed to touch me. I was happy only when dancing with him. I looked up at him when we danced because then our faces almost touched each other. Was ever any girl so foolish and so wicked? I am ashamed and frightened because I doubt whether he felt the same way. I thought of Amiel's words on the ways of men, who can absorb themselves into all manner of things besides their love, while woman was ever wholly wrapped up in it alone. The night was filled with Hugo's presence and none other. I talked little, and laughed less, but no one noticed it. If he moved away from me, my heart bled. If he moved toward me, my heart leaped. Most of all I feared talking to him lest he should read in my eyes and in my voice the grave tenderness overflowing in me, the longing which filled me with inexpressible sorrow. These feelings of mine are new to me. I scarcely understand them, yet I trust them because *he* arouses them, he has awakened them in me, and he is Hugo.

I am posing for painters who have studios in the region of Washington Square, and for others who isolate themselves in remote parts of the city. More often I find myself on West 57th St., or on 67th St., where the aristocratic studios are. I see my face on the magazine covers, in the newsstands. I went to exhibitions where I saw two paintings of me, and one won a prize. I pose in the Watteau costume, in the Egyptian one, in Spanish shawls. I look to the right, and to the left, and full face. I am turned and studied until there is not a gesture or an expression of mine which someone has not tried to catch. For the illustrators I have to act. I crouch on the floor in a torn shirt, riding trousers, and dusty boots, with my hair loose and wild, looking frightened and speechless for hours. I was supposed to have been thrown from my horse, and some dark Arab was about to snatch me away. But until he came I had some strenuous posing to do. I have posed for a sculptor, in flowing white robes. He measures me with sharp-pointed compasses, and says my proportions are good. The most difficult moment is when the rest comes. Then they turn on the phonograph and ask me to dance, which is only an excuse to hold me and try to kiss me. The faces of the painters change then. I hear cynical words, and see the faces transformed. The painters telephone to the club and ask for a type. Then I have to go to the address given me.

Today when I rang the bell a man opened the door with a palette in his hand. The hall was dark and the light of the studio was behind him. It outlined his silhouette, that of a small man

with shaggy red hair. He engaged me abruptly and closed the
door. In the vivid light of the studio I found he had green eyes
and thick lips. While he worked he chewed tobacco, swore and
sang coarse songs. He said he could tell I was a virgin. He had
sullen, mocking glances when he said this. His bed was right in
the studio, and unmade. The sheets looked soiled. I was so de-
pressed and miserable I never returned. I had a happy day posing
for Luis Mora, who painted me exactly as I looked the day I came
to see him, in my black velvet dress and blue hat. My enthusiasm
made me forget the hours, and I posed until my body trembled
with fatigue. On snowy days, when I pose for poor painters, I
suffer from cold. Their efforts to warm the room end in a place
full of smoke. I posed until I was blue with cold. One of them
could not afford to pay me, but I enjoyed the coffee he made, his
laughter, his love of his work. An hour after posing for Luis
Mora, who was a real artist, I was posing downtown for an artist
who drew subway advertisements, wearing satin slippers and
Kayser stockings. When he tried to touch me I slapped him, and
I had to leave without my money. Posing in a school for young
boys was sweet. They adored me, considered me a goddess, showed
me their work, gave me their photographs, asked me for mine.
They lined up at the door to take me home. I posed for Neysa
McMein, a young woman famed for her magazine covers.[1] Her
walls were covered with photographs of actors and actresses. She
had humorous blue eyes, and kept her wild hair wrapped in a red
handkerchief. She wore bedroom slippers and a blue blouse. She
worked surrounded with people and taking part in the conversation. I met many celebrities there—F.P.A.[2] and Heifetz. It was so
enjoyable, so bright and lively, that when I was finished posing
for her and she was about to pay me, I said to her: "It was so
wonderful, posing for you, I hate to take the money for it." "Oh,
they all say that," said Neysa McMein bluntly and ironically.
And I felt a flush of anger at the way she took my remark.

March 5. Days follow days, weeks follow weeks, and my experiences have reached such vast proportions that they rise like mountains and their peaks are lost among the clouds, unattainable,
awe-inspiring, unconquerable. No amount of writing can cover the
limitless space of my discoveries, my adventures and my reflec-

[1] *See the photograph of the* Saturday Evening Post *cover for July 8, 1922.*
[2] *Franklin Pierce Adams.*

tions thereof. So I can but choose a grain of sand from the beach and offer you a brief peep into the most crowded of lives and the most talkative of hearts.

I mixed my metaphors, a sign of deterioration among the literary regions of my spirit kingdom. No matter. All things seem mixed in my head. The time of calm and patient disentanglements has passed. Law and order in diaries are good when one has long days to find the proper place for each thing, and the proper language.

But today! Ah, today it is a question of being in possession of 60 precious minutes in which to write of 335 precious hours—or thereabouts. No matter for mirth, you can well understand. Rather too heavy a burden for so light-headed a person as I tonight. Happiness has the most disastrous effect on me; it does away with my habitual dignity and leads my pen into the paths of nonsense when I intended it to spread its flow of ink along serious channels. I wait disconsolately for a sober thought—and it has come.

I shall leave a large blank space where the story of my activities should be theatrically presented, as once was my custom. I am not interested in what is happening to me but in someone whose power over me is deepened by every meeting. Since my birthday I have seen Hugo once. We had an evening to ourselves last night and heard Wagner's Walkyries. Again I felt that whatever we *do* is of small importance, which is the true test of perfect understanding, for the joy that we find in talk and in each other's presence seems more than sufficient—whatever else is added to it only changes our means of expression. Wagner's superb composition, strong, fantastic, stirred fresh currents in our talk and set our emotions vibrating to new notes, just as Erskine's poetry did, or the sight of the sea at Long Beach, or our walks through the woods.

Afterward we returned home by some strange way, and were lost about Richmond Hill, and walked through the mud and mist and drizzling rain like two creatures in fairyland, perfectly contented, light of heart and finding beauty in the blurred lamplights, in the glistening streets, in the stillness, in everything. And what strange little things I notice. What foolish little things please and touch me. How he looks at me, what he says to me, how he does this and that. I wrote once that I watch his eyes continually for the soft gleam I worship and need. I find it in them oftener now. He loves me, yes, but I would like to know how much, and whether he loves me enough to want to have me by his side always. And a thousand other things—whether he dreams of me as I do of him, and thinks of me at all hours of the day as I think of him, and whether he writes as I write—and enough.

March 6. Immediately upon taking part in ordinary life I jumped to the unreasonable conclusion that I would equally participate in the ordinary mental lethargy which appears so invariably to be a result of it. I followed unquestionably the example set before me by the others: Frances, Eugene, Hugo, are too busy to write and therefore it should be the same with me—this is what I thought. Then it was more than I could bear, this silence, this crowding of thoughts without hope of setting them down some far-off day in the future. Ah, no. There were many drawbacks. A longing for dreamless and thoughtless relaxation stole upon me the first nights and silenced all others. Weariness of body hovered about my spirit like a shadow and tinged every effort I made with the sadness I strive so eagerly to conquer and which I know to be without cause. I was deeply discouraged by these signs. I doubted whether I would ever write again as I once wrote, and spoke of that far-off day with longings. Tonight I made my first effort, intent on turning my eyes inward and anxious to find words to describe what I saw. Assuredly my head is not as clear as on those bright mornings long ago when I could follow Amiel's Road unwaveringly for hours. It is dulled by one long day filled with sounds and scenes and incidents, and worn by hours of concentration, but then we can think of my thoughts as having wandered much before they paused at the little home for shelter— haggard, weary, dust-laden thoughts worthy of pity and of a little corner in these pages.

Gradually the effort I make to write will become tempered by habit. After all, it is not a matter of time but of gathering courage and setting your mind to work when it would more willingly be idle. Or at least, this is what I believe now; I may retract this statement upon closer investigation.

March 13. Alas, the courage, if it be courage, I need to write at night has failed me all this time; I am tired when the day is done, and too often distressed and perplexed and unwilling to probe the deep wells of sorrow I find in my heart. I am absorbed in my work in a way that surprises everyone. The thought of *necessity*, of Mother's troubled face, urges me onward, fires me to an ever increasing ambition. All my efforts are bent upon one fixed task.

I am awake to every opportunity and watch keenly and eagerly for possibilities. More than that: I do not wait for things to happen and to come my way; I seek them out, I spring upon them, I throw myself into the very dragon jaws of Chance.

I visit the painters who have bad reputations and whom the other models keep away from. I suggest new poses, invent pictures for them, participate in their work with all my own ideas, seek new costumes, persuade and win more and more work. I face the ugly sides of my work. I hate to pose for the catalogue illustrators. They work in offices, they rush, they smoke cigars while they draw, I get no rest in between, I wear kimonos and slips, and stockings and shoes, and dresses. It is all ugly and prosaic. One man pretended I had only posed three hours, paid me for three hours, and when I came out of the place, exhausted, I looked at a clock in the street and I had been working five hours. It was cold. I was shivering with fatigue.

But after work, as my reward, I have my Magician of Happiness. Not books, not walks, not writing, but Hugo. Hugo and Eugene came last night. We discussed all kinds of things, and so well. I walked to the station with them. Eugene was to walk back with me and leave by way of Richmond Hill. Walking, with Hugo's arm under mine, and his voice so near, I experienced strange feelings and was tempted to quote him some lines of Shelley: "I am as a spirit who has dwelt / within his heart of hearts, and I have felt / his feelings, and have thought his thoughts and known / the innermost converse of his soul, one / unheard but in the silence of his blood."

For that is what came to my mind as we walked. I was dwelling in his heart and "unlocking the golden melodies of his deep soul." How keenly I felt my isolation when we separated and I walked back with Eugene. Hugo gone, I felt deprived of the treasured glimpses into his warm heart, a spirit truly locked out from paradise. I missed his step in rhythm with mine, his voice, his laughter, yet I had Eugene, who loves poetry as well, and has great thoughts and fine feelings. So that after all, I like Hugo for his very own sake.

While I dream of him, however, a thousand things are happening. I am to pose for Charles Dana Gibson, which is considered an honor among models. I was told to go and see him because I was the type he likes to draw, the face of 1900. I was timid when I knocked at his door. But he soon put me at ease, saying: "By God, by God, you're swell to draw, by God, what a girl!" Luis Mora finished a marvelous painting of me in my black velvet dress. He says I look Spanish, but the old Spanish type, the one in paintings. I wonder why I am being painted and told at the same time always that I look like a painting. I have made two friends (in the light sense of the word).

Of the great change in my life I can hardly write. I long for the day I may spend describing it, for what I see and hear and do surpasses the wonders of fairy tales and novels. I have very little time to talk with the other models. We sit waiting in the parlor of the club when we have no engagements there for the week, but I have been so busy that I have only once sat there, to be called by the woman at the desk for James Montgomery Flagg. Over the telephone he had been very insistent about wanting shapely hands and ears and shoulders. When I went to see him he kept his feet up on his table, kept answering the telephone, and cursing in between because nobody had decent hands or ears, and asked me to show mine, and then made me pose right then and there.

While we wait, the girls talk about the painters. About studio parties. I go upstairs in the dressing room to powder myself and fix my hair. On the top floor there is a room full of costumes. I have sometimes waited there after dinner, because either Hugo or one of my new friends (Boris Hoppe, who is Russian, and Edward King, who is Irish) come to take me out. Once, to go out with Hugo to the opera, I had to rent a coat from the costume room, which is forbidden.

March 28. It is because I love Hugo that I grow restless and unhappy when I see him seldom, and am deprived of his magic presence by his other obligations. Last week, following his visit with Eugene, I felt such longings and loneliness as would appall the bravest heart. I went about my work strangely absorbed in memories of Hugo and vainly seeking peace from this imaginary companionship.

Friday came, and with it a masquerade dance to which Boris Hoppe was taking me. I had told Hugo by telephone during the week that I wished he might be there also as I had a costume he would like, but he answered regretfully that he could not—and my heart sank. You might laugh here, and say that I am more foolish every day, but I must write the truth, and this is it. Yet, if this be foolishness, Hugo is foolish too, for he passed by toward midnight just to see me, and I came upon him unexpectedly and read pleasure in his eyes. Afterward he told me that in my Egyptian costume I looked like the women in the Rubáiyát. Of the entire evening, Hugo's little visit was what I dreamed of later. Boris Hoppe, Edward King's admiration, other people's attentions, were all forgotten.

Then Saturday we met on the train. I had passed him by and he had quickly abandoned his seat to follow me. I felt him coming behind me, and looked back. Later we tried to explain what made me look back and pause suddenly. This little fact seemed important in our eyes. I do not know what Hugo thought, but I, in my heart of hearts, recognized love. The trip, of course, passed like one minute. Tired, oppressed by strange impressions, I found the sight of Hugo like a breath of heaven, and I wondered how it would seem to have him always near me at the end of the day. He was tired too. I could have kissed away the shadows under his eyes if he had let me.

And now you may ask why I should write all these things when there are so many things which might seem to be more interesting. I am happy writing of Hugo and I am happy thinking of him. The posing often brings me sadness. I have to struggle so often to refuse to pose naked. I cannot tell the painters why, for fear they should laugh at me.

March 27. The tender, unearthly magic of the Spring has crept into my heart. I hear the song of birds, I smell new odors, see new colorings, and the softness of the air melts me. And I feel. Oh, God, how deeply I feel, and grieve and rejoice. More than ever in my life before, more than all I felt during childhood, and that was a great deal, more than all I felt during girlhood, which I thought nothing could surpass; I stand on the threshold of the world itself, and a new life has taken hold of me.

All day I work, and all day I dream. The big studio windows are open now. I am posing for illustrations of a fairy tale. I wear the most poetic costumes, I lie on Persian shawls, I hold an opium pipe, I carry a bird on my forefinger as in the Persian prints. I read out of enormous books. I gaze at the stars. It is really a dream which I take seriously while I pose. I imagine myself in the story. The painters always tell me they find it easier to work with me, that my interest helps them. I return home with a heart so full that it speaks in whispers only to its own self—never to paper as it once did in its days of idleness and irresponsiveness. Also, I find I no longer need to come to you to do my thinking. I have learned to do it as I go along, learned to deprive myself of the luxury of pen and ink. Yet remember, though I write less, I feel more, more and each day more! And what I think would fill more books than I would have time to read.

That he loves me now I am certain. But how much, and why? He came last night with Eugene. Saturday afternoon we saw the play Liliom together. His eyes tell me things I long to hear him speak.

April 9. I have found this concerning sadness and joy: the first isolates you, and the second binds you to the entire world and makes you a sharer of its secrets. Sadness gives you a greater knowledge of soul, and joy a knowledge of what is tangible and real in life. The beauty of Spring stabs me. It is piercing, indescribable. My soul is one great harmony of magic sounds and scenes and scents. Skies, fresh woods, fields wrapped in mists, and everybody moving in a glamour of romance and fairy tale—these are but a few of the things I feel, and notice, and can name. All within me trembles in the hold of a mighty wind—its name is Love. But of this I cannot write.

April 11. Out of an infinite number of hours crowded with incidents and emotions, one dropped out, a quiet, sweet hour of repose and meditation which I somehow dared not capture in writing and yet refused to let slip by unnoticed, unsung. Knowing that I can write but badly at such a time, after such a day, what moves me to write, and yet to commit nothing short of a sacrilege? Gratitude—the very gratitude I feel for being granted this precious moment to look into my heart, and because I am so filled with it, I must write, as some creatures weep when they despair, or as we laugh when happy; to write is the same to me, the most natural of mediums. Never did a heart behave so strangely, I assure you. When I come to you I hear a thousand voices and one among them crying out: "Write about your work! Tell about your posing, of the knowledge of painting you are acquiring, of your widening views and growing understanding of people, of artists . . ."

"No, no," cries another voice, a deep, manly voice. "Write of me. Tell what you think of me, Edward King, your new friend. Count how often we have been out together, and what we have talked about. Tell about the way I fell in love with you. When I was sick, recovering from an illness I can't tell you about, I used to watch you walk by my house, on your way to the station. I fell in love with your walk. I used to sit on the porch every day waiting to see you pass. And by your walk I knew you. You don't know what my life has been until now. I was so surprised the other day that you trusted me enough to walk with me along that lonely country road. It makes me so angry to think that you are posing. Painters are no good. Tell about the time I took you riding along the speedway at night, how we heard screams from women, and I wanted to drive on, how you made me stop and get out of the car, how the two girls came running up to us and how you made me drive them all the way home when I was worn out."

"How can you be so fickle?" exclaims Eduardo's voice. "Write about my visit to you, of our talks and walks. Think of the night we took a walk with our own fancies, and exchanged dreams, and gently allowed our confidences to melt into one another. Tell of the concert we heard together, of what you read in my Journal."

Boris Hoppe's smiling face is thrust before me, and he speaks with a Russian accent: "Remember the long walk we took one Sunday, and I tried to embrace you. Remember the time we went to the theatre, and supped, and danced, and I made love to you all evening."

"Write of me," says Hugo quietly. He does not tell me what to write. Love transforms all we do together into exaltation.

Then comes another voice which says: "I am Spring. Fill your pages with the story of my magic. Speak of the budding branches, the golden wealth of forsythia, of all that grows and blossoms, of sweetly scented fields and whispering woods, and of the incessant song of birds which fills the air, of blue skies and flaming sunsets, of melodious April showers, and mystic twilights, and long moonlit evenings, and fleecy clouds. Write of all that is musical and tender in coloring and of a beauty surpassing dreams."

And I sit here and wonder, wonder, wonder and write nothing. Gradually the voices die down.

How strong Life is! How marvelous are People! How inadequate are words to describe it all! In spite of all I might do, they will not tell enough, they will not convey the smallest conception of this explosive torrent of experience by which I am swept to incalculable heights. Tamely, conventionally, I set down the outlines of things. A long time ago, I wrote better than I lived. Now I have learned to live—and have forgotten how to write.

April 12. I feel that in the midst of this bustling life I have lost the power of readjustment I once had. I remember so well at the end of each day I was able to give things their proper name, place, and meaning, and I cannot help comparing the orderly, calm, collected explanations and descriptions I wrote in the past with what I write now. It seems as if I can no longer *see* clearly. My vision of things is blurred and the result, to say the least, chaotic.

Yet something tells me that this effect of activity on my writing is only temporary, that what I am learning now is worth all sacrifices. Later on if I do write, it will be repaid by knowing that I am not merely setting down dreams and filling pages with my fancies, but recording ideals that have passed the supreme test. That is what I must think of when I look back regretfully to the days I once spent writing until I had no more to say. I still have thoughts. They are never affected by outward temperatures and evolutions. Changed slightly, yes, in that they have taken on a more speculative form instead of being constructive. But even though I have ceased to reach the heights of an imaginary wisdom, I feel that I come nearer Truth than I have ever before.

April 14. There are a thousand things in me which I do not understand and can never explain, but one of the strangest perhaps is the extraordinary change that has taken place in my sense of values. Just as the life of thought and introspection had made Amiel unfit for practical life, so had it dulled me in the appreciation of human relationships. In the past I filled my journal with abstract truths, theories, principles, concepts—with throbbing life, individual characters, the story and workings of human hearts, never! Now suddenly I find that what I attached most value to at the time has lost its power over me, and I am powerfully attracted toward the very things I passed over and scarcely ever noticed.

All this, of course, is a preliminary to a confession. I feel sometimes I ought to come to you with the story of what I am learning and discovering and thinking in terms of abstract and general, detached conclusions—in terms of ideas, I mean. And yet I no longer can do it. I have ceased to be the Outsider and Onlooker. I am *part* of what I wish to describe. I live! I live! I live! And one of the subjects dearest to my heart is a thing I do not pretend to analyze or explain. Take it as you will. I count it higher than all things and treasure its phases as much as the very mysteries of Souls or Religion I used to ponder on. For its sake I leave all else unwritten. Somehow I feel that it is worth my worship, my great interest, my absolute devotion to it. I am even proud of being swayed by it, and so held by it that all else should seem trivial in comparison. Indeed, I have often written that the day I should be called upon to act a part in Life I should be above all else thoroughly a Woman. And now I work, I write, but above all things I am woman and my heart and soul are lost in the wonders of love, for love is the thing I mean, of course. Hugo's love for me and mine for him.

In my writing it is clearly revealed because it is a reflection of my truest thoughts. At first I was ashamed to allow myself to write of what seemed always at the tip of my pen: Hugo. But now I let things run their course, and am contented now and then to mention "changes in my sense of values," etc., merely to satisfy my old standards of how a philosophical heart should behave itself. The last vestiges of stoicism have vanished. Next I shall write of Hugo without preliminary warnings, excuses or preparations (I give you a choice of terms).

I happened to reach this conclusion because I wasted the little time I had to write tonight in what you might call the introductory paragraph. And now just as I introduce you to the all-absorbing subject, I find it is time to bow myself out by order of the Queen of the Household!

April 15. I am not superstitious, and yet it seems to me that every time I prove untrue to my inclination for unsociability I am punished. Last night, moved by this all too vulnerable heart of mine, I exalted Hugo and depreciated what used to possess all my attention and devotion. I abandoned philosophy, introspection and analysis to lay my offering at the altar of love. I could scarcely refrain from raving of Spring, which would have proved, if nothing else had, the irretrievable heights of my madness, the extent of my perversity! I write lightly. I try to take it lightly, but I am truly hurt, and by Hugo. How sorely I am tempted to return to my shell, to my books and my philosophy (my stoicism, which I never had) and my independence. Have I lost the precious key? Am I condemned to wander forever in the world of men and women when my refuge is in ideas? I must retrace my steps. I have not the courage to go further knowing I shall meet but Pain. Sad thoughts I do not fear. But I cannot bear that my Ideal should act in a way so far beneath his station and by the most trivial act fall short of my expectations, my trust, my faith. Yet with Hugo I am more tolerant than with anyone because I love and respect his ideal, his expectations, his trust and his faith. But does he love and respect mine when he so often grieves me, when I never, never cause him pain? I am to see him tomorrow night. He may efface this sad impression, as he effaced all the others— by his utter proof of innocence, his complete ignorance of how his actions trouble and perplex me, which I read in his frank, clear, confident eyes. Surely I must be acting under the spell of a strange enchantment to be so angelically forgiving and forgetful when he is there, though I might have wasted vast quantities of paper and no end of indignation in a fit of passion only two minutes before his coming.

Later. I am resolved to develop a sense of humor at all cost. And I could not have chosen a better profession than that of modeling. I am eternally on the choicest seat of observation, watching the most extraordinary performances. At times I catch myself writing parodies. Artists' lives lend themselves to as many forms of description as there are artists themselves. You may be dramatic, intense, tragic, as is my custom. You may be slightly mocking, optimistic, bohemian, light and frolicsome, as is my ambition. But whatever you choose to be, you cannot help being dominated by Enthusiasm. I love my work. I love artists and their ways. I love the studio life, the studio pathos and the studio humor. I love the ridiculous and the admirable. When you sum up the great and the small, the noble and the ignoble, the sublime and the seamy, you have Life. Add more than an ordinary share of beauty, add genius, and talent, and the charm of the unexpected, and you have the Artist's Life. It has everything of the ordinary life doubled in intensity and size. And it has Soul. I mean that while you move among them you feel the presence of spirit, spirit expressed by genius or distorted by the unskillful, distorted but recognizable. Spirit expressed sometimes in ambitious phrases, pathetically powerless aspirations, or more often fully revealed in successful creation. Whoever has the last spark of understanding can but glory in the watching of these things and is bound to feel every one of them in sympathy with the artists who experience them.

It is no wonder that at the end of each day I should be filled with wonder and gratitude. Notice that I wrote of failure as well as success, that I mentioned the real artist with the bad artist. This, because I have come to believe that all things teach and help us, whether great or small, noble or ignoble. In the beginning

I rebelled against the life that brought me such sad revelations and keen pangs of regret. I trembled to see my conception of the world so blurred and unreal beside the clear mirror held before my eyes in which Reality reflected itself. I trembled for my faith, and looked back to the days of utter ignorance. Yet I was thirsty for wisdom and thirsty for truth. Gradually I learned to readjust my doubts, fears and desires to the course of experience and recognized the blunder I was making by standing in its way with my foolish prejudices, weak dreams, and unreasonable expectations. And I no longer railed, and struggled, but watched, listened and grew to love and value what I once feared, and learned to long for what I once despised. I can speak now of life as painters speak of their pictures. Lights and shadows, both intermingled, neither one able to express anything by itself and alone. Beauty and ugliness, joy and grief, perfection, imperfection; speak of them as lights and shadows. Picture the world without them—weak, monotonous, uninteresting. No deepenings, no mysteries, no contrasts, no changes. Our souls would know no desires, no ambitions, no ecstasies, no progress and, therefore, no life.

When I look over the many notes I took since I began to work, I am tempted to throw away those I made at the beginning. I realize now that I understood extremely little at first, only half perhaps of what I saw and heard, even this I looked at through the eyes of others—what people had said of artists, of studios and of models—not what *I* thought. Now all this has changed. I dare do my own thinking and interpret all things in my own way, and as far as I can see, my understanding has reached unbelievable dimensions and I find meaning in everything. The doubt that it may not be the right meaning does not trouble me. I think of Emerson. When my faith in myself shows symptoms of deterioration, I close my eyes tightly and repeat solemnly two or three times: "Self-trust is the essence of heroism. Self-trust is the essence of heroism." And the charm works, except when the lurking suspicion comes into my mind on the question whether Emerson was amusing himself when he wrote this, knowing and meaning to say that it really takes a *heroic* mind to believe in itself! At this the tide of humor invariably wells inside me. And surely the efforts which always follow the heroic effort only increase it. On the whole, the question of self-reliance and self-depreciation cannot be treated solemnly. One is too much in danger of acting the fool in both parts. I wish all life's problems could appear to me in such an undignified light. How simplified existence would be without the alarming and appalling procession of unsolvable, unfathomable problems that pass year in and year out before the most timid minds—minds which afterward are responsible for the writing of such books as *Main Street*. But all this has nothing to do with the story.

Again I appeal to Emerson. He said a great soul had nothing to do with consistency. I like to be certain of my grounds before I give you a proof of my inconsistency. (Had Emerson said the contrary, I should have been obliged to look up another quotation—this is a perfect example of self-reliance!)

All this by way of preparation for a confession. Though I praised shadows, I will let them fall on these pages as seldom as possible. What is more, I will voluntarily ignore them. I cannot bring myself to write in accusation or condemnation of anyone or anything. It is enough that I should have seen envy, pettiness and prejudices; to write of them, to libel creatures guilty of them, I leave to those who seem to glory in belittling humanity and presenting it in its most bitter phases. Whatever anger or disappointment I might have felt after the first shocks which unveiled my eyes to sin and misery, I directed toward I know not what—a power beyond human understanding or human reasoning—and never allowed it to alter my faith in the Divine idea smoldering in every human being. I will not write of my very first days of work. At that time my impressions were far too vague and childish. And besides, I was all pride at that time, proud of being able to work for Mother, proud of the strange, nay, incredible, discoveries I was making about myself. It was only after I grew used to hearing the artists rave about me that I gathered enough self-possession to look around, figuratively speaking.

And I have done nothing else since then. The studio atmosphere became familiar to me. The sight of books, statues, pictures and draperies, paint brushes, easels and palettes at first excited my curiosity and then became almost commonplace. I learned an infinite number of things relating to the metier, the way to criticize a picture, the language to use and what not to say (which is more important because that is just what everyone is bound to say), all the peculiar expressions used by the painters among themselves. Exhibitions became a momentous factor in my life. Also at the beginning I believed literally what painters said about one another, and now I have learned to reverse it in order to know the truth. The wonder and charm of it all is that each day is different from the other. Not one studio is really like another, and the posing is characteristic of each painter's way of working. Now I understand their moods, their whims, their likes and dislikes. The qualities I had to cultivate most arduously were patience and facing facts, because I had understanding and sympathy and enthusiasm already.

Gradually I realized all the poetry there was in my work, and the knowledge it would give me. I learned to distinguish the artist from the man and learned to please both. The artist wants beauty, inspiration, material to work with. The man wants interest and understanding and *feeling*.

Poetry I find in everything—in the immense windows showering light on you all day and through which I can often watch the clouds; in the work itself; in the beauty that is to interpret an idea, an idea I can watch glowing in the eyes of the artist; poetry, too, in the characters that are revealed to me during the long hours of united efforts, in the surroundings, in the sense of coloring and composition one gradually acquires by constant contact and hearsay; poetry, above all, in watching the artist at work, in seeing vague splashes of color assume lovely shapes, in the wonder of the mind giving its visions color and form and immortality.

It is no wonder then that with all these things I should think so much and long to write. Their wonder is too great for utter silence. I can tell no one. I simply say, "I love my work." Why I love it and how much, I keep a secret here. Not one girl I know seems to see what I see in it. No one seems thrilled by it. No one turns over thoughts to ask if they are right or wrong. No one mentions the poetry of knowledge in connection with it, so I have concluded that it is the very life of introspection that has so transfigured the world for me, so that I find the secret doors to deeper meanings everywhere I go—I, who feared it would make me unfit for ordinary life!

April 17. Once more all narratives are abandoned before the supreme subject; I cannot write of artists and of work when my mind is full of Hugo, and my heart bleeding.

And the trial goes on. I no longer know my own feelings. Hugo's conduct maddens me. It is strange that at this period Edward King should have become my friend. Can it be possible that the Fates should want my eyes opened to the folly of my choice, the folly of my heart's desire? Who shall say?

Edward King is an extraordinary young boy who has suffered

much in health, and consequently his mind is old. His face is serious, rarely illumined by a smile or laughter, but out of his eyes shine goodness and frankness and understanding. He is moody and sometimes brusque and mystifying, but I have learned to understand him well and we have passed many happy hours together, although he talks but little and most of his character has been revealed to me by little actions, glances and only a few confidences. It is his generosity, his thoughtfulness, his constant wish for my company, that have touched me so. He sends me flowers and candy and takes me out continually and comes to see me and demonstrates in every possible way his appreciation and his interest.

By contrast, Hugo's conduct is inexplicable—Hugo in whose love I try to believe. His comparative indifference startles and grieves me. I see him once a week—three hours! Even Mother, who is Reason itself, shakes her head and disapproves.

Oh, that the love I had valued so highly should fail me! That Hugo, my Hugo, should prove unworthy. Mother says that I am too young to know my own mind and know nothing of men—and adds that I must wait, wait, wait. And as if to prove her words, Edward King's ways return to my memory and I ask myself desolately: "Is it possible, is it possible my heart could have been mistaken? Can I no longer trust myself to see Hugo and love and other men as they really are, but always through the eyes of dreams and of my eternal idealism?"

Oh, it could not be. Hugo's face haunts me now as I write. I wrong him, I wrong him by all these accusations. If I could be certain of his heart . . . and his love!

To Eduardo:

I promise you that if you write often, I won't become spoiled and pout when you pause for breath—and inspiration . . . I find my Journal blossoming and flourishing once more. . . .

April 18. A strange thing happens to me in regard to Hugo and reasoning. I try to analyze my feelings and seek to reason myself out of what I sometimes term my "folly," but when I believe myself prepared to write coolly and deliberately, Hugo's face need only appear before me with one of his characteristic appealing expressions and I am swept away by a wave of tenderness and unable to write a line.

April 23. Hugo's family show by every possible means that they dislike me. Frigid English hearts. What have I done to deserve their taking part in my life? What has placed my Love among them so that if I should win him, I must suffer the very sorrows I most feared—that of being transplanted like a wild flower from a sunny garden in a warm and tender climate to some arid, frozen waste of gloom and neglect? Oh, if his love is not strong enough to protect me, if his heart is not opened to me for refuge and strength—I shall die.

April 24. Tonight I remembered Amiel's words: "Is happiness anything more than conventional fiction?" There is no happiness in the world, no peace and no justice—this is what I am forced to believe. Yet I might forgive all, and this restlessness that is eating my heart would cease, if only my one best-loved Ideal of Love had proved possible.

Like all others, it has failed me. Love, for which I waited so long, Love, which filled my girlhood with thrilling visions, Love, around which my unknowing heart had woven the most perfect tales—all enchantment, exaltations, magic hours—oh, it does not exist in the world! There is a flaw in everything, a worm in every fruit.

I wanted romance, I wanted to be lifted above earth for one precious hour—no more. I wanted happiness and it mocks me. I wanted to taste the pleasures of life, and these are denied me.

And I suffer because I am powerless to do more than I am doing now. I work, savagely almost, with desire burning within me. The shattering of my Love Dream has given birth to a new ambition. I shall, from now on, cease to pursue all my childish fancies, and bend all my energies, heart and soul, upon this one purpose: Work for my mother and brothers, that they might have all that can give them happiness. I shall no longer think of myself. Life holds nothing for me but sorrow.

And Love? Ah, I shall learn to do without it!

May 7. Before writing, I read these last pages and was roused to a keen sense of shame. They have but one explanation, and that is that they prove how from time to time the strength of my trials exceeds the limit of my endurance and my share of courage—a thing for which there is no excuse because courage and power should increase with the size of all that is to be conquered and should be at all times ready to meet and master it. But I am not so much ashamed of my loss of courage as of the futility and foolishness of my bitterness, for it was all born of a trick of my own fancy—born of that strange element in me which is continually distorting my view of the world. I see as if through a multicolored lens—through moods and false doubts and perverse imaginings. At times my thoughts become petty and critical, like those of a sick child. Fortunately, a mere breeze can carry me to the very hilltop of existence, where the air is clean and the sun pure and dazzling, so that my heart is instantly healed and I can trust it once more and listen to its daily songs of life and hope.

Days ago I wrote moved by an indescribable sense of injustice only half-spoken in those few words. What I truly thought and could not bring myself to write was like a great fire burning within me and consuming me. I suddenly saw the world black, black with misery and cruelty. Then my Healer came and swept me off my feet, bore me to the very heights and showered upon me countless hours of enchantment and exaltation—all flawless and noble and beautiful. My Healer! If I thought I loved Hugo before, then I can only say I did not know how to love because what I feel now surpasses all, and it is a thing so deep, so piercing and so mysterious that I am wrapped in it, heart and soul, lost in the wonder of it.

Since I last wrote here I have seen Hugo only three times, and each evening we spent together seemed to me more perfect than the other. To be certain of his love is all I ask, and during those hours he showered proofs of love upon me. It glowed in his face, it gave warmth to his voice and an indefinable magic to every word he uttered. I felt truly as if I had "unlocked the golden melodies of his deep soul."

And meanwhile the life of work and *wants* and misery and injustice drifts on without hurting me because I hold in my hands its most precious gift, its one divine gift to man—Love. And can one ask more? Oh, let me be deprived of all things, of all other pleasures and smaller blessings, but give me love, give me love to its fullest measure!

May 18. I no longer know what to believe of Hugo. I have never been so shaken and pained and tormented by anyone as I am by him. Time after time I have forgiven him the one thing I find to blame because I love him. Oh, I should *hate* him for playing with my faith so, a faith that is born of love. I love him and he hurts me, he whom I thought good and tender! And my patience is exhausted. He shall know now that I am not all sweetness, that there is fire and anger, pride and rebellion in me and that he has fanned them to white heat by his conduct. If I could only believe a little longer. My love for him is so great that if he came to me soon I might still forgive him.

May 30. Following my exclamation of despair when I wrote that I might still forgive Hugo if he came soon, I sat one evening on the porch with Mother, brooding disconsolately. Hugo telephoned and came, having found time, by the merest chance, and completely oblivious to my state of mind. One glance at his face revealed this to me and almost disarmed me. I struggled with myself—at war with my habitual softness and my determination to be loyal and truthful at any sacrifice. In order to do this I had to cause Hugo pain, and it was at this I hesitated. Then a strange impulse came to me and I told him everything.

We both suffered, and struggled to express ourselves, and to understand each other, yet throughout it all we felt we were adding a stronger link to that chain that binds us so closely. His hands tightened around mine and mine clung to his, as if we wished to help each other sustain what we were forced to inflict upon each other. Hugo explained, and I understood long before we separated, but our hearts, once unlocked, continued to pour out what had been held back so long. We had walked to a spot on the outskirts of the woods and sat there for hours. Hugo spoke of his sorrows, his dreams, his desires, and I listened, moved beyond words, trembling—all littleness again, all fire, and deep, piercing vibrations. And the calm, soft night all about us helped to heal our tormented hearts. We returned, laughing a little—not too much because we had been so close to grief. Hugo had not only understood and been surprised, but he was incredibly penitent. "I feel as if I had been trampling on a flower," he told me. And then: "You are so sweet, Anaïs, how could I be such a . . ."

"Hush," I said quickly. "You did not *know*." I cannot bear to hear him belittle himself.

Ever since that strange night, Hugo has been marvelously good to me. We have arranged to meet on the train whenever possible; he has telephoned; he pleaded until I agreed to go with him today to Forest Hills, where I watched him win a tennis match; and he is coming tomorrow! And that is all I asked—the attitude I sought to win from him. Happiness, frail and winged, has smiled upon me. I doubted its existence, nay, I denied it.

One thing troubles me greatly, and that is Edward King's love for me, which I have watched slowly unfold and shine in his eyes. I have learned to like him a great, great deal for his marvelous character. He is so devoted and thoughtful; he has given me so many happy hours in his own characteristic way, utterly unselfish and good and high-minded. He has ideals too, dreams of a Christian home, of a clean, fresh life in the country—things which he has told me quietly during the long walks and long rides we have taken together. All the deep and quiet feelings of friendship I have in me go out to Edward King. But my love goes out to Hugo, fully and unhesitatingly. I wish I had more to give, I wish I had the power to distribute happiness to those that deserve it and love to all who need it. There is nothing that moves me so much as a longing or a need in others. To hear someone in want is, of all things, what gives me the keenest pangs of pain. I want to give, sacrifice myself, immolate myself, tear my heart into a thousand pieces, if it could fulfill someone's dream and answer to his needs. And saddest of all is the need of love. There is so much in me that I could give away to all who need or want it, yet strange and mysterious laws force us to restrain it and give it other names. And probably the day I shall tell Edward King: "Here is my friendship instead of the love I cannot give you," he will say: "That is like giving a loaf of bread to a man who is dying of thirst."

Did not Enric and Marcus and other boys express the same thing? I can love that way so well, with a love made of intangible things—ideas, dreams . . . I cannot tell just what. A love that makes it possible to share things, the devotion to books, or nature, for instance, that helps you to bear sorrows and to rejoice—simply an exchange of knowledge, an unselfish union of qualities and minds. There is so much pleasure in these things, and yet it can never be had without the human element, which instantly *demands* possession, security, the assurance that this love must be imprisoned, and selfishly hidden from all other eyes. Well and good. Liking a million other people will not diminish my love for Hugo—and liking none, as long as they do not let me do it in my own way, will give me time to love Hugo better, perhaps. As if such a thing were possible.

June 16. The young girl whose heart has been reflected here has ceased to be. She has passed from the state of conceiving to that of fulfillment, from wondering to that of deciding, from aspiring to that of choosing and making terms with life. All that has been was in preparation for the dawn of young womanhood to come— all that is to be, the story of its existence and consummation. Hands that knew only how to shape desires and aspirations, which were ever stretched to receive, now hold a man's happiness, are responsible for the molding of his destiny, and are stretched to *give;* to hold life's most precious gift; to comfort and sustain, and lift and to *steer*. This is no longer *My Diary!*

Journal d'une Fiancée[1]

June. Woodstock. I can still see him sitting by my side on the sand. I can still hear the waves breaking at our feet and feel night's soft enchantment all about us. We had been talking, both strangely moved by feelings far tenser and deeper than we had ever experienced together. A force—invisible, irresistible, divine— drew us nearer, nearer, until our lips met, and promises, longings, hopes, all leaped from within us and were mingled.

What a love ours, oh, God, when it gave him the courage to hurt me in the midst of our first moment of tender ecstasy, and I the strength to bear his words.

That night he told me he loved me, but not with the love he deemed worthy of me; part of him was not yet ready for the high pitch of devotion he intended to give me, and he begged me to wait. He was tired, so tired, and all things were quiet in him, subdued by a lifelong restraint and holding-back.

For one fleeting second the soul of the woman, expectant, soft and weak and tender, winced; then made a supreme effort and joined itself to the other—the soul that *comprehends* and grasps all, reaching out toward the ideal at whatever cost, the soul capable of visualizing aspirations and sacrifice all for the fulfillment of them. From that moment, our love became essentially *intelligent*. All disappointment and hurt fell from me, unworthy, put to shame by Hugo's brave appeal to my own worship of the ideal, by his trust in me as a woman of understanding. My own expectations were stirred. Deep within my own self I knew that I was not ready yet. I knew that, although my heart was satisfied because its one desire was love, its only need love and, being truly woman, I let the desires and needs of my heart dominate my life, later my mind would regain its influence and recognize we had

[1] Journal of a Fiancée, *the title A.N. gave to this volume of her Diary, June 1922 to January 1923.*

not touched the heights Hugo's far-reaching idealism had conceived. Yes, I knew, but only vaguely, and at the time was certain only that I trusted him, so that when he asked me if he had a right to ask me to wait thus for him, I was silent and looked up simply into his eyes that he might read in mine of the great love he had kindled in me.

I did not sleep all night, and, as I afterward discovered, neither did Hugo. We were deeply startled and shaken. I spent the time *marveling* and seeking a "point d'appui"[1] for these thousand new emotions that had been aroused, those new dreams suddenly unfolded before my eyes, for the great confusion in me, and the fears and the trembling hopes. At times I was flooded in a divine peace, floating in worlds of soothing and harmonious feelings. The certainty that I loved and was loved brought me hours of the most perfect happiness I have ever known. But at others an oppressing shadow lay over me and I was haunted by things unexplained, by the dread of losing him, by a vague uneasiness, a hunger for I knew not what.

The hurt hovered very close to my happiness. I burned at the remembrance of his kisses and trembled and shivered at the thought of his dissatisfaction.

This and more I felt, and dreamed, and thought through the night, and dawn found me transformed by the Great Adventure, a young girl no longer—a woman and his betrothed.

I remember coming home dazed, white-faced and with eyes shining as they had never shone. I remember hearing Mother question me as if in a dream: "It is done," I said. "We have kissed . . . we love each other."

And in order to make her happy I told her what Hugo thought of me and dwelt on the stories he had told me concerning the very beginning of his interest in me; how he wrote in his journal of *thrilling* when he saw me on the porch (a year ago in June) and called me the "lovely one" then, and was learning to love me long before I ever knew or imagined. Like a girl still, I laughed to think of my anguish and doubts and blunders, laughed for not having read his soul sooner. But how was I to know? I was a child then, and so was he, and I was timid, as he was, and unknowing because he was unknowing.

At the end of my story Mother bade me sleep with a true mother's unfailing thoughtfulness.

[1] *Base.*

"Let me just ask you one thing," I pleaded.

"Well?"

"What date is this?"

"The 8th of June."

This I heard and treasured.

All of this passed, and since then much has changed, things invisible, intangible and subtle, of course, on which our love is chiefly based, and of a kind most difficult to write or speak of. Hugo and I have been much together; we have talked and felt our way with words and striven to explain and to make all things clear, as much as it is in the power of human creatures to tell another of those formless dreams and visions haunting them.

My own tenderness kindled such response in him as often surprised and startled me. I discovered deep wells of hidden sentiments, and felt the fire and intensity of his nature. He found joy in conquering and holding, and I in yielding and giving. Love's power of *completeness* appeared then to me in all its radiance and perfection.

Content in the realization that he was wrapped in love as much as I myself and feeling myself moving in the glamour of a tenderness for which I had long hungered, I turned all my thoughts to one purpose: to understand his moods so that mine should never oppose and hurt them. I feel certain now that I have tuned myself to the nature of these moods and can at least cease to wrong him by a misconception of them. We did this together, and I told him of the things he did which shocked and hurt me, and he with his limitless understanding met my explanations halfway and promised to work with me.

Of our hours together he writes me: "I have been thinking of these last few perfect evenings down in Kew when we seemed, my dear one, to flow together sometimes, senses and minds joined in perfect union."

In spite of this, however, there came the day when I was moved by a strange and powerful impulse to accept coming to Woodstock to pose. My choice was unwaveringly made. Something told me I should do it for him. And he, without a word of mine, *knew*.

Saturday, after many hurried preparations, accompanied by Mother and Eduardo, who had come from school before going to Cuba, sustained and spurred by the warm and glowing memory of my last evening with Hugo, I boarded the train and was off, as Hugo says "upon the road of my great adventure, as seemly an adventure as ever fair ladye dared for true love's sake."

July 1. On the train, speeding onward to Woodstock, I was fired by the adventurous spirit of the conquest, lover and explorer. My imagination gave vivid shapes to all that might happen, and to all that was bound to happen as a result of the change in environment and condition, and to the break I had made in the systematic, regular course of my life by my own free will. The sense of what I was moving to and approaching was stronger than of what I was leaving behind me, although I did not escape entirely those moments of softened musing and recollection, of clinging to the old, which is so strongly imbedded in me, as you know.

I jotted down some impressions roughly, called things by their names as I passed them because I loved them.

On one side water, the long, blue rippled river. On the other, trees, vegetation, fresh green things and scattered houses. Long stretches of beach with little waves lapping the sand gently in the sunshine, and across the water, an endless line of hills with red roofs showing now and then through the thick clusters of trees. Green hills against a pale-blue sky and seeming to rise above the blue water, passing in endless processions. A boat sailing by, cool and white and shining in the sun, disturbing the water and sending angry little waves to break on the shore. Purple, yellow and white flowers cling to rocks by the shore, are swayed gently by the breeze and reflected in the river.

When we turned away from the river I was too lost in wonder at the sight of the mountains to continue jotting. I was struck by the grave harmony of their long, sweeping lines rolling into one another and unfolding against the sky. The quiet, soothing charm of so much greenness and freshness enveloped me. My fancy lost itself in the mere enjoyment of things and fell into a state of luxurious idleness. I have never ceased to feel, since I have been here, that I am absorbing intensely instead of giving out, absorbing color and sound and scent and sensation. I have been drinking beauty and quaintness in long draughts and feeling that glow and thrill of life penetrating me through every sense, touching heart and imagination without arousing any visible reaction in my intellect. Of course, I know this will not last. Even now, a thought will come from time to time, but it will be a simple one, in tune with the simplicity of the life of those around me, and the microscopic size of their problems and situations. When the habit of philosophizing has taken hold of one, it will be satisfied with any subject—from infinity, time and space to the lowliest animal on a farm. At times I found my interest arrested by discussions on the ways of chickens, and the habits of a certain cow, and began wondering and moralizing, then caught myself in time and mocked myself out of that mania for dissecting all things in order to find the why and the how, the cause and effect of them all, great or small.

Who was it said that Youth is an experimental stage? I might add also that it is also the time when most mental energy is wasted in unnecessary questioning and pondering, and is an essentially uncomfortable state besides, generally speaking, when one considers the superfluity of such questions as Why? and How?

Once in Woodstock, alone in my little room, a great flood of determination swept over me, together with a *sense of power* such as I have never known.

Now is the time to test yourself, I exclaimed inwardly. Now is the time to set all your forces at play and to *act*. Knowledge of practical life, art, of planning and wise carrying-out, strength of moral character, self-possession and independence—all this is to pass through the crucial test, all this and more.

Alone, suddenly deprived of Mother's guidance and sane counsels, thrown upon my own resources, here my real self must appear and assert itself.

It did, and making its acquaintance thoroughly amused me and gave me a sense of security and ease. I am in safe hands while I trust to myself. I mean this new individual now ruling me, a firm, resolute, grave, almost sensible creature exulting in her solitude, and in the belief that she can handle life and not be handled by it—in plain language, a creature become almost troublesome with her overflowing sense of power and the longing to use it, whose fingers ache to create, whose spirit yearns to reach and move upward and onward, whose constant outcry is: I *can* and I *will!*

Heavens, how revolutionary my description of her sounds! She might be a virago, a monster, by the way I use such words as strength, power, will, desire. They are the words that move mountains, but when they stir in the heart of woman and kindle such fiery energies, well, then, she *might* make—shall I say it?— a good wife, perhaps!

What an intense happiness I have found in this life I am leading here! I rise in early morning, don my bathing suit and run barefooted over the dewy grass, across fields and a stretch of dense woods, to the pool. The glory of dawn is still in the air, and so is the thrill of youth eternal, and the glow and tingle of new life, and they are all revealed to you in their dazzling brightness at such an hour and in such a place.

After swimming in the pool, I run back as if with winged feet, feeling strong, buoyant, clean. I walk to breakfast and I walk to work and from work, drinking in all the beauty of rural life. The quiet green pastures, the farmers at work in the fields, brown, tawny, sun-beaten and windburned men, the bleat of a sheep, a crowing cock, the ruffled cackling hen, the lazy cow ruminating and glancing up as you pass, fields dense with berries, branches charged with singing birds, all these were things to make the heart rejoice, and their simplicity touched responsive chords in me.

And then the mountains, ever new to me in the light of their transformations, gray and shadowed, or half-veiled in mists, bright and green in the full midday sun, purple, massive, vague at dusk . . .

Freedom unbounded, indescribable, is felt to the point of ecstasy here. Freedom from conventions, from walls, from drudgery, because labor is sweet when done beneath the sky.

One becomes, in Stevenson's words, "reconciled to life," nay, even attached to it, when seeing it made up of such as these to balance the others.

The radiance of these pages shall be my torch henceforward, to enlighten me through darker passages and through sorrows.

It is at night that my greatness drops from me like borrowed wings. I become all littleness and tenderness once more, and it is in truth a mere slip of a girl who steals softly into her bed, one wrapped in loneliness and in need of those she loves. I cling to memories for comfort, and my fancy brings Hugo close to me. Wave upon wave of love and yearning ebb from me and surround him, so that it is a mystery to me he should not feel them, even being so far from me in reality.

This is yet bearable, for it is but womanliness and a thing within control, but what I can truly compare to what Hugo calls "the evil that walketh by day and the terror that flyeth by night" (from which he would like to protect me) is the persecution from

Man, my only evil and terror upon this earth, men and their unwelcome attentions and admirations, their peering, prying, inquisitive eyes. I can no longer go to the pool. I was in a real danger the other day when one painter, Gerald Leake, took me in his automobile to an exhibit and then pretended the car had broken down and we should sleep in the grass all night. I walked home, for eight miles. He did not believe I would do it. In the studio I have to be on my guard every moment. I have to struggle to assert my independence, to demonstrate forcibly and yet gently that I am not at all flattered—quite the contrary! Finally I have won a certain degree of freedom, but at the cost of my work. The painters have talked among themselves; they have laughed at the predicament of Gerald Leake, who made me come here thinking I would be always with him—in fact, live with him—and for whom, the second day, I would no longer pose. So where I go I am received with ironic glances and given less work. But I do not care. I am unapproachable and unsociable toward those who would steal from me the few and precious hours I have to dream or walk, for reading or writing. I like to talk with painters, with Mr. Chase and Mr. Emerich, the stranger, and Dean Cornwell, and with Mrs. Snider, in whose house I live.

Hugo has written me a letter fulfilling my highest expectations, all beauty and tenderness and wisdom. I answered it as best as I could, but felt somehow that my pen was powerless in the hold of my love's glowing guidance and caught but rays from the light that burns so strong and clear in me. Things such as these are but echoes of things intensely felt.

To Hugo:

A vast, undefinable awakening has taken possession of me, beloved, the approach of an infinite knowledge coming to me, knowledge of you, and of love. . . .

I have had moments of sacred exaltations which have lifted my mind into regions of pure divination during which I have felt and feel the presence of that strange disquietude I believe to be yours. . . . It is the *passion* for *perfection* that is moving us both so strongly.

Meanwhile, you can do no more than write me as you have done, dearest one, for your tenderness and your thought of me are my greatest joy and sustain me when the feeling of being alone steals upon me. . . .

This separation will give us time to comprehend and to grasp our love's inspiring mysteries, its possibilities, its power, its purpose.

And then, speaking of what I have here, I tell him that he is the one who needs these things and that I would be much happier if he had them. An unsatisfactory letter as a whole, and yet I pray it may not seem so to him.

Were I to give way to feeling without thought, I would write like this: "Dearest, I want you here by my side, with your arm about me and your cheek against mine. And all the beauty around me here I would fain exchange for one moment with you pressing me close to your heart . . ."

July 3. I made Mother come here for three days that she might rest and find recreation in change and novelty. But for one evening we have been extremely happy together, walking, swimming, chattering and teasing each other. In that one serious talk we had, it was inevitable that we should touch upon the question of the future. Having woven my usual fairy tale about it, careless of the possible and the reasonable, I was appalled by Mother's presentation of it, and the tragedy of her life was revealed to me all at once in a way I had never grasped before.

She sacrificed all as a young woman to follow the man she loved—and he proved unworthy. Then she turned to her children and spent all of herself on them, labored and slaved as no mother has ever done, showering all the gifts in her power to give, immolating herself and finding in them her one and only compensation, her only source of courage and perhaps the one and only reason of her reconcilement to life.

And now? Now that she is no longer young, and is tired, now these children, one by one, must leave her, for such are the laws of nature. And it is against these laws that Mother rebels most bitterly. I tell her she shall never be alone and that we will never be entirely separated. But she wishes more than a promise of nearness. She will have us all in the same house; she will have me directly under her watch and care and guidance. And at this, in spite of my great love for Mother and although it would be my life's greatest sorrow to feel that by my own fault her life's best-loved dream (and she has so few) should not be realized, in spite of all this, I say, something much stronger in me moves me to maintain an attitude which seems unbelievably cruel and selfish, but I cannot, I cannot adapt my ideals to her plan; my whole being revolts in the very effort. A desire almost beyond my will, vast and burning and absolute—a desire which is a purpose, rules in me: that of wanting to shape my own life, with Hugo, and to have our own house, however small and poor, and humble, to be alone, the two of us, and to be near, but not with, those we love.

A divine law compels woman to leave all behind her at the time of her marriage. A more divine law binds me to die rather than to be a cause of grief to Mother. Oh, time will solve our problem and bring her compensation. I wait most anxiously and watch and pray. Is it my fault? Am I not ground and pressed in the turning of a wheel far beyond my control? Is it not the inevitable change and evolution simply working out their eternal round of destruction and separation and estrangement, forming new attachments and dissolving the old, giving birth to higher duties and trampling on those of the past, seeming to shatter only to build again, to destroy in order to make space for more?

What injustice, oh, God, what incredible cruelty. And these, the works of a plan designed by a benevolent and divine being!

The whole story of Mother's life is one of heroic struggle against adversity. At her age, the little source of happiness she had won for herself by untold sacrifices, devotion, by work and endurance and incessant strife, is taken from her by others who have no other right than Love's.

And I, who should slave for her, live for her alone and die loving her alone, I feel all my love and devotion deepening about one whom I have known but a year! Maddening problems are continually set around us like traps, by which all of us, victims at one time or another, are tortured to the very end of existence.

And yet—oh, if it were true!—by widening my circle of love I might bring to Mother but a warmer radiance, bring more to love and cheer her than just myself. Yes, I hope. I hope . . . and trust!

At the end of our talk I lost control of my feelings and sobbed desperately in Mother's arms. I told her I had not thought of these things, that they had all seemed so simple to arrange and plan.

"Yes, yes, I know," Mother said. "You do nothing but dream, dream, dream, fifille, and it is just that which frightens me for you. And with such a temperament as yours you are going to make yourself very unhappy. You know nothing of life, everything shocks you . . ."

And later: "Quel enfant tu es! Rien qu'une toute petite fille *naïve* et *ingénue,* et j'ai si peur pour toi! La vie sera difficile et tu auras besoin de ta Maman."[1]

Incapability, the need of another's strength and knowledge of life, a harmful childishness which makes me helpless in the face of reality, an ingenuousness which leaves me forever unprepared and shocked by life's unexpected turns and difficulties. This is Mother's diagnosis of my malady. But I, deep down in my heart, feel that what she conceives is what her mother's eyes alone can see, and the things she finds lacking are those by which she believes she can hold me to her. My love for her will keep me by her, but as to the other, I long for an opportunity to prove to her that I am not helpless, and that I can and will do all things, endure all things, learn to adapt my dreams to the possible and reasonable and practical.

It was strange how quickly the crisis passed in us. Its very strength was like the fury of a storm soon spent for reason of its very power. As I write now, Mother rests and looks at me now and then, smiling and contented. She is leaving me tomorrow, and I am to return home Sunday perhaps. Together we waited for the mail, and I read her Hugo's second letter, which has again made me supremely happy.

Oh, life, life. Who shall say what your eternal contrasts were meant to teach us!

July 4. Morning. "Overmastering pain—the most deadly and tragical element in life—alas! pain has its own way with all of us; it breaks in, a rude visitant, upon the fairy garden where the children wander in a dream, no less surely than it rules upon the field of battle, or sends the immortal war-god whimpering to his father; and innocence, no more than philosophy, can protect us from the sting." So says Stevenson, but he might have said more and taken in account youth, who, quick at feeling and detecting pain even when it only exists in its imagination, is also capable of quickly conquering and ridding itself of it. It must be youth that makes me feel so hopeful and confident today, and so humbled at my outburst of denunciation of yesterday. My last vision of Mother was one to gladden the heart.

Afternoon. Just now, as I sat answering Hugo's letter, an artist came to see me and offered me an engagement for posing

---

1 *"What a child you are! Nothing but a naïve, ingenuous, tiny little girl, and I am so afraid for you! Your life will be difficult and you will need your Maman."*

which should last ten days, but only beginning Monday. What I felt, I wrote Mother in these words: "Vraiment, il n'y a pas de détermination qui résiste la possibilité de 15 jours de plus toute seule. Même si j'avais une bibliothèque et trois journals à écrire."[1]

And to Hugo:

Oh, my beloved, if I felt free to write you whenever the impulse takes me, some few words would reach you every day, and by the help of them you would follow me in fancy through the story. Your thoughts, weary and worn perhaps, might mingle with mine that are penetrated with the freshness and strength of this new life. And you might see me beckon and would follow me through fields and woods, that you might taste with me the selfsame boundless freedom to the point of ecstasy and be flooded in the same divine peace.

Yet how much I miss those long exchanges of inexpressible feelings through the eyes and by the voice and changes in expression. . . . You must tell me what you think, sweetheart. I want to know and cannot act unless you tell me. Something moved me to come away, but nothing seems to detain me here any longer than this coming Sunday. An endless chain of gray and misty days and spells of rain, though lovable and beautiful in their own way, have seriously interfered with my work. I was looking forward with secret pleasure to discarding my pen, and although I loved the self you revealed to me in your letters, I wove fairy tales about the one I would meet upon returning. And now—now I am asked to remain ten more days, and given work to completely fill my time. Shall I stay? It means in all fifteen more days. For love's sake tell me your true feelings. If I knew that you will rest and feel the need of more time, then I stay. Tell me, and tell me immediately, I beg you . . . Bien aimé, à celui qui aime il ne semble jamais qu'il n'y est plus d'une langue, les mots se dépouillent de leur forme et ne conservent que l'essence dont l'esprit créateur les a chargé. Quand même, soit en français, soit en anglais, ce sont toujours les plus tendres de ces mots qui s'envolent vers toi.[2]

[1] "*Truly, there is no determination that can withstand the prospect of two more weeks all alone. Even if I had a library and three diaries to write!*"
[2] *Beloved, to one who loves, it never seems as though there is only one language. Words are stripped of their form and keep only the essence with which the creative spirit has endowed them. Just the same, whether in French or English, it is always the tenderest of words that fly to you.*

Being in Mrs. Snider's house is a great advantage from an artist's point of view, provided one is not particularly devoted to any one of life's comforts, such as undisturbed sleep at night, uninterrupted reveries by day, and the blessing of harmonious sounds falling upon one's ears when there is sound at all, and peace and quiet the rest of the time. The artist, then, who can overlook the lack of comfort, can dig deeply every hour and is certain to find an ever increasing amount of material upon which to fasten, temporarily at least, his concentrated interest. Under his creative fingers, the spectacle unfolding under his very eyes assumes the shapeless form of marble gradually being molded and becoming an intelligible idea—an idea captured and confined and become fact. Not being an artist (though aspiring to become one) and yet keenly conscious of the privilege attending the possession of a window overlooking Woodstock's Main Street, I shall, instead of making profound dissertations and a work of art with the material on hand, simply tell the story as I see it and name whatever I see passing by. And somehow I cannot help believing that a little loss of sleep, and a little endurance of unmelodious sounds, such as automobile horns and rumbling carriage wheels and children's war cries, are all small prices indeed to pay for the sight of such quaint and bizarre characters as I have seen.

I am grateful to the people of Woodstock for their disregard of conventions; it spells the true heroism and the calm supremacy of Individuality, the triumph of personal freedom over fear of public opinion. And the spirit is contagious because of its sincerity. No sooner did I feel myself attuned to it than I demonstrated my approval by wearing flowers in my hair.

Having then established myself as one of them and planted my emblem of defiance beside theirs, I proceeded to observe them closely and quietly. They never suspected it—in fact, I do believe they thought they were observing me, and that I did not know it. But so it is always in this world: the people who honestly do things do not show or speak of it, and it is those who are incapable who emphasize their activity and success and boast and make a show of it—probably to convince themselves as well as others. Please do not mistake me as belonging to the second class. I am not boasting now, I am simply explaining.

The first discovery I made was that in this noble fraternity of independents there were perhaps half absolutely on the outside of the circle, though believing themselves in it and believed by others to be in it. Those were the ones who appear everywhere and in every society and who stand like a shadow behind every idea, every creed and every leader of this earth. I mean the ones who accept the *form* of things but miss its essence by reason of their lack of intelligent comprehension. They cannot interpret, they cannot adapt, and they cannot be rational. You speak to them of throwing off convention, of having faith in their individual beliefs, of being original and adopting personal instead of public opinion—and then do you know what they do? A stout, plump, ungainly, massive, uncompromisingly monstrous woman will dress as a man in shirt and knickerbockers and heavy square boots and offer to glaring publicity what a little of woman's art and feminine trickery might so easily soften and conceal. And yet I could wager she would not dare use such artless power simply because others will think her old-fashioned and fearful of modern methods, or perhaps not intelligent enough, too narrow-minded to approve them.

Excess, excess, and due to nothing but stupid conceptions and hypocriticial handling of the *same* material from which others will draw a real use.

This may be a harsh denunciation but there are times when one's own mind is bound to beat upon the locked doors of others in despair, perhaps with the mere hope it may yield . . . and be saved. And even this is but in certain cases; at other times one takes it calmly and is saddened without being indignant. This happens when one finds the door of a mind closed fast, but not through the unknowing creature's fault. And when it is not closed by vanity or shallowness or hypocrisy or willful blindness and evasion, then it is pitiable, but God forbid that anyone should condemn.

I know of such an instance, to compare with that of the woman I mentioned. Some days ago I sallied out for a walk late in the afternoon after work, seeking rest and courage to return to my lonely room. Unconsciously I set out toward the mountain and came upon a hill (there is no moral in this) which dominated a wide expanse of fields and woods. At the very top of it I found myself facing a little farmhouse whose roof shone in the sunshine, and whose white walls were half-covered by a wild growth of climbing roses and ivy. On the doorstep sat a little old man smoking a pipe, and out of his wrinkled face shone, very dimly, faded and haggard eyes. I fancied they questioned me, and smiling, I walked as if to turn back.

"Good day, Miss," he said affably in a very old, broken voice. "Been here long?"

Somehow, his gentle smile held my interest, as did his pipe and his farmer's clothes and his weather-beaten face. I paused, and after slightly raising my voice when I discovered he was hard of hearing, I fell into talk with him.

From the top of that hill we could see the most enchanting scenes, the mountains, the fields, the woods, all lying in the glory of the sun, and other farms and pastures and little white cottages peeping through the trees. You felt as if you could touch the clouds with your fingers. I was overwhelmed again by a sense of infinite freedom and infinite perfection.

Yet as I talked I read in the old man's eyes that he was absolutely unconscious of these things.

"Don't you love this life?" I asked him.

"Hard work," he answered, grinning and showing me his hands, which bore all the marks of the toiler, the man who plows and plants and weeds.

The scent of sweet grass was wafted to me by the breeze. I breathed deeply. "Your grass smells good," I could not help saying.

"It's good for the cows," he replied.

And here he had lived all his life in the midst of things which meant so much to me and gave me glimpses of heaven, and all he knew was that the season had been a good one, that he had sold his eggs well, that his cows were the best in the town, that corn grew well at the foot of the mountain . . . And he sat there basking in the sunshine, smoking, with vacant eyes fixed on nothing, resting from his hard day's work, without thoughts, without feelings, a creature truly but half-awake and deprived of life's greatest treasures . . . No response in his eyes, not the faintest glimmer of understanding or consciousnes, he was simply existing with half of himself in darkness, a thing as dead, as thoroughly dead, as if it were lying in that little cemetery there on the side of the mountain.

I returned home lost in thoughts, struck by the mystery of it, telling myself: the man is happy. He does not think or feel or know there are such states, and yet . . . One thing I knew. The barrier between the old farmer and me I would never touch were I commanded to do so by all the earthly powers. It is God's doing, this distribution, and it has its reason.

To find his mind locked did not disturb me; it puzzled me,

yes, but I would not knock there, however softly, without feeling I was committing a sacrilege. Neither vanity nor shallowness nor hypocrisy had their place there.

Why I was led to wander so far from my subject, I hardly know. In pursuing thoughts, it is like pursuing butterflies—the one which appears most beautiful to your taste will lead you far from the rest. But now I have that pinned down, and wishing the collection complete, I return to the others!

Half of the pleasure of seeing strangers lies in the speculation —or in simpler language, the fancies—your imagination can weave about their person, provided they give you some legible signs and outward marks betraying at least the outline of their personalities. There are great possibilities in the game, and the goal consists in making as little of a fool of yourself as possible.

Well, I begin. The first creature who attracted my attention was a middle-aged man whom I met on my walks now and then and who never noticed me. At least here is one original man, I thought to myself with a sigh of relief; he lets me alone.

He wore very torn and untidy clothes, a blue shirt and brown knickerbockers and dusty boots. His hair was rumpled, the expression on his face moody and bitter and aggressive, invariably, rain or shine; the weather did not affect him. He was always in my favorite places, by the side of brooks, under trees, in shady nooks, but seemingly absorbed in writing, so that my heart softened to him with the pity one prisoner will feel toward another, or a tramp toward another tramp—brothers in misery, I mean. And I would steal away without claiming my rights.

Then I heard him named and was told that he was unsociable and lived in a log cabin all alone up on the mountain. This completed my judgment of him and finished my picture. I decided he was a genius because he wrote. That he had a great intellect and force of character and a knowledge of what was truly wise because he did not notice woman. That he had great thoughts and a deep appreciation of nature because he loved to sit by the brooks and under trees and shady nooks. That he had a rare nature and beautiful spirit since he loved and could endure solitude, and great power since he could thus tower above the needs of ordinary men for society and company. Of course, the artistic temperament was easily detected in the rumpled hair and moody face. Once so much had been said, it was easy to add a touch of heroism and courage based on the aggressiveness of his face. You might even suspect a tragic life, and people trampling on his childish faith, and the world shattering his youthful illusions, to explain the bitterness of his expression. From this point, it was easy to rave on. He was an admirable character, a great man, one I would be proud to have surrendered my seat by the side of the brook to . . . Enfin! a hero!

Then I was introduced to him.

"Ha, ha," laughed the introducer upon presenting him. "Here you have one of the most famous composers of musical comedies. He comes here and works for a time, doesn't see anyone and then goes back to the city, sells his music, makes money and spends it well on Broadway. Some stepper, eh, I'll say."

And the hero agreed, with mischief in his eyes and a grin, which in one flash exterminated all my well-ordered notions about "rare nature" and "beautiful spirit." And what is worse, the artists' wives, speaking of him, say he has "to make every woman in sight."

It took me some days to recover. For some time whenever I saw an interesting stranger, I wondered whether he would turn out to be the owner of a cracker factory, a bar or some other monstrosity comparable with a Broadway musical show!

Evening. Well, the tide of cheerfulness is spent. I sit alone and feel my loneliness most deeply. I have mailed my letters to Mother and to Hugo and wait. What Hugo will say and how he will say it is what I long to hear.

It takes more courage than I thought to do without the warmth and sustenance of home, without my mother and little brothers, without Hugo's visits. I miss the faces I love, the sound of voices, the tread of feet, Thorvald's teasing and Joaquin's pranks and all the noises which once disturbed me when I wanted to write and which I find I value far more than all this pile of paper.

Intellect, you might say. True. I can wrap myself in thoughts and read and be lost in the world of mind and even exult in a solitude which makes real thinking and writing possible. Did I not say myself I felt I could write something if I were left alone? But the woman in me clings to affection, secretly ashamed, and praising hard, strong natures in awed silence—yet knowing full well that happiness must be the possession of both the Writer and Woman when they are so equally mingled and neither will be submerged.

If to be wholly woman means to be an incomplete, imperfect writer, well then I know which way to set my course. I shall

be Woman, in all its entity and perfection, and succeed in that—
and the other will come of itself and follow like a satellite and
never be quite lost or quite recovered or quite perfect, if you will,
and yet not quite dead either.

And there you have it, whether it be true or false, only time
will say.

I have thought deeply and long about marriage these days,
remembering all I have been told with no little scorn and what
I have read, only to make my own selection. Stevenson as an adviser is entirely out of the question: he is too sarcastic. Unfortunately he is the only one I have by me now. I must trust my
general impression, and that is a most discouraging one. Mother
simply repeats that marriage is not made of the same stuff as
dreams. "C'est une chose tout à fait terre à terre,"[1] she told me.

And I have talked of it with Frances. She concluded, and I
agreed feebly, that the *glamour* of love has its spring in novelty,
and novelty ceases to exist with familiarity.

"But not so with a love based on what each one *thinks* and
on moods, for these are ever changing and ever new," I told
Frances.

"Not as changing as you believe," she answered. "One mind
will grow accustomed to the workings of the other and anticipate
all its reactions and grow to know exactly how it is moved by
every condition. After a while no thought or mood can be a surprise."

"Well, even if the glamour and thrill do fade, love in itself,
turned into devotion, cannot be entirely gone and might be per-
petuated or transferred through the children. Or the love of children can replace the other, if as you say, it must be lost. But oh,
Frances, don't you sometimes rebel at what people say, and feel
that you can make your marriage *different*, as I feel I will make
mine?"

Frances has never laughed at my naïveté, but she made me
feel it sharply by this remark quietly made: "Our mothers said
their marriages would be different, and so did our grandmothers
and great-grandmothers, and they all thought they would be
happier, and that their husbands were the best. Yet in the end,
they are all alike."

Mother told me the thing I believe most important to remember, and that is: "The mistake most women make is to expect their

[1] *"It is something entirely down to earth."*

husband to continue to play the part of the *lover*. Once a man has won his bride, he has more serious things in his mind than to compliment his wife. The very fact that he has chosen her for a wife implies that he believes the best of her, and what need is there of repetition? He has to support her, work for a home and children, to keep them in comfort, and it is all he can do. And woman, unreasonably, expects flattery and constant attention besides."

The fairness and sense of this struck me immediately. I promised myself I would never forget. And if our marriage is not different and does bring tribulations and difficult moments and sorrows to overcome and crises to be passed, it will only be natural. But I love Hugo, I love him so that all my life shall be spent in giving him happiness. I shall strive to please and comfort and inspire him; I shall serve and do all things for him, and seek for more to give, and make all his dreams of woman come true in me, and maintain myself as far as possible worthy of his devotion; and I shall hold his love until Eternity.

I promise he shall never be hurt through my fault. I promise never to allow an angry word to pass my lips. I promise to be ever patient and sweet and thoughtful.

I promise not to let my moods make him unhappy. Unreasonable feelings I shall conquer—all the whims I have and my unsociability; my tendency to evade ordinary talk and intercourse, which he does not approve.

I shall think first of him and then of my desires, and teach them to become his.

If he be cold, I shall not complain. If he be weary, I shall comfort him. I shall not burden him with my moments of sadness, unless they have a cause, and be ever strong, even-tempered, reliable and utterly unselfish.

And then if his love for me dies, I shall steal away without a word and never return . . .

We do what few lovers have ever done. We dare to think, and we dare tell each other what we think. Though less peaceful, our love should be much stronger and greater because of that.

The tone of Hugo's voice still rings in my memory the time he said: "We are going to be happy together, Anaïs."

Other words of his surge in my memory too. Once he took my face between his hands and, gazing on it long and intently, whispered awed: "You are so utterly, so utterly beautiful . . ." Later, when we are married, I shall read this and be consoled!

What he said repeatedly were words which echoed a great longing in him—a longing for a thing he has never had and found in me: "Oh, I can rest with you, Anaïs," and I knew it was true.

"You have given me the greatest gifts: love and understanding, Anaïs. Think of yourself as a sea of beauty, and of me diving into the deeps, seeking to get to the very bottom of it. Besides my love for you as a woman—for your womanliness—I admire you as I would a man, for your courage and your strength. It is not only your understanding of me, but your understanding of life, of books, of poetry, of everything that I love."

All this I heard and treasured.

July 5. I am now in a golden cage which I have made for myself, just twittering to pass away the time until Hugo throws open the little door and gives me back my freedom. How quickly I shall fly home! Meantime, I must twitter loud and long so as to keep my wings from drooping.

I am resolved to believe in the permanence of interest in marriage while people consider each other's spiritual development as a source of attraction and are in sympathy with each other's thoughts and fancies, which are like an ever changing and fascinating panorama, forever to be unfolded before one's privileged eyes.

Early afternoon. A few false notes played on the instrument called life should not frighten one into eternal silence and inaction.

Oh, be strong and laugh, heart of mine, laugh at blunderings and disillusionments, and learn to look through the facts at the essence of things, through material happiness at those intangible sources of inward peace and tranquillity. Rise above the confusion of mortal warfare, master anguish and draw from grief only such spiritual and moral wealth as one does from all experience in general.

There is no other punishment on earth for High Expectations than that of finding them unfulfilled. On the other hand, to some it brings about the discovery of riches never possibly found without earnest and diligent research. High Expectations are maps to Treasure Islands throughout the world. They help us to raise our sails and set a course on life's high seas—and sometimes bring us safely to port.

In some persons there is an eternal change of currents and points of view and attitudes. Theirs is a continuous struggle for readjustment, harmony and peace. They are keenly conscious of at least three strings of thought vibrating in them. There is the feeling of detachment from reality, a sense of the ghostliness of existence, which results in passionate dreams and conceptions hardly to be realized and remaining simply stagnant in the form of moods. There is the absolute grip over actuality, the power of swift and clear decisions moving in perfect accord with instant action, accomplishment, fulfillment, the type of thought that moves and reaches. And then, towering above these two, detached equally from both, is the artist and critic who describes and approves, condemns and understands both perfectly. These three are ever at war with each other, ever seeking the order and reason of things, each in his own manner. Whether by dream or acts or criticisms, the purpose, conscious or unconscious, is to reach a state of absolute understanding and classification of all the forces of the universe which disturb, perplex or weaken us.

Such persons know but one fear, and that is the one of suddenly being revealed to themselves as hypocrites. The very fact that they do not feel *whole*, being moved by so many divergent powers, appears to them as an act of insincerity and inconstancy. The war continues because the three are of equal strength, and it is waging in me now.

If the writer in me requires a life that will supply food to the imagination, will it survive between four walls and in caring for home and husband? It matters little to me now because I love, and my love is greater than my ambition.

It is a strange thing to be thus alone for a whole day. I have exchanged in all perhaps ten or fifteen words with people, have walked in silence about two hours on the open road, have eaten in silence and whiled away the afternoon in reading and in desultory thinking. I feel like a person in a trance, one moving in an unreal and shapeless, formless world. It is as if I were conversing with ideas and moving from one into the other, passing through them as through stages, dropping them, assuming another character and viewing things from an impersonal and purely transitory elevation all the while. In one day I seem to have alighted upon every subject and passed through every mood, seen all my transformations in the penetrating light of the latest one, judged and corrected according to my newest standards. Yet somehow, I am deeply dissatisfied. The purpose of thought is to reach a conclusion, to attain a limit, to grasp something, to establish a fact—and in this sense I have wasted an afternoon in utter idleness. All I have done is voice things, give them words and make them substantial and tangible and fixed. And this, by the little I have written here and the great quantity I have merely jotted in my notebook and on scraps of paper. None of it was created today. They were old thoughts I dug out of my mind as one visits a drawer of forgotten things. I simply pulled them out, glanced at them and gave them a name.

My one hope is that so setting order in one's head might make room for fresh ideas. I hold idleness in great contempt, but it is the calm, lazy, restful spirit of this place that has corrupted me.

Later. The finite human mind must of necessity remain baffled by the infinite mysteries of religion. That the intellect should question, probe and doubt is only natural, but when it strikes upon the wall of its limitations, it should take refuge in interpretation through a faith guided by the highest instincts in human nature—those of *need* and *trust*.

My ideal of love is an appeal to the soul of man so strong, so powerful, that the appeal to the senses should follow as if in harmony, unnoticed almost, as one, upon seeing a bright light, remains dazzled and unconscious of the object holding it.

The substance of what the world tries to teach woman is this: If you have a mind, make a secret of it, or bury it in some secret place, but for heaven's sake do not *use* it. It is of no use to you in religion; it will spoil it for you and stands in the way of your piety and virtuousness. It is of no use to you in love, for men detest women who think, and like meek, gentle, ignorant spirits. And women, fearful of losing what is dearest to their hearts, learn to pray and sew and cook and the art of pleasing and being good and useful. The one who defies such teaching (I!) revolts and willfully chooses to follow her inclinations, is constantly beset by difficulties and has her moments of tremor, when it seems as if she had made an irrevocable choice between what is dear to her as a woman and what is said to satisfy philosophers, writers and artists—between affection and devotion, and knowledge and creation.

Yet in the end she conquers. And among the gifts showered upon her is that of a love that surpasses all loves and contains in itself all the beauty and wisdom and glory of creation.

Humility is, after all, only the result of being uncompromisingly honest with ourselves. A dose of self-depreciation administered not too frequently is extremely salutary. When we take long strides and great leaps toward the end we have set ourselves without ever pausing, there comes a time when, in our overconfidence and supreme satisfaction with self, we lose sight of the true value of things, of the importance of time, the necessity for incessant and earnest labor, the sacredness of our mission and purpose in life. A little musing on our limitations and lacks will set us forth upon the road again with greater attention and intentness, desires sharpened by the realization of the distance separating us from them, and in a mood, generally speaking, for greater appreciation and deeper capacity for understanding our doings.

If you have a perception fond of playing tricks on you and which makes you see the ridiculous, the absurd, the weak in a character as swiftly and as clearly as the commendable traits and lovable qualities, I think it is better to keep it out of sight, for it is a thing which hurts without doing the least good. Leave mockery and scoffing, sarcasm and irony in the hands of a genius who knows how to use them and who, with them, is able to correct, teach and reform.

The human in us is subject to mistakes and fallacies. But we can have faith in the divine that is forever struggling to assert itself.

Intellect we admire, but it is beauty we love, and it is beauty that receives the tribute of youth and the poets. And it is also beauty that wins love, but it is only beauty united to intellect that can *hold* love.

Evening. Just returned from another long walk through flower-scented fields. This place has become incredibly dear to me. I think it is because in it I have found the fulfillment of all the poetry of nature I have ever read. Knowing the intensity of my love of nature, I am awed when I find that it has no hold on me, in spite of what it arouses in me. I cannot become entirely absorbed in it, as I once did, because a greater love has taken its place, a greater love calls me, and at its bidding I would sacrifice all this instantly.

July 6. Early morning. In this seclusion with a few books, an ink bottle, pen and paper, I feel as if I had detached myself from all reality and become but a wandering spirit intent upon seeking and pursuing a haunting desire. I feel as if I could better see and reach after I have dropped the occupations and obligations of the tangible world which hamper me and make my voyage slow and difficult, my purpose less distinct. Here I have been and lived as a spirit all these days, and having seen more clearly and traveled with greater ease to understanding, and given my desires a definite form and a name, now I long passionately to reassert my real self and to return to the world of action, that I might test its power.

Later. Hugo sends me Ibsen's *Doll's House*, but he cannot have realized to what an extent the story would pierce me. Sharply, clearly revealed in Ibsen's words, I have found defined the Thing I have escaped and which instinctively terrified me all these years while I struggled to *understand* everything about me and myself. My one blind hope was that my education would make me worthy of love and marriage instead of being an obstacle to the realization of them. Oh, now I am certain; I know and believe heart and soul that Nora and Thorvald's failure shall not come to Hugo and me. Even in our love we have "sat down in earnest together to try and get at the bottom of things." (And used the same words even.)

Nora struggles when she says: "I must try and educate myself. . . . I must stand quite alone if I am to understand myself and everything about me . . ." and "I believe that before all else I am a reasonable human being, just as you are. . . . I must think over things and try to understand them. . . ."

Hugo and I—each an individual, above all things, with equal understanding, equal knowledge of things, of *work* and life and its problems and difficulties and its *seriousness;* with equal realization and acceptance of its sacrifices, difficulties and responsibilities and obligations . . . Oh, ours shall not be a Doll House, nor our marriage all playfulness, nor shall we be strangers to each other and each live alone as a man and a *doll* are bound to live alone, spiritually and morally.

Afternoon. I took the book of Ibsen's plays with me on my usual ramble but quickly abandoned it after reading *Ghosts*. Besides my natural hatred of ugly things, my horror of sin, my fear of the revolting and unclear aspects of life, it was impossible and almost a violation of all sacredness in sentiment to read of them in the very midst of so much purity and beauty. It was with the most unutterable gratitude that I gave myself to the contemplation of fields and mountains to calm the anguish which that play gave me.

I have had time to think of everything and time to find all manner of new thoughts, but cannot write of it all, nor half of what I would wish to write. Even the little I do write does not satisfy me, simply because the more I tell, the more I find untold, and the more I name things, the more words I find to rename them and regret having been so thoughtless as to use the first word that dropped from my pen! I wonder what good all this pondering, sifting, dissecting, will do me when I begin once more to *live*.

Evening. The power to twitter has gone from me; I must sing out my song of intolerable loneliness. No one will hear it or be hurt by it. The writer in me can thrive on solitude and seclusion and is satisfied. But my woman's heart is starving for affection. I can feel the two most clearly and know so well the power of each and how far its domain extends. The mind will rule quietly, undisturbed for a whole day, finding joy in every moment, sustenance, life itself, in contemplation, in the use of its force, in scrutiny and considerations of all things great and small. Then in one moment, caught unawares, a flood of feeling will submerge it and reign supreme. Then it is I realize how passionately and wholeheartedly I love. Too well, perhaps. It is then, also, that I wonder if it is a thing to subjugate and control, this intensity of affection toward the few in my circle of devotion. For as you know, there are not many, and I would not wish them greater in number for fear of being consumed with love.

Tomorrow, tomorrow is the day I have set for the coming of my Deliverer. Pray that his words may open the door of my cage in a way that might compensate me for what I have endured and give fire and strength to my wings. Dear heart and most beloved, call me back.

July 7. Morning. After mail time. Not a word! What anguish, oh, what doubts assail me!

Later. Mother said to me while she was here that I *deserved* happiness, love, care and protection. I answered her that if anyone had ever been worthy of all the good in the world, it was she, and yet she had been given none of the love, happiness, care, protection, hers by right, and that things in the world were not distributed according to one's worthiness.

Whenever I think of Mother's life, a burning rebellion and bitterness is roused in me. That such self-sacrifice, such abnegation, such wasting of youth and beauty and devotion upon a man devoid of all sense of what is noble and right—that all this should exist! One sorrow upon another, one struggle after the other, an endless chain of suffering. Compensation? Oh, yes, so we try to make ourselves believe, and it is nothing but deceit and lies, of which we should be ashamed. No, there is no compensation, and there is no justice, so that if it falls to my share of things to be given a cup brimful of sorrow, I can but drink it to the bitterest end; whether I deserve it or not is what least concerns the world, or myself for that matter.

What if I do love more than I am loved? What if I give more than I am given? What if I do *waste* youth and devotion? Well, then, I will have lived and suffered no more than a million others and given and lost no more than most women and received no less of life than the rest, who also, perhaps, deserved more.

True, my spirit will never *bow* to these things; it shall forever cry against them, fight them, libel them; it will remain unchained when all else around me or in me is chained. I shall not shrink from anything, nay, I shall teach my body, and the outer envelope, to *endure*, and to appear *resigned*, and neither by word nor by look shall I betray the fire within me.

Only let me write, let the agonies of my mind flow into you. I can be silent before the world and silent before those I love, but I cannot stifle thoughts and feelings, and in this communion with my own soul I find the freedom of utterance, the freedom to cry in my pain, which is all I dare ask of life and which can hurt no one but myself. I can restrain myself from all things except the speaking-out of what I believe to be *truth* and the condemnation of injustice!

The Critic ventures upon an observation: Instead of gradually reaching various states of mind, you leap from the highest to the lowest, from peace to despair, from philosophical passivity and satisfaction to the most bitter abysms of grief. Beware of this; it is the evil sign of *absolutism*. You never consider, you never make allowances, you never pause to question how far you are speaking against your own theories, how you act in utter disregard of your own set and fixed ideals. Beware of your hotheadedness and your inconsistencies. You yourself a few days ago wrote: "Rise above the confusion of mortal warfare, master anguish and draw from grief only such spiritual and moral wealth as one does from all experiences in general."

Be true at least to your own teachings!

And the Dreamer, not yet descended from any heights, untouched by doubts or sorrows, murmurs gently like a child: "He will write, he will write."

Veritable wisdom is not, like truth, usually found in wells. It is in one's own soul and above all in the dream. It is the Dreamer, therefore, who waits and trusts.

Afternoon. Mrs. Snider thinks I am writing a book. She has

the most unbounded respect for the looks of my poor insignificant journal. This morning she demonstrated surprise at the decrease of ink in my bottle and would not believe that it had been mostly used by evaporation while I waited for inspiration.

July 11. Kew Gardens. The wisdom that is in dreams! I waited for the thing that was to come like one on tiptoes, prepared to catch something that flew high and might be missed. And when Hugo's letter reached me, in which he did not call me back, I nearly failed in grasping it and only by a supreme effort succeeded in touching it—but the mere touch was the fine thread of sympathy upon which understanding could weave a stronger link.

In it he climbed a step higher, dared another thought, and I, though the road he had taken seemed dark and rough to me, followed, determined to ignore the bleeding of my heart and the cutting stones. He revolutionized my entire soul by his words, stirred fresh desires and restlessness and destroyed in one blow the balance I had regained and so firmly established those few days. And I loved him for his daring, and promised to ever stand by him in this pursuit, this complete, absolute devotion to the ideal at any price, because at the time I believed it was only through *thought* that we could obtain it.

I could not help, however, realizing sharply the pain and torture brought about by the constant mental activity at its highest and strongest pitch and longed at times to find a refuge from this heartrending state of mind, from the immensity of our self-made problems and difficulties. Yet I would never, never hold him back, for it is in me also, the *habit of thought*, a thing so strong that, united to his and carried too far, was leading us to intolerable depths.

It was to Hugo that the revelation came; he was struck by the same need and the knowledge that thought carried to such an excess was not necessary and was depriving us of happiness. He came to me one night, and during our talk the solution blazed forth, radiantly beautiful. We promised not to *think* any more!

It is always the simple return of wisdom that speaks invariably through this pause I have so often made, after excessive thought and only thought and thereby all loss of equilibrium, the return to balance and normal distribution and reasonable sharing to replace that exclusive and blind absolutism by which nothing can be gained and so much lost.

This was indeed our fairy-tale night. For the first time Hugo became my own Prince Charming, my Knight of Knights, saving me from the jaws of the Dragon, bearing me away on his steed to El Dorado, to the land of Joy and Romance.

July 12. It seems incredible that our minds should be so much alike that we should be able to pass from one state to the other together and able to know and name them, conquer them when necessary, as in the case of our exaggerated excess of thought.

Since I have returned I have seen him every evening. For each evening I would wish a month to explain—the astounding number of revelations, the worlds that are discovered, the new feelings that are aroused.

Hugo's letter reached me Friday afternoon; Saturday I left Woodstock with so many varied feelings in my heart that all I can do is allow them to remain memories. Home, I found Mother weakened, broken down by worry and trouble and difficulties. Ever since I returned, I have felt the Shadow of Responsibilities growing heavier upon me, gripping me with a hand of iron, but at the same time the thought of self has entirely vanished. My only dreams, my only joy, comfort, sustenance, are the time I spend with Hugo. The rest is all submerged in a passionate desire to help Mother and to live only to serve her, so that there is nothing I would not sacrifice to reach this end at the cost of all pertaining to me.

And now I can truly say: "To love and to labor is the sum of living."

I love, I love with all my heart and soul, and I labor with all my strength and power. Nothing can stand in my way; nothing can turn me away from the two things for which I would willingly die and, what is more, for which alone I live now.

I can say now, with Carlyle's Wanderer: "Ever from that time, the temper of my misery was changed: not Fear or whining Sorrow was it, but Indignation and grim fire-eyed Defiance."

I defy everything. I challenge the whole world. Indignation shall spur me, and adversity, calamity, shall be lifted from Mother's weary shoulders, and whether they choose to fall on mine instead, *I do not care one whit*.

Thus the pursuit is on, and a hot fiery race it will be because the result of all that pondering, sifting, dissecting, I did in Woodstock is a wild and powerful loosening of all the forces in me for Action!

Hugo has given me another piercing and revealing book. In *The Woman Question*[1] I have found little pieces that fitted me, but I was startled more by the great quantity both unknown to me and contrary to my ideals. Again I can say: there is no one, no book, by which you can explain or classify me. It could no more be done by reading French traits or Spanish character than by this collection of Essays on Woman.

This I liked, describing one of the women of today: "The maiden of the other type carries in her blood an oversensitive chastity barometer. There is a very large group of women—and I have observed that they are usually the finest minds and noblest souls—who instinctively guard with fear and trembling, their inviolability; nothing is to them so distressing, so debasing, as to feel a stain upon themselves, stained by everything imaginable; by the glance of a man to whom they are utterly indifferent . . ." (And I add: by the attentions of such men, by their very presence!) "In many cases this super-sensitiveness is nothing but unrestrained maidenliness; the woman jealously reserves her entire capital for the great bliss of an individualized self-abandoning love for the one man destined for her."

I called this, when I discovered manifestations of it in myself, an exaggerated sense of honor and partly chided myself for it, yet today my one supreme and perfect joy is the knowledge that I have come to Hugo in all purity of heart and body and as stainless as a virgin; that he was the first to kiss my lips and the first to read my heart in my eyes.

And then of this same type of woman it is said: "In her, all passive womanly qualities—desire to love, devotion to man, reflective intelligence, faithfulness, solicitude, loyalty—have, as it were, stepped from their home in the spinal cord and formed a closer communion with the brain . . . A third characteristic is the warm, full, nourishing passion which she wraps about man, fostering but not scorching . . . There is in this love of the grande amoureuse . . . a love without repletion, a love of unlimited surrender, of intellectual devotion . . . a love in which the physical is transformed without loss into vibrations of the soul; finally a love of long duration, a joyful self-surrender to one man."

All this I feel and believe I am.

But I go further. I find a little of myself in the description of the "cérébral" type. She thinks and she judges; she is always giving reasons. She has become critical.

[1] *By Thomas Robert Smith.*

But for this, I love all the better, and not less, as it is said of the modern woman, who because "she cannot forget herself, cannot lose consciousness of herself, cannot surrender herself in ecstasy, cannot subjugate herself . . ." cannot love! Somehow *I* can do both. The cerebral woman began by expecting to find something, and everywhere she finds nothing. Gradually she loses her desire for love and becomes desirous of knowledge.

In this I differ, because I only consider that knowledge would make me worthy of the great love of my dreams. And I expected everything and it has come to me. For me it had to be body, intellect and soul, or nothing.

And then the more I read, and live and think, the more I see of men, the more convinced I am of the divine beauty and completeness of our love, and the more I marvel at having reached it, because Hugo is the only one I could ever have loved, the only one who could pass untouched by judgment, criticism and every motion of my mind, the only one who could satisfy my woman's heart and whose soul would harmonize with mine, and last, whose touch could convey to me the unutterable joy of a perfect union. I am awed to think such love has come to me, for I realize how high my expectations were and how rarely such expectations are fulfilled. All I can do is marvel.

July 15. Love and labor! That is now the sum of my life. My love grows deeper every minute; at times when Hugo holds me to him, I feel as if I could die of happiness.

And as to the other, I have fulfilled my promise. I work as much as I can possibly bear. I found I was not making enough money for what was needed at home, so I have taken a job modeling in a "coat and suit" shop during the day and I pose during the evenings.

I am in truth a creature set on fire, as it were, and burning with the greatest intensity and strength, using its power and activity to the fullest measure.

I look back to the quiet days at Woodstock as one does to a fragrant dream. Now I move among hard realities. I touch, and whatever I touch bruises and wounds me physically and spiritually. But what am I but an instrument whose use it is to be played upon, to produce until all within it and without snaps and crumbles? Whoever has any love or pity for himself is indeed a blind fool.

July 16. Now I am confined long hours between bare walls in a group of rooms in a gray building. The first room is large and well lighted, and in it the head of the firm and his salesmen receive the buyers, offer them comfortable chairs and then call out orders into the small back room where all the dresses are kept, hanging in a row against the wall, and where we sit waiting. dressed in black satin slips.

"Quick, get into number 409, 410, 411, 412," comes the command, and the four of us have to put the dresses on quickly and then come out, walking slowly and affectedly before the critical eyes of the buyers. Too often their interest wanders from the dress to the girl who wears it, and I wince under their gaze, realizing how different their looks are from those of the painters.

What a sharp contrast to the posing! I miss the painters, the change of studios, the bohemian life, their kindness. The customers lick their lips, rub their hands and invite me to dinner.

The long back room is narrow and dark. Between customers we all sit huddled together on a bench, rearranging our hair, studying our faces in the mirror, and the girls read the latest scandals out of the newspapers and discuss men.

They belong to that class of well-dressed girls who know how to make the most of their prettiness. Just like the chorus girls, they are all waiting for a rich man to marry them or for a job on the stage.

We are adored by the office boys and flattered by the head of the firm.

I conceal my feelings, and I keep reading *Jean-Christophe*,[1] weeping over his dramas and difficulties, forgetting myself in that marvelous, rich life. But I am suffering. Jamais la vie ne m'a semblée aussi laide![2] Things I never knew existed I have been brought face to face with. All my innocence, my ignorance of evil and baseness, are gone from me. I *know* life now, human nature, man. There is not a sensibility in me that has not been violently shocked, and my entire nature has undergone passionate storms of revulsion and disgust and bitter disappointment. I am haunted by the ugliness, the littleness of things. I feel now when I look at a child's face that I could take him into my arms and shield him forever from what I have undergone. Poor, poor little ones. Once,

[1] *By Romain Rolland.*
[2] *Never has life seemed to me so ugly.*

I looked into children's faces and felt like a child myself and would have kneeled there to play with them, so utterly unconscious was I of all but the world's *purity* and *beauty*. The thought of danger, of self-protection, never crossed my mind. Are my eyes still clear? Can I forget all I have learned of truth, harsh, unrelenting truth?

It is like a jungle of leering faces, of men waiting to touch me, grasp me. The other day when Hugo telephoned me, the salesman took advantage of it to walk up from behind and slip his hand into my breast. I kicked him so hard he howled with pain.

May I laugh and lift my head until the very end—and *never* become bitter or bow before the weight of reality.

I should not take it so dramatically, but it is too much, too much, too much in just one short year, and I have not learned yet *not to be startled* by the trivial! Meanwhile, I suffer through my own fault. I wish I could take my sensibilities and stifle them one by one. Have I not succeeded already in trampling upon my own pride—a pride so strong in me that the very glance of a passer-by would set my blood on fire with anger? I do not let other girls feel any difference between us. When one is poor, it is no time to consider one's feelings or to remember one's ancestors. I want to get close to them, but I can't while they read the Daily News and I read *Jean-Christophe!* I can't while they talk to me about the policemen and the firemen they go out with on Sundays! I can't when they are willing to stay one night with one of the buyers for the sake of a dress.

August 5. It is impossible to write when one feels incapable of explaining, and yet I had a great longing tonight, and I wished merely to tell you of things and let it go at that. I realize that if I could explain the aspect and form life has suddenly taken in my eyes and describe the attitude I have adopted toward it, the extraordinary transformations in my point of view, sense of values and interpretation that I have undergone, it would be as great a miracle as if I solved every mystery and problem concerning the universe. And this, for the simple reason that I am still too deeply involved to know what is precisely taking place—too *near* the Thing—and only in time shall I be able to judge coolly and name with accuracy.

Meanwhile I am conscious of a vast stretching and widening of my horizon, meaning that the world in itself seems to have increased in size and with it, a hundredfold, all perplexities, difficulties and sorrows. Most of all I am conscious of intensity and speed. Tranquillity and restfulness have dropped from me. In my ears sounds a continual din—love, love, love, live, live, work, work, work.

Sometimes I close my eyes and seek to bring back the dreams I had in those carefree days when I knew so little and did so little. And all I can remember is something resembling a fragrant garden within whose sheltered precincts moved a child's heart wrapped in the glamour of fairy tales.

A self that is never to reappear except in dreams. I know. One of those parts that one can play but once in life. By contrast, now I am a troubled and restless creature, deeply startled by the discovery of things which arouse indignation and regret—a creature perpetually in ferment. I wish for the power to absorb in an orderly manner. In some way there has grown upon me lately a confusion that passes all classification. I am full of contradiction and excess, swinging from one extreme to the other—disgust and enthusiasm the dominant moods. The world is full of mysteries, elusive facts, changing scenes, whose meaning I struggle in vain to grasp clearly. And all things happen, pass on, disturb me profoundly, arouse an intensity of emotion and variety of sensation and leave me with a great longing for unity and harmony and a desire to subdue this piercing, consuming activity. To be perpetually at war with one's self, with the world, with everything, is to choose willfully the most difficult and dangerous road. But passivity in any form is repugnant to me.

August 6. There must be some way of arranging one's life so that there should be time for all things; it is not possible that it should thus remain filled to the brim with work alone. My one hope is that once the habit of work grows upon me and my body becomes accustomed to constant effort and exertion, it will cease to demand or to feel such an excessive need of rest and inferior recreation. So far its weakness is an obstacle to my every wish and dream. I am still overwhelmed at night by weariness, and my mind refuses to be roused. It saddens me to see the days drop away into eternity in this careless fashion—not wasted, of course, according to ordinary standards, but not enriched either (as they once were) by reading, thinking and writing. If I could but believe that it is being enriched by *experience* in place of all those other things. Perhaps it is a vague, instinctive faith in this idea which moves me to regard such a life as Eduardo's without envy.

He, having no need of activity in the practical sense of the word, can devote all his time and energy to the pursuit of the things he loves. His life is one long worship and discovery of beauty, unhampered, unfettered, by Necessity and Responsibility. And yet his life cannot be complete, and whatever his mind produces cannot be strong, having known no trials, no griefs, no true and piercing sorrows. I have but just come to the full realization of the vast contrast between his share of things and mine and must not judge their respective values too lightly or overestimate mine for the sake of peace.

August 7. One thing I know: if I cannot conquer the great habit of sorrow now so strong in me, I will fly from the entire world and hide from those I love because I do not want them to suffer through me and by my own failure to understand life in their sane, balanced, wholesome way. I have lost the will to live and am oppressed by a terrifying darkness. I seem to have tasted of all things and have found them bitter and poisonous. Yet, no, I cannot blame the world or blame people. I know too well there is in reality no cause for the fierceness of my despair—*it is all within myself.*

But if it were only a phase—a transitory stage, if I could conquer or pass *through* and *away* from it . . . Is my whole life to lie in a shadow thus? Is a struggle endured by so many to prove too much for me? What weakness is this, what contemptible cowardice! No longer the will to live because the world is ugly?

August 8. The world has assumed a monstrous shape in my eyes. I am working myself up into a state of volcanic anger at all things in it. I walk about raving and exclaiming inwardly, consumed by indignation, looking at all things with the utmost scorn and contempt. I cling desperately to my conceptions; I struggle against the facts forcing themselves upon me, against the prosaic, the commonplace, the *animal* in life, against which my whole nature rebels violently.

Most of all the ugliness of the city overwhelms me. When I walk and I am not lost in reverie, I am sharply conscious of discordant sounds, the rumble of traffic, whistles, bells, drabness. Conscious of evil smells, dust, smoke and roar. People pass me hurriedly, walking awkwardly with anxious, strained gait. I scan their faces earnestly and find only restlessness and viciousness and sorrow.

It is the workers' lunch hour and they are standing idly on

the corners. Catching their eyes, I find mirrored in them the ugliness, the misery, the hunger and slavery of life. I do not even judge by their outward appearance, their coarse features, their shabby clothes, their bestial play of expressions, but beyond that— yet even then, that is all I find!

Farther on, a little fellow is selling papers, barefooted, in tattered clothes. His body is little, but he is no longer a child. I am deeply startled by the look in his eyes. Hard, miserable, hungry eyes. Life is no fairy tale to him. A wave of pity and tenderness surges in me, a longing to protect the poor, frail and worn-out little boy from the misery and ugliness forced upon him. Does not God feel such a desire, such a pity?

Some other day I came upon two men quarreling. Their faces were distorted by anger. It is the word money they shout at each other. Money! One throws a handful of change to the other, cursing him. The other gathers it eagerly and, muttering, walks away, gloating over it.

The people everywhere are incredibly ugly and poor and sad. The looks on their faces are looks of the dead. And I am divided between immense pity and intense revulsion.

I came face to face with two lovers whispering in the shadow of a doorway. She is small, with a thin, colorless face and straggling hair. He is a brutish-looking man, towering above her. They hold each other's hand and smile into each other's face, a grotesque smile, a distorted caress.

These things, all of them must be, I murmured to myself. Must they?

When I arrived at the place where I work, the boss was waiting for me. He said: "See here, you're getting a salary to be pleasant to the customers. I told them you were posing for painters before. When they ask you to dinner, see, you got to go with them. If you don't, you'll lose your job."

So I lost my job and had to look for another place.

At night when I am posing after dinner, my body begins to shake all over from fatigue. My eyes are blurred.

One night I came home at midnight. Bob[1] had telephoned my home and found on what train I was coming. He was waiting for me at the station. At the sight of him waiting there, at the idea of not having to walk twenty minutes home, I broke into tears.

[1] *Unidentified friend.*

August 14. To love is to know the greatest suffering as well as the most sublime joys. Hugo and I have discussed many things. Our ideals of conduct, code of honor, thoughts and feelings, with all their differences (natural to two distinct characters), are bound to clash at times when we reach the necessity to decide upon a step—an *Act.* Without love these discussions would be most bitter, but we have such an infinite desire to *understand,* such a respect for each other, such tenderness in the handling of each other's feelings, that we invariably reach a happy compromise and solve our problems.

Hugo wounds me deeply by some of his ideas. I am still discovering him and finding him utterly bewildering. I want to *understand* his point of view without *accepting* it. There is no need of surrendering one's idea to obtain harmony, but one must make room for others. And that is the result of our conference.

Happiness, I find every day, lies in the recognition of others' natures, and in sympathy. One must conform to the existence of hostile or merely contrasting characters and accept the fact that they have an equal right to assert themselves.

If I love Hugo, I must not expect him to mold himself into my conception and become as I would want him. He must be himself above all, and I must either sympathize with, recognize, this self and adapt my own character to it or else realize I must lose him entirely and be left only with the man my imagination has created.

But I love him more than my life, and I must tune my nature to his and cease to condemn anything that is his by right, whether it be a principle or a dream, a way of loving or a vision!

I must above all things make him happy, and he cannot be happy if I insist on my ideas and assert my wishes without considering and respecting his.

And now, in writing this I am struck by the fact that I can use the same attitude not in love alone but toward all things. Mine would be a stronger and nobler character if I could learn tolerance and reasonableness and charity instead of continuing to walk about with clenched fists, searching for what I might condemn and criticize.

Instead of the words "I want, I ask, I seek, I expect," use "I have, I give, I give!"

One cannot live so eternally at war with every fact, law and reality of existence and with oneself, unless with the one redeeming purpose in mind, the desire to make better, to redress, to re-create, to reform; without these, mere rebellion is like the anger of a child, futile and unreasoning.

Later, fired by this new thought (new to me, or at least resuscitated) I sallied forth from work and spent a repentant hour noticing whatever I had before ignored in my stubborn sorrow and realizing how much I had exaggerated through this most culpable and powerful imagination of mine, which is the cause of both my joys and grief.

August 15. Hugo has the magic power. He can dispel all my sadness; he can lift the heaviest clouds; he can subdue the sharpest pain. Last night he came to me and his love kindled new life in me. *I had been wishing for death.* My life seemed a failure and I had even trembled for my love simply because Hugo had unknowingly hurt me. In one moment his presence gave me warmth and courage. A wholesome, normal joy sprang in me, and laughter and contentment.

The tide of love welled higher than ever. I want to live! I want to succeed! I am young, I love and am loved! I want to live only for my Beloved.

August 18. An overwhelming shame gripped me when I opened *The Quest of Happiness.*[1] In this book I found most piercingly described and condemned the state into which I was sinking.

True, long before reading it I had been brought to reason by my own thoughts and by my love, had recognized my attitude was utterly wrong; the book only confirmed my idea and only helped me to retrace my steps, as I do each time I reach another crisis.

In recognizing a failure, thus I am humbled, and it is with greater fire that I renew my life, purified and intensified by the ordeal.

Today I have undergone the last transformation and stand on the threshold of a world bathed in new light. And all this I owe to Hugo. As I write even now it is the burning memory of his understanding, his energy and strength which kindles me. His love is life to me—oh, more than life, for he makes me believe in God, in all that is divine and everlasting, and in Beauty. While I have him, his love, his heart, to read, no evil can touch me and no sorrow, and I shall never surrender to any hostile force, to any element, to any calamity, or to any death of the spirit, of the soul, by despair, which is by far worse than the other.

[1] *By Philip Gilbert Hamerton.*

August 25. I made a curious discovery through an editorial in the papers. It seems that I am only one in a thousand passing such a crisis as I described some days ago, so that my reactions are exactly those of an ordinary young girl in the midst of common occurrences. These are the phrases which struck me: "It sometimes seems as if the sentiment were becoming these days more common that life is too much for us . . . It is a ghastly thing if, with all our culture, we arrived at last only at the end that would make life so complex and terrible a thing that death would be preferable. The contempt of life seems to be rather an important cult . . . Pessimism is a by-product of self-indulgence. Cynicism is the shadow of a disordered and masterless mind . . . The prevalent sentiment among the younger generation, that the greatest calamity of all is sorrow and that the negation of life is better than a life of trial, is indeed alarming . . . Not the least alarming symptom is that so many people seem happy only during the few brief moments of escape from the problem of life as though life itself contains no inherent joy."

Thank God, I have passed *through* all these things, as through any other experience, and am soaring far beyond that.

[*August ?*] Written at odd moments in New York. It was while reading the Introduction to *Sartor Resartus* that I came upon a full and uncompromising realization of my mistake. In seeking to know myself and the world and to put my knowledge into words, I have neglected to give my material a human shape, a reality. I have put forth ideas without a body, described emotions and given them no proper setting. I move in a world of abstract thoughts, and because I am at ease among them have neglected to give them substance by which I might reach others' understanding. I have neglected symbols by which others reach the essence. I have gone directly at the heart of things, *through* the envelope, and no one can follow me because the sign by which they might have recognized the idea and been led into it, is not there, and they are lost in a world of vague generalizations and disconnected observations and criticisms. Mine is the story of the soul, of the inner life and of its reactions to the outward life.

This in itself is a grievous fault. Apart from the consideration that it makes my writing useless to others and to those many unwilling to use their own imagination and set their mind to work, unwilling to pursue or struggle to grasp truth from evanescent suggestions, images, impressions and other unrealities, it weakens it as pure expression of thought for its own sake. It is as if I were using a language long discarded, and risking to be lost myself in a world of phantoms, spirits and souls. And to lose strength, to lose my grip and hold on the palpable would end in disaster.

And yet somehow I feel that even if I am too much inclined toward the dangerous state, this tendency of mine can easily be subdued, and my thoughts can be made to flow along more human and approachable and practicable channels and become duly invested with their proper clothing (as Carlyle would say).

By looking so much beyond these clothes, I had forgotten their existence . . . and I apologize most humbly (and yet secretly promising to do the same again) as one does at Court when one has bowed to the Poet and forgotten the presence of the King!

One thing saves me, and that is that now and then I do use physical symbols. When I compared the world to a round, grinning face, how Hugo laughed and praised me for it. Having done this once, I may do it again.

I still maintain that it is far better to start from where I have started and work outward (what most have to do), which is to pierce the coarse outer texture in order to penetrate the inner.

Like Amiel, sometimes I feel more each day that "I am becoming more purely spirit; everything is growing transparent to me. I see the types, the foundation of beings, the sense of things. All personal events, all particular experiences, are to me text for meditation. Facts to be generalized into laws. Realities to be reduced to ideas. Life is only a document to be interpreted, matter to be spiritualized. Such is the life of the thinker."

Now and then I fall in the mood of repentance during which I acknowledge my blunders and omissions, and I turn the full, pitiless eyes of criticism upon myself instead of upon others. A most salutary practice! And it is then I can judge my own writing.

I do get tired of the eternal repetition of the personal note throughout this, but I feel I am practicing on myself as one does upon an instrument, and when I have become adept in the sounding of souls, in the emission of the choices of its harmonies and of its discords, I may proceed upon my task of concept-going, and I shall make heard all the music I can now hear through the habit

I have of listening to and anticipating *some sound* from everyone; whether good or bad is the least of my considerations.

August [*?*]. At the time I read *Jean-Christophe*, I used to be carried off by the story of his life and forgot my surroundings and myself completely and could only be brought back by my work or the talks that shocked and disgusted me so profoundly.

I was terribly saddened at the time by the manner in which the world of sin and license and immorality was being revealed to me, but I believe I was more sorrowful than was reasonable because I was taking Jean-Christophe's sorrows upon my own shoulder—so real and unutterably near was he to me and so completely had he gained my sympathy and love and pity.

Jean-Christophe, however, is in part an exemplification of the attitude in life I believe wise to escape and ignore. I stand by him in his sincerity, his furious libel of hypocrisy, his constant attacks on sham, his positive hate of ugliness, baseness, etc. But there are times when he looks at the world through eyes blinded by grief and stubborn revolt, and is far too intolerant. He truly represents the man who repudiates passivity, and he puts to shame those who shut their eyes and say: "I will not see—it hurts." He does not care how deeply he is wounded, but he *will see* everything, naked, bared, bleeding . . .

If I push this description of Jean-Christophe further, I shall reach my Great Question: Should we look at the world so and sacrifice happiness? Does it lead you anywhere to spend your whole life in condemnation and denunciation? God knows there is enough injustice and falsity, decay and ugliness and baseness without our emphasizing it. If we let ourselves be demoralized by an intellectual war against intangible but nonetheless piercing and torturing evils and crushing forces, then such a war is wrong, because we were made to act and create to the utmost of our capabilities. If the contemplation of wrong and of things in general throws us into such a state of fierce, burning anguish and consuming grief, goading us to despair instead of action, to morbid apathy instead of purposeful struggle, then it is an act of the mind that is harmful, and one which is therefore to be conquered.

There are people in whom the flare for the dramatic, the sense of the artistic possibilities of human behavior, is so strongly developed as to become an actual power in their life, serving as an incentive for some of their actions and as a guide to all of them. They do all things, consciously or unconsciously, with the purpose of the storyteller who desires his audience to be struck by an effect, or who loves to have events and changes fall in their proper place at the proper time in harmonious accord with a plan whose climax is arranged long beforehand and whose power to appeal, move or convince is kept in sight during the very formation of the material.

If it be instinctive, inborn and unconscious, it is a gift which enhances the charm of the poetical and dramatical qualities of life. If it be calculated, forced, purely acquired and used by design for purposes other than simple artistry, then it is an unpardonable fault because it extinguishes all traces of sincerity— sincerity without which life is a mere bauble in our hands, a foolish, fragile toy out of which we cannot fashion even the merest shadow of a noble act.

If, after passing through all the stages of experience, we were given to choose the one best to our liking and permitted to remain in it permanently, all would be well. But the pity of it is that, as we pass on from phase to phase, we lose the last forever and are robbed of the privilege to return to it.

How often we speak of the loss of innocence and girlishness! How often we look back into the past and muse on our youthful conceptions of the world—and this is, in turn, replaced by curiosity, by wonder at the new discoveries, by disgust, rebellion and a last flicker of enthusiasm toward the small part that is worthy of admiration—and then dismay, discouragement, disillusion and, in the end, skepticism and indifference. Is this not a current story of a life?

How refreshing the sight of my old self would be to me today, my trusting, innocent, high-minded self! And that is one of the charms of diary-writing. It gives one the power to return for a moment to some old transformation, some past state of soul, some loved emotion which under no other condition can humanly be experienced again.

The storyteller lovingly preserves his story, and I find such joy in this document of life as one finds in a story, the more so if it is of my own making! And so through writing one does away with the impossible. One no longer needs to say, "I can never feel like this again or ever again entertain such thoughts. I am changing even at this very moment, and whatever *was* shall never be mine again."

No. There are no obstacles, no earthly barriers, no outward conditions, no considerations of the visibly possible or impossible, which can interfere with the freedom of the mind to come and go, to assume old transformations, to revisit old haunts, to rediscover the world, to bring the past into the present or to outstrip both in order to conceive the future.

In reading over my Journal I am confronted with the question: Is all this sincere? Have I honestly meant all I have written at a moment and meant what I did? Can I truly have lived such experiences as I have recorded, uttered such words as are reflected here, entertained such thoughts? Are these glowing pages of love reflections of a *true* love?

Yes, Yes, a thousand times yes! All this was true, intensely, heartrendingly, overpoweringly true at the time it happened. I have sorrowed, rejoiced, felt even more than all I wrote. But that is the tragedy of change. It all passes, it falls, crumbles, vanishes into nothingness with time, and instantly new loves, new joys, new sorrows, replace the old ones. Hot, passionate emotions, intense love and devotion, promises, desires, resolutions, expressions of sentiments one might believe eternal—they all pass and change, and life flows on, sweeping it all along in its course, floods of memories piercingly sweet and agonizingly painful and heartrending, giving away before the powerful tide of the new which demands room and claims its right to absolute reign.

How clearly one sees the birth, the growth, the flowering, the decadence, the decay and death of all things, tangible and intangible, beautiful and ugly. Not one can resist the destroyer; youth and hope, strength and knowledge, beauty—all alike are swept into oblivion.

It is of no use to pause and to lament. The forces bear you on and on; even while you are writing, life rushes onward with its tragic changes and transformations.

And I stand with hands extended in supplication, and I wait breathlessly on the threshold of every new Chapter of what I please to consider a story—a story whose end and purpose and moral is yet unrevealed and even unsuspected.

Work teaches one to drop dreaming, thinking and meditation with unbelievable rapidity, and to become again keenly conscious of surroundings and of what is to be done next, at instant notice. It is an art to be able to pass from one thing to another, however contrasting, without losing one's mental poise and calm sangfroid.

Why am I repulsed by talk of sex and mention of whatever is animal in us, when coarsely and frankly dealt with? The animal in man, it seems to me, can be refined and spiritualized. If only we ceased to vulgarize through speech things which should come most naturally to us, and become beautiful through their naturalness and spontaneity and unconsciousness, through the purity of the creative desire—and through their *wordlessness!* The act of reproduction should not in itself occupy so unwholesome an interest.

Oh, for the magic touch, the power of enchantment words and names can render to the commonest objects and phases of existence. Why I evade books such as *The Woman Question* is because natural and inevitable things are given crude and repulsive shapes. Sensitiveness to language and treatment is found far too seldom, alas. Most minds are callous to the beauty of suggestion and, in the search for truth, clothe it with their own coarseness and bestiality or, to put it mildly, their lack of artistry, making repulsive materialism out of a subtle, delicate web of facts.

Having known sorrow, I promise myself no one shall suffer through me, or suffer if it is in my power to alleviate their pain. Having seen my ideal conceptions flung aside, trampled on, cruelly disregarded, and having known agony, I will spare others and never inflict equal pain upon them.

Experience, if it embitters instead of sweetens, softens, melts, if it weakens instead of inspires us, if it degrades and debases instead of ennobles and purifies, has then proved stronger than our character and superior to our intellect. We should pass *through* and *above* it, enriched and not impoverished by the crucial test and lifelong struggle.

August 26. The one subject that occupies my whole mind and heart is the one I have avoided all this time for fear of it. My beloved is sailing for Europe the 13th of September. The thought is agony to me, but this absence, this trip of three months, is absolutely necessary. He has had a breakdown and his health is seriously impaired. I am torn between the full realization of this fact and my selfish love for him, which makes me cling to him, ready to give my life only to keep him by my side a few months more. But the other love, the love that sacrifices and understands, shall win.

I count the days. I shower on him now all the love it is possible for me to give. The day I am deprived of his presence, something in me will die—oh, I must not think of it, I must not think of it.

Our last days together—we must crowd in them all the happiness, all the charm and tenderness, they can hold. How we shall hunger for their return; how we shall live upon the memory of them! It seems incredible, but the thought of losing him even for three months gives me the greatest pangs of pain I have ever known.

September 15. Hugo has gone and I have three months in which to make the supreme decision of my life. I shall bend all my energies to the solving of my question. I spend my days in thought; I have never scrutinized life as closely or as intently, have never listened for the voices of inspiration with so much earnestness and never lived under so sorrowful a cloud of persistent and willful brooding and questioning as I have lately. And all because Hugo in his unconscious way made me feel during our last days together the greatness of the sacrifice I make if I marry him. And I am torn between the desire to say these words: "Leave me. I have a greater duty to myself." Or, "I love you. I am strong enough to bear the burden of sacrifice."

Too often, in moments of disappointment so inevitable to dreamers, have I doubted my choice and tortured myself with the fear that I did not love Hugo, that it was all a trick of fancy, that I was again the dupe of too vivid an imagination.

He is not as I thought him to be; he is no god but a man like all the others He is the opposite of all I had conceived and dreamed. And yet I love him. I love him in spite of his shortcomings. I love him beyond these, and I seem to be capable of seeing Hugo noble and great through these faults of his.

What he can rise to be at his best moments, what heights he attains from time to time when, like one inspired, he acts precisely as I had longed to see him act—then I see him transfigured; I see the Hugo of my love dreams, the man within the man.

Nothing he does afterward seems to correspond to the character I endow him with. Then it is he disappoints me profoundly, and I accuse him of being crude and matter-of-fact and of bringing me "down."

I can explain this better by an example. When he confided to me that he had loved someone before me, I felt he was tearing with thoughtless fingers one of my best-loved dreams of him.

How often I had dwelt on Hugo's purity of heart, secretly prizing this quality in him as highly as I did his intelligence or his understanding. It was a cherished ideal I worshiped in him— but could he grasp all this? Could he correctly interpret the nature of my disappointment? Alas, whatever he attributed it to, jealousy or piqued vanity or pride, I do not care to know. It was enough to realize he could not grasp the most extraordinary and the most characteristic of my fancies.

"I wouldn't be human . . ." he ended.

That is just it. Hugo is *human*. I would have liked that he should have come straight to me with a heart never stirred before. It suited my ideal conception, my fanciful fabrications, my habit of weaving stories . . . and by the way, my habit for picking the impossible as the only reality.

Fortunately, I recognize the fault as lying in myself. I am romantic, imaginative, poetical and practical; I am loving and devoted and consumed by the desire to understand, but I am not *human*, and it is the human in others which I am at a loss to understand.

I must learn to fashion my dreams out of clay, to descend in order to rise, because I am repudiating the human, I am repudiating the roots of divinity. What *is* is what I must learn to love.

September 16. Hugo is essentially a purely physical being above all else. He lets the flesh control his emotions and moods as well as his love. And it is that which separates us. I live more on the mental. I have a control over my body which is so potent that the physical seldom influences me or is responsible for my acts. It is not that I forget the fact that it is at the basis of all things and that my physical being is at the root of all the spiritual, or that I do not realize how often my own moods and sadness spring from weariness of body. No. It is that at the crucial moment I can always rise above it all and act, sustained by some inner and invisible force which is beyond the human. Hunger or cold, weariness or illness, through all these my will can pass untouched and the Thing could move me to action until the very breath of life fled from me.

This, for which I have no name, Hugo lacks.

The night of our leave-taking he wounded me most deeply, not for the second or even third time but for the thousandth! He was going to Europe. I felt him thrilled and eager, and this alone should have opened my eyes to his thoughtlessness. It was in his power to leave me a sweet memory of our last night together. One expression of feeling and regret, a little warmth and tenderness, might have given me enough happiness to treasure during his absence. He was going to be happy, and I, left alone, and yet, even now when his love for me should have been at its highest and inspired unselfishness and kindness in him, it moved him only to demand more from me, to expect that I should understand when I felt no response to my tenderness and sadness.

He was tired, he told me. I was exhausted that night also, and yet my love was beyond that, and I *forgot* myself in him, while he remembered himself only and himself above me!

Is his a love worthy of my own?

This casual manner at the moment when I had greater need of a proof of his best nature left me with a sense of irretrievable loss and gave me the greatest agony of my life. I sobbed bitterly and desperately, called him back to tell him never to return to me.

In Mother's love I took refuge, and in Mother's love I found balm. Had it not been for her that night, I would have died.

Had I asked too much, expected too much that time also? Ah, no. His love is small, small and selfish, and each test of it reveals it more in that light.

Evening. From the moment he left me until an hour or so before sailing, when he telephoned, I suffered what it is beyond my power to describe. I talked with my own self and struggled to regain control. I talked to Hugo, despite the furious agony of my soul, as quietly as if he were listening to me and I would not say too much lest I hurt him.

"All I have asked of you is love. Others demand more—a home, protection, comfort, none of which you are able to offer me and which I hunger for. Yet I was satisfied, and love to its fullest measure replaced whatever gifts were not in your power to grant me. But love gives itself at least without thought of its own self, and marriage can only be made happy by the care and devotion of one for the other, not each for his own self. And Hugo, it is this devotion I find lacking in you, so that life with you would be an immolation of myself. And who are *you* that you should expect such a sacrifice? A man . . . and I shall not waste my life on a man when I can employ it for the service of humanity."

My thoughts were all at war with one another. My heart was fire and ice by turn. His last words to me had been: "Be strong!"

Be strong, to bear the wounds of his own hands!

Then he telephoned to hear my voice again. His own was joyful and thrilling. I could visualize the boy's expression lighting his face at the moment. The thoughtless, rough-hearted and happy boy—I forgot all my sorrow. I shared his satisfaction. My whole body shook, my voice trembled and sounded far off, but he never knew or guessed. Nor shall he ever know that "me" who is beyond his understanding and whose love he shall never possess.

My last words for him were: "Be happy! Be happy!" I want him to come back well and strong and happy, even if it is not to me that he is returning.

Before *that* day was over, I almost believed I loved Hugo more than myself and that I would sacrifice *all* for him. It is in his rugged nature with its inherent selfishness that my own has found a sympathetic chord. It is to this man that a great force draws me.

After all, I am weary of seeking a perfect harmony of souls. It does not exist. We are all destined to an eternal solitude. Love only relieves this solitude by moments of utter and sublime communion and unity, by fleeting touches and a sense of nearness both rare and frail.

And there is more to consider than our own happiness. Hugo would be a good father to my children, a loyal, conscientious and dutiful husband. Can I expect, *besides* the altruism and devotion of a Great Lover, gentleness and tenderness, response to all that is feminine and soft and reliant in me?

Alas! "The ideal has poisoned reality for me." I was never meant for happiness. I cannot be happy in such a world among such people. But at least I could redeem the failure of my own heart by making others happy and become purified and ennobled by the task. The question is: would my marriage to Hugo mean happiness for him?

If it did, at least my life would not have been in vain, as it otherwise would be if I chose rather to live only for myself and my writing and to seek only peace and a life free of responsibility, all fetters and duties; a life of pure thought and study, arid of affection and untouched by humanity, and by all sorrows of the heart, therefore, which are so much harder to bear than the sorrows of the intellect.

Meanwhile, of one thing I am certain; I shall let Hugo

regain his health and drink his cup of pleasure to the last drop. He shall not be troubled with the faintest inkling of my struggle and shall only know the outcome.

These are the strongest and saddest days of my life. I am overwhelmed by a sense of desolation and the futility of existence and the worthlessness of it all and by the realization that nothing is worthy of either interest or emotion—and still less of tears.

At loss for a way to relieve myself of the pressure of life, seeking an outlet for the overwhelming tide of sentiment, enclosed on all sides by a multitude of problems and difficulties, I take refuge in my old habit of writing.

I leave all action behind me, I fly from the visible world into that of thought and plunge into phrases hungrily, hoping the making of them will abate my suffering and serve as a balm for the fever and anxiety consuming me. I escape in no way from what is hurting me because my grief comes from within myself. I *am* sorrow, my thoughts are sorrow, and I cannot fly from my own thoughts. But I believe that treating all this as a writer, turning realities into material for artistic creation and for observation, the practice necessary to literature, I may smooth the agony of *actual* living through my interest in it as a thinker and critic. I may learn to detach myself somewhat, and the pangs, having become a subject of mere literary curiosity, must of necessity be felt less personally.

And this I do not feel to be cowardice, because I do *not fear*. I am at the end of my strength when I most need it, and if I can retain my balance, I may retain my moral hold on life. Knowing that it is through writing that I usually find my balance, I want to make use of it as a means more than as an escape.

How often I have found balance after sifting all my facts and fancies through my ink bottle.

September 17.
Cher Papa:[1]

I have hesitated a long time before answering your letter because what I have to say is going to hurt you. Above all, I want you to know that in spite of my love for you, I am obliged to write you the sad truth.

Your wish to see us cannot be realized, or at least not in the

---

[1] *Letter translated from the French.*

way you thought. After all the years that Mother has spent struggling for us, laden down with responsibilities and worries, now she is weary but has her reward. Thorvald and I have reached an age at which we can join our strength to hers, and we are working with her to support the family that you created and that you should have supported. You never realized that your children would suffer so much, be deprived of so many things, and have lives filled to the brim with difficulties and sacrifices and need—because of you, through your fault. We have never complained. We have never said to one another, when we saw other children's fathers: Why doesn't our father work for us? Why doesn't our father give us what all fathers give their children?

No. We have never complained, because our mother gave us everything she could, while teaching us we could be happy enough with that. And she has never let us feel the great gap you left in our life by depriving us of all that you owed to us, your children. By her great courage, by her strength, by her energy, by that tenderness combined with intelligence from which children draw the inspiration essential to life, our mother was able to replace your duty, your presence, your influence.

The man who ceases to maintain and serve his home is like a creator who abandons his work . . . and loses it.

Now that Thorvald is a young man and I am a woman, we are ready to share the burden. Now you ask us to come to you. Are we to leave our mother at a time when she needs our support and our energy? A thousand times no!

We are carrying out the mission that you did not accomplish. With our young strength, we are paying the price of the obligation you ran away from.

Your son has had to sacrifice his dearest dream. He graduated from school with highest honors, and in addition won a prize that would have admitted him to an advanced school where he could have begun studying for his career in engineering. Instead he is working, already in harness instead of studying and enjoying himself. When he should be leading the life of a young lad, he is leading the life of a man. So soon!

Also, your daughter is engaged.

If I seem hard on you, oh, Papa! think of all the sorrow I have felt in realizing, little by little, the extent of your mistakes against us. Our whole childhood was darkened by you. Our whole youth is difficult, hard, sad, because of you.

That is all I have to tell you. If you understand, fine. If not, nothing I can say will help you to see something that depends on your interpretation of: Justice.

Your daughter, who suffers for you and with you,

Anaïs

Some time ago I wrote to Eduardo, and before throwing away the scrap of paper on which I first planned the letter, I want to keep this: "It is well for you to escape Action and keep your soul roaming idly in utter freedom, absorbing sunshine, so to speak, and remaining unsoiled, unstained by darkness. But surely that day will come when higher things will call you, as they have called me, the need to love and to live and work for others. And then you will have to work and act among practical men and women and win your bread from the same pitiless soil and shoulder the same pitiless responsibilities. Be strong then, as strong about that side of life—actual, visible life—as you are now about the intangible thought life. Only conquering both makes the complete man or woman.

"Do not think of me, however, as one who has stepped from one creed into another. I hold your life of the mind in both my hands and shall never let it go. But both my feet are on the ground.

". . . However, it seems to me there is little need for me to spur you on. You are well off upon your road and advancing at a splendid pace. It gives me deep pleasure to see you thus set on fire and so utterly devoted, so single-hearted in the pursuit of your goal. Through your letters I can watch the formation of your character as well. I am proud of you, and I want you to know it!"

Eduardo was here three days before leaving for school in August. We were together only one evening, for when he came again to see me, Hugo, Eugene and John Guiler[1] were here.

On that first evening we had the same kind of talk as "of old," except that Eduardo and I were both changed by a multitude of experiences, and we found greater charm in rediscovering each other's heart. How good, how *lovable* and noble he is! I treasure his friendship and it inspires me.

He has already written. Once more we dream together and feel together. The second evening was devoted to heated philo-

[1] *Hugo's brother.*

sophical discussions in which Eduardo took little part, voicing now and then my very own thoughts, the result of my teaching!

September 18. Today I come to you humble and repentant. It is with the most profound shame that I have read the preceding pages. Truly, I, who write so much of conquering the physical and of meeting experience by strength, let myself be mastered by most unreasonable sadness. It is beyond my understanding to grasp what in my nature moves me to see everything so tragically, what it is which awakens in me such deep, solemn and distressed responses. Have I no humor, that I cannot realize my own foolishness? Have I no eyes to see when things are worth despair and when not?

I resolve today to do all in my power to control this tendency to the tragic, and this I shall do first of all by laughing at myself, laughing at my seriousness, my weakness of spirit, my lack of courage and all the absurd ways I have of interpreting life and the world, as if they were grim and fierce forces, acting but to destroy—when the whole thing is, in truth, but a little play of most short duration and thoroughly amusing and interesting when one has the wit to find it so.

But I must not waste time. Whatever I write thus each day is the product of a few spare minutes I have following my lunch—a half-hour or so, which I spend in a hotel lobby in the midst of chatter and confusion. It seemed difficult at first to shut myself away from sound, to retire within myself in order to hear the voices of my own mind, but having once reached the seclusion of my own chamber of thoughts, I find it easier day by day to remain in it undisturbed until the moment of my departure. It is the clock alone which upsets me, pointing irrevocably to the hour when I must close this book and return to work. But it will be good practice for me to be forced to say only what is most necessary. I can no longer allow a few minutes to elapse between each thought and watch them strolling in deliberately, one by one—nor can I take so long about the choice of them. They must pass quickly and be caught at hazard. Whatever is displeasing to you shall henceforward be blamed on the surroundings, the hour, the circumstances.

By talking much with everyone, I have discovered many things and gained the finer knowledge of people. Gradually the life of all those with whom I work has been partly revealed to me. Theirs is a life of arduous toiling. Each evening finds them tired;

they have longings, too, and days of sadness and discouragement. Listening to their talk of life and work and love, I had an insight into their homely philosophies, into their needs and their limitations. I heard sighs and complaints and expressions of envy and of self-pity, and I heard, too, one encouraging the other, smiling, telling her it did not pay to take things too hard. That day my heart went out to the girl who had lost courage under the weight of her burden. I wish that she would understand the look I gave her; I could find no simple words in which to convey a sympathy at which, I am certain, she would have been most surprised.

Homely philosophies, undramatically expressed, and yet they struck me, and I shall remember all they taught me.

That is where the poorer classes, who have missed the blessings of education, surpass us. They waste no time endeavoring to put things into words—they live them. They keep one another materially, they encourage each other by acts, they are satisfied with a few commonplace phrases. Sparing words and fine phrases, theirs is a less complicated life. No need of explanations and subtle searchings for the perfect name of things. Simple, direct words will do, and to even these they attach small importance. Yet this is the primitive, inarticulate stage from which we have struggled to rise, and it would be a weak creature indeed who would exchange progress for ignorance, for fear of the complications it brings into one's life.

It is the girl who works who truly possesses a heart. It is in the girls who work that I have found the greatest kindness and discovered the best qualities.

My days in Jaeckel's, apart from the great weariness they brought about, were very happy ones. I have learned to love the girls there and experienced among them all the sweetness of comradeship and mutual love of service. They are always doing little things for one another, and when they do little things for me my heart overflows with gratitude, and when I can do something for one of them I feel akin to bliss.

How well I could love people and how I want to love! I am at heart no savage, and if I have been rather a recluse, it is because I do not know how to get to people, how to pierce the distances and reach their hearts, because of shyness on my part. And now that this shyness is wearing off, I find a great joy in being close to girls of my age and to people in general. I am ever ready to give affection, but it is often smothered or frightened away by the other person's poise and apparent indifference; indifference above all else is what most quickly silences me.

How happy I am today and how *warmed* I am by my relations with other models. We have talked about clothes and the customers and our admirers and our ambitions, have given one another remedies for tired feet and advised each other about the color of our next dress . . . simple expansiveness to which I respond simply and under which I glow. I love those girls and I hope someday to give them the praise they deserve—in a book perhaps, that the world might know all there is of soul, gentleness, devotion and kindness in a mere model, and of how they plod under their tired, unselfish, well-filled life. I remember Beatrice Otten, Betty Ware, Miss Heller and Miller, Helen Eagen, Melisande.

Helen Eagen is a statuesque beauty. She has the most classical head I have ever seen, clear, strong features and a massive, sculptural figure, which gives no sense of throbbing humanity or of softness, flexibility or warmth, but of a thing carved by centuries of care and art in stone. Impassive beauty, one you would never imagine capable of chattering or laughing, and it always surprises me to see bursts of humor appear in her eyes and rippled laughter issue from those chiseled lips; it makes one think of a marble statue come to life.

Helen tells me that, when in repose, my expression is placid, restful and contented, a great contrast to the other girls'—hard or anxious, strained, discontented faces.

Probably she noticed me while I was dreaming! Thank heaven I still can dream. Oh, of all gifts, let not the power of dreaming be stolen from you, and you may conquer all things. The power to lift oneself above one's surroundings and to imagine, to create, to visualize, to invent, is a charm against despair and discontent, and it can disarm the greatest sorrow.

To be capable of imagining! What a world of power lies in the one word. I imagine . . . and in one bound my mind is freed from earthly fetters. It no longer hurls itself against locked doors; it soars along vast stretches of spacious, endless imaginings, it flies, it roams, it expands . . .

And then, to dream is to see through the appearance of things, where truth alone can dwell, for truth is ever hidden and disguised, and to see truth is to see goodness, and to see goodness is to see all beauty, all perfection . . . the ideal. As others are saved by their sense of humor, I am saved by my idealism.

It is a religious feeling that is returning to me. I repudiated its forms and it comes to me pure and unfettered, not the appearance but the feeling itself, formless, invisible to human eye and revealing itself to the mind alone, in all its penetrating sincerity. Oh, I have reached a ray of truth, of divinity. It all comes to me through the gift of seeing beyond the facts, beyond the human world, into the thing itself, stripped of form and name. That is what truth *is!* I am still and shall forever be alone in my sorrows, because they are always deeper than the normal and reasonable and can be neither shared nor communicated to others. But at least no sorrowing creature shall feel alone with me, because I shall always *know* and my heart will forever go out to whoever suffers; nor shall anyone's grief pass beyond my understanding. I want to love the world. I want to develop more kindness, to subdue the critical, to be tolerant. And in order not to burden others with the sight of my sorrow, I will feign passivity in all its forms so that by no word or act of mine shall I betray the war being waged perpetually within me.

[*September ?*]. *Women's Beauty* (At Jaeckel's). Life among mirrors reminds me of a quotation expressing the belief that woman spends hours in contemplation of her reflection moved by an unconscious desire to understand herself. Does it not, in appearance, seem sensible that one should seek knowledge of one's self through a close scrutiny of the outward mold?

How infinitesimal is the knowledge thus gained!

Beauty of face and form is a thing apart and detached from spirit. True, an expression from within might illumine an otherwise meaningless set of features and through this medium translate an emotion better than words.

But gravity of bearing, ease of manner, softness of contour, fineness of features, all might mean everything—or nothing. Some relation between the physical and the mental might exist in some isolated cases, approaching the ideal, but not in a general instance.

Somehow one cannot refrain from considering the body as the clumsiest medium of expression in our possession. And poor are the means, indeed, which entrust an imagination, an intellect or a kind heart to the shape and coloring and texture or quality of our outward envelope and render them dependent on these material signs for translation and demonstration.

One cannot say absolutely that the physical may not be an

expression of the spiritual (considering exceptions), but one can state with a high degree of assurance that it is rarely a fitting and perfect expression.

What thoughts can pass through a head and leave the face impassive, masklike, impenetrable! What secret laughter or gentle raillery can fill a heart to overflowing and never appear on the surface or betray itself in either word or look. No trace of inner joy or suffering need ever speak through eyes or quivering lips if these have been trained in unconscious self-control.

Woman, instead of gaining a better knowledge of herself, may become more confused by a thousand conflicting reflections gazing back at her from the rippled surface of her soul. Sweetness and anger, vanity and disinterestedness, gratitude and disdain, compassion and coquetry, thoughtlessness and emotion, fidelity and fickleness, all opposite, passing like so many clouds, dissolving, vanishing—replaced by love, by ambition, by visions, by faith, by submissiveness and pride. Forever passing in an endless procession, looking out from within, appearing on the surface and submerged by an ever changing, ever increasing tide of sentiment and thought.

September 20. Back to the little writing table amidst chatter and confusion . . . the only thing which has not yet changed about me, and I cling to it for an assurance that I am *real* and that everything is *real.*

Yes. Here you are and here is the table and here I am, but the rest of the world, the picture I was gazing at so intently, the state of things I was struggling to explain . . . what has become of them all? With the rapidity of lightning, the world offers me a new face, and I cannot find in it the vaguest trace of the old. What has happened? Where am I? What does this new face mean, and what has suddenly made it turn full upon me?

I can decipher with no difficulty the meaning of the "ensemble," the whole expression in general, not the details. It all spells in magic, glowing letters: Opportunity.

Tia Antolina is taking me to Cuba. One of Mother's dreams is to be realized, and through me. Besides, Tia Antolina finds herself given the opportunity to return her sister the good she has done her.

I can regain strength and health, which I so sorely lack now, and return better able to help Mother. This great plan is pleasing to everybody; the only sadness of it is the fact of my being separated from Mother, but she is the first to wave that aside, and I want to prove to her I too can be sensible.

Consider all the good that comes of it. I can be of use to Tia Antolina, and I can make Mother happy. I can please Mother by success and contentment. I am free; I can rest and play and teach myself that cheerfulness and lightheartedness I miss in myself through lack of proper training and (again!) *opportunity*.

I can return to Mother with renewed courage and energy. Working as I am now, I feel as if I could never live through the Winter. My life has been too serious, too cramped, too intense, and everything about it has only helped to exaggerate the tendencies in my nature most to be condemned and mistrusted. Now I can be happy, and only in a wholesome and balanced state can one be fit to serve those one loves.

I have a great plan in my mind by which I can make Mother happy and lift the tremendous burden from her shoulders.[1] I have given my word. The decision is made and I am resolved to make the most of the miraculous opportunity. If I cannot make a success of my life now when so much is offered me, I never shall. And life is, after all, only worth living in proportion to *what we can do for those we love*, to what we can give and how much we can serve.

This shall be my creed henceforward and the law by which I shall abide. Every action of mine shall be criticized and viewed under that light, wanting or satisfactory in measure with its bearing upon this belief. And who shall not say with me after this: "I believe in fairy tales, I believe in miracles, in chance and luck and in all that is impossible, the improbable, the incredible, unexpected and unbelievable."

Evening. Inherent idealism alone bears me safely through these dangerous and despairing mental crises. While I express doubt, something in my nature secretly and tenaciously maintains its faith and loyalty. While I speak of being struck by a sense of the futility and smallness of existence, part of me is melting with love and an all-embracing pity and the desire to live.

Nevertheless, I am astounded by my capacity for grief and feel a thing akin to fear toward the unfathomable depths I find in myself, the intensity of my despairs, my passionate outbursts and my intolerable sensitiveness.

[1] *A.N. had decided to sacrifice herself by marrying a rich Cuban.*

September 21. I cannot believe love to be true if, for a time at least, it does not soften the failings of the beloved. While there is criticism without forgiveness, there is a weakness somewhere in the affection, and its stability and duration cannot be trusted.

Looking over the beginning of this book, I am surprised at the strength of the love which inspired it. Can such a love ever die? I ask myself. Can such a love ever be changed or forgotten?

And yet . . . it seems to me that it is when love is strongest and most passionate that it most quickly ceases to exist if the object of it proves unworthy or falls short of its expectations. Love, like warm and quiet love, will accept its disappointment with greater indifference because it is the lesser love. But love, so infinite, so self-abandoning as I have felt, if Hugo disappoints me, will die far more quickly and far more completely than any other. And how long can my love for him last if so much of what he does I can criticize without forgiving? God help me!

It is not that life is proving too much for me mentally, but it is the physical burden of existence that wears me down. What I feel is more than a transient weariness, and these last days I realized how inevitable it was that I should go with Tia Antolina for a time at least and conform myself to an indefinite sojourn in Cuba.

Why am I not strong and energetic like so many others? Why must work play such havoc with my endurance and threaten to ruin my health? Shall anyone foretell the outcome of this decisive step—its influence upon my whole future? It may determine what my life is to be henceforth; it may save me from a treacherous blunder; it may unshadow my whole existence; it may be the cause of much regret—or much happiness.

And meanwhile the play goes on, interminable, and keeping the end as the mystery of mysteries . . . And we cannot pause to demand an explanation or to think; we must live on and on and on.

With what hopes and tenderness and pride I wrote on the first page of this journal: "Journal d'une Fiancée." And it is this very book which contains the story of Hugo's departure for Europe and of mine for Cuba. He, in the very midst of the first year of our love, can leave me.

Only a miracle can make our marriage possible, and I have strange forebodings that we are being separated not for weeks or months or years but for eternity.

I have kept myself so occupied, have filled every hour so well, that I can honestly say I have not missed Hugo an instant.

No sense of loss has yet come to me, and I feel no longing for him. Is this the result of such self-control that I become and feel what I *should* be instead of what I am naturally?

September 23. Today the sound of a street organ reaching me in the midst of my work suggested to my willing imagination freedom and sunshine and health. The homely little music held me spellbound, floating amid a host of dreams.

I looked at the other faces and was tempted to tell them: "Oh, I wish you were all going to be free with me! I wish you could all rest as I am going to rest." Why was I chosen by fate from among all them to be made happy? I who did not deserve it, because I have not been good, I have not been noble—I who cried out against my fetters when I had promised to bear so much.

But I know how to make amends for all this. There is one thing I can do for Mother and my little brother, and if it depends on me alone, it shall be done. I do not want to write of it yet.

September 24. Today is one of the days when my power of vision is sharpened to its finest edge and my ideas are incredibly vivid and clear. I cannot suppress the tide of thought swelling within me and the overwhelming desire to write which always follows in its wake.

I had so many of those days long ago! I could not move away from my writing table; the fever of composition would take hold of me and burn in me with passionate intensity. And what joy to feel the return of such a state! To feel keenly alive and to know for certain that one is not yet buried beneath the ruins of skepticism and self-destroying speculation. I have passed through all my sorrows as if they had been necessary steps in my growth and expansion. And I feel enriched by every incident, every thought, every emotion that has visited me; and what is more, I feel enriched by every *doubt,* every misstep and fall as well, so that whatever I have recorded in hurried moments, even if I be tempted to term it the history of mistakes, still stands as a thing of merit, inasmuch as it has served its purpose.

Life on a day like this is brimful of hope and renewed expectations. Old dreams spring up again, and youth turns all it touches into gold. It is the Spring of the soul, which comes not once but as often as it triumphs over its miseries during its one year of inward progress.

This morning I stepped forth with H. W. Mabie's little book

tucked under my arm, sensing the chill in the air. I became intoxicated by the thrilling, vibrant charm of Autumn and remembered what he had written: "The sense of pressure, of limitation, so constant and often so oppressive in the routine or ordinary life, vanishes and then comes in its place a sudden exhilaration."

I hummed as I tripped along in the glittering sunlight and overflowed with youth and joy, gratitude and confidence.

Last night I dreamed of Hugo. He came back to me and kissed me repeatedly and fervently as he used to do and talked to me of his ideas of life. I awoke wrapped in the glamour of a love I thought to be dying. Memories of Hugo rushed upon me, and I experienced the first pang of longing since his departure. I want him back. I want the Hugo of my dreams back but without those things by which he wounds me and which estrange us.

Yearning for the ideal again, sighing for the impossible! Hugo cannot change for my sake. There is an element in his nature toward which I feel an instinctive antagonism, and I must bear it in mind when the romantic mood comes to me and when I see him as I want him to be and not as he *is*.

October 1.

Dear Eduardo:

. . . Above all else I want to give you my opinion of your sonnet. Eduardo, it is an exceedingly beautiful piece of work and expresses a true knowledge of "the inward sphere of things," a sensitiveness to the spiritual meaning, a power of vision extending far and deep—in short, it expresses the gift of *interpretation* through spirit, which is as rare as it is precious. I wish I could say more, but whatever I have felt while reading it has remained vague and formless, more like the flow of an emotion than the shaping of a definite idea.

And now, while you continue to indulge your inclination and to drink deeply of the Cup of Knowledge and Poetry and Philosophy, I, your "mere elusive spirit," am set forth to wander in "El Mundo de los muñecos"[1] and to have my taste of the Cup of Pleasure and Frivolity. I am being transformed into a butterfly. a sunflower or whatever you may wish to call me. I must hide beneath brilliant wings a heart most weary with problems and difficulties. And Eduardo, I am going to be spiritually in utter loneliness, and I am counting upon your letters to help me to

[1] *The world of the puppets.*

keep my wings fluttering and to sustain me through my Great Pretense—for I shall pretend to be everything that I am not and betray to no one that creature of serious thoughts and intense ideals and hermit instincts which you know so well!

The Great Pretense! The brooding heart silent beneath the light and careless chatter, the ever active mind disguised beneath frivolous acts. Do you judge me ill for keeping my real self only for the few who understand? I am certain you approve, either boisterously or secretly (and with a quiet chuckle) or mildly and hesitatingly—it does not matter as long as you approve a little. By and by I shall convince you that I *am* right.

. . . In spite of what I say, Eduardo, I believe I am going to be quite happy there, and I *am* looking forward to it all as one does to a great adventure. . . .

Oh, Hugo, you are my dream, and yet you seem intent on doing all to prove your self the very opposite! One thing I know; I shall never cease loving you, I shall never love anyone else. Whoever has had a glimpse into the ideal, however fleeting, can never be satisfied with anything smaller or inferior. You gave me such a glimpse, and for it I can forgive the actions which veil my visions and leave my expectations unfulfilled.

You are the embodiment of harsh realities of existence, and yet you are all my poetry. You have a way of forcing plain facts upon me and yet hold in your hand the power to enchant, transport and touch me.

Alas, tonight I feel capable of proving the extent of my love through marriage. I am strong enough, I am strong enough to love him in spite of all his faults. Yes, my love can outlive my illusions and my dreams!

But, my own Hugo, my beloved, it is too late, too late . . .

It is when I judge Hugo with my mind rather than with my heart that I see his faults. When he did something that displeased me, I soon forgot it under the spell of his nearness, and whatever anger I felt melted before his glance, and I was instantly disarmed by the very touch of his hand on mine. The woman's heart muses lovingly on the times when he reached the heights of nobility, generous and kindly impulses, and sees him at his best, and even now, when I find a thousand proofs of his selfishness, his egoism, surrounding me, I tell myself with the characteristic, womanlike logic: *all* men are selfish egoists—why should not Hugo be so too?

October 2. This evening Joaquin sat at the piano and played the accompaniment to Madame Butterfly. (Un beau jour,[1] etc.) while Mother sang. At first I listened to the glorious notes with a feeling of pure admiration for Mother's voice, and then suddenly the music penetrated to my inmost being, and its plaintive, sorrowful quality pierced me. I imagined myself in Havana, far, so far from my little mother, far from Joaquin and Thorvald, deprived of the joy of seeing and hearing them all . . . going forth alone, leaving behind what is dearest to me in this world, what this little old home holds now within its humble walls, all my joys, my love, my very life!

From my heart welled burning, desperate and bitter tears. More than the pain of separation commonly felt by ordinary creatures, mine was agony, agony because I love so much, so much, and even now as I write, my hand trembles and my whole being is ravaged by a sorrow I must control, knowing too well that it lies far beyond the bounds of reason!

I leave on the seventh, I believe, and it is a marvel that in the midst of so much hustling, preparations and confusions, I should find time to write; but it is my one source of calm. When my nerves become stretched at their highest tension, then I drop things and I write, and I am soothed as by some soft melody.

Last week I left Jaeckel's, where I worked but a few weeks, and all I have done ever since is sew and remake and create and shop and prepare the thousand and one things which go to the making of a lady's wardrobe. I am with Mother all I possibly can be. And my feelings are a weird mixture of regret, despair, and gratitude and expectation. One moment I am filled with apprehensions, another, with exultation and confidence. I have asked Mother a million times: Are you satisfied with this plan? Does it make you happy? And she, my darling, always says yes, and we kiss more fondly than ever, telling nothing of what it costs us to view our separation reasonably.

I hear with a sad and mysterious smile what everyone has to say about this and what they wish for me: they envy me, they tell me to make good use of my opportunity, to return married to wealth so that I may help Mother. What clumsy, thoughtless, stupid things people are wont to say. And little do they know how closely they touch ideas which I do entertain but which in

[1] *The aria "Un bel dì"—One fine day.*

the workings of my own mind appear less crude and less repulsive. To hear someone say that the only solution to Mother's difficulties is in my marriage to money shocks me profoundly. To me it can become beautiful and an ideal. Under the touch of my fingers it loses every vestige of baseness. I transform the ugly thought into a passionate prayer, an offering, a renunciation. Let others take it as they will, see it as they must, being what they are, but within me I bear the assurance of the act made right through the intention, sanctified through the purity of the *desire*. Within me I bear my self-made standard of nobility and my way of measuring the greater or lesser duty, the higher or lower call . . . and I judge by no others.

Others will judge me by their own standards, making wrong what I believe right. Suffice it that I myself approve and that I do not forget to judge others by their own standards. These days, I realize how few are those I regret leaving, outside my home. Not a soul in Kew Gardens but Bob, whom I have remembered as I passed by his house, and then Frances . . . and then?

October 3. Following many discussions on our contrasting ideas of life, one night I resolved to tell Hugo that it was impossible for him to change me, that I did *not want* to change and that I thought we should better separate than continue this opposition of opinion with so much obstinacy on both parts. Somehow *all* our ideas had been touched upon, and we had reached a summary of our philosophies and realized how far they were from harmony. Among the many things which hurt me, there was the fact that I understood Hugo to be driving me away from my ideal of a "home" and talking to me of outside ambition and achievement. His persistent talk of mastering the practical of life, etc., seemed to encompass a sphere I had no desire to reach.

And then he forever brought before me the idea of completeness in one being when I talked of completeness reached through love and marriage. I meant that he should excel in his line of work and be monarch of his world of affairs and practical administration—that I should excel in my own line as woman and give more time to the things most needed and most fitting to my place, and devote my energy to the pursuit of the thing I love and toward which I feel an inclination, even as I believe he should, instead of distributing his time among a thousand pursuits, none of which he fulfilled particularly well.

This we found applicable to the little things as well as the great ones of our lives, and therefore it is natural that it should have assumed such importance in our eyes. We were planning our life, and our plans did not correspond.

I struggled with these conflicting thoughts and sought a solution. After our long talk, I spent the night wide awake, in high fever and tossing continually; the fluctuations of my own heart and mind were intolerable. Finally I reached the decision which seemed like the signing of my own death sentence.

I sent for Hugo, and he came in the evening. I had made myself ill with sorrow and spent the day in bed, and I met him with a white, white face and cold hands. He had a surprise for me. At the first words I uttered, I felt him deeply shaken. His voice became as unsteady as my own, but he rose very quickly, searched his pocket and brought me a letter.

"The other night when I left you, Anaïs, I could not sleep and I wrote you this because I wanted to explain it all better. Whatever moved me to do it . . . how glad I am now. Listen."

He began in those moving tones by which I recognize his deeper feelings. Often I have hesitated to tell him things so as not to see the hurt look in his eyes or hear those strangely touching and appealing tones. The reading of that letter I shall never forget, for it was Hugo at his best. And I want it copied here because he wrote it in pale pencil and it is nearly effaced:

"I thought of a way to make this idea plainer and more workable for you. You know I said it was a vital affair for us, and I think you know what I meant by that—that it affects directly our mode of living, and upon it we will begin acting tomorrow morning and the next morning and each day of our lives. And our lives are a trust which is not alone ours, but for which we are to be held in the end responsible. It is what we are and what we do that tells our own thoughts. This is what holds the character of children, for I believe it is not until they are quite grown that words begin to have some meaning for them. The first and most decisive molding, however, is accomplished by the silent, wordless persuasion of the mother's personality. What she has decided to be and is will determine more than anything else the child's fate for better or for worse. No chance of her advocating one course of action while she herself is acting another, for we can conceal nothing from the child. No use to be urging the little one to be self-reliant in even little things, to become skillful in handling the machinery of life, if we do not exhibit ourselves as successful masters in the art. I am assuming that we have arrived at the conclusion that it is not possible to carry out the idea of selection from life which you spoke about to the point of excluding skill in handling the machinery. I am assuming that we have the courage to grasp this clay of ours in all its apparent ugliness and with our hands mold it into something strange and beautiful.

"Anaïs, I wonder if I have been really honest with you about my character. I have tried to be enough times, I know, but each time it seemed to shock you so much that I have had to be silent about it for fear of losing your regard. It has almost seemed sometimes that I would have to be someone other than what I thought my best self in order to come up to your ideal of what I should be. I think again and again of Carlyle's conclusion in the *Everlasting Yea*, when he was satisfied with a simple home and homely pleasure and they made up the sum of happiness for him. I feel that your reaction to my talk of perfection has been that I am traveling from this idea of simplicity, but if I had only spoken more plainly to you, you would have seen that it is not so. These things for the house, these little things, *are* what I crave and they are my poetry. If you love them too, Anaïs, as you say you do, then just show it in the little ways that mean so much. That is why I have felt hurt when you spoke of selecting the high peaks of life and not, as it were, soiling your hands with the common, practical things. Anaïs, dear, a house is a little world in miniature, and it is here more than in any place that there is a heavenly mandate for wife and husband, side by side, to work with a holy joy, for the perfect ordering of practical things. Over and over again, we have spoken of these practical things, and the most you concede is that they are necessary evils and when we speak of them we are 'coming down,' as you express it. If it shocks you to come down in this way, to do these yourself, Anaïs, will it not be too much to ask you to devote your life to using your mind in the preparation of food, in teaching little hands to do the common daily tasks, as well as in arithmetic, in managing and organizing a household even to its finances, in taking charge of its relations with other households, in doing, in fact, each of these things which you appear to avoid, even while having an interest in them, in theory at least?

"My dear one, what is it you dream of when your dreams are of a home, as I know they are? Are they of some indefinite, beautiful existence which takes no exact shape but which lives on love alone? I spoke, you remember, of about three-quarters of our life being occupied with these common things. It will be more than that in the house, and if you do not find happiness in doing them, then I cannot see that you will be happy in a constant effort to flee from them."

Before Hugo even finished reading, he knew that he had misunderstood me, just as I had misunderstood him. I talked to him of how I had grown to think of a house exactly as he described it and that I did love the humblest duties of women and that I was willing to be practical . . . And he, in turn, expressed anger at the clumsiness of words and at the way they turned against me and became evil instead of a help to us in this struggle to understand each other. And we charmed each other's pain away with fervent kisses and promised to talk about all these things and write about them until they became clear to us both.

Side by side, thus, under the spell of love's illusions, we whispered with sublime confidence: "We *were* made for each other. No, our love is not a *mistake*."

Alas, that night Hugo was at his best. Only a few days later one of those faults through which I suffer so greatly would appear more glaringly than ever, and I would be plunged again into the realization that only a miracle could bring about our marriage.

October 4. Before such a letter as I received from Hugo, all *reasoning*, all judgment, vanish, and nothing is left in me but overpowering pity and tenderness. To Hugo, suffering, sad, tormented, unhappy, my love goes out once more in the form of a letter. While I have love to give him, it is all his. How unimportant are my displeasures and my disappointments compared to his need of me, his need of love and devotion!

My dearest Hugo:
Think of me and I will feel it, just as you must feel my thoughts about you, my desires for your happiness and my hope that you may find rest and that quiet satisfaction you so greatly need . . .
P.S. (At Midnight) Eugene has just left me. I have never seen him so talkative and so brilliant. He was truly at his best and charmed me by his clear eloquence and his knowledge. O beloved, if you had been here, I know you would have been pleased, because among the many things we touched upon in our talk, Eugene, almost unconsciously, showed me the relation between

economics and literature—economics and humanity. It flashed upon my understanding so clearly, so vividly, and I instantly saw and made this truth my own forever.

We talked too (in abstract terms) of people who express their thoughts and feelings by symbols, by words or gesture, and of those who do not. The first class, comprising the Latin race, will label the lack of expressiveness as a fault and the person guilty of it as one having missed a precious artistic gift. They have the love of symbols as artists. The second class, comprising the Anglo-Saxons, will say that understanding *beyond* symbols, understanding without form, is a proof of higher intelligence and higher culture which makes the symbol both primitive and superfluous. Now, both ways have proved successful and fully satisfactory to each race, and both, by themselves, are happy in the broad sense of the word. It is only when the two individuals meet that the difference is so sharply felt and that there is danger of misunderstanding. Now, Hugo, you see how natural is the impulse that moves me to write as I have done toward the end of this letter. It is the sense of *need*, the need of something which you can hardly conceive. Expressiveness in your writing makes itself felt in other ways than in words. And through an effort of the mind, through reasoning, I shall struggle to reach unimportant forms so dear to me because your happiness is far more in my eyes, and after all it was only because I believed it would be increased through these things that I so persistently sought to kindle them in you. It is always thus, with both of us; all we do seems so unreasonable, so thoughtless, to the other for whose sake it is done.

Eugene said he would write to me. Whatever the motives (and if it be through friendship for me I am only too glad), [it] does not matter as long as he writes. I feel that his ideas and knowledge are so valuable that they should be preserved, and it would be a great joy to me if I could get him to sustain a regular correspondence. No one can outlive me at writing letters, so if he follows my example faithfully, I can assure you much shall be preserved . . .

On reading all this over, I wonder that I should have so completely devoted these pages to Hugo when I was in the midst of my preparations for this change and clinging with infinite regret to my last days with Mother. I believe I was seeking to evade the subject which truly most filled my heart and mind by plunging into thoughts of Hugo.

October 7. On the train. Night. How strange, how unreal it all seems. What unutterable emotions fill my heart, what confused thoughts cross my mind as I lie here to dream before falling asleep, and to write, because by doing so I come to *realize* what is happening and to assure myself of the reality.

I am on my way to Cuba, bearing within me the warm, sad memory of my little mother. The pain it gave me to leave her, to kiss her tear-stained and tired face, was far deeper than any I ever felt, and I know for certain now that my love for Mother is greater than my love for Hugo, and there is nothing I would not do for her. I hope my little brothers will fill my place. . . .

This was my only sorrow, for this long day of traveling has brought me nearer to my adventure, and I have spent much time dreaming scenes in my mind's eye and speculating and fabricating stories and weaving fairy tales, but of a kind tinged with moderation and a little wisdom—and I struggle to shape my world now with more tolerance, more understanding and less illusion.

And so, to the shaking and rolling of the train, my hope and dreams are rocked no more tenderly than the movement and evolution of my new life.

October 9. Finca La Generala,[1] Luyanó, Havana.
To Hugo:

I have been transported to Fairyland, I now live in an Enchanted Palace! All my sadness and apprehension fled the moment I caught sight of Havana, and as the ship neared the harbor, I was thrilled beyond words at the strangeness of all that was happening to me. You can hardly imagine what it is to see a new city, to hear a new language, to see the faces of an altogether different race and yet to recognize all this as belonging to part of you. Whatever is Spanish in me has now come to the surface, and in every glance from large dark eyes I read feelings to which I can respond and characters I understand as well as my own. The spell of the south is upon me, and I feel the soft, caressing air and the warm, vibrant touch of its twilight, and my thoughts are lulled into dreamy indolence . . .

To Eduardo:

I had promised myself not to weave about my change of home and my new adventure, and so I approached Havana very soberly

[1] *The ranch of Tia Antolina, who was the widow of General de Cárdenas.*

and with many misgivings, knowing too well the penalty one pays for illusions and determined to live henceforward with as few as possible. And the gods, therefore, showered their gifts upon me. I find myself living in the most beautiful of houses on the outskirts of the city, one which seems a palace to me, most exquisitely furnished and decorated, surrounded by an enchanting garden. And all about us are unfolded the sloping fields of Cuba, fertile and rich under the ever shining sun.

And the air is soft and balmy and the tall, straight, infinitely graceful palm trees are outlined everywhere against a most brilliant and colorful sky. Everything seems penetrated by some hidden warmth and softness and one feels the spell of the south—languor and fire by turn steal upon you through spirit and senses.

All these days I have been in appearance like one dazed by the strangeness and novelty of my surroundings, because I could not write as well or talk as much but I was simply observing intently, absorbing all things, gathering experience and impressions in order to understand and explain better later on. You now know why, Eduardo, today I send you but a short letter and one filled with the outward appearance of things, description of the tangible and visible things only. The thoughts will come later; they lurk in the background, half-fearful of I know not what, but I am contented to see and hear and feel meanwhile, and to write in the manner of ordinary creatures.

Yes, I will give expression to the wrath your intended-to-be poem kindled in me, but not now, for I am in the mood for gentleness, and if you were here, you would be treated with extraordinary consideration. And the more so when you are so far and I wish to coax you into writing a heart-satisfying letter to your "cuisine" whom the world has abandoned on an island to perish in solitude. Mimi

Still dazed, still unable to believe that it is true. First I have known Cuba through the medium of nature, her fields, her sky, her sea; every scene has filled me with mute wonder, and a feeling akin to tenderness has crept into me when I have looked about. seeing beauty in the things so many have passed unnoticing—a beauty which has touched me and which I have understood in a purely miraculous way.

And then I have seen the city from the lowest to the highest houses. I have become familiar with its strange little houses painted white and yellow and pale blue and rose; have distinguished a quaint charm in a mass of bizarre coloring, in the narrow streets. One passes over the dirt and the laziness and the vivid, vulgar ornamentations and the primitive, barbaric traits that cannot be denied, and finds much that appeals in its inhabitants. The poor are desperately poor; the rich are ostentatiously rich, but one feels in sympathy with both. Whatever repels is redeemed by much that is touching.

Havana strikes me as a city of extremes, of contrasts, or it may only seem so because it is comparatively small. It seems all to be condensed in a handful, so to speak, and can be so easily observed.

Now I have begun to know Havana through its society. Nature I saw and felt; the city I saw and judged by its appearance. But society I shall absorb and through it understand all of Havana in unity, for are not the people the most complete and convincing proof of the character and temper of a city, of its traits as a whole, its main faults and virtues?

October 17. Today is the beginning of my second week here. And I come to you humble and repentant for having told you so little, so little of what is happening within me. But I evaded you for fear of rousing, with the scratching of my pen, the little demon who sleeps in me these days, the demon Sadness, the Sadness you know far too well and which is made of infinite longings, intense restlessness and *thirst*.

The other night as I returned home with Antolinita, following some visits, an uncontrollable anguish seized me and I knew the little demon had opened one eye and was blinking at me. But tonight as we were all talking in Tia Antolina's room, an intolerable sense of suffocation overwhelmed me, and I realized he had opened the other eye and become fully awake.

Now this is what I must conquer above all things. I had promised to play my part well and I have done so until now. I, the incurable hermit, have displayed the greatest sociability, and my solemn ways, pensive moods, deep reveries and fits of abstraction have been relegated like old furniture to the musty chambers of the past.

Can I do more? I shall reserve my lamentations for my ink bottle and give my sad thoughts the freedom to roam about my writing table and no further, so that I may quickly find them when the time comes and lock them up safely while I go about my business the rest of the day. It is to be a battle between Sense and Sensibility.

October 19. Yesterday as we returned from a long ride on horseback, seeing that the shadows were falling fast, and fearful of arriving late, we galloped homeward—the wind on my face, the hills and fields assuming strange shapes and color in the dusk, the palm trees swaying against a sky in which burned the last red ghost of sunset. I fancied myself on an Arabian steed galloping through a desert and all the fancies of the Arabian Nights filled my mind with their fantastic charm. I was thrilled beyond human words, held utterly spellbound in a fairy tale of my own making. And the fancy lasted until my cousin spoke and the horses, pausing, resumed their cantering and their commonplace appearance, and the world its placid, prosaic state. But the red glow in the sky and the palm trees gave my dream a semblance of reality to which I have clung ever since.

To Eduardo:

. . . It is, as you say, most difficult to recapture an impression after much time has elapsed. I cannot forgive myself for not having written an answer to your old letters when the spirit moved me . . .

Happiness is a small consideration and seems of little value. I feel a joy beyond joy in the midst of my sorrows, and what I feel while suffering is far beyond contentment, beyond peace—it is something nameless which approaches the divine. In agony, in torment, in despair, through burning tears I thank heaven that I am suffering because through the purifying fire of sorrow I shall see the ideal and I see God. I repudiate ordinary happiness. I want martyrdom and sacrifice, I want something *greater* than human happiness.

And so, Eduardo, in this sense I can tell you: I am happy because I am suffering. And if I describe my pain, you will understand that I do not want deliverance but that I accept sorrow, nay, that I now seek it instead of fearing it as others seek happiness of another kind and contentment I despise . . . Mimi

October 26. Mental development in any degree can be the cause of acute suffering and yet bring at other times such perfect joy to both heart and intellect. The pleasure is equaled in intensity only by the sorrow.

The most complete example of this has just come into my own life. The story of it first opened on those sunny and solitary days I spent in Woodstock and came to a close here a few days ago. The first chapter of it consisted of a letter, as does the last. They cover a brief span of months and are both enclosed in this very book.

Hugo wrote me a letter [in Woodstock] spurring me to the consideration of my individual ambition and desires beyond love— our love. In it, he voiced a disinterested regard for me as an Individual, one he refused to detain on its supposed course of life in the fulfillment of its purpose and plan.

Womanlike, I threw myself on my bed and sobbed desperately: He does not love me, he does not love me!

Then a faint light dawned upon my troubled, tempestuous mind. This was the result of my own ideals. I sought the man devoted to ideals, I demanded intelligence, and I found one capable of upholding an ideal before me, regardless of the infinite pain he was causing me and himself!

Through pain and the littleness, the womanly that is mine, I understood that Hugo was but stirring anew desires I had always had, revealing me to myself, uncovering the secrets of my soul, which I believed I had buried so deep. Had I not dreamed at night of what I might have done had I not come to love him? Had I not suppressed my desires to *be* and *do* and resigned myself with a sigh to the "common fate" of a woman because I knew my love to be greater than this desire?

Why was I weeping then because he made me *dare* what I had stifled for his sake?

But why could we not work together I, protected by his name? I had fully satisfied my desire to be true to myself by pursuing all my inclinations, by developing such faculties as I wished developed, by daring all in thought, and I had come to the conclusion that marriage did not imply a surrender of mind. That it would not interfere with my love of writing except in changing its importance in my eyes and rendering it but a secondary instead of an absolute motive. What need was there of each pursuing a course of life apart from the other?

But, womanlike, I kept all these things to myself and we never spoke of this again and became absorbed in the thousand other problems and difficulties our habits of thought created for us.

But neither one of us had forgotten it. It smoldered in both our hearts and needed but a word to burst once more into flame, and within me the pain was not abated, though well concealed, for such wounds, even when ignored and forgiven, are never entirely cured.

And then, months afterward, Hugo himself writes me, Hugo who alone has come to the same realization, Hugo whose mind has worked slowly but unwaveringly toward the very same decision.

And mine is the joy to have watched for him, waited for him, and stalked by his side, phantomlike; and finally to have known the ecstasy of feeling his mind once more work in harmony with mine!

". . . There has come to me . . . a great thankfulness that with the restoration of my tired body I am now able to know how blessed I am in your love, my sweet, my own Anaïs. Do you remember those letters I sent you when you were at Woodstock? I want you to forgive me for them now. I could not write like that again. At the time I was groping about with an idea that each of us should have a destiny which transcended love itself. I suppose there is a grain of truth in that, in general, but I can't understand why I did not see that you had just such a grand future in your writing. I feel that literature is to be my calling, and if it is to be yours too, what a glorious prospect to work out our destinies together!"

How long it took him to say it! And through my infinite joy and supreme satisfaction quivers but one red-blood arrow of unutterable pain, for it is too late, too late, too late, my own beloved, my dearest, too late!

October 31.

To my Beloved in answer to the letter in which he tells me he loves me at last, with all that is in his nature, and begs me to become his wife someday and wonders whether he has not forfeited my love by his actions:

You know I love you, my own Hugo. I have done all to prove it. I love you and I would ask no more than to live only for you and for your happiness. But those words I have waited for for so long have come too late. O my darling, I must not and I *will* not think of my own happiness now, for in depriving me of strength and rendering me unable to remain by Mother's side to help her in the struggle for existence, heaven demands of me a sacrifice by which I may redeem myself. And I am struggling now with a problem greater than I have ever known before. I must find a way, I must with time make a supreme decision. I told you once I would not give a thought to myself until I had accomplished these things: placed Mother beyond want, now that her strength is failing her at the close of so stormy a life, give Joaquin the opportunity to develop his talent and get Thorvald through college. I failed in one, but it was perhaps beyond reason, but I wanted to succeed in the others, alone, through my own efforts. . . . Now I may remain here with my aunt as long as I desire if I were without pride or without ambition for those I love, which urges me forward, always forward. And *apart from all this* I am considering your own happiness, too, for if I were certain that it is bound to mine, my love would sacrifice my courage, I fear, but this I doubt, my beloved. And it is all this which moves me to say today: I cannot promise to become your wife. I could have pledged myself before, but not now. Please darling, do not blame. Trust in me in this struggle as I have trusted you, to do all in my power for you, even if it exacts of me that I should shut myself away from my only hope, my only joy.

Oh, I can't say more. Love me, help me only by trusting me. If you were here, I could tell you everything that I cannot write. The most I can do is to assure you of my love, which has survived all my discouragements and disappointments and proved strong and deep, a love which had *vision* and was beyond pride at the time when I might have sent you away and misunderstood you—a love that was patient and waited and hoped, and a love that shall be yours wholly completely, everlastingly. . . .

And when Mother told me your love was not worthy of mine, my heart sank; for I knew the love you showed *then* was not, but the other, the one of my dream would be—and if she could wait . . . Mine was so purely visionary and uncommunicable a faith!

Tell me that the assurance of my love compensates you for the promise I cannot make.

But, beloved, we can make believe. Ask of me things as if you were certain that someday we would be together, as if sometime we might gather in a little home all our most cherished dreams and find perfect harmony and be no longer alone as we are now.

I am sharply conscious of the contrast between my past and

present life. Long ago, it seems to me, beloved, I was rich with life's intangible gifts: love, understanding, unity, talent and intelligence . . .

Daily I thank the gods I belong to no country, that I love none enough to be blinded to its faults . . .

November 1. My love wrote me a letter so beautiful and glowing with so passionate and true a love that I can hardly write of it without feeling the most exquisite pain, as if my heart would burst with so much suppressed happiness and pride. At last he has come into himself, and he loves me as he wanted to love me and reached the ideal in love he spoke of from the very first.

"Will you wait for me until I love you as you deserve to be loved?" he asked me. Since then I waited. I hoped, I suffered intolerable anguish and doubts, I warmed him in the light of my own love, I was patient and despairing by turn, and what alone sustained me was that vision of the love that might be.

All that I have complained of in silence, in writing, was the result of his physical condition. Fortunately, when I failed to understand, I wrote that I could never feel anger toward him—my love was beyond anger—and so he has been spared the agony of my disappointments and my doubts. And now we have come into our divine kingdom and our love for each other is equal and unsurpassed in beauty, in vision, in power.

But what he asks me, I refuse: I do not promise to become his wife—he has my love alone.

A new joy has penetrated me. I am transfigured by love, by happiness, and I am glowing with health and the ecstasy of youth. Far away looms the sacrifice, but I do not fear it, and until the time is ripe for its consummation, I want to gather strength through joy and share with my beloved a life which is his until the last. Oh, we belong to each other in a way that no human obstacles can prevent or subdue. Our souls have met and touched and are irrevocably linked—and to be separated materially will only emphasize the pain of the spiritual loneliness we are condemned to suffer without each other.

I boasted too soon of having at last found time to write and was immediately punished by the gods. My aunt (who is watching over my welfare) believes I write too much and has taken matters into her own hands. She has made plans to keep me busy with other things—pleasant things, they call them, of a kind which does not wear you, etc. As I cannot hope to convince her that writing is to me the very breath of life, an incomparable pleasure, the joy of joys, and the very source of youth, strength and hope, I am doomed to write at odd minutes, stolen minutes.

I take it philosophically and have begun to believe I might apply myself to the development of humor and the practical things of life instead—and to the best advantage.

To Eduardo:

I have discovered another thing we have in common. Listen: we fall into a mood, a mood intense and powerfully sincere at the moment. We write of it [in a letter]; we believe in a permanent state; we call it either that or a conviction, a belief, a conclusion, a philosophy. And we send our [letter]. And then the mood passes; we repent. It has become an experiment and we believe ourselves a little wiser for having passed *through* and beyond it.

But the writing? In black and white, irretrievable, beyond recall, it has traveled fast, unwaveringly to its destination. And what can one do but send more words, more words to give the others the depreciation they deserve. . . .

I am no longer sad, and I no longer suffer, and all that talk of martyrdom, etc., was but the last cry of anguish from a heart that has now found peace and joy and come into its share of normal happiness.

But I mean what I wrote. That is, I believe in those ideas about sorrow and I shall uphold them when sorrow does come to me. But I did not admit then that there was a respite from sorrow, and that is what I wish to do today. And I am resting from sorrow, and my heart is light. So rejoice with me! . . .

November 8. Resting from sorrow! Free from pressure and limitation, soaring above the oppressive phantoms of self-inflicted agony . . . And with this, the desire to write becomes more intense, the joy of composition becomes ecstasy, and I surrender to its delicious domination.

November 9. The one great privilege attending this state of rest from sorrow is the turn the mind takes once freed from its subjection to the one emotion, and how it branches out and embraces the entire situation, and can once more profit from experience and be enriched by it in general, universal terms.

It is in such a state that I have rediscovered Havana. Havana, en masse, vaguely stirs in one memories of pictures of ancient Moorish cities—cream-white stone houses, flat-roofed, with arched doorways, columns and balconies, all linked, following the fantastic curves of narrow, irregular streets. Or it rouses faint recollections of old Spain, and vestiges of Spanish dominion are distinguishable everywhere, in the homes of the middle class, with their plaster-walled, high-roofed, stone-floored rooms; in the Cubans' dress, taste and customs.

Tradition hangs about the quaint furniture, and nothing within the commonplace home is either modern or even moderately up to date. And tradition walks about the streets, too, and one is strongly tempted to plead thus: for less tradition and more cleanliness!

Shops, cafés, etc. open out upon the streets. Misery is more apparent since one can see into the inmost heart of the houses through wide windows and doors flung open—across rooms to the very backyard. A habit of inordinate hospitality fostered by the climatical conditions and atmospheric pressure!

Poverty stands fully revealed, naked, a striking, repulsive sight to a stranger until all feeling of condemnation melts into an all-absorbing compassion.

In the walk of the people about the streets is reflected a peculiar indolence. It is a slow, dragging step, a deliberate, swinging movement, a gliding, serpentlike motion, something speaking indefinably of that characteristic laziness of the tropics and a something else which might be called a state of mental apathy, a universal malady of Havana, at least to my mind. Mental idleness, vacuity, are what I read in most passing faces. Eyes seeming to wander forever, alighting on everything but carrying no thoughts to the mind, eyes devoid of vision, gleaming alone when the senses are pleased . . . All this with a few exceptions, but it strikes one as universal in comparison with the expressions on the faces of any other crowd or mere passers-by of other cities.

Traces of religious bigotry—a deep-seated ignorance and superstitious slavery to custom—the total absence of individual will, intelligence, understanding, a faith of childish simplicity, all these are still found in some women here. And in most cases she does not even fulfill the demands of beauty, for she lacks grace and charm and culture. Vanity is her all-absorbing passion and only interest, and whatever else conforms with the character of the doll that she is. If she is sweet and submissive, it is the submission of unconscious inferiority. All this, with exceptions and taking into consideration that the younger girls, educated abroad are returning with knowledge and ideals, so that for Havana, as for every city, one can count on the gradual influence of progress.

The Latin race, outspoken, expressive, generous, hospitable, exemplifying "largesse" in every sense, would be better appreciated and loved but for its sad deficiency in dignity and fastidiousness. One trained in English reserve and delicacy is bound to look with arrogance and disdain upon that unrestrained conduct, that carelessness in regard to propriety and reserve in individuals and family life, so strangely visible throughout the city. The frank, irresponsible, uneducated Cuban appears unintelligible to those who possess instinctively that quality, elusive and indescribable, which might be called culture (for lack of a better term) or innate refinement—all that includes personal appearance, manner of speech, manner of living, through which good taste or lack of it is irrevocably expressed. In these an unsubdued coarseness distinguishes the Cuban, a state of primitive vulgarity, man uncultivated, and unsuspecting of his failing, which silences reproach.

November 11. I have struggled to mark the distinctions between the thousand kinds and forms of happiness in the world, have gone so far as to term sorrow the most divine happiness and the one pursued by ordinary mortals and their material craving, commonplace, unworthy. And I have struggled to distinguish true from false joy, the valuable from the worthless, to separate the low from the high, the noble from the ignoble.

But I have gone no further than a thousand others who, each in turn, gave his own name to what he loved and placed his own value upon things he praised in the innocent sincerity of his soul, and in the end made things no more or less right than they were before, nor more or less believable, beautiful or noble.

Can anyone efface the individual note that rings so through all such utterances? Can no one voice a universal, all-embracing teaching and be heard? Well, then, shall I be silent? I wonder at all this because my words struck me with their uselessness, their helpless bondage to the eternal "I," which renders them as lifeless to the others. My desire now is to gradually move away from the personal and individual. I wish to merge myself into the universal experience.

Shall I ever find the all-revealing light? By my desire I breathe so close to its own sacred existence that if it should ever shine, I would be the first to feel its warmth . . . I wait.

November [?]. Notes on a Visit to the Convent of Santa Clara.

Through a curious architecture, twisted to meet the need of aggrandizement, a whole world lay enclosed within the high, forbidding outer wall, a world of many houses linked to one another by passageways and little wooden bridges, forming spaces and courts in so immense and confused a plan that no clear conception of it could be gained in a short visit.

Quaint and unforgettable details could be gathered on the way, suggesting bygone centuries—old lanterns; arched colonnades; wide windows, heavily barred with iron, opening upon the street; heavy, imposing doors creaking on their ancient, rusty hinges or locked by ancient, rusty locks; and every stone, every step, old, worn and yellow.

It was sad to have its historical sacredness thus violated by the intrusion of unfeeling strangers. To the poet or the dreamer the place was filled with traces that he could recognize and by which he could reconstruct the broken web of many human documents.

One could imagine the old garden in the tender sunlight, calm, serene, and nuns gliding about, softly murmuring their beads; or moving across the frail wooden bridges and bending over the wooden banister . . . shadows crowding in one's mind, fantastic characters of one's own making, moving, giving a semblance of life . . . praying, laboring and then at night perhaps retiring into their bare, cold cells to sleep on their beds of board. And the candlelight perhaps trembling in the still night and throwing the shadows of their window bars upon the stone floor—the symbol of their voluntary exile and imprisonment.

Days later. Since then I have heard many stories about the old convent which have supplied the last touch of reality to my fantastic imaginings—stories of folded love notes found in the crevice of a door, of drawers in the kitchen wall through which the nuns did their marketing, of secret tunnels under the chapel leading out into the city for the escape of the nuns at the time when they lived in constant fear of the pirates and of pillages (to protect their treasures, the walls were built so high and so forbidding and the windows barred and the doors massive, strongly locked), of the well in the center of the court, dating back as far as 400 years, and of the "poseta," or kind of public bath.

Some are in possession of documents and diaries in the handwriting of the nuns themselves, strange, romantic stories of girls seeking refuge in religion, the seclusion of the cloister against the cruelty of parents forcing them to marry against their inclination; stories probably of unrequited love, of disappointments, of separations by violence or misunderstanding—of all the causes, in short, which can turn a creature against the world and move her to total renunciation of it. It is curious to notice how few are the people who have faith in the vocation—in a pure, religious spirit, in a truly pious inspiration. With their small minds they cannot conceive a disinterested and purely unworldly sacrifice. To them it must be a human reason, a lower incentive which can move a man or woman to retire within these austere walls and to seek forgetfulness and peace in religion. Not a love and devotion to God but an unhappy experience with the world.

And as I heard this I was struck by disgust—a disgust toward all things, toward life, human nature, toward myself for being human. I suddenly saw all action reduced to nothingness where before it signified growth—all nobility shrunk to calculated, selfish motive. Alas, contact with Skepticism, a glimpse of those ignoble depths of others' hearts, in which Doubt sits enthroned, gave me a sense of absolute loneliness in my faith, my conceptions, my aspirations . . .

November 12. A letter from Eduardo brought me to a full realization of the strangeness of my creed in relation to sorrow. It has profoundly disconcerted me to notice that I have not lived in keeping with it, that I have proved inconsistent by admitting the return of normal happiness. I believe what I wrote, most firmly and absolutely, but what might be questioned is the practicality of such a belief.

In the first place it bears a not *inhuman* semblance, for ordinary life cannot accord with divine aspirations, and sorrow, the admitted burden, is never accepted, but is borne only with the resignation taught by religion. If I have known and sought the ecstasy of supreme pain in moments of exalted aspiration toward nobility, I have at other times, as a normal girl, been satisfied with simple, ordinary contentment. No higher state is a permanent one except in the case of saintliness.

Whether by reading or by personal experience, I hope to reach the truth of this soon. Meanwhile, I feel no shame for my inconsistency. Who am I that I should make a statement and expect to live unfalteringly and unwaveringly by it when so many

of the strongest fail and allow their actions to belie their words—
and more, their whole life, the quality and theme of their most
ardent teaching?

Inconsistency! Has a human mind ever freed itself from it?
Its very human temper and limitations have given birth to the
word. True, sometimes one may write as if one were not human,
but only to declare one's self defeated in the face of a purely human failing.

And the sum of it all is that a creed that is neither human nor
practical, even if it be divine, can remain but an aspiration—and
I wish mine to be more than that. Perhaps both *divine* and workable.

To Hugo:

. . . It seems to me you will approve my reasoning when I
tell you how I have decided to carry out your own wish—that we
each should grow in strength and intelligence for love's sake. If
one finds joy a source of health, it is reasonable to profit from a
respite from a sorrow that weakens one, is it not? We can gain
meanwhile "un élan," a new power, that we may use later on if
it is so willed that obstacles should forever bar our way to each
other. Thus I struggle to let the future take care of itself and am
interested only in making a veritable use of the present. It even
seems to me when I laugh, when I dance, when I am joyful, that
I am doing it for you and not to hurt you. Now, can you understand this? . . . I am gaining in courage, in clearness of perception, in vision: I shall be ready for the decisive step, for the act!
In keeping with this philosophy, I refuse to be discouraged from
dreaming and I am making believe all day long, dear Hugo. Must
I give you an example? Then prepare yourself for a surprise.
Aunt Antolina. All the refined simplicity, the charm of hospitality, all the dainty detail of woman's humble art that appeals to
me, I see practiced every day, and I follow her about, and I ask
questions and I make resolutions, and I store a precious knowledge . . . (and I cook etc.). Oh, I am intent on dissolving all
your fears of the "high peaks of life" habit which so distressed you
in bygone days! I shall load [you] with such tremendous proofs of
my substantiality that you shall beg me on bended knees to return
into my old self and resume my old airiness!

A sharp realization has struck me in the midst of this life.
There is a carelessness and a lack of taste sometimes for which
circumstance and not will is to blame. Such is the case with our

home, which so poorly expresses and reflects our ideals except in such intangible ways as you may have felt—for all the rest of it, materially, is naturally within criticism by those ill-fitted to judge because they will not penetrate beyond appearances. Through all this, in spite of such disadvantages whose importance human nature has rendered great, in spite of what you may say, you have reached and touched the heart of things, but not without pain. Those who feel envy for subtle riches they do not possess emphasize the lack of proper setting and appearances in their efforts to belittle and to efface, if possible, these qualities. I am generalizing, but you know what I mean: you had to endure criticism for which you had no answer, suffer accusations you could not battle, because they were dealing with facts . . . Your judgment I never doubted, but I have sometimes suffered with you for things I understood and could not speak of. I knew so well what was lacking!

Thus has grown in me a desire to have you come here, that you may see me here. This in all ways is nearer the ideal, and I wish you to have a taste of it, my Hugo. . . . It is your pleasure, your satisfaction, I dream of. It is your compensation I am planning with all the tenderness and art that love can give. I wish to enrich your life with all there is in mine to give. I wish to say wherever it is in my power: Hugo, here is a scene, a situation, a phase of life, as near perfection as can be obtainable. Enjoy it, possess it; it is yours and for you . . .

November 20. Now and then my self-control weakens, for my liking for society is purely an effort, a tremendous effort, and sometimes when we return from dancing and laughing, I sit silently in a corner of the automobile and I dream a little sadly and look into my heart and see the love of other things lying there, calm, subdued, but waiting only for a sign to burst out again into glorious flames . . .

To my dearest One:

. . . When I can explain to you the cause of my hesitation, you will understand and believe that it is my very love for you that is drawing me away from you, away from what I cannot live without, for I love you and need you, and I do not hesitate to tell you *that* a thousand times—not until the last day—though even after that I shall love you—not until I am deprived of more than life itself, deprived of the power to prove and to live my love for you. You tell me in your last letter all I have longed to hear, you rouse a thousand secret dreams I do not dare approach, you kindle such hopes, such visions of a future. Oh, together, yes, we could do all things and live with that fullness you desire, but alone . . .

But then, if you trust me and if you can find happiness in what is yours now, it shall be easier for me to understand what I must do. That is the assurance I need now and which I am waiting for, my darling.

It is no wonder that the other day I sat talking to a Cuban lady and could hardly suppress an inexcusable hilarity, for as she sat before me, rocking herself wildly in her characteristic rocking chair, fanning herself, gesticulating to emphasize her loud words, rolling her eyes expressively, and sought to impress me with the fact that life here was deliciously restful and soothing and calm and so different from the hustle and bustle and nervous tension of New York, I was struck too forcibly with the humor of it all and nearly betrayed [it]. When the mocking spirit left me, I saw another side. I compared what the nervous tension had achieved, the marvelous result of that restless activity, with the achievement, the state of civilization and progress in restful Havana. A most unfortunate comparison! (Description of Havana in full.) If this seems too *English* a criticism, beloved, remember that I am impregnated in English literature and ideals and that there is more beauty, in my eyes, in an exaggerated reserve than in misinterpreted frankness and naturalism. And if you find it on the whole unkind, then I shall paint you an enthusiastic picture of the sea, the sky and the palm trees and the gardens and of society, which overflows with culture and all the other charming products of super-civilization, to counterbalance it. But I maintain that you should appreciate my impartiality and cool, impassioned judgment. I, who am forever passing from one state of ecstatic, blind enthusiasm to another, and who, in my own way, love all those countries that have given me a little of themselves! But enough of this, you must be getting sleepy. . .

November 22. A day of my life is no longer lived, has no sooner become an experience, than it flows into ink and becomes a letter. And all the energy that once went in my journal is now spent upon an arduous correspondence. It is the only way I can remain by Mother's side, and the only proof I can give her of my devotion; to replace my talks, my presence, I must send her voluminous descriptions of all that may please, entertain and accompany her. It is also the only way I can prove to Eduardo that the light of our friendship is in no way dimmed by the radiance of love. And it is the only way I can prove to my love the infinite tenderness with which I follow him in his wanderings. And so you are abandoned, and for once I am gladdened by the thought that you are not human, that you are soulless, for you cannot feel the desolation of desertion or miss my confidences.

I have honestly come to believe that between my experience and me there is an immense magnifying glass colored too by a variety of moods. Or else how can you explain the *fullness* which I feel each day more intensely and the ever changing aspect my life assumes whenever I am about to describe it? That fullness in joy, in sorrow, has become a part of my character in so pronounced a way that I sometimes envy those tepid, lukewarm, passive temperaments. And that changefulness is a serious obstacle to my old habit of diary-keeping, for if I must wait until the rare evenings I may devote to it, I cannot for the life of me preserve one feeling for more than a minute without seeing it replaced by another. But I take this philosophically, as has become my acquired tendency, and I merely scribble all day in pencil in a notebook.

In the very midst of the hot excitement of the keenest living there creeps into me a vague desire, a secret thirst for retirement and solitude. traces of my old self no earthly powers can efface!

November 25. I wonder if there exists a God of Writers whose justice is distributed only according to what is for the good or evil of literature, for in this case my actions nowadays shall be judged with mercy and looked on perhaps approvingly, being all, as a matter of fact, entirely dedicated to the service of literature. Without this I can most easily be condemned as a confirmed and callous hypocrite, a coquette on the road to eternal perdition.

Will anyone (besides myself, be it understood) believe and admit the possibility of this, that a woman should employ her power in the pursuit of psychological studies and researches? Right or wrong in others' eyes, I must not waver. It seems right to me and I shall await only the verdict of the God of the Writers.

It all comes to this: that with a true love in my heart I am nevertheless flirting outrageously, excluding no kind word or act or pretense that may reveal a human heart to me and bring about intimate contact with a character. Thus I make use of all my power to bring about me many friends. I even go so far as to play the part of a coquette with a *vulnerable* heart, which no one can resist.

Strangely enough, I am not devoid of pity, sympathy or interest. I play with feelings with all the gentleness imaginable, and I make believe without losing my control over the situation, which I can fashion to my own liking—that is, giving pleasure in exchange for a knowledge of people, in which I now exult.

It seems to me that my true heart remains untouched by these literary pranks, and my sincerity is unweakened by them. At least I experience no pangs of conscience, and until now I could rely upon that conscience as upon the strictest guard on my actions.

One can force accidental opportunities into the service of the ideal, turn every situation to the benefit of our highest aspirations. I no longer want to sigh for what I do not have. I want to make an immediate and practical use of whatever material is now lying about me.

I wonder how I can explain the thrill one receives from being loved by anyone. In society, is it the novelty which makes it interesting for me to receive homage and be courted? I wish to maintain myself a spectator, and yet I am moved by diverse sentiments when a face is turned full on mine and eyes search mine and words, voice and expressions all tell me: "I love you." I have no ideas, no thought at the moment. I hear, see, understand and am touched by the fact as if it were a simple, inevitable, natural thing—sad, too, and pitiful.

But there is an undeniable charm to it all. Balzac would attribute it to pleased vanity; yet it has never occurred to me to be flattered. I consider it too impersonally to fall into that commonplace state.

And I weave a little story about each fancy, each passing attachment of which I am the object, studying beginnings, developments, climaxes, with the joy of a storyteller; dealing lightly and gently and tactfully with all the phases so that my various little sham loves should never pass beyond the bounds of pleasure. And I hurt no one, and if anyone threatens to be serious, I thoughtfully lead him into other channels.

Charles [de Cárdenas] tells me frivolity and the frivolous life serve only to bring out the beauty of the other life, and I agree with him. And at present I am utilizing my contact with society to gain a knowledge that will enrich that other life. Now my solitude is crowded with scenes and incidents and memories most salutary and serving to the balancing of my overserious nature. And I am happy and grateful for this experience.

Charles seems to understand. He watches me as one watches another going through a thing he himself has passed beyond. And he knows now the ultimate end and has already discovered what he believes I am about to reach. What he does not know is that I see that end even while I am in the middle of my road. That I see at this very moment far beyond the present. I have no love of frivolity for frivolity's sake, no love of society for society's sake. I love it all as writer, as artist, but I wish to love it, even in this respect, well, and not appear like the others, but better than the others in their own type of life.

I do it all so intensely that I have come to mean it, to be it. It is all *real*, sincere, at the moment, and it is only when I begin to write, when I detach myself from actual living, that I see it all as transparent play, a role, an act.

Thus I cannot say that I suffer any of the hypocrite's pangs of conscience, and yet I am tasting all the joys of the make-believe. What a curious life! What a curious state of mind! And what will come of it? Will I lose myself in these labyrinths of personalities, assumed yet unassumed, sincere and yet unstable, real and yet fictitious and purely invented, the product perhaps of too active an imagination?

I have experienced a great appreciation of the time granted me in which to readjust my ideas, plan my life and see it all more clearly, for during the time I worked in New York I had reached a state of confusion and despair due to my loss of energy and health and my physical impotence. Here I can more clearly judge all things and be at last ready for my Act. I am so placed as to be totally incapacitated to act immediately; I cannot force the situation. I must give it time to form itself, but I can think, I can plan, I can grow in physical endurance and gain a better knowledge of life and practical results, of *facts*.

It is a curious phenomenon to trace the progress of my transformation. My aunt tells me I once had a faraway, dreamy gaze she could not understand, that I appeared utterly unconscious of my surroundings, uninterested in all but mysterious thoughts. She went so far as to suspect me devoid of intelligence. And now she tells me she notices me alive; she knows I am listening when she speaks to me; I am interested in everyday life, in everybody, in everything; I seem better able to grasp and understand.

My own faith in self-improvement, self-teaching, self-control, all I advocate so ardently, I now can say to have experimented with, on my own self, and obtained palpable results. By my passionate desires to better myself I have at last emerged from the vaporous clouds of dreams and move about with an ever increasing poise and an ever growing wisdom in the world of realities.

There is at bottom only one honest reason for my joyous acceptance of society. My life has become incredibly difficult. *I fear my own thoughts* and I wish to escape myself, for oh, to you alone I confess that to do what I must do I must forget myself entirely; I must become selfless. And I am driven out upon society because I must seek forgetfulness. All these dissertations with which I fill these pages are what lies furthest from my heart; I struggle to maintain myself on the *surface* of all things. I talked before of appreciating the time granted me in which to *think;* I must not think, I must not think!

Hugo's love, as I know it today, cannot bring Mother happiness. And Mother's happiness is the first desire of my heart. I do not speak of Hugo's suffering because in relation to his love it shall not be very great. There are the facts. I can go no deeper than that. Today, at least.

Though I may never bring forth a work, though I may fail to fulfill materially the mission of one in whom the creative spirit burns, I can truly say that I am blessed by all the compensations, the ecstasies, the numberless joys of a creator's inner life. The deep, the infinite, the indescribable pleasure writing brings me! Even with its difficulties, its arduous, exacting phases, requiring efforts from every faculty, physical labor, patience, writing is, in my eyes, wrapped in radiance, a subject of devotion, of an almost unearthly exaltation.

And life itself at its lowest moments has become invested with a peculiar sacredness since I consider it a mere human document and I a chronicler whose mission it is to complete faithfully and at all costs this life of a soul.

In joy, in sorrow, I can come to these pages and find with whom to share all things and a relief for my torments. I repeat what I wrote here in the beginning: only let me write, let the agonies of my mind flow into you. I can be silent before the world and silent before those I love, but I *cannot stifle thought,* and in this communion of my own soul I find the freedom of utterance, the freedom to cry in my pain.

November [?]. Havana. The Spanish is essentially the poetry of the senses, of a purely physical beauty. The English is fragrant with loftiness and nobility; and whereas the former makes for restless reading and leaves one troubled and dissatisfied, the second serves as balm to the soul. Its refreshing purity, its delicacy— which is the essence of strength—its subtle power of converging thoughts and depth of feeling, may not captivate the imagination at first, while the brilliancy of the Spanish does; but following the glamour comes the void felt by the intellect, and it is then that the appreciation of English poetry comes to me, bringing a deep and enduring enchantment besides which all the evanescent qualities of the Spanish, the fire, the passion, the enthusiasm, gradually fade.

Silence as Argument. Why is it there comes a time in one's life when discussion becomes distasteful and all wrangling, all argumentation with those who do not comprehend, is clearly revealed as futile. A profound silence takes hold of one's whole nature before all spoken opposition—a silence that is not surrender, that is even more like a sense of right, so certain of itself, so positive, that it has no need of display or of asserting itself. And before hot words no angry retort comes. To indignation one responds with passivity; to passion, with a semblance of approval. And in the end what might be taken for weakness, betrayal, is but a shelter that has served to let one reach in silence an all-embracing absolution.

One has risen above the human vanity which prompts one to make a show of one's belief, risen above that childish desire to have the world with us and to win the approval of the majority; and, by the way, one has learned to control one's temper.

December 6. I have finally promised Hugo to marry him. I sent him a cable after receiving a letter which completely revolutionized me. All the generous sentiments, the devotion, the supreme understanding, are at last roused in him . . . I had a vision of a truer happiness for Mother. God help me!

December 20. Now I am completely at loss for the words to interpret to any other than myself the meaning, the importance, the influence of these last days upon my life. Guided by an unseen force, by a reasoning which is now above doubt, by an instinct beyond personal faith, I have taken the decision which makes me Hugo's betrothed. And yet, I am assailed by a thousand other kinds of doubts, torn by intolerable conflicts and indecision—God help me, for I have done what, with my human mind and its sad limitations, seems right to me, and I have taken a step whose importance no imagination, however exaggerated, as mine is, can magnify too well.

Oh, God will not permit that I should make a mistake so fatal to all those I love. God cannot allow that I should have had the opportunity to serve Mother and have flung it aside under the false illusion of the true Gift.

A thing has happened which I may never write of, and all has tended but to augment my doubts. Today I cannot say I know myself. I cannot know the truth. If I am allowing sentiment to rule my reason, if I am the cause of Mother's unhappiness instead of her peace, I shall never forgive myself. I prefer death.

I doubt *myself;* I doubt my motives, my judgment, my sincerity, my *love,* everything. My thoughts when I am alone are all against myself, crushing me, accusing me, pointing out my folly, my blindness, my weakness. O God, deliver me from this heartrending indecision, from this self-depreciation. I am not worthy to live for myself. Inflict all pain upon me, but let me be the instrument of Mother's happiness. Torture me, but give her peace. Immolate me, but bring upon her the fruits of compensation, peace, all earthly joys.

And the bitterest thought of all is that now it is too late; I fear that my love for Hugo has waned, and not through his own fault. He must come, he must win me; I cannot be the cause of so much suffering. I could not tell him.

And all this shall become worse through *thinking.* I shall write no more of it until I have a fact to communicate. And I shall seek distractions to occupy my mind and dwell on other topics.

Though most moods tinge one's view of life and color it with their own peculiar character, there are times when, impersonally, one can see life as clearly as through the purest, clearest crystal, when, moodless and selfless, truth alone reveals itself to man. It is a universal element, truth, a thing so great that it cannot be encompassed within one soul, so dazzling that it cannot be seen wholly by the eyes of one mere man, except in such moments of intensified vision as come with the utter forgetfulness of self, of sentiment, of prejudices, of human ties, of vanity therefore.

I have proved the wisdom of my objection to secondhand information in regard to life and love and fame and human nature, etc. In nearly all things I have gone against the general belief, and I have found myself right. It is senseless to abide by general statements, for no experience ever resembles another, and the best in the world is composed of exceptions to these classifications and conclusions.

To begin by discrediting all things is to begin with an open mind, free of prejudices or obstinate preconceptions, and it is simpler for truth to penetrate one in such a state than to do what it is generally forced to do—to filter a drop at a time through thick, dense opposition and unwillingness, at the risk of crowding at one of those microscopic byways and finally leaving the rest in utter darkness.

It is, at least, in such an open mood that I have discovered intelligence in many who have been thought stupid, sparks of comprehension sometimes in seemingly ignorant, uneducated natures, flashes of natural ability in habitually selfish creatures, treasure after treasure in the form of a rare and valuable quality too often unperceived because it is so unexpected, too often crushed by cynicism or lack of kindness, too seldom helped to flower.

Every passing day increases my faith in a contrary opinion. I would prefer the risk of drowning rather than follow the common current—when that common current leads me downward into abysses instead of into the higher spheres of the ideal.

December 27. And Eduardo's letters come to me, laden with sweetness, with peace and serene beauty and faith. And I bless that tie through which the bitterness of my experience is softened by a precious share of his! *Through love, through friendship, a heart lives more than one life* and is made joyful or sorrowful by the experiences of many others. It is sweet to share all things thus and give and receive comfort and give and find inspiration and sustenance. What one lacks, the other supplies, and life lived in that rich harmony and unity becomes complete.

Eduardo's charm and romanticism, Eugene's knowledge and wisdom, Charles's clear thoughts and judgment, I appreciate them all, all, and for each of them I have something within myself to give in return. Tonight this thought has thrown a consoling radiance about my isolation.

Woman, primitive and animalized, who rises no higher in her estimation of life than in seeking its physical joys and no higher in her relationship to man than to desire to please his senses—what an obstacle she is to civilization! And she is the one who brings upon our heads the first accusation of insignificant mentality and the incapacity even to carry out well the one task and responsibility imposed on her by heaven, for what children can one such as she give to the world?

It is her kind, alas, that outnumbers that group aspiring to the divine fulfillment of its human mission. Intimacy with so low a type of womanhood only urges one to greater efforts, as the sight of grossness gives one a greater longing for delicacy and finesse. And so it should be with all we term degrading. It is the weak in us which yields to the lower influence. The strong is strengthened.

When a man admits the power of beauty, the woman with intelligence wonders if he can be detracted from her faults by the charms of her femininities. She would like to be judged apart from them, and yet she knows full well that it is simpler to be loved and served and worshiped as woman than to be criticized as mind to mind.

December 28. Analyses and criticism turned upon one's self spell self-destruction. I am in danger of stifling all shadows of happiness by my questioning and examination and dissecting, and of reaching a state of such intolerable consciousness as to threaten to exterminate every vestige of sincerity and every natural impulse. I alone am the one who creates doubts and oppositions within myself. I am the very cause of every internal trouble and confusion. And it is only by my constant thinking that I am losing the strength of my own convictions. I myself am the genie who each day uncovers the jar and frees the demons with which it is filled.

Again, I humbly recognize the fault to lie in me. Again, with an effort I propose to retrace my steps, having reached another "crisis."

In this mood I draw my eyes away from inward life and fix them upon that outer world which is at the moment so fascinating, so varied, so spectacular, as to deserve all my attention and interest.

December 30. I cannot follow in one unchanging story of this life of mine because there is more than one unfolding itself within me and all at the same time—my inward life, my outward life, my experiences as a society girl, as the member of a new household, as one fond of thinking, as a writer . . . Yes, a thousand lives, facts as well as fancies to record, happenings as well as reactions, scenes and the moods through which they have been observed, people to describe in the light of personal intimacy, and others in the superficial and flattering lights of society . . . pleasure— frivolous, artistic, spiritual; pain, discoveries, conclusions . . .

My eyes would see all as a whole instead of becoming lost in details. Force of habit draws them inward. The sense of how it should be bids them fix themselves upon the outward. Youth too has its say; it flavors experiments and observations with the thrill of actual living.

And so I should, by right, keep three or four diaries. Habit bids me not to change the tone of this.

Some dates do not even appear here which were once lovingly dwelt on. Christmas is one of them. Remembrances held back my pen when I was about to write of it. The contrast startled me.

A year ago, in my little house, the Christmas tree with its trembling light of a thousand candles, and holly and mistletoe, and the midnight Mass, and the family, closely united, sitting around the fire, and the sweet, cheery spirit through it all, the holiness, the simplicity, the profound joy . . . feelings one can never forget and beneath which our hearts expand and the noblest in us flowers.

This year, while others prayed, society danced and supped and expressed joy in a revelry which lasted until three o'clock. The luxurious ballroom brilliantly lighted, the tables covered with roses, which were afterward flung about and trampled on, the exquisite music, with its quick, gay rhythm, the rich coloring, the beauty and taste of those jeweled, silk-gowned women, the perfume, the laughter, the animation, the dazzling splendor . . . Having seen and heard this, can anyone forget it?

A beautiful spectacle which left the heart hungry and cold, and when, at midnight they struck the hour on a harmonious bell, the laughter died on my lips. As through a transparent veil I recognized Frivolity tragically playing the part of absent Happiness. And how many, lifting a glass of sparkling wine to their lips with a cheer, must have felt, perhaps at the same moment, the pang of that spiritual thirst consuming them which they cannot abate or understand.

To one who is unaccustomed to this life and who has succeeded in taking part in it through a great effort, there is nothing more natural than that immediate deviation from it, as if, delivered and exulting in its deliverance, the mind were eager to absorb itself in other things. Hence the exclusion of such a life from the preceding pages when it may well have been expected to dominate them. Yet I shall seek to atone for my seeming lack of interest.

Certain pictures detach themselves more clearly from the mass and make a decisive impression on one, and of these I chose the simplest.

At night I have been struck by the quaintness of carts coming home, following their rambling country roads by the light of candles in paper bags. And peasants walking by, singing with peculiar dragging tones, trills and a strange monotonous repetition of the lingering notes.

At night, too, I have seen lovers acourting their ladies, listening behind their iron-grilled windows or leaning over their balconies.

The countryside assumes a sad aspect, for the little houses of the poor are lit by dim candlelight and their animals are left to stray about in the road. Farther on, the city, though not so bright as in the dazzling sunlight, becomes more pleasing to the eyes—its miseries, its defects, its dirt, are charitably softened by the darkness.

❧ *1 9 2 3* ☙

January 19. There are many gaps in this human history which shall never be filled. They will mark the beginning of that supreme effort by which I shall gradually wrench myself away from the personal note—an effort I imposed upon myself as the result of reasoning, born of a conclusion I have forcibly reached and only lately admitted to myself. And now, besides all other reasons, such as I have annotated in various parts of this book, I have another for cutting short this study of life.

It was well, and worthy of approbation when it saved me as the very source of faith, for my life was loyal and I believed in loyalty; it was pure and I believed in purity; it was sincere and I believed in sincerity; I had faith because I lived in faith—this faith I communicated to my writing; the reading of my own words kindled, maintained and sustained it in all the beauty of its first ardent birth. I raised human nature because I had not yet fallen myself. To come to my white pages was one and the same as to describe a blameless heart.

Yet now I turn my eyes from it all with a profound disappointment. I have failed in loyalty—I have committed a fault.

Peace at last has come to me through strength and through love. Strength because I conquered a weakness and have risen above the tyrannical sway of my imagination and thrown off poisoned imaginings . . . Love because I have found my *soul* upon earth, and I have read the commands of my destiny. And now I love more truly than woman ever loved, and I am loved as truly. My Beloved is coming to me and shall win me once more. And all the rest shall be buried in my heart, serving only to kindle a more profound compassion and tolerance in me toward weakness and to render me humble and kind.

January 26. I surrender to this overwhelming tide of happiness. It has swept over me, borne me away into the blessed regions of delicious forgetfulness. The world moves about in a continuous and thrilling harmony. Waverings and hesitations and mental warfare are submerged. My eyes open upon a vision of marvelous possibilities.

I render thanks to heaven for my experience, my sorrow, my failings and falls, my disappointments, disillusions and despair. Out of these my soul has risen, cruelly tried yet triumphant, risen out of thought and observation to embrace action. My life has begun. I have just emerged from strained and intense schooling and from a self-inflicted bondage. The first intoxicating touch of strength born of keen struggle has electrified me and plunged me into a burning state of enthusiasm. Hunger for unity, my restless search for harmony, are paling in the vivid light of more tangible desires. I wish for Mother's happiness and for the right to dedicate my life to Hugo.

I often cry out in my agony against that sensitiveness which renders me so susceptible to all impressions, which kindles so deep a response in me every moment of the day, which has given the smallest thing the power to thrill me, to move me, to throw me into despair or bear me into the heights of ecstasy. But, often, too, I am thankful for that very intensity; that very extreme consciousness and susceptibility is what makes my life so full, so fascinating. I live a thousand lives in a moment through this limitless capacity for thought and emotion. It is thus I find more cause for suffering, but I also enjoy more. It is life simply carried on in a wider, deeper way.

Perhaps because I have by habit been preoccupied by the outflowing of my emotions, I can more easily divine those of others, and in every gathering of people I seek to follow the fascinating undercurrents of the invisible beneath the visible.

Lost in the contemplation of the two, which these last years have become more difficult to separate, my admiration at times reaches boundless spheres.

The fullness of the world, its variety, its mysteries, its coincidences, associations, its romantic and adventurous qualities, are all a perpetual source of wonder and interest. Would that I could maintain my opinion on this level, but alas, this is one phase of it, and there is yet another, the one which the cynicism of the period is revealing to me and forcing me to comprehend. And I turn, shrinking from the revolting sight with a sorrowful sense of the inevitable, unwilling to see, yet foreseeing! Is it the pain I fear? Why do I cling so tenaciously to the beautiful and the noble?

My faith has flickered and trembled these days—this blood-red flame of faith which I have tended with such tenderness and worshiped so passionately; it has paled and disappeared, yet in the end it ever revives, defiant. But I shall live only while it lives, while I know that my soul is growing toward perfection and not descending.

February 7. I stand with arms outstretched, pleading with Life: "Oh, flow not so swiftly, bear me not away before I may understand what is happening to me!"

Heedless of my supplications, Life flows on. I see the approaching month looming on the horizon, heavy with mysterious significance. I am at once awed and thrilled.

My love is coming to me, and our marriage time is approaching, and all this will seal the beginning of my New Life.

No longer shall you know me as Child Heart or Dreamer Girl or the frail and wavering Nature, bowing beneath the weight of experience, but as Young Woman, Hugo's wife-to-be, preparing to enter the Kingdom of Kingdoms and to fulfill her earthly mission.

At last the fullness of love has returned to me. When, through the very excess of suffering I had to endure, I taught my heart to suppress its outflowings, I dreaded having stifled its habitual spontaneity and expressiveness.

Mother alone I dared to love with full adoration. And now, in my reawakened love for Hugo I find all the strength, the fire, the depth, of other days to which are added the intolerable longings of a long-repressed tenderness.

The end of another book, well filled and yet but a pale reflection of the sweeping and thrilling current I am borne on.

Destiny working out its plan surely and mysteriously toward an end which is to the human mind impossible to divine; the wheel of evolution turning, turning with a blinding swiftness—out of this I weave my Story, which is like a tribute to the wonders of the Mystery, gathering thread by thread with infinite and loving care, because its workings move me so profoundly; because its significance is becoming clearer to me day by day; and because, above all, the Force that lies behind this plan has instilled in me Consciousness, the desire to communicate it and to awaken it in others.

February 10. Finca La Generala, Havana. How wondrous the web I hold in my hand! Extending far and wide over the world, unbroken and complete, stirring alone when a change is made, while I watch every trembling and fluttering with anxious heart, striving to bring my best loved ones to me, striving to hold my friends, handling the fragile tracery with infinite care lest it should break.

Some day I may write a chapter in which all the characters meet. Meanwhile, as is the way with reality, they are dispersed, coming, going, meeting, separating.

My Love is on his way to me. I pulled the fine web toward me with all the wisdom my love could teach me, but I have promised myself our ships shall anchor together and he shall steer both on our journey toward the fulfillment of our Dreams.

Mother shall come later, Mother for whom my love grows day by day . . . and, ah, how I tremble for this tender thread.

And I have met Enric after an absence of two and a half years, Enric with the last faint glimmer of an old love still smoldering in his eyes; changed, graver, older, disenchanted, moved by one ambition: to sustain his mother and sisters—and unsuccessful, according to the world, struggling.

Eduardo, in college with his books, dreaming, poeticizing, his inner life most vividly reflected in romantic, enthusiastic letters

. . . in need of stimulus, in danger of losing his active hold on life through vaporous imaginings.

Frances, Eleanor, Eugene, Mr. Richard Maynard[1] . . . These, the ones you know. And there are others. My new friends, my fresh collection of characters, which I believe most interesting.

This is a Chapter of Recollection mingled with a description of the present and a suggestion of the climax. But the dominating feeling is the one of Anticipation for Love. And for a long while its dazzling light shall by far outshine the others!

Oh, there is nothing, nothing, so sad to a woman's heart as the sudden revelation of having caused pain instead of pleasure, the realization that she has taken away more than she has given. If I could but cry out my story and let it serve as a warning to all women. If I could describe the feelings which have come to poison all my happiness. I am torn by regret, by shame, by pity, by the desire to atone, to soothe, to console.

And I must be silent. And all because in my naïve trustfulness I believed my society was bringing joy to a person who is rarely happy—and my heart had gone out to him in sympathy because he was sad, because he was friendless, because, like me, he had dreams of ideal friendship. And then my presence disturbed him, and too late, too late I became aware of the love that had been kindled in a noble, worthy nature. I hate myself for all the qualities that have appealed to him. I hate the face and the ways and the talks that have seemed lovable in his eyes . . . not that this is the first time that this has happened, but because now I have hurt someone who was nobler and better than the rest, and through my very own fault, for I drew him away from his books by my own interest in him, and allowed him to see me. Had I known, alas, but because of his seriousness, his lack of interest in society and women, I believed him invulnerable and insensible. If all I have that is worthy of love might only pass unperceived by all but the One for whom it is destined.

I shall henceforward become so fearful—with each glance or word I shall experience a secret tremor, for I could not endure the thought that together with the power to please I am cursed with the power to wound. To me, whose chief preoccupation is the alleviation of others' suffering, it would be an intolerable punishment. May God give me wisdom to evade this wrong.

And then Hugo. He must not suffer by my thoughtlessness,

[1] *A sculptor for whom A.N. later sat.*

my childish trustfulness. My faith in friendship is fortified and exemplified by Eduardo and Mr. Maynard. If the human turns things against me, makes of friendship a disguise for love or offers me love when I expect friendship, all I can do is retire once more into my shell and seek the ideal in solitude and love alone.

Why I have this great interest in people I do not know. My heart seems to go out to everyone that my mind deems worthy; I can love in a thousand different ways, loyally, truthfully; I cannot suppress this warmth and largeness of feeling which so quickly kindles sympathy and interest in me. But if it is to be a source of grief to others, it is wrong and I must seek some other expression of these feelings which are to me so natural and so innocent of wrong.

Perhaps under the vivid impression of so recent an incident, I am struck too exaggeratedly by the tragedy of it (as is customary!) In a saner light I may find the solution to my little problem. But the face of the one I have wronged haunts me, and I must above all redeem myself.

In a large garden court beneath the warm southern sky, society assembles on Sunday afternoons for tea and dancing. The tables are massed in a circle, some beneath large English umbrellas, others beneath the light of large and quaint Japanese lanterns all soft, wavering lights, illuminating a crowd most gorgeously dressed. Near the music a bit of water in which green and red lights are reflected and statues and the delicate jets of fountains, all steeped in an air of distinguished splendor, beautiful, fairylike scenes.

A soft breeze sometimes quivers and the lanterns tremble, the surface of silks and satins ripple, and feathers quiver; and cheeks, flushed and burning with the dance, are touched as by a caress and refreshed.

How thrillingly alive and yet so superficial—the surface of life, brilliant, polished, attractive to the senses—soft to step on and simple to follow by gliding, gliding . . . And the depths are forgotten, and feelings become dulled, and emotions pale, like some weak flame. How strong the temptation to keep the depths unruffled, to let the hours gently and lazily slip by in this state of semiconsciousness, content to lounge and dance and laugh, unconcernedly, unfeelingly. Society, apathetic and but half-awake, basks in the sunny cheer of a life simplified by fortunes, in the comfort born of others' arduous struggle, of these others who toil, who suffer, who endure, while they lie back in ease and luxurious enjoyment. In those moments, when the scene bears a semblance to the motionless, the inanimate, like a picture to be admired, the artist is awed and can contemplate with reverence. But when the drowsiness and indolence of luxury, like the heavy perfume of too rich a flower or the taste of too sweet a food, steals insidiously through the veins, the thinker sharply realizes and turns away from the revolting sight.

Is it stupidity to continually believe the good and the miraculous in people? In spite of those who tell you that it is unreasonable to expect impossible virtues from men and women, from ordinary human nature, who tell you that by the use of intelligence you judge better and with more security, expecting little and not being, therefore, ever brought to grief.

Sentiment might be compared to an optical illusion voluntarily accepted through charitable motives; for worldly wisdom, clear insight into human nature, produces unkind suspicion and skepticism—this, if you have no faith in the divine spark that slumbers in that human nature, if you have neither imagination to anticipate its awakening nor enough vision to sustain that faith and communicate it.

Can one reach an understanding of humanity, of the universal, from self-analysis, working from the particular to the general? I may prove the Yea or Nay of this by my own experience. But when I reach the conclusion, it will be too late for me to retrace my steps—if it be necessary—and will it serve others?

February 18. Wind and rain—a gray, sulky, oppressing day, a fitting scene for my anxiety and uncertainty, for this is the eve of his coming, and I have had no word from him since the frail cablegram which long ago announced the date of his arrival here. I know not why, but I cannot believe I shall see my Love tomorrow. My heart is heavy . . . I have lost my confidence in life. Now, at every turn of the road, I expect to see the sinister face of Sorrow mocking me. And tonight, consumed by a burning impatience, trembling while my destiny unfolds itself, I thirst for love and peace and for the day when I may say with Amado Nervo:

> Ya no tengo impaciencia
> Porque no aguardo nada . . .[1]

[1] *I no longer am impatient / Because I expect nothing . . .*

Morning. Waiting for life and love . . . in vain!

Afternoon. As if to shame me for my fears and doubts, heaven has ended my despairing agony. He is coming Thursday.

It is never the same to describe a thing too long after it has happened; although Stevenson justly explains that we can see it more clearly, the sincerity of the emotion is altered and the point of view varies.

We are perhaps at first blinded by the heat of the moment— we might see more clearly later, in the light of a cooler observation, but we have lost later that fleeting quality that distinguishes all emotion described in its very first outburst, an unquestionable, unwavering truthfulness.

We are tempted to consider what most flatters us—and many fall victim to this temptation; we may modify according to a judgment that is in turn born of the knowledge of what things *should be* instead of what they *are*. Let us say then that what is perhaps but roughly written at the moment has its value as the truest. And what is written afterward has its value as a product of super-civilized judgment, which is so greatly composed of hypocrisy, self-love and reserve at the cost of frankness, naturalness and spontaneity.

What comes forth in a moment of enthusiasm or of anger or of any emotion is truth—too passionate and extreme, perhaps, but nevertheless *truth*. What comes afterward is but a disguise suited to the personal standard of conduct and ideas, in turn influenced by culture and education, more subjected to the aspirations than an unconscious flow of natural qualities.

Dazed by the course of events, I piercingly seek the significance underlying them. In solitude I question myself and read my soul. I dread that shroud which imprisons me, which moves me to see all things through the vaporous clouds of dreams and imaginings. I seek to look upon the face of reality. It awes me. I place my fingers upon the throbbing pulse of actual life, repeating to myself: Hugo is coming. We may be married soon . . . married, married . . .

Oh, I have lived too long in a world of my own making and I have suffered by the destruction of it. Do I know the truth of things *now?* Do I know love, and wedded love? Am I true woman? Has life, the Fairy Tale, been dimmed by the life of falsity, evil, corruption, deceit and baseness which has been revealed to me? One by one these have passed me by and cried: Look at me—I exist. I am part of the world, part of the air you breathe. And

I have heard and seen them and have sorrowed. Yet I feel untouched, untainted, free from the low contagion. And I believe those I love are free.

God help me, for I am entrusting all to love and binding my very soul to the fulfillment of my human mission. And while the knowing ones whisper: "Love passes, Marriage is a failure, Man is selfish," I stand unwaveringly, in expectation, my soul filled by visions which elevate me above myself.

❦ *Glossary of Family Names* ❧

Ana: Ana María Sánchez; a cousin, daughter of Bernabé Sánchez and Anaïs Culmell

Anaïs, Tia: Anaïs Culmell de Sánchez; Rosa Culmell's sister

Anaïs, Anaïsita: Anaïs Sánchez; a cousin, daughter of Bernabé Sánchez and Anaïs Culmell

Antolina, Tia: Antolina Culmell de Cárdenas; Rosa Culmell's sister

Antolinita: Antolina de Cárdenas; a cousin, daughter of Rafael de Cárdenas and Antolina Culmell

Bernabé: Bernabé Sánchez; a cousin, son of Bernabé Sánchez and Anaïs Culmell

Charles: Carlos de Cárdenas; a cousin, son of Rafael de Cárdenas and Antolina Culmell

Coco, Tia: Aunt Edelmira

Cuca: Caridad Sánchez; a cousin, daughter of Bernabé Sánchez and Anaïs Culmell

Edelmira, Tia: Edelmira Culmell de Chase: Rosa Culmell's sister

Eduardo: Eduardo Sánchez; a cousin, son of Bernabé Sánchez and Anaïs Culmell

Enrique, Tio: Enrique Culmell; Rosa Culmell's brother

Fifille: Nickname for A.N., meaning "little girl"

Grandfather: Joaquín María Nin y Tudó; paternal grandfather

Grandmother: Angela Castellanos de Nin; paternal grandmother

Graziella: Graziella Sánchez; a cousin, daughter of Bernabé Sánchez and Anaïs Culmell

Joaquín Nin: father

Joaquín: Joaquín Nin-Culmell; the younger of A.N.'s two brothers

Juana, Tia: Juana Culmell; A.N.'s godmother, Rosa Culmell's sister

Linotte: A.N.'s nickname for herself, literally "linnet," meaning "featherhead"

Lolita, Tia: Dolores Culmell, first wife of Thorvald Culmell

Marraine: Tia Juana, A.N.'s godmother.

Miguel: Miguel Jorrín, younger brother of Tio Enrique's wife, Julia

Nuna, Nunita: María Teresa Chase; a cousin, daughter of Gilbert Chase and Edelmira Culmell

Rosa Culmell de Nin, Rosita: mother

Thorvald: Thorvald Nin; the older of A.N.'s two brothers

Thorvald Sánchez: a cousin, son of Bernabé Sánchez and Anaïs Culmell.

❧ Index ❧

Murray, Dr., 33
Musardises, Les (Rostand), 376
Musset, Alfred de, 238, 244

Nervo, Amado, 526
New Arabian Nights (Stevenson), 100
New York, N.Y., 37, 46, 53, 56, 57, 65, 68, 69, 71, 85, 89, 105, 107, 115, 124, 234, 294, 359, 510, 513
New York Journal, The, 69
Nin, Anaïs
  artists' life, 421–22
  at eighteen, 149–50, 324
  at nineteen, 408–09
  being a woman, 445–46, 450–51, 483, 499–500, 517–18, 524
  books and reading, xv, 169, 237–38, 249, 387–88
  describing and living life, xv, 292, 296, 419
  dream of Cathedral, 179–80
    of "Divine Idea," 251
    of Hugo, 374, 487
  fame, 313
  family dinner described, a, 51–53
  father, life with, 86, 87, 192, 477–78
  first meeting with Hugh P. Guiler, 154–55
  friendship between women, 171
  husband imagined, 140, 161, 164–65
  illness, 87–88, 104, 120–21
  introspection, 207, 366, 461
  language, 5, 96, 98, 203, 242, 291
  "Linotte, Mademoiselle" (A. N. as), viii, xiii, xv, 16, 17, 18, 29, 30, 31, 32, 33, 34, 35, 37, 40, 41, 42, 44, 45, 50, 53, 57, 68, 70, 71, 72, 79, 82, 89, 90, 92, 99, 102, 103, 107, 110, 111, 116, 128, 135, 137, 152, 160, 181, 185, 192, 209, 217, 358, 403
  living in Barcelona, 89
    in Berlin, 85
    in Brussels, 85–86
    in Neuilly, 82

  at 158 West 75th Street, New York, 106
  looking for work, 367
  love, 175–76, 184, 216, 305, 322, 370–71
  men and women, 218, 303, 328, 362, 394, 446–47
  money, 63, 300, 353–54
  nature of, 141–46, 152, 163–64, 274, 289, 306–08, 320–21, 369–70
    split personality, 102, 448–49
    tendency toward sadness, 479, 497
    transformation, 513–14
  plans to marry rich Cuban, 484, 486, 501
  ready to marry Hugo, 488, 515–16, 527–28
  religion and Catholicism, 28–29, 72, 219, 224–25, 226, 236–37, 303, 342–44, 482, 507–08
  sadness of the city, 462–63
  sex and animalism, 471
  starting a "new life," 201–06
  surrender to happiness, 521–23
  trip to Cuba, 483, 489, 495–96
  visit to Convent of Santa Clara, Cuba, 506–07
  writing, 139, 293–94, 334, 336, 338–39, 340, 352, 353, 389, 398, 413, 419, 466–67, 476
  working as model, 410–11, 414, 415, 416, 423–24, 459–60, 480–81, 511–12
Nin, Joaquin J. (father), viii, 22, 30, 41, 65, 68, 81, 82, 83, 85, 86, 87, 89, 90, 92, 97, 98, 101, 104, 109, 123, 133, 141, 144, 145, 182, 211, 227, 242, 313, 327, 346, 376, 380
  letters to, 16–18, 64–65, 126, 131–33, 184–85, 242–43, 344–45, 406, 476–78
  quarrels with, 86
  requests divorce, 101, 145
  with A. N. in Berlin, 84
    in Brussels, 85
    at Villa "*Les Ruines*," Arcachon, 88

[*Index*]   537